TOWN HOUSES OF MEDIEVAL BRITAIN

TOWN HOUSES OF MEDIEVAL BRITAIN

Anthony Quiney

PUBLISHED FOR THE PAUL MELLON CENTRE FOR STUDIES IN BRITISH ART
BY YALE UNIVERSITY PRESS, NEW HAVEN & LONDON

Designed by Ruth Applin
Set in Baskerville MT by SNP Best-set Typesetter Ltd., Hong Kong
Printed in Singapore

Library of Congress Control Number: 2003112642

Endpapers
John Nordern, *View of Medieval London Bridge*, 1597–8, © Museum of London. Detail of Fig. 27

Frontispiece
Greyfriars, Friar Street, Worcester

Illustration on p. x
The Tower of Babel, under construction, as shown in the *Duke of Bedford's Book of Hours* (*Bedford Missal*). © British Library. MS Add 18,850, 17v. Detail of Fig. 1

CONTENTS

PREFACE

This book began as a challenge. Reviewing Pierre Garrigou Grandchamp's *Demeures Médiévales: Cœur de la cité* in 1993 my old friend Andor Gomme concluded that any criticism was rather out of place since, so far as medieval town houses in Britain were concerned, there were only tantalizingly brief chapters on the subject, including one of mine, but no complete study. Could I be persuaded, he asked, to fill the gap. Imagining this task to be a welcome antidote for teaching three or four hundred students each year, I was persuaded, and the head of my school backed me, as he so often did. John Nicoll, the managing director of Yale University Press, accepted my proposal, so I had his valuable support too.

I consulted another of my old friends, Malcolm Airs, who welcomed the idea and suggested that I should include guildhalls, hospitals and other civic buildings. As ever, he stood by me until the end; he read my text and offered valuable criticism as well as photographs to fill gaps. So the concept of house came to include more than the ordinary dwellings of town people that I had at first envisaged. Monarchs and magnates would be included, as well as clerics, professionals, merchants, artisans and the urban poor. Religious houses would not be included, since these are already well covered under monastic architecture. The domestic establishments of bishops, nevertheless, have a central place. I still had to find some kind of boundary between town and country, and decided, as a general rule, to include the smallest of settlements that gained borough status in the Middle Ages, but to exclude the largest of villages that did not. Similarly, I had to fix boundaries for the Middle Ages. The collapse of Roman Britain in the fifth century was an easy choice for the start, since this really marks a new beginning for domestic building. No substantial buildings survive from the first five hundred years after that, although the few documents for this period are supported by a growing archaeological record. The terminal boundary needed a bit more thought. The accession of the Tudors in 1485 was too early as a social boundary, so this became the English Reformation of the 1530s. But not for Scotland, where I extended the period beyond the Scottish Reformation of 1560 to James VI's ascent of the English throne as James I in 1603. This would round off the story, and a story I mean it to be.

This is a building history, so it is about those who commission, those who build, and those who occupy, as well as the buildings themselves. The fabric of buildings is important: their structure gives them their form and their lasting qualities; their planning relates to how people use them; their architectural style, most important of all, expresses their owners' self-esteem and displays their worth. These are the strands that I have tried to string together as a tenuous narrative thread.

I was soon surrounded by people who could help me. For thirty years the Royal Archaeological Institute has given me a valued context for studying building archaeology and history. The wide scope of the Institute's interests extends from the archaeological remains of all periods to their multifarious social and physical causes. I was lucky since it has a tradition of meetings and lectures that, for a century and a half, have taken its members to practically every British town as well as, recently, to Ireland and France. I could find nowhere better to meet all kinds of people working close to my subject and seeing it from widely differing viewpoints. I therefore owe a debt of gratitude to my fellow officers and members of the Institute, and in particular to the indefatigable Brian Dix, who has recently arranged much of this programme of meetings. The large number of articles that the Institute has published in the *Archaeological Journal* and the many drawings that, with the Institute's permission, I have reproduced here is just a little evidence of its value to my work.

Like a second pillar of Hercules in my academic world, the Society of Architectural Historians of Great Britain provided another forum of friends and ideas, one that again gave me the opportunity to set out and argue many of my ideas. Andor Gomme's review had appeared in the Society's *Newsletter*, and his support, personally as well as through his editorship of its journal *Architectural History*, was essential, not just to initiating the project, but in supporting it right through to the end. Moreover, he came to my rescue with many of the photographs that illustrate the text. He deserves my special thanks. The Society's conferences, particularly those in Lincoln and Stirling, were timely, and I am particularly grateful to Anne Riches for help with matters relating to Lincoln and Scotland.

With so much to find and so much to read I would have been at a loss without the library of the Society of Antiquaries of London, where five minutes is worth at least an hour anywhere else. The librarian Bernard Nurse and former librarian and continuing denizen John Hopkins were always ready with answers to abstruse questions and help with illustrations. I am deeply grateful to the Society for permission to reproduce these, and to Adrian James who coped with my frequent requests for reproductions. Two further societies lightened my load. The Society for Medieval Archaeology published W.A. Pantin's significant article on town houses as long ago as 1963, and every study since then has built on this sound foundation; its journal *Medieval Archaeology* has been second only to the *Archaeological Journal* for the value of its reports on town houses, particularly those investigated by archaeological excavation. Meanwhile the Vernacular Architecture Group was invaluable to me, particularly for the publication of plans of buildings visited during its conferences and of the results of dating timber buildings by an analysis of tree rings (dendrochronology).

Anna Eavis and her colleagues at the National Monuments Record and the staff of the British Library answered many of my questions with particular alacrity: it would be invidious to single out individuals there and in other archives I have used, yet they all treated me with individual care. Nevertheless, I must particularly mention several of my colleagues who shared their thoughts with me and gently put me right over some of mine, namely Panos Arvanitakis, John Ashdown, Brian Ayers, Martin Biddle, Leslie Burgher, Laurence Butler, Jonathan Coad, Nicholas Cooper, Catherine Cruft, Roger Evans, Tom Fenton, Eric Fernie, Richard Gem, Kate Giles, John Goodall, Patrick Goode, Jane Grenville, Geoff Holman, Peter Howell, Tom Beaumont James, Stanley Jones, Frank Kelsall, Grace McCombie, the late Nicholas Moore, Robina McNeil, David and Barbara Martin, Martin Millett, Patric Morrisey, Julian Munby, Sarah Pearson, Dominique Pitte, Carol Rawcliffe, Peter Ryder, Tim Schadla-Hall, John Schofield, James Simpson, David Stocker, Richard Suggett, Tim Tatton-Brown, Michael Thompson, Ian Toplis, Blaise Vyner, Christopher Wakeling, David Walker, and Stanley West. I am also grateful to Hemantha Perera who prepared many of the drawings for publication by adding and removing details and making other time-consuming changes that would have defeated me, and introducing me to the thrills and spills of computer drawing; to Liz Smith who copy-edited my text and suggested several improvements; and to Ruth Applin who prepared the text and illustrations for publication. Despite all this help, there are bound to be errors and omissions. The responsibility for these is mine, but may I ask readers to tell me of any they find?

Books are unkind taskmasters. They require a particular kind of concentration, devotion and reflection that enforce solitude. This one became an addiction, as I only realized when eyes met eyes during my lengthy explanations of how far I had progressed. I therefore owe a debt to my family who put up with all of this. It was not the first time, but my family has grown, and now extends to children and step-children, their partners, and now to grandchildren, as well as various menageries. All of them suffered at one time or another from my obsession as I tried to interest them in my task in hand and shake it from my head into my word-processor. I found them an inspiration even as I vaguely wondered why they couldn't be more like me. My wife endured this manic phase with the greatest fortitude and patience every single day. A writer herself, she perhaps understood my condition, although her abilities are known to a different and much wider audience than mine. She read through the text twice, greatly reducing its obscurities and suggesting several improvements to its structure in the process. So my greatest debt is to her: to her and to the rest of my extended and extending family I dedicate this book.

INTRODUCTION

In the beginning was the Word

> Towered cities please us then,
> And the busy hum of men[1]

As they came from the east, the families of the sons of Noah found a plain in the land of Shinar and built there a city, a city of thoroughly burnt brick, with a tower that reached up to heaven. (fig. 1) Thus, we are told, began the civilization of the world. This ancient story embraced a remarkable idea, one that, long afterwards, the Romans were quick to recognize in their language: the city and civilization are, literally, indispensable to each other.

Fearing that nothing would in future be restrained from Noah's descendants, the Lord decided to confound their language so that they would not understand one another. They stopped the building of Babel, as their towered city was called, and, according to Judaeo-Christian belief,[2] the Lord scattered them abroad upon the face of all the earth. The Lord, of course, brought down endless trouble with this petulant action, but in one respect He was too late: humanity was not to be restrained, whatever different languages He determined its various tribes should speak. There would be cities.

For all that these far-off events recorded in *Genesis* would carry the weight of biblical truth in medieval Europe, they hardly touched ancient Britain, or indeed much of western Europe at the time. Not a word of whatever language the inhabitants of Britain then spoke has been recorded. The tribes that sparsely populated this island knew little of the idea of a house, let alone a house in a towered city. While their culture nevertheless developed over the succeeding millennia, the island remained uncivilized until the advent of Rome. After that, as they say, everything is history.

Just as the Roman conquest of Britain brought with it the civilization of urban life, so the collapse of Roman rule removed it. The second attempt at civilization was to be more lasting. It took many years to take root in England, more still in Scotland and Wales, but did eventually lead to humming cities, replete with towers, that not only lasted but also in the course of time outgrew Rome itself, and set the pattern for the unrestrained urbanization of the modern world. (fig. 2)

The Lord's Church was hard put to restrain the worldliness of these new medieval citizens, whose livelihood depended on craft, trade and finance. Its doctrine was at odds with the economic necessity that gave cities their life, and, in fact, with its own temporal needs – for churches, furnishings, vestments and relics. These items were costly, but were the very foundation of its worldly power. 'Render unto Caesar' was fine for the Bible, but not for the real world. Despite this source of conflict, for twelve hundred years the Church thrived, even though, as the Middle Ages proceeded, it found itself more and more often at the Devil's supper table.

Craft, trade and finance were a secondary matter: salvation in heaven counted first and last. (fig. 3) This attitude to the ultimate purpose of life characterizes the Middle Ages above all other ages. Western Christendom, from Iceland to Sicily, from Ireland and Portugal to Hungary and Poland, looked to this world for day-to-day survival, but the weight of Last Things directed deeper motivations towards the next. Christianity governed society and it governed politics. 'In the realm of government the teleological principle upon which any society

1. The Tower of Babel, under construction, as shown in the *Duke of Bedford's Book of Hours* (*Bedford Missal*). While it is made of stone, rather than brick as the Bible states, and is clearly fanciful, this is a fairly accurate record of medieval building practice in the 1420s. © British Library. MS Add 18,850, 17v

2. Constantinople, the successor to Rome and for nine centuries the greatest city in Christendom until in 1204 rampaging Christians sacked it during the fourth Crusade. This illustration in the *Luttrell Psalter*, *c*.1340, shows it in the form of a medieval English town, with its stone church and timber-framed houses encircled by embattled walls and turrets. © British Library. MS Add 42,130, 164v

must needs rest, operates through the principle of functional qualification.'[3] While Mother Church succoured society, he who was qualified to translate the purpose for which society existed into everyday terms and measures was its ruler, namely the pope, by virtue of his succession to the chair of St Peter in Rome.

The Church had come of age when civilization in western Europe was threatened by the collapse of the Roman Empire. Its first task was missionary, as it struggled with surrounding

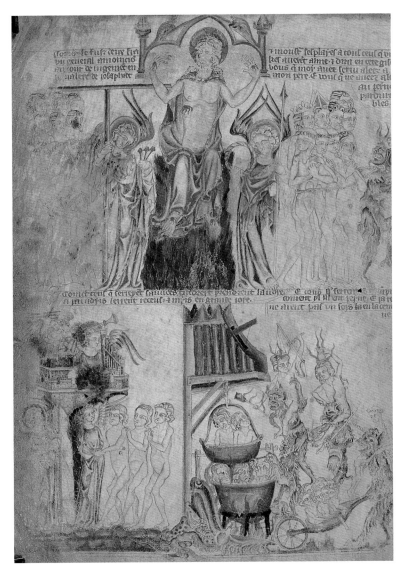

3. The Last Judgement, as depicted *c.* 1330 in the *Holkham Bible*. The choice for every Christian – kings and bishops as well as ordinary men and women – was clear: damnation and the fires of hell lay one way; salvation, celestial music and the eternal bliss of heaven the other. © British Library. MS Add 47,682, 42v

4. King Athelstan, portrayed *c.* 934, and thus the earliest contemporary representation of an English monarch, shown in the role of protector and benefactor of the Church, presenting a holy manuscript to St Cuthbert. Parker Collection MS 183, 1v. © The Master and Fellows of Corpus Christi College, Cambridge

barbarism; conversion achieved, its second was social reconstruction, with itself the ruler of the political institutions that made this end possible. The establishment and maintenance of the supremacy of the office of Pope as Vicar of St Peter over western Europe's secular rulers is a recurrent theme of early medieval politics. The Emperor Constantine had, so the Donation of Constantine stated, conferred on Pope Sylvester and his successors not only the ancient title of *Pontifex Maximus* but also the temporal possession of Rome and imperial rights within it. Thus, through this forged eighth-century document, western Christianity eventually freed itself from the old pagan Empire, from Christian Byzantium, and from the Church in the east. In the words of St Ambrose, 'Ubi Petrus, ibi ergo ecclesia' ('Where Peter is, there must be the Church').[4] Since the western Church was founded on Rome, the shrine of St Peter, *Romanitas* and *Christianitas* became indivisible.[5]

This view of the purpose of society and the legality of its governance was promulgated by every decree of the Roman Church, an all-pervasive view which had largely triumphed by the ninth century and was imposed on secular rulers through canon law, with the ultimate sanctions of excommunication on those who opposed it, and interdiction on whole states. The pope came to rule the western Church as its monarch, the Church being the one body of Christians, embracing both priests and laymen, united by faith. Priests were qualified by the special authority of being ordained, this giving them their particular spiritual function, and one that did not necessarily preclude their involvement in secular affairs as well. Laymen were not thus qualified, although they might dispute this, and emperors, kings, princes and dukes, for all the magnificence of their worldly powers, could not readily sustain a claim before the pope to full monarchy for the government within their own sway. The prime function of secular authority was to protect and

3

defend the Roman Church. (fig. 4) Holy Law should determine its actions: the Sword, when necessary, would enforce them. Thus, in accepting this, Pepin the Short became through the pope's authority *patricius Romanus* and his shaky claim to be king of the Franks was duly legitimized. His son Charlemagne did better, being crowned the first Holy Roman Emperor.

Society as a whole was governed on a rigid class basis. Divine authority required it to have its priests, warriors and servants. Lay society must therefore have both its rulers and its ruled – 'lords whose parents were the Lord knows who',[6] and men, tied to the soil as another man's serf. Between these must be the various gradations of man and woman, each in an allotted place, each with a distinct purpose. This was ordained in heaven where, ultimately, the reward for fulfilling one's role, however high, however low, might be attained.

So, more than a faith, Christianity ruled society and became an entire culture. The city that enshrined the body of St Peter was the geographical expression of western Christianity itself. Its culture took Rome as its *fons et origo* and its Latin language became the language of learning and discourse between peoples of different tongues, just as Greek and Arabic were to be the *linguae francae* in the east. Rome, moreover, was not simply the Christian city of the incumbent of the papal chair, but the classical city of Constantine, the emperor who had embraced Christianity in the first place and given it legitimacy. (fig. 5) However distant the passage of time would make that Rome seem, its inspiration was never forgotten.

As well as the Sword, the Church had a second powerful weapon, the Word. Through its grip on culture the Church monopolized the accounts of the time, causing, for instance, the Venerable Bede to condemn the unholy alliance of the professed Christian King Cadwalla and the heathen Pendar of Mercia for resisting the Christian convert King Edwin of Bernicia, and defeating his forces with terrible slaughter at Hatfield in 633.[7] A differently motivated view of these events might prefer to see Cadwalla and Pendar resisting the expansionist policies of a petty ruler who had conveniently espoused a winning cause for the purpose of self-aggrandizement. But such a view, were there one, was condemned to silence by the Church's control of the written word.

The rule of Christianity was defended and promulgated not only by law, but also by the powerful grip on people's minds of saints and angels, who interceded with God to provide the possibility of access to His heavenly city, and through whom God worked His miracles. (fig. 6) Such intangibles promoted the need for saintly relics and an immense and growing armoury of symbols, of which Rome was one of the most potent. The faith itself was fully armed with its own, starting with the bread and wine of the Holy Eucharist that symbolized Christ's body and blood sacrificed on the Cross to redeem mankind. But the everyday world was also garrisoned by rank upon rank of symbols that enlightened and, in a sense, protected every facet of life. Some of these, like the round-arched Carolingian and Romanesque styles of architecture that sought to remind people of their lasting inheritance from the Eternal City, do not require a

5. The Arch of Constantine, Rome, which commemorates his victory at the Battle of the Milvian Bridge in 312, when his soldiers triumphed under the sign of the Cross, and thus paved the way for the conversion of imperial Rome to Christianity. While the first Roman triumphal arches predate Christianity by two centuries, the popes also staged ceremonial processions from the twelfth century onwards in which they passed through temporary arches of a similar kind erected for the occasion

6. St Mary's Hall, Coventry. Saints, woven on a fifteenth-century Flemish tapestry that also depicts the Assumption of the Virgin Mary, the Twelve Apostles and either Henry VI and Margaret of Anjou or Henry VII and Elizabeth of York together with a host of angels. © The Herbert Art Gallery and Museum, Coventry

7. Iffley church, Oxfordshire. The meaning of the rich carving around the doorways has not been deciphered, but is surely more than an expression of wealth and art for art's sake. Drawn by F. Mackenzie, engraved by J. Le Keux, and published by J. H. Parker in 1834

8. Colston's House, Bristol. Decoratively carved roof timbers of the great hall of a lavishly finished merchant's house, as recorded in the middle of the nineteenth century. From Dollman & Jobbins 1863, 2, Pl. 62. © Society of Antiquaries of London

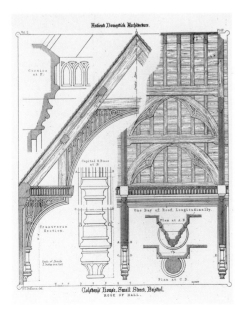

great leap of the imagination for their understanding, while the meaning of others, such as the arcane iconography of Iffley church in Oxfordshire,[8] can only be guessed at today. (fig. 7)

The Church, therefore, claimed to be the heart of civilization. This attitude persisted to the end of the Middle Ages, despite the changing social and economic circumstances that attended the accumulation of wealth. This reached a peak in the thirteenth century, before an ensuing collapse in the fourteenth century with its associated pestilence. But increasingly the Church became 'an immense vested interest, implicated to the hilt in the economic fabric'.[9] The essential dichotomy in the Church, which needed this world for its control of the next, threatened a schism even greater than that which divided pope from antipope. Understandably, Bernard of Clairvaux railed against the worldly riches of the Church: 'wealth is drawn up by the ropes of wealth, thus money bringeth money', he wrote in the 1120s; 'O vanity of vanities, yet no more vain than insane! The Church is resplendent in her walls, beggarly in her poor. She clothes her stones in gold, and leaves her sons naked'.[10]

Yet the Church survived, despite its wholesale venality and disputed Papacy. Only when Luther protested at the sale of indulgences for the forgiveness of sins in 1517 was the first effective broadside fired into this ancient hulk of Roman Catholicism. Britain's first action came soon afterwards, but the process of Reformation was only finally laid to rest in 1690, its work completed, with John Locke's forthright proclamation of today's democratic secular state: 'The great and chief end therefore, of men's uniting into commonwealths, and putting themselves under government, is the preservation of their property'.[11] He did not mean, as the medieval Englishman, Scotsman or Welshman would have meant, that ultimate property, namely a promised place in the Celestial City. For Locke it was what one means today – a house.

The medieval house, however desirable as physical property, is also an expression of culture. (fig. 8) It accommodated the primary social unit, the family, to whom its appearance granted a measure of status. This is difficult ground, harder to determine than the means by which it might also satisfy the needs of *firmitas* and *commoditas*. Although the ten books *De Architectura* of Vitruvius were hidden from most medieval eyes, his insistence on building with due regard to firmness, commodity and delight (*venustas*)[12] have universal applicability. Whether in the palaces of royalty or the cottages of journeymen, these three qualities were the aim of medieval builders, even though the widespread loss of Roman constructional skills put them out of range until they had learned anew. While delight is the least tangible of the three, it is at once the most inspiring. In the last analysis, architecture exists in order to make a visual, icono-

9. The King's Head, Mardol, Shrewsbury. A late fourteenth-century timber-framed merchant's house, now an inn, with eye-catching cusped panels and window tracery that might indicate that it was carved by the best carpenter in town, and, more significantly, could have demonstrated a now-forgotten connection with some other monumental work; the facade was originally gabled, and the interior was finished with wall paintings

10. Archaeologists at work in 1981 excavating a Norman house at St Martin-at-Palace Plain, Norwich. The surviving, lower part of its flint walls incorporates the base of a garderobe chute (left) and one of two entrances (centre). The remains are now preserved beneath a new magistrate's court. An impression of the complete house is shown in Fig. 196. Photograph Brian Ayres. © Norfolk Museums and Archaeology Service

graphic point.[13] The constructional skills that allowed a medieval mason to raise a high vault are clearly marvellous, but the ultimate reason for his doing so – the glory of God – emphasizes the radical difference between the transcendent aspirations of his world and the materiality of ours.

As the Church sent out its missions into every corner of western Europe, and economies revived, the most developed building skills went first into the construction of churches, eventually to give them substantial stone walls, lofty vaults and a chance of longevity. The faith was everlasting: so should they be. Moreover, churches were, after all, the focal point of society: longevity was thus a double imperative. The miracle is that there was stone and timber enough for providing the mundane comforts of decent houses as well.

Nevertheless, houses did become the object of substantial building skills, though in England not until after the Norman Conquest of 1066, so far as we can tell from the earliest survivors. These included the palaces of kings and bishops; the houses of magnates and merchants; the houses devoted to such institutions, religious and secular, as monasteries and colleges, and those devoted to the succour of the poor and needy, as well as those to the hospitality of travellers; the dwellings of more ordinary people who found their livelihood in town; and, of course, the most numerous of all, those of the countryside that sheltered all kinds and conditions of man. For all of these there slowly developed both suitable and often characteristic plans that fulfilled the needs of usage, and forms of decoration and other kinds of enhancement that satisfied the more symbolic needs of the age – in short the very stuff of architecture.

So, firmness is in many respects a matter of record, though the need for it is not necessarily self-evident. Commodity, again, is more or less visible in the planning of rooms, but, while urban house plans are related to rural ones, often descended from them, and may be constrained by restricted sites, what these plans meant in terms of everyday usage is rather harder to determine. Finally, there is delight, expressed visibly as style and decoration – those qualities that today's house agents glibly explain away as 'kerb appeal'. (fig. 9) This glib explanation is of little service to our understanding of medieval houses, but appearance had a meaning then, as it does now, and this meaning is certainly not always obvious.

Hardly a century after the end of the Middle Ages, the busy hum of the City had grown so loud that King James I cried out in despair, 'London will be all England'.[14] Such royal prescience is the more surprising since London at the start of the seventeenth century was just one

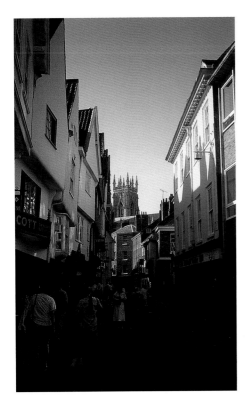

11. Low Petergate Street, York. The jettied and gabled fronts of medieval timber-framed houses face the regular brick-faced fronts of Georgian houses in one of the best-preserved medieval cities in Britain

12. Watergate Street, Chester, as recorded in 1829 by the topographical artist George Pickering. Less tumbledown now and much renovated, this is still recognizable as the street of today. From a print in Chester Archaeological Society Library

of many European cities of comparable size, having grown populous enough during the Middle Ages to enter the second, and just perhaps the first European league. Yet James was only giving word to an already established fact. From the tenth century onward London was Britain's greatest city; from the thirteenth century it had become unassailably dominant, and this lead has grown ever since. His own city, Edinburgh, was very small indeed, and all other Scottish burghs were hardly more than villages in size.

The London that King James knew was still largely a medieval city – in its fabric, if not its mind. His grandsons Charles II and James II saw it all reduced to ashes in the Great Fire, leaving London's landowners, developers, builders and occasional architects to replace it with the grandeur of what would become Georgian London, the capital of a now thoroughly secular state. Far more of that survives than of medieval London. The nineteenth century set about rebuilding the City and its suburbs with such determination that it swept aside practically all that remained from the Middle Ages, and, as a result, at last exceeded ancient Rome in both size and population.

Poor medieval London! What the Victorians so vigorously pursued, the *Luftwaffe* and hungry developers of the twentieth century have completed. Any study of medieval houses in British towns is therefore like Shakespeare's *Hamlet* without the Prince. Only seventeen fragments of medieval houses survive in the City, and there is little more in its medieval suburbs and in Southwark.[15] Yet, as in a glass darkly, there is at least the picture which can be built up from the graphic and documentary records that put London's great medieval structures on to the map and into the mind, along with the growing evidence of archaeological excavation in many towns and cities, which has transformed ideas of the past in countless ways since the war that destroyed so much evidence of a more immediate kind. (fig. 10)

Despite the wartime ruination of great swathes of several other British towns – Bristol, Canterbury, Coventry, Exeter come to mind – many, like Chester, Oxford, York and St Andrews, have fared better. (figs 11 & 12) Although it is not always clear what their surviving medieval houses signify without the evidence of princely London, it is from the evidence of these towns and many smaller ones that a picture of the medieval urban landscape may be drawn.

Those medieval houses that do survive, do not do so unaltered. When unrestored they tell as much about the centuries following their construction as that of their birth, and when restored, as much about modern notions of what the Middle Ages were like as of the Middle Ages

7

themselves. These notions, for all their attempt at accuracy, are bound by law and modern sensitivity, and tend, therefore, to portray a sanitized view of the past. They do nevertheless serve an ancient purpose: by referring to the past, they give the present a validity it would otherwise lack. Just such feelings characterized the past too, and these crop up throughout the Middle Ages from the time that Christianity was first accepted, both as a religion and as a culture.

For all their survivals, few of these towns boast the number of medieval houses or even the quality that several ancient towns of Britain's Continental neighbours still display. Modern desolation is one reason, but not the only one. British medieval towns were small by European standards and it is the rebuilding and growth of later centuries that have given them their his-

14. Smarden. Granted borough status in 1332, this remarkably prosperous but hardly populous village never assumed an urban character, despite the wealth of its burgesses and a cluster of houses by the parish church

toric centres. Those centuries had less effect on the historic medieval centres of many European cities. (fig. 13) While they did bring about the wholesale reconstruction of much of Paris, one of Europe's largest medieval cities, they left an extensive medieval legacy in, for instance, Gent, another great city which was comparable in size to Paris and London. Despite the terrible destruction of the Second World War, much survives in Germany, thanks to its later industrialization and to a greater and more effective desire to protect its old stock of houses as part of its modern culture. Until the 1970s Britain was far more careless of its past inheritance,[16] preferring myth to what remained of the reality.

While London was hardly a small fish by medieval European standards, Britain's provincial cities and towns were mostly minnows. Many were no larger than villages, and some – Lydford in Devon and Smarden in Kent – are villages still. (fig. 14) What has always made them seem unlike towns is less their modest populations than their lack of perceptible urban centres and clearly defined boundaries.

If Lydford and Smarden are extreme cases, many British towns were hardly more populous by the end of the Middle Ages, although their urban qualities were more apparent. Several medieval towns eventually boasted walls, and others felt the presence of notional walls that defined their boundaries. (fig. 15) These were not simply topographical limits, but boundaries between worlds set apart by their different social and economic circumstances. Medieval rural life was by and large fixed: customs and services, and, above all, the agricultural calendar set the pattern. Merchants and craftsmen, by contrast, needed freedom and mobility in the pursuit of their livelihood. These they greatly prized, among other reasons because they gave them liberties not generally possessed by the rural peasantry, who owed a clearly defined allegiance to their ruling lords. The freedoms that towns offered could not be limitless: religion, government, even society at large would not have allowed it. So urban liberties had to be defined more or less clearly both by legal charter, royal or otherwise, and by physical boundaries within which, for example, markets might be held only at fixed places and on specified days.[17]

Whether towns had walls or not, their urban qualities were most visible in their tight street layout, usually incorporating a market place, causing the houses to form a distinctive nucleus. While licensed markets and borough charters distinguished towns legally from villages, their different economic and administrative status might also be evident in their buildings. Some of these were specifically urban, such as market houses, the halls of guilds, commercial and lordly inns, and hospitals. Once again, these were occasionally built in villages,[18] but size and compactness usually differentiated towns. The resulting pressure on land in their centres, where costs might be ten times as high as in villages, affected their houses, which, already by the late twelfth century, had to respond in their planning.

Despite the restrictions, most towns still contained much open space, particularly on their peripheries, and this was usually put to agrarian or pastoral use; and the houses, for all their proximity, were sometimes quite rural in character and might back on to extensive gardens. (fig. 16) This beau ideal of *rus in urbe* only exercises the modern mind: rural husbandry was practised in towns because economic need required it, and they were never entirely filled with buildings – fields, pastures and gardens were an abiding feature of the medieval urban landscape, together with their crops and animals. So a craftsman by day might milk his cow before nightfall and a burgess one day might reap grain the next. Urbanism, in the most extreme sense, was not a very British quality in the Middle Ages, just as it is not even today.

15. A carved timber panel from the Market Cross, New Buckenham, representing the palisaded walls of the castle or a small town with a fine gateway and towers – features that this modest new town may have aspired to but never gained

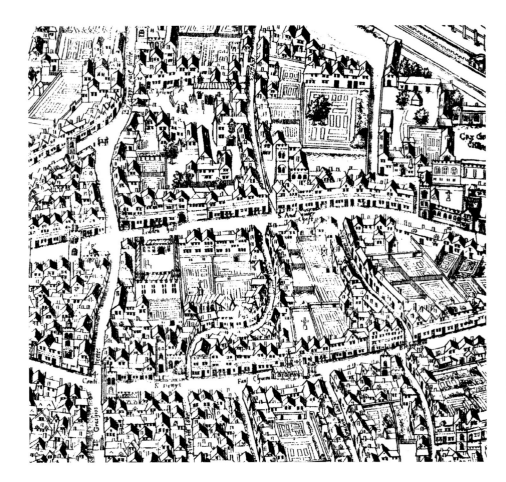

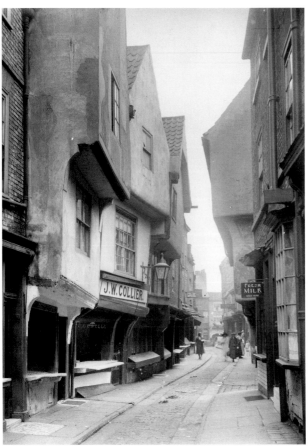

16. Gardens in Elizabethan London. Part of the 'Copperplate' map of London, of *c.* 1553–9, showing properties to the east of the present Gracechurch Street (Grachios Strete) and Bishopsgate, many of them having gardens laid out with formal paths and beds, and the occasional tree. © Museum of London

17. The Shambles, York. Laid out conveniently behind the market place where meat was sold, it was already sanitised for modern sensibilities when this photograph was taken early in the twentieth century and is today the epitome of a medieval street. © National Monuments Record

A village, equally, had its craftsmen and traders, but the scale of their operations in a rural economy set a village apart from a small town, though both might count their inhabitants in only a few hundred. These people, in any case, would enjoy rather different legal status. A villager might complain of subservience to a manorial lord, but would also be glad of the protection gained in return; the same person in town would enjoy various liberties from feudal dues, but still had to pay tax when this was demanded and was far more at the mercy of economic circumstance.

Occupations, specifically those in trading and manufacture, took on an urban character as much through their variety and scale as through their specific type. Some of these made far from ideal neighbours. A fire in a mint was blamed for burning down Canterbury Cathedral in 1174.[19] Mints were specifically licensed, and then only in a few towns. Slaughter-houses were not. The street that today is most evocative of medieval York in all its picturesque disorder, the Shambles, is so named not because its narrowness affected how people walked along it, but because a shambles was a place where butchers slaughtered animals and sold meat. (fig. 17)

The twentieth century has learned to keep these unsavoury places out of sight and sound, and the scheduling of urban land has segregated noisome uses of this sort from places of dwelling so as to ensure that offensive occupations do not threaten everyday notions of decency and hygiene. These notions first became of prime concern in the nineteenth century, largely because of the deepening offence caused by industrialization; the unbearable increase in scale of its slaughter-houses made these places, with their associated tanneries and tanks of urine, a thoroughly objectionable feature of British towns.

Nevertheless, while medieval towns mixed together cheek by jowl what today would be considered unsavoury and what would be considered picturesque, they also excited prospects of untold wealth, hence their attraction to anyone tired of the everyday grind of peasant life. So it was that wild and impossible chimeras tempted a small minority of people to migrate to town in search of golden-paved streets and economic salvation from the hard world that they inhabited, or to petition for the granting of a charter to give their village borough status. Their houses are the subject of what follows.

PART I

AND THE WORD WAS MADE FLESH

Venerable marks of antiquity

The Anglo-Saxon inheritance

By the start of the Middle Ages several traditions of building had already emerged in Britain. The most sophisticated of these had been imported by the Romans and grafted on to the old Celtic traditions of the Iron Age. The Anglo-Saxon invaders brought further traditions as well as turbulence to the national melting pot. This established, in building as in other matters, two main cultural ingredients: the classical and the barbarian, the Roman and the Germanic, with a pinch of Celtic seasoning. These were not necessarily in opposition, despite the centuries of bloodshed, and certainly not in the way perceived in the nineteenth century when romantic nationalism attached all sorts of spurious virtues and vices to each culture in a partisan endeavour to raise one above the other.

There was a form of dialogue between these cultures, allowing continual modification and change. While 'the language, institutions, culture, and material resources of the Romanized population virtually disappeared'[1] as a consequence of Anglo-Saxon invasion, Christianity reintroduced Roman culture, albeit with a new face. This eventually had the better of the dialogue, perhaps because of its universality, possibly because of its Christianity, and certainly because of its literacy. The Romans were the first to write extensively about Britain, and this defines the boundary between British prehistory, which is known almost only through archaeology, and history proper, where the written word illuminates the physical record. The power of words gave the Romans the great advantage of publicizing their achievements, and set up Rome as a standard by which all things might be measured for a millennium after the city fell to the barbarian invaders.

Both words and archaeology make it clear that the Romans have the distinction of introducing to Britain the first recognizable towns. These had a layout which was new to Britain and often based on a grid of streets. Rising from within this pattern, new kinds of buildings served the needs of the large populations that towns attracted. Walls formed well-defined boundaries; streets defined building plots.

Since biblical times towns have always been founded to serve variously as military strongholds, administrative or religious capitals, or centres of manufacture and trade. If towns were to survive, nature had to provide a strategic site and fresh water, and man – and woman – had to provide a sound economic basis. Many Roman towns in Britain took the place of Iron Age hill forts, as Durnovaria apparently superseded Maiden Castle in Dorset, after Vespasian's victory over the Celtic Durotriges in AD 44. Some Roman towns superseded the *oppida* of the Belgae. One of these large defended strongholds, Wheathampsted in Hertfordshire, which was perhaps the capital of the Catuvellauni, Cassivellaunus tried to defend against Julius Caesar in 54 BC. Another *oppidum* was Camulodunum in Essex, which the Romans converted into their first legionary fortress, or *castrum*, after the successful invasion of AD 43.[2]

Some Roman towns developed from *castra*, notably Lindum and Glevum, particularly when a civilian settlement or *colonia* was attached to them, or, as in the case of the Roman Camulodunum, replaced them. Others developed from *principia* or administrative centres of a civil region or *civitas*, such as Verulamium and Corinium Dobunnorum. Then there were those towns that primarily developed from the needs of commerce and industry. Londinium stands

18. Caerwent Roman town (Venta Silurum). Plan, showing its grid of perpendicularly aligned streets, set within more or less rectangular walls and defining twenty island building sites (*insulae*), numbered I–XX. At the centre, *insula* VIII contains the forum and its enclosed square, opening on to the main east-west street on its southern side, and backed by the town basilica on its northern side. To the east in *insula* IX there is a small temple and opposite in XIII a suite of public baths. After a plan drawn for Cadw, and published in *Archaeol. J.* 150 (1993) sup. 20, fig. 5. © Royal Arcaheological Institute

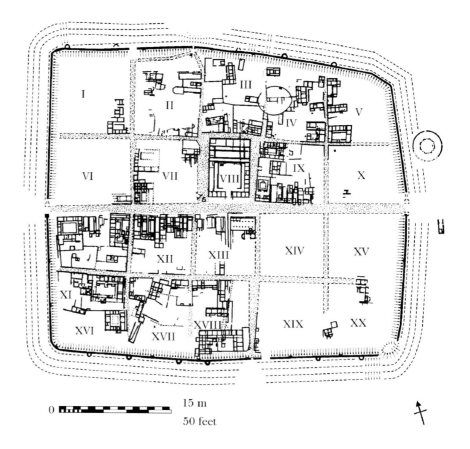

0 ▮▮▮▮▮▮▮▮▮▮▮▮ 15 m
                50 feet

at their head; being well placed by a river and at the centre of the Roman road system, its development into an administrative capital soon became irresistible. More typical were small towns like Clausentum, a port on the Itchen estuary, from where Mendip lead was exported to the Continent. A few towns originated as a result of their special natural qualities, particularly springs of water, which became the focus of cults. The name of Aquae Sulis commemorates Sulis, the Celtic goddess of the hot springs, as well as the waters themselves.

The largest Roman towns sheltered populations that exceeded 100,000, and lesser towns readily reached 40,000 during their heyday in the third century. Londinium, a distant provincial capital with a population of hardly 30,000 at its peak and probably very much less, was half the size of the modern City of London, and covered 330 acres (134 ha); Venta Belgarum and Durovernum Cantiacorum reached about 130 acres (53 ha), but 80–90 acres (33–6 ha), the size of Ratae Coritanorum, was the norm. These sizes are similar to those of the towns of Roman Gaul. The greatest English towns of the Middle Ages, by distinction, were eclipsed in both size and population by what the Continent would show, London and Norwich apart.[3]

These planned, large-scale Roman settlements were quite alien in form to what had gone before, even though their purpose was in many ways similar. (fig. 18) The Romans gave them walls and forts for defence; strong gateways for entrances; markets, shops and warehouses for manufacturing and commerce; basilicas and public squares for justice and administration; temples and shrines for religion; baths and theatres for entertainment; as well as apartments and houses for the inhabitants. All this they did within the confines of carefully laid-out streets that imposed order on the buildings and put them into an easily comprehensible context.[4]

The recall of the legions in 410 fatally weakened this unrivalled civilization, and undermined its already failing traditions of building. The collapse and subsequent invasion affected much of western Europe, not just Britain.[5] This collapse was particularly severe in those lands whose waters drained into the Atlantic, leaving the south with more of the past on which to build. Parts of the Mediterranean got off lightly. The Roman population of Phoenician Barcino quickly came to terms with the Visigothic immigrants in what would become Barcelona, and the rule of law and commercial activity continued in a way that was impossible further north. Being an island, Britain was especially vulnerable.

The collapse in Britain shows in the decline of wealth. The Anglo-Saxon seaborne invasions brought chronic poverty. A crude measure of this is population. The Roman population of Britain, which, at its greatest, amounted to some 3 or 4 million,[6] had fallen to around 1½ to 2 million by 1086, the time of the Domesday Survey,[7] with Wales and Scotland adding perhaps 200,000 or 300,000 more. All this was despite the immigrant Anglo-Saxons, then Danes and Norsemen, and, finally, a scattering of Norman lords. The causes of this depopulation are not hard to find. Violence was one, but not as important as the more insidious social and economic causes of mortality. The Roman economy was ruined, together with the political stability that supported its concomitant high standard of civic and domestic hygiene.

Even where occupation remained unbroken and the old Romano-British character merged into Anglo-Saxon, as perhaps it did at Abingdon,[8] the basis of urban life failed. Vanished markets took away the incentive to repair the breaches made by disrupted cultivation, broken tradition and the ignorance of newcomers. Production fell; so did productivity. This hardly mattered: demand had fallen. Writing from a briefly peaceful vantage point in the middle of the sixth-century, the British historian Gildas recalled in his *De Excidio et Conquestu Britanniæ* twenty-eight cities in Roman Britain, all in ruins.[9] Those inhabitants who remained in the twenty-one major Roman towns were no more than camping in them. Much the same happened elsewhere north of the Alps: until the eighth century, Vienna was little more than a camp site measuring 220 by 550 yards (200 by 500 m), and the Roman walls of Cologne surrounded a group of farmsteads.[10] When these old Roman towns revived, as some like Canterbury and Eboracum soon did, and when new ones were founded in the following centuries, King Alfred's burhs, for instance, and the Danish Five Boroughs of the eastern Midlands, they took a long time to reach the size and importance of their Roman predecessors.

There had to be a fresh start. When it came, the new order, brought by the sword of invaders and, later, by the steadying hand of the Christian Church, set off in a very different direction. The Anglo-Saxon immigrants from northern Germany and Denmark were agriculturalists. They traded by barter, not money. They lived in villages, not towns. Even so, the Roman legacy of urbanism was not entirely lost with the failure of their rule, as was the legacy of their rural villas. Reflecting the troubled times, many of the first medieval towns started life as military strongholds, but then followed the direction of Civvy Street with mints providing new coins to further their trade. A different route could be taken when, in later times, a town's foundation was initiated or augmented by the presence of a religious house, a likely event when worldly Benedictine monks were at hand, though hardly at all when the monks were the solitary Cistercians of the twelfth century.

Finally, there were the remains of the abandoned Roman towns: these did not simply vanish with the legions; most of them were eventually reoccupied, although in a very different way. Thus Durnovaria was re-founded as modern Dorchester, Camulodunum as Colchester, Lindum as Lincoln, Glevum as Gloucester, Corinium Dobunnorum as Cirencester, Aquae Sulis as Bath, Ratae Coritanorum as Leicester, and so on. Many of their new names end in a corruption of the Latin *castrum*, as a reminder of their Roman origin, regardless of whether they had military connotations or not; in Wales, similarly, they have the prefix *caer* as in Caernarfon, Caerwent and Cardiff (Caerdydd). Scotland missed out. The Romans had marched all round the Highlands during the long days of summer, tempting the natives to engage in pitched battle, but, after their first exuberant advance and attempted settlement of the lowlands, they preferred not to stay over winter and did not found any towns there to inspire the future.

At first the early invaders were confined to the eastern half of England. This, in the account given by the ninth-century monk Nennius in his *Historia Britonum*, came about at the start of the sixth century, perhaps in the year 516, through King Arthur's final defeat of the Anglo-Saxons at Mount Badon. This event, whether it really happened or not, became a potent symbol for the future. Arthur (fig. 19), successor and perhaps nephew of the Roman Ambrosius, himself reputedly a descendent of the great Constantine, kept alive the old civilization and defended the Christian faith which had been brought to Britain, according to legend, by Joseph of Arimathea, together with the Holy Grail. Thus, through his claim to Roman blood and Christian faith, Arthur became the bridge spanning past and posterity – a kind of lay pontifex. Thanks to Nennius and, three hundred years later, to the authority of William of Malmesbury,

Arthur's memory lived on, his deeds now shining forth all the more brightly in the fitful light of legend. Geoffrey of Monmouth's account of his revered life[11] led eventually to Malory's fabulous *Morte d'Arthur*, printed by Caxton in 1485, a timely publication all set to legitimize the future Tudor dynasty.

Despite Arthur's twelve victories, which allowed the west to remain largely British for at least a generation, the new English were pressing on again well before the sixth century was out, eventually to establish their seven kingdoms, known as the Heptarchy. That split the British between the West Country, Wales and Cumbria, the last of which became part of the Scottish kingdom of Strathclyde.

The new English settlements achieved a certain stability, and this brought a revival of trade, of wealth, and of towns. In their wake came Christian missionaries, but the holy men were unable to convert all rulers and to stop the rivalry between the new petty English kingdoms, which often led to skirmishing and war, to saintly martyrdom, and in the goodness of time – of course – the just destruction of heathen tyrants.[12] As a result, towns were razed, but, equally, they were founded for the strategic purpose of defending and stabilizing territory. These towns, some new, others Roman revived, symbolize the slow beginnings of British regeneration. Their existence might result from the gradual enlargement of a small settlement, or a conscious act of planning, or indeed from the two processes overlapping; but some of these defended settlements, like the earlier Roman *castra*, did not necessarily become towns at all in the fullest sense of the word.

Kent led the revival. About 430 the British leader Vortigern had decided to enlist Saxon mercenaries to engage invading Picts and Scots. The cost was north-east Kent. It became the fief of their leader, Hengist. He eventually rebelled and founded a separate kingdom named after the Cantiae, its ancient inhabitants. The *Anglo-Saxon Chronicle* for 473 records that the Britons of Kent 'fled from the English like fire', and so they may have done, but Kent was soon to prosper.[13]

The rich agricultural land around the North Downs encouraged settlement: trade exploited the proximity of the sea, abetted by navigable rivers and the short crossing to France. While Roman Durovernum fell to pieces, Hengist's mercenaries started its reconstruction as Canterbury – the borough of the Cantiae – by building *Grubenhäuser*.[14] (fig. 20) This common, imported Germanic form of sunken-featured building could, like Iron Age round houses, be put to any use, whether it be domestic, industrial or agricultural. If this were an unpromising start for a capital city, within a century the old standards of wealth, based on the twin pillars of political power and trade, did re-emerge. Already, by the end of the sixth century, regeneration was so advanced that, though Kent was hardly more than a promontory of a small offshore European island, its powerful King Ethelbert could make a politically advantageous marriage to the Christian Princess Bertha, whose father, Charibert, was the king of the Franks, north-west Europe's most powerful and wealthy people. The marriage led to St Augustine's mission in 597, confirmation of Kent's prime importance to Pope Gregory's desire to establish the Christian Church in Britain as a dependency of Rome.[15]

Money, as well as ritual, is crucial to the promotion of faith, as the Church fully realized. (fig. 21) Canterbury minted Britain's first silver pennies, and in the seventh century was minting gold coins as well. Trade, the circulation of currency and the foundation of new towns made increasing progress in the footsteps of Christianity. All over England new towns bear witness to this, although progress was neither speedy nor assured. Within a decade of Augustine's arrival, Bede records,[16] Ethelbert had founded cathedrals in Rochester and London, and these would eventu-

19. King Arthur, depicted on the Winchester Round Table. This representation was probably painted in 1516 to resemble Henry VIII as a means of reinforcing the Tudor succession as British monarchs and defenders of the faith. From a photograph by R. K. Vincent jnr, in Biddle 2000, Pl. XXIII. © Winchester Excavations Committee

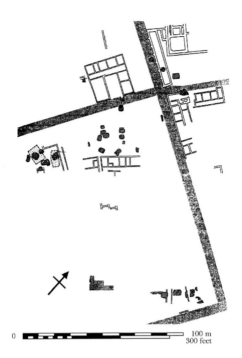

20. Canterbury. Plan of the Marlowe Theatre and adjacent sites, excavated between 1960 and 1982, showing part of the Roman road pattern (shaded), the remains of rectangular Roman buildings, including a large town house to the west of the crossroads (top), and, hatched, over thirty *Grubenhäuser*. After a plan published in Canterbury Archaeological Trust 1982–3, p. 11. © Canterbury Archaeological Trust

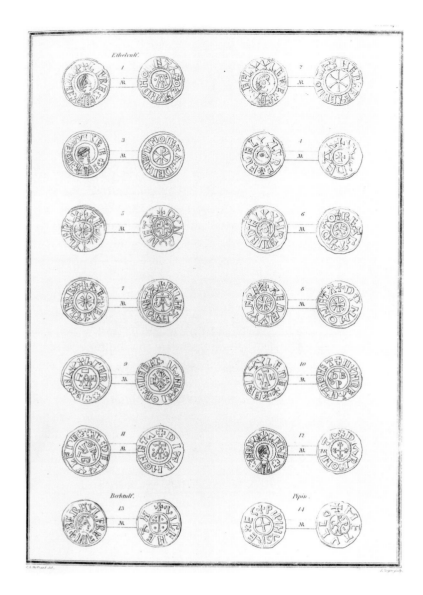

21. Anglo-Saxon coins from a hoard found at Dorking in 1817, now deposited in the British Museum: silver pennies, obverse and reverse, of Ethelwulf, king of Wessex and Kent (d. 858); of Beorhtwulf, king of Mercia (d. 852) (bottom, left); and of Pepin the Short, king of the Franks (d. 768). From Taylor Combe 1821, Pl. 10. © Society of Antiquaries of London

ally open the way to trade in people and ideas as well as goods. Yet, for a while, the old Roman City of London in its revived form was a centre for religion and administration, not trade, this finding a new site upstream. Early in the tenth century these circumstances had changed: Canterbury then boasted seven mints, four the king's and three the Church's, and there were three more in Rochester; but London now did better with eight mints.[17] Closer to home, one of the early archbishops of Canterbury founded the new town of Fordwich, first documented in 675, to serve as Canterbury's port at the limit of navigation on the Great Stour.[18]

Possibly the Church attracted royalty, or possibly royalty attracted the Church, but either way, by the middle of the eighth century Northampton had come into being with a remarkable timber building of palatial magnitude. More remarkably, this was rebuilt in stone a century later, but in what circumstances and with what consequences it is impossible yet to say in this time of, at best, muddled and partial record.[19]

In the north, Christianity revived Eboracum. It had been the seat of a Roman bishop as early as 314, and perhaps this stirred Paulinus on his mission to Northumbria to baptize King Edwin there in its first church in 627.[20] So York became a royal capital, retaining the old Roman name for its ecclesiastical role right up to the present. It was to be the seat of a bishop, and from 735 of an archbishop who would claim the North and even Strathclyde for his see. A monastery was founded here, soon to be a centre of learning famed throughout Europe, thanks to its most celebrated son Alcuin, who became Charlemagne's mentor.[21]

The arrival of monastic communities, which spread Christianity throughout the land, provided another stimulus, though less certain. About 700 the all-powerful King Ine of Wessex founded – more probably re-founded – Glastonbury Abbey, surely recognizing the site's 'venerable marks of antiquity', which struck Daniel Defoe 'with some unusual awe' a millennium later.[22] Its monks believed it to be the oldest monastery in the land, with the first church too, the *Vetusta Ecclesia*, or so they persuaded William of Malmesbury in the 1120s. And had not Joseph of Arimathea brought the Holy Grail here in Roman times, and founded a Christian settlement? Was this not Avalon, the burial place of King Arthur? Out of legend was created not just an abbey, with all the necessary means of validating its status and interests, but a living town, and on this legend it still thrives.[23]

Much Wenlock, by contrast, may originate in St Mildburga's foundation of a convent there about 680, encouraged by an already existing settlement. She worked miracles, but these did not embrace the foundation of towns; the Danes destroyed her convent some two hundred years later, and it was not until about 1079 when the powerful Norman lord Roger de Montgomery re-founded the house as a Cluniac priory that the town began to develop, and it received its charter as a borough only in 1468.[24] By then the settlement was flourishing in a modest sort of way, as its surviving medieval houses demonstrate.[25]

Ports were vital to trade, particularly since most goods travelled more easily by water than land. Kent soon had several around its long coastline, including Dover, the old Roman Portus Dubris. Where there were none, a rich hinterland or a flourishing industry would make a new one imperative. By the middle of the seventh century, if not before, the thriving kingdom of East Anglia had Ipswich.[26] Its sheltered site at the head of the broad Orwell estuary had attracted small settlements in the past, including a Roman villa, but never a town. So Ipswich became the first English town to take root without a Roman predecessor. At first there was a small settlement by Stoke Bridge, built up with a number of *Grubenhäuser*, and in the ninth century a grid of streets was laid to the north. Ipswich pottery was a valued speciality, and this was exported to the whole of eastern England and across the North Sea. Goods were shipped to and from the Continental estuaries – the Rhine, Somme and Seine – and foreign traders established themselves here, as they did wherever a profit made their presence worthwhile. Soon Ipswich had joined the ten greatest Saxon towns, and encouraged the foundation of several more new towns on the back of trade.

By the eighth century, London was once again 'a trading centre for many nations who visit it by land and sea', as Bede recounted.[27] The old Roman City still lay prostrate, even though its walls sheltered Ethelbert's episcopal church of St Paul's, a bishop's palace, and possibly a royal palace as well; this was Lundenburh. Beyond, on the further side of the river Fleet, new settlements were humming with business. These lay on the northern bank of the Thames around the modern Covent Garden, where the Strand connects the City to Westminster. They are probably commemorated in the name Aldwych, or old *wyc* (a trading post), hence the other London – Lundenwyc.[28] It was nevertheless a small business by the European standards of such cities as Naples and Paris, and it had a trading rival on the south coast.

This was Hamwic, which perhaps King Ine had founded about 700 on a strategic site beside the river Itchen and opposite the Roman Clausentum. (fig. 22) Like the Orwell estuary, this was an ideal place for an entrepôt, and far closer to France. Hamwic became one of Saxon England's wealthiest towns, and indeed one of Europe's leading trading centres, with goods going up to Mercia as well as across the sea. Beside the river a rectilinear pattern of streets, the first evidence of planning since Roman times, filled some 104–29 acres (42–52 ha), making it well above the average size of Britain's Roman towns. This was no Roman town, however, for the streets gave access to a complex sequence of *Grubenhäuser*. By the end of the eighth century the town had a population of at least 4,000, many of them foreign merchants. Business and local industries brought the construction of several larger buildings rather like those found at Dorestad in Holland, which had a similarly large mercantile population.[29]

Trade was equally vital to York. The Anglian city grew up around three interdependent centres: firstly the old Roman fortress of Eboracum, where the royal minster was sited; secondly the monastery, apparently sited in the suburb of Micklegate on the further side of the river Ouse, which had been the old Roman *colonia*; and thirdly Fishergate, to the east of the confluence of the Ouse and the Foss, which became the commercial heart of the new Eoforwic. (fig. 23) Probably subservient to the authority of the minster, but equally protected by it, trade flour-

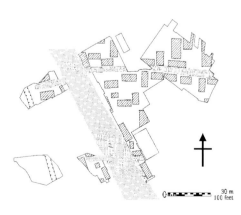

22. Hamwic, Southampton. Plan of excavations at Six Dials between 1977 and 1986, showing part of Saxon Hamwic, including the remains of thirty-six timber buildings (shown hatched), aligned along a street and two lanes (stippled). After *Medieval Archaeol.* 31 (1987), 137–9, fig. 2. © Society for Medieval Archaeology

30 m
100 feet

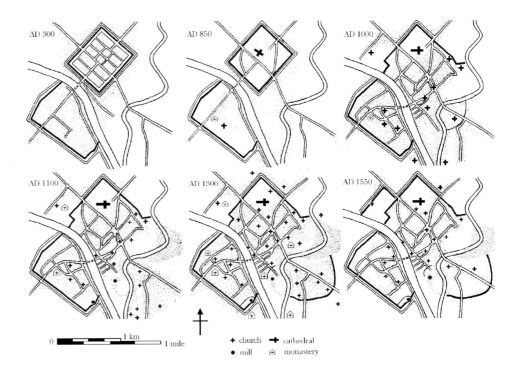

23. York. Plans showing (left to right, top to bottom): Roman Eboracum in AD 300 with its *colonia* across the river Ouse to the south-west, their built-up areas shown stippled; the cathedral in AD 850 amid the decaying road pattern, with a church and a monastery in the former *colonia*; the progressive development of the two areas with a proliferation of roads, churches and religious houses between AD 1000 and 1300, the construction of two castles, and the extension of the city south-eastwards along Fishergate towards the junction of the two rivers; and, finally, by 1550 the contraction of the city and the loss of its monasteries as a result of pestilence, economic depression and the Dissolution. After plans by Kate Biggs in Hall 1996, fig. 15. © York Archaeological Trust

ished here. Thanks to its strategic siting beside road and river routes leading across the Vale of York and to the sea, Eoforwic came to rival Lundenwic, Hamwic and Ipswich, and similar centres across the North Sea such as Dorestad, and Ribe in Jutland.[30] There was a colony of Frisian merchants here in the early ninth century, tempted by the trade in metal, glass, luxuries, leather, bone, cloth, wooden goods and pottery.[31]

The spread of Christianity in the seventh century brought murder and mayhem as well as piety, as Bede recounted in his *History*. Worse was to come. In 787, the *Anglo-Saxon Chronicle* records the first Scandinavian raid, and raids continued sporadically, but lethally for several of the new English settlements, as violent bands of Danes, Norsemen and Vikings despoiled the land for booty. Then, in 865, conquest and colonization became the main purpose of the Danes. Once again, political boundaries were established only to be redrawn after furious bouts of warfare.

At first the Danish conquests brought more destruction than construction, but, in promoting the power of the great Alfred, king of the West Saxons, they instigated such diverse long-term achievements as the foundation of the English navy and the revival of education and learning, which the early raids had greatly depressed. Alfred taught himself Latin, believing the Latin culture of the previous century to be the highest achievement of learned endeavour, and his own translations into the vulgate spread learning from the Church into a rather wider society.[32] As importantly, he set up a system of local defence based on fortified strongholds or burhs, which both served Wessex well and promoted the cause of urban life.

Meanwhile, in 866–7 York was attacked and fell to a 'great army' of Vikings, subsequently picking itself up to become Jorvik, the capital of their northern kingdom. Similarly the advantages of Hamwic tempted the Vikings, and their seaborne raids began to decimate European trade. Hamwic's days were numbered, as were Dorestad's. The Danish conquests which followed ruined monasteries and destroyed their learning, and pillaged towns and wrecked their trade, but at once gave them a new strategic importance. This did not save Hamwic as it did York, but it did promote Winchester.

Winchester, like Canterbury, had, as Venta Belgarum, been the capital of a flourishing Roman *civitas*, with a grid of streets set within a rectangle of stone walls. It, too, decayed in the fifth century. The Roman south gate collapsed, leaving what little traffic that went that way simply to push through the rubble. Early in the seventh century Wintanceaster, as it became, seems to have achieved enough importance as a local centre of authority for a new south gate to be constructed, just to the west of the old one. Attracted, the Church in 635 duly sent a missionary, Birinus, to convert Wessex. He was successful and became bishop of Dorchester-on-

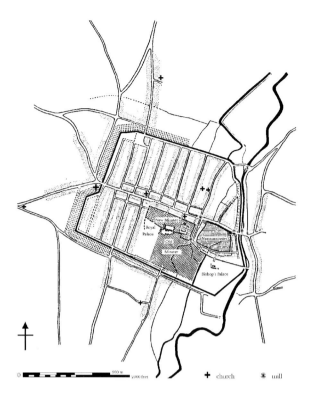

24. Winchester. Plan of the town in the early eleventh century. A new grid of streets fills the area within the old Roman walls, and already these are built up with houses (stippled), and yet more houses line the suburban streets outside the walls. The south-eastern segment (hatched), meanwhile, is the royal and episcopal quarter. After Biddle (ed.) 1976, fig. 25. © Winchester Excavations Committee

25. Wallingford. A winter view looking north of the south-western sector of Kine Croft, *c.* 1890, showing part of the Saxon embanked defences surrounding the town; the three-storeyed house (Stone Hall) faces on to High Street, a short way to the right of the site of West Gate, and beyond it lies an even larger open space. The centre of the town is out of the view to the right. Leafless trees are growing out of the ditch formed by digging the embankment. © Oxfordshire County Council Photographic Archive

Thames, eventually dying there. However, both the immense see and his body were transferred to Winchester, which in 660 became the seat of Bishop Wine, and boasted a minster. Eventually it became the administrative centre of Hampshire. This role it apparently took from Hamwic, or Hamtun to use its alternative name, after which Hamtunscire or Hampshire, England's first recorded county, was named. So Winchester's political and ecclesiastical *raison d'être* became ever more distinct from Hamwic's trade.

Even so, the Vikings found it hardly less tempting. In 860 they attacked. The long-term consequences ensured Winchester's future as the greatest of the Anglo-Saxon burhs and, later, as the capital of all England. The Roman walls were repaired and built up, and the town was defended in earnest. (fig. 24) A new High Street was laid out, starting at the Roman west gate, but on a slightly different alignment from the Roman street, to reach the river Itchen near where the Roman bridge had been. Back lanes ran parallel to the High Street, a significant change implying a new form of land holding with an attendant new pattern of building; and perpendicularly across these were laid a series of streets that gave Winchester its second grid in a thousand years. As in Roman times, this filled most of the town, albeit with a different shape. Only the south-eastern quarter was excluded, and this was given over to buildings that served the burh's political and ecclesiastical needs: a palace, a mint, a minster and religious houses.[33] By the powerful Æthelstan's time, the city had six mints, a sign of prosperity putting it third in the Saxon league.[34] So Winchester eventually became the jewel in the Wessex crown, even though the *Anglo-Saxon Chronicle* only records Alfred's having made a single visit – in 896.

The tenth-century Anglo-Saxon document known as the Burghal Hidage lists thirty-one burhs which Alfred the Great founded, or at least inspired, before his death in 899.[35] They formed a defensive bulwark along the Thames and to its south, protecting Wessex against the Danes, and, in Devon, against the British. They stretch from Lympne and Lewes in the east to Exeter, Totnes, Lydford and Barnstaple in the west, with London, Windsor, Wallingford, Oxford and Malmsbury facing north. Many were fortified with rectangular earthworks on the pattern of Winchester, making use of either the remains of Roman walls or what their builders understood Roman defences to have been. Of these, Wallingford was second only to Winchester. (fig. 25) It lies on the west bank of the Thames, a short way upstream from the Goring Gap, and thus could block the route to Danes driving westwards. A great earthen bank, much of which survives, was thrown up to enclose a rectangle, which was then quartered by streets. The open space in the south-western quarter, known today as Kine Croft, since it has

26. Queenhithe, the City of London's first wet dock, photographed at low tide in 1967, then still serving as a dock and overlooked by nineteenth-century warehouses (now all rebuilt for a different use) which were separated by lanes running down to the river from Thames Street

served as a pasture from time immemorial, was probably designed equally as a refuge for local communities if the Danes threatened.[36]

Lewes and Shaftsbury, two more of Alfred's burhs, are sited on commanding spurs, one overlooking the Sussex Ouse, the other the Vale of Blackmoor. They were also well sited for trade, and would soon have two mints each.[37] In 880 Alfred uniquely favoured Shaftsbury by giving his daughter Æthelgiva as its first abbess to the Benedictine house he founded there. She ensured the political stability of the burh and laid the foundations of her abbey's economic success: the nuns would become the richest in England.

More importantly, Alfred took London from the Danes in 886 and reformed it as a burh. Its Roman walls became the basis for his revived stronghold, which successfully withstood the Danes in 994, 1009 and 1014. The old Lundenwic had decayed, and trade now reverted to the City, which became the entrepôt for landlocked Mercia. The small wet dock of Queenhithe, (fig. 26) first recorded as Ætheredseshyd in 889, served this revived trade, both up and down river, until a new London Bridge was constructed downstream, thus requiring a new dock at New Fresh Wharf, further downstream still. The bridge was designed to block invasion fleets penetrating up river, as occurred in 994 when Viking ships were stopped dead in the water, as well as to restore communications and bring Southwark within the defended perimeter.[38] (fig. 27) Only now could London regain its former lead to outstretch by far other British towns in size.

27. Medieval London Bridge. John Nordern's view from the east of 1597–8; this shows not the Anglo-Saxon bridge, nor the repulse of a Viking fleet, but the point is nevertheless clear. © Museum of London

The *Anglo-Saxon Chronicle* mentions a good twenty further burhs that were established in the first two decades of the tenth century by another of Alfred's daughters, Æthelflaed of Mercia, and by his son and successor, Edward the Elder. Chester and Runcorn guarded the north; Bridgenorth, Ludlow, Hereford and Gloucester guarded the west; while Stafford, Tamworth and Warwick faced the Danelaw further east. With the Danes' retreat, Edward was finally creating or redefending burhs as far apart as Manchester and Bakewell in the north, Stamford in the east, and Hertford and Maldon in the south.[39] Once again, several were resurrected Roman towns, such as Manchester, Exeter and Towcester, but most were not, and several of their names have the suffix 'bury' instead, signifying their burghal origin. Likewise the five burhs of the Danelaw: Leicester and Lincoln were formerly Roman, as were their bases at Cambridge and Colchester, but Derby, Nottingham and Stamford were new, and so was their base at Huntingdon, although there had been Roman settlements nearby.

The Scandinavian lords of Jorvik set up a new trading centre in Coppergate to take the place of the abandoned Fishergate. This practically virgin site was carefully set out with defined building plots, many of whose boundaries survive today. These were closely built up with houses and workshops and became the home of numerous craft skills, particularly in leather, glass and metals. Gold and silver were made into jewellery, as were jet and amber, while silk and leather were worked into clothing. The manufacture of household goods was important enough to be recalled by the name of Coppergate, 'koppari' being Old Norse for cup-maker, 'gate' for street. Jorvik entered a golden age of prosperity, becoming, after London, England's second city. Political changes there were, mainly caused by the inability of the Anglo-Saxons of Wessex to co-exist with the Danes and Scandinavians of the north. But Jorvik survived its loss of independence in the tenth century and continued to thrive, as it would do once again after 1066.[40]

The establishment of a burh was strictly for the protection of political power. Expediency often saddled an earlier trading centre with the trappings of a burh, and when this was not the case, trade soon arrived to serve its inhabitants. Even so, several burhs never became full towns, a reminder that this was not their purpose. A small number, a few with unplaceable names such as Bremesburh and Scergeat, were presumably weaklings and fell to oblivion, while rather more – Chirbury, Eddisbury, Thelwall – never reached urban status. Portchester, for all its Roman origin and resurrection as a Wessex burh, succumbed to better-sited competition from both Portsmouth and Fareham. Lydford developed strongly with a mint, and Burpham, one of Alfred's Sussex burhs, similarly developed as a port; both kept going, Lydford indeed until well after the Conquest, only to fail, leaving their archaeological record and proud churches as lone witnesses to the magnificence of their past.[41] (fig. 28)

Long before that, the great Hamwic had failed. During the early years of the tenth century, its harried inhabitants removed to a new, higher and more readily defensible site, overlooking the river Test. But their new Southampton remained a backwater and had to await the Norman Conquest before it would flourish. The history of Romney is more peaceful than Hamwic's. Old Romney's port, close to the mouth of the sluggish river Rother, silted up and became unusable. By 960 this had led to the foundation of New Romney, by the receding sea some two miles (3 km) to the east. A long grid of streets was laid out alongside the estuary, and the town flourished well enough to need its own mint.[42]

Two of England's greatest medieval towns emerged during this period of late Saxon prosperity – Bristol and Norwich. Bristol, like London, grew up on an obvious site for a town, one that, somehow, the Romans missed. Its name is a corruption of bridge-stow, the place of the bridge, over the river Avon, so it was at once the hub of overland routes connecting the western Midlands with the West Country and a port for boats using the Avon and its tributary, the Frome, and equally the Severn and the route to the sea down the Bristol Channel. Bristol's gain was Cirencester's loss: the latter lay at the crossing of the old Roman Ermine Way and Foss Way, but it gained little from the river Churn that piddled through the town on its way to the headwaters of the Thames. Bristol, meanwhile, looked to Europe's Atlantic coast, to the Mediterranean, and eventually to Africa, India and America.

28. Lydford. Plan, showing the defensive nature of the site on a promontory set between the river Lydd and a tributary, with an earthen bank completing the scheme on the north side; the main street is crossed by lanes to form irregular *insulae*. The stippled areas have been excavated. After Radford 1970, fig. 35. © Society for Medieval Archaeology

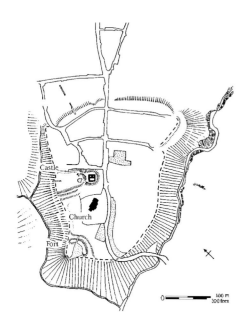

Norwich never looked that far, but it took what the older Thetford once had. At the time of Domesday Thetford had a population of over 4,000; it was first mentioned in 869 as a wintering place of the Danish army, then grew on trade via the Little Ouse with the Wash ports and the North Sea. There was a mint already in Edgar's reign, and about 1071 the East Anglian see was transferred here from Elmham.[43] This marked the height of its fortune, decline setting in after Norwich took the see in 1094. The population fell and never reached its old level until after the Second World War.[44]

Norwich had a better site: favourably astride a crossing of Roman roads as well as the river Wensum, it had access to both Norfolk's wealth and the North Sea at Great Yarmouth. Already established by the sixth century on the gravel terraces flanking the river, two small sites, one at Westwic and the other at Coslany, merged to become a substantial settlement by the eighth century. For some unexplained reason it was only in the period of Danish control in the late ninth century that Norwich at last grew into a town. As well as holding a flourishing market, it minted coins, those of Æthelstan being inscribed 'Norvic', the first appearance of the name. This referred to another settlement on the north side of the Wensum that, perhaps, subsumed the other two. By then there were timber wharves along the river front at Fishergate, soon to be joined by others on the south side of the river. On the eve of the Conquest these were served by timber warehouses and workshops and a large market at Tombland, making the town the third largest on the east coast after London and York, its trade extending to the Continent, particularly the Rhine and Scandinavia. With a population of probably 7,500 it was way ahead of Thetford and all set to grow further.[45]

Political power, the establishment of the Church and the growth of trade were inextricably mixed together in the foundation and development of these towns. King Edgar's confirmation in 972 of Oundle's right to hold markets, the first record of the town's existence, could have been motivated as much by a desire to improve his local political support through granting favours as to improve his finances through taxation.

With the reconquest of the Danelaw, the kings of Wessex used every means to extend their authority. One of these was through the Church. Edgar himself is the most likely royal sponsor of the mid-tenth-century reforms that removed churches from the control of unreliable aristocratic Wessex families, who counted on them as a source of profit, and put at their head the saintly Benedictine monks Oswald, Æthelwold and wily Dunstan. Winchester's canons and eventually the entire English episcopate were replaced by Benedictines, establishing both the monastic duality of English cathedrals and the loyalty of the Church in England to the Crown. Edgar gained the blessing of the pope and in 973 was crowned by Archbishop Dunstan at Bath. During the ceremony Dunstan anointed Edgar, a significant ritual usually reserved for the consecration of a priest. If this symbolized the power of the Church over secular rulers, it also raised Edgar above other British rulers, who, duly impressed, assembled before him at Chester and acknowledged his supremacy.[46]

One great advantage that the reforms gave to the Church was greater control over its economic affairs. Abbot Wulsin VI of St Albans speculated in urban development by diverting the old Watling Street, which ran through Roman Verulamium, leading it eastwards across the river to his abbey gate and then back to its old course, nearly a mile (1.5 km) from where the diversion began. Two new churches marked the start and finish of the diversion, and a third church marked a new triangular market place laid out to the north-east of the abbey. As an enticement, he offered free timber to all who would build themselves houses on his new streets.[47]

Nowhere was the secular power of the Church greater than in Durham: its bishop, at once its secular prince, wielded vice-regal power, so crucial was the need to present a strong face towards the north and Scotland. The rocky crag rising from a tight bend in the river Wear on which Durham lies was more readily defensible than the old settlement at Elvet, a necessary consideration in the troubled north. In 995 St Cuthbert's body was brought there, and three years later Bishop Alhun consecrated a great new stone church as a shrine. At the same time, a new town grew up, just to the north, complete with accommodation for leather workers and a market place to serve the region's economic needs.[48] (fig. 29)

The credit for founding a town before the Conquest very much depends on the authorship, Church or Crown, of the surviving record, just as it was for the foundation of monasteries.

29. Durham. The bishop's castle and cathedral seen from the river Wear and Framwellgate Bridge

Dunstan, Oswald and Æthelwold are recorded both as notable church builders and promoters of towns, Æthelwold physically – and nearly losing his life in the process – at Abingdon Abbey; but so too are the kings Edgar, Cnut and Edward the Confessor. The ultimate responsibility for Peterborough and Bury St Edmunds may be an open question in an age of sparse records, but an economic alliance of royal power and ecclesiastical zeal is probably the likely answer.[49]

Either way, trade was the great temptress. The Domesday Survey records over seventy-five bakers, brewers, tailors, launderers, cobblers, robe-makers, cooks, porters and intendants, all serving the everyday needs of the great abbey at Bury St Edmunds in 1086. Trade was flourishing to such an extent that the abbot was planning to double the size of the town so as to gain from the augmented rents he could charge. Long before the Conquest, abbeys brought trade on an encouraging scale. This was increasingly the rule in the comparatively settled conditions of the late Saxon period, which reduced mortality and allowed the population to rise. The monastic reform gave religious houses new opportunities of exploiting the land by setting up agricultural granges; more hands in the fields reaped greater harvests, and found a market for them in town.

2

New masters in ancient places

Norman and Angevin England

After the Conquest, economic activity struck out at a greater pace, thanks to the Norman settlement.[1] The vigour of William's new regime ensured that the lowlands of the south, the Midlands and east became rich and populous, as they had been in Roman Britain. Similarly, the bleaker and more barren northern and western fringes lagged behind, except where special circumstances prompted unusual development. The Normans fully understood the value of towns from their long sojourn in France, and William himself had already founded two boroughs at Caen. In England and, soon, in Wales too, both Crown and Church were at work promoting new foundations, and, above all, so were Norman lords. This in turn prompted the Scots to make amends and to start promoting towns of their own.

Of the secular Norman lords who came to England, the most energetic was William's kinsman, Roger de Montgomery, whose name crops up all over England – he gave his Norman name to a castle he built on the Welsh marches, and his descendants played a major role in the colonization of Wales. In the north and west came the Lacys – again, they were active as marcher lords on the Welsh frontier. Almost ubiquitous in southern England, in south Wales and across the sea in Ireland were the Clares, a powerful and extensive family that took its name from a modest borough they founded in Suffolk, and finally gave it to an Irish county and a Cambridge college.

For many of these men, as for the king, the establishment of their temporal power depended on the construction of a castle, and, for its legitimation as well as their salvation, the foundation of a monastery or some other major ecclesiastical establishment. Before the twelfth century was out, some 124 of these joint foundations had been established, the political and administrative means of ordering society thus clearly being seen beside the concrete expression of its ultimate goal in heaven.[2]

These necessary political and administrative objectives were most readily achieved in a town, and, where one was lacking, through the foundation of a new one. There was another simple reason for this: profit. However profitable a rural manor might be, its income depended on what its agriculture could produce. That in turn required either the organization of vast numbers of feudal villeins to work the fields, or the collection of rents from free peasants. The conversion into a town of a space no larger than a corner of an open field, and then one whose fertility or lack of it was immaterial, involved at most the loss of a few acres and of rents amounting to no more than shillings. It provided two welcome sources of greatly augmented income – that from the rent of individual building plots, and that from tolls and dues charged on markets and fairs. A town might fail, but this posed less risk than that of the natural vagaries which constantly threatened harvests. Moreover, the establishment of a successful urban economy stimulated the local rural economy, the two nourishing each other and providing marketable goods in return.[3]

William's thank-offering for victory at Senlac was his foundation of Battle Abbey. The four monks he brought over in 1070 from Marmoutier to set up a monastery on the Wealden ridge overlooking the field of battle were dismayed by the prospect of furze and forest, only relieved by a few homesteads in small clearings. Nevertheless, they vigorously promoted agriculture, both locally and on the six poor manors William had provided as their endowment; moreover,

30.   Battle. Aerial view from the east, showing the site of William's victory over Harold on Senlac Hill (1), the abbey centre on the crest of the hill (2), with the extant gatehouse facing the triangular market place (3), from which High Street (4), lined by typical burgage strips, runs towards the top right-hand corner; Upper Lake lies out of the view below the parish church(5). © National Monuments Record

William granted them the right to hold a Sunday market, free of dues, 'to be entirely under the management of the monastery'; on this basis the town that grew up to the north-west of the abbey gate modestly prospered.[4] (fig. 30)

The majority of the other southern foundations were ports, partly required for maintaining communications with Normandy, partly for shipping goods to and from the region. Hastings was a re-foundation, necessary because the old Saxon burh was already drowning in the English Channel, just as Cnut's foundation of Old Winchelsea was to drown two centuries later. Before that occurred, Old Winchelsea's exposed position prompted the birth of Rye. Like Hastings, Rye was founded by the rich Norman abbey of Fécamp, which owned it in the eleventh century. It was sited on the first inland island rising above the wandering waters that drained the soggy eastern Weald. This was a foretaste of the hilltop site chosen for Edward I's New Winchelsea in 1288, when the sea finally claimed its predecessor.

Then there were Roger de Montgomery's Arundel, which began its slow dispossession of Saxon Burpham, and New Shoreham, which another Norman lord, Philip de Braose, founded after William's death to replace the old borough, whose port on the river Adur was silting up.[5] Further west, Jean de Gisors set about developing his manorial estates in collaboration with Southwick Priory by founding a new chapel in what would become Portsmouth. The inlet of water that surrounded the island of Portsea had all the makings of a fine harbour, a point which Richard I rapidly appreciated: in 1194 he granted the town a charter, formed a dock just to its north, and established his fleet of corsairs there. In 1495 the world's first dry dock was constructed, and the town's naval role has gone from strength to strength ever since.[6]

The decision of the synod of Windsor to move the seats of bishops to towns set the scene for the transfer of the East Anglian see from Elmham to Thetford about 1071, and then in 1094 on to Norwich. Similarly, the seat of the vast midland bishopric which stretched from the Thames to the Humber was moved from its strategic site on the border of the former Wessex and Mercia at Dorchester-on-Thames to Lincoln. This had a new strategic motive since it greatly strengthened the route from London to York in defiance of Danish aggression. New sites for cathedrals disrupted towns and demolished houses, but the political as well as the ecclesiastical advantages brought a financial increment as well as prestige and pilgrims. Norwich and Lincoln soon entered the premier league of English towns.

The post-Conquest rise in population and wealth, for the most part rural and agricultural, promoted the foundation of new boroughs as never before. This process was more obviously continuous than ubiquitous. Despite the arrival of Battle, the Weald of Kent and Sussex remained a wooded wilderness, as it had been in Roman times, until pressure of rising populations in neighbouring regions brought in colonists and eventually a few towns. The New Forest was another wilderness, like the northern stretches of Norfolk, which remained undeveloped, despite the presence of Norwich and the newly founded Lynn.

Mountain and marsh kept their grip on the wastes around the coast and the north and west. Cornwall's windswept land was not a conspicuous asset. Being an earldom with a non-resident lord, what little profit could be gleaned from its poor soil left the region, and its inland markets were pitiful. About 550 – well before the advent of Augustine – the Celtic Saint Petroc's missionary activities in Cornwall had culminated in his foundation of a hermitage on Bodmin Moor. This unlikely association allowed Bodmin to struggle into existence as a poor inland market town. Between the time of the Conquest and the Domesday Survey, the Conqueror's half-brother Robert of Mortain founded Launceston on a steep knoll on the south side of the river Tamar by removing a Saxon market from St Stephen's on the north side, and building a castle both to demonstrate his power and to protect the wealth promoted by the new market at its foot. (fig. 31) The earl had a second go, transferring a market from St Germans to Trematon, but this never took wing.[7]

Fishing and the export of its minerals, mainly tin, nevertheless brought numerous small boroughs to the Cornish coastline, at least one to each estuary, and several more where a sheltered indentation made a suitable haven. Ultimately no county had more boroughs for its size, but they were all very small, their houses of the meanest.

The same was nearly as true of Devon. More successful than most of its boroughs was Tavistock. Its Benedictine abbey, which received a royal charter in 981, eventually became the wealthiest and most powerful in the south-west. The town that grew outside its walls soon matured on the export, down the river Tavy, of the region's agricultural goods, especially wool, and, after the Conquest, of tin. Early in the twelfth century a market and an annual fair were held here, and later the town was incorporated as a borough. It went from strength to strength. In 1305 Tavistock became one of Devon's four 'stannary' towns, named after the stannary court which regulated the manufacture and sale of tin, and its prosperity continued, not just to the end of the Middle Ages, but to the present day.[8]

For all their number, these western ports, even Tavistock, were small business compared with Lynn in East Anglia, (fig. 32) and also with Boston, another foundation on the east coast that

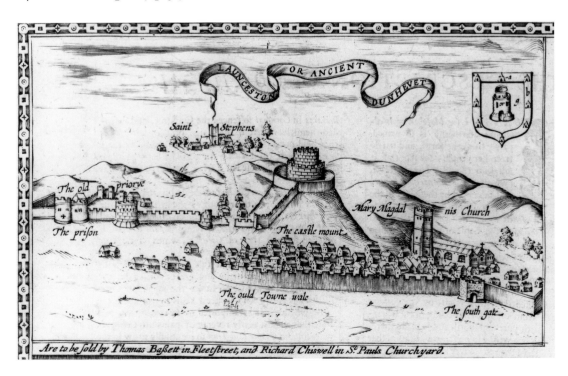

31. Launceston. The castle mound surmounted by a round tower and surrounded by a later stone wall, dominating the town, which lies at its feet. From Speed 1676, vol. I. II. © Society of Antiquaries of London

32. King's Lynn, from William Faden's *Plan of the Town of Lynn* of 1797. Founded by Bishop Herbert de Losinga in the late eleventh century, the original Bishop's Lynn (Lynn comes from 'len', an estuarine lake) comprises the southern half of the town, between the Mill Fleet and the Purfleet, and extended towards the river Ouse only as far as the curved streets (Nelson Street and Queen Street) that mark its former bank. The northern half of the town was founded separately in Bishop Turbe's time (1146–74) with its own market, and extended as far as King Street. The dumping of spoil to extend the quays, and hence the town, westward followed in the later Middle Ages. See V. Parker 1971, 19–29

33. Hull. Speed's bird's-eye view of the port on the west bank of the river Hull to the north of its confluence with the Humber, with a loose grid of streets within the town walls and its huge parish church of Holy Trinity on an island site in the centre. Speed 1676, vol. 1. 41. © Society of Antiquaries of London

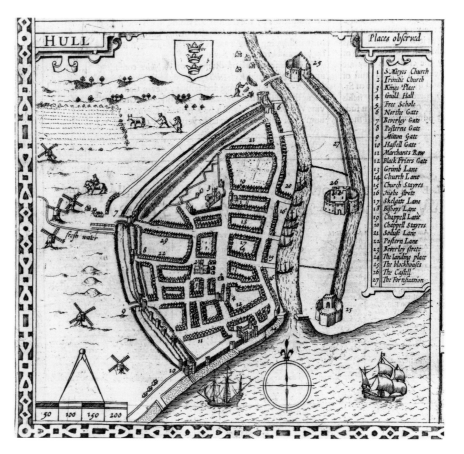

34.   Norwich, from Cuningham's view from the west of 1558. The river Wensum is marked QQ; the town wall and its gates D, I, P, Q, T, V, W, X and L; the cathedral E; the French borough on the site of the Saxon market lies just below the cathedral; the new market EE; the castle on its vast mound CC; King Street runs just below the churches marked FF, GG, HH and KK; the church of St Martin-at-Palace F, with the Plain to the left; the Great Hospital is between E and D. © Norfolk Heritage Centre

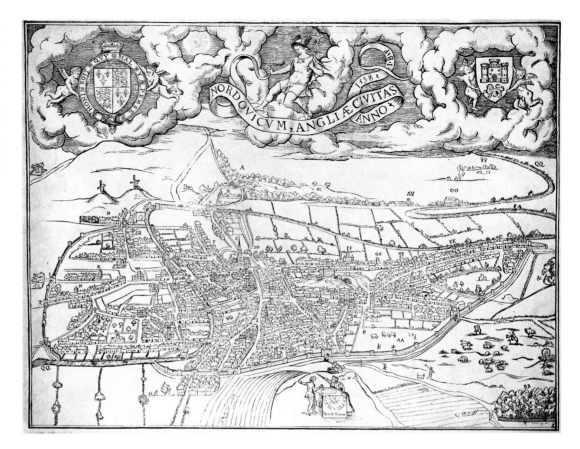

followed the aftermath of the Conquest and was carried to dizzy heights in the thirteenth century, alongside the greatest of Britain's medieval ports.[9] Both grew on the export of corn and wool, as, further north, Kingston upon Hull would do after Edward I had taken over Wyke, one of the few Cistercian promotions, and enlarged it 'to increase the fitness of the port for ships and traffic'. This took time to come into effect: Hull was still 'a meane fischar toune' in Edward III's day, but soon its 'first great increasing' came about 'by passing for fisch into Iseland, from whens they had the hole trade of stoke fisch into England'.[10] (fig. 33)

More evident than these commercial ports in the early days were the strongholds that confirmed William's political control of England. For this reason the Crown played a major role as a founder and developer of English towns before 1100. Even so, Norman lords did better: political control was vital to their existence too, so they built castles, and the payment of rents and tolls from the towns that sprang up below them topped up their feudal coffers.[11]

The Conquest was in the first instance a disaster for the inhabitants of Norwich. (fig. 34) The town suffered the imposition of a castle, probably but not certainly on the site of the present one, which apparently required ninety-eight tenements to be emptied to enable its construction. Preparations were also put in hand for a new cathedral, which required yet more land, causing the old Saxon market at Tombland to be removed to a new site by 1094. The mound of the present castle spread itself further, all these works inaugurating a major centre of provincial government.[12] Consequently, there was a hiatus in Norwich's economy until the city had adjusted to this monumental reorganization of its land, which laid down a pattern that is still recognizable today. The economy then picked up causing Norwich to become England's foremost provincial city, boasting 130 different trades. When its walls rose between 1297 and 1334, they embraced an area significantly larger than the City of London and a population in the region of 10,000–15,000, and by some calculations even as high as 30,000. Statistically more curious were its 52 churches and 365 taverns, no doubt a weekly penance and a daily joy for the bibulous.[13]

The Vale of York suffered the worse disability of being the centre of Danish independence, a threat William could not tolerate. In the winter of 1069–70 he marched on the Vale and laid it waste, destroying Danish power in England once and for all, and securing the strategic route further north. Following this 'harrowing of the north' he gave the land to his allies, William de Percy, Ilbert de Lacy, Hugh fitz Baldric, Roger de Busli and many other powerful lords. They

enforced a policy of resettlement on the peasantry by uprooting them from the Pennines, where they might still have caused trouble, and transplanting them to the ruined lands of the fertile Vale. So the plains, which had borne the brunt of the attack, were the first to revive.[14]

The lords reaped the rewards, and, like Norwich, York became a prosperous provincial capital. (fig. 23) The remains of Roman Eboracum formed the basis for a growing population that eventually spilled out beyond the old eastern limits of Norse Jorvik to fill all the inhabitable land between the rivers Ouse and Foss, and a trading centre grew up on the south bank. The Roman city walls still continued to determine the north-western limits (fig. 35): the old Roman gate became the medieval Bootham Bar, and Petergate, as far as Stonegate, and Southgate, southwards, took the course of former Roman streets. The minster, meanwhile, following the example of Winchester, obliterated the remains of the northern quarter of the old Roman enclosure. To the east William had seen the construction of two mottes each side of the Ouse on the south side of the city – these, as in Norwich, requiring the destruction of numerous houses. Both mottes were devastated by the Danes in September 1069 and then rebuilt before that fateful year was out.[15] York became a bastion against the Scots, and remained so. Edward I's failure to deal with them, as he had succeeded against the Welsh, kept York's military importance alive as the royal head-

35. York. The Multangular Tower of the late third or early fourth century marks the western corner of Roman Eboracum, recalling the polygonal towers of Constantinople's Theodosian wall, and was extended upwards in the thirteenth century

quarters of the northern armies. They continued to feed York's economy past the turn of the thirteenth century until well after the tide began to turn against the Scots in the later fourteenth century. So York prospered from the king's military needs.

Then there was weaving. In the twelfth century York's gild of weavers paid £10 annually to the Crown – a higher sum than any other guild – in return for recognition of its trading privileges within the county. Their cloth was justly famous and in great demand.[16] For much of the time York enjoyed the status of being a staple town, and the town council was dominated by mercers, who took the biggest share of the profits. Competition in the thirteenth century spoiled this trade, as it did for many other towns. But the fourteenth century once again favoured York's cloth industry, which advanced rapidly, particularly during the second quarter of the century. This gave work to more than weavers. Apart from masters, journeymen and apprentices, all sorts of craftsmen flocked into the city in the hope of living off their skills, and with them came traders and all the people who serviced their needs, such as victuallers and bakers and brewers. The influx continued long enough to be recorded as late as 1371. Ten years later, records of those who paid poll tax returns show that there were over 250 craftsmen working in the textile industry in some way or other, as well as a further 164 in leather, and 136 were serving their needs by working in the food trade.

Despite this great thriving community in York, the northern uplands remained poor and empty. The most northerly boroughs, all of them recorded in 1086 as within the county of York, were Penwortham (which defended the Ribble estuary, just west of the later Preston), and Pocklington, Bridlington and Tanshelf (later called Pontefract). Further north, and outside the survey, there were the strongholds of Durham and Newcastle upon Tyne. Beyond them lay Scotland and hostility. York itself had its share of Scotsmen, 'vile and faithless men, or rather rascals'; Chester had a bad name too, 'on account of the desperate Welshmen'.[17]

Apart from York, Chester was the only firm island of wealth in this northern sea of poverty, repeating its Roman past by growing fat on the needs of its garrison. To the south there was Lincoln, now the seat of the immense midland see. Here its first bishop, Remigius, set up within the Roman walls of old Lindum overlooking the commercial settlement to the south, and built himself a great tower – now incorporated within the west front of the cathedral – whose size, shape and position were both strategically ideal and symbolically imbued with a thousand years of conquest and power.[18]

The Domesday Survey recognized 111 boroughs in England between the south coast and Yorkshire and Cheshire, and also included Rhuddlan in north Wales, which was administered from the powerful border town of Chester. Nearly 90 more boroughs had received charters by 1200, and as many again were chartered in the years up to 1334, particularly in the Midlands and north. Meanwhile, some 40 pre-Conquest boroughs had lost their charters, leaving an aggregate of about 240.[19]

As symptomatic of the new prosperity was the foundation of planned towns as opposed to the recognition through the granting of charters to boroughs that had grown piecemeal from lesser settlements. Forty planned towns were founded in England during the sixty-five years between the Conquest and 1130 at a remarkably consistent rate, and nearly half as many again in Wales. These became significantly more successful than later foundations by establishing themselves at the start of a long period of economic growth. There was a marked pause in the number of foundations in the 1130s and, particularly, the 1140s, a consequence of the anarchy of Stephen and Matilda's contested reign, when civil war devastated central England. Recovery was quick, and the old pattern re-emerged until the 1190s. Then, with post-Conquest economic expansion at its greatest, the rate of new foundations nearly doubled and remained high until 1230.[20]

So, what William started, his successors and, even more so, his lords continued. Rufus took possession of Cumbria with the result that Lancaster, Appleby, Church Brough and Carlisle became at once defensive strongholds and centres of commerce. Boroughs sprang up along the eastern routes to the north – Tickhill, Scarborough, Richmond, Durham, Newcastle upon Tyne, Alnmouth. Norman lords established themselves to the north of Hadrian's Wall, particularly the Percys. They had to contend with the Scots, who claimed Northumberland as theirs. Lacking a tradition of founding towns, the Scottish kings quickly learned from the Normans, and produced a pattern of development of their own that was remarkably distinct from that to the south. Moreover, as in Roman times, they were just able to maintain their independence.

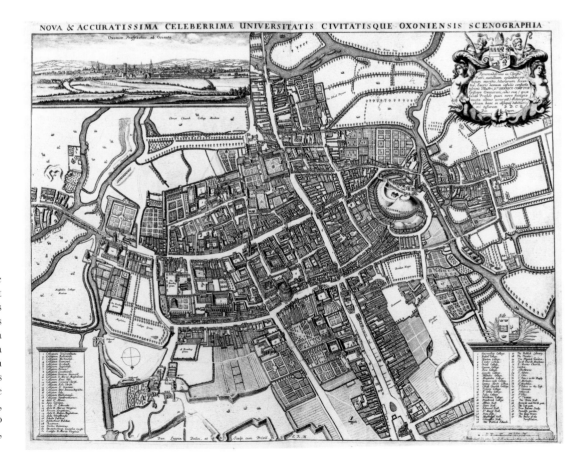

36.   Oxford. Loggan's bird's-eye view from the north of c. 1670, showing the castle to the west (right) with the town walls extending eastwards to embrace four main streets, lined with shops and inns, crossing at the centre (Carfax) and a rough grid of streets based on them, and a further extension eastwards to embrace Merton College, New College and several others (left). Long, thin burgage plots characterize most of the town that is not in university use, particularly the streets that lead out of town to the north, south and west. Loggan 1675, vol. 2, 1. © Society of Antiquaries of London

Their Celtic cousins in Wales, again as in Roman times, were not favoured in this way. They were indisposed towards founding towns, but the Conquest inexorably forced them to adopt English practices, even while they asserted their independence. Like York and Chester, Shrewsbury, Bridgnorth and Ludlow did well as frontier towns. Shrewsbury had succeeded the Roman town of Viroconium, the present village of Wroxeter, which lies five miles downstream; exploiting a strategic loop in the river Severn, it was defended by a castle founded by Roger de Montgomery. Ludlow was laid out in the early twelfth century in the shadow of Roger de Lacy's castle, begun in the 1080s to defend the border. Here the Council of the Marches set up its headquarters.

Two ancient English market towns differed from all others, not because of any advantage in their location or the goods their markets dealt in, but because they became centres of learning. Quasi-monastic institutions devoted to learning had taken root in Italy, where the University of Bologna had come into existence in the eleventh century and could claim 10,000 students within two hundred years. The pleasures of student life spread to France, and from there to England and Scotland: by 1098 Robert of Étampes was lecturing in Oxford, but it was the quarrel between Henry II and Philip Augustus of France in 1167 that closed the doors of Paris University to English students and set Oxford on its path to match town with gown. Students and masters lodged where they might, and a full century elapsed before colleges were founded to house them. (fig. 36)

Cambridge was founded in 1209 after a dispute in Oxford in which two students murdered a prostitute and were consequently seized by the town's officials and hanged. This unwarranted defiance of university privilege sent Oxford's outraged East Anglian students back home to found their own university in a little market town south of the fens and model it on Paris. The two first colleges, Merton in Oxford and Peterhouse in Cambridge, both followed the example of the Sorbonne, the one in 1264, the other in 1284. When in 1347 Mary de St Pol, Countess of Pembroke, founded Pembroke College at Cambridge for thirty scholars, the Royal Licence of foundation barred them in perpetuity from 'drunkenness, taverns, contentiousness, lechery and notable viciousness', and fellows were expected to converse in Latin, or, failing that, in French. Although these and other similar rulings were noticeably ignored, at least by a minority, as indeed they still are, learning took root in both places, competitively, and to such an extent that, long afterwards, one poet, having left the other place, remarked: 'I find Cambridge an asylum, in every sense of the word'.[21]

Both universities were indeed universal, and took in students from all Christendom, not just from England. (fig. 37) While they had an international flavour students from particular countries tended to congregate together in 'nations'. In Oxford the Scots favoured Balliol College, the first of many so-named 'Scots Colleges', but, following Edward I's invasion of their homeland, the Scots abandoned England for their ally, France, and tended to favour Paris. Here in 1326 the bishop of Moray endowed what became the most famous of Scots Colleges for students from his diocese.[22] It would be a hundred years before the Scots had a university of their own.

37. New College, Oxford. A misericord from the chapel stalls (West End 5) carved with a representation of the founder, William of Wykeham, who appears on the left side, welcoming students to the college, centre; meanwhile, graduating students emerge from it, as though from a medieval sausage machine, on the right. © National Monuments Record

3

Beyond the borders of an easy life

Wales and Scotland

Scotland took to urban life slowly. Wales was little quicker: it had only a poor legacy of towns from Roman times, much of it military and a consequence of its generally low economic worth. Like the Roman towns of England, these were all deserted following the recall of the legions. Unlike them, they were not to be reoccupied within a few centuries. It was not a simple matter of poverty. The native Welsh remained steadfastly rural in habit and mind. Only in 921 would military needs give Wales Clwdmouth, its first and only Saxon burh.

This was a false dawn. The Welsh provoked the real dawn by reacting against the Conquest with a series of border raids. Thus began the Anglo-Norman conquest of Wales, an intermittent tussle that lasted for two centuries. The first acquisitions of territory caused towns to be planted along the frontiers as a deliberate policy whose initial purpose was military and administrative. While these towns straddled the boundary between the traditions of the indigenous rural Welsh and the alien urban English, the Welsh began to appreciate their attendant economic and social benefits. They consequently founded a few towns of their own. Nonetheless, most Welsh towns were founded by their conquerors. By the first quarter of the fourteenth century, eighty-four new plantations had given Wales every town it would have before the Industrial Revolution changed their purpose.

About 1073 the earl of Chester replaced Clwdmouth with Twthill, which included a church, market, mills and fisheries as well as a castle; and these, in their turn, Edward I replaced in 1277–80, at the start of his Welsh campaigns, with Rhuddlan.[1] The Norman incursions in Wales required castles for their defence, and planned boroughs were laid out at their gates. The keep which William's close political colleague and companion in arms William FitzOsbern raised at Chepstow between 1067 and 1075 was the first of these, and indeed is the first datable secular building of stone, not just in Wales, but in the whole of Britain. (fig. 38) Its fabric, significantly, appears to make conscious references to Rome through its reuse of stone and tile, probably robbed from Roman Caerwent, a few miles to the west.[2]

Chepstow opened the way to operations further west. In 1081 the Conqueror marched across south Wales, leaving Robert Fitzhamon to begin the construction of a castle over the ruins of Caerwent, the Roman fort at Cardiff, thus founding what became the largest of medieval Welsh boroughs. In a similar way, Cowbridge, Brecon and Builth, Monmouth and Abergavenny were the fruit of this first incursion of Norman lords during the last decades of the eleventh century. Henry I's acquisition of the plains of south-west Wales, and his foundation of Carmarthen in 1109 and, through the agency of a bishop of Salisbury, of Kidwelly, opened the way to west Wales. No castle was greater than Gilbert de Clare's Caerphilly. His ancestors colonized Pembrokeshire, beginning with the reconstruction of Arnulf de Montgomery's castle at Pembroke and the addition of a single broad street below it, all within a curtain wall. (fig. 39) Haverford West was probably their next foundation, and Tenby possibly another,[3] though there may have been a Welsh fishing village here already.

By the middle of the twelfth century the Norman conquest of southern Wales was complete, and military needs were less imperative. The few Welsh landowners who accepted English dominion founded a few boroughs, and possibly three or four more were founded by Welsh

Chepstow Castle belonging to his Grace the Duke of Beauford.

princes in emulation of the invaders.[4] Numerous towns on the south coast and also Newport in Dyfed and Cardigan on the west coast followed, but mid-Wales and the north remained Welsh territory until Edward I's campaigns.[5]

Military needs were less paramount in those parts of Wales further from Norman influence. Nefyn, Dolgellau and Wrexham owe their origin and continued existence to markets. Many of these towns were consequently as unpopulous as their poor rural surroundings, six of them having less than twenty burgesses in the thirteenth century, and twenty of them with less than thirty. Even Dinas Mawddwy, which had thirty-five burgesses in 1393 had been reduced to only fourteen two hundred years later.[6]

The princes of Gwynedd were responsible for encouraging the development of a number of towns that grew up beside their palaces or *maerdrefi*. Llanfaes on Anglesey had grown into a flourishing town by the end of the thirteenth century, with fish-traps along the shore of the Menai Strait, a harbour and a main street leading first to a market square and then on to the parish church, beside which lay the palace. So successful was the town that Edward I would not allow it to continue so close to his new castle of Beaumaris, which, for strategic reasons, he planted where the Llanfaes ferry landed. So he transferred its economic role to the castle and its population to the site of another *maerdref*, Rhosyr, in the south-west of the island, which was then renamed Newborough.[7]

Wales counted many towns so small that they are untraceable today, and many others that have decayed so far that their business has quite vanished. Llawhaden was once a significant borough, dominated by a palace of the bishop of St David's, and included, at some distance from the palace, a parish church, a hospital and a mill; but today this is a place of country lanes that give no clue that $174\frac{1}{2}$ burgages were recorded here in the early fourteenth century.[8]

From 1277, Edward I based armies of both soldiers and craftsmen at Chester so that his conquest of north Wales could be consolidated with the construction of a chain of castles around its peripheries.[9] Chester became a boom town, and its Rows still bear witness to this. In Wales itself, castles at Ruthin, Rhuddlan, Flint and Builth, and the fortification of Montgomery began the process close to the border, with a further castle at Aberystwyth overlooking the Bay of Cardigan to guard the sea route. In the 1280s the start of mammoth military works at Hope, Denbigh, Conwy, Caernarfon and Harlech impressed Edward's rule on the Welsh for good, works that reached a climax with Beaumaris, and gave them boroughs on the English model.[10]

Edward's Caernarfon is imbued with all the symbolism of Rome. (fig. 40) As a means of furthering his political purpose he seems to have consciously given substance to the ancient Welsh romance of Macsen Wledig recounted in *The Mabinogion*, which associates the ancient Roman fortress of Segontium, overlooking the town, with the Roman emperors Constantine and Magnus Maximus. Maximus (Macsen), according to the romance, dreamed of journeying from Rome to a fair land of high mountains where a river flowed into the sea opposite an island; here he found a fortified city, resplendent with multicoloured towers, and a hall containing an ivory throne emblazoned with twin golden eagles. This would be the site of the greatest of Edward's Welsh castles, the pre-eminent symbol of his power. It therefore differs from his other castles in north Wales in having polygonal towers instead of round ones, and walls banded with differently coloured stone. The resemblance to the polygonal turrets and

39.   Speed's map of Wales, together with his marginal bird's-eye views, left and right, of the principal towns founded as a result of the early Norman incursions and Edward I's conquests. Speed 1676, vol. 2. 1. © Society of Antiquaries of London)

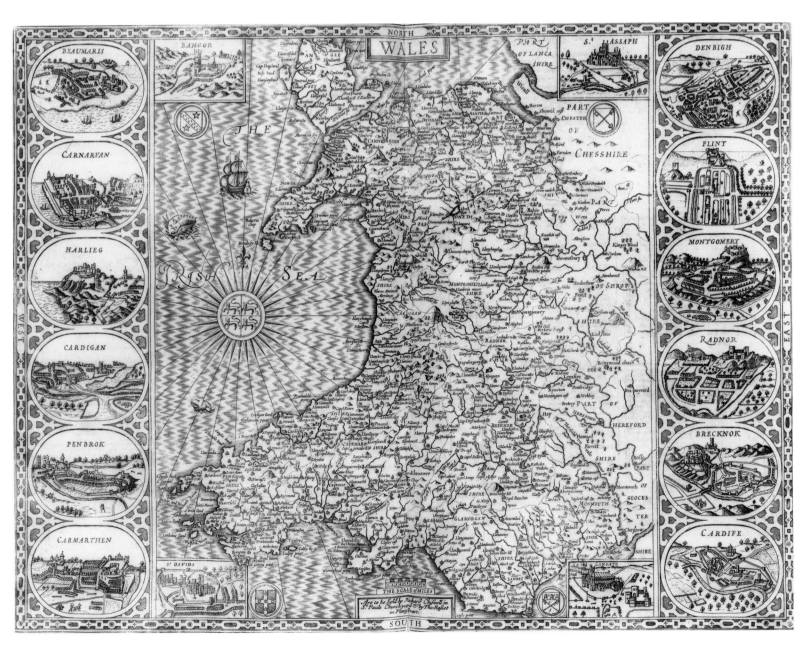

tile-laced Theodosian wall of Constantinople is uncanny, so much so that it can hardly be the workings of chance, any more than can the appearance of imperial eagles adorning the triple turrets of the great western tower, the first to be completed. In essence, here is a new Constantinople, an imperial city, dominated by a palace for the vice-regal throne of its Plantagenet rulers.[11]

With Wales conquered, but Caernarfon far from complete, Edward turned his sword on North Britain. This was a harder nut to crack. On the face of it, Scottish towns are different from English and Welsh towns only in detail. Their origin and history, however, are quite separate. For all their brief occupation of Caledonia, the Romans did not found towns in Scotland. Its inhabitants continued to occupy tribal centres that were much the same as the Iron Age centres south of the Border, and these outlasted Roman rule in Britain. What followed lacks the light of even the comparatively sparse documents that illuminate the English Dark Ages. North of the Border, dark means the black of their winter days, not the white of their summer nights. There is no equivalent of the Domesday Survey, and the paucity of records extends right through the Middle Ages.

Only in the fifth century did the Scots set up military strongholds which would eventually give rise to Edinburgh and Stirling as centres of the Gododdin kingdom, and to Dumbarton as the capital of Strathclyde, which extended far south into Cumbria. While the Christian Church began its settlement of Caledonia in the fourth century, there is little physical evidence to show for it. St Mungo (alias St Kentigern) had an episcopal church in Strathclyde towards the end of the sixth century, and this may mark the beginnings of Glasgow – or perhaps Govan.[12] St Andrews had a monastery in the mid-eighth century to which the probably mythical St Regulus had brought some bones as a relic of Scotland's patron saint.[13] (fig. 41) This flourished and eventually became the seat of a bishop who exercised primacy over all others in the land. By the end of the eighth century, Abernethy and possibly Dunkeld were centres of further bishoprics, although, like St Andrews, not towns in any recognizable sense. That was on the eve of the Norse incursions; thereafter only fitful light illuminates the blasted heath of Scottish affairs, until, as in Wales, the Normans started to press against the Border.

By the middle of the twelfth century the Normans had reached a line snaking across the Cheviots from the Tweed to the Solway Firth. The Scots reacted by defending the Border. Earl David founded Berwick and Roxburgh as strongholds before his accession to the Scottish

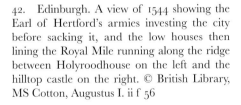

41. St Andrews. The eleventh-century tower of the church founded by St Regulus to contain the relics of St Andrew

throne. Long before he succeeded his brother Alexander I as king in 1124, he had determined to achieve the same political and ecclesiastical autonomy for Scotland as any other state enjoyed in western Christendom. He began by endeavouring to free the Church in Scotland from the clutches of the archbishop of York, who claimed suzerainty over it. In 1110 or shortly afterwards he succeeded in persuading Pope Paschal II to appoint his tutor John Achaius as bishop of Glasgow without reference to York. This act of independence was more generally confirmed in 1192, when Pope Celestine III decreed that the *Ecclesia Scoticus* was a *filius specialis* of the Apostolic See.[14] This gave Glasgow a cathedral, begun by John's successor, and later still a palace within its precinct overlooking the Clyde and the commercial centre that would grow below it. Meanwhile, David initiated the settlement of lowland Scotland in a way comparable to William's settlement of England and Wales, and ruled it on Norman feudal lines. He gave charters to maybe fourteen more royal burghs with exclusive trading rights before his death in 1153, most of them with castles to promote defence, strong administration and the collection of rents from the burgesses. Thus he entered the ranks of Scottish heroes.

David's prime achievement was Edinburgh, which he founded as a royal burgh about 1130. (fig. 42) In 1140 he gave leave to the canons of the Abbey of the Holy Rood, itself founded twelve years beforehand at the foot of the hill on which Edinburgh stands, to found their own burgh of Canongate. In both cases the aim was to attract merchants and craftsmen who would pay rent for individual strips of land on which they had to build a house within a year and a day. Similar foundations were concentrated on the fertile plains between the rivers Forth and Clyde – for instance Dunfermline, Stirling (fig. 43) and Linlithgow, with a few more further north, Perth on the river Dee, and Montrose, Aberdeen, Forres, Elgin and, perhaps, Inverness, defending the east coast. Peebles and, probably soon after David's death if not before, Lanark and Jedburgh guarded the routes from the Border into the lowlands.[15] Both the Church and the Scottish barons joined this promotion of burghs in a modest way, so that by the end of the twelfth century Scotland could boast over forty burghs in all.

Scotland's economy was based on wool, and the best part of its trade was with Flanders and Artois. By the end of the thirteenth century Scottish merchants had their own quarter in Bruges as a means of promoting this. Already David had encouraged barons from France and Flanders, and even from hostile England, to settle on large Scottish estates, which they would rule in his place. This he successfully achieved, and prevalent among the early Scottish burgesses are several men from Flanders. In 1144, or shortly afterwards, Bishop Robert of St Andrews issued a memorandum to the effect that he had founded a burgh at St Andrews and had appointed as its provost Mainard the Fleming, previously one of David's burgesses at Berwick. He hoped that the new

42. Edinburgh. A view of 1544 showing the Earl of Hertford's armies investing the city before sacking it, and the low houses then lining the Royal Mile running along the ridge between Holyroodhouse on the left and the hilltop castle on the right. © British Library, MS Cotton, Augustus I. ii f 56

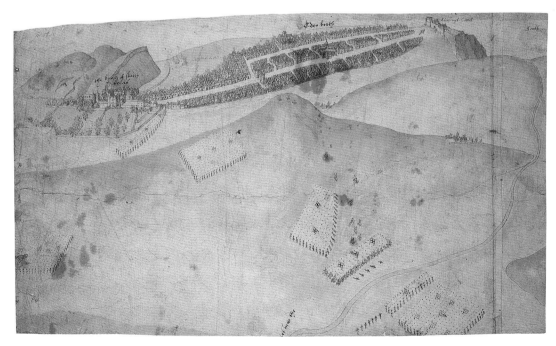

43. Stirling, seen from the east. Like a miniature version of Edinburgh, the town overlooks the river Forth from a rocky outcrop, crowned by the royal citadel that guards the route into the Highlands

44. Anstruther. The port was reputedly a mean town, hardly more than a large village, inhabited by fishermen and sailors, but, blessed by Fife's fertile fields and the fish-rich waters of the North Sea, it flourished, and was created a royal burgh in the 1580s

town's trade would support the cathedral, and indeed this was admirably justified.[16]

The east coast did well from these foundations, particularly Fife with its numerous ports from Culross to Crail and round the headland of Fife Ness to St Andrews. Trade with England, the Baltic and the Netherlands, and the export of its coal, salt, fish, grain and wool set up many a burgh, although many attained royal status only towards the end of the sixteenth century. Despite their tiny size, James II called the East Neuk ports 'a fringe of gold on a beggar's mantle'. (fig. 44) The west coast was small fry by comparison. Trade again brought a few Spanish merchants to its fishing ports, and Spanish iron ore was landed at Ayr,[17] but the ports remained little more than unpopulous villages.

When Edward determined to reduce Scotland, as he had Wales, his first target was the line of fortified burghs that David and his successors had founded to defend the east coast. These Edward systematically attacked. He marched as far as Elgin on the Moray Firth, but could not sustain the advance and had to deal with the Scots. His forays into Scotland continued, with summer successes reduced by winter failures, everything he grasped slipping from his hands. His son Edward II tried again, but met Robert Bruce and defeat at Bannockburn in 1314.[18]

This reverse let the Scots into northern England, where they brought death and destruction. The anarchy of the northern Border remained a problem for the English, and indeed the Scots too, as it had done for the Romans, and not even the Union of the Crowns in 1603 entirely staunched the anguish and bloodshed. York and Carlisle continued to profit from the trouble. Berwick, which Edward I captured in 1296 but his son lost to Bruce, came into prominence as a bastion of defence, but lacked the impregnability to avoid changing hands some fourteen times as the ferocious tide of war ebbed and flowed.

4

Money makythe the man

The commerce of towns

The variety of goods on which a town's commerce was based was no more than a reflection of the success of its citizens, whether they be mercantile magnates or common labourers. This was crucial. Industry could be based anywhere, provided that sources of raw materials and capital, power and labour, and a ready market all came together, and did so with greater economy than anywhere else. In their various ways towns generally met most of these needs rather better than rural parishes did, even if some of their overhead costs were higher.

For ordinary town people, the most important individual privilege that success might bring was the right of burgage tenure. This allowed a tenant or burgess to hold a more or less standard plot of land on the payment of a fixed money rent, customarily a shilling a year, and freely to alienate it or to pass it on to whomever he or, occasionally, she chose. Other privileges often allowed a burgess to bequeath goods without paying a death duty or heriot, unlike a manorial peasant, and, similarly, a burgess might grind flour, bake food and brew ale without hindrance. The recognition of a borough or its establishment by royal or lordly charter gave its inhabitants a valuable freedom from all the other common feudal dues, particularly labour services in the lord's fields or a monetary payment in lieu, as well as rights to trade at weekly markets and annual fairs, all of which were denied to their rural cousins.

Thus in 1314 Gilbert de Clare, as Earl of Gloucester, charged his burgesses in Tewkesbury 12d a year to hold their burgages free of heriot, allowed them to bake bread and brew ale for sale, gave them a monopoly of trade over outsiders within the town, and, finally, freed them from the jurisdiction of the shire court.[1] The burgesses of Scottish royal burghs enjoyed similar privileges, with an established local monopoly and rights to foreign trade, unlike the burgesses of the burghs of barony, which were essentially inward looking and local in scope.

Some of the more important towns gained a further privilege, one that would be greatly extended after the Middle Ages and become the norm in the second half of the sixteenth century. When the success of their economy had given rise to a large and prosperous bourgeoisie, they might gain a measure of autonomy from their principal landlord, and their most prominent burgesses become in effect a governing oligarchy of aldermen. London led the way before the Conquest, and such provincial centres as Norwich, York and Bristol followed. By the thirteenth century some lesser towns like Exeter, Gloucester and Salisbury were in effect self-governing, this being confirmed by their borough charters.[2]

Towns were often created when, through the industry of their inhabitants, settlements were promoted to borough status by the grant of a charter. When this happened its inhabitants immediately gained in status, as, for instance, the ninety-one villeins did overnight when they were newly enfranchised as the first burgesses of Higham Ferrers in 1251.[3] Industrious inhabitants had to attract a landowner in this way, and pay small annual rents. Such were the freeholders. Their privileges and the fortunes they could make from these then attracted all manner of immigrants from the surrounding countryside who preferred the chance of quick profit through practising initiative to the slow slog of rural life. This was fine for the few, but too risky for the majority, whom the annual passage of the seasons had taught the hard but beneficial lessons of caution. The price of civic freedom meant giving up a sizeable acreage of agri-

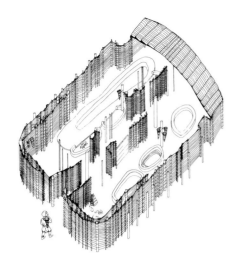

cultural land for the right to sell one's labour or to practise in a craft or trade so as to pay one's way. Wages were low compared with food prices in the twelfth and thirteenth centuries, but craft skills produced goods for which the expanding population provided a ready market, and that helped the trader too. For the most part these retail traders operated a money economy, but the manufacturers of wholesale goods among them could turn to credit and barter among the merchants and traders whom they supplied. Immigrants might make enough from their skills to enable them to lease plots from the freeholders. Eventually, a migrant might be touched with luck, and be able to afford a burgage rent.

The foundation of new boroughs is one measure of success, but their overall prosperity is ultimately more significant. Whatever specific causes brought boroughs into existence, whether they were principally political, religious or commercial, they either became centres of trade or failed. Soldiers, clerks and clergymen needed food and clothing like anyone else, and the local rural population could have a similar need of imported food and clothes which it paid for by exporting its own produce. Given the difficulties of medieval transport and the perishable quality of many foodstuffs, trade in food usually gave a town a fair livelihood provided that there were no competing towns too close by. To avoid this potential source of economic conflict, a borough could establish a local monopoly by securing a charter in return for a payment to the Crown.

The development of a specialized market alongside its trade in everyday necessities was the surest way to success, although specialization only came fully into its own in the late Middle Ages. Specialist foods gave many a market its name and many a town its reputation. Chester and Shrewsbury made a living from Cheshire cheese as well as garrisons. Ports such as Hull had locally caught fish as well as imports and exports to keep them busy. Great Yarmouth, for instance, was known for its herrings, and also for salt. Salt, the most important food preservative, was Maldon's speciality. King's Lynn made a living from salt, and so did Droitwich. While King John gave its burgesses the '*vill cum salsis et salinis*' (the town with [its] salt and salt works) at the time of its charter, when Leland visited the town about 1540, 'thoughe the commoditie thereof be syngular great, yet the burgesses be poore for the moste parte; bycawse gentelmen [hathe] for the moste parte the great gayne of it, and the burgesses have all the labowre.'[4] The three Cheshire salt towns of Nantwich, Middlewich and Northwich are first recognized in Domesday, when at least eight salt or *wich* houses were recorded there. The remains of two such houses with stake and wattle walls, the later one with the additional support of posts set into the ground, typify the surroundings in which brine was boiled for the production of salt in the twelfth century in a part of town especially reserved for this purpose. (fig. 45) Leland was particularly taken with this industry: 'They sethe the salt water in furnesses of lede, and lade

45. A wich House at Nantwich, hypothetically reconstructed, showing stud walls and internal partitions and brine tubs. After McNeil 1983, fig. 8. © Society for Medieval Archaeology

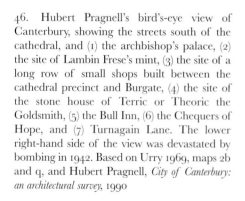

46. Hubert Pragnell's bird's-eye view of Canterbury, showing the streets south of the cathedral, and (1) the archbishop's palace, (2) the site of Lambin Frese's mint, (3) the site of a long row of small shops built between the cathedral precinct and Burgate, (4) the site of the stone house of Terric or Theoric the Goldsmith, (5) the Bull Inn, (6) the Chequers of Hope, and (7) Turnagain Lane. The lower right-hand side of the view was devastated by bombing in 1942. Based on Urry 1969, maps 2b and q, and Hubert Pragnell, *City of Canterbury: an architectural survey*, 1990

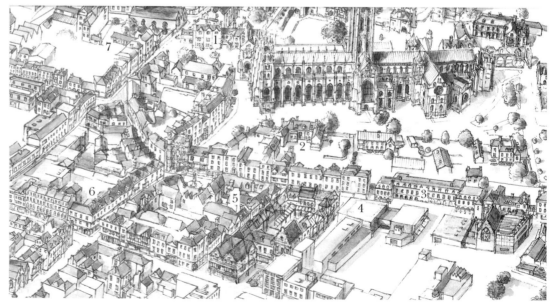

47. Church Street, Tewkesbury. A row of houses with shops at the front built at the end of the fifteenth century, with the abbey, whose possession they were, in the background

out the salt some in ca[ses] of wiker, thorough the wich the water voydith, and the salt remaynith.'[5]

Second to food was clothing. This began with wool and leather. Beverley gathered in the wool shorn on the Yorkshire Wolds before its merchants sent it down to the Humber for export to Italy and Flanders. In the fourteenth century the little Hampshire town of New Alresford was one of the ten greatest wool markets in England, wool being shipped down the canalized Itchen to Beaulieu.[6] Newcastle upon Tyne exported hides as well as coal, and imported furs from the Baltic. Inland, Leicester was, in Defoe's words, a 'vast magazine of wool', shorn from sheep that he, a self-proclaimed expert in such matters, described as 'without comparison, the largest, and bear . . . the greatest fleeces of wool . . . the finest wool in the whole island'.[7] This was an age-old reputation. Four hundred years beforehand, wool had been paramount in Leicester, but was only one well-established part of the town's diverse economy: there were also a weekday market, a Saturday market, a hay market and a horse fair.

The larger the town, the greater the number of markets it could sustain, these dealing in the widest variety of goods. Edinburgh is a prime example: Lawnmarket was reserved for cattle and sheep, butter, cheese and wool, and also cloth and haberdashery; beyond, in High Street, there were separate markets for grain, poultry, flesh and salt, as well as clothing; below the castle, Grassmarket again served cattle and, here, cutlers and smiths set up trade.[8]

In Canterbury during the 1230s there were at least two hundred small lock-up shops, about 6 or 7 feet (2 m) wide, open for small business of all kinds.[9] Many of them were on the fringes of the cathedral, where they would attract pilgrims with souvenirs as well as more usual necessities. (fig. 46) It was a short step from a stall to a permanent shop, and many were built on the fringes of Church lands. (fig. 47) By 1300 Chester was a booming trading town with 270 shops.[10] In the first half of the fourteenth century, Winchester's traders, like those of Edinburgh, fell

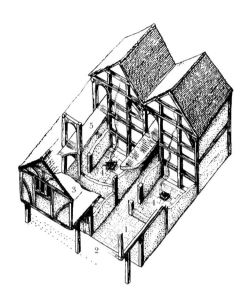

into specialist groups along High Street according to the goods they sold: starting up near the West Gate, there were fishmongers and then saddlers on the north side, parmenters or skinners on the south, followed by gratery and more skinners on the north, with goldsmiths and spicers on the south, then butchers on the north and drapers on the south, and finally cutlers on the north with dubbers or dyers opposite.[11] Even in the years of decline, over half the city's houses incorporated a shop, (fig. 48) and over a hundred stalls or selds did business in the High Street. Hardly a town was without its shops, all clamouring for business in a way that would seem very foreign today.

London, of course, had everything. London Bridge was lined with 138 shops in 1358.[12] (fig. 49) Cheapside became a shopper's paradise: goldsmiths, spicers, saddlers, girdlers, chandlers, ironmongers, cutlers and spurriers had their shops down each side of the street; hawkers filled the street itself with their wares; and established traders set up stalls to sell corn, bread, fish and meat, leather goods, and wool and linen cloth. Meanwhile, founders, wiredrawers, buckle-makers, purse-makers, button-makers, hosiers, hood-makers and embroiderers were at work in the nearby lanes, giving them the appearance of an eastern souk in all but one aspect: men and women worked there side by side, and intimate personal services were on offer as well as goods.[13] (fig. 50)

Towns had room for many of the rural crafts and countless others too, and in this lay their attraction. In 1185 Baldock's citizens included a blacksmith, an ironmonger, a tailor, shoemaker, tanner, mason, cook, carpenter, mercer, weaver, saddler, goldsmith, merchant and vintner.[14] This was not Cheapside, but they had access to a good market, one of eight in Hertfordshire founded since Domesday.[15]

Markets were generally regular events, but annual fairs took over whole towns for days at a time, giving them a festival air. St Ives had the most famous of all. Ramsey Abbey, which owned the town, obtained a licence in 1110 for an Easter fair. This brought all manner of goods up the Great Ouse from Lynn, along with Continental merchants; and across the river lay Ermine Street and the road from London. The traders are recorded in the names of Barkers' Row, Spicers' Row, Skinners' Row and Canvas Row, while Ypres Row, French Row, Lincoln Row, Beverley Row and Leicester Row recall cloth and wine merchants from the Continent and wool merchants from three English towns too.[16] Here one could purchase anything, reputedly from wives to kittens, all in sacks of seven, and seven times seven; such was its reputation. But the Stourbridge fair at Cambridge eclipsed it in the fifteenth century and became the greatest of all, lasting for three weeks in September, and specializing in ironmongery, wool, cloth, leather – and books. Reading was becoming a recognized way to knowledge, even among students, some of whom were willing to spend their paltry pennies at the fair.

London not only led the way, but also grew proportionally throughout the Middle Ages until James I despaired at its overweening size.[17] It became the only British city to rank with Europe's greatest. The poll tax returns of 1377 suggest that its population was in the region of 35,000–45,000. It may have been more still. Even so, this was way behind that of Naples, and no more than about half that of the great northern Italian cities and Paris. London was well short of Gent's population, too, but it was at least on a par with such northern towns as Bruges, Brussels and Cologne, and the four largest towns in Spain.[18] No other British town, with the possible exception of Norwich, reached this second order in Europe of towns with around 20,000–30,000 inhabitants, such as the Baltic ports of Lübeck and, eventually, Danzig, and the great inland cities of Augsburg, Magdeburg, Nürnburg and Strasburg. York and Bristol probably exceeded 10,000 by a fair margin; otherwise Lincoln and Oxford kept their places among the most important of inland boroughs, but their populations only amounted to a few thousand each. By comparison, Scotland's burghs were tiny, many of them hardly making a thousand, and the same was true of Wales.

The fortunes of boroughs increasingly depended on manufacture, particularly weaving, to provide the wealth to keep them growing. The newly sited Salisbury, planned and re-founded by the brother bishops Herbert and Richard Poore in the years up to 1219, leapt forward on the profits of weaving. Coventry grew to equal stature from even less, again on the profits of its weavers. Shrewsbury continued to grow, less in spite of than because of the pacification of Wales, as the market place for Welsh cloth. For all their fairs and markets, Winchester and Gloucester, county towns both and lacking staple industries, settled into a pattern of life that allowed others to overtake them. Another county town, Northampton, settled further, and singularly failed to live up to its early promise.

Ports probably suffered greater swings of fortune than did inland boroughs. Southampton maintained a long-lasting trade in wine from Saintonge, to which was added oil, iron and wines from Malaga, linen and canvas from Normandy, timber from the Baltic, hides from Ireland, haberdashery and household goods from the Low Countries, silks, spices and dyes from Italy, and salt from the Bay of Bourganeuf.[19] The new settlement on the south-west of the promontory between the Itchen and Hamble slowly revived on the export of wool from the bishop of Winchester's vast estates, reaching a peak of prosperity in the early fourteenth cen-

50. Cheapside, in the City of London, shown in the centre of an eighteenth-century copy of a lost mural painting from Cowdray Park of the coronation procession of King Edward VI in 1547. The street is lined with shops, including those of goldsmiths, whose cups and flagons are prominently on show. Above the shops are fashionable long bands of windows, filled with onlookers. To the right is the spire of St Paul's Cathedral, to the left the tower of St Mary-le-Bow, and beyond, London Bridge and, on the Southwark bank of the Thames, St Mary Overie. © Society of Antiquaries of London

51. Wool House, Southampton. The wide arch-braced roof of a fourteenth-century two-storeyed warehouse, built of stone, traditionally associated with wool, but suited to any goods that had to be kept dry

tury. (fig. 51) So Southampton just scraped into England's top twenty wealthiest boroughs, but then suffered from the decline of wool exports attendant on the wars with France. The variety of its import trade is exemplified in the record of soap, green ginger, linen cloth, madder, woad, hemp, oil, salmon, stockfish, salted eels, lath nails and even frying pans all being landed on one day in 1469.[20]

Typically, the south coast was dotted with small ports, many of them importing goods like these and exporting wool and grain. (fig. 52) Only Plymouth came near Southampton's standing. Of Kent's eight boroughs recorded by the Domesday Survey, all but Canterbury were ports engaged in both fishing and trade. In the middle of the twelfth century a number of them challenged the power of the Church to control their affairs and to levy dues. By claiming ancient privileges enshrined in various charters granted by the Crown in return for naval service as opposed to burghal taxes, they established the right to govern themselves as the Cinque

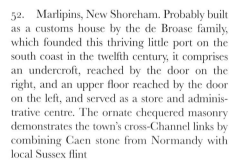

52. Marlipins, New Shoreham. Probably built as a customs house by the de Broase family, which founded this thriving little port on the south coast in the twelfth century, it comprises an undercroft, reached by the door on the right, and an upper floor reached by the door on the left, and served as a store and administrative centre. The ornate chequered masonry demonstrates the town's cross-Channel links by combining Caen stone from Normandy with local Sussex flint

53. Quay Lane, Faversham. A late medieval timber-framed warehouse, close-studded, like a typical Kentish house, but accommodating two open floors for goods

Ports.[21] Sandwich, by far the largest of them, was allied with Dover, which served passengers crossing the Channel, and with Hythe and New Romney, and Hastings in Sussex. Looking for a share of the spoils, a number of lesser ports became attached to one or other of these as Limbs. Thus Fordwich became a Limb of Sandwich, Faversham (fig. 53) a Limb of Dover, Rye, Winchelsea and Seaford all Limbs of Hastings.

The loss of Normandy in 1204 gave the Cinque Ports added strategic importance and the excuse to engage in general piracy on both sides of the Channel. In 1252 Henry III ordered the men of the Cinque Ports to cease interfering with the trade of Southampton and Portsmouth. Raiding the French coast did not bring royal disapproval, but the tables were soon turned: the French grew stronger, and sacked Sandwich in 1216, the first of many raids. Edward I gave the Cinque Ports a charter in 1278 which confirmed their right to trade freely, a cause of great envy elsewhere that led to the occasional sea battle. The Hundred Years' War brought the French back with bloody results. Less vicious but more final was the older enemy, nature. Silt had blocked most of their harbours by the seventeenth century, leaving Sandwich with the small jetty that remains today, and only Dover of the original five eventually to build on its past.

Dunwich, on the Suffolk coast, was perhaps England's wealthiest port after London in the middle of the twelfth century; two centuries later what Leland called 'the rages of the se' had washed it away.[22] Torksey's decline was less dramatic but hardly less complete. An Anglo-Saxon burh, it owed its success to its position beside the river Trent, sixty miles from the sea, but connected to Lincoln by the Fossdyke, a canal of Roman origin. Here goods were transhipped, particularly wool and lead from Lincoln, and this brought prosperity and wharves to the river bank.[23] But Boston took its trade, and that of several other eastern ports, to join the main league, along with Great Yarmouth, Newcastle upon Tyne, Bristol, and, of course, London. By the end of the Middle Ages Torksey was no more than a large village; today it is a church, a ruined castle, a pub and a couple of farms.

The great successes were Boston and Lynn, which grew prodigiously on the export of grain and wool, and their by-products, malt and ale, and the luxurious cloths woven in Lincoln and Stamford. King's Lynn had been founded by Herbert Losinga, bishop of Norwich (1091–1119), on the Great Ouse between Purfleet and Mill Fleet, and was based on its Saturday market and the church of St Margaret. Prosperity caused its expansion northwards into the New Land up to Fisher Fleet, which was planned by Bishop Turbe (1146–74), thus opening up a further stretch of river bank for wharves.[24] From both here and the wharves of Boston, ships went up and down the coast, to Berwick and Scotland, across the sea to Flanders, Zealand and

Brabant, to Norway, Denmark and eventually to the Baltic and Iceland. Small but valuable cargoes of lead and salt augmented their exports, and in came Gascon wine, fresh, salted and dried cod from Bergen, Swedish herrings, Baltic timber and Arctic furs.[25]

In the thirteenth century, the expansion of both agriculture and the population it fed reached a culminating point. By the middle of the century the rate of town foundation had diminished, simply because there were enough of them. They were remarkably evenly spread, with a tendency for their numbers to increase along the fringes of the south-western and Welsh uplands. This was a consequence of accessibility, the plains allowing speedier journeys to market, and therefore greater distances there and back in a day's ride than were possible along the more tortuous routes of the hill country.[26]

This happy conclusion to six centuries of town building hid a fatal weakness in the national economy. By concentrating on the two great interdependent agricultural staples – grain and wool – the thirteenth-century led its rural population into a cul-de-sac, hedged in by demands for products that were less and less efficiently produced. High grain prices ploughed up the most marginal of lands, ultimately with ruinous results. For the while, landowners reaped profit as famine reaped peasants. When the crisis came, it was not just the countryside that suffered. Many towns reeled at the blow to their economies, and, in doing so, allowed a few others to grasp new opportunities.

The crisis might have been averted had the economy diversified. That was not to be, and nature took its course. The foundation of new towns as a means of stimulating the economy lost its attraction; nor were the needs of defence, administration or religion a temptation, as these were served already. The failure rate among new planned towns in England increased so that in four decades between 1230 and 1350 it exceeded 25 percent. The foundation of new towns as a whole again rapidly fell away. There were only nine new foundations after 1300, nearly all of them around the extremities of the kingdom.

Though decline came later, the story in Wales is similar, despite the rush of foundations attendant on Edward's conquest. Just eight or perhaps nine new towns originated after 1300, the last seemingly the lonely little town of Rhayader, which had markets and a fair, first recorded in 1360.[27] In a sense, the economic life of Welsh towns had been marginal from the first. Caernarfon owed its existence to Edward's castle and political expediency: it served the castle and without it would have quickly vanished, so unimportant was it to the local economy. In varying degrees, much the same can be said for all the other medieval Welsh foundations.

The last new town in England was Queenborough in Kent, founded in 1368 to accompany Edward III's new castle, which defended the Thames estuary; the wars with France had started and her navies sought reprisal. The previous foundation had been New Eagle, planned in 1345 on the Foss Way between Lincoln and Newark, and a failure from its very inception. That was just before the Black Death struck. The next foundation would not be until Falmouth – in 1613.[28]

5

WHAT IS THE CITY BUT THE PEOPLE?

The society of towns

Medieval European society was based on the family. In classical times this meant the household, and indeed still did: it was not confined to husband, wife and children alone.[1] The Church spoke of itself as a family, meaning all Christians bound together by faith; but, as in prehistoric times,[2] the basic family embraced all the occupants of a single medieval dwelling. In a religious house, therefore, the family comprised the abbot or abbess and monks or nuns; in a secular house, similarly, the parents and children, attendants and servants, of both sexes.

Society was dominated by men, as most societies always have been. This was particularly evident in the higher ranks of society. The Middle Ages were born in blood. Strength counted – on the battlefield, certainly, in bed too. Even so, the ambiguous evidence of the times cannot readily pinpoint war between the sexes. Women had to apply their wits to counter their weakness, but sword and spindle were not locked in mortal combat; both had their place. The Church confirmed this. Carnality, dangerously close to sin, was shrouded in a veil of decency that gave rights to men and penalties to women – but also a measure of reverence and protection. (fig. 54)

The Church, itself the mystical Bride of Christ, whatever claim the 'real' Mary Magdalen may have had, venerated the other Mary, Mother of Christ, for her virginity. Its ordained priests, who were symbolically married to the Holy Church, therefore vowed chastity and preached the tempering effects of marriage on 'men's carnal lusts and appetites'. So marriage was advocated as 'a remedy against sin, and to avoid fornication; that such persons as have not the gift of continency might . . . keep themselves undefiled members of Christ's body.' Men should love, comfort and honour their wives and forsake other women; women, however, should also obey and serve their husbands, heeding, first, that marriage 'was ordained for the procreation of children'.[3] Conspicuous adulterers and fornicators were pilloried, both literally and metaphorically, and that included priests.

So the Church came to formalize its patriarchal view of marriage and men's dominant role within it. This embraced everyone, for everyone had had parents, even if they were lost, and all belonged to that greater family enshrined by the Church. Each family embraced a married couple and their children, its head – usually the husband – also being father to the servants and guests who made up the household. This hierarchy was the foundation of medieval society, and became the accepted norm. To stray beyond it, particularly to satisfy lust, would at least set tongues wagging, and, at worst, bring down on the offenders opprobrium tantamount to wholesale persecution.

Pity the women who preferred kissing to spinning:

> In daunger hadde he at his own gise
> The yonge girles of the diocise . . .

Despite his denials, Chaucer's Summoner readily blackmailed any lass he caught with her knickers down, and threatened young lads with betrayal to the archdeacon for a similar purpose. Nevertheless, he 'wolde suffre, for a quart of wyn, A good felawe to have his concubyn'.[4] So a likely lad could get off lightly, but not a maid-no-more. As for those outside this order of things – Jews and Moors – they were just that, outside and beyond redemption.

Then, as today, sex was an abiding fascination, and, whether for the procreation of children or the satisfaction of carnal lusts and appetites, was tamed by binding it with the conventions of decency. Decency meant privacy and privacy was rare, particularly in town. Night brought a flimsy cloak, but that was easily lifted, and a chamber was a false security that opened to any peeping Tom. In fact, privacy meant little more than curbing blatancy enough to spare the blushes.

What a bower gave a king took a long time to descend to the base level of society. (fig. 55) The small size of most houses and their lack of rooms limited availability, and so did the nature of households. By the late Middle Ages, this impediment was somewhat reduced, even in ordinary houses, by the distinction between service rooms and chambers. Even so, that only favoured the head of a household and his wife. Just as they would sit on chairs at table while the rest of their household made do with benches, he and his wife would sleep together, alone in their chamber, while the rest slept where they could – and it was his business to know exactly where.

So far, so good; but even the privacy of a chamber was prejudiced by how far servants and apprentices had the general run of a house. In Chaucer's *Miller's Tale* Robyn the apprentice and Gille the maid had to be sent packing from the carpenter's house at Oxford so that his young wife Alison and the student lodger Nicholas could cuckold him in secret.[5] In the hilarious bedroom farce of *The Reeve's Tale*, Chaucer turned the tables on millers and threw sleepy dust into the eyes of all who put their trust in the privacy of darkness. The socially pretentious miller of Trumpington and his wife shared their chamber with their plump daughter of twenty years, though she had a bed of her own, and there was a cradle for a baby son. 'Myn hous is streit',[6] he was forced to admit, because, unusually for men of his standing in the later fourteenth century, there was only one place to sleep. So, when two lusty Cambridge students begged shelter for the night, another bed was set up in the chamber for them. Snoring kept them awake until the lure of the daughter's 'buttokes brode, and brestes rounde and hye' became irresistible.[7] What followed is best left to Chaucer, but the story concludes at dawn with one student in the miller's bed, his wife in the students' bed, their daughter contentedly alone in hers, like the cat who got the cream, and the baby still asleep despite the comings and groanings.

While the smaller medieval household in the main comprised two generations of parents and children, and, because of high mortality, a household of three generations was a rare thing indeed, it also included its unrelated members. The households of most merchants and craftsmen comprised about a dozen people, those of lesser people, labourers and journeymen half as many or fewer – often just those parents and children whom early death had spared. Conversely, the wealthier the household, the more numerous it was. On average a knight's household grew fourfold from about 15 to 60 members between 1250 and 1450, and that despite the plague; meanwhile, a noble or episcopal one similarly grew from about 40 to 160.[8]

Privacy in these large lordly households was circumscribed by the cohesion of its members,

55. King David spies on Bathsheba in the bath, sends a messenger for her, commits adultery with her, and then sends for her husband Uriah; from a mid thirteenth-century French or English manuscript. The general message, apart from the illustration of a biblical tale (2 *Samuel* 11), is that privacy in the Middle Ages was largely for the rich and powerful, and not for lowly, vulnerable women who might live over a shop. Pierpont Morgan Library, New York. MS 638 f41v. © The Pierpont Morgan Library/Art Resource, New York, USA

who comprised all ranks. 'Not in front of the servants' had no meaning; everyone but the head served someone, and everyone was everywhere, all bending their backs to the lord's various needs. The lordly household might provide the manpower for military service for the physical maintenance of the lord's power. It certainly provided the executive, administrative and judicial processes through which its power was more peaceably wielded. It demonstrated this power through elaborate formalized rituals which mixed the secular with the religious, particularly at the time of feasting in the great hall. (fig. 56) Finally, it displayed its opulence by keeping open house, dispensing hospitality to all who would avail themselves of the lord's table — literally if they were of suitable rank, at his gates if they were too poor and indigent to be allowed entry.[9]

56. Duc Jean de Berry, seated at his high table, exchanging Christmas gifts, *c.* 1413. Feasting in the hall and the whole hierarchy of the family revolved around the high table and the lord who sat at its head; everyone else took their place, according to strict protocol, determined by their rank and status, right down to the lowliest, who sat nearest to the doors leading to the service rooms. Interestingly, the blazing fire is behind the duke, and a large wickerwork screen shields him from it, possibly confusing the focus, the fire representing hospitality, and the duke lordly power. From January, *Les très riches heures de Duc de Berry*, f2r. Chantilly, Musée Condé, © RMN – R.G. Ojeda

The larger these households became, the smaller proportion of women they contained. The lady of the house, her daughters, her attendants, a few personal maids and nurses might add up to little more than a twentieth of a large secular household. Apart from his servants, the lord was attended by knights and retainers, who also had their own servants, and there were invariably numerous guests, again with their attendants, all of them males. If the women be pitied in this fearsomely masculine company, so should the large bands of virile young men that attended a lord.[10] Everyone of every grade in the household knew what everyone else was doing – and with whom. Frustration honed their bitterness: when they all sat down to eat in the great hall, among them, talk of the Devil, sat Pride, Covetousness, Wrath, Envy, Gluttony, Sloth and Lechery.

The circumstances in which people were born, grew up, married, procreated and died only becomes clear in the closing years of the Middle Ages. Procreation in the lower levels of society might produce a small and readily manageable interdependent unit. In towns this was usually an economic unit as well, but social differences imposed variety. Wealth and status were decisive factors; inheritance was a vital consideration.

Medieval society was largely rural and ranged from the extremities of the landed aristocracy to those of the landless peasantry. Both lived in families, but the one was pressed at all costs by a need to maintain the family as a continuing entity, generation by generation, the other by a need to maintain its members alive, season by season. Between these poles was an infinite range of men and women whose family character took on a different hue in town from that of the countryside. It must also have taken on differing shades as the Middle Ages progressed, but this is only visible towards their end.

So important to a family was a house that in parts of France the same word, *domus*, was used for a peasant's family as for his house.[11] In Britain, the word 'house' was usually applied only to those families with a pretension to antiquity. In this context it meant the family line – the dynasty – as well as those who occupied the building at the centre of its estates; thus it embraced not only those alive, but also its dead ancestors, who gave it its pedigree (as Arthur did for the royal line), and its descendants, who would safeguard its status and property in the future. Such families were bound by the necessity of putting lineage before person.[12] This produced a hierarchy centred on the head of the family, to whom all its members owed allegiance. He, and just occasionally she, held the key to the dynasty's political and economic power. This was vitally important in a dangerous, violent age, when other families could easily be not just competitors but deadly enemies. The lengthy feud that divided the Houses of Lancaster and York was certainly not cricket.

Dynastic necessity raised problems that had all the makings of a dilemma. The family head must preserve the estate intact; he must ensure the continuity of the family line; and he should endeavour to improve the inheritance through political alliance or the acquisition of further property. Marriage was the key. There must always be a male heir, so a suitable wife had to be carefully chosen for the eldest son from a family of similar degree and status, and particularly one that might cement political alliances as well as give a valuable dowry. This arrangement, determined by the families of both sides acting communally, and with no thought of romantic attraction, produced a marriage that for the most part was acted out communally within the family and with little private intimacy. Mortality being what it was, the newly married couple had to produce several offspring to ensure the line; but, lest the bulk of the estate be dispersed, inheritance had to be restricted by primogeniture to the oldest surviving male. That left the remaining children without property or prospect.

The privilege of birth into an aristocratic family therefore came at a high personal price. The eldest sons had to wait in the wings, to be married as early as feasible to a wife not of their choosing, so they might breed as vigorously as the family required; but otherwise they waited on the deaths of their fathers before they could come into their own and take centre stage. Younger sons suffered different pressures. They had no claim on the family estates, and the more sons there were, the less their share of what inheritance lay outside the estate. That put a curb on their chances of marriage, so they might also loiter in the wings in case their older brothers either died before their fathers or eventually died childless. Were these hopes unrealized, they would in the end face hard choices, ones that would in all likelihood lower their status. They must leave the theatre and forsake their home. Then they might choose between attending on another lord, taking holy vows and entering the Church, setting their brains to learning and entering the law or some other profession, or risking all, either by emigration to town or by engaging on a chivalrous life of adventure.[13]

The pressures on aristocratic daughters were worse still. They might hope that a tempting dowry would win a suitable boy and carry them into a family equal to their own, where they would be set to childbearing. Lacking such a dowry, they might choose between spinsterhood or the veil, since marriage beneath them would heap disrepute on both themselves and their families. A nunnery could offer power, almost on a par with men's; a lordly bed outside wedlock might be a similar temptation for the few who would wager their reputation for high stakes; otherwise spinsterhood was just grey duty.

So the English aristocratic family system developed a peculiar ruthlessness to its kittens, if not drowning them, indifferently casting all but the first born into the water to see how they would swim. The heirs had to swim too. Failed political acumen and unwise alliance might drown an individual, or even the entire line. The old Norman aristocracy found it hard to keep its head above the buffeting waves stirred up during the regal contest between Stephen and Matilda. John's reign brought fresh storms, and the Wars of the Roses a tempest. A failure of economic acumen had the same result, even if this were slower. The fourteenth-century famines and plagues changed the economic climate by raising wages and lowering rents, stranding many a landowning aristocratic line, 'immobilised in sumptuous appurtenances, at once splendid and unrealisable', and the great Tudor price rise put paid to those that survived the Middle Ages, trapped by 'the magnitude of their commitments and the rigidity of their incomes'.[14]

The wonder was that this aristocratic way of life appealed to lesser classes. Although Kent and some eastern and northern counties preferred the equitableness of partible inheritance, elsewhere most lesser landowners, tempted by a whiff of power, accepted primogeniture, settled their estates on the eldest males of the next generation, and did their best to follow the county families. Society and the Church kept an eye on them: appearances mattered. Towns benefited so far as they took the enterprising cadets of these lesser families, but they might still lose out since the ultimate aim of making a fortune in town was to spend it back in the countryside.

In the fifteenth century, much of north-west Europe's middling and lower classes of both sexes tended to marry many years after reaching adulthood, whether they lived in town or country. These late marriages had probably been commonplace since the thirteenth century, if not well before. Teenagers might be lovers, but by the sixteenth century men contracted their first marriages on average at the age of twenty-seven or twenty-eight, and women at twenty-five to twenty-seven.[15] The specific reasons for this hesitancy are unclear. One cause must be the teaching of the Church through the Catechism, which tempered romance and gave gossips a field day when its commandments were flouted. Another cause was that legal consummation depended on the ability to set up house: a husband – a house bondman – and a housewife were not so called without reason. A marriage required a separate home since it was not the custom in north-west Europe for a married couple to live with one or other set of parents, as they did in the south. An inheritance, a gift or purchase allowed a couple to set up as householders, and these social and economic imperatives rather more than moral or romantic ones finally determined when a marriage would take place.

Frustrated romance thus became the baggage of every poet:

> My peyne is this, that what so I desire,
> That have I not, ne no thing lyk therto;
> And ever set Desire myn herte on fire.
> Eek on that other syde where-so I go;
> That have I redy, unsoght, everywhere,
> Me ne lakketh but my deth, and then my bere.[16]

Those who would get on in the world must put desire behind them and await their turn. There were few ways around this predicament. The poorest were unlikely to come into property, and had to fend against social deprivation as best they could. Marriage and legitimate children were largely beyond them. In the thirteenth century, when land hunger was acute in many rural areas, young men sought out widows with a title to land as marriage partners – and the older the women were the better. That way they might soon die, and the men, now established householders, would still be young enough to marry again and start a family.[17] It was not unknown for young women to try it on too, but the risks were great and the penalties damaging: they could find themselves left high and dry. Not all young women could enjoy cuckolding their aged husbands so readily as Chaucer's Alison – but she lived in town.

Late marriage meant small families, and high mortality made them smaller still. A newly married couple might start to have children at once, but low fertility limited marriages to perhaps eight pregnancies at most. (fig. 57) Not all would reach term, and uncounted numbers would end in stillbirth or death soon afterwards. One child in five was likely to die before its first year was out, and a second would never reach maturity, so monstrously high were the hurdles that bacteria set up between infancy and adulthood. Families teeming with children were not unknown, but neither were they common. On average, perhaps only half the pregnancies resulted in a grown adult.[18]

These survivors were enough to allow the population to grow slowly and more or less continually from the Norman Conquest until the end of the thirteenth century, the period of anarchy in the mid-twelfth century excepted. How this growth was spread throughout the country is unclear, although it was not a feature of towns. Poor and crowded housing, contaminated water, continuously present bacteria, monotonous unbalanced diet, starvation and other

57. Childbirth, from Guido Bonatti de Forlivio's *Liber Introductorium ad Iudicia Stellarum*, made for Henry VII in 1490; the baby, bound tight in swaddling clothes, will also be bound by the fortunes of its natal star, shining overhead. © British Library. MS Arundel 66 f 148 r

hurdles put paid to many a life. The mobility that differentiated town from country helped to spread disease as though it were a particularly desired luxury on sale in the market place. In Norwich infant mortality was 65 percent higher than in the countryside at the start of the twelfth century, and an adult male would not expect to live long beyond thirty-five years, a woman rather less.[19] Other crowded towns suffered similar disabilities. The plague years of the fourteenth and fifteenth centuries aggravated this beyond remedy. While infant mortality was particularly cruel, death culled the whole population, not just the newborn and the aged. Between them, disease and late betrothal curbed the duration of marriage, which seldom outlasted the twenty or so years that a couple devoted to reproduction and upbringing. A quarter and even a third of households contained children from whom death had taken a mother or father, leaving not just fairy tales populated with step-parents, cruel or otherwise.

The various diseases that brought early death were believed to result from a soul infected by sin, the outward signs of disability and physical deformity being just retribution. Recalling a visit to Ireland in 1184, Giraldus Cambrensis was appalled by 'so many individuals who were born blind, so many lame, maimed or having some natural defect', and concluded that this was the consequence of adultery, incest, illegitimate births and marriages, and indeed a lawless nation in which Nature herself was foully corrupted by perverse habits. Not only should such people be pitied, but – and here was the rub – they also carried a dire warning. God had permitted their sickness and suffering to purge their sins on earth, and they would reach heaven more quickly as a result. Cruelty and suffering were therefore seen as part of God's order and not to be avoided. Nevertheless, it was an act of charity to relieve these, as it also was to relieve poverty, since the poor and oppressed would eventually share God's throne and help to determine the fate of those who on earth had enjoyed the trappings of wealth.[20]

While many acts of benevolence were cynically motivated in this way, particularly in the two waning centuries of the Middle Ages, the genuine charity of Walter Suffield, 'of venerable memory', is well attested. As bishop of Norwich from 1245 to 1257, he wielded power over matters of both Church and state with political acumen, demonstrating an ability to compromise without slipping from the bedrock of his Christian principles, which 'blossomed with renowned virtues, holy deeds and devotion to God', exemplified by his gifts of alms to the poor, the sick and the needy for humanity's sake, not heavenly reward.[21]

The parable of Dives and Lazarus[22] weighed particularly heavily on Henry III, who went far beyond common acts of hospitality whereby the poor were fed at the gates of a lordly hall. Four of his great halls were decorated with depictions of the parable, so that all rich men who entered would be warned of the penalties of hell for failing to feed Lazarus at their gates. Moreover, Henry commanded that two or three thousand paupers, mainly the elderly and infirm, should be fed on the high feast days of the Church within Westminster Hall. The records of payments for these alms show that on at least two days in 1243–4 the numbers reached 10,000.[23]

For all these acts of charity, this was an age of ingrained cruelty. Seemingly as cruel as natural deprivation was the practice of sending off children when they reached puberty to serve in other households, where they would learn the ways of life. As a result, households of even a modest sort included a servant or two taken in from this source. Some might end up in towns. If they were lucky they entered a seven-year apprenticeship with the master of the house, at once becoming a member of his household on equal social terms with his own children. Less fortunate servants might move from family to family as circumstance dictated until at last they came into an inheritance or had saved enough to attain some kind of independence, or even had found a marriage partner who could take them out of their servitude. Lucky the diligent apprentice who caught the eye of his master's daughter and only child!

While death and this peculiar practice of teenage servitude fragmented the medieval population as a whole, one of the abiding features of urban populations was their mobility. People were drawn in, seeking a fortune. English and Welsh burgesses came in the first instance from the immediate locality of their towns. Coventry's founding fathers were mostly Warwickshire men, and in the mid-thirteenth century this was again true of Stratford-upon-Avon: perhaps 90 percent of the burgesses of this fifty-year-old foundation had come from within a radius of sixteen miles; and other Midland towns tell a similar story. Towns in Scotland were less attractive to natives, and King David looked to Englishmen, Frenchmen and Flemings to provide their first burgesses.

While English towns usually attracted locals, the reputation of a booming town might be so great that some of its burgesses were drawn from far afield. Reputation, however, diminished with distance, just as the difficulty and expense of travelling grew. Nearly half of Winchester's population in the thirteenth and early fourteenth centuries seems to have come from no more than a long day's walk or twenty miles away, perhaps a fifth from two days' walk, another fifth from three days', hardly a tenth from four days', and the remainder from further still.[24]

Generally, the larger the population, the greater the need of immigrants. London's numerous commercial and administrative openings attracted people in droves to the sweet jingling of silver, and therefore outstripped all other towns. So its pattern of immigration differs from Winchester's. Few came from ten miles away or less, and although nearly half originated from no more than forty miles away, a good quarter came from some forty to eighty miles and even more from over eighty miles away,[25] so great was the pull of its reputation. Its streets were paved with gold, fabulously, as that famed migrant Richard Whittington discovered; his journey, were it from his likely birthplace at Pauntley in Gloucestershire, was over a hundred miles.

The attractions of London were repeated by many county towns, though on a smaller scale, but, when these were hit by recession, the proportion of enterprising people drawn from afar would fall, as it did in Canterbury in the middle of the fourteenth century. Once, only a third of its burgesses were of Kentish origin, but this proportion rose to 93 percent during the quiet years when opportunity was no longer knocking at the door. So a general pattern emerged in which country people who lacked a likely inheritance but not trade or craft skills migrated to small towns, and from here, if they were successful, they went on to more important towns, with, perhaps, London as an ultimate destination.[26] Moreover, these migrants were mostly of the middling sort, neither from the families of abject serfs, nor of noble blood; their wealth lay not in deep purses but in enterprising minds bolstered by a certain familiarity with a chosen trade. Nevertheless, for success, they had to practise all their skills, and do so in such a way as to build up the funds to pay for an apprenticeship.[27] If luck deserted them, they joined the poorest of labourers, who, when they could find work, only earned a penny or two a day. These people had to live wherever they could – in crowded tenements, in single-roomed hovels, or, if they could afford it, in lodgings; but they had no economic worth and nobody would want to make much space for them, let alone build houses.

Just one class of poor did prompt the construction of buildings: the 'holy poor'. For a short while after the Conquest, various churchmen, seeking to reduce the torments of purgatory by their acts of charity, founded hospitals that would accept patients solely on the basis of need; but, as poverty became an overwhelming problem, they gave relief only to deserving individuals, not those who had fallen sick or into destitution through their 'owne foly' or 'rytous lyuying'.[28]

An ambitious and talented migrant might step over the sudden and catastrophic pitfalls that dogged all roads and become an apprentice in a specific trade or craft, serving a master and living in his household for seven or eight years in return for being taught its secrets. When this was successfully accomplished, the next stage was to set up on his own as a journeyman, whereby the practice of these secrets could be put to use for a daily wage. Journeymen could earn between 3d and even 6d a day, so they had money to spare for more than the basic necessities of life. Finally there was the promise of becoming a master and paying an entry fine to a guild. That achieved, the doors could open wide. They had a good chance in the heady expansive days of the thirteenth century, although by the fourteenth century urban depression was reducing the chance of achieving this.

Town people seem to have formed the first guilds some time before the Conquest. These were fraternities of affluent people, women as well as men, who came together for their mutual benefit by promoting acts of charity and welfare, including the provision of funeral rites and perpetual masses for their souls, together with the prayers, candles and bells that would ease the journey ahead through all the pains of purgatory. They organized religious festivals and such social benefits, common in village life but not otherwise in towns, as the care of widows and children. While guilds were often dedicated to saints, they looked after the needs of this world with regular feasting, which was supposed to symbolize Christ's Last Supper, and they made monetary and other loans to their members.

Guilds always insisted on exclusivity, which at first was based on social standing, and later on an established position within a trade or craft. Chaucer describes a haberdasher, a carpenter, a weaver, a dyer and a carpet-maker, united in their membership of an influential guild, 'clothed alle in o lyveree of a solempne and greet fraternitee'.[29] The gentility of trade made them acceptable to each other's society, for their fraternity served their social needs, not their trades. By the fifteenth century, when plague and strife brought depression to towns and minds, the incorporation of guilds for charitable purposes was commonplace. Self-help was their motto, and bequests for the worldly comfort of their brothers and sisters kept alive memories and guaranteed prayers for the soul after death. Chartered in 1441, the Fraternity of Corpus Christi had already existed in Maidstone since 1422, when John Hyssenden granted to twenty-five 'elderly and discreet' men 'a certain edifice, to be called the Bretheren Halle' together with a cloister and other buildings.[30]

In 1447 Ralph Lord Cromwell and Thomas Thurland founded a perpetual guild in the parish of St Mary, Nottingham, dedicated to the Holy Trinity, and comprising an alderman, two wardens and parishioners, 'for the maintenance of two chaplains to celebrate divine service for the good estate of us and Margaret our consort while we shall live and of our soul when we shall have departed this life'; and they were to put the profits of their property towards 'the relief of the poor and feeble brethren and sisters of the said fraternity'.[31]

A century after the Conquest, guilds were beginning to promote trades and crafts in individual towns, and, so as to achieve this, were paying the Crown sums ranging from a few shillings to several pounds to maintain rights of control within the town boundaries. Lincoln had a weavers' guild by 1129–30, and this was soon followed by others at London, York, Winchester, Oxford, Huntingdon and Nottingham.[32] York had a more general association of traders by 1130; there was a guild of leather workers by 1181; and eventually the city counted some eighty guilds in all, serving its various trades and crafts.[33] The most powerful of these was the Company of Mercers. Entry was not cheap: when William Katryk entered the Company in 1435 as the son of Thomas Katryk, already a member, his entry fine amounted to 3s 4d – about a week's earnings.

In the thirteenth century Lincoln had two important guilds: the Guild Merchant, which was essentially a trade cartel, and St Mary's Guild, which cared for its members' social and reli-

58. St Mary Redcliffe, Bristol. 'The fairest, goodliest, and most famous parish church in England', thanks to William Canynges, who paid for the raising of its clerestory and high vaults

59. The tomb of William Canynges and his wife, in St Mary Redcliffe, Bristol

gious needs. So as to accommodate its feasts and other festivities, St Mary's Guild purchased an impressive hall, possibly built a century beforehand for royal use. By the fourteenth century the guild had become so exclusive and grand in its ways that Corpus Christi Guild was founded in 1350 specifically to care for the 'common and middling ranks'.[34] Another Corpus Christi Guild, that of Cambridge, joined with another town guild, St Mary's, in 1352 to found a college in the town for the accommodation of students because, in a singular act of enlightenment, they recognized the benefits of learning. While many affluent guilds either purchased or built impressive halls, such as those at York, lesser guilds simply made use of a hall in an inn, for instance the Peacock at Chesterfield. Many towns had small guilds of this sort. The burgesses of Much Wenlock looked to the Guild of Our Lady, which supported a number of chantry priests on the rents of its properties in the town, but had no known hall of its own.[35]

Ludlow's burgesses favoured the rich and powerful Palmers' Guild, a quasi-religious foundation of the mid-thirteenth century with branches throughout England that ostensibly welcomed anyone who had made the pilgrimage to the Holy Land and brought back a palm as a souvenir. While the Palmers promoted pilgrimages and the salvation of souls, later, like so much else within the Church, they became heavily involved in commerce and land to pay for their activities.[36] The Ludlow guild was apparently served by ten priests in the town, paid for out of rents from its properties there, and soon after 1411 they built for their feasts a fine guildhall in Mill Street, which was notable for its aisles as well as the ornate cusped and carved trusses of its timber roof frame.[37]

At the start of the fifteenth century, Winchester boasted twenty-five trade and craft guilds to serve the interests of the city's butchers, bottle-makers, card-makers, carpenters, chandlers, cobblers, cooks, coopers, curriers, doublet-makers, dressmakers, glovers, goldsmiths, hosiers, innkeepers, masons, parchment-makers, quilt-makers, saddlers, skinners, smiths, spurriers, tailors, tanners and tilers.[38] In 1422 there were 111 separate trade and craft guilds listed in London.[39] Increasingly, as economic depression circumscribed trade in the fourteenth century and far more so in the fifteenth, these guilds endeavoured to establish monopolies; they hedged around their affairs with restrictions, formalizing their practices and endeavouring to protect their members by the imposition of a policy of exclusivity. The rewards were great. The most successful guilds became extremely powerful and, in some cases, grasped the reins of civic power. Once in, a master-craftsman might be promoted to the ranks of aldermen, as Chaucer's craftsmen hoped to be, and the next step was to become mayor. So a town's more important guilds fed its governing oligarchy.

For all this thriving activity and charitable care, towns could only sustain their populations through immigration rather than reproduction. Despite their wealth and privileges, burgesses seldom enjoyed long lives and notably failed when it came to sustained procreation. Some made fortunes and returned to the countryside as gentry, hoping to establish a dynasty; others failed and eventually moved on or died. This was never so true as it was in the years of urban decline in the later Middle Ages, when plague tipped the balance even further against urban continuity. That said, some families did establish themselves in towns and, through alliances with other families, were able to maintain themselves as a bourgeoisie, and to wield power and exert influence for several generations. But such vital families, content with urban life, were exceptional, and there were limits to their wealth: England, let alone Wales or Scotland, never produced its Medicis. London had no great patrician families who spanned the generations.

London and many another town nevertheless fostered the rise of such magnificent citizens as the draper and merchant John de Pulteney. Like his, the names of dozens of wealthy men of the fourteenth and later centuries are remembered and indeed still celebrated in the street names of many towns, their tombs and houses occasionally bearing witness to their achievements. Even in the thirteenth century, merchants such as Walter le Fleming, John of London and Roger Norman are recorded as piling up fortunes in Southampton, and William of Doncaster likewise in Chester. Their names are significant, suggesting the origins of their families and their immigrant status. In the fourteenth century they were followed by such Salisbury wool merchants as Robert of Knoyle, John Aunger and Robert Woodford, who were also ship masters as well as being deep into property.

60. Chipping Camden church. The brass commemorating William Grevel and his wife Marion. © National Monuments Record

In the fifteenth century, there were few who could rival William Canynges the Younger of Bristol, who employed a workforce of eight hundred on his fleet of ships and another hundred – masons and carpenters – at his properties in town. His house in Redcliffe Street, largely demolished in 1937, once proved the point, and the upper parts of the church of St Mary Redcliffe still do (fig. 58). He paid for these, perhaps fearing for his soul, and, after the death of his wife, took holy orders in 1467. So it is that one of his monuments in the church shows him as a rich citizen, but the other shows him as dean of Westbury, pious and ascetic, in his priestly habit.[40] (fig. 59)

Beautifying the Church was never more demonstrably a way to heaven than in the fifteenth century. William Grevel of Chipping Camden was described as a 'citizen of London and flower of the wool merchants of all England' on the splendid brass in Chipping Camden church that records his death on 1 October 1401 and that of his wife Marion on 10 September 1386. (fig. 60) He gave 100 marks 'for the new works to be carried out in the church'; but what marks him out today is his ostentatious stone house in the High Street, which he occupied following his return to his native town.[41]

These wealthy men dominated their respective towns and cities to such an extent that when they were assessed for tax they accounted for a sizeable proportion of what the whole borough owed. In his day the clothier Thomas Horton paid 70 percent of all the subsidy owed by Bradford-on-Avon, and it was common for a small group of burgesses to pay the bulk of the tax because they owned the bulk of the wealth.[42] For all that, none of these men founded great dynasties to rival those of Florence or Augsburg, or, for that matter, many a Continental city. Urban mortality cannot therefore be the only cause, since this was not a specifically British condition. More a British condition was a widespread attitude to urban life which saw it as a temporary means of accruing wealth that would be spent later elsewhere. 'Elsewhere' was the countryside, since the only sure basis of power was ownership of land and the allegiance of all who tenanted a country estate and paid rent; landowners, not merchants, were the dominating class.[43] So, when burgesses made their fortunes, and especially when they produced heirs, they or their descendants preferred to get out while the going was good. Sentiment may have pulled them back to the land of their birth. A stronger desire for power pushed them out of town to set up country estates, and their heirs went into one of the professions until they came into their inheritance.

Many lesser families that did rise to prominence in towns maintained themselves there through fruitful marriages. Between the mid-twelfth and early fourteenth centuries the families of St Laurence, Bulehouse, Isembard, Fleming, Bonhait and English successfully intermarried and kept their hands on the tiller of Southampton's economic and administrative affairs.[44] By 1263, over two thirds of London's recent aldermen came from a web of sixteen interrelated families, whose menfolk were united by the attractive idea of being Something in the City.[45] Similar circumstances prevailed to a lesser degree in other towns and cities – Bristol, Canterbury, Exeter, Gloucester and Hull. Money and power rubbed shoulders and attracted suitable daughters to continue a few of these lines.[46]

So far as can be gleaned from tax returns, these wealthy men whose names are known were in a tiny minority. While wealth isolated the richest from the poorest, and a rich man's house might insulate him from the wretchedness of poverty, he did not generally occupy an exclusive neighbourhood of like houses, but was surrounded by the houses of all conditions of men. (fig. 61) His city mansion typically faced inwards on to a courtyard, but its outward face was lined with small shops and tenements. Crosby Place – which was occupied progressively by Caetano Pinelli (a Genoese merchant), the rich wool merchant Sir John Crosby (who rebuilt it), the Duke of Gloucester (later Richard III), followed by Burgundian ambassadors, and, later still, several mayors – was just such a mansion, its entrance from Bishopsgate lying between rows of common messuages, with several more surrounding it.[47]

The chance of striking gold may have tempted the bulk of the migrants to medieval towns, but wealth was spread with extreme inequality. Luck favours the well prepared, but more preparation was needed than craft skills and an enterprising mind. Most burgesses did not join the executive club of the extremely wealthy, and the more ordinary inhabitants of towns and cities, for all their abilities, clung on to their precarious livelihoods as best they could. Few are

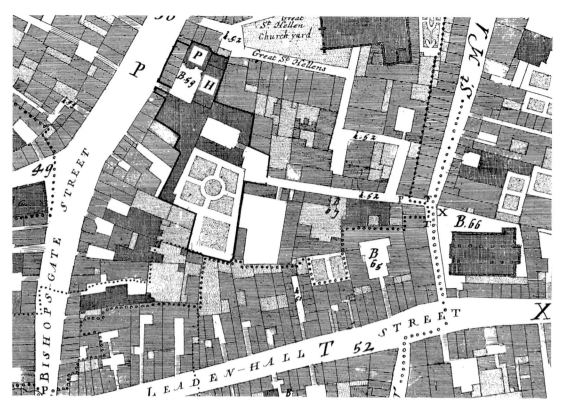

61. Crosby Place, City of London. Plan based on John Ogilby & William Morgan, *A Large & Accurate Map of the City of London*, 1676; the black outline indicates the extent of the property (marked *B.59*) comprising: an entrance from Bishopsgate Street, between one tenement to the south and five to the north; a front courtyard flanked by a parlour (*P*) and great hall (*H*), of 1466–75 (taken down and rebuilt in Chelsea, 1908–10, after the remainder was demolished); a rear courtyard and a further yard with a back entrance; and an extensive garden, the whole surrounded by small houses fronting Bishopsgate Street, Leadenhall Street, St Mary Ax and Great St Hellen's Churchyard. Based on Schofield 1994 [22]

62. Gerard's Hall, City of London. The undercroft of the Gisors mansion, as painted by C. J. M. Whichelo in 1810, still apparently in use for the storage of wine. The hall was first recorded in 1290 when both it and the undercroft were probably new. © Museum of London

as well known as their rich neighbours, but in many towns and cities, such as York, their names are recorded, and the streets where they lived, and even on occasion their houses too, are known, and in a few cases survive.

Only the poorest are unrecorded. Some had fireless lodgings, often outside the town walls. Others lived on the streets, practising patience, the beggar's virtue, just as many of them do today, memorable to those with pity but faceless to history. Their record may be found in the individual act of charity for their relief, and in the fraternal charitable works of the hospitals and guilds. But the poor were always with us, never of us.

Unlike the richest men, the lesser people who made up the bulk of a town's population tended to live in particular quarters that related to their trade or status, just as immigrants from some countries tended to live in quarters of their own. This is remembered in street names, like the common Mercer Street and the less common Chandler Street. Salisbury, curiously, had its Wynman Street, Carterstret, Melemonger Street and Chipper Street (the street of the market men).[48] Gradations of wealth marked out individual streets, such as York's Goodramgate, which was definitely for journeymen, and Stonegate, which was for craftsmen and therefore rather superior. The carpenters of Oxford lived by the hundred near the east gate where Merton Street joins High Street, and the smiths, who were not out of quite the same drawer, lived just outside, happily setting the scene for Chaucer's *Miller's Tale*.[49]

Apart from the migrants from within the kingdom, there were those from abroad. Since Bede's time foreign traders had always stood out, partly because they attracted attention, and thus came to be recorded. The Conquest encouraged large numbers of Normans to settle in Britain. A whole new borough was given over to them in Norwich. Between 1071 and 1075 Earl Ralph de Guader laid out the old Saxon market at Tombland, west of the cathedral, for the *Franci de Norwich*, and here they started to build stone houses, the remains of two of which have recently been excavated.[50] Among the new Norman traders, the Gisors family lasted as long as any. They presumably came from the eponymous Norman frontier town, capital of the Vexin, and are recorded in London by the late twelfth century. The first John Gisors was a flourishing wine merchant, becoming a City alderman in 1243 and twice mayor; and for three hundred years the family prospered as vintners and property owners.[51] (fig. 62)

The loss of Normandy to the French in 1204 set up lasting barriers and an end to this immigration. The possessions of the English Crown in Aquitaine made good some of the deficit, particularly with the flourishing Gascon wine trade. The Gisors family quickly stepped in here, and so did Chaucer's ancestors, who apparently came from France in the middle of the thirteenth century and traded as vintners.[52] They set up in London, and Chaucer's father, John Chaucer, was for a while deputy to the king's butler in Southampton. Many vintners favoured Southampton, where their cellars still survive: the rich south-west quarter of the town gained an Anglo-French flavour still recalled by the name of French Street, and there was 'the French street known as Bull Street', namely the present Bugle Street. Significantly, today's High Street in the poorer south-east and poorest north-east quarters was known as English Street in the Middle Ages.[53]

Good business had always attracted foreign traders in specific goods from specific places, even though only a minority of them settled down and married British women. Wool headed the list and encouraged large numbers of Flemings, smaller numbers of Italians. Communities of these traders tended to live in quarters of their own. Flemish weavers, for instance, occupied a quarter on the south-east side of Beverley.

While the rather uninformative evidence of people's names in Winchester shows a sharp decline in Norman names by the middle of the thirteenth century, a continuation of other names suggests the origins of other citizens in Aquitaine, Lombardy, Spain, Poland and Antioch, some of whom perhaps arrived quite recently. Inquiries in 1440 put the number of aliens at 118, some 3 percent of the city's population, of which well over a quarter were householders and therefore at least semi-permanent immigrants. Not surprisingly, Southampton, being a port, counted 145 aliens.[54]

Christian doctrine was not quite certain about all this trade, far less so about the money that made it work. 'Labour – the common lot of mankind – is necessary and honourable; trade is necessary, but perilous to the soul; finance, if not immoral, is at best sordid and at worst disreputable.'[55] Even so, it was less an inclination towards morality than a failure of the British to be first in the field that put banking into the hands of foreigners.

The cleverest money men were Jews. They were quite outside the ordinary run of foreigners and society as a whole.[56] They came to England with the Conqueror because he needed their business prowess. Many came from France, where they were already well established, and yet others from Germany. They were soon settled in the more prosperous towns, but were forbidden to enter trade or craft guilds, since these required their members to swear an oath to the Holy Trinity. There was a chink in this wall of restriction: because canon law forbade Christians to lend money on interest, Jews were able to exploit this impediment by oiling trade with their capital and charging very high rates of interest. William and his successors protected them, but treated them as personal possessions by taxing them more heavily than ordinary people. Jews were still able to flourish in these peculiar circumstances. They provided the capital equally for building cathedrals and waging war, as well as for engaging in the everyday processes of trade, and all this so successfully that they controlled a large proportion of the country's coinage. This made them at once popular for their usefulness and despicable for their wealth.

Jews could nevertheless be on good terms with their neighbours. The Church respected them as people as well as for their uses, and this feeling was returned. In 1189 the Jews of Canterbury prayed in their synagogue for the besieged Benedictine monks of Christ Church – then embroiled in a bitter dispute with the Cistercian Archbishop Baldwin over, among other things, the funding of his college at Hackington – and gave them food and drink.[57] (The synagogue, incidentally, was built on land held from a Canterbury citizen who himself held it at an annual rent of 4d from the monks of Christ Church.)

By the end of the twelfth century Canterbury's Jews were third in number after the colonies in London and Lincoln, if their payments to free their king can be taken at face value. When in 1192 Richard I was taken prisoner during his return from the third Crusade and held to ransom for 150,000 marks,[58] the London Jews stumped up £486 9s 7d, those of Lincoln £287 4s 11d, and those of Canterbury £235 19s 4d, so anxious were they for the return of their protector. Jacob, the 'Rothschild of Canterbury Jewry', himself subscribed £115 6s 8d.[59]

Winchester, as an important royal, administrative and financial centre, had a large Jewish population that may have been fifth or sixth at the time of Richard's ransom, but grew in the following century to become third. Like Canterbury's, Winchester's Jews were on good terms with their Christian neighbours. Almost uniquely, one Jew – Benedict – was admitted in 1268 to the guild merchant of the city. Henry III was deeply indebted to them since they allowed him to avoid demanding grants from a difficult parliament. Their houses were concentrated around their synagogue at what today is the south end of Jewry Street, close to the trade of High Street, but successful Christian traders were just as keen to live there too.

Jews in Colchester again congregated around the High Street, among the town's traders. Similarly, in London the Jews were well entrenched in the streets between Wood Street and Old Jewry, behind Cheapside's busy markets and near the Guildhall, and so were rich merchants. This seems to have been generally true of most towns with Jewish populations: while the Jews congregated in colonies, and sometimes were required to do so by law, these were by no means ghettos since wealthy Christians lived happily among them, cheek by jowl. There was apparently a widespread network of Jews based on the wool trade between Southampton, Winchester and the market towns to the north. Even more than ordinary merchants, Winchester's Jews seem to have sustained this contact with Jews in other towns, often travelling between them and sometimes maintaining lodgings for the purpose. Trade and the transfer of capital required no less.[60]

Because Jews commonly dealt with money, both bullion and tallies, they had to protect themselves and their property from the ravages of conflagration and common envy by living in strong houses of stone, whose remains are still visible in Lincoln and Norwich as well as in Normandy. It was once believed that these houses were built of stone specifically for this purpose and were known as Jews' houses accordingly.[61] The house in Steep Hill, Lincoln, once called Aaron's House, is one of these, but Aaron himself lived more grandly closer to the cathedral. Nevertheless, it was possibly built by another Jew, Moseus of York, whose wealth was less but whose needs were similar.[62] (fig. 63) Wealthy gentiles lived in these houses too, and it seems that stone was as much an expression of their wealth as a means of defending it.

During Henry II's reign, Jewish wealth and influence reached a peak, but after his death in 1189 a century of persecution ensued. In part this was a consequence of Christian xenophobia stirred up by the third Crusade, but the chance to wriggle out of inconvenient debts to Jewish financiers was also responsible. The anguish started in 1190 with the mass death of York's Jews besieged in Clifford's Tower by a Christian mob. On Palm Sunday rioters in Bury St Edmunds killed fifty-seven Jews, and Abbot Samson expelled the rest of the Jewish community from the town later the same year.

Individuals were harassed too. Jews were often accused of the ritual murder of Christian children: a case was reported in Winchester as early as 1192, and in 1255 the Lincoln Jews were said to have crucified the boy Hugh, whose body was reclaimed by the dean and chapter and given a martyr's burial in the cathedral choir.[63] The Jew Pictavin, allegedly involved in this murder, was dispossessed as a result. There were worse punishments for lesser crimes against property: the Jewess Belaset, who lived at Jew's House in Lincoln, was hanged in 1290 for clipping the king's coin.[64]

These continual acts against individuals were matched by others against whole populations: damage to Jewish property in Winchester was countered by a royal edict for their protection in 1270, and the cathedral priory paid up £100 in damages. In 1275 there were anti-Jewish riots in Southampton. Already the Ordinances of 1253 restricted Jews to those communities that had already been established in King John's time, and decreed that worship in synagogues should be subdued 'so that Christians hear it not', and placed all kinds of limits on intimacy between Christians and Jews.[65] Again in 1275, Edward I, who cared little for Jews, ordered the removal of Marlborough's Jewish inhabitants to Devizes, citing his mother's wishes, and similarly the Jews of Gloucester were to be transferred to Bristol, those of Worcester to Hereford, and those of Cambridge to Norwich, 'without doing any

63. Aaron's House, Lincoln, recently renamed Norman House, since Aaron in fact lived elsewhere in the city

64. An Italian moneylender, depicted in a fourteenth-century manuscript, engaged in the formalities of a transaction, including a proper show of hospitality, that attend the deal. © British Library. MS Add 27,695 f7v

damage to them in respect of their persons or their goods'.[66] Despite that injunction, no doubt more honoured in the breach than the observance, the end was near. In 1290 Edward expelled them. All physical remains of their existence in England were quickly expunged: their synagogues have all but vanished, the possible remains of a few of them being a matter for debate,[67] and only two inscribed fragments – one from a ritual bath in Bristol, the other from a tombstone in Northampton – survive today.[68]

The Jews' value in facilitating trade was again quickly expunged. Merchants from Lucca and soon other Italians – Friscobaldi, Bardi and Peruzzi – learnt the arts of usury from the Jews and pinched their business.[69] (fig. 64) Lombards were in London before the end of the twelfth century, lending money on pawns and on sums owing to the pope. Lombardy became synonymous with banking, and that meant making money from money – even clipping coins on occasion as the Jews had done. Bankers were, in short, indispensable. London consequently gained Lombard Street, though not without protest. Bishop Grosseteste of Lincoln, a stern critic of the indulgent Papacy, rebuked the Lombards for their activities in facilitating the capital's trade. The bishop of London went further and expelled them, but they were soon back, thanks to papal protection. Later on in the thirteenth century, Archbishop Peckham refused to pay the Italians interest on the very Christian grounds that it was his 'duty to take strong measures against such lenders', but he was forced to relent when Pope Nicholas III threatened excommunication.[70] Langland, who, a century later, lived in London close to this trade of 'Eschaunges and chevysaunces',

> . . . lerned among Lumbardes a lesson, and of Jewes—
> To weye pens with a peis · and pare the hevyeste,
> And lene it for love of the cros, to legge a wed and lese it[71]

Credit was not in pennies alone, pared or otherwise. From at least the later thirteenth century wool was exported on credit, even when capital was not directly involved.[72] If strapped for cash, a monastery might well accept payments from an Italian merchant on the basis of the wool still on the backs of its flocks. By the fifteenth century wool had almost taken the place of gold, at least so far as accounting was concerned, and the use of credit was so advanced that it strung a chain of transactions between merchants, exporters, weavers and yet more merchants that could link a fleece on the Cotswolds to a garment on the back of a Spaniard or Pole. This was not barter, since the transactions involved no exchange of goods; nor was it usury, since no interest was charged; but there was an interest assumed by all parties in this advancement of trade. 'Bargaynes' and 'chevyssaunce' – that was the key, as Chaucer well knew.[73] This wealth, in origin the product of rural husbandry, needed the commercial skills of urban middlemen. Many of them died leaving their physical wealth evenly divided between stock and cash, but these together might be only a small proportion of what they were owed as a consequence of the deals they had set up on credit.

Credit was no longer a dirty word, least of all in Rome. The Church had long lost her virgin-white integrity. The Papacy was, among other things, Europe's greatest financial institution in the Middle Ages, receiving monetary payments from all western Christendom. This might violate its teaching – indeed grossly, according to the moralists – which, they said, now followed 'not the gospel according to St Mark, but according to the marks of silver'. A wail of condemnation rose up against the iniquity of the Church, which seemed to have substituted avarice for the cross on its altars. The temple should be swept clean, but it was too late. The word 'cross' itself became slang for the gold coin that bore a cross on its back, and those who succeeded by trade temporized. They put their faith in Thomas Aquinas: 'It is lawful to desire temporal blessings, not putting them in the first place, as though setting up our rest in them, but regarding them as aids to blessedness, in as much as they support our corporal life and serve as instruments for acts of virtue.'[74] Money spent judiciously on desirable goods would lead to the profit that would make virtuous acts possible. Money spent virtuously on acts of charity would surely find favour with God and a place in heaven.

Thus did merchants reason, and long before Aquinas put words to the thought. Christianity, after all, preached divine ordination, but, to ensure their place in heaven, merchants set to, founding churches and chapels, chantries and colleges, all to expiate mercantile avarice. In the expanding boroughs of medieval England these came to be seen as units of property, belonging to lords secular as well as ecclesiastical, and to fraternities of burgesses and even to individuals. They might be private property as often as communal property, so keen were citizens to establish and to be seen to be establishing their credentials with Almighty God, and equally served parishes, monasteries, hospitals, fraternities and chantries.

Unlike the countryside, where a single parish church served not only a village but also its outlying hamlets and farmsteads, in most pre-Conquest towns churches and chapels had already proliferated to such an extent that their over-provision ultimately became an embarrassment. London's City churches, numbering over a hundred by the start of the fourteenth century and by no means all of them rebuilt after the Great Fire, are still thick on the ground; (fig. 65) those of Norwich, reputedly one for every week of the year, but in fact several more, tell the same story; and Winchester, again, once had as many.[75] Wales tended to follow the English pattern on a smaller scale,[76] but Scottish burghs, meanwhile, had only one church, although this was strongly attached to the needs of the burgesses.[77] New foundations fell off after the eleventh century, and the numbers of churches in some towns even began to decline in the later Middle Ages.

Yet in many towns all over Britain the arrival of the friars in the thirteenth century started another campaign of church building. In particular, the Dominican Blackfriars and Franciscan

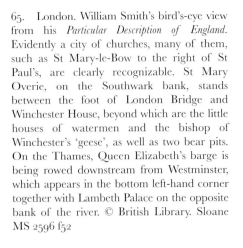

65. London. William Smith's bird's-eye view from his *Particular Description of England*. Evidently a city of churches, many of them, such as St Mary-le-Bow to the right of St Paul's, are clearly recognizable. St Mary Overie, on the Southwark bank, stands between the foot of London Bridge and Winchester House, beyond which are the little houses of watermen and the bishop of Winchester's 'geese', as well as two bear pits. On the Thames, Queen Elizabeth's barge is being rowed downstream from Westminster, which appears in the bottom left-hand corner together with Lambeth Palace on the opposite bank of the river. © British Library. Sloane MS 2596 f52

66. Tiverton Church. The Greenway Chapel carved with merchant ships, anchors and other symbols, and a far less prominent frieze adorned with scenes from Christ's Passion

Greyfriars chose urban sites for their houses, usually just outside the walls, where they could expect the greatest financial as well as spiritual increment.[78] Their houses and hospitals, as well as colleges and fraternity and chantry chapels, added to the great numbers of churches. This gave towns a very different character from that of the countryside: they were full of sacred buildings, and the air rang with the silvery tones of a thousand priests singing masses for the wealthy dead.

So great were the advantages in their transactions that many a merchant would invest in land. Canterbury's leading citizen, Robert son of Richard, owned so much land in the city about 1200 that he gave, firstly, four shops in Burgate to Christ Church to establish his anniversary, and, secondly, land worth an annual rent of 10s to St Augustine's to found another anniversary, this time for both himself and his wife.[79] Stephen Cornhill, a London draper and wool exporter, left property in London valued at over £33 at the time of his death in 1295. A century later every London merchant of substance was also a landlord: in the middle of the fourteenth century William Eynsham, a wealthy wool exporter and cloth merchant, owned over seventy tenements in London to the value of some £110.[80] When the vintner and five-times mayor of Oxford John Gibbes died in 1386–7 his property in the city included Knaphall – a wine tavern next to the Guildhall – and Ducklington's Inn, both in St Aldate's, a house, tenements and shops at Carfax, and a site in Cornmarket where he was building New Inn and a row of five shops with rooms above.[81]

The motive for investing in property might be less for profit than for social advancement, and, of course, for eternal salvation. William Wyggeston (1467–1536), Leicester's richest citizen in the late fifteenth century, gained his wealth from the county's wool by selling it through the staple at Calais, where he was four times mayor; in 1511 he founded a chantry in the Newarke church for two priests who would pray for the salvation of his and his brothers' souls, and in 1513 he founded a hospital for Leicester's aged and decayed citizens, twelve poor men and twelve poor women.[82] John Greenway, Tiverton's richest merchant, similarly beautified the parish church, (fig. 66) adding his initials to the luxuriously decorated porch he gave it, and when he died in 1529 his will provided for the foundation of almshouses for five poor men in Gold Street, each with two rooms and a garden, as well as a chapel which was a plainer version of the one he added to the church. Just a few were content with unostentatious humanity in these threatening times. One, according to the inscription on his tomb, was Allaine Dister, who died in 1534:

A Clothier vertuous while he was
In Lavenham many a yeare.
For as in Lyfe he loved best
The poore to clothe and feede
So withe the riche and all the rest
He neighbourlie agreed
And did appoynt before he died
A special yearlie rent
Whiche shoulde be every Whitsuntide
Amonge the poorest spent.

There was no greater name in fourteenth-century London than that of Sir John de Pulteney. He was a City draper and merchant, four times lord mayor in the 1330s, and financier to Edward III, his loans probably paying for the campaigns that led to victory at Sluys and Crécy. By today's standards he was a multimillionaire, one who could have bought out a handful of noblemen. He built a princely house in the City,[83] and, feeling the call of the shires and perhaps desiring to found a dynasty, purchased from the moribund de Penchesters their ancient manor of Penshurst in Kent. He obtained a licence to crenellate in 1341 and proceeded to build there the county's finest surviving hall. So much for this world. For the other he founded a chantry, a college and a friary. His patronage of the City parish of St Lawrence Pountney gave it its name. This attention to things of the soul was timely. In 1349 his worldly hopes were all brought to nought, since that year he died, probably of the plague.

While Pulteney reached the highest position a burgess might achieve in the capital, burgesses themselves formed the upper levels of urban society generally, with only kings, princes and lords above them. For the most part they were men and the heads of their households, but women could also reach this position, either as widows or in their own right. Women probably enjoyed greater equality in Anglo-Saxon England, few of royal birth after the Conquest – Queen Matilda aside – attaining the heights scaled by Alfred's daughters. The Normans, with their feudalistic trappings of militarism, were less favourable towards women as equal partners, so ambitious women had to achieve power through men rather than directly. They could nevertheless establish a separate and even an independent economic position in society, although this seldom led to the merest fraction of Pulteney's riches.

Women were often heads of households where men were lacking, and sometimes became burgesses too, just as they could rise to higher rank in the Middle Ages – even in the Church. The Church was suspicious of women, having never quite forgiven Eve for tempting Adam. Even so, medieval nunneries had their share of powerful and brainy women, after the Conquest as before. The Church was not their only refuge. Medieval women, at least in London, were often educated and could obtain a training in a trade, as well as being independent householders.[84]

Women's names appear in rent roles alongside men's, but always less frequently and usually occupying smaller and cheaper burgages.[85] For instance, there was Athelisa of Canterbury, a tenant of Christ Church who in the 1160s paid an annual rent of 4s for land near the city wall, leased out some of it for 7s and thereby made a profit of 3s. Then in 1234 a list of arrears includes the tenants of at least nine shops apparently belonging to Susanna de Planaz. As the daughter of a wealthy landowner in Kent, and learning young, she had long beforehand made a name for herself in Canterbury by wheeler-dealing in property.[86]

To own buildings was not so great a rarity among medieval women as to build them, yet there are several records of women working in the building industry. An account of 1327 records masons, carpenters and plasterers being paid daily between 4d and 5d in York, while women doing unspecified tasks were paid 2d – double the usual female rate. Unskilled female labour was apparently fairly common on building sites. In Scotland, 103 male ditchers were employed at Linlithgow in 1302 at 2d a day, and no less than 140 women worked with them for 1d. Female labour did not always suffer this gross discrimination: in Ripon in 1392 a woman assisting a dauber was paid 3d, that is 1d less than his rate, and in 1400 women were paid 4d when the daily wages for masons, carpenters, plumbers and slaters was just 5d.[87] Women not only

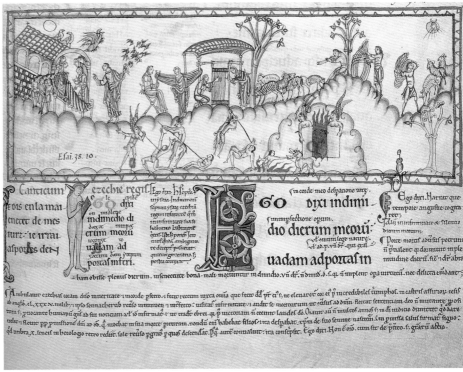

67. The smith's wife forging nails for Christ's crucifixion at a waist-level hearth, as portrayed *c.* 1330 in the *Holkham Bible*. © British Library. MS Add 47,682 f31

68. Women working a mid-twelfth-century, two-beam loom (for making hangings, rugs and coverlets), set up within a weaving shed, in a scene that illustrates the writing of Hezekiah as told in *Isaiah* 38, 12: 'Mine age is departed, and is removed from me as a shepherd's tent: I have cut off like a weaver my life: he will cut me off with pining sickness: from day *even* to night wilt thou make an end of me.' Eadwine's Canterbury Psalter, MS R.17.1, f.263r. © The Master and Fellows, Trinity College, Cambridge

worked in the building industry but sometimes provided its materials. Constance Tiler supplied tiles at 10s (50p) the thousand in York in 1327, and sixty years later Katherine Lightfoote supplied 2,000 tiles for the king's bathroom at Sheen.[88]

Perhaps the most surprising trade in which women made their name was as blacksmiths. Less surprising, perhaps, is that working with the fires of hell gave them an evil reputation. According to the *Northern Passion* it was a smith's wife, 'a fell women and full of strife', who forged the nails for Christ's crucifixion after her husband feigned an injured hand.[89] (fig. 67) The far-from-fallen Katherine of Bury learnt the blacksmith's trade from her husband, Walter of Bury, who had been the king's smith for nine years; in 1346 she was paid 8d per day to 'keep up the king's forge in the Tower and carry on the work of the forge', because her son Andrew, whose task this was, had left to campaign at Crecy. She was paid at exactly the same rate as her son, and did well. She was probably the very same Katherine the 'smith-wife' whom the king employed at Westminster in 1348 for 'steeling and battering the masons' tools.' Another smith-wife, Agnes Cotiller, promised in 1364 to train Juseana as an apprentice, 'to feed, clothe and teach her, and not to beat her with a stick or knife.'[90] These tasks may have been more managerial than physical, yet an account of 1408–9 shows that female muscle could equal male, but not for equal pay: among the tasks allotted to a 'smytheman's' wife were helping to break up rock, blowing or working the bellows, and helping at the bloom hearth, but for these she received only one penny for every shilling paid to her husband.[91]

Occasionally women achieved the full status of a merchant or craftsman and enjoyed its legal privileges, and so became members of guilds. In the building trades, as in others, women were accepted as members of a guild just as soon as their husbands or fathers became masters; they attended feasts, though were charged less on account of their smaller appetites, but a fully paid subscription gave their souls an equal right to a sung mass.[92]

Women far more commonly found roles in the clothing industry, where several activities were specific to them. Medieval illustrations of carding, spinning, combing and weaving almost invariably show women at work, not men. (fig. 68) These activities made 'spinsters' of women and their sex 'the distaff side'. Women were also cloth-cutters, dressmakers and glovers. They worked with silk, which was imported for the luxury trade; spinning it, embroidering it and making braid. Much of their labour was in the convent, where their embroidered and braided copes, amices, orphreys, frontals and palls satisfied the clerical dandy. From at least the thirteenth century there was similar work outside the cloistered wall in city workshops to satisfy the demands of court.[93]

Cloth-making was a woman's preserve in Saxon England, but the Conquest brought improved tools and looms, and, with these, professionalism and male domination. Yet, while Chaucer's Good Wife of Bath may have owed her business to her husband, it was she who maintained it and made it famous:

> Of clooth-makyng she hadde swich an haunt
> She passed hem of Ypres and of Gaunt.[94]

In many a family business, the husband might devote his time to manufacturing while his wife managed the shop and the whole process of retailing. (fig. 69) Women were cooks and bakers, they brewed ale and managed taverns, using charm to attract custom as well as business acumen to maximize profits.

It is not necessarily a denigration of female business skills or an accusation of inferior morality, as the Church so readily believed, to suggest that women would augment these by using their appearance in this way. Kitt the tapster of Canterbury's Chequers of Hope welcomed Chaucer's Pardoner 'with a friendly look, al redy for to kiss',

> And he, as a man y-lerned of such kindenes,
> Braced hir by the midell, and made hir gladly chere
> As thoughe he had y-knowne hir al the rather yeer
> She haled him into the tapstry, there hir bed was maked:
> 'Lo, Here I ligg,' quod she, 'my self al night al naked,
> Withouten mannes company . . .'[95]

Much she promised, but little gave, and, for his troubles, took his purse.

Neither is it a denigration of either tapsters' skills or male powers of bargaining that a certain susceptibility led to the practice of that oldest profession of all. Official attitudes were determined by fear, particularly of underhand methods. In 1351 a proclamation in the City of London attempted to stop 'common lewd women' from wearing noble attire. This was a vain

70. The rape of Dinah (*Genesis* 34), curiously recalled by the fourteenth-century *Egerton Genesis*, as though this were the consequence of gratuitous shopping: a group of women are shown beside a stall, tempted by a display of belts, knives and purses, unaware of the greater threat to virtue lying at their very feet. © British Library. MS Egerton 1894 f 17)

endeavour. How else could the alleys off Cheapside have gained their notorious reputation and such graphic names as Popkirtle and Gropecuntlane?[96] (fig. 70) Nobody missed the pun in Cocks Lane, and Flower de Luce Alley was for those who had no doubt where delight really lay.

Here and elsewhere, inns and taverns were as good a place as any to start looking for a whore, because they employed women who were anxious to supplement their income and welcomed travellers in need of relaxation. It was not only the taverns of Eastcheap that had their Mistress Quickly and Doll Tearsheet. Entering a City tavern Langland's Gluttony found

> Cesse the Souteresse sat on the benche.
> Watte the warner and his wif bothe,
> Tymme the Tynker and tweyne of his [knav]es,
> Hikke the Hakeneyman and Hugh the Nedlere,
> Clarice of Cokkeslane and the Clerk of the chirche,
> Sire Piers of Pridie and Pernele of Flaundres,
> Dawe the Dykere, and a dozeyne othere—[97]

Pernele and all the other Flemish streetwalkers so offended respectable citizens by 'the illicit works of their lewd flesh' that in 1417 an ordinance was made for the abolition of stews within the City.[98] They were even refused lodging there, and were supposed to keep themselves to 'the places thereunto assigned, that is to say, to the stews on the other side of Thames, and Cokkeslane'.[99] Thus enfranchised, Southwark embraced visitors to London like nowhere else: its inns and taverns were the best of all, and entertainments of all kinds augmented the wealth of its service industries. 'The ale of Southwerk' induced tales of harlotry;[100] its riverside brothels delighted all London, tempting priests and monks as well as the lay population's lustier and sadder members. Its excitements were dangerous, condemned for their wickedness and, in the same breath, condoned for their convenience.

All this their landlord well knew. How else could the Southwark girls have been called the bishop of Winchester's geese? The back streets of Winchester, as again he knew, had a similar reputation. The city's brothels were liberally scattered around within the walls. In the fifteenth century *les horizontales* especially favoured Hyde Street on account of its large numbers of small cottages and its freedom from city jurisdiction, being outside the northern gate. The lax attitude of the landlord, the abbot of Hyde, can only have encouraged the trade that paid their rent. A little later Gold Street, within the walls, gained a similar reputation simply on account of its isolated rows of cottages.[101]

Despite their vows, clerics did not themselves always live 'reverently, discreetly, advisedly, soberly, and in the fear of God'; they even braved public opprobrium and behaved 'like brute beasts that have no understanding'.[102] Clerical debauchery is scattered throughout English literature, often to make fun of hypocrisy. It was, however, a moral point that Langland made in recalling the priests who openly went out with Clarice and her like. By the early fifteenth century, at least for those of them blessed with divine prescience, the fear of God was intensified by a new fear, if the corpse of a young woman seemingly buried by the Blackfriars of Gloucester is valid evidence: her skeleton is marked by an advanced stage of syphilis.[103]

6

From plague, pestilence and famine

The late Middle Ages

It was the agricultural profits of the thirteenth century that fulfilled the promise of the Norman Conquest, even though the rich became very rich indeed and the poor became indigent and starved. The population reached some 5 or 6 million, probably a higher figure than in Roman times and a size not to be repeated until the eve of the Industrial Revolution in the eighteenth century. People must be fed, but in some rural parishes the pressure on land was so great that little remained for cultivation beyond infertile dust. Scarcity of land pushed people into the towns, where they arrived hungry, destitute and homeless. A few took to urban life and profited from its opportunities. The masses huddled in rookeries or on the streets, a prey to disease, awaiting the fires of purgatory in the hope of a seat in heaven.

London's population was pushing 80,000, possibly even 100,000. Far outstripping all other British towns and cities, it compared at last with the dozen or so great cities of Europe from Constantinople to Cordoba that looked to the Mediterranean, and the handful of newer cities of the north – Paris, Gent and Cologne. London's gain and Europe's gain were Britain's loss, or, at least, that of her towns. Their single largest industry was cloth, but the highly organized Continental industries in Italian and especially Flemish towns became so fiercely competitive in the thirteenth century that England turned to exporting raw wool rather than supplying its home manufacturers. However one interprets the causes and effects of the economic state of the nation at the start of the fourteenth century, crisis lay around the corner.[1]

During the second decade of the fourteenth century this had shown itself, and by the 1340s the old conditions of rising grain prices and cheap labour had been reversed. Foul weather and crop failures in 1314 and 1315 brought starvation and scattered corpses all round Europe.[2] In Britain, this upset the balance of labour, production, prices and trade, by entering full graveyards and empty granges into the account. In the period 1324–6 floods struck, and so ravaged flocks of sheep that their numbers never recovered. Exports of wool, as a result, rapidly declined from the peak of 46,000 sacks, or 6,000 tons, recorded between Michaelmas 1304 and Michaelmas 1305.[3] Market towns and ports had to seek new goods or fail.

On top of this natural disruption there was already the cost of fruitless war with Scotland. This strained royal finances and aggravated the already difficult economic conditions of the time. In Scotland this state of affairs was all but lethal to its burghs. These were not much by English standards, but the campaigns of Edward I and his ill-advised, wayward son Edward II were met by a scorched-earth policy, one that successfully denied Scotland to the English and at once the benefits of urban life to the Sots. What little they could lose, they lost.

To aggravate the waste, the first skirmishes of the Hundred Years' War broke out. In 1338 Edward III, claiming its crown, invaded France. The French immediately responded with a raid on Southampton, leaving houses in flames.[4] They attacked Rye in 1339, and it was their target again in 1377 and 1385. They burnt Teignmouth in 1340,[5] and sacked New Winchelsea in 1359, destroying half its church. (fig. 71) They burnt Yarmouth on the Isle of Wight in 1377 (given a charter in 1135, the town had fifty houses, which made it pre-eminent on the Isle of Wight at the start of the fourteenth century, but this role was now at an end[6]). In 1403 it was the turn of Plymouth. All the southern ports were at risk, even after the war formally ended in

71. New Winchelsea. Air view from the north-east of the town founded in 1288, showing (with roman numbers) some of the thirty-nine quarters surrounding St Thomas's church (1), and, further from it, some of the quarters that are now empty; the land falls sharply at the bottom of the view, below Strand Gate (2), which provides one of the two original entrances to the town; meanwhile part of a wide street was used as a market place (3). See M. Beresford & St Joseph 1979, 238–41.
© National Monuments Record

1453. The French had already attacked Sandwich twice before, destroying its suburb of Stonor in 1385, when in 1457 a party of 4,000 landed behind the town, breached its defences, murdered the mayor and left half of it in flames. This was the reverse side of the campaign medals struck with the glorious names of Crécy, Poitiers and Agincourt.

The south coast was not the only war zone. In 1333 Edward III had retaken Berwick. Not surprisingly, the Scots allied themselves to the French against their old enemy, and recaptured Berwick, thus starting a century and a half of marching and counter-marching which only ended with the English finally taking the town for good in 1482. Even the Welsh joined in, headed by Owain ab Gruffydd, Lord of Glyndwr and Sycharth (Shakespeare's Glendower). When his former master Henry IV succeeded to the throne in 1399 he rebelled, and, allied with the French, remained a thorn in the English side for nearly a decade.

With war on two fronts, and occasionally three, England became isolated from Europe, artistically and economically. Trade was upset, and poor European silver production aggravated the decline. By the 1320s the population had stopped increasing and, perhaps, even before the outbreak of the wars began to fall as a result of famine and uncertain food supplies. Definite changes were in the air. Before they resolved into a new pattern there came the Black Death.

The arrival of bubonic plague in 1348 marks the great turning point of the Middle Ages. Death opened 10,000 doors for men to take their exits. Overall, Britain lost a third of her population, perhaps more. Many towns lost half their people owing to the great risk of contagion. Some monastic communities were even more afflicted. Young monks, fresh from the countryside and unused to the contamination of urban life, lay down in their crowded dormitories to sleep and awakened before the even more crowded gates of heaven. Death reaped Westminster's monks to a man.[7]

After two years the plague died down, but its cull was not complete. Some sort of recovery gathered way in the 1350s; then the survivors had to bear further visitations. Between 1361 and 1485, thirty years saw fresh outbreaks of plague, each lasting a year or two. Twelve affected the whole country, but, as time went by, the plague satisfied its appetite on the insanitary conditions of the towns, leaving the countryside more or less free; eight visitations were confined to London alone.

The consequences of poor harvests, starvation and then plague were far from uniform, but eventually they undermined the growth in population that characterized the twelfth and thirteenth centuries. This unbalanced the old order of cheap labour and expensive foodstuffs that had so favoured agrarian landowners. Some villages were abandoned while others were hardly touched. Yet, for all the greater threat of their plague-bearing vermin, towns still attracted migrants; the countryside needed fewer hands to tend the harvest because the demand for food had fallen, while emptied houses and the promise of employment were an alluring feature of some towns. Though many towns nevertheless went into decline, this was more through economic failure than an inability to sustain their populations.

The Hundred Years' War wrought great changes in Britain's economy. The disruption of imports of cloth transformed weaving at home. Partly through government action forbidding exports of wool, weaving quickly became a domestic craft, and soon a rural industry wherever pastoral farming had flourished. The West Country, the West Riding of Yorkshire, the Weald and East Anglia all hummed and creaked with spinning and weaving.

The new centres grew up not so much where there had been old ones, nor where sheep were herded – land which was generally under strong manorial control and lacked a good water supply – but where pastoral economies allowed yeomen with a little capital to spare, time on their hands after tending their cattle, and a good water supply, to organize an efficient home industry. So effective was their competition that weaving ceased to be concentrated in such towns as Coventry and Salisbury that had specialized in it, but in individual farmsteads out in the countryside. Cloth merchants were increasingly now natives, not foreigners, and they grasped their chance and looked abroad for new customers.

This brought a new agricultural and mercantile class into being, one that distinguishes the late Middle Ages from the era before the plague. Towns were not favoured as they had been, and had to change their roles or face decline. Lincoln declined rapidly, at first because the plague had bitten so deeply, and then because its vital waterways – the Fossdyke to the Trent and the Witham to Boston – were failing. This contraction removed pressures to rebuild. Many of its rather small stone houses, built in the heady days of the twelfth century, consequently survived until the nineteenth century did away with them, whereas in a more successful city they would soon have been replaced by larger and more adaptable houses, built of timber. In Nottingham decay meant more still: not picturesque stagnation, but houses themselves decaying and their sites falling empty.

The decline of Winchester, which had reached the peak of its fortunes by the end of the thirteenth century, is particularly marked by its failing population. Within a few years of the outbreak of the Black Death this had halved. Although there was some recovery, the population never reached its medieval peak again until the middle of the nineteenth century. A petition of about 1450 records ten deserted streets and a thousand empty houses. In Lower Brook Street even fairly new houses were abandoned, but, despite this, others were being constructed in High Street, a prime site where there was still enough business to require some renewal. The design of these new houses, however, shows no evidence of bowing to the changed circumstances. If the failing demand made land cheaper, houses were not built larger accordingly; failing demand also reduced the amount builders would be willing to invest in houses even where there was still a small profit to be made.[8]

Seventeen churches lacked priests, and the church of St Mary Tanner Street was entirely abandoned. Fifty-four parish churches had served Winchester in 1300, but, by the Reformation, nine out of every ten had closed for want of a congregation. Moreover, the Black Death killed off nearly half the clergy in the diocese. The Church as an institution was less affected. The bishop of Winchester was possibly England's greatest landowner, his sheep still the most numerous. The profits flowed in, to be reinvested in buildings of the utmost magnificence. William of Wykeham founded Winchester College in the 1380s with the express intention of educating fresh clergy to replace those who had died of the plague. (fig. 72) At the same time he founded New College, Oxford, on land made derelict by the plague, giving both institutions buildings that were as advanced in their planning as they were sumptuous in their decoration. He continued with the modernization of his cathedral's nave, remodelling its ancient Romanesque form into up-to-date Perpendicular. For all the money ploughed into these works, and for all the revival of royal interest in the city – Henry IV marrying Joan of Navarre there in 1403 – the decline was not to be reversed, and the city's cloth industry suffered continual vicissitudes.[9]

72. William of Wykeham, the founder, with the fellows and scholars of Winchester College, which appears in a recognizably accurate form in the background. Chaundler MS 288 f3r. Reproduced by permission of the Warden and Fellows, New College, Oxford. © Bodleian Library, Oxford

However badly the plague struck Oxford, it is full of buildings of both town and gown that date from the later Middle Ages, thanks to Wykeham and his like. Learning triumphed similarly at Cambridge, where the first outbreak of the Black Death may have killed half its students. Contacts with Europe spread disease, but also provided the stimulus to replenish numbers with fresh faces in the unique academic environment that the two towns nourished.

The plague dealt York a blow, as it did other towns, but York suffered a greater decline through the failure of its cloth industry. This continued to expand throughout the fourteenth century, despite the plague, the finished goods being exported through Hull, which had previously taken bales of wool. All of this is evident in York's rich heritage of timber-framed houses, but their survival is due to the decline that followed in the fifteenth century. In 1334 York was England's third largest provincial town, and, while it had yielded second place to Bristol during the later twelfth century, the fifteenth century was a period of unprecedented contraction as its ranking among English towns fell to the obscurity of eleventh place. Its weavers failed to compete with Pennine yeomen, who were able to combine weaving with their traditional pastoral farming. Worse, York's political and strategic importance as a bulwark against the Scots declined as English military successes reduced the threat from beyond the Border.[10] The slump in York's cloth exports troubled Hull, whose problems were aggravated by competition from the port of London and opposition from the Hanseatic League in the Baltic.

London, of course, survived. Its unique size helped, and the City, with its diverse population, could easily suppress competition from nearby towns. While its ancient craft industries were impaired, a taste for luxury kept it afloat, and, moreover, the old professions were drawn to the court which spent more and more of its time at Westminster.

Both wool and cloth still had to go to market, although to find different purchasers. Burford's and Cirencester's merchants continued to profit from trade in Cotswold wool, but were now selling to English weavers from as near as the Stroud valley or as far as the Pennines, though no longer from Flanders and Italy. Chipping Camden readily made the transition from selling to Italians and Flemings to selling to the English. William Grevel may have been the flower of English wool merchants, but, alongside him, Robert Calf, William Bradway and a host of others kept the market humming with business and saw the bales of wool packed off to rural weavers.[11]

Clare and Sudbury lay at the receiving end of this trade, needing the water of the river Stour, which divided Suffolk from Essex but united their weavers in a new prosperity. Their churches, together with Lavenham's, show that cloth might buy as much fine masonry and indeed timber as wool could on the Cotswolds. Soon after the Guild of Corpus Christi was founded in Lavenham in 1529 it erected its magnificent timber-framed Guildhall in a dominant position overlooking the Market Place.[12] This was a *folie de grandeur*: (fig. 73) the Lay Subsidy of 1524 had placed Lavenham, unluckily, as the thirteenth town for wealth in England, a position from which it fell to oblivion in barely thirty years.

73. Lavenham Guildhall, built in the guise of a grand merchant's house, as it was a hundred years ago. © National Monuments Record

74. Tenterden, photographed about 1900, with the grand late fifteenth-century tower of St Mildred's church overlooking the market place where High Street is at its widest

75. Grevel's house, Chipping Camden. The oriel window lighting the high table in the hall, and a visible status symbol for all the street to see

Tavistock, which had grown on the export of wool and tin, now turned to cloth, indeed so successfully that the parishioners added the Clothworkers' Aisle to their church in 1442. This was as well, for tin failed them at the end of that century. Tiverton similarly benefited by turning to the weaving of fine kersey. The buttresses of the parish church are decorated with carvings of the ships that exported the town's cloth and brought its merchants their wealth. The richest of these, John Greenway, added a new porch and south chapel in 1517, and had their walls lavishly decorated with yet more ships, and woolpacks, staple-marks and heraldic panels that quite outshine the finely carved scenes of Christ's Passion.[13] In a similar act of piety and civic pride, the rich clothier William Stumpe saved the nave of Malmesbury's abbey church at the Dissolution and gave it to the town as its parish church.

There was less civic pride in Kent. Edward III gave Cranbrook, Smarden and Tenterden charters in 1332, recognition of the growing importance of the Weald. They all retain wide streets where markets were held. Tenterden's seems credible enough today, (fig. 74) Cranbrook's more or less so, but Smarden's not at all; it is no more than a small village, and a scattered one at that. It can never have been more, even though its unusual wealth is expressed in a score of surviving medieval houses, all of them magnificent but quite rural in character.[14] If their householders were burgesses, they were also yeoman-clothiers, living on enclosed farmsteads and more attuned to rural ways that actively discouraged the growth of nucleated villages, let alone towns.

The new wealth from weaving, therefore, found expression in the construction of substantial houses. It did little to encourage the foundation of new towns, but it did fill boroughs that until a day before had been villages. New houses lined their streets, a few of which, like Grevel's, survive alongside their aggrandized churches as monuments of the new wealth. (fig. 75)

The changes in the clothing trade had an immense effect on the fortune of towns. London, Boston, Hull, Yarmouth and Southampton sent the bulk of English wool to Continental weavers at the time of its greatest export at the start of the fourteenth century. Two hundred years later, wool exports were a mere trickle, and London, Boston and Southampton handled most of them. Instead, cloth exports had taken the place of wool, principally through London once again, with Exeter and Bristol exporting the West Country product, and Southampton, Hull and a newcomer, Poole, sending the bulk of the rest.[15]

The once-mighty Boston and Lynn suffered from both the changes in trade and the way it was conducted. Merchants from the German Hanse towns took control of the Baltic and then the North Sea coast of mainland Europe, and finally attempted to edge the English out of Iceland. The first crisis came in the middle of the fourteenth century with the start of the Hundred Years' War, the second a century later when the English cause in France was in full retreat. At last in 1475 the Treaty of Picquigny established peace with France, and a deal made with the Hanse that year ended another feud, though very favourably for the Germans. Stable times returned to Boston and Lynn, and brought in an imposing variety of imported goods designed for a newly affluent middle class, but this was on a scale so small that it bore no resemblance to the striving days of the thirteenth century.[16]

While individual towns and cities faced the snakes and ladders of fortune, the Church seems to have increasingly looked to its urban property in the fourteenth century, rather than its immense agricultural estates, simply because of the effects of rural depopulation. If expensive labour and weak agricultural markets threatened to empty the Church's coffers, expensive labour engaged in non-agricultural occupations could pay good rents. The Church was not in a position to respond to its weakened agrarian position simply by calling a halt to its material obligations. Its existing buildings had to be maintained. They had to be modified and extended for new uses. New ones had to be built to meet changing circumstances. The clergy had to be accommodated. New forms of religious devotion required a material response, for instance the building of chantry chapels where priests could pray for the souls of their founders. Moreover, these priests had to be trained and supported.

So it came about that the needs of both this world and the next were expeditiously combined when the Church built houses for rent on its urban land so that it could gain from a new source of income. Ultimately, the Church had the economic clout and could command the skill to manage such large financial ventures, as well as the experience of building on every possible scale. It also understood the problems of designing domestic accommodation of all sorts. This gave it the edge over other landowners both to invest and to innovate.

The problems experienced by English towns during the fourteenth century were felt in Wales too, and these were exacerbated by the start of Owain ab Gruffydd's rebellion at the end of the century. Only after his demise was peace restored. This brought a small renewal of prosperity, as exemplified by the construction of Alberconwy House about 1420. It is the first of many houses to be built around the principality marking a revival in Welsh affairs.

In Scotland the revival was rather later. Neither the thirteenth nor the fourteenth centuries had been fruitful for towns. The creation of new royal burghs fell by a half, and other creations did not fill the gap. Following Robert Bruce's expulsion of the English in 1314 there was a recovery in the number of non-royal foundations, as well as an intensive rebuilding campaign to make good the destruction, but this fell away again after 1350, partly because of mortality attendant on the plague. Only with the English finally thrown out of France and turned against themselves in the Wars of the Roses did the foundation of Scottish towns recover. Despite weak kingship and civil disorder, the burghs attained a degree of self-government, and nearly 150 new ones were founded in as many years after 1450, thanks to strong trading and cultural links with Continental Europe.[17] (fig. 76)

Scotland's political links were the prime reason for the foundation of her first university, and the Great Schism in the Papacy gave this the final push. Like her ally France, Scotland supported the popes at Avignon, not those at Rome, who had the support of Germany, Italy of course, and England. In 1408 France abandoned the Avignon Papacy and followed a course of neutrality. All the while Paris filled up with feuding Burgundians and Armignacs, who made life impossible for foreign students. The Scots returned home and in 1410 set up school in the little but thriving town of St Andrews, which was informally the ecclesiastical capital of Scotland on account of its influential bishop and splendid monastery. In 1411/12 Bishop Henry Wardlaw granted them a charter. More was needed, and it came. The Avignon Pope Benedict XIII, now exiled in Spain, needed political support among the nations of Europe. The masters and students of St Andrews needed full recognition. An approach was made, and it was irresistible. Six papal bulls arrived from Benedict in February

76. Dysart. Created a burgh of barony in 1510, and attaining the status though not the legality of a royal burgh in 1535, this little port thrived on salt-making, and the export of coal and fish, as did many a town on the Forth estuary

1413/14 confirming the school as a *studium generale*, or university, and were promulgated with solemn rejoicing.[18]

Although it is a Scottish trait to equate plain living with elevated thoughts, Paris soon regained its attraction for Scottish students. To counter this, Bishop James Kennedy founded St Salvator's College in 1450, (fig. 77) and three more colleges followed in the sixteenth century, all of them with the intention of training clergy. It was probably not a means of countering Scottish seriousness, but merely coincidental, that a frivolous game of hitting a small ball about with a long stick developed here at the same time, spreading the name of St Andrews around the world even more famously for golf than its university.

This late Scottish development is quite distinct from English and Welsh experience. Even so, many of these new Scottish burghs remained little more than villages. This was particularly true of the so-called burghs of barony, which accounted for the majority of the later creations. They served the self-sufficient closed estates on which they were sited, and, unlike royal burghs, were debarred from foreign trade.

Few were so pitiable as Rattray, which lies on the north-east coast of Aberdeenshire between Fraserburgh and Peterhead. It had probably been founded as a burgh of barony by William Comyn, Earl of Buchan, in the mid-thirteenth century and, for a while, prospered in a very small way on agriculture and fishing. The settlement grew up between castle and church, a stretch of some 600 yards (550 m), but always seems to have lacked the economic basis of a town that would have favoured merchants and craftsmen, despite once boasting a market place. Worse, its ownership was disputed by two feuding families, the Hays, earls of Erroll, and the Keiths, earls Marischal, and this resulted in its creation as a royal burgh by Mary Queen of Scots in 1563/4. Title and reality were poles apart. It was never more than a manorial village, and, at the height of its prosperity between the thirteenth and fifteenth centuries, when some of its inhabitants engaged in small-time iron-working and pottery as well as trading along the coast, its economic lifeline lay in its fields and the sea. The ports of Fraserburgh and Peterhead were too close, the routes inland tortuous. So competition from nearby towns, themselves hardly more than villages, brought Rattray to nought long before sand dunes blocked its way to the sea. This may be an extreme case, but in general burgh status was fine in law but less so in reality.[19]

By the end of the sixteenth century, Scotland enjoyed a remarkable concentration of burghs on the east coast from Dunbar to the Forth, and from there right up to Inverness, even though most were tiny. Like England's West Country, nowhere was more than a ten-mile (16 km) ride from market, which was about the practicable limit for the coastal grain trade. A similar concentration crossed Scotland from Dumbarton up the Clyde valley and across to the Firth of Forth. Along the west coast of Ayrshire there was a smaller concentration of burghs, and there was another on the coast of Dumfries and Galloway.[20]

Like the Romans on their summer marches, the line of new towns passed by the mass of the central Highlands, and only a few scattered ports like Dingwall, Cromarty and Kirkwall occupied a place in the far north. The bleak hinterland could not produce enough goods to fill a market, and the routes to the south were too lengthy to sustain an urban economy. A further disincentive aggravated the similar conditions in the great empty spaces that stretched across southern Scotland from Ballantrae to the Cheviots. Here natural poverty was reinforced by the violence of a disputed Border.

David's Berwick, lost to Edward I and regained by Bruce, was lost and retaken again and again, before it was irretrievably lost to the English in 1482. This left the Border hanging between the English strongholds of Berwick and Carlisle across the wildernesses of the Cheviots. Known euphemistically as the Debatable Lands, these were occupied by English and Scottish confederate groups, the so-called 'surnames', who owed allegiance to neither crown. They were 'bold and brought up in Theft, spoyle and bloode . . . Neither have they anie other trade . . . but stealinge; which they Accompte not shame, but rather as grace and Creditt unto them'.[21]

The violence turned particularly nasty in Elizabeth's reign when gangs of villainous heroes like Jock o' the Side, Hobie Noble and Kinmont Willie kept the Border garrisons on the *qui vive*, and Carlisle's gates routinely locked at night.[22]

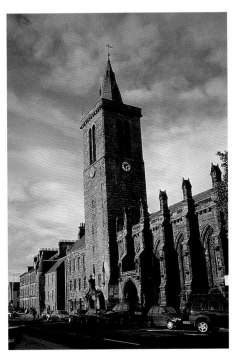

77.   St Salvator's College, St Andrews. The gate tower flanked by Hebdomodar's Building (left) and the chapel

Now Liddesdale has ridden a raid,
But I wat they had better hae staid at hame;
For Michael o' Winfield he is dead,
And Jock o' the Side is prisoner ta'en.[23]

But Jock was snatched from Newcastle jail on the very day of his execution and restored to his 'ain ingle-side', free to plunder on.

Matters came to a head in 1603. Four days after Elizabeth's death there began what came to be known as the 'busy week': mosstroopers from the Armstrongs, Elliotts, Grahams, Hendersons and Nixons rode down upon Carlisle, burning, spoiling and robbing for ten days, finally reaching Penrith before soldiers from Berwick drove them back. Their excuse to King James was that evil men 'did perswade us that untill yor Majestie was a crowned kinge within the realme of England that the law of the same kingdome did cease and was of no force'.[24] Such likely innocence was of no avail, but that is why the Border lacks towns between Berwick and Carlisle, and the two nations maintained an often hostile independence until long after James VI went to London as James I, king of England.

Eventually exile drew the teeth from the lawless surnames. The savagery of plague, again, declined. Already by 1500 the population had steadied at perhaps half its peak of some two centuries beforehand. Slowly it began to grow again, in the towns as well as in the countryside, as people lined their pockets with the profits of urban life. The Middle Ages left behind all the means of regenerating the towns, but, after two centuries of decline, regeneration meant rebuilding, and much of this would destroy the past, leaving Britain's surviving medieval urban houses far more a rarity than their rural counterparts. While much of what had been built beforehand had decayed and fallen, in those towns where economic activity continued or even grew apace a new legacy of buildings came into existence and these survive in such numbers, ironically, as to suggest that the heyday of the British medieval town was in the fifteenth century rather than in the eleventh, twelfth and thirteenth centuries, before plague hit the land.

In Scottish towns the pattern is different. For all that survives, the Middle Ages seems to have achieved nothing but a handful of lordly houses with a defensive face. That is due to the belligerence of the English, and even the sixteenth century could only point the way towards the great stride forward that the kingdom would achieve once its monarchs went south in exchange for a modicum of political harmony.

7

For the common utility of the City

The regulation of towns

The pattern of boundaries, streets and open spaces that give towns their form is far clearer evidence of their history than the buildings that line them. Towns may be devastated by invaders and burnt in conflagrations, but the pattern survives beneath the rubble of mere buildings above. Even London, despite the Great Fire, the Industrial Revolution and the *Luftwaffe's* bombing, still retains the impress of the Roman walls that Alfred reused and many of the medieval streets that replaced the Roman ones during the years of post-Conquest prosperity. Despite uncountable amalgamations, medieval property boundaries still abound, even though only a dozen or so fragments of medieval houses remain. The reason is clear. Patterns of ownership cannot be readily extinguished. For all his vision of ideal town planning, Christopher Wren could not reform what the City's burgesses owned, and rebuilding after the Great Fire of 1666 hardly changed the streets or the holdings that lined them.

Even when towns and suburbs were newly laid out on green land, ancient patterns could remain. Although new towns might take whatever form pleased their landowner, give or take the limitations imposed by topographical obstacles, many of them made further accommodations that still persist, centuries after the reasons for them have been forgotten. Simple things such as field boundaries and even paths across fields became frozen, and mark the map long after their purposes and destinations have blown away.

The first aim of a new town may have been to exploit the natural advantages of the site for its better defences – a ridge or cliff, or a loop in a river. (fig. 78) The second may have been good communications, existing roads, a likely port or, once again, rivers. Then came the provision of suitable locations for its principal monuments. But ultimately there was always the underlying motive of providing a suitable number of building plots or burgages, for on these the town's economic activity would be based and the landowner's rents charged.

In whatever way each plot might be built up, the street front was its public face and therefore gained in status, while the rear remained private. The front was for shopping and display; privacy or no, the various uses confined to the rear might need separate access, and were therefore served by a back lane. The simplest town plans have no more than a main street and back lanes, like those of Henley-in-Arden, which is strung out along a pre-existing road that leads to Stratford-upon-Avon.

Expecting rents and dues from a market, most landowners would allow for a market place. (fig. 79) This is an abiding feature of towns everywhere, whether it be a full square like the market place at Cambridge, or a widening of a street, like Broad Street in Oxford. Both of these were acts of conscious planning, lying outside the boundaries of the first settlements. Chipping Campden's market was held in its main street, which gently sweeps across the contours in a long descending curve, broadening out to accommodate the great wool sales that gave the town its fame, while two back lanes divide the town from its enclosed fields, where the sheep were gathered at shearing time. The market at St Ives occupied a main street that links the parish church with the priory, becoming ever wider along its course until it spans forty yards (36.6 m); on one side there is a back lane in the usual way, and on the other is the river Ouse, ideal for the landing of goods.[1]

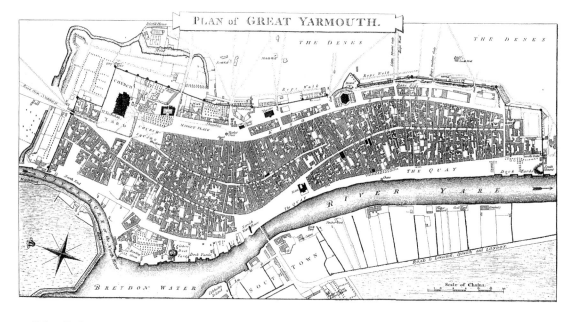

78. Great Yarmouth. William Faden's plan of 1797, showing the town lying along a low spit that separates the dunes facing the North Sea from the river Yare. The town wall, begun in 1285, faces the dunes and has a main gate to the north (left) that leads to the sinuous streets that run through the town; these are lined by long, thin burgage plots, the Rows. Just to the south of the parish church of St Nicholas (a favourite dedication in a port, since he was the patron saint of sailors) lies the market place

79. Faversham. Market Place was once open and lined with medieval shops, such as those on the left, but many of these were replaced in the sixteenth century, when the Guildhall (right) was built as an open market hall in 1574 to shelter traders; it was converted to a guildhall in 1604 and its upper parts were rebuilt in 1819

Like St Ives, a town was often laid out at the gates of a monastery or castle, with a single wide street acting as a market place. Pembroke lies at the foot of its castle, and the market place and main street run down a ridge. On each side, beyond the burgages, lie the twin arms of the Pembroke river, once again providing access for trade, and also for the English conquerors – a recurrent theme of the Welsh plantations. Appleby's main street and market place run directly downhill from castle to church, as though this descending relationship – State, Trade, Church – symbolized the harsh facts of survival in a dangerous border region. Edinburgh is the prime example of a market place set before a castle. Lawnmarket and High Street run down from the castle along a hog-back hill directly to Netherbow Port and the start of the originally separate burgh of Canongate. Here the street continues on its way as far as the Abbey of the Holy Rood, and all the while it accommodated markets of various sorts.[2]

When Bishop Roger planned his new burgh of St Andrews in the middle of the twelfth century he began with the ancient Kinrimund, the church on the king's hill, which had been built within a double enclosure or *cashel* overlooking the sea. (fig. 80) Its outer precinct was split into three: the central part was for the use of the archdeacon, the more southerly part became a pilgrim's hospice and later part of the university, and the northerly part was the centre of the municipality or, in Gaelic, *clachan*. A market was established here at the start of one of two streets that followed long-established paths, and radiated westwards from the central focus of the new burgh, where the cathedral would soon rise as the shrine of its patron saint. This imbued St Andrews with a dignity second to none among Scottish burghs.[3]

On a more mundane scale, some towns, such as Richmond and Aberdeen, have a fully fledged market place in the shadow of their castles, or, like Battle, their monastery, with the town lying beyond. Chelmsford's market lies just south of the parish church. Often a town's first market was held in its churchyard, and was then moved to an adjacent site. Here it is at the junction of routes going north, south, east and west, these routes being an important reason why the bishop of London founded Chelmsford at this site in 1199. Ashbourne and Swaffham similarly exploit a junction of routes to form a market place at their heart. Wallingford's market lies immediately south of the town's crossroads, embraced by St Mary's Street and St Martin's Street and overlooked by St Mary's church, a classic symbol of the Church's early interest in trade.

As in the case of Canterbury, York and Winchester, a Roman origin might determine the boundaries of a town for some time, but, even when the old Roman streets were used for a while, they often gave way to a new pattern that nevertheless still recalled Roman principles of town planning. Canterbury's medieval walls are based on their Roman predecessors.[4] A few of York's Roman streets survive along part of their length, notably Petergate and Stonegate, but the overall pattern was renewed. London was something of an exception: Alfred's revived defence went as far as reusing all six of the Roman gates as well as the walls, and even the streets survived until after the Conquest.[5]

80. St Andrews. Aerial view from the east, showing the rocky headland (bottom and right) at low tide; the tower of St Regulus (1) and the ruined cathedral (2) in the yard that formed the central part of the *cashel*; the radiating streets, South Street (3), North Street (4), and Market Street (5), which was formed between them to supersede the original market just beyond the cathedral; St Salvator's College (6); the archbishop's castle (7), and the Royal and Ancient Golf Club (8). © Aerofilms

81. York. Part of the city wall – at 2¾ miles (4.5 km), the longest in Britain – built in 1250–1315, perhaps replacing a palisade on the summit of the ramparts, using Magnesian limestone brought from Tadcaster

82. Bootham Bar, York, built on the site of a Roman gate in the late eleventh century and then raised, its twin bartizans being post-medieval additions

The boundaries of many towns were marked out with walls. Alfred's burhs needed them for defence, even though they might comprise no more than an earthen bank with a ditch from which the earth had been taken on the outer side. The defensive capacity of a wall might be improved by palisades set on the crest of the bank. In both cases gates had to be provided. Canterbury's flint walls were first raised in Roman times, and were largely rebuilt along the same lines from the twelfth century onwards. The demands of defence and a desire for status caused stone walls to replace many banks or to be raised upon them in place of palisades, as they are at York, and likewise the gates were made into prominent features, often incorporating towers. (figs 81 and 82) Walls also served the economic function of delimiting a town's jurisdiction and performing the task of a notional customs barrier, so that goods entering the gates incurred the payment of a toll.

The planning of London's riverside was typical of many ports in that a major street ran along the top of a bank overlooking the waterfront, from which narrow lanes and alleys ran down to the water and the landing places.[6] (figs 83 and 84) This gave rise to Eastcheap and its westward continuation roughly along the line of the present Cannon Street and Queen Victoria Street, together with such former alleys as Lovat Lane, Pudding Lane, Fish Street, Garlick Hill and Huggin Hill, running down to the Thames. Post-Conquest reclamation, caused by pushing wharves well out into the river, started the process all over again with Upper and Lower Thames Street being formed over the earlier wharves, and a fresh set of alleys – Swan Lane, Vintners Place, Bull Wharf Lane, Trig Lane – leading to the new river bank.[7]

Far removed from London's scale – and typical of such Norse towns as Stavanger in Norway – Kirkwall, the capital of Orkney, has a long meandering main street, with alleys, or 'vennels' in local parlance, running down to the old shore line of the Peerie Sea to to its west, while, away from the shore to the east, lie the cathedral and bishop's palace.

83. King's Lynn. A lane reached through an opening in a fifteenth-century range forming 7 and 9 King Sreet, with a fourteenth-century open hall at the back whose Georgian re-fronting appears on the right. The lane was progressively pushed out towards the receding Ouse and lined with warehouses, two of which can be seen on the left

84. Part of the 'Copperplate' map of London of *c.* 1553–9, showing the streets north of the Thames between the Steelyard (shown as 'STILIARDS', bottom, left) and London Bridge (bottom, right). The more northerly street running across the map is Cannon Street and its continuation as Eastcheap, these being a former river bank, from which lanes led down to the river, but now linking it to Thames Street (Tamys strete), a succeeding river bank, from which yet more lanes run down to the river. © Museum of London

All these various plans are influenced in some way by pre-existing features, natural or man-made. The idea that a town should have a predetermined rational plan, rather than respond to various individual imperatives, took some time to mature. The slow repopulation of Romano-British towns was not an ordered process. While Roman streets apparently served for a long time, as they did in London, their original buildings were robbed for their materials and allowed to decay; thereafter, they were never again lined with regularly arranged buildings. The siting of Canterbury's early *Grubenhäuser*, often within the ruins of collapsed Roman buildings, paid so little heed to what remained of the street pattern that this was no longer used in getting about town. It was well into the Saxon period before new tracks were laid down.[8]

The most distinctive form of predetermined town plan largely disregards the previous landscape. This is the grid, in which one row of streets crosses a second row at right angles. Historically, the grid is the most continually used of all town plans. Indeed, it is as old as towns themselves, being found throughout the classical world and in much of the Orient. Medieval Europe adopted the grid, from where it has spread like a badge of imperialism right round the world. The individual streets of a grid enclose a series of rectangular blocks known as islands, following the term *insulae* used in Roman towns, or sometimes as quarters, and at Salisbury as chequers. (fig. 85) The plan was very easy to achieve, the surveyors sometimes marking out the squares with a rope to ensure equality. This, in turn, made for equal areas, and, finally, plots of either equal size, or sizes readily calculable in terms of the whole and thus to be leased for an equitable rent.[9]

In England, Winchester began the practice by attempting to follow its Roman predecessor, and Wallingford, Wareham and Oxford show the practice continuing among those of Alfred's burhs where there was no Roman predecessor. The port of Ipswich expanded northward away from the Orwell with a grid of streets in the ninth century,[10] and New Romney was similarly

85. Speed's bird's-eye view of Salisbury as it was *c.* 1600, showing the chequers and the system of watercourses that ran down the streets. Speed 1676, vol. 1. 14. © Society of Antiquaries of London

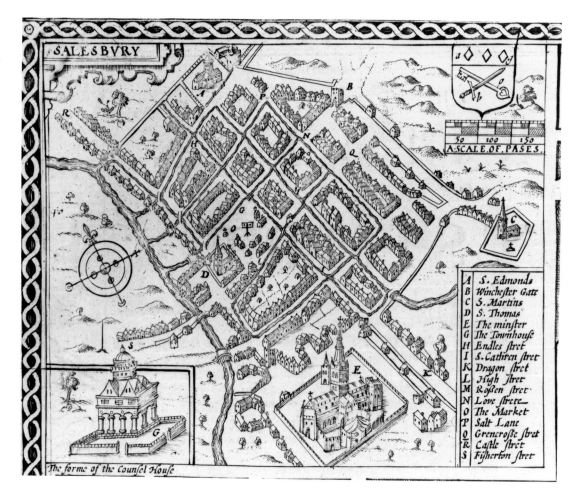

planned in its entirety with a grid in the tenth century. At least twenty-five further English towns, London among them, were laid out with a grid plan after the Conquest, if only in part. In Wales, a similar number bears witness to the preponderance of planned towns in the principality, the grid of eight islands at Caernarfon possibly resulting from Edward I's knowledge of Aigues Mortes in Provence, which he had passed through in 1270 on the way to his abortive Crusade.[11]

Scottish burghs were less often laid out as grids, perhaps because they were small and had little need of planning. St Andrews gained a grid of sorts, although far more imaginative in concept, as a result of the re-planning that followed the foundation of its cathedral on the headland in 1126. Two great processional avenues lead westward from it, *vicus borealis*, or Northgait, and *vicus australis*, or Southgait, and these were bisected by *vicus burgensium* and *vicus piscatorum*, which later became Castle Wynd (or street). Other streets followed, including Marketgait, which runs between the two radiating streets, and, later, Swallowgait or The Scores, which follows an east–west path further to the north past the castle, and further cross streets were laid out as the town spread inland.[12]

Following its foundation, Perth slowly developed as a grid between the thirteenth and sixteenth centuries.[13] Similarly, the town that grew up to the north of the precinct of Dunfermline Abbey took on a loose grid between Maygate and Queen Anne Street, with High Street running between them. The royal burgh of Burntisland, which James V founded in 1541 beside an improved harbour, again has a loose grid based on its High Street, crossed by Kirkgate, which leads to the parish church.[14]

So obvious is Salisbury's overall grid that it is often described as the only medieval planned town in England. Nevertheless, Bury St Edmunds, Portsmouth and the first phases of Ludlow preceded it on a handsome scale, and numerous small towns such as Rye and Bawtry are evidently based on a grid, though not as extensive. Less evident is the grid with which Liverpool began life as a planned town in 1207. Then there are the smaller towns and failed towns, villages now, which began proudly with grids, like those of Lydford, New Buckenham and New Radnor.[15]

Some grids hint at the earlier history of their sites, such as, perhaps, the line of the watercourses that once drained the meadows on which Salisbury was laid out.[16] The funnel-shaped layout of Burton-on-Trent recalls a former drift way for cattle coming down to the village from their pastures in Needwood Forest. Nowhere do these hints of past use show more poignantly than at Stratford-upon-Avon. In 1196 its lord of the manor, the bishop of Worcester, granted it the right to hold a market. As a result the village rapidly spawned a town on a gravel riverside terrace. This was laid out with three streets crossing the line of High Street and Corn Street at an oblique angle that reflected the form of the terrace. These streets, the four islands formed by them and, indeed, the house plots, each 12 perches (198 feet or 60m) long and 3.5 perches (57.7 feet or 17.6m) wide, that fill the islands are slightly curved towards their ends, thus fossilizing the lines of the ploughed strips of the open field taken to make the town. Moreover, the first houses to be built on these plots, whose remains have been excavated in Rother Street, were distinctly rural in form too, having the plan of a long-house, in which farm animals as well as human occupants share the building and enter by a common doorway.[17]

Despite its seeming rigidity, the grid was adapted to all kinds of circumstances, allowing changes in alignment and different intervals between streets to be readily embraced. Hedon, for instance, has a grid adapted to serve its needs as an inland port: one cross street connects three streets running northwards from the canalized stream that forms a notional second cross street at the base of the grid, and three further 'water streets' run northwards from it to form havens for shipping. But, for all this ingenuity, as Leland noted, 'Treuth is that when Hulle began to flourish, Heddon decaied.'[18]

Devizes has the extraordinary plan of a quasi-grid based on two flattened, more or less concentric semicircles with radiating streets linking them. These result from following the curve of a motte raised by Bishop Roger of Salisbury in the 1120s. An inner half-ring at the foot of the motte swells to accommodate a market, and is embraced by a second, outer ring, in a separate parish of its own, with the smaller Monday market half-way along it. The very name of Devizes (*burgus de devisis*) recalls this division between two parishes, but not how it has given the town a unique plan.[19]

Some of the islands within a grid could be left free, for a church or market for instance, and surrounded by houses of a suitably superior sort. New Winchelsea reserved a whole quarter for its parish church and another for a friary, but the Monday market was confined to a length of widened street.[20] A single island of Abbot Baldwin's new borough of Bury St Edmunds was reserved for its new butter market, which supplemented the old market on Angel Hill, hard beneath the abbey walls.[21]

The space within a town's walls would take time to fill up, and even in many successful towns never did. Wallingford still has its open Kine Croft, land which was never built on before the town preferred to expand outside its walls after the close of the Middle Ages. During its thirteenth-century heyday, Canterbury had a well-developed suburb along Wincheap, the route outside Westgate leading to Ashford, even though there was plenty of open space within the walls, some of it waste, some garden.[22]

Gardens of the rich were there for pleasure, but lesser citizens grew fruit and vegetables. (fig. 86) Leeks and parsley, and, to a lesser extent, onions, beans, peas, vetches, sage and hyssop filled Winchester's gardens in the later Middle Ages, and apples and pears came from its orchards; the bishop had vineyards at Wolvesey, while suburbanites grew madder and teazels for the specialist needs of the City's dyers and fullers. This picture of *rus in urbe* was augmented by the sounds of farmyard animals: the grunting of pigs, the crowing of cocks and hens, the cackling of ducks and geese, the bleating of sheep on the city's meadows, and the neighing of horses and lowing of oxen in the streets.[23]

Some towns were famous for their gardens and orchards. In Nottingham they survived until the Industrial Revolution made slums of them. The fields, orchards and gardens of Louth remained to inspire a nineteenth-century panorama from the top of the church steeple. This

86. Gardeners at work in a walled herb garden, perhaps in Boulogne, from the late fifteenth-century *Le Livre de Rusticon des prouffix ruraulx, compilé par Maistre Pierre Croissens, Bourgeois de Boulogne*, a French translation of an Italian treatise. © British Library. MS Add 19,720, 165

87. Leadenhall Market, London. Partial, cutaway view of the angle of the north and west ranges showing the two floors of warehousing built over an arcade. After Samuel 1989, fig. 10. © Society of Antiquaries of London

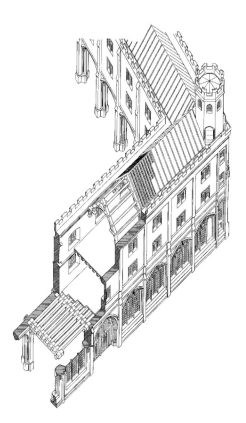

can still be seen in the town hall, as well as readily imagined when walking round the town. In most towns these spaces slowly filled piecemeal with the back extensions to houses facing busy streets, places where local crafts and manufactures took up more and more space as trade increased. Churches, which had been built in spacious yards, allowed stalls to be set up facing the street, as happened all along the south side of Canterbury Cathedral; if these impermanent structures did good business, it was hard not to let them become permanent, thus improving business and rents, an increasingly widespread practice throughout Europe.

Occasionally in the largest towns, covered markets were built, either for the convenience of traders or for specialized purposes. Leadenhall Market in the City of London was the finest. (fig. 87) Built between 1439 and 1455 around a great trapezoidal courtyard, facing Leadenhall Street, it comprised four arcaded ranges, with stair turrets at the corners leading to two upper storeys of grain warehouses; on its eastern side there was a small chapel and a grammar school, endowed by the rich mercer Simon Eyre, mayor in 1445–6, who initiated the whole scheme 'for the common utility of the City'. Whatever his motives, this act of both charity and shrewd economic sense was dressed in the most up-to-date Perpendicular style.[24]

Just as open spaces in many an ancient town filled up with encroachments, vacant spaces also appeared, often as a result of decay. Winchester was already in decline before the Black Death struck in 1348 and its open spaces demonstrably increased between 1300 and 1550. The city's tenter grounds where finished cloth had been hung to dry reverted to meadow as most of its weavers gave up, and where there had been building plots now there were orchards. By 1490 a hop garden close to High Street was giving the lie to William Caxton's old saw 'Ale of England; Byre of Alemayne'.[25]

The principal unit of medieval urban land was the burgage, in Latin a *placea*, and known in Scotland as a rigg or toft. This was a parcel of land which, with as many more or less equal parcels that the landlord chose to provide, he leased out for the annual rent that gave him a proportion of his income. Towns imposed a major restriction. Because of demand, land was comparatively expensive, so it had to be used as efficiently as possible. Before the Conquest, a burgage might embrace several acres (2 or 3 ha) and be coincident with an urban manor. As time passed, open space near the centre of town increasingly became a great luxury and, as a town matured, could only sparingly be provided. A market place would pay its way, but this need equally applied to streets. Unless they, too, were given over to a market, they produced no rent by themselves. This put a heavy premium on frontage since shops were best placed facing the street, and profits depended on this.

The more plots a landlord could fit in within reason, the more his potential rents would be. This had the general effect of restricting frontage to between 13 and 26 feet (4 and 8 m). So an adequate area for a burgage could only be gained by depth, resulting in most plots being characteristically long and thin. At the bishop of Winchester's New Alresford, founded in 1200, there are thirty-three burgages 350 feet (107 m) long; and at his other foundations, the burgages varied from 165 feet (50 m) at Newtown, Isle of Wight, to 440 feet (134 m) at Hindon in Wiltshire.[26]

The plots, or *placeae*, into which the islands of a grid were divided could run from front to back, thereby ignoring the two side streets and causing one street to become in effect a back lane, as occurs in Winchester. Alternatively, they could run inwards from all the streets, causing difficulties at the corners and centre, and making internal back lanes difficult or impossible, as at Salisbury and New Winchelsea. There were advantages, nonetheless, since various shapes and sizes of plot could be accommodated. In Winchester itself the plots of Alfred's burh seem to have been larger than they would be after the Conquest, perhaps because, as demand rose for land in the centre of town, plots were subdivided, and, once these had been substantially built upon, the pattern became permanent. The narrowest plots are therefore in High Street, where the busiest trade brought the greatest demand, but the side streets have wider plots for the double reason that demand was less and economic decay in the late Middle Ages brought greater dereliction there than in High Street. The plots consequently merged into haphazard patterns for less intensive uses.[27] A similar pattern of haphazard change caused York's building plots to be aligned on boundaries, not on streets. House plots perhaps started 18 feet (5.5 m) wide and included a lane down the side for access to the rear, but later varied from 12 to 20 feet (3.7 to 6 m) and were already closely built up by 1066.[28]

Because the pattern of long, narrow plots was imposed by a simple expedient designed to maximize rents, it is common wherever settlements were planned along streets. This also includes some villages, such as Appleton-le-Moors in North Yorkshire, as well as towns, and it includes towns abroad as well as in Britain. Parts of numberless medieval cities across Europe from Aachen to Zurich were characterized by their long narrow plots. So too were small towns: Fåborg in Denmark was planned in the first half of the thirteenth century on the shore of the Lille Balt, with long narrow burgage plots lining a single street that broadened to accommodate a market square and church in a pattern that could as easily have been produced in Britain.[29] The narrow plots that characterize the quayside at Bergen, long to begin with, extended ever further each time the quay was pushed out into the fjord taking the plots with it.[30] Exactly the same extension of plots occurred at Sandwich, where the town plan comprises a central section flanked by two sides. The westward side has short, broad plots, but those in the centre are particularly long as a consequence of their extension outward towards the river.[31]

When a street was particularly broad, for instance because it was designed to accommodate a market, it was common practice to encroach on to it, at once reducing its width and increasing the length of the facing burgages. This widely adopted means of improving property when other pressures were insuperable might be the final phase in determining the line of a street that had begun with houses set well back, then slowly edging forward through progressive stages of rebuilding, and finally taking over the fringes of the street itself where impermanent stalls were customarily set up. In Bristol, for instance, encroachment on to Broad Street in the fifteenth century provided extra space for adding new three-storeyed fronts.[32] A similar process could add even more on a corner site, where shops might face both ways and so double the commercial benefit. In 1404 the Palmers' Guild capitalized on the corner of Broad Street and

King Street in Ludlow, which had been established with rows of framed houses in about 1360 and leased to mercers: on the site of the market stalls that once stood outside the houses they built four permanent shops with rooms over them and hence extended the corner well beyond its former point.[33]

It was not always possible to find extra space in this way, and sometimes the opposite happened: streets were widened to allow for new or expanding markets. St Andrews was rapidly laid out with riggs along North Street and South Street, and their back lands met along a narrow lane between them. At some time in the thirteenth century these back lands were reduced so that the lane could be widened for a new civic street and market place called Mercatgait.[34]

The riggs of Edinburgh were set within a topographical straitjacket. Castlehill, Lawnmarket and High Street run precariously along the crest of a ridge, and the adjacent riggs become ever steeper as they run downhill each side. Between the closely spaced houses facing the street run narrow gaps known as closes, wynds or vennels depending on whether they were closed, private passages, open, public passages or winding passages. The buildings or, in Scottish parlance, the lands erected on the riggs needed to be near the street and could not extend very far back because the slope became too precipitous. The only recourse when commercial pressure prompted expansion was to add galleries to extend them outwards as they rose, and to build upwards to inordinate height.[35] This restriction gave Edinburgh's houses a character of their own, and accentuated a divergence between Scottish practice and English practice that ultimately found expression in quite different forms.

The order implied by regularly laid-out burgages was readily achievable in newly planned towns, but in old settlements, particularly where topography presented difficulties, this was impossible or, at least, unlikely. In Lincoln, the slow process of transformation from Roman to Norman England caused the lower town to be laid out within the old walls on the slopes of the Lincoln Cliff and beside the banks of the Fossdyke and river Witham. This resulted in a maze of streets that formed irregular blocks of building land, some more or less square, others polygonal, with no apparent rhyme or reason, but, no doubt, conforming to some long-forgotten pattern of fields and paths. Even the comparatively rectangular blocks, such as that bounded by Danes Terrace, Flaxengate, Grantham Street and the Strait, were parcelled out into an irregular pattern of burgage plots. While they tended to run from west to east, their boundaries incorporated numerous cants and angles, and they were of all sizes, a reflection of multi-ownership and a long period of buying and selling, amalgamation and division. This came to an end with a general re-planning and rebuilding of blocks of land that consolidated boundaries in the later twelfth century, and there was little further change until the nineteenth century.[36]

Canterbury's gradual growth gave it a sort of regularity, despite the meanderings of the river Stour's millstreams within the walls and the rather different meanderings of numerous lanes through what might once have been conceived of as a grid. By 1200 the old Roman grid had vanished apart from alignments just within the city gates. Many plots were approximately square, with frontages commonly of 60 feet (18 m) and more, reflecting the wealth of so many of its citizens, but these were matched by depths that were in general only slightly greater and sometimes less. Jacob the Jew amalgamated three plots, each of some 20 feet (6 m) frontage along High Street, but these extended less than half their total to the rear along the aptly named Hethenmanne Lane (later Stour Street). The lesser plots in Canterbury were more characteristic of burgages elsewhere, long and narrow, but they had a regular pattern only when subdivision had occurred. This was often the case where shops were set up, such as those in Burgate: along the north side a frontage of 12 feet (4 m) was standard for long rows of them, but opposite Buttermarket this had shrunk to 10 feet (3 m) or less – but still more than enough for a shop. Successful traders such as William the Cook might occupy three shops, and Lewin the Carpenter had a plot 21 feet (7 m) wide.[37]

New Winchelsea's quarters varied in size from 1 to 3.75 acres (0.4 to 1.5 ha). The smaller quarters might only carry a handful of houses, but several of the larger ones had over thirty houses each, and one of them had forty-two. Individual plots varied in size from a sixteenth to half an acre (0.003 to 0.2 ha), and annual rents per acre, which averaged between 48d and 56d (119d and 138d per ha), rose to over 60d (148d) for the more valuable plots. Even higher rents reached 69d and 75d (170d and 185d) for plots close to the market and the main gate through which foreign merchants would enter, with the top rate of 81d (200d) being paid for those plots that fronted the market itself, on the grounds that these might be used for stalls as well as permanent buildings.[38]

Landlords normally leased out a newly formed burgage plot on the understanding that the tenant would build a house on it within a year and a day. A clever tenant might then divide the plot, build on one half, and lease out the other at a greater rent than the whole. In Stratford-upon-Avon, where wide plots of 3.5 perches (57.75 feet or 17.6 m) were leased out at a rent of 12d, it was the practice to lease out half of a divided plot for 18d while building on the other half.[39]

How plots were built up is a measure of a town's maturity. Before the Conquest houses were usually set well back on their plots in a way that remained common in villages throughout the Middle Ages. In the earliest towns, indeed, the relationship between house and plot was haphazard, and between house and street non-existent. The layout of Danish Thetford from the ninth and tenth centuries was partly based on a wide metalled road with a subsidiary road running towards the Little Ouse, and, while there may have been some form of zoning of its industrial and commercial activities, its buildings were not clearly related to the roads nor was there a recognizable attempt to build up the frontages. While this might follow the Danish practice of such contemporary urban settlements as Birka and Hedeby, it may simply result from its citizens having no pressing need to attempt any form of communal planning.[40] The contemporary Saxon sunken-floored houses or *Grubenhäuser* of Lydford were nevertheless apparently arranged systematically within the plots defined by the lanes that divided up the length of the main street into three and probably five or six separate islands on each of its sides.[41] By contrast, when Flaxengate was developed in Lincoln from the late ninth century onwards, it was always lined with houses until the Conquest brought a reordering of the site, after which the houses were built to front Grantham Street instead.[42]

As frontage increasingly mattered with the growing pace of economic activity after the Conquest, houses were built facing the street, particularly to provide for retail shops. Although they were set back for a while, additions at the front soon brought them right up to the street line. Timber buildings already lined the crowded Bow Lane in the City a decade before the Conquest, and in the following two centuries stone houses were built hard against the street in many prosperous towns. Despite large areas of waste land, the streets in the centre of Canterbury were well lined with houses by 1200.[43] In Winchester, before houses were generally set hard along the street frontage, there was sometimes a narrow space of some 8 feet (2.5 m) which at first was taken up with subsidiary structures.[44] This practice was widespread in Europe as well as Britain, and suggests a common response to the need for efficient use of space at a time of economic expansion. It may nevertheless reflect changes in people's social attitudes for which there is no direct documentary evidence: it is possible that a greater sense of security following the Conquest led to a willingness to face directly on to the street without the insulation of boundary fences and private open ground before the entry into one's home.

At the same time, plots came to be subdivided, and where land was particularly short in the centre of prosperous towns even alleys between plots might become narrow plots in their own right. Building and rebuilding again and again could lead to individual properties overlapping and boundary lines between plots becoming obscured, as they do in parts of Norwich;[45] but, for all that, the pattern that they fell into at the time of the great twelfth-century fruition of Norman wealth tends to survive. In Stratford-upon-Avon, for example, the plots are still 12 perches (198 feet or 60 m) long, but have been subdivided into halves, thirds or quarters.[46]

The prosperity of post-Conquest England and Wales, and indeed contemporary Scotland, varied to such an extent that the main streets of some lesser towns were never completely lined with houses. The fourteenth-century borough of Cranbrook still has many of its first houses set well back from the street, particularly those like The Studio, a hall-house whose four bays run parallel with the street, with no thought to economy of frontage either. (fig. 88) Much the same pertains in Tenterden; and in Smarden, despite the obvious prosperity of its newly enfranchised burgesses, the old rural ways remained, and hardly a single house reaches the street.

88. –The Studio, Cranbrook. A Wealden hall-house, built in two stages parallel to the southern-end of High Street, with an enlarged, gabled service end (left), and a wagon entrance punched unceremoniously through the formerly open hall. As photographed at the end of the nineteenth century by Galsworthy Davie and originally reproduced by the collotype process in W. Davie and E. G. Dawber, *Old Cottages in Kent and Sussex*, London, Batsford (1900)

There was profit enough in the local economy without squeezing the last drop of value from the available land, but it was rural custom, not urban fashion, that won the day.

As towns grew and streets were built up with contiguous houses, it became clear in those towns that had governing bodies of aldermen that, without regulation, overcrowding could lead to chaos and disaster. In 1189 the *Assisa de Edificis* was set up in London, and this was both effective and much copied. It recognized that 'in past conflagrations many dwellings had been saved by the presence of a single stone house which stood in the way of flames.'[47] The introduction of stone walls would certainly reduce the risk of fire, a common hazard when most building was in timber and roofs were thatched in straw, but stone was expensive and beyond the reach of all but the few. The risks continued. The fire of 1212, however, prompted regulations covered by the Assize of Building which required thatched roofs to be covered in fire-resistant lime and stone party walls to be at least 3 feet (0.9 m) thick. A measure of their success is the absence of widespread fires thereafter in the City until 1666.[48]

Several towns adopted an assize of this kind. Newcastle upon Tyne had a Building Assize, compiled in a Black Book in the later sixteenth century, but which certainly predates 1535 and is thought to be much older. Its main aim was to enforce the use of stone for the ground and first floors, and specified that the walls should be at least 3 feet (1 m) wide and 16 feet (5 m) tall. What little evidence there is of its effectiveness is positive: the first phase of building of The Cooperage, undated but apparently late medieval, roughly conforms with this specification,[49] and so does the party wall between 41 and 44 Sandhill (Milbank House and Surtees House), which again may date from 1400.[50] The towns of east Devon did without an assize, Tiverton reputedly losing 400 houses in the fire of 1598, and 600 in the fire of 1612, and only after another 298 houses had been burnt in 1731 were thatched roofs finally banned.[51]

London's Assize of Nuisance, which was again in force from about 1200, dealt with more mundane matters.[52] By the start of the fourteenth century the City aldermen were appointing respected masons and carpenters of national standing as Viewers who would inform them of complaints about building works, usually brought by one neighbour against another, so that these might be settled. Common complaints were about water penetration, leaking sewage,

89. Canterbury Cathedral. Plan of the monastic water supply, the numerous channels (coloured red) threading their way around Lanfranc's cathedral into the monastic buildings, which include the surviving Lavatory Tower, shown within the great cloister in the centre just below the cathedral

90. Canterbury Cathedral, Lavatory Tower. Built before 1160 and figuring in the waterworks plan, its appearance was transformed by the Perpendicular windows of the rebuilt upper storey. A cistern fed water to wash basins in the upper storey and drained through a central hollow pier

drains, gutters and cesspits, and other problems relating to disputed boundaries, encroaching fences, noxious chimneys, dangerous overhangs, and threats to privacy caused by disputed rights of access, encroaching doors and misplaced windows.[53]

Of nearly six hundred cases heard by the Assize of Nuisance in the fourteenth and early fifteenth centuries, nearly a quarter of the complaints dealt with drains, gutters and water disposal, rather more than a sixth with the positioning of doors and excessively low and unglazed windows impairing privacy,[54] and rather less than a sixth with various obstructions. While the task of the Viewers was to investigate disputes between two parties that might result from shoddy construction, this did not extend within plot boundaries to construction as a whole. Yet the Viewers were consulted on standards of good practice and seem to have encouraged proper standards of construction for both public and private buildings.[55]

Water supply and sanitation, a major concern of the Assize of Nuisance in London, were harder to arrange in many towns than in the countryside by virtue of their dense populations, and towns were slow to adopt the services that had given Rome's huge population its long lease of life. A clean water supply was crucial to health, but bacteria were unrecognized, and taste and smell were the only guides to hygiene. Rivers, streams and wells were customary sources of water, serving the needs of both drinking and washing as well as those of numerous industries. While these sources were a focus of society, they were similarly a focus of dissent when water was short. Like many a civic problem, it was the Church that found the first answers.

Monasteries were invariably laid out with a good supply of water, which flowed from the highest part to the lowest, providing drinking and washing water before flushing out refuse and excrement. As early as 960 Abbot Ethelwold had ordered a series of water channels to be laid at Abingdon, probably for drainage. The sophisticated water system of Canterbury's cathedral-priory (fig. 89) was inaugurated by Prior Wibert before 1167. This had springs supplying a conduit house, from which water was taken by underground pipe to five reservoirs or settling tanks, and thence to wash-basins, one of which was for the use of the townspeople, while other pipes took water to the refectory Lavatory Tower, (fig. 90) scullery, kitchen, bake-house, brew-house, bath-house and guest hall. Meanwhile, some of the waste water fed a fish tank, and the more polluted water, flushed out by rainwater, was channelled to the city ditch.[56]

A similar system served Durham, where

Within the Cloyster garth, over against the Frater House dour, was a fair Laver or Counditt for the Monncks to washe ther hands and faces at, being maid in forme round, covered with lead, and all of marble, saving the verie uttermost walls; within the which walls you may walke round about the Laver of marble, having many little cunditts or spouts of brass, with xxiiij cockes of brass, rownd about yt.[57]

What monks required for their daily lives as a matter of course could readily be achieved through their firm government, the open rational planning of their monasteries, and their wise choice of sites on sloping ground close to springs and rivers.

In towns where the supply of water might be particularly difficult the Church took care of its own. The Priory and Hospital of Spital in the north-eastern suburb of the City of London had a water supply that carefully separated clean water from dirty with a system of cisterns and dams.[58] By the end of the thirteenth century, Exeter had a complex system of water conduits and drains serving the Blackfriars and the cathedral. In 1259 Bishop Bronscombe licensed an aqueduct to branch off from the Blackfriars' water supply and to run along the inside of the town wall to his palace. It apparently took the form of a lead pipe housed within a stone culvert laid on an earthen base.[59] But for common people, water was delivered by the bucket, as the name of Waterbearer Street, first recorded in 1253, implies.[60]

By the start of the thirteenth century, washing and bathing was common among royalty, Henry III laying on vast waterworks at Westminster on the monastic pattern so that he could wash his head. Washing was soon taken up on a more modest scale. Occasionally there was a basin or laver close to the hall of a substantial house so that its occupants could wash their hands before eating. Like many prosperous citizens, the Flores of Oakham were accustomed to washing their hands at a laver set in the passage before their hall, which was fed from a lead cistern by way of a pipe.[61]

Towns were usually served by wells and rivers, but, lacking the authority of monastic government, their burgesses invariably allowed the rivers to be used for all purposes, upstream and down, and this continued to be so until cholera struck in the nineteenth century and forced government to pass the first public health act in 1848. (fig. 91) The City of London enjoyed the broad flowing Thames, which only became a noisome sewer with the industrialization of the

91. The Stour, which meanders its way through Canterbury, and part of The Weavers, 1–3 St Peter's Street, which overlooks it. Picturesque now, the river was a convenient drain for slops as well as a source of drinking water

eighteenth and nineteenth centuries, and it could also benefit from numerous rivers that flowed down from the north. London's first water main was inaugurated in 1237 when, at the request of Henry III, Gilbert de Sandford gave permission for water from his springs at Tyburn to be fed via a conduit to West Cheap. By 1350 some grand houses were paying water rates and presumably took a private supply from the conduit. This also fed a public fountain that was specifically intended to provide drinking water for the poor – anyone with a penny to their name drank ale, and the wealthy drank wine. It also supplied water for cooking, but regulations failed to stop brewers, cooks and fishmongers from overusing it.[62]

The upper part of Winchester was fortunate in its water supply, even the smallest cottage having its own well sunk through the chalk. The low-lying parts made do with streams and public brooks, still remembered in the name of Brook Street. Most houses with a street frontage were served by water channels running through their front rooms, rooms which may have resulted from encroachment on to public spaces beside the street. John Skynner had a 'water howse', perhaps in just such a front room in Silver Street, and this also included cisterns and distilling equipment. There were no wells here, but this part of Winchester had had them in the tenth century and before, perhaps because the elaborate system of brooks had yet to be constructed.[63]

Salisbury's flat, gently sloping site beside the Avon made a complex system of watercourses relatively easy to achieve. Surface channels, probably originating in the former watercourses that crossed the meadows, took water from the Mill Leat to the grid of streets: 'through the midst of them runs a little rivulet of water which makes the streetes not so clean or so easye to passe in', Celia Fiennes recalled after her visit about 1685; 'they have stepp's to cross it and many open places for horses and carriages to cross itt – it takes off much from the beauty of the streets'.[64] Beautiful or not, the water could be taken for both household and industrial use, while deeper watercourses and drains took water at a lower level from further down the Mill Leat to flush refuse through the system down to the meadows at Bugmore Water, and on into the Avon well below the city.[65]

During the fifteenth century, conduits became increasingly common in many towns and cities. London and Westminster tapped the northern tributaries of the Thames, the Tyburn, Fleet and Walbrook. To the south of the river the land was flat and marshy, and, even well into the nineteenth century, tides simply filled up and emptied the numerous channels and ditches around Southwark and Lambeth twice a day, which otherwise took the waters of the Nekinger, Peck and Effra slowly to the Thames. Along their courses many a pond was used as a stew where fish were kept for the table.

Water was drawn from river, stream or ditch, and refuse tipped in, and, where properties overlooked these, garderobes drained into them too. In the twelfth century Exeter had its Shitbrook, which drained into the river Exe well downstream of the city.[66] In 1415 the means of removing filth from the Walbrook by 'a watergate called a scluys or a spey' seems to have failed, and hence orders were given for the removal of a common latrine which was believed to be the cause. Elsewhere refuse was simply tipped into the streets or back lanes, and only carted away when complaints and smell equally became compelling – and even then not invariably. In 1321 Ebbgate in London was blocked by the discharge from overhanging latrines '*quarum putredo cadit super capita hominum transeuntium* [from which filth falls on to the heads of passers-by]'.[67]

Parliament passed a sanitation act of sorts in 1388, prohibiting the pollution of rivers and other watercourses, but this only gave ineffective national force to what local by-laws already were failing to achieve in most large towns. Other complaints that commonly went before the Assize of Nuisance, such as dressing skins, tanning and brick-burning, were addressed by banishment to the outskirts, and there were even attempts to limit the use of coal, so acrid was its smoke.[68] In London, as in most towns, the mess of refuse and excrement was aggravated by horse dung, fertilizing a rich breeding ground for insects and beetles and a feeding ground for mice and rats. Crows pecked at putrid garbage, while, overhead, hawks hovered on the lookout for lunchtime snacks, and kites wheeled in the heavy air to prey on carrion.

For all the filth, cesspits were probably incorporated within many of the houses of Winchester's poor; an excavated cottage had a large cooking pot set into its floor, perhaps to serve as a urinal, although it was more probably used to collect urine for use in fulling cloth. The priv-

92. Governor's House, Newark. A privy, squeezed into a tiny space, less than 3 ft (1 m.) square, beside a staircase, and typically containing a small seat with a round hole cut into it, with a cover, and a chute, draining outside

ies of better houses emptied by way of a chute either into a pit or a drain. (fig. 92) Or, for those who preferred to keep the smell of excrement outside, privies were erected well away within their gardens. These were common later in the Middle Ages and for centuries afterwards, and comprised little huts with a seat with a hole in it set over a crude unlined pit. Stone-lined cesspits, which could more easily be dug out, were often provided in the crowded parts of the city.[69]

London householders commonly sited cess pits as near property boundaries as they dared and as far from the street as possible. The Assize stipulated that garderobe pits should not be closer than 3.5 feet (1.05m) from a neighbouring boundary unless they were lined, in which case 2.5 feet (0.9m) would do.[70] From at least 1160, several tenements shared a single privy. Being inclined to leak, private cesspits constantly offended neighbours whose complaints in the fourteenth and fifteenth centuries filled the rolls of the Assize of Nuisance.[71]

Such amenities in the end depended on who would bear the odious and odoriferous task of cleansing them, a task that no civic authority ever satisfactorily accomplished in later centuries. Nevertheless they tried: many town authorities employed 'gongfermors' to 'fey' their cesspits, the removal of tons of excrement being commonplace. Hence the church wardens of St Mary-at-Hill paid 5s 4d (26.5p) 'for voyding of ij tonne owte of a pryve in Harry Williamson house' in the City, and, in 1500, 10s (50p) 'to Donyng, gong fermere, . . . for fermyng of a sege in George Gysborow the clarkes chamber wherin was v tone, at ij[s] the tone'.[72]

Understandably, it was always easier to site privies and latrines over the town ditch or beside its river. In 1237 'the necessary house built at Queenhithe at London by Maud formerly Queen of England [Henry I's widow] for the common use of the citizens' was extended to ensure that it would continue to drain into the Thames.[73] Exeter, similarly, had its 'Pixey or Fairy House' on the Old Exe Bridge.[74] Sometimes neighbours clubbed together in Winchester to provide a common latrine over running water, as occurred in Buck Street on the south side of Bollebrigge. Public latrines such as this served visitors to Winchester, some being discreetly sited near the market. The inhabitants of the lower part of the city may also have made use of these since they had no other themselves, circumstances which are still widespread in parts of Africa and Asia, even, for instance, in the centre of Beijing to this very day.[75]

8

SQUARED STONES, EVENLY JOINTED

Walls, floors and roofs

Roman buildings in Britain made full use of a wide range of materials, both natural and man-made. Architect-builders, educated at least to some degree in the way that Vitruvius had promoted in his ten books *De Architectura*,[1] were responsible for supervising their design and construction, and, as occasion demanded, could do so with the highest order of technical and artistic skill.

Medieval Britain had to start again. The Anglo-Saxon immigrants brought various skills with them, but their abilities were modest when set beside those of Rome. At least their skills had the advantage of simplicity. They were specifically developed to exploit natural materials; hence earth and straw, and stone and timber remained in use, while, in the first instance, manufactured materials such as brick and tile were used only when they could be robbed from Roman buildings. The manufacture of these was forgotten and only revived later in the Middle Ages, and even then brick was made only in parts of England. Cement, which had a central place in Roman building, vanished from the scene altogether, not to return until it was reinvented at the start of the Industrial Revolution; builders had to make do with lime mortar instead.

Constructional methods similarly changed. The failure of an adequate economic base ruined the old Roman craft of carpentry and severely curtailed masonry, even though half the land could quarry stone if it chose to do so, and most of it could cut timber. These were to be the major constructional materials with which medieval Britain would rebuild itself. The choice of which one to use all the while depended on such rational considerations as availability, cost and suitability, as well as the irrational whims of taste and fashion. How these materials were put to work depended on design and that, so far as the most important buildings were concerned, was determined by those who commissioned them, and the ability of their craftsmen to interpret and achieve their desires. Only towards the end of the Middle Ages would building-craftsmen call themselves architects, but the meaning of this term was vague, and the separation of design from construction belonged to a later age.[2]

For the while, buildings lacked durability, and the materials used in their construction and the methods of construction themselves reflected the impermanent nature of society as a whole. Not all buildings required a designer, nor even, if it comes to that, a builder in the modern sense of the word.

Walls in the main were of two types. They were either solid, with their materials building up to form a more or less homogeneous mass, or they were framed, usually with timbers set at intervals to support some kind of light-weight panel or cladding. Timber posts or planks could be butted together to form a kind of homogeneous mass walling, as they do for the stave-walled nave of Greensted church in Essex, a unique survivor of a Saxon or Nordic tradition apparently built between 1060 and 1100.[3] Stone might be used, indeed commonly, to form great arched openings which could be glazed, as in the late medieval church of St Mary Redcliffe in Bristol, although it could hardly be described as stone framed. But generally the two kinds of walling fall into the respective orbits of the two kinds of material.

Earth, the most primitive of materials for raising a mass wall, has an illustrious history. Loam, clay, gravel and sand, in all their various forms and combinations, are among the oldest building materials, and in some ways the best. Medieval ramparts were invariably begun by piling up earth. Readily available practically everywhere, cheap and easy for the raising of walls that are warm in winter and cool in summer, earth is full of advantages. Mixed with a binding material of straw, bramble, or animal hair, it can be used to build a vertical wall simply by piling up more and more of the mixture until the requisite height is reached, and then by scraping the sides more or less flat. This process needs little skill beyond an easily acquired measure of practical experience, which anyone can learn when the time comes to build a house. All that is necessary for durability is a waterproof base, a sound roof, and a coat of lime-plaster to proof its surface, since damp is its main enemy.[4]

Earth has been used since ancient times to form solid walls by being simply piled up in this way, or by being rammed down between shutters to form *pisé de terre*, or by being shaped into bricks. Unbaked earthen bricks have been used since the fifth millennium BC. In Egypt they form the earliest pyramids and the earliest extant arches, and today they can be seen in the exotic towered city of San'a in Yemen. Unbaked earthen bricks may have been used in medieval Britain since Saxon times, but the first certain evidence is from Norwich, where such brick, later known in Norfolk as clay lump or clay bat, was used for partition walls in the fifteenth and sixteenth centuries.[5]

Even in so wet a land as Britain, earthen buildings were ubiquitous in the Middle Ages. A few of these survive in Cumbria, the Midlands, East Anglia and the West Country, their thick walls providing strength, durability and amelioration of climatic extremes. Their construction was probably a communal task, as it was two hundred years ago in Cumbria when whole villages turned out to run up a house for a newly married couple, since this needed much labour but little skill.[6]

In English towns earth, when used alone, was formed into floors, the walls of undercrofts, sleeper walls for timber-framed buildings, boundary walls and occasionally external walls and internal partitions within buildings. Few earthen buildings in medieval London are well attested, although they were probably common: the London Assize of 1212 records the term 'torchiator',[7] probably meaning a builder of earthen walls;[8] in 1293 an earthen wall was condemned as a nuisance;[9] and there certainly were boundary walls of this material right through the Middle Ages.[10] In Scotland earthen walls were probably far more common, even as late as the sixteenth century. An Edinburgh court book records a house in 1570–1 that comprised 'ane eird [earth] hall, ane chalmer, ane stabil, ane fore buith'.[11]

Few medieval earthen buildings survive in British towns, even in those regions where they are still fairly common in the countryside. Fashion required a change, so, in Devon, where cob, the local term for earth, remained the principal building material in much of the county until comparatively recent times, it was slowly replaced in towns by stone or timber. Yet in Exeter a fifteenth-century house, partly of cob, survived in Egypt Lane until it was bombed in 1942.[12] In Barnstaple, remarkably, there are still not only boundary walls of cob but even a few cottages in the back streets, although these are not medieval. However, at Silverton, once a small market town that boasted a fair, 4–12 Fore Street were built in the late Middle Ages with walls of cob and roofs thatched with straw, and these survive.[13] (fig. 93) Similarly, one or two earthen buildings can still be found at another small town, New Buckenham in Norfolk.

There is a little evidence that medieval houses of earth existed, at least on marginal sites on the north side of Norwich where Alms Lane runs into St George's Street: at the start of the fifteenth century industrial buildings were replaced by three clay-walled houses, which were extended and probably raised into upper storeys in the second half of the century.[14] A mixture of earth, pebbles and clay rammed down into shuttering – *pisé* – was used for the walls of a house uncovered in Wimborne, Dorset;[15] walls made of earth and faced in plaster are recorded in Southampton in 1312 and Bridport in 1483; and in 1478 a malt-house was added to a tenement in Exeter with 'x fote of mudwalle'.[16]

However poor a material earth seems, it was not restricted to small, poor buildings. Excavations at Wallingford Castle unearthed a comparatively large cob-walled house of the late twelfth or early thirteenth century which had been buried by spoil when the castle bound-

93. Fore Street, Silverton. A row of houses built of cob *c.* 1500, two of which retain evidence of their former open halls in the soot adhering to the underside of the medieval base coat of their thatch, and several have chimney-stacks built into their front walls in the characteristic way of the West Country. © M. W. Everett via National Monuments Record

ary was extended. Its ground floor was divided into three rooms, all of them with fireplaces, that together measured 28 by 41 feet (8.5 by 12.5 m).[17]

Floors of rammed earth, particularly when hardened with ox blood or milk, could take a polish of sorts. These can still be found in many parts of the world. In Britain the remains of earthen floors often turn up in the early levels of archaeological sites, for instance in Norwich where chalk floors and the remains of hearths were excavated from pre-Conquest levels near King Street and Rose Lane. The earliest, pre-Conquest houses excavated at St Martin-at-Palace Plain had earthen floors, and those that followed had floors of rammed chalk and clay.[18] The houses of Danish York were floored with stone rubble and sand, levelled and finished with lime mortar;[19] the first houses in Durham were floored in hard clay;[20] and in the City of London 'a lood of lome to ovircast the flore' was delivered in 1479 to St Mary-at-Hill.[21]

While these floors might be polished, they were also covered with straw, rush or reed to preserve the surface and to reduce the cold. This encouraged slovenliness. To sweep a problem under the mat had a particularly English meaning, as Erasmus complained when he described an English house:

> The floors are all of clay, over which marsh rushes are so repeatedly renewed that the foundation often remains for twenty years, harbouring spittle and vomit, dogs' and men's piss, spilt beer and the remains of fish and other unspeakable filth.[22]

Earth was largely superseded as a walling material by stone and timber after the Conquest, and became obsolete even though magnificent multi-storeyed buildings made of it can be found in south-west Asia and north Africa. There has never been anything in Britain to compare with the thousand kasbahs of the Dadès Valley in the High Atlas. The difficulty of raising high walls of earth without their becoming very thick may have been one of the reasons for this obsolescence, particularly in town, where space meant money; but, as stone and timber came to replace it for expensive buildings, earth became associated with poverty, and this reduced status was probably more responsible for its decline than any practical reason.

Earthen walls were often made thinner by giving them a core of stakes, a method that in England was already used in the Bronze Age.[23] The stakes were set into the ground, and perhaps joined together by either withies (flexible branches) or basket-work, and the earth was applied to both sides. While this made an efficacious wall, it reduced its durability. A solid earthen wall might stand indefinitely if properly maintained and protected from damp, but the wood within a composite mud-and-stud wall would rot or succumb to insect attack within a generation or so, thus bringing all to nought.

This composite method would nevertheless have its day as a means of filling the panels between the main timbers of a framed building. The filling took the form of either wattles sprung between the framing members or studs housed into the framing, and these were covered in a daub of earth reinforced with straw, bramble or animal hair, and finally weatherproofed with plaster. Because it can be kept dry, wattle and daub may last for centuries, and has the additional advantage of being flexible enough to cope with the movement inevitable in a framed structure.

Stone has always led the hierarchy of building materials.[24] Enviable and expensive, its attractions hide its disadvantages: it is not available everywhere; it needs skill in the quarry to find the best seams and to cut them; it taxes transport to the limit because of its weight; it takes time and experience to raise it into a wall, still more to carve attractive mouldings and ornate sculpture; and even then, despite its structural strength, the ability of some kinds of stone to last is not necessarily greater than that of other materials. For all this, its appearance is crisp and colourful when new, and the best stones can be raised up into monuments where size matches durability. In short, stone means status. (fig. 94)

The Church quickly realised this. Durability was appropriate to buildings devoted to the eternity of faith, and if stone were robbed from Roman buildings and laid in the Roman way, it would also symbolize the rock on which the faith was founded.[25] According to Bede, Benedict Biscop was the first to introduce into England 'builders of stone edifices and makers of glass for windows'. This was in 674–5 for his monastery at Monkwearmouth, the craftsmen being sent from Gaul with the express purpose of building in the Roman manner.[26] So the craft of masonry slowly revived after the collapse of Roman rule, but, because of its cost, stone was seldom used outside the Church. Masons and churchmen between them were the first designers of buildings, the latter explaining what they wanted in some detail, often through personal experience of what they had seen abroad, perhaps in their native countries or even in Rome. The masons put this into practice, and increasingly became learned in design, to such an extent that, by the later centuries of the Middle Ages, master-masons and their fellow master-carpenters might fairly be called architects.[27]

Before the Conquest the use of newly quarried stone seems to have been slight. There were numerous Roman buildings waiting to be robbed, which not only provided a source of good stone, but also satisfied the symbolic need for continuity in a Christian context. Alfred the Great, who built in stone and wood,[28] removed masonry from his royal residences in order to build others at more appropriate places. The stones may have represented an intrinsic regality,

94. Building Hunstanton, from John Lydgate's *Life of St Edmund*, a manuscript presented to Henry VI in 1433, in which St Edmund is shown superintending the construction of his royal town of Hunstanton: a mason dresses stone with an axe, another lays stone on a pier, and a plasterer finishes a completed wall; in the background, perhaps symbolically meant to indicate their lesser status, two carpenters carry a timber beam to a framed building. © British Library. MS Harley 2278, 28v

even if the main reasons for their transposition were economic. A similar reason may account for the rebuilding in stone of the palatial timber hall excavated at Northampton.[29]

Even after the Conquest, Archbishop Thomas's new cathedral at York made extensive use of robbed Roman stone since there was still plenty there to take.[30] Certainly, the recycling of stone continued throughout the Middle Ages. Roman stone also supplied complete parts, such as the impressive tower arch at Alkborough church. Practical advantages accrued, but so did the symbolic ones, as is borne out by the reuse of a Roman monument in the tower of St Peter-at-Gowts at Lincoln, apparently to demonstrate its intimate connection with the ancient source of the faith.[31]

The tortuous and often bloody route from Roman Britain to Norman England did less to promote the construction of secular buildings than it did for churches. English monarchs commanded the building of several stone churches, although when Edward the Confessor built his new abbey at Westminster of 'squared stones evenly jointed all round',[32] this was remarkable enough to be recorded. Royal palaces, by contrast, were generally made of timber.

Following the Conquest, builders required stone in unprecedented quantities. Timber churches were rebuilt in stone and minsters were doubled in size as well; stone castles superseded many a wooden tower; and in numerous towns where merchants had been content with timber for their houses they now turned to stone too.[33] Moreover, soon after the Conquest most of the best sources of stone in England were being exploited, and some stone, particularly fine oölitic limstone, might be carried up to seventy miles for an important building.[34] While the stone for many grand projects came from far afield, the immediate locality best served smaller buildings on account of the cost of transport. On average, a journey of 12 miles (20 km) by land might cost as much as the stone itself, and the labour involved in loading, unloading and local cartage could soon undermine the advantage of transhipment by water.[35]

Lincoln could sport large numbers of stone merchants' houses by the end of the twelfth century since the city was well served by as many small quarries of inferior oölite as it needed, and Roman sources were probably still available.[36] Stone supply is nonetheless only part of the reason; fashion and status meant much. Canterbury, where supplies of good local stone were poor, could, notwithstanding this, count some thirty stone houses by 1200. Before the loss of Normandy a few years later, the main building stone for the cathedral and other important buildings was brought by sea from Caen,[37] but local flint served lesser buildings, although these would need a fine stone such as Caen for quoins (corner stones) and other dressings forming window openings and doorways.

Similar circumstances prevailed in Norwich: the remains of a twelfth-century stone house excavated at St Martin-at-Palace Plain were of flint, and its dressed stone probably came by river and sea from Barnack.[38] Apart from the Music House, no others survive, but fourteenth-century records account for sixteen stone buildings of similar size, mostly houses, although one was a synagogue. Many of these buildings were in King Street bordering the river Wensum, so stone could easily be brought in by boat and landed nearby.[39] Poor local supplies of stone proved perhaps less a break on building than a temptation to spend ostentatiously.

York, like Canterbury and Norwich, had poor local sources, even though there was for a while enough Roman stone waiting to be robbed. Despite the discovery of stone foundations for an eleventh-century building in Petergate,[40] stone probably took nearly a century after the Conquest to descend to the level of York's burgesses. The first record of this is a deed of about 1150–61 that mentions Alan's stone house,[41] but this is only matched by the remains of a single stone house of c.1170–80 behind Stonegate.[42] These are of Magnesian limestone, and, if this is not of Roman origin, the cost of transport from the nearest quarries around Tadcaster called for a journey by water of some twenty miles.

In Winchester, which lacked a decent local supply, stone was in regular use well before the Conquest for the two minsters, but was rarely used for complete houses at any time in the Middle Ages. That aside, it often lined the undercrofts that supported framed buildings, and it was sometimes used for the halls of larger houses that were otherwise timber framed. The walls of these comprised a rubble core of rough shelly limestone, imported from the Isle of Wight, together with local flint that was then faced in fine, square-cut ashlar. For this, a soft greensand from Selborne was the best stone available. It was possibly introduced in 1222 for works at the castle, and by the end of the Middle Ages was so common that it even served as hearth stones. With little else readily available, chalk found its way into building, particularly in foundations, the core of walls and the vaulting of cellars. Mixed with earth or clay it made a good flooring material too. Stone walls between houses reduced the common hazard of fire, but after the twelfth century this became a far less common feature of Winchester houses.[43] Stone party walls did nonetheless separate medieval framed houses in the West Country, as indeed they do, for instance, in many parts of France.[44]

A significant difference in the way stone was used distinguishes Norman masonry from what went before. Saxon stonework comprises well-cut stones that form complete walls, face and core alike. Norman walls often have a core of rubble or inferior stone bound with mortar and a facing of finely cut ashlar, or, at least, some stone of better quality. Moreover, these walls tended to become very thick, particularly in buildings of any height. Where a Saxon wall might be 1.75 feet (0.5 m) thick, a Norman one would be double that. The great disadvantage in this was that, if the mortar failed, as it tended to do, the core lost its strength, throwing all the weight on to the ashlar facing and thus imperiling the whole structure. Nevertheless there was a singular advantage in these thick walls, since they could be hollowed out to make space for galleries within their thickness.[45] These provided access routes to the roofs in great churches. Eventually space was found in the walls of castles and houses for flues, chutes, newel staircases, and even privies and narrow chambers. This was a convenience that timber-framed buildings could only achieve by other means.

The thirteenth century marked a definite shift away from stone for the construction of houses. The development of carpentry together with a comparative reduction in costs slowly gave it the edge over stone, which thereafter was rarely used for ordinary houses, except in towns near good quarries. Even then, so fashionable was timber framing in the later Middle Ages that it invaded many towns which were in traditional stone country. This is unusually evident in Wales. While the marches with England were typical timber country, and many houses in such towns as Presteigne, Llanidloes and Hay-on-Wye were built accordingly of timber, further west, for instance in Dolgellau and Conwy, which are in stone country, timber became the fashionable material for houses in the later Middle Ages.[46] Nevertheless, the cachet of stone was so great that it always remained the *ne plus ultra* for the richest buildings or their richest parts.

Brick became an alternative to stone towards the end of the Middle Ages. The firing of a mixture of earth, clay and other material to make brick was as old as antiquity. The Romans had introduced it at the same time as the production of cement from chalk and clay. Bricks, the British quickly discovered, were not only durable and fireproof, but could be cheaply manufactured in many parts of the country, and were light enough to be more easily transported than stone. Despite these advantages, bricks and brick-making were abandoned, together with other Roman building methods, and were robbed until this supply dried up.

When the manufacture of brick was revived towards the end of the Middle Ages, it was Continental practice and imports of ready-made bricks in the thirteenth century from the Baltic and Low Countries that spurred the revival. For this reason brick was known as Flanders tile, and under this name (*quarelli de Flandria*) was imported by the hundred thousand for the Tower of London in 1278 and 1283.[47] Yet, despite a number of fine brick-built monuments dating from before the fourteenth century, it was only after 1500 that bricks came into common use, and many western counties had to wait another hundred years for their first brick buildings. (fig. 95)

Reused brick robbed from Roman buildings is particularly evident in Colchester, but the first use of newly made native brick was in London and a few eastern towns such as Beverley and Hull. The city walls of Norwich, raised between 1294 and 1343, had their flint arches, window openings, arrow slits and copings finished with brickwork, and the towers and a staircase were vaulted in brick too. What proved itself in these civic works soon came into wider use, particularly in the vaulting of many of Norwich's numerous undercrofts.

Norwich had no local stone, and neither did Beverley, so both turned to brick vaults with stone ribs in their great churches. There was no such difficulty with stone supply at Lincoln, yet the Exchequer Gate was similarly vaulted in the early fourteenth century with stone ribs and brick webs. Here, it seems, fashion triumphed over tradition. Hull's town walls, together with

95. A mid fifteenth-century Flemish drawing of brick-making. In the background a labourer is shaping bricks by hand; these are then set to dry before being taken by barrow to be laid out for firing; the bricks will be packed with charcoal and covered with earth to form a make-shift kiln. Meanwhile, to the right, fired bricks, now bright red, are stacked up ready for use. © British Library. MS Add 38,122,78v

96. The North Bar, Beverley, though patched and restored, still retaining much original decorative brickwork, notably that of its trefoiled window arches

its four gates and some thirty towers, consumed well over 4 million bricks between 1321 and 1400. Michael de la Pole had already built three houses of brick as well as his palace at Hull before his death about 1389, and this set the pattern for the town's new houses in the fifteenth century.[48]

The earliest bricks were far from uniform in size, and, if they were to be laid in courses, their variable thickness required much mortar to fill out the gaps. Similarly, variable length and width made the development of regular bonds difficult and favoured the laying of lengthwise courses of stretchers upon crosswise courses of headers – in short English bond. Where large quantities of brick were made on a regular basis, the bricks were shaped in moulds; consistent sizes followed and so did improved quality. Where only small quantities were needed, these improvements took place well into the sixteenth century. In Kent, where brick had already been used in 1365, progress was remarkably slow. At Sissinghurst Castle, the standardization of brick sizes came only with a second building campaign between 1558 and 1573 when Sir Richard Baker raised his great tower.[49]

By the middle of the fifteenth century, bricks were moulded, cut or rubbed into various shapes so that they could form decorative string-courses, corbels, arches and foils, these already appearing on Beverley's North Bar as early as 1409–10.[50] (fig. 96) Similarly, vitrified bricks whose surface had become glazed and darkened during the firing process were used to form decorative patterns of diapering when laid among plain red bricks. This first decorated a wall in England at Stonor Park in Oxfordshire in 1416–17, where, significantly, the craftsmen were Flemings.[51]

For all its utility, an element of fashion prompted the choice of brick, and in the last two centuries of the Middle Ages so did the matter of cost: a timber house was far cheaper.

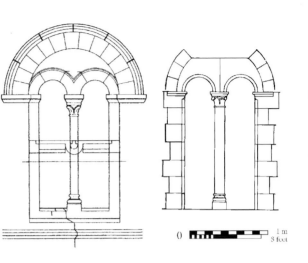
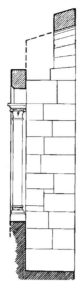

97. Two twelfth-century windows compared: from Norman House, Cuckoo Lane, Southampton (left), with a superimposed section showing the rebate in the jambs and central shaft for shutters; and from Norman House, Stonegate, York (centre), with a section through the wall (right). Similar windows are found across Europe from Spain to Germany. Redrawn after Faulkner 1975, fig. 17, and RCHME *York* 1981, fig. 142. © Crown Copyright)

98. 82–3 Church Street, Tewkesbury. Medieval glass was expensive and therefore conferred a degree of status, so ostentatious builders sometimes glazed the whole width of a house, as here, where Perpendicular tracery adds an extra ornate touch beneath the jetty of an upper floor. Because this offended later sensibilities as well as making the interior unduly hot or cold, depending on the weather, the windows were usually filled-in or replaced with smaller casements or sliding sashes

Consequently, grandees, for whom cost was less important than appearance, used brick first. In Winchester, where brick was late on the scene, its first public appearance came in 1441–2 when bricks were purchased from makers at Bishop's Waltham to fill the panels of a framed wall at Wolvesey Palace. Shortly afterwards the fireproof qualities of brick brought them into use for the construction of ovens in the city, and only after 1500 for fireproof chimney stacks. Houses entirely made of brick did not appear until well after the Middle Ages.[52]

While the most primitive houses were lit only by what light might enter through their doorways, windows seem to have been universal in all but the meanest of houses long before the Conquest. These openings were no more than rectangular gaps in walls, which, if more than about 2 feet (0.6 m) wide, were protected by bars and perhaps closed by hinged or sliding shutters.

In the later Middle Ages windows were sometimes made in the form of hinged casements so that part could open.

> He rometh to the carpenteres hous,
> And stille he stant under the shot-wyndowe . . .
> Unto his breste it raughte, it was so lowe . . .
> The wyndow she undoth, and that in haste.
> Have do, quod she, come of, and speed the faste . . .
> Derk was the nyght as pitch, or as cole,
> And at the wyndow out she putte hir hole . . .[53]

Such windows, the anatomical evidence of *The Miller's Tale* suggests, might be 2 feet (0.6 m) wide or more, and their sills 4 feet (1.2 m) from the ground. This singular documentary source is silent about whether or not the window was glazed, but the need for it to open implies that it was filled with translucent material of some kind.

Glass filled windows in Roman times, but like much else of that period fell out of use. While Bede records that Benedict Biscop brought glass-makers to England, their purpose was to furnish churches. Two methods of manufacture were known to the Romans. These involved either the spinning of discs of glass to produce what became known as crown glass, or the blowing of balloons of glass that were worked into cylinders and then cut to produce plate glass. In fits and starts, both were revived in Britain to be the mainstay of window glass until the nineteenth century.[54]

Glazed windows may have been a feature of some Saxon domestic buildings in Hamwic and Thetford, and also of the royal palace at Old Windsor.[55] This was not universal. Despite the lesson of Hamwic, glazed windows were unknown in Southampton's twelfth-century houses; many of these had round-headed two-light windows with a central shaft and a round relieving arch above, well executed to a common pattern, but these were simply shuttered, and not in

99. St Mary's Hall, Coventry. The Perpendicular north window of the Great Hall, filled with late fifteenth-century stained glass depicting seven English kings; as a demonstration of royal legitimacy, these are flanked, significantly, by King Arthur (left) and the Emperor Constantine (right), and include the most recent kings, Henry V and Henry VI. © The Herbert Art Gallery and Museum, Coventry

the first instance glazed.[56] (fig. 97) Glazing remained uncommon in Winchester throughout the Middle Ages.[57] Many ordinary houses may have turned to translucent oilcloth or parchment as a poor response to the problem of keeping out harsh weather but not light. Reed or withy mats could achieve the same effect, but, like cloth curtains, were probably more likely to be hung behind glazed windows.[58] Another method was to ensure that a building should not be too deep, thus allowing its windows to be shuttered on the windward side, but not on the leeward.

The widespread use of glass in domestic windows probably dates only from the thirteenth century, and then seems to have descended the social scale until, at the end of the Middle Ages, quite ordinary houses had a glazed window or two. Because of their framed construction, late medieval timber houses might have long bands of windows, the upper parts carved with tracery, just like the stone windows of a church. (fig. 98)

> And, sooth to seyn, my chambre was
> ful wel depaynted, and with glas
> were al the windowes wel y-glased,
> Ful clere, and nat an hole y-crased,
> That to beholde hit was gret joye.[59]

From the tenth century onwards glass was coloured and subject to prodigious art. The windows of royal and magnate's houses and collegiate halls were eventually glazed too, and the glass might on occasion be as brightly and artistically coloured as that of any church.[60] (fig. 99)

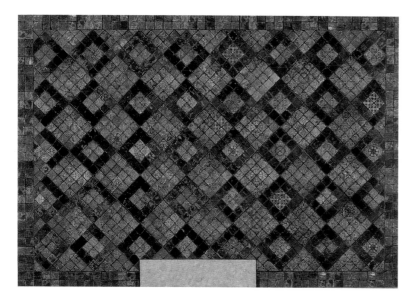

100. Patterned floor tiles from Canynges's House, Bristol. © Copyright The British Museum

101. Clifton House, King's Lynn. The medieval tiled floor awaiting conservation

102. White Hart Inn, Newark. The two upper storeys of the street range, as restored by Freddie Charles, with their restored late medieval scheme of painting and new glass behind the traceried windows

While earthen floors downstairs and timber boards upstairs served the majority of town houses, a few of the more important ones emulated churches and were floored with tiles. Nottingham had a commercial tilery in the fourteenth century. Tylers Hill, outside the city, served Canterbury, where patterned tiles in the Poor Priests' Hospital depict flowers and tendrils. Barnstaple tiles were sent all round Devon, and Malvern tiles were famed even further afield than Worcestershire.

While few houses went beyond plain quarries for their floors, patterned and differently coloured tiles of the kind that were commonplace in church were laid in royal palaces, those from Clarendon being the only survivors.[61] The houses of a few of the wealthiest citizens sported patterned floors, and these too are now museum pieces. William Canynges's house in Bristol had a paved floor with an arrangement of tiles in which patterned squares of four and sixteen tiles were set within a frame of plain tiles. (fig. 100) Clifton House at King's Lynn still has an array of alternating patterns comprising four squares, with differently coloured patterned and plain tiles forming chevrons, all set within a plain border one tile wide.[62] (fig. 101) These paved floors of the last decades of the Middle Ages are great rarities, and probably always were so.

The colour that tiles gave to a floor was often matched by colour washes applied to masonry and plaster, both inside and out. Almost nothing survives except for valuable fragments hidden in recesses or beneath later coats of paint. While it was common to whitewash even the best ashlared masonry and then line it out to represent the masonry that had been covered over for its protection, even bricks were sometimes covered in a wash given the colour of bricks with reddle, and, again, lined out to represent jointing. A framed building might well be limewashed too, leaving it gleaming white, and the plastered infill strongly coloured with reddle or ochre, or a vegetable dye with a pronounced blue or green colour. The most remarkable scheme on any medieval house is the restored paintwork of the White Hart Inn at Newark, where fragments of ancient paint prompted the current colours. (fig. 102) The studs beneath the windows on both of the upper floors are coloured with reddle, their brattished bases are picked out with green and their moulded cornices with black and white bands and tendrils; meanwhile moulded panels depict coloured figures under gilded canopies. Rare today, it is probable that many an establishment with a desire to catch the eye was similarly coloured.[63]

Interiors were coloured too:

> And alle the walles with colours fyne
> Were peynted, bothe text and glose,
> Of al the Romaunce of the Rose.[64]

A few schemes survive in medieval churches, fewer still in houses. The occasional hospital or guildhall preserves a little of this painting, for example the pattern of hexagons and lozenges enlivened with fleurs-de-lis and a frieze of hearts and knots in Aylesbury's Brotherhood House. (fig. 103)

While earth became the common burgesses' floor and poor people's walling material, thatch became the equivalent for their roofs. From the earliest times, reed or straw was available everywhere, either as a by-product of arable farming, or growing wherever the ground was damp and marshy. Confusingly, the terms straw and reed were sometimes used indiscriminately in the Middle Ages as if they were synonymous, while at others they meant specifically corn straw or water reed. Other forms of vegetation were pressed into use as well; heather, bracken, broom, gorse, sedge and rushes among them.

Bundles of reed or straw, tightly bound into tapering 'bottles', 'yelms', 'bats', 'gavels' or 'bunches', so-called region by region, were applied to the roof to make a waterproof and warm covering that would last a generation at least. The first bundles were laid on the slope of the roof with their thinner ends upwards and their thicker ends along the eaves so that, together, they formed a horizontal layer. The next layer was then laid above so as to overlap, and then another until the ridge was reached, all the while covering obstacles such as roof valleys and hips.[65]

Thatched roofs are implied by the archaeological remains of countless medieval town houses, before as well as after the Conquest, if only because of the insubstantial nature of their walls and the absence of fragmentary tiles or slates among the finds. Wooden shingles and boards may also have been used, since these again would have left no trace. Similarly, thatched roofs are well attested in written records, again often by implication. Hull was probably a town of thatched roofs in the Middle Ages since it was only in the latter half of the sixteenth century that its citizens were forbidden to 'theake with straw, reade, or hay, or otherwise than with thacke tyle'.[66]

Thatching in straw or reed was so universal throughout the Middle Ages that the word 'thatch', or 'thack', was originally synonymous with roof,[67] but was eventually confined to roofs of straw, reed or other vegetable material, thus excluding roofs of tile, slate or lead. A 'thacker' or 'theacker', nevertheless, was synonymous with a 'sclater', and meant a roofer, generally, without implying one who laid a roof in a particular material.

Like all building materials straw and reed thatch has its disadvantages. Bede recorded two miracles involving the burning of thatched houses, one in 428 when earth from St Oswald's burial place saved a beam within a house from being consumed by flames, the other the next year when St Germanus was visiting the shrine of St Alban's and was saved from a fire that swept through cottages thatched with reeds.[68] Hardly a town or city avoided devastation at some time or other during the Middle Ages when a fire swept across its thatched roofs. London was terribly burnt in 1077. In 1087 the Saxon St Paul's was burnt, together with much of the rest of the City, long before its successor was more famously consumed in the Great Fire of 1666. The disastrous extent of that fire is well enough known, whereas many a medieval fire, often associated with the hand of God or some other natural or supernatural cause, was often exaggerated for effect. London burnt in 1161, as did Canterbury, Exeter and Winchester. Canterbury was in flames again in 1174, Winchester in 1180, Glastonbury in 1184, Chichester in 1187, Worcester in 1202.[69] Clearly God was still incensed by the Tower of Babel.

Regulations promulgated in London in 1212 stipulated that roofs could not be covered with reeds, sedge, or any kind of straw, and existing roofs covered in these materials were to be plastered so as to reduce the risk of fire.[70] Having learnt the hard way in 1174, the monks of Christ Church, Canterbury, insisted that properties close to the cathedral should be tiled, not thatched.[71] Other materials than thatch, particularly tile, were then becoming available, and these for the most part were far more proof against the spread of fire. During the fifteenth century Coventry, Salisbury and Worcester banned thatch, but legislation was neither systematic nor ubiquitous. Edinburgh's roofs were mostly thatched in the middle of the sixteenth century, the remainder being tiled.[72] Norwich still appears to have allowed a fifth of its houses to have thatched roofs early in the eighteenth century, and there was not much difference a century later.[73]

That was in a county where tile was readily available. Even so, presumably 80 percent of the roofs in Norwich were tiled. In some towns that proportion of roofs would signify a marked change from the past. Thatch remained a popular roofing material in the towns of east Devon until well into the eighteenth century, despite recurring fires that consumed hundreds of houses; and this continuing reliance on so combustible a roofing material may be why so few medieval town houses survive in that part of the county. The west of the county had slate, and this presumably helped to keep fire at bay since a few medieval houses survive in the towns there.[74] The disfavour shown to thatch elsewhere was particularly marked in rich counties like Kent, and even more so in towns generally. By the later Middle Ages thatch had started a long, gradual decline, now all but complete so far as towns are concerned. Only here and there in such towns as Dorchester and Shaftsbury in Dorset has time stood still, picturesque qualities saving their few remaining thatched roofs.

London probably heeded its thirteenth-century regulations and, apart from the suburbs, had abandoned thatch well before the end of the Middle Ages:[75] it was too dangerous and, besides, stood for poverty as it eventually would everywhere. In France, significantly, the word for thatch, *chaume*, came to suggest a poor cottage, *chaumière*, and the same notions persisted in Britain until recently.

Indeed, really expensive buildings were seldom roofed in thatch after the Conquest. Castles, needing a fireproof roof, avoided it and used stone or lead. Apparently since its construction in the 1090s, the roof of Westminster Hall was covered in shingles, essentially tiles made from oak that were laid on battens and pegged in place in a way similar to that used for fixing fired clay tile; and the shingles were regularly replaced throughout the thirteenth and fourteenth centuries.[76] In Winchester, where thatch was outlawed in the later fourteenth century, oak shingles had been in regular use for even mundane buildings since the eleventh century. Early in the fourteenth century blue slate was being imported from Devon and Cornwall, and this and shingle were then regularly used in place of thatch, sometimes together on one roof.[77]

Slate, which was imported by sea, was not cheap; lead was very expensive; and tiles were not yet manufactured everywhere. Lead sheeting may have been common enough for great churches, but its use on even expensive houses was so remarkable that in the City Leadenhall Street perpetuates the memory of its use on a long-gone roof.[78] Moreover, both lead and tile, unlike thatch, required not only substantial rafters to bear their weight but also accurate carpentry in the roof framing.

During the thirteenth century the price of oak shingles began to increase. In the 1230s shingles cost 2s per thousand to make in Marlborough, and clay tiles 3s. By 1329 shingles purchased in Croydon for use at Westminster now cost 9s 4d for a thousand, but in 1386 this price had risen to 13s 4d, far more than the equivalent price of clay tiles, which were thought expensive if they cost above 5s per thousand.[79] Tile consequently made rapid headway, particularly in the south-east and east of England, and in several other regions where good supplies of clay facilitated production.

Fired or ceramic tile was another Roman importation that fell out of use when its production ceased. Roman tile was still being robbed for occasional symbolic use after the Conquest, as it was for Chepstow Castle in the decade following the Conquest;[80] but pressure of demand

and probably knowledge imported from Normandy soon revived its production, and tiles came into general use much more quickly than brick, even though the process of shaping the tiles and firing them was similar.[81]

Clay roofing tiles do not retain the warmth of a building as well as thatch does, but that disadvantage is reduced when tiles are laid on a thin covering of straw or theaking, and moss plugs the gaps between them. With wooden pegs to hold them in place tiles last far longer than thatch, provided that they are not caught in a tearing gale. They also last longer than shingles. Longevity and their bright colour conferred an element of esteem too.

Tiles were already in use on London roofs in the twelfth century, and these at first were either curved and flanged, like Roman *tegulae* and *imbrices*, or took the form of shouldered peg-tiles, the roof ridges, meanwhile, being finished either with curved tiles or especially made decorative tiles. Both of these types of tile fell out of use in the late twelfth and early thirteenth centuries when they were superseded by standard peg-tiles, which were plain and had a small flange in place of the shoulder. A century later, production embraced shaped tiles designed for ridges, hips and valleys, and these were now in widespread use in south-eastern England.[82]

Southampton roofs were covered in flanged *tegulae* in the late twelfth century. These were supplanted by plain tiles at least by the middle of the thirteenth century, with the bishop of Winchester's kiln at Highclere in production from the 1290s, if not before. Royal works led the way, followed by those of lesser magnates and manors, so that, by the early fourteenth century, records of purchases of several thousand tiles at a time show how far Hampshire had turned to their use. Kilns at Petersfield and, just over the border, at Farnham in Surrey, were spreading red roofs across the south before the end of the fourteenth century. A tilery at Nackholt in Surrey was producing 100,000 tiles annually in 1355, and had almost doubled this output twenty years later. Salisbury was largely roofed in clay tiles by the early fourteenth century, even though western and northern parts of Wiltshire and eastern Somerset preferred tiles made from stone.[83]

Lincoln's first stone houses of the 1170s were apparently tiled from the start with plain roof tiles and ridge tiles, some of which were crested.[84] While most of Canterbury's houses were thatched before 1200, thanks to the fire of 1174 tile was already making steady headway four years later according to a lease of shops near the cathedral.[85] By the middle of the fourteenth century both the Benedictines and Cistercians were promoting the manufacture of tiles in Kent. Battle Abbey owned a huge tilery at Wye which, like Nackholt, had an annual output of 100,000,[86] and London obtained the bulk of its great needs from tileries at Woolwich, although Smithfield satisfied some of these.[87]

104. A fired clay finial in the form of a moulded mask. © Copyright The British Museum

In Winchester clay ridge tiles made their appearance in the fourteenth century, if not earlier, yet plain roof tiles of clay only started to make deep inroads on the shingles and slates a century later.[88] Ridge tiles were sometimes given a moulded or decorated crest, perhaps with raised triangles called cocks comb or with cut steps or loops. Such tiles were costly: 'riggetyles' or 'crestes' could be ten times as expensive as plain tiles, and when they were specially decorated even more – John Pottere of Chayham was paid 1s each 'for two crests made in the fashion of mounted knights'.[89] Similarly, ridge ends were sometimes decorated with finials in the form of spikes, carved or moulded faces, or standing or rampant beasts.[90] (fig. 104)

There was an organized slate industry in south Devon by the twelfth century, and slate was exported by sea for important buildings in south-east England, but exactly when its use on the roofs of ordinary houses became common is less clear.[91] Stone tiles and slates seem to have come into local use in the thirteenth century wherever suitable quarries could provide a supply, and it took a further century before they were exported widely for general use. Expensive houses and even small peasant houses on the Pennines had roofs tiled in stone – so-called theakstone – in the fifteenth century, but the cost of carriage and a desire to be fashionable kept York tiled in fired clay. Theakstone came from numerous small quarries, which were opened up for a few years even to supply the needs of a single roof, before being abandoned and lost to sight.[92] Stone taken from quarries at Cheglow, Chilmark, Corsham, Haslebury, Hindon and Frome was used in Wiltshire and Somerset. It was simply soaked in water and exposed to frost over winter, following which it readily split into suitably thin layers. Stone tiles were nevertheless more expensive than those of clay, so they were generally used where trans-

105. Jew's House, Lincoln, its front stack, replaced above the eaves, rising over the entrance, between the characteristic twelfth-century windows of the upper floor; the remains of the shouldered arch on the left-hand side of the ground floor once spanned a shop window (from T. H. Turner and Parker 1851–9, vol. 1)

106. King John's Palace, Southampton, now the home of a rebuilt fireplace and chimney-stack taken from 79½ High Street

port put an excessive premium on clay tiles. Cheaper buildings, though, remained wedded to thatch.[93]

The ridges of many hall roofs were pierced by louvers – openings that were designed to allow smoke from an open fire to escape without letting in rain.[94] These were usually made of timber and built into an opening in the rafters over the hearth. Square, hexagonal or octagonal, they rose like a small lantern over the ridge, with slatted sides and a small cap. The slats might be hinged allowing them to be opened and shut, according to the direction of the wind, by pulling on strings. Louvers of this sort with adjustable runners controlled by rope on each of their four sides were once common, even, in Winchester, on the smallest houses.[95] The louvers of small houses were usually quite simple: the timber base for a louver at 7 West Street, Dunstable, suggests little more than a vent protected by its own roof.[96]

Being vulnerable, and eventually made redundant by chimney stacks, few louvers survive, but documents are full of them, and many a medieval hall roof, like those of the Deanery at Salisbury and the Prior's Lodging at Ely,[97] still retains the timber base, just below the ridge, on which one was mounted. The original louver of Gainsborough Old Hall, dating from the 1470s, is exhibited within the house: a storey high, it is in the form of an octagonal kiosk with moulded posts and mid-rail, and an overhanging roof terminating in a ball finial. Most louvers were removed when chimney stacks were inserted, but occasionally they were retained as highly decorated lanterns to let in a little light to the roof space, at others simply to enliven the ridge.

Despite the evidence from Winchester, most ordinary houses did without a louver, the smoke simply finding its own way out of the roof by escaping through the tiles or a vent in a gable. The underside of many a hall roof is consequently blackened by soot, even when a small hole

107. The Merchant's House from Bromsgrove, Avoncroft Museum, Stoke Prior. A timber and plaster firehood, serving as a cheap alternative to a brick chimney-stack to remove the smoke from a hearth

108. A late medieval fired clay chimney pot with crested ridges. © Copyright The British Museum

in a gable, just below the ridge, allowed smoke to exit. The advent of tile reduced the need for louvers since smoke could readily find a way through the gaps. Occasionally, slightly curved tiles were used in that part of a roof immediately above an open hearth to ease the path of the smoke.

With the arrival of roof tiles in the thirteenth century, pottery louvers came into fashion. These were sometimes for decoration as much as utility, as seems to have been the case in Winchester, where none of the surviving fragments is smoke blackened.[98] The plainest of these louvers were little more than slightly raised ridge tiles with side vents, but they might be elaborated to look like miniature castle towers, or even like one of about 1300 found at Goosegate, Nottingham, which is over 1 foot (0.3 m) high and rises, pagoda-like, with diminishing tiers of flanged and canopied apertures beneath a tiny spire to keep out the rain.[99] Another form of louver looked like a chimney pot and sat upon a round hole in the roof, and, similarly, could be decorated with patterns of canopied openings, or even take the form of a standing figurine.[100]

Norman town houses usually eschewed an open hall and their fireplaces were placed against a wall in an upper room. To ease the removal of smoke, a hood set over the hearth led to a flue and a chimney stack, continuing it upward and often prominently sited rising from a front wall. (fig. 105) The earliest stone castle walls were laced with flues, and occasionally stacks still rise above them. These were round, square or polygonal, and often had decorative tops if old illustrations and the few survivors are representative evidence. Indeed a chimney stack was a status symbol at a time when most people were content with an open hearth, given that some houses appear to have lacked even that. (fig. 106)

Since there was no need for a chimney in the standard medieval open hall they were late arrivals in ordinary houses. Winchester's twelfth-century stone house had a fireplace and chimney, but later hall-houses were heated by open hearths set against a wall or partition. A masonry or tile fire-back or an iron reredos may well have protected the wall and helped to throw the heat out into the room, and possibly a plastered timber firehood funnelled the smoke outside, but no archaeological evidence of the latter has been found. Chimneys serving enclosed hearths first appeared in Winchester's ordinary houses in 1506–7, becoming common only after the 1570s,[101] although part of a single medieval chimney pot has been found in the High Street.

The smallest houses seem to have had no provision for heating at all, but larger ones were sometimes fitted with hoods and chimneys. (fig. 107) A specification of 1335 states that the upper room of houses to be built in York were to be fitted with a plastered chimney (*caminum*), 5 feet (1.5 m) wide under the mantel, with a louver or flue (*luuarium*) to remove the smoke. By the end of the Middle Ages some form of flue had become a necessity in those parts of Britain where coal was taking the place of wood as household fuel, owing to its acrid, poisonous fumes. In 1370 a row of eighteen houses in London were to be provided with brick chimneys, eight of them with doubled flues to serve two houses each, and they were to rise 1 foot (0.3 m) above the ridge.[102]

Pots of fired clay were already in use in south and south-east England in the thirteenth century. The surviving fragments show that they were about 1 foot (0.3 m) high and about a third as wide, and some of them quite a bit larger. In general they resemble inverted flower pots with a central opening, and sometimes other openings around them below the top. Some are decorated with a variety of ridged or gouged patterns, but few are glazed.[103] (fig. 108)

For all their apparent advantages and evident status, enclosed flues surmounted by chimney stacks were apt to cause a strong updraft and thus make a wood fire burn too quickly. This simply increased the draft further and any warmth was reduced to unpleasant radiation that burnt faces and left backs cold. A good fire was kept going with a little dry wood burning slowly on as large a pile of hot ash as could be maintained. A wide and deep hearth served best, as well as providing space for cooking, while the hood allowed for the installation of hooks and chains on which spits and pots could be hung. Possibly the evident disadvantages, together with common prejudice, reduced the introduction of chimney stacks to such a slow pace that two centuries passed before first smoke bays and then chimney stacks had generally superseded open hearths.

Writing in 1577, William Harrison remarked on the multitude of chimneys 'latelie erected', but noted that this was a cause of complaint: smoke from an open hearth ensured that 'our heads did neuer ake' and would 'keepe the goodman and his familie from the quacke', whereas 'our tenderlings' now suffered 'rheumes, catarrhs and poses' because chimneys had removed the smoke.[104] As late as 1632 the lawyer turned mathematician Edward Howes was still grumbling about the introduction of enclosed hearths set against a wall with a chimney stack which increased the draft or let smoke billow out into the room:

> I like well the old English and still Irish buyldinge where the roome is large and the chimney or herth, in the middest [i.e. where an open hall has a hearth in its centre]. Certainly thereby ill vapour and gnatts are kept out, lesse firinge [fuel] will serve the turne, and men had then more lusty and able bodies than they have nowe.[105]

Such conservatism delayed the substitution of chimney stacks for open hearths until well into the seventeenth century in affluent rural Kent,[106] and this required the hall to remain open. But the pressing need for space in town hastened its decline, and in this, as in much else, urban fashions were well ahead of the countryside by the end of the Middle Ages. Besides, there was a new fuel available, one that would distinguish later centuries from the Middle Ages and town from countryside. This was coal, and its smoke was not just black but poisonous as well: to burn it safely, an enclosed hearth was essential.

9

Like season'd timber, never gives

Framed walls and roofs

No building material contrasts more greatly with inert earth than live timber. Most surviving medieval houses are framed in timber, the bulk of them in oak. Its utility was second to none. Timbers could be used roughly and unsquared, poles being simply lashed together. Squared and joined by lap-joints and mortises and tenons, timbers could be quickly erected into a substantial frame, a few weeks being time enough for a large hall, and, similarly, this could be deconstructed as quickly, and its timbers reused elsewhere. This was cheaper than stone and, in many places, no more expensive than earth. Timber could be carved with mouldings or figurative sculpture just as stone could, and its posts, studs and braces could be disposed in pleasing patterns that implied status and conspicuous expenditure.

Britain's natural woodland was once the source of supply. Oak flourished wherever deposits of clay gave its roots the heavy, damp soil they need. These conditions were widespread in the Weald of Kent and Sussex, in the Thames basin and in the western Midlands. Because of its hardness, its resistance to warping and splitting, and its lasting qualities, oak became the most highly prized building timber and the most widely used.

Other trees played their part in building too. Sweet-chestnut, which had been growing in Britain since Roman times, was a good substitute for oak, but only used in the Middle Ages on rare occasions. Ash was used for wheels, including those of hoists, and alder found a niche in scaffolding. Elm was occasionally used where oak was scarce or where its greater length was an advantage. Because it lasts particularly well when submerged in water, it has been used since prehistoric times for piled foundations below the water-table, and famously for coffins.

By the fourth millennium BC, agriculture was advancing so rapidly in Britain that clearances were denuding the landscape of its natural woodland. Trees were so extensively used in manufacturing and building, as well as for implements and fuel, that woodland had to be specially managed to ensure adequate supplies. Coppicing, a process whereby trunks were cut just above ground and allowed to regenerate by growing new shoots that could be harvested almost indefinitely, produced straight poles, ideal for light building work as well as for fencing and fuel.

When especially long and stout timber was needed for a particularly large building, this would come from mature trees chosen from well-wooded parks or forests. For more ordinary building work, the trunks of younger, standard trees generally served. These grew naturally in woods or hedges, but, so great did the demand for building timber become, they were eventually cultivated in managed woodland, where they grew quickly and straight upwards among underwood.[1] (fig. 109) From the thirteenth century onward, this demand set builders to look abroad for supplies, particularly of timber from wildwood, which had become scarce in England and Wales. The Baltic became a traditional source of supply, mainly of broad, flat timbers used for wall planking and floorboards.[2]

This much is understood about timber supply, mostly by inference from standing and excavated buildings, and from the few documentary and graphic records that survive. While the craft of carpentry produced magnificent timber buildings right through the Middle Ages, its skills only turned in the twelfth and thirteenth centuries to the development of frames that

109. Hounds hunting a wild boar in wood-land, from a Flemish illustration of *c.* 1530, which also shows tall standard trees growing out of the underwood, with shorter coppiced trees in the background. © British Library. MS Add 18,855, 108v

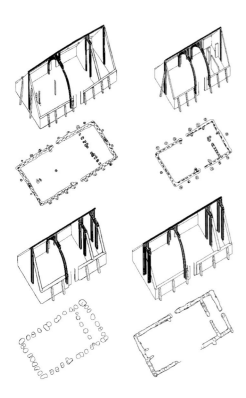

110. Plans and hypothetical reconstructions drawn by Simon James of two halls at Cowdery's Down (top) and two at Chalton (bottom), as interpreted from the patterns of earth-fast posts (bottom, left) and posts and sleeper trenches. After James, Marshall & Millett 1984, fig. 7. © Royal Archaeological Institute

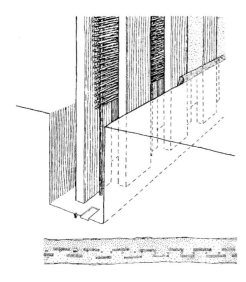

111. Plank construction of a wall drawn by Simon James, interpreted from the excavated archaeological pattern at Cowdery's Down. After Millett & James 1983, fig. 61. © Royal Archaeological Institute

could have a chance of long-term survival. Everything of earlier date must be conjectured from written accounts and tenuous excavated remains, for the most part restricted to a discolouration of the soil where once a post was held fast in the earth. (fig. 110)

The earliest houses, the *Grubenhäuser* and halls of the Anglo-Saxon immigrants, depended on timber posts for their support; these were possibly squared, like their predecessors in Roman Britain, and may have had the benefit of lap-joints and perhaps a few mortises and tenons, lashed or pegged together so as to form a sound frame.[3] Because the timbers were set into holes in the ground, the firmness this gained was at the cost of a short life, perhaps no more than a generation or so, owing to the onset of rot.

By the end of the sixth century, an alternative building method that employed timber planks was used for halls as great as those at Cowdery's Down and for numberless very ordinary houses too. The planks were either set up vertically in trenches, or mounted on sleeper beams, also laid in trenches, which were then filled in. The planks were arranged in various ways to support either horizontal planks and boards, or an infilling of wattles daubed with an earthen mixture.[4] (fig. 111) This method of building was widespread, appearing beyond the North Sea at Emden and on the Baltic at Lübeck, and it seems to have lasted until at least the thirteenth century and probably longer.[5]

Where the ground was unusually wet or waterlogged, as it was in York, builders used two methods of preparing foundations, either setting the walls on oak piles or on stone-filled sleeper trenches. The timber frame of a Danish industrial building excavated at 27 High Ousegate was supported on piles and had a brushwood floor set on a timber raft, and merchants' houses only differed in that they had floors of stone made flat and level with a mortar finish.[6] The walls themselves were either of wattle and daub mounted on posts, or of post and plank, the two giving each other mutual support.[7] Some sites offered comparatively dry and solid foundations for timber posts. In Hartlepool, for instance, eight pre-Conquest timber buildings excavated at Lumley Street were built with squared timber posts founded in continuous narrow trenches cut into the underlying Magnesian limestone.[8]

Between the late ninth century and about 1200 Lincoln's timber buildings were supported by round posts irregularly set into the ground and perhaps clad with horizontal weatherboarding,[9] as they also seem to have been in Coppergate at York. Earth-fast posts were used in Bristol near St Mary-le-Port Street,[10] and again in Winchester by the tenth century. Here, the corner posts measured 8 inches (0.2 m) square and were set about 3 feet (1 m) into the ground, with slighter, subsidiary earth-fast posts between them. These buildings were probably of no more than a single storey and weatherboarded, which added a further element of rigidity.[11] Lesser buildings were more poorly constructed. In Durham, single-storeyed buildings were constructed of strong wattles staked into the ground, and these accommodated leather workers until the later eleventh century brought their destruction.[12]

In later pre-Conquest Thetford, the posts of a particularly long building were rather irregularly laid out in both alignment and interval, and set in shallow sockets; this was followed by a later building that had pairs of posts set opposite each other as though to form a cross-frame, but errors of 5 degrees in what should have been perpendicular eventually accumulated, resulting in the need for an extra post at its south-east corner.[13]

Already by the Conquest constructional methods had advanced far enough for the posts of some of Lincoln's buildings to be regularly aligned in pairs, suggesting that they supported a tie-beam. This improvement continued after the Conquest.[14] In Winchester massive timber posts, up to 16 inches (0.4 m) in scantling, were mounted on roughly cut timber sole-plates placed in the bottom of trenches, and aligned in pairs, some 16.5 feet (5 m) apart, to form bays, with about 8 feet (2.5 m) between each pair, and, again, these were clad in boards, now perhaps grooved to allow for an overlap. Such methods produced great strength, but they consumed large amounts of mature timber, and still the buildings were doomed by the onset of rot.[15] The construction of bays was nevertheless an important advance, since these came to form a basic constructional unit as well as a unit of design.

By the time of the Domesday Survey, England was one of the least-wooded countries in Europe, its woods haphazardly covering less than an eighth of the land. The supply of timber

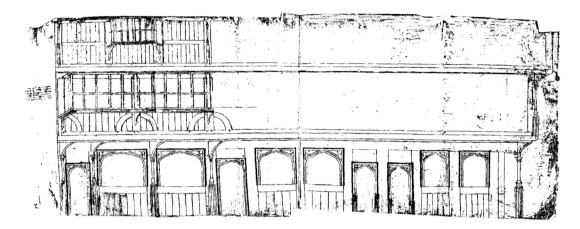

112. An architectural elevation of framed shops and two upper storeys of chambers, shown in a worn and faded sixteenth-century drawing that was reused to bind a register belonging to Bishop Ghinucci of Worcester. After Charles & Down, 1970–2, Pls 8–9

FACING PAGE

113. Noah preparing to build the Ark, from a fifteenth-century illustration that shows the tools of his trade: an axe, an augur, a chisel, a drill, a saw, a square and a reel of cord for measuring, as well as straight, curved and elbowed pieces of timber awaiting assembly. © Bodleian Library MS Barlow 53r

was increasingly in the hands of woodmen who grew and cut timber commercially, and so efficiently that they met the great demands of the richer southern, eastern and midland counties of England, right to the end of the Middle Ages. There were scarcities, even so, and these were aggravated by the generally poor state of roads: a journey of fifty miles could double the cost of a load.[16]

It was the carpenter's task to select the trees for a proposed building. These were then felled and stripped of bark and branches, which were sold for such purposes as tanning and fuel, leaving the trunks to be squared for use as posts or beams, or sawn down their length to make boards or studs. These straight and comparatively slender standardized timbers were crucial to the design of framed buildings. As increasing prosperity and a building boom in the twelfth and thirteenth centuries pressed forward the development of carpentry, it quickly embraced a new tradition based on this timber with a set of rules tantamount to a complete grammar.

This grammar facilitated the process of design. Many houses and other common buildings made such use of standard forms that they were designed only so far as their sizes and number of bays were specified, with standing houses perhaps providing exemplars. In York, for example, a contract of 1335 between the parishioners of St Martin's, Coney Street, and the carpenter Robert Giles required him to build six houses that were to have a continuous roof, be of a specified length and breadth, 'and conform in all ways with the house of Richard de Briggenall in North Street'.[17]

When a house was unusual, or when some forgotten circumstance dictated, its design could be set out with drawings of plans or elevations. Thus in 1436 the carpenter John Berewik of Romsey undertook to erect a house in Middle Brook Street for the Warden of Winchester College 'as the trasying schewith y drawe in a parchement skyn'.[18] This was probably unusual, and only one such drawing is known to survive – an early sixteenth-century elevation of a three-storeyed row of houses with shops on the ground floor.[19] (fig. 112)

However the design was made, these new framed buildings were prefabricated in the carpenters' yard, where the timbers were cut to size and their joints shaped.[20] (fig. 113) Most localities where resources of timber were good and there was a continuous demand for framed buildings probably had a small carpenters' yard, but for major buildings it was necessary to go further afield. When the master-carpenter Hugh Herland rebuilt the roof of Westminster Hall between 1394 and 1401, the extremely large timbers needed for the job came from royal woodland at Odiham and Aliceholt in Hampshire; more came from Stoke d'Abernon in Surrey, and two hundred oaks for the rafters were brought from Hertfordshire. These were cut to shape in a yard called The Frame near Farnham, some thirty-five miles from Westminster as the crow flies, and a good deal more when transported by water, along the river Wey to the Thames.[21]

When cut, each major part of a timber building, large or small, whether a wall-frame, a cross-frame, or, as for Westminster Hall, a roof-truss, was then assembled flat on the ground, and checked for fit; the timbers were made flush with each other on the side that faced upwards, the joints were adjusted, and the peg-holes were then drilled and the individual timbers inscribed on the upper face with a mark as a means of identifying them and easing their final assembly on site.

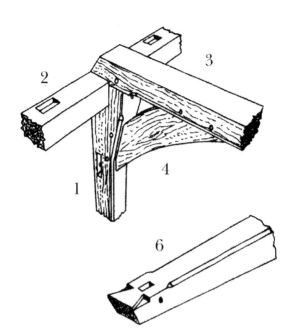

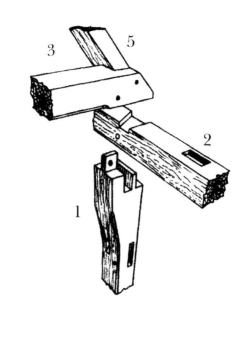

114. Edgar's Farm, Stowmarket (re-erected at the Museum of East Anglian Life). An arcade-post of an aisled hall, carved with a capital beneath the springing of the curved braces that rise up to support the arcade-plate (running from left to right), and the tie-beam above that; beneath the common rafters, a so-called passing-brace stiffens the framing of the aisle, on the left, and the main span of the roof above

115. Assembly at the top of a main-post, assembled (left) and exploded (right and below): (1) jowled top of main-post; (2) wall-plate with open mortise to receive bottom ends of rafters; (3) tie-beam; (4) brace; (5) lower end of rafter; (6) underside of tie-beam showing dovetail to engage wall-plate and mortise for upper tenon in main-post. Detail from 21 High Street, Canterbury. © Canterbury Archaeological Trust, 1988

As carpenters refined their techniques in the thirteenth century, this process became ever more crucial. By carefully jointing the horizontal and vertical timbers, and triangulating their joints with braces, a timber frame could be raised on to pad-stones or timber sills mounted on a waterproof base. In the first instance this was achieved through a multiplicity of braces and several extremely long timbers. But, during the thirteenth century, carpenters progressively reduced the number and length of these separate timbers, and employed types of joint that were more efficient. This left no room for mistake: it was no longer possible to add parts to an assembled frame if these had been forgotten during the proper stage of their assembly. They could now set a timber-framed house of two, three or even more storeys on a waterproof plinth or over a stone undercroft, which simply supported the sole-plates or sill-beams on which the frame was raised. This immediately removed the old problem of decay, since rot could be avoided, as well as providing economies in timber.[22]

The earliest buildings framed by these new methods adopted a wide centre divided by arcades of stout posts from lower and narrower aisles. One of the first great surviving aisled halls was built for Bishop Foliot at his palace at Hereford with timber felled in 1179.[23] Its remarkable round-arched timber arcades are in essence copying the form, though not the structural integrity, of stone arcades.[24] Most aisled halls had plainer arcades of posts and beams. These carried continuous roofs with no break between nave and aisles. (fig. 114) The carpentry techniques made use of methods known to Rome, but their immediate source was France, where the techniques may have come northward from the Mediterranean.[25] Whatever the origin of the aisled form, it seems to have brought with it an element of esteem, perhaps because aisles were associated with great churches, or just with size.

The all-important junction of a vertical post and the wall-plate or arcade-plate that it supported in the longitudinal plane and the tie it supported in the lateral plane was crucial to stability. The means by which this was achieved seems to have been entirely of English origin. During the thirteenth century, carpenters devised a crafty compound joint that employed a lower mortise and tenon to hold the plate, and an upper mortise and tenon to hold the tie, which was then lap-dovetailed over the plate, thus tying it in place. (fig. 115) This practice so satisfied carpenters that it lasted some six hundred years. No other method was so universally applied in Britain, despite others being common on the Continent. It indeed worked well, but shrinkage of the green timber as it dried out could strain the joints to such an extent that the head of the post might split. Yet this compound joint became an essential feature of the carpenter's grammar, seemingly understood without question equally by the woodmen who produced the timber and the carpenters who cut it.[26]

116. Perspective of the box-frame of 70 Castle Street, Canterbury. The frame is mounted on a timber sill, and has two bays, and two storeys; the further side has a projecting jetty, the nearer side (in which some floor joists are omitted) extends into a rear aisle; the roof comprises a series of common rafters, halved and pegged to each other at the apex, and supported by collars (omitted from the drawing except at each end and in the middle); the collars rest on a crown-plate, which runs down the length of the roof space, and is supported by crown-posts that rise at bay intervals from the tie-beams.
© Canterbury Archaeological Trust, 1988

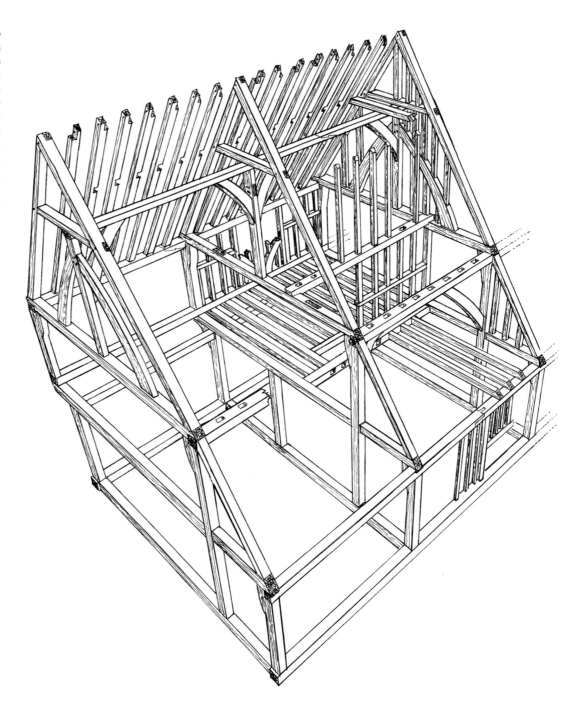

Lateral stability in these early aisled structures was provided by bracing together the centre and aisles with very long straight timbers, and applying large numbers of subsidiary timbers to add a degree of stiffening. During the thirteenth century, carpenters learnt how to dispense with these and frame their buildings and roofs with fewer, shorter timbers of uniform section or scantling, which greatly eased the problems of supply and their ability to mass-produce buildings. This inaugurated the so-called common-rafter roof, which comprises pairs of rafters, pegged at their apex and often braced by collars about a third of the way down, all made from timber of common scantling. (fig. 116)

Although arcades brought the status of the wide halls where they had first been developed, arcade-posts interfered with the internal space, and so were slowly abandoned in the later Middle Ages in nearly all buildings that did not need to have a span of more than about 22 feet (6.5m), or the length of a readily available beam of oak. This left at its simplest a timber box, framed on a rectangle of sill-beams, with four corner posts that carried the weight of all above, namely wall-plates and tie-beams, all suitably braced together, and, mounted on them, the roof

frame and rafters. This box-frame became one of two basic forms of timber building from the late thirteenth century onwards. It comprised a series of units or bays that could extend lengthwise, bay by bay, as far as desired. This bay system links the structure with the plan in an immediately comprehensible way that is not found in other forms of building, whether of timber or stone.[27]

The box-frame was applied to the construction of houses in which the main room, the hall, could be of one, two or more bays, and the subsidiary rooms could be the same, or even of half a bay. Moreover, when the hierarchical arrangements within a room such as a hall or principal chamber so required it, the bays were not of uniform size. In fact, most two-bay halls consist of unequal bays, the longer one containing the high table, the shorter one the entrances. Bays could be arranged to form angles, making winged plans shaped like an L, a T or an H. Less easy was to add ranges of bays in depth, firstly because this required multiple roofs, each range of bays usually having a separate roof of its own, which caused problems with drainage between them; and secondly, because daylight in so deep a building might not fully illuminate the centre. Nevertheless, a building of two bays in depth was acceptable in town, where limits on space often made it necessary, and was used, for example, for the large halls of some guilds.

One of the features of the bay system and the spaces embraced by one or more bays was a means of emphasizing the superiority of one of these spaces over another, or one of the sides of a frame over the other. This was achieved by erecting a frame with its so-called upper face in the more prominent position. Because of the flush finish of the timbers on the upper face and the fact that the pegs had been driven home on this side, it had a more finished appearance than the lower side, where differences in the thicknesses of the various timbers would show, and the pointed ends of the pegs would protrude. Being more visible, the outside face of a wall was usually also its upper face. A frame spanning a hall, where both faces were equally visible, would be set up with its upper face towards the high table, its lower face towards the service end. Similarly, the frame behind the high table would have its upper face toward the high table once again, and the lower face toward the chambers beyond. A whole set of rules based on the hierarchy of spaces thus governed the way each frame was set up.[28]

An important development in box-framing, which had all the advantages of a highly visible status symbol, allowed a frame to accommodate an upper floor. This solved the problem of fixing both ends of the floor-joists without interfering with the assembly of the main part of the frame. It was achieved by tenoning the inner end of each floor-joist firmly to a bridging-piece, or bressummer, and simply resting its outer end on a second bressummer at the front and projecting it forward to produce an overhang or jetty. (fig. 117) This avoided the difficulty of jointing both ends, and, as a bonus, the projecting jetty provided around 2 feet (0.6 m) of extra width on the floor above. The jetty would also advertise the existence of the upper floor, and, when such floors were still not universal, this would confer a fashionable degree of status.

117. (top) Tudor House, Palace Street, Canterbury. A medieval house, re-fronted in timber at the end of the fifteenth century, its jetty is supported at the corner on a grotesque bracket, and the ends of the jettied joists themselves are concealed by a fascia carved with a guilloche moulding adorned with roses, white and red, to represent the Houses of York and Lancaster, united under the first of the Tudor monarchs

118. (bottom) 13 Stonegate, York. A dragon-post carved with a well-endowed angel

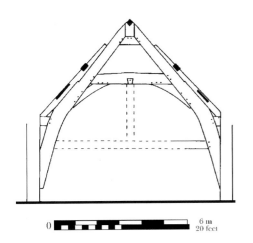

119. The cruck-frame between 25 and 26 Barrow Street, Much Wenlock. The crucks are joined by a braced collar, from which hangs framing (now mostly removed) that forms a partition. The crucks carry a ridge-piece and principal rafters that carry purlins, and are attached to the upper part of the walls with stubs. After Moran 1992. © Vernacular Architecture Group

0 ▮▬▬▮▬▮▬▮▬▮▬▮▬▬▬▬▬ 6 m / 20 feet

Jetties were made to protrude on adjacent sides of a frame simply by projecting a diagonal beam, or dragon-beam, at the corner into which the floor joists could be tenoned at an angle on each side so as to project forwards and perpendicularly sideways. Already by about 1250–80 the cross-wing of 48–9 Churchgate Street in Bury St Edmunds was built with adjacent jetties projecting from a dragon-beam, mounted on a corner post, or dragon-post.[29] Because of their prominence, dragon-posts soon came to be specially carved, either with bases and capitals in the manner of timber columns, or with grotesques. (fig. 118)

Jetties were apparently first used in crowded towns where upper floors were becoming a necessity. They appear at a similar time on the Continent, so the idea may well be an import. London's first recorded jetty[30] was already causing a nuisance in 1246 in an alley leading off Ironmonger Lane, probably because it stuck out. By 1300 jetties were common in English towns, York's oldest surviving timber houses, Lady Row in Goodramgate of 1316, having a jetty down their whole length. (fig. 311) Jetties became a means of articulating the floors of a house, which could rise by two jettied storeys and then a third into its gabled garrets. Moreover, the ends of the jettied joists might be grotesquely carved and supported by carved brackets, or hidden by decoratively carved fascia boards, although these were only common in the sixteenth and seventeenth centuries. Wherever houses were framed in timber, jetties became popular. The earliest jetty in Wales to be securely dated is at Conwy, where Aberconwy House, of about 1420, according to tree-ring dates, has stone lower floors and a jettied, timber-framed upper floor, extending round the corner. The jetty is all the more remarkable because each joist is ostentatiously supported by a bracket resting on a stone corbel in a way that suggests an origin in the projecting timber hoardings and their supporting machicolations temporarily erected on top of castle turrets. North Wales is of course pre-eminently a land of ostentatious castles, Conwy Castle among them. Scotland has its castles too, but jetties eventually came into use in a more ordinary urban context there, as the rare examples of Edinburgh's John Knox House and Huntly House show[31] (figs 199, 361 and 363).

Shortly after the middle of the thirteenth century carpenters adapted a form of roof that had been developed in French cathedrals whereby vertical struts held down the ridge against any tendency to distort when wind buffeted the roof. This led to the adoption of the so-called crown-post, which was centrally mounted, bay by bay, on the tie-beams to support a longitudinal plate that kept both the collars and the common rafters that were coupled to them in place. The crown-post was highly visible from the ground, and could be given an appropriate architectural prominence. Possibly for this reason, as well as for its use of standard scantlings, the crown-post roof dominated carpenters' practice in much of medieval England, even though it was neither particularly efficient nor the only method open to them, and was only finally superseded by other types in the early sixteenth century.[32]

The alternative method of framing bays, which again came into prominence in the thirteenth century, carried the weight of the roof independently of the walls on a cranked A-frame.[33] This comprised a pair of curved or elbowed timbers, known as crucks, joined together at the apex and braced by a collar. (fig. 119) The mystery of its obscure origin is all the deeper since crucks appear to be quite absent in many parts of eastern England, and the boundary between where they are common and where they are absent is remarkably sharp.[34] A series of cruck-pairs, linked by lengthwise timbers carried on their backs, formed the basic frame of a cruck building. Unlike the box-frame, the cruck frame is inherently stable transversely and has little need of either extensive bracing or sophisticated joinery. Assembly is easy: a pair of crucks, assembled on the ground, can be reared upright, to be followed by more pairs as building proceeds, bay by bay.[35]

Despite these advantages, crucks serve best in relatively small buildings, otherwise they must be very stout and long if they are to do their job. The availability of suitable timber therefore set limits to their use. While they can reach a little over 33 feet (10m), as they do at Pershore Abbey's unequalled barn at Leigh Court in Worcestershire, this needs massive bowed timbers of a similar length to its great span, and with a maximum scantling of well over 1.6 feet (0.5 m). Such timbers were way beyond what woodmen could quickly cultivate, and very large cruck-framed buildings are consequently rare. Even ordinary crucks of, say, 20 feet (about 6m) in length probably came not from the young trees of managed woodland, but from the trunks

120. The north-western end of High Street, Thame, photographed *c.* 1900. The nearest house (on the right), 87 High Street, a three-bay medieval cruck-framed house probably dating from the late fourteenth century, characteristically is both lower than its later neighbours and devoid of external evidence of the use of crucks; again typically of such houses, it was built close to the extremity of the medieval town, rather than the centre where economic pressures eventually required houses to be larger and higher. Photo via Malcolm Airs

121. 83 West End, Kirkbymoorside, section showing the roughly shaped cruck frame rising from the walls of a poor house that has a low ground floor and garret. After Hayes & Rutter 1972, fig. 28. © Scarborough and District Archaeological Society

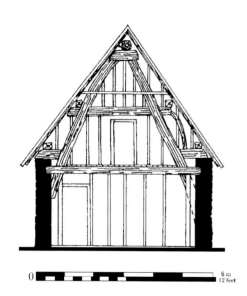

and a low curving branch of more aged trees that had to be specially selected. Crucks could, nevertheless, be used and reused because they could be as easily dismounted as raised.

By 1981 over 3,000 cruck-framed buildings had been recorded in England and Wales, and a few hundred more in Scotland.[36] No more than some two hundred of these are in towns. Because the height and width of a cruck-framed building are usually much the same, the headroom of a standard frame is limited to a single storey and garret. Although the height needed by most storeyed town houses might be obtained by raising crucks of a standard length well above ground on the walls, this rather defeated the reason for using them, namely to free the walls of bearing the weight of the roof. So there was a penalty. Worse, having no external signs that confer status, unlike some other forms of framing, their use in town is largely restricted to places where a desire for status was nullified by poverty, and utility was all.

Perhaps only a score of medieval cruck-framed town houses survive today. The difficulty in dating crucks may be partly responsible for this, but it is also due to their unsuitability. There were once substantial numbers of cruck-framed houses in towns where a single storey and attic were not an evident waste of space. Thus in Ludlow in 1272, Peter Gelemin was crushed to death by a falling cruck (worth 6d.), and, in the suburbs, a cruck-framed hall in Corve Street appeared in a legal case of 1296–7. In 1373 a tenant agreed to build a small house with four crucks in Le Fere Street, a minor street in Coventry.[37] Poor single-roomed houses built in the late twelfth century at 75–87 Main Street, Cockermouth, with timber posts set into holes, were rebuilt about 1400 with clay walls and cruck trusses to support the roofs, and these in turn were replaced by rather better stone houses three centuries later.[38] While crucks were probably fairly common, this lowliness put paid to the bulk of them.

Out-of-the-way towns like New Radnor in mid-Wales perfectly exemplify this. Radenore Nova is first recorded in 1277, but its heyday was in the early fourteenth century when its rapidly expanding population held a weekly market. Its earliest buildings had earth-fast posts, but these were now being replaced using either box-frames or, more probably, crucks. One two-bay cruck-framed hall-house indeed survives at 8 Church Street, but it probably dates from the fifteenth century, that is after Owain ab Gruffydd had sacked the town in 1404 and its economy had long lost its glitter. Never particularly urban in character, rural qualities were reasserting themselves, so that by the end of the 1530s Leland noted in his *Itinerary* that its buildings were 'in moste part but rude, many howsys being thakyd', and depopulation and decay were claiming even those.[39] Similarly, at Much Wenlock the small St Owen's Well House and 25–8 Barrow Street, a row of single-storeyed dwellings, again exemplify poverty associating with cruck frames in the earlier fifteenth century.[40]

Notably, several medieval cruck-framed houses survive at Aylesbury, Thame and Burford without associations of poverty.[41] (fig. 120) The upper Thames valley is well endowed with medieval crucks, some of which are of the greatest antiquity. This may account for two of Burford's eleven cruck-framed buildings, Pethers in the High Street and Bull Cottage in Witney Street, which were both apparently built in the fourteenth century with cruck-framed open halls. These may be accidental survivals of what were once status symbols in a remarkably well-preserved market town, since there are other surviving medieval houses here, without cruck frames.[42]

The general unsuitability of cruck frames to any but the poorest urban houses is borne out in the small market towns around the Vale of Pickering, where crucks are still common in the poorest houses. At Malton on the south side of the vale there were once ten cruck-framed houses,[43] all lowly and now reduced to three. There is a record of no less than sixteen very small thatched and whitewashed cruck-framed houses in Kirkbymoorside, (fig. 121) and in Pickering itself seventeen (fig. 122). Their lowly status also shows in their planning, which suggests that some of them originated as long-houses in which one end contained a cattle byre. None is medieval, but there is little to differentiate them from the long-houses of nearby villages, such as Pockley, and the moors to the north of the vale, which are medieval in concept if not in date.[44]

Possibly a lack of suitable timber in the face of a strong tradition caused the West Country to turn to jointed crucks, that is crucks made of two lengths of timber pegged together at the angle. Again these are only rarely found in towns. Two jointed cruck-trusses frame a very small hall of about 1400 at the back of 62 Fore Street, Topsham, and once more suggest what was probably common in the small ports of Devon and Cornwall before wealth and a desire for greater space and height reduced their numbers.[45]

122. Castle Gate, Pickering. A cruck-framed house with a single storey and a blocked doorway that may have once been used for cattle as well as people

123. Leicester Guildhall. The nearest truss, forming an arch, employs a pair of base-crucks; the further two trusses and the end truss have common wall-posts and braced tie-beams, and consequently lack the height and hence the prestige of the base-cruck truss

How base-crucks are related to common crucks is far from clear,[46] although they perform a similar constructional function. Combining the curved form of a pair of crucks with a tie-beam, base-crucks again support the weight of a roof free of the walls, but they also provide width without needing such long timbers. While the first survivors[47] are contemporary with the first crucks and date from the mid-thirteenth century, they are likely to be a development of the basic form which, if these survivors are a guide, originated in Gloucestershire and the western Midlands.[48] Within a century they had been widely adopted, for instance in Essex, Kent and Lincolnshire, where there are no true crucks, as well as in the west, but were never commonly used.[49] As an opulent substitute for an aisled frame, they removed the encumbrance of arcade-posts in both large barns and important halls.

Few of the 115 buildings with base-crucks recorded by 1981 are in towns, the most significant being in the mid-fourteenth-century Leicester Guildhall, where the base-crucks are used instead of arcade-posts. Through the rarity and bravura of their form, they add a good measure of status as well. (fig. 123) Exactly the same occurs in the hall of Hamden at Smarden, which is thoroughly rural despite the grant of borough status in 1338. One of the most extraordinary uses of base-crucks is in the so-called Pilgrims' Hall of 1310/11 within the cathedral precinct at Winchester;[50] here a base-cruck truss is combined with an aisled truss, a raised aisle truss and two hammerbeam trusses, as though the master-carpenter responsible for its design wanted to build an exemplar of his range of accomplishments.[51] (fig. 124)

Raised aisle trusses involved the odd idea of raising all the framing associated with an aisled structure on to a very long tie-beam. Such a frame was used in 1299–1300 for the roof of the hall in the Warden's House at Merton College, Oxford,[52] which is a little earlier than the Pilgrims' Hall, but its real future lay in ornate church roofs rather than in secular buildings. By

124. The Pilgrim's Hall, Winchester. The restored cut-away perspective (bottom) shows, right to left, trusses I–V; I–IV are shown in sections above. Truss I (top left) has arcade-posts and aisles, right and left; II (top right) has base-crucks; III (middle left) has raised aisles set over a long tie-beam; IV (middle right) has hammer-beams with curved braces supporting both them and the upper tie-beam. After Crook 1991, figs 1, 7, 8, 9 and 10. © Society of Antiquaries of London

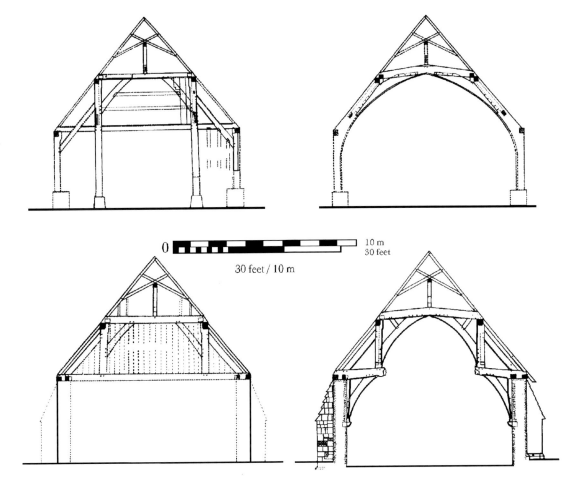

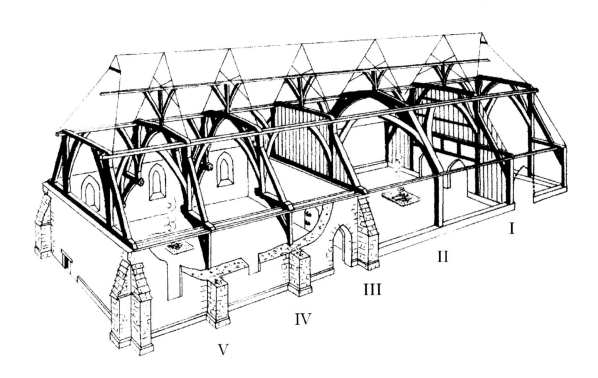

125. The Pilgrim's Hall, Winchester. The hammerbeams of truss IV

the simple process of cutting out the centre of the tie-beam between the two raised arcade-posts of such a truss, and cantilevering the stubs that remained, a carpenter would arrive at the hammerbeam roof. This was far more spectacular, and was to have an illustrious future, as the Pilgrims' Hall clearly shows (fig. 125).

The hammerbeam seems to have been an English invention, at least so far as there are no Continental examples to prove otherwise.[53] Hammerbeam roofs again had a great future in churches, but they graced several spectacular halls including Edward IV's great hall at Eltham Palace of 1475–83, and, combined with arches, the master-carpenter Hugh Herland's unequalled roof of Westminster Hall, of 1394–1402.[54] (fig. 126) Seemingly based on Herland's magnificent design is the miniature arched hammerbeam roof of the hall at 8–9a The Close at Exeter, a remarkably opulent courtyard house built for a cathedral canon at the end of the fourteenth century.[55] (fig. 127)

By the sixteenth century the hammerbeam roof had been exported to Scotland. The Great Hall of Stirling Castle was completed with a hammerbeam roof in James IV's reign, probably to the design of the king's principal carpenter John Drummond, who was active between 1507 and 1541. That roof has gone, and so has the possibly similar roof of the great hall at Linlithgow, but it may have been Drummond who roofed Edinburgh Castle's Great Hall with hammerbeams too, and these survive. (fig. 128) This decidedly odd roof, with its mass of short, thin bracing timbers forming polygonal arches, is very similar to Drummond's design at Stirling. Even so, just when it was raised is open to doubt because the monogram of James IV, 'IR4', which appears on one of its supporting corbels as well as on payments for timber in 1496 and slating the roof in 1511, do not easily relate to the antique classical motifs carved on the scrolled corbels, which are evidence of an extremely precocious Renaissance taste.[56]

Much more ordinary buildings than royal halls were occasionally given the crowning glory of a hammerbeam roof. There were two in Salisbury, firstly at 27 Winchester Street, a court-yard house built by the wool merchant John Balle between 1377 and 1387. This was subsequently owned by or leased to nine mayors, before falling on hard times and being subdivided and finally demolished in 1962. The Plume of Feathers Inn was the second, and again owed its fourteenth-century origin to mercantile wealth.[57]

These great roofs show how far carpenters developed their skills in the thirteenth century. A more mundane development, achieved about 1300, was the decision to institute trussed roofs in place of common-rafter roofs. In these, stout rafters rise over the tie-beams or base-crucks to

126. Hugh Herland's arch-braced hammer-beam roof at Westminster Hall. Based on Waddell 1999, fig. 3. © Society of Architectural Historians of Great Britain

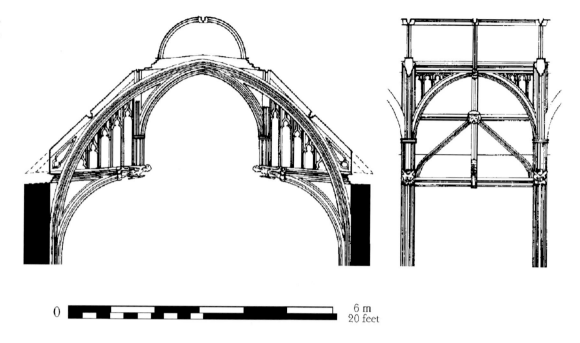

127. Hammerbeam truss at 8–9a The Close, Exeter, and elevation between two trusses. © after D. Portman 1966, fig. 6

0　　　　　　　　　　　　　　　　　6 m
　　　　　　　　　　　　　　　　　20 feet

128. Great Hall, Edinburgh Castle. Hammerbeam truss, restored to its assumed state before alteration, showing its seemingly archaic multiplicity of bracing timbers, and decoration restricted to carved beasts on the ends of the hammerbeams. © Gifford, McWilliam & Walker 1984, 96

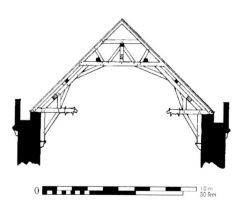

0　　　　　　　　　　10 m
　　　　　　　　　　30 feet

support purlins, which bear the burden of the common rafters set between them, thus removing the need for the collars linking pairs of rafters. Purlins first appear in cathedral roofs in the second half of the thirteenth century as an importation from France, for instance in the nave of Chichester, and also in the bishop's palace there.[58] By the fourteenth century, the trussed roof complete with purlins became typical of western carpentry and would be the principal alternative to the common-rafter roof. (fig. 129) The north quickly took to the form as well, the first surviving domestic example being at 12–15 Newgate, York, a row of houses built in the late 1330s.[59] Both here and even in the west the older form of common-rafter roof survived for a short while if the evidence of what was probably a canon's house, built in the mid-fourteenth century with a crown-post roof at Hereford, is significant.[60]

A great advantage of the side-purlin roof over the common-rafter roof was that it left most of the roof space free of intrusive collars and plates. Chaucer's Oxford carpenter must have had a roof like this in the 1380s:

> He hadde yboght hym knedyng tubbes thre,
> And hadde hem hanged in the roof above,
> And that he preyed hem, for goddes love,
> To sitten in the roof, par compaignye.[61]

With so much space for hanging the tubs, he could have floored over the roof to convert it into a usable garret.

By the early fifteenth century this was becoming common, and windows set into gables show this exploitation of roof space. By 1500, new houses often had their roof space partitioned as well to form separate chambers, just as Paycocke's House at Great Coggeshall shows with its two garret chambers, divided by a central partition along a roof-truss and each lit by a gable-end window.[62]

Trussed rafters were usually supported by collars, as common rafters were, and the collars could be supported on struts, either in the centre or, more usually, at each end. Alternatively, the tie-beam might be replaced by timber arches rising from the main-posts to support a collar. Already in the 1230s the Greyfriars of Lincoln had raised a common-rafter roof whose collars were braced by round arches rising from sole-pieces over stone walls,[63] and in later church roofs arches were substituted for tie-beams so as to make headroom for stone vaults. Whether these influenced the later arch-braced roof, which was often raised over stone walls, or whether the

129. Merchant's House from Bromsgrove, Avoncroft Museum, Stoke Prior. The solar chamber and its trussed rafter roof. This comprises a tie-beam, on which are mounted a king-strut and collar to support the principal rafter, and these in turn carry purlins and curved wind-braces to support the common rafters

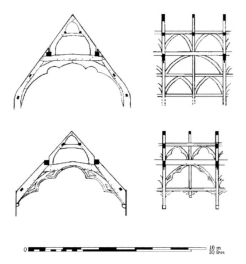

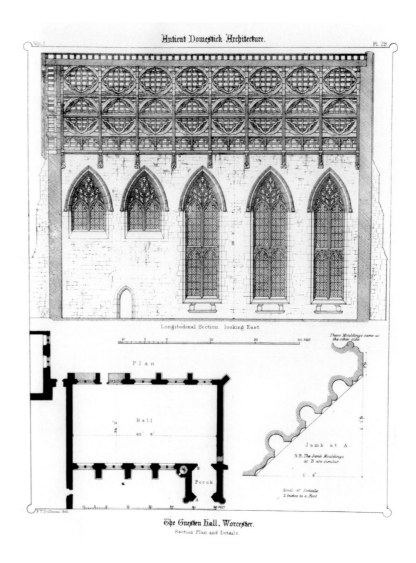

Longitudinal Section looking East.

Plan

Hall

Porch

Jamb at A.

N.B. The Jamb Mouldings
at B are similar.

Scale of Details
2 Inches to a Foot

The Guesten Hall, Worcester.
Section Plan and Details.

130. Two arch-braced roofs in Wells: at the Priory of St John (above), where arch-braced base-crucks support a collar that carries a miniature cruck truss in the upper part of the roof; and at the King's Head Inn (below), which is similar except that the base-crucks have shrunk to plain principal rafters. Both roofs have tiers of curved wind-braces (show on the right) to support the purlins. After a survey by R. G. Gilson and E. H. D. Williams in Penoyre 1998, fig 4. © Jane Penyore

131. The Guesten Hall roof, showing in elevation its cusped wind-braces. After Dollman & Jobbins 1861, 1, Pl. 29. © Society of Antiquaries of London

cruck truss was the point of departure is unclear, but it is significant that arched trusses seem to have started in the west, and rapidly extended eastwards until the majority of stone-walled halls were roofed this way.

Two early arch-braced roofs were built at Wells in the early years of the fourteenth century. (fig. 130) In about 1315 the open hall of what was probably the guest house of the Priory of St John was spanned by base-crucks and collars in the usual way, but these are braced by highly decorative cusped arches. Closely following this is the truss spanning the hall of what is now the King's Head, where the cusps are even more prominent, the likely inference being that the same carpenters built both roofs.[64]

One of the finest arch-braced roofs was built at Worcester in 1320 for the Guesten Hall, where the prior received his guests. This stood to the east of the cathedral chapter house until, unsafe, it was demolished in 1862; but the roof was saved and for a century served a church, until a second removal took it to the Avoncroft Museum of Buildings. Its arches support collars and cusped struts just below the apex, and this cusping is taken up by wind-braces above and below the purlins, all to make a highly ornate roof in line with the prior's opulent architectural taste. (fig. 131)

Far less opulent is the arched-braced roof of the mid-fifteenth-century hall of Owain Glyndwr's Parliament House at Machynlleth, and there was another medieval arch-braced roof in Dolgellau until in 1885 it was removed to Newtown for the Cwrt Plas-y-Dre (Quaker Meeting House). The eastern counties of England also preferred less flamboyance: the fine arch-braced roof raised about 1465–70 over the hall of Gainsborough Old Hall comprises plain, moulded arches that rise effortlessly from the walls to carry two tiers of purlins, the lower

ones themselves further supported by curved wind-braces in the form of arches, rather like those of the Guesten Hall, but lacking the cusps that are such a feature of western roofs.[65] (fig. 132) The arch-braced roof of the Old Hall of Lincoln's Inn is again similar, but here the wind-braces take the form of drawn-out S-shaped double curves, which look pretty but structurally not quite sound.[66]

Like most medieval roofs, which were designed equally to carry thatch or tile, their pitch was relatively high, 50–60 degrees being the norm. Roofs covered in lead or the heavy stone tiles of the Pennines needed a lower pitch and put a different strain on the rafters. Probably as a result of this, rafters set at a low pitch for this purpose were not simply pegged together but were fixed to a ridge-piece, which required the support of a central king-post set on each tie-beam, and the purlins might again be supported by posts. (fig. 282) This form was often used on lead-clad church roofs, but was otherwise characteristic of the north. So two schools of trussed roof appeared, one originating in the west and one in the north.

The western school ultimately won the day. From the fourteenth century onwards it slowly pressed eastward towards London until even Kent finally succumbed in the 1520s. This new form, however, required stronger and thicker principal rafters, which had to come from older trees, and this is probably why the hard-pressed supply of anything but standard timber in the wealthy south-east delayed the change for so long.

By the late thirteenth century the lavish use of timber for new building works, exacerbated by the need to replace the large number of buildings that were failing because their earth-fast posts were rotting, was forcing through all of these advances at an ever-increasing pace. This may have been quickened by a wholesale reorganization of the source of building timber that produced more or less standardized scantlings and lengths or increased its cost.

Winchester's house carpenters, like many others in much of southern and eastern England, adopted these new forms of timber framing fairly quickly. By 1300 they were adopting the French forms of roof framing that had penetrated the south, as exemplified by the roof of

132. Gainsborough Old Hall. The arch-braced hall roof with its single tier of curved wind-braces

42 Chesil Street,[67] but these gave way to a variety of roofs, many of them employing crown-posts and common rafters, and others with struts, collars and side purlins.[68] They now set their frames on unmortared flint ground sills.[69] Through economic necessity they turned to shorter timbers of standardized scantlings, in lesser quantities, building by building, than they had used beforehand. They no longer needed the extra rigidity that boarded walls had given their buildings, since the new carpentry techniques provided that in full measure, and wattle and daub were better for insulation.

Winchester's new houses of the fourteenth and fifteenth centuries comprised a series of bays formed by pairs of posts set 16.5 feet (5 m) apart with a bay length of 8 feet (2.5 m) between each pair.[70] So successful were the city's carpenters in the production of such houses that they became its most important building-craftsmen. They could oversee the decoration of the front of a house with ornate framing and elaborately carved mouldings, friezes and tracery, and

ensure that it was built rapidly and cheaply. They could run up a house in as little as ten weeks, even if twenty were more normal, and £15 was the price of a fair-sized house, 70s (£3.50) of a cottage.[71]

In the face of such prices it is little wonder that stone was increasingly reserved for the inordinately wealthy and for those buildings, churches in the main, where ancient tradition required nothing less. The timber frame was better suited than stone to domestic buildings, being not only cheaper but also more readily adaptable to change, particularly as the circumstances and needs of the occupants altered or their numbers grew. Carpentry could similarly make greater use than brick or stone of a confined urban plot, for instance through its overhanging jetties. Moreover, from the fourteenth century until the end of the Middle Ages, indeed for a good century afterwards, timber framing retained its fashionable cachet, and came to be used even where timber was hard to find and stone easy. Devon's rural buildings were seldom made of timber, stone being plentiful and cob a good substitute where stone was too expensive, yet many of its towns, even Moretonhampstead on the edge of granite-strewn Dartmoor, looked to timber in the later Middle Ages, if only for jettied front walls where it would show, leaving the stone party walls as a sensible fire precaution but largely out of sight.[72] Timber was similarly favoured in parts of Wales where stone was easily found.[73]

So successful had they become by the fifteenth century that Winchester's more prominent carpenters came to be known as *architectores*: having worked their way through the carpenters' yard, they now combined the arts of design with the entrepreneurial skills of a contractor, and could see a building through from commission to completion, the only implements they physically wielded in the process being the compass and scribe. With skills like these, it is also little wonder that master-carpenters such as Hugh Herland could scale the heights of the building world. He was an architect in the fullest sense of the word even though he described himself by the name of the trade he served.

In essence Herland's abilities extended a whole world beyond those of today's high-tech architects, who rely on engineers, computer-aided methods and other means of arriving at their breath-taking designs that put simple implements such as the compass and scribe in a museum, where they belong. Nevertheless, they cannot match the lifelong understanding of a single material and the long tradition of using it that Herland and his like could call on. Nor are their works the product of little more than the axe, assisted by the adze, augur, chisel, drill, plane and saw, all powered by muscle alone. (fig. 133)

Yet most building carpenters were not Herlands, and had to practise many skills. While the masters at the top of the craft might employ others of lower status such as sawyers, carvers and turners, who would be paid at various rates below the usual 6d a day,[74] even masters might have to turn their hand to small works, or works far removed from the ordinary processes of designing and erecting buildings. Their status, like that of the material they worked, was generally held to be lower than that of the mason, though this was not necessarily true of their wages. This lower status was exemplified by the Carpenters' Company which sought to represent them. It was a late arrival, being incorporated in 1477, and a small affair when set against London's more illustrious companies. Its attempted exclusivity failed, and carpenters practised in London regardless of its existence. They preferred to belong to a wider fraternity, joining other companies of men of different callings but similar rank and understanding.[75]

PART II

A HOUSE APPOINTED FOR ALL LIVING

10

The shadow of a fleeting dream

Impermanent houses

No houses remain from before the Conquest. What is known of them only comes from buried fragments and literary and graphic records. The Romans had introduced sophisticated planning and construction to Britain, finally ending the seemingly eternal rule of the round house, which had sheltered prehistoric Britons for at least a millennium, if not two. Most round houses were grouped together, each one serving as an individual room with a distinct function, such as a bedroom, work room or kitchen. They were slowly giving way to the rectangular buildings that Belgic immigrants had brought with them, but these had made few inroads into domestic planning before the arrival of Roman civilization in the first century AD.

Roman houses, by distinction, were divided internally into separate rooms, each serving a different need in a sophisticated way, and these were set out in specific, comprehensible patterns. (fig. 20) None of this suited Anglo-Saxon England, neither its purse nor its temperament. The newcomers, like all the peoples of Germany, had never lived in cities or set their houses close together, as Tacitus had recorded over three centuries beforehand.[1] Their villages, he wrote, were not laid out in Roman style, with buildings adjacent or interlocked. Everyone left an open space around a house, perhaps as a precaution against fire, he suggested, or perhaps because Germans were such inexpert builders. The social needs for open space between individual buildings, however important, were lost on Tacitus. Being agriculturists and warriors, the Germans spent most of their waking lives out of doors. They presumably felt a greater need of the open air than Romans did, and distrusted complex buildings as their migrant descendants would do in England.

Their buildings, Tacitus continued, made no use of even small blocks of stone or tiles. What served their purpose instead was 'ugly timber, both unimpressive and unattractive'. Thus spoke the civilized Roman. But he did recognize qualities of the noble savage among these German barbarians: they were not indifferent to art, and might smear some parts of their houses with 'an earth so pure and brilliant it looks like paint or coloured mosaic.'[2]

The internal divisions favoured by the Romano-British must have seemed impenetrably labyrinthine to the newcomers. Once again single-roomed buildings became the norm for a family's domestic accommodation, but with one major difference: these buildings were now rectangular, not round. Anglo-Saxon invaders found the collapsing Roman towns at once threatening and tempting: they were dangerous, yet infused with the power of their vanished builders. So when they came to build within these towns they began tentatively, their urban constructions no different from those within their villages. This attitude faded but was never entirely lost, and medieval town houses can be readily related to their rural counterparts.

These first Anglo-Saxon buildings belonged to the ancient Germanic traditions that the invaders imported from beyond the Roman pale. They did not adapt the houses the Romano-British had occupied, but, using 'unimpressive and unattractive' timber, and thatch for roofs, built types that were quite new to Britain. One of these developed into the medieval hall. Pre-eminently Germanic and apparently the antithesis of everything Roman (the basilica possibly excluded), the hall would stamp its mark on England and Wales throughout the Middle Ages. In doing so, it provided an alternative to other forms that were developed from the chaff and

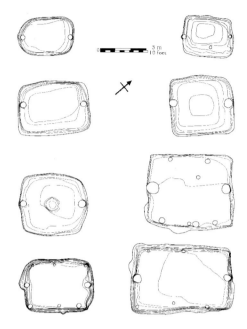

134. Contoured plans at 3-inch (76 mm.), intervals of the archaeological remains of eight *Grubenhäuser* excavated at Mucking, all of them apparently with large posts to support their end walls, and some with additional subsidiary posts at the corners or along the sides. After M.U. Jones 1979, fig. 2. © Royal Archaeological Institute

ruin of ancient Rome. Another new type of building, apparently known as a bower, was smaller, less clear in form, perhaps of two storeys, and served in an ancillary role. Finally there was a further type, far more distinctive though shorter in lifespan, namely a sunken-featured building, or *Grubenhaus*.[3]

The *Grubenhaus* had been a common component of Germanic settlements for some centuries before the invaders set up house in England. Tacitus did not record *Grubenhäuser* specifically, although he did mention the German habit of hollowing out cellars underground for storing goods.[4] The Anglo-Saxons started to build *Grubenhäuser* in eastern England as soon as they arrived, notably at Mucking, on the Essex shore of the Thames estuary east of Tilbury, where the remains of over two hundred of them have been found.[5] These buildings were cheap, easy to build, and, above all, useful.

Although they were essentially rural, their archaeological remains have been found in several towns. Some were built as dwellings, others as workshops, cowsheds, barns, granaries or general storehouses.[6] Their size varied from 33 by 20 feet (10 by 6 m) down to 8 by 6.5 feet (2.5 by 2 m). (fig. 134) The largest, at 660 square feet (60 m²), have the floor area of small family houses, but most have the dimensions of individual rooms, and were largely used as such. Their sunken area was dug to between 0.8 and 3.2 feet (0.25 and 1 m) below ground level. This may have formed the floor of some *Grubenhäuser*, since it was covered with boards, but in many cases the sunken area was also floored over at ground level, again with wooden boards. These would be kept dry by the flow of air through the space beneath them, which might be used as a store. From the sunken area rose two timber posts, one in the middle of each of the shorter sides to support the end walls and roof ridge. The larger and deeper *Grubenhäuser* had three posts set along each of the shorter ends, while the sides of the sunken area were lined with wickerwork or timber planks to stop the earth from caving in, and the floor extended further outwards beyond the sunken part.

Their supposed form and construction have been tested at West Stow in Suffolk, where fifty *Grubenhäuser* were excavated in the 1960s.[7] With this for guidance, various forms of experimental *Grubenhäuser* were built on an east–west alignment, like those on which they are based, so that one long side faces south. (fig. 135) The larger ones were given an entrance on this side, and this provides plenty of daylight within for craft-work or plain domestic convenience. Smaller and lower houses, lacking side walls, have an entrance in a gable end and, being darker inside, could only be used as stores, animal houses, or bedrooms.

The latest hypothetical reconstruction, unlike earlier ones whose poles were lashed together, has squared timbers cut with lap-joints, mortises and tenons, and fixed together with pegs, on

135. West Stow. Hypothetical reconstructions of *Grubenhäuser*, most of them with very low side walls, and entrances in their gable-ends

the grounds that these may not go beyond the techniques of people who had built *Grubenhäuser* for generations and could also build wooden ships strong enough to carry them and their goods across the North Sea.[8] It has centre posts and corner posts as well, these slightly inset so that a cross-beam can be lapped and pegged between them in such a way as to project well outside the sunken area on each side to stabilize the walls, which are clad with vertical boards. With eaves about 6 feet (2 m) high, an entrance door in the centre of the south side is conveniently high enough to avoid stooping. The whole floor is boarded, while a trap provides entry to the sunken space, and a stone hearth is placed towards one side, but far enough from the walls for safety. There is plenty of space to accommodate a large family, but no privacy.

The limiting factor in the lifespan of these buildings is their lack of resistance to rot. Being sunk in the earth, the feet of the posts that support them are affected by damp and therefore liable to rot fairly quickly. Possibly the sunken area was designed, among other reasons, to reduce the effects of damp, particularly when the walls and roof extend about 3 feet (1 m) further outwards. Even so, the expected lifespan of the reconstructed West Stow *Grubenhäuser* is little more than twenty years, and this seems to be borne out by the condition of the older ones. This may not seem long, but it was certainly long enough to suit the circumstances of the times, and both the adult working lives of their original builders and the likely lifespan of a marriage.

West Stow was no more than a village, but the archaeological remains of *Grubenhäuser* have been found in the wreck of several Roman towns. Their distinctive archaeological pattern is easy to spot, and the appearance of *Grubenhäuser* is often the earliest evidence of renewed occupation. Hengist's mercenaries built large numbers of *Grubenhäuser* at Canterbury in the fifth century on open spaces within the decaying pattern of Durovernum's Roman *insulae*, thus ensuring a continuity between the old and new civilizations of a tenuous kind.[9] (fig. 20) Some were large, others small, some with single end-posts, others with three, and a few with six as well as three intermediate posts along the sides. Their construction continued through the sixth and seventh centuries, until the eighth century, by which time their form had become more developed. By the tenth century, there is evidence of the digging of full cellars instead.[10]

Grubenhäuser were often the first buildings to be constructed in many new Anglo-Saxon or Danish towns, as, for instance, they were at Lydford,[11] and at Thetford, where four *Grubenhäuser* apparently formed part of a neighbourhood of artisans.[12] The *Grubenhäuser* found in Ipswich provided only about 215 square feet (20 m²) of space, and must have served as individual rooms.[13] A ninth-century *Grubenhaus* excavated in Milk Street in the City of London had an entrance from one of the dilapidated Roman roads – yet another sign of continuity of a sort, and the last of such evidence before a new road system came into being to replace the old. Measuring about 15 by 10 feet (4.5 by 3 m), this *Grubenhaus* had a hearth, which with other finds suggests a domestic use.[14]

What was common practice in England was again common in Germany, their homeland. Here, too, the *Grubenhaus* became urbanized, as in Braunschweig, and remained in use until about 1000 or so.[15] In England the archaeological evidence suggests an earlier decline. After the seventh century more solidly constructed buildings were probably superseding *Grubenhäuser* so that by the fourteenth century they had all but vanished from the scene.[16]

At West Stow, groups of about six or seven *Grubenhäuser* were typically centred around a larger rectangular building, which lacked a sunken floor.[17] These groups seem to have belonged to people of substance. For typological rather than documentary reasons the larger, central buildings have been called halls, even though they probably had no formal role as a royal hall had, but would serve as a family gathering place. These were large rooms, open from floor to roof, with a hearth somewhere in the middle. Occasionally, as at Chalton, they were rather more developed and had a small subsidiary space partitioned off at one end, perhaps for storage.[18] (figs 110 and 136) Much larger than usual and clearly more sophisticated are the buildings excavated at Cowdery's Down near Basingstoke. These belong to the sixth and seventh centuries and had a constructional complexity that is open to as many interpretations as their possible function.[19] Several of them were over 1,000 square feet (100 m²) in area, that is to say the size of a modern family house, and the largest of all reached 2,090 square feet (194 m²). Not only may some of them have had small spaces partitioned off at each end, but one may have had a

136. Two of R. Warmington's hypothetical reconstructions of halls at Chalton, the lower one with a partitioned room at the nearer end. After Addyman, Leigh & Hughes 1972, figs 15 & 16. © Society for Medieval Archaeology

137. French School, *King Edward the Confessor (c. 1003–66) giving his instructions to Earl Harold,* wool embroidery on linen, 11th century. Edward is shown enthroned in what is probably his hall at Winchester Palace, as depicted in the first scene of the Bayeux Tapestry. Musée de la Tapisserie, Bayeux, France

boarded floor raised above the ground. The grandeur of these buildings and their social importance are unmistakably aristocratic.[20]

This suggests a descent from the Germanic halls of tribal kings. These are known to have been large open buildings organized in a formal way. St Paulinus described the Bernician King Edwin's banqueting hall where he sat in winter to dine with his thanes and counsellors in the comforting glow of a fire, while two doors on opposite sides provided access.[21] This early seventh-century hall, built on the Cheviots high above Yeavering in Northumberland, was accompanied by several smaller buildings, perhaps private quarters or bowers belonging to the queen, thanes, counsellors and servants.[22] Such arrangements were age-old: a tribal centre with a magnificent hall, called Heorot, plays a central role in the Old English poem *Beowulf.* Heorot was a place of government and justice, and of customary feasting and drinking to the strains of the minstrel's harp and the epic words of the bard. Lesser nobles and servants slept within it while the leaders retired to the privacy of separate bowers.[23]

How these ancient beginnings gave birth to the medieval domestic hall can be traced through a wide range of pre-Conquest halls, known through documents and archaeology, to the earliest survivors, which date from the twelfth century. Apart from the royal hall at Yeavering, and another excavated hall at Cheddar, which had bowed sides like those found in large halls north-east of the Rhine,[24] there were three royal halls of the Anglo-Saxon kings at Westminster, Winchester and Gloucester,[25] and several lesser buildings that functioned in a similar way, being courts and places of assembly and formal dining.[26] Another may have existed at

Northampton, where the excavated remains of an immense eighth-century timber hall also suggest the unusual combination of wealth and status appropriate to a royal establishment.[27]

Apart from the remains at Cheddar and Northampton, practically nothing of these later pre-Conquest royal halls survives, and even the site of the royal hall at Gloucester is lost. However, the Bayeux Tapestry apparently illustrates both Westminster and Winchester. In the opening scene of the Tapestry Edward the Confessor appears enthroned in what may be his hall at Winchester. (fig. 137) This is shown as a large open building with turreted corners and a round-headed window in its diapered end wall with arcading above. Later in the Tapestry, Edward is shown at Westminster, seated beneath rich hangings in what again looks like a large open hall; overhead there are two turrets and also perhaps a louver rising over its roof, although no open hearth appears below.

Second to the Crown was the Church. During the late 960s and 970s Bishop Æthelwold reformed the see of Winchester and completed his works by building a new palace.[28] He ordered the enclosure of 8.6 acres (3.6 ha) of land in the south-east corner of the city which became known as Wolvesey. By the turn of the century a hall and attendant bower occupied the site, as well as other buildings that may have included a chapel and a prison. Together with the royal palace nearby, the Old Minster, the New Minster, and a monastery known as the Nunnaminster, these formed the 'first great ceremonial centre of the Anglo-Saxon state.'[29]

The Church also built hall-like refectories where monks dined together. These appeared in the first monasteries of the fourth century, even before communal eating became enshrined in the Benedictine Rule. Benedict Biscop's monasteries at Monkwearmouth and Jarrow may have incorporated refectories in long narrow buildings lying parallel with the churches on their south side.[30] (fig. 138) The celebrated early ninth-century St Gall plan shows a refectory in the form of a rectangular hall, again lying to the south of the church, and beside a cloister. The entrance is in the middle of one long side, with the abbot's table at one end and a doorway leading to the kitchen at the further end.

A similar arrangement was adopted at Cluny, following the abbey's foundation in 919. Cluny became so rich that its influence spread far beyond Burgundy and also religion. Its abbots advised popes, emperors, kings and princes. Three stood out for their zeal; the third and most famous of them, St Hugh, became abbot in 1049 and led the influential Benedictine confederation until his death sixty years later. All the while he strengthened the order throughout Europe, embellishing its ceremonies with formalities, its liturgies with music, its priests with rich vestments, and its churches with splendid symbols. St Hugh's rebuilding of the abbey church of Cluny made it the greatest in all the west. Already by 1050, a long narrow refectory was sited on the south side of the cloister in such a way that its entrance was at its west end beside the doorways leading to the pantry, bakery, kitchen and cellar.[31] (fig. 139) The notion

138. Plan of the excavated parts of the Saxon monastery at Jarrow. The church (1) lies to the north, with monastic buildings beyond a cemetery (2) to the south; the larger of these may have been a refectory (3) with an attached annexe (4) to its west and a detached suite of rooms (5) to its east. After Cramp 1976, fig. 30. © Royal Archaeological Institute

139. Plan of part of the monastery at Cluny as it was in 1050: the long refectory (1) lies centrally on an east-west axis with an entrance at its north-west corner between two cloisters (2 and 3); to the north (left) lies the abbey church; to the west (below) lie service ranges including an aisled cellar (4), a pair of kitchens (5) and a bakery (6); to its east (above) lie domestic ranges. After Conant 1959, fig. 26.

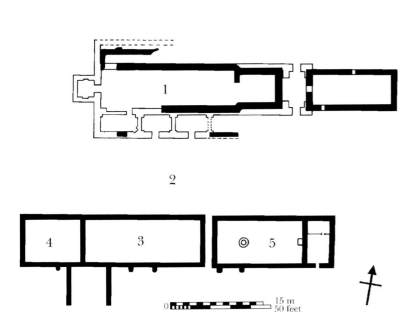

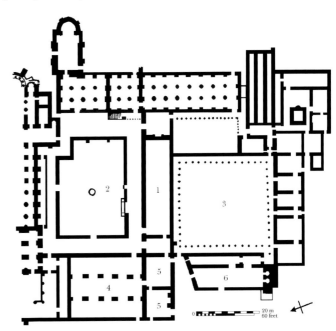

ʰIC EADVVARDVS:REX
IN LECTO:ALLOQVIT FIDELES:
ʰIC
CC
ET ʰIC: DEFVNCTVS EST

140. French School, *King Edward the Confessor (c. 1003–66) on his Deathbed*, wool embroidery on linen, 11th century before 1082. Edward lies on his deathbed in his bower at Westminster Palace (above), and (below) his body is carried away for burial, as depicted in the Bayeux Tapestry. Musée de la Tapisserie, Bayeux, France

that one end was reserved for dignitaries and the other for entrances and services would become a dominant feature of English halls after the Conquest.

Anglo-Saxon and indeed post-Conquest halls were invariably accompanied by subsidiary structures, these apparently serving in ancillary roles as work rooms, private rooms, bedrooms and stores. Some of these probably had at least one upper floor, and some may have been bowers after the fashion of the *brydbur* in *Beowulf*. This was a separate building, reserved for sleeping, for women, for junior members of an extended family, or for guests.[32] Following the scene at Westminster Hall in the Bayeux Tapestry, Edward takes to his bed, placed in the upper room of a bower, which has pentices each side and an attached tower; (fig. 140) and, following his death, his body is carried out from the ground floor to the adjacent minster. After the Conquest, these bowers came to be called *camerae*, or chambers.

There were nevertheless other uses for these upper rooms, and they could be large enough for small gatherings. According to the *Anglo-Saxon Chronicle* for 978, an upper room at Calne collapsed under the weight of an assembly of King Edward's councillors, leaving Archbishop Dunstan, uninjured, stranded on a high beam.[33] Was this room a substitute for an open hall, or

HIC HAR

141. French School, *Earl Harold dines and then sets sail*, wool embroidery on linen, 11th century before 1082. Harold dining with his knights in an upstairs room at Bosham, as depicted in the Bayeux Tapestry, apparently in a building with an affinity to the Königshalle at Lorsch (see fig. 163). Musee de la Tapisserie, Bayeux, France

merely used in lieu of an open hall that happened to be unavailable that day? This important question may also be asked of another such room, which the Bayeux Tapestry depicts at Bosham, showing Harold dining among his knights. (fig. 141) This seems to be a gallery or a first-floor hall, reached by an external staircase, and supported by an arcade of three round arches set on columns, with taller, articulating columns rising between the arches and at each end in the old classical Roman way. The origin of this building is as obscure as its form, but it may have been similar to the Carolingian Königshalle at Lorsch, (fig. 163) and hence part of a complex of buildings that had no need of an open hall, and served in its own right rather than as an adjunct to a more important room.

After the Conquest, the hall and separate chamber block were to become one of the main elements of domestic planning, representing a Germanic strand in the increasingly complex pattern of medieval building. Below them there were already several lesser forms of urban building that comprised little more than a single room, some of which included a hearth, open to the roof. They have left traces in many towns. In later pre-Conquest Thetford a number of

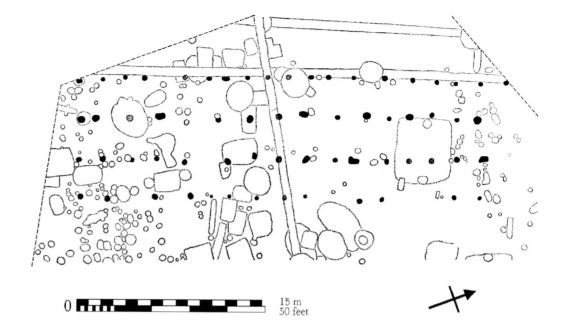

142. Pre-Conquest Thetford. The rows of black marks suggest the post-holes of a long hall (once thought to be aisled), known as Building G, amid other archaeological evidence excavated at Thetford. After Davison 1967, fig. 43. © Society for Medieval Archaeology

0 ▮▮▮▮▮▮▮▮▮▮▮▮▮▮ 15 m
50 feet

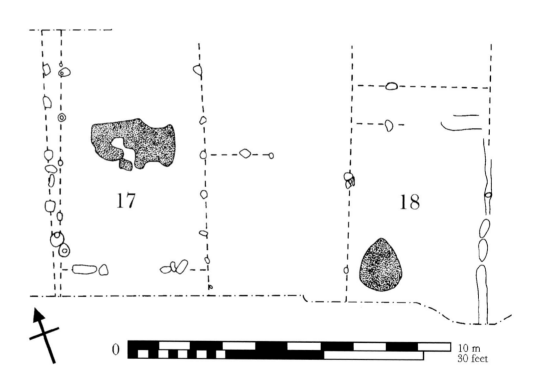

143. The remains of two flimsy structures, 17 and 18, excavated at Flaxengate, Lincoln. These may be houses on account of their hearths (stippled), which show up more clearly in the archaeological record than their confining walls. After Perring 1981, fig. 32. © Lincoln Archaeological Trust

17

18

0 ▮▮▮▮▮▮▮▮▮▮▮▮▮ 10 m
30 feet

timber buildings were erected with boarded walls, one with a permanent hearth. The longest was in the form of a great hall, 110 feet (34 m) long, apparently lacking internal partitions, (fig. 142) and other buildings around it probably served in an ancillary capacity.[34] In Hamwic the first Anglo-Saxon *Grubenhäuser* were replaced by a series of far larger buildings to serve the needs of business and local industries.[35] They measured about 65 by 20 feet (20 by 6 m) and appear to have had bowed sides like those of the royal hall at Cheddar. They are also very similar to buildings found over a long time-span in Germany, Norway, Denmark and Sweden, and most significantly at Dorestad in Holland.[36]

Similar houses, called long halls, are known in Scotland. Three comparatively grand long halls have been excavated in Perth, one of them dating from about 1250. It was 38 feet long and 18 feet wide (12 by 5.5 m), and well framed in timber with twin arcades forming side aisles. This house burnt down, to be replaced by a rather larger house with plank walls that was

divided into three rooms, perhaps a chamber, hall and kitchen, with an attached privy.[37] This was already becoming a standard arrangement.

Archaeological remains of the smaller common dwellings of poor people have been found in many English and Scottish towns. Flaxengate at Lincoln was apparently laid out in the ninth-century after the Danish conquest as a planned settlement with a series of small timber houses. The oldest of these had hearths open to the roof and were of a single storey, about 33 feet (10 m) long and 13–16 feet (4–5 m) wide. In the eleventh century, many of these houses burnt down, to be replaced by a series of buildings that were rather wider and perhaps at least half as long again. They were more elaborate since they had entrances in the middle of the long side, where possibly a passage across the houses divided them into two parts, one with a hearth for domestic use, the other without and probably for crafts, which seem to have included glass and metal working.[38] (fig. 143)

At Ipswich, the early *Grubenhäuser* were superseded by larger structures set on undercrofts which were dug up to 6.5 feet (2 m) into the ground and these, as the evidence of their stout posts suggests, carried one or even two upper storeys. Their floor area was nearly double that of the old *Grubenhäuser* too, and, given two floors of up to 375 square feet (35 m²) each, enough to provide for a complete family house.[39] Comprehensive excavation at Winchester shows how the city was built up from the start with timber buildings, such as those lining Castle Street.[40] In the eleventh century these houses were built either lying along the street or end-on to it. Like the Lincoln houses, they were about 16 feet (5 m) wide. The smaller houses were aligned with the street and might be up to 25 feet (7.6 m) long, but not more, while those set end-on took up less frontage and could stretch to 35–37.5 feet (10.5–11.5 m) in depth. In front of those houses that were set along the street there might be a narrow space of some 8 feet (2.5 m) which was taken up with subsidiary structures.[41]

Some two hundred small houses have come to light in Scotland, mostly at Aberdeen, Inverness and Perth. These generally had wattle and daub walls, supported by stakes, measuring about 20–6 by 10–13 ft (6–8 by 3–4 m). The quality of their construction varied too, from the roughest and poorest to the relatively substantial, some of them being built with oak posts and employing sill-beams. The best houses were attractively roofed with stone or glazed tiles and crested ridges. The walls were only about 5 feet (1.5 m) high, but with a pitched roof, usually supported by a ridge-pole and centre posts, there was plenty of headroom inside. The plank doors, set towards one end, were fitted with locks that gave some security. While many of these houses had internal hearths, a few had these outside, and the same is true of their privies, those inside apparently being screened from the main room for modesty's sake.[42]

While all of these houses were utilitarian, some of them had finer qualities, which rot eroded as it ate its way into their construction. When Wallingford Castle was extended in the thirteenth century, the earth-works buried a building of the late eleventh or early twelfth century which had been solidly built of earth with a tiled roof. (fig. 144) Its major room was about 28

144. Archaeologists at work in 1972 on a site at Wallingford Castle where they have uncovered the lower part of the earthen walls of a late eleventh-century, three-roomed building. The presence of a hearth in each room suggests a domestic use, perhaps as a house or an elaborate kitchen. © Robert Carr

feet (8.5 m) square, externally, and there were two end rooms, about 10 feet (3 m) square, all of them with hearths, plastered walls and wooden-framed doors. This was spacious and comfortable accommodation, even without an upper floor.[43]

Its plastered walls may have been coloured with an earth so pure it resembled paint. This suggests that decoration was commonplace in these early houses, even though impermanence has removed nearly all the evidence. A twenty-year span, after all, was an age in the eyes of many people, and decorating the house an age-old instinct hard to resist.

11

Vaultes stronglye and substanciallye wrought

Undercrofts

When New Winchelsea's increasing number of empty quarters were recorded in 1570, the surveyor found 'maney costly vaults, arched and sett forthe with pyllers of Caene stone, as meant to have houses built over them meet for famous merchants'.[1] Whether these vaults had originally supported houses or not, that had been the intention. By the late Middle Ages, a vault and the house above it were often separately constructed, the one of stone, the other of timber. That was not the case earlier in their history: vault and house were integral, though the evidence of separate entries suggests that their uses were separate even then.

These vaults, known today less ambiguously as undercrofts, are among the oldest form of secular urban building still extant. Their earliest remains are from the tenth century, and they have been a distinctive feature of urban building ever since. They may have developed from the older *Grubenhäuser*, as the large, deep sunken buildings which first appear in London and other towns in the tenth and eleventh centuries appear to have done. These early undercrofts could measure 50 by 20 feet (15 by 6 m) and were dug over 7 feet (2 m) into the ground, and so could provide extensive storage space. The fragmentary remains of one of these commodious sunken-featured timber buildings, probably dating before 1000, have been found on the west side of the newly laid out Bow Lane, while others followed on the east side in the second half of the eleventh century.[2] Like the sunken parts of *Grubenhäuser*, these were lined with planks, held in place by posts set into trenches or, in the later ones, mounted on sill-beams. They were apparently ceiled-over with an upper floor of planks set on joists, and so could have supported a substantial superstructure.[3]

By 1100, undercrofts were usually lined in stone, and were not always dug deeply into the ground. Undercrofts built more or less at ground level beside Bow Lane and at Well Court, Milk Street, had stone vaulting and probably served as a kind of podium to support two further storeys above.[4] This suggests a second tenuous line of development originating in the church crypt. Neither this nor a line of descent from the *Grubenhaus* is confined to British shores. The parallel evidence of undercrofts in such important trading towns as Bruges and Lübeck shows that the process of development from primitive *Grubenhaus* or ecclesiastical crypt to fully fledged undercroft is as likely to have been prompted by Continental as British practice, coming in as yet another import along with the foreign traders who did business in Britain.

From early Christian times, chambers or crypts were formed beneath the main floors of churches, but not necessarily underground, and used as shrines for valued graves or relics. In Britain, Wilfred built his incomparable church at Hexham about 675–80 with a crypt, flanked by passages and a vestibule, made all the more precious by its reuse of Roman stones. Soon after the Conquest the great new abbey church at Gloucester, and also the cathedrals at Winchester, Worcester and Canterbury were laid out in a way already common in Rhineland churches with aisled crypts underlying their eastern parts.

Their heavy, round arches, springing from short, cylindrical piers with block or scalloped capitals, are typical of the universal European Romanesque style then current. These forms are found in a number of secular undercrofts, notably those of the Burgundian pilgrimage town of Vézelay, where, perhaps romantically, they are said to have been constructed as hostels

145. Drawings by E. P. Loftus-Brock of the twin-aisled 'Norman Crypt' discovered at Corbet Court in 1872. See Schofield 1995, figs 29 and 30

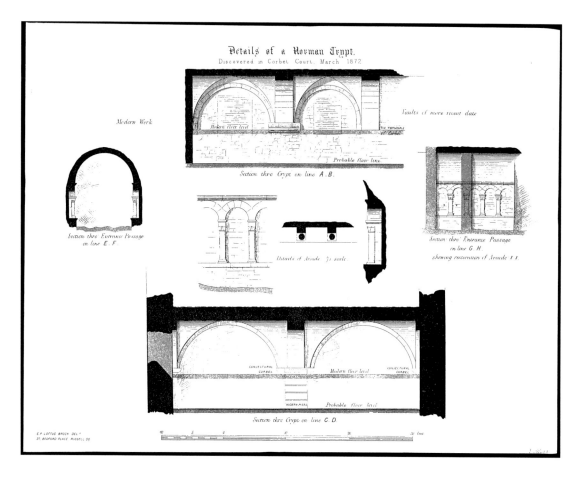

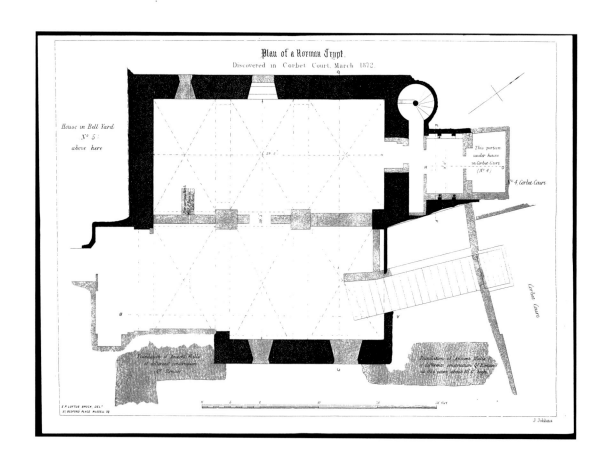

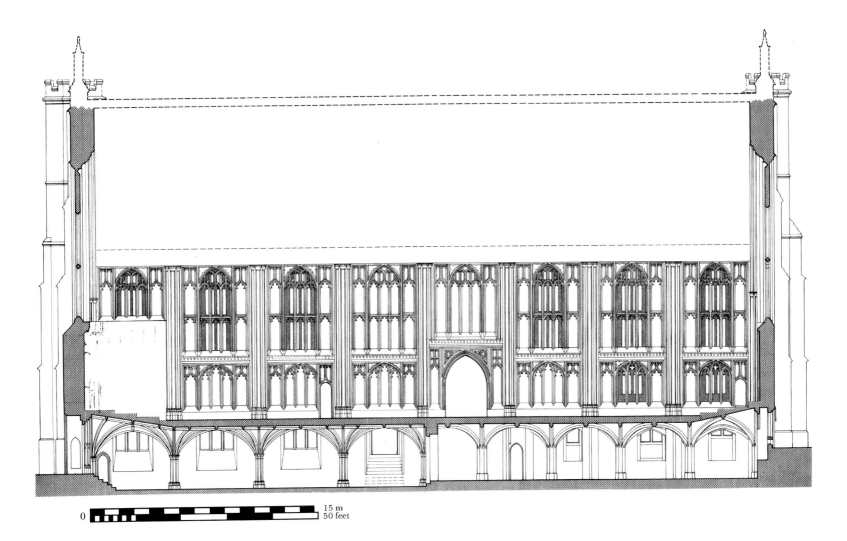

for pilgrims. Deeply cut into the limestone, some of them by as much as 16–20 feet (5–6 m), they may reach a height of 15 feet (4.5 m) to the crown of their vaults, and are sometimes so wide as to need an arcade dividing them into twin aisles.[5]

In Gloucester a similar aisled undercroft was built under a prosperous merchant's house at what became the Fleece Hotel. Many of London's undercrofts were similarly wide, needing the round columns and scalloped capitals, as well as the broad, unmoulded arches that characterized the vaults of the so-called Norman undercroft in Corbet Court, Gracechurch Street, recorded in 1872.[6] (fig. 145) Its grandeur is reflected in a rather later undercroft that can still be seen in Mark Lane, which has carved capitals, moulded ribs, and arches enriched with chevron mouldings suggesting its construction about 1140.[7]

The Church built several aisled undercrofts in the twelfth century. These supported its houses, both in and out of London, for instance the demolished Abbot's Lodging at Chester and the surviving Vicar's Hall at Chichester, and they became commonplace in the thirteenth century beneath the houses of bishops and abbots.[8] While cathedral crypts are the most obvious model for these undercrofts, the same must be true of the smaller number of ornately arcaded undercrofts that originated among the laity. By far the grandest are the pair of undercrofts beneath the City Guildhall. (fig. 146) The earlier, west vault of the late thirteenth or early fourteenth century (reconstructed in 1973) has five bays of quadripartite rib-vaults. The later east undercroft, which continues the line of the earlier one, was built about 1411 to 1425 by the mason John Croxton, who rebuilt the hall above them, and is magnificently decorated with Purbeck stone shafted piers, and lierne vaults in the best ecclesiastical style.[9]

By the middle of the twelfth century, undercrofts had become widespread in British towns, just as they were on the Continent from Burgundy to Normandy, and along the Channel to the North Sea and the Baltic. They supported all sorts of buildings above them from the commonplace to the palatial. Illustrations of London's undercrofts show how similar they were to the many survivors in Canterbury, Chester, Coventry, Southampton and Norwich. (fig. 147) Undercrofts are far less common where marshy ground or a tendency to flooding jeopardized their use, for instance in Hull, Salisbury and York. Notably Winchester's thirty undercrofts are almost all sited away from the river on rising ground.[10] Seemingly against the odds, the undercrofts of Portsmouth, all that remains of the town's medieval houses, are sited on low ground liable to flooding. Several undercrofts were dug into the sandy spit on which Great Yarmouth is built, and mostly lined with brick or flint cobbles. The undercroft at Clifton House, King's Lynn, was dug out of land reclaimed from the river Ouse (fig. 148). Whatever the threat of flooding, these undercrofts were probably designed to provide a firm, level base where the natural surface of the land offered neither.

Like New Winchelsea, the aspirations of many a failed town or stagnant town, such as Seaford, can be read in its surviving undercrofts. The Pembroke historian George Owen remarked of Wales that 'most houses of any accompt were builded with vaultes verye stronglye and substanciallye wrought', and these can be found in Pembroke itself, as well as in Haverfordwest and Tenby, but not in those parts of Wales where Anglo-Norman culture was lacking.[11]

There are several undercrofts in St Andrews in Scotland. The inspiration for these may have come with the Flemings who settled in Scottish towns. Well before the end of the twelfth century, Dean's Court was raised over a barrel-vaulted undercroft, 21.5 by 19 feet (8.8 by 5.8 m) internally, and set within massive stone walls 4 feet (1.3 m) thick. There are possibly others of that date in St Andrews, but many of those in North Street and South Street were dug out in the middle of the fifteenth century when the establishment of the university prompted a general rebuilding in stone.[12]

Aisled undercrofts were not necessarily vaulted. The fragmentary twelfth-century undercroft at Deloraine Court at Lincoln has the remains of a central arcade of round piers, but this carries a timber joist to support a long west range.[13] The undercroft at 32–4 Watergate Street, Chester, has a single arcade formed by three stout posts, known as samson-posts, which carry a bridging-joist.[14] By the fourteenth century, arcades of samson-posts dividing pairs of aisles had become comparatively common in Chester. (fig. 304) The undercroft floors are hardly 3 feet (1 m) below the level of the four main streets that they front, on account of the solid bed of rock that lies just below the surface, but their further ends are almost entirely below the level of the back lanes because of the build-up of the terrain towards the rear.

A number of arcaded and aisled undercrofts are no wider overall than those that have a single vaulted span, and were probably built for effect. The twin aisles of the undercroft at 115 High Street, Guildford, span about 20 feet (6 m) together, and there are others like this in Lincoln's Bailgate and at Stamford.[15] (fig. 149) Effect was also achieved by elaborate decoration, although

147. The remains of a five-arched undercroft at 21 High Street, Canterbury, supporting a later framed building the ground floor of which has been rebuilt; the jettied upper storey has a characteristic crown-post and common-rafter roof. © Canterbury Archaeological Trust, 1988

148. The brick-lined undercroft of Clifton House, King's Lynn, with one of the octagonal piers that carry the plain rib-vault. The floor, now much higher than it originally was, conceals the base of the pier

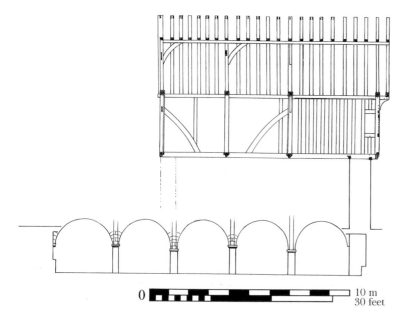

149. The undercroft at 13 St Mary's Hill, Stamford, showing the circular pier supporting the vault and its plain chamfered ribs. © National Monuments Record

damp and destruction has spoiled most of it. The early-thirteenth-century crypt of Lambeth Palace chapel has two aisles of four bays, and stone walls where fragments of painted plaster show that it was lined out in the medieval way to look like regularly laid ashlar. The Dominicans' south dorter range at Blackfriars was similar, and the finest of all was probably the arcaded and rib-vaulted undercroft of Gerard's Hall of about 1290. Its decoration reflected the status of the already long-established Gisors family, by then rich importers of Gascon wine, but it was used as cellarage for wine and the embellishment was designed to impress would-be buyers.[16] (fig. 62)

Notwithstanding the evident display of wealth in this undercroft, twin-aisled undercrofts were uncommon in London's secular buildings. The small but ornate undercroft of about 1300 at the junction of Leadenhall Street and Fenchurch Street, which had two aisles of three bays, was among the last in London. Most vaults in the City were narrow enough to avoid arcades altogether; after 1300 the construction of twin-aisled undercrofts was apparently discontinued,[17] and that seems to have been true of all towns from then on, as well as the capital. Whatever their status had been, it was now on the wane.

While a few of Southampton's early undercrofts were aisled, from the late twelfth century onwards they were regularly built with a single-vaulted span to a fairly standard width of about 20 feet (6 m). They could be from two to nearly three times as long and from 8 to 16 feet (2.5–5 m) high. Typically, they were sunk 6–10 feet (2–3 m) below the level of the ground. (fig. 150)

These more common un-aisled undercrofts often have vaulted roofs: barrel-vaults for the plainer or earlier ones, rib-vaults for the more ornate later ones, leaving the remainder with timber roofs. None of them was cheap. Stone became a necessity for their walls on the grounds of permanence, until the advent of brick in parts of eastern England. In many places stone had to be imported, so adding to the cost. The arches of the earl of Warenne's undercroft in Southwark were said to be of Caen stone, and other substantial undercrofts were built in part with stone imported from Normandy. In Canterbury, where stone of good quality was not readily available, local chalk, lined with flint and occasionally finished with Kentish ragstone, gave the city's undercrofts thick, lasting walls.[18] The use of strong stone walls equally applied when the undercroft was finished with a timber ceiling. Although all Chester's undercrofts are lined with stone or brick, many have solid timber ceilings rather than stone vaults. The samson-posts at 32–4 Watergate Street support a floor 2 feet (0.6 m) thick, comprising flags and a packing of rubble laid on thick boards.[19]

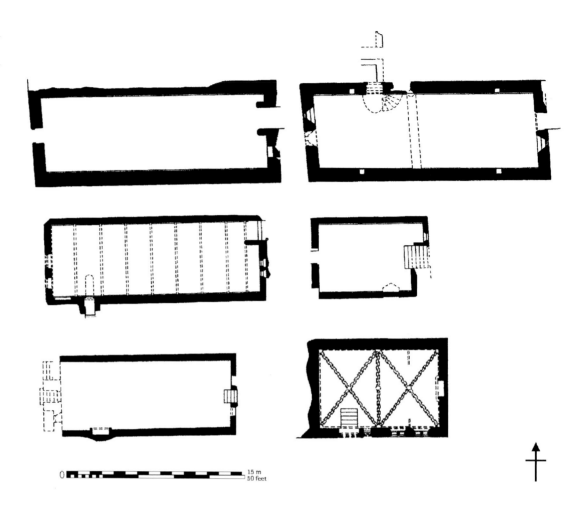

150. Southampton undercrofts, plans, from left to right, top to bottom, of: 88 High Street; Quilter's Vault; 94 High Street; 104 High Street; Woollen Hall; and The Undercroft. After Faulkner 1975, figs 21, 22 and 28

0 ▮▮▮▮▮▮▮▮▮▮ 15 m / 50 feet

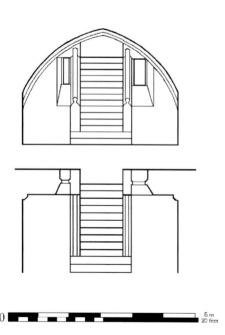

151. The entrance to an undercroft in Winchelsea, plan and elevation from within. After Faulkner 1966, fig. 3. © Royal Archaeological Institute

0 ▮▮▮▮▮▮▮▮ 6 m / 20 feet

Most undercrofts were built flush with the street as they are in Chester and again in Canterbury so as to serve trade. Generally, they run back from the street to conform with the pattern of burgage plots, and are entered at one end; but they may lie along a particularly wide plot in the manner of the undercroft of Tackley's Inn in High Street, Oxford, and these were entered from the side. (fig. 303) Entrances from the street were often through a wide doorway down a flight of steps, and only in special cases was there access from the building above. Often the entrances and the steps were treated ornately as a demonstration of status, even when the decoration did not extend to the vaulting.

The undercroft at 17 Palace Street, Canterbury, is less usual in having a small yard in front of it with a way down through an arched door. Again, at 43 Burgate, the site of a great, early-thirteenth-century stone house, the undercroft was entered from a central courtyard. The undercrofts of large houses like these were exceptional since they were often part of the establishment above, and might be directly linked to it by a staircase.[20]

New Winchelsea's many undercrofts are typical. They are aligned perpendicularly to the street so as to fit the individual plots. One of them, typically, measures 13.5 feet (4 m), the width of the plot, and extends 28.25 feet (8.6 m) to the rear, with Caen stone walls supporting nine pointed arched ribs giving it a height of 10 feet (3 m) above its beaten earth floor. Its only entry was from the street down a flight of stone steps within an arched stairway, which was divided from the undercroft by a thick stone wall, some 5 feet (1.5 m) high.[21] (fig. 151)

This provided security, but lighting was always a problem. Apart from that which came down the stairs and possibly through windows in the end wall, there was no natural daylight at all. If the sides of the undercroft were unrestricted by adjacent buildings, and it was high enough above ground, there might be windows set just below the vault, as the undercroft of Tackley's Inn once had along the side that faces the street. The Undercroft at Southampton

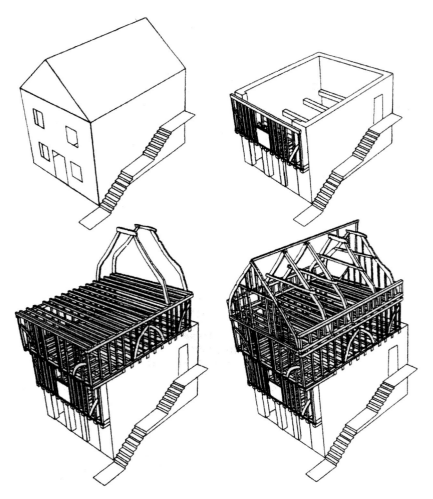

152. The Cooperage, Newcastle upon Tyne, built and rebuilt in at least four phases from the late Middle Ages onwards, at first in stone (top, right), with an undercroft dug into the hillside overlooking the waterfront, and a single upper storey, and steps leading upwards beside it; and three successive later stages in which the upper parts are re-fronted and extended upward in timber. After Heslop & Truman 1994, fig. 4. © The Society of Antiquaries of Newcastle upon Tyne

153. The Cooperage, Newcastle upon Tyne. The front after various campaigns of rebuilding and extension upward, but the ground-floor undercroft, built into the hillside overlooking the River Tyne, is essentially medieval

was similarly lit, and that was important because of its unusual decoration, which extends to corbels, carved with heads, from which spring moulded ribs intersecting at carved bosses, with a hooded fireplace and lamp brackets terminating in ball-flower ornaments.[22] This ornament suggests a public use, distinctly separate from the house above.

While merchants could use undercrofts as adjuncts to their houses, a lack of direct communication between the two in 85 percent of them strongly indicates (but does not prove) separate occupation.[23] Undercrofts were therefore probably let out to tenants for all kinds of commercial uses, just as lock-up shops were. This was common practice in France, for instance in Senlis, Beauvais and Provins, as well as in Burgundy.[24] So too in England: of the forty-odd undercrofts in Winchelsea only three directly communicated with the houses above. Quilter's Vault at Southampton, which dates from about 1170–80, was divided into two, suggesting double tenancy, with one part entered from the High Street, the other from a back lane, and both separate from the house above.[25]

Those with direct access from the building above were probably stores. Castle Vault at Southampton, which had direct access to the castle quay, was well placed to be a warehouse for goods in transit between sea and land, as were the stone undercrofts built on the Thames waterfront at New Fresh Wharf in the twelfth century.[26] The steep stairway of most undercrofts would impede this use, despite wide doorways, and the dog-leg stair of Quilter's Vault in Southampton would make the entry of bulky goods particularly hard.

Like Southampton, but rather later, Newcastle upon Tyne, close to the North Sea trade, established a tradition of building on undercrofts so as to provide storage for goods landed on the adjacent quays. The only substantial survivors are the stone undercrofts of The Cooperage (figs. 152 and 153), Milbank House and Surtees House on the landward side of The Close and

Sandhill, where the river bank rises rapidly to the upper town. The undercrofts, which may date from 1400, are dug deeply into the hillside, allowing the front entrances to open directly on to the quay, but steep steps ascend beside them to reach further entrances into the largely rebuilt storey above and the properties further up the slope.[27]

The fireproof qualities of a semi-subterranean building constructed of stone were particularly valuable, as was the more general security offered by such a strong building. Undercrofts were therefore well suited to the storage of those goods where security from fire and theft was paramount. The twelfth-century undercroft at 36 High Street, Canterbury, is traditionally said to have been one of the city's mints. The undercroft that the Canterbury moneyer Lambin Frese built in 1175–80 may have had a similar use. By 1200 there were some thirty stone houses in Canterbury, all of them with undercrofts, many of them belonging to merchants, others to moneyers and a few to Jews who needed their security. Jacob the Jew, Canterbury's wealthiest financier, owned an undercroft whose six bays lay beneath the County Hotel in High Street until their destruction in 1922, and there were others belonging to Henry the Goldsmith, Terric a goldsmith and financier, and Wiulph a moneyer.[28]

Those who built undercrofts were certainly wealthy. The Church built them for its own use, and urban manors, the guilds and their richer members were builders too. The undercroft of Moyses Hall, in Cornhill, Bury St Edmunds, was probably owned by the abbey and leased out, although tradition puts it in the hands of a rich Jew. (fig. 154) One of the most influential Jews in Norwich, Jurnet Ha Nadib, like the even more successful Aaron of Lincoln, loaned money to Henry II. He is associated with the Music House alias Wensum Lodge in King Street, yet, it turns out, it was not he but his son Isaac who purchased the house, undercroft and all – and from a gentile.[29]

Security aside, the cool, even temperature and shade of the interior were essential to the storage of wine, as the undercroft of Gerard's Hall exemplifies. Despite steep stairways, barrels could be rolled inside down removable runners, just as they are today. In London the remains of vintners' undercrofts have been uncovered facing the Thames,[30] and others are known in Coventry.[31] Many undercrofts, for instance several in Rye and Winchelsea, are associated with the wine trade and this may have prompted the construction of inns above them. At Rye both the Flushing Inn and the Mermaid were built in the fifteenth century with their timber frames founded on thirteenth-century undercrofts with hollow-chamfered transverse arches, and so were the Salutation Inn and the New Inn at Winchelsea. In Southampton some undercrofts were rented to wine merchants for very short periods, sometimes for only a fortnight, which was just enough for them to take in and dispose of a shipment of wine.[32]

The Church, being both allied to the wealthy guilds whose members were likely users, and involved in the control and sale of liquor, often built undercrofts for leasing to licensed victuallers. Tackley's Inn at Oxford was built by Roger le Mareschal, parson of Tackley,[33] and its undercroft was used as a tavern.[34] The undercrofts of both the Checker at Abingdon and the Angel at Guildford served as taverns in their own right. Bristol has several undercrofts, particularly in Broad Street, many of them serving in exactly the same way as the French *cave* does. Fireplaces added warmth to their hospitality and decoration some character. For instance, the walls of an early-fifteenth-century brick-vaulted undercroft at the White Swan Inn in St Peter's Street, Norwich, were painted with birds, rosettes, and an armoured figure on a prancing horse.[35] Undercrofts were furnished with seats and tables, and, for a little privacy, these were set in cubicles partitioned from each other with lattice work. Tapsters drew the wine and ale directly from barrels stored towards the back, where it was cooler, and took it to the drinkers at the front.[36] In Winchester, where the Vine was a celebrated drinking hole, the terms cellar and tavern seem to have been interchangeable, and there, as in Southampton, the architectural differences between the front and rear of undercrofts used for these purposes appear to reflect the respective status of drinking at the front and cellarage at the rear.[37]

As wine, so ale. The waters of the Trent went into many a brew, and ale is synonymous with hospitality, as Defoe recorded:

The town of Nottingham is situated upon the steep ascent of a sandy rock; which is consequently remarkable, for that it is so soft that they easily work into it for making vaults and

154. Moyse's Hall, Bury St Edmunds, undercroft. Photograph by Andor Gomme

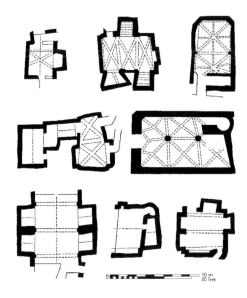

cellars, and yet so firm as to support the roofs of those cellars two or three under one another; the stairs into which, are all cut out of the solid, though crumbling rock; and must not fail to have it be remembered that the bountiful inhabitants generally keep these cellars well stocked with excellent ALE; nor are they uncommunicative in bestowing it among their friends, as some in our company experienced to a degree not fit to be made matter of history.[38]

While cellarage for wine or ale was their most frequent use, there were too many undercrofts, placed too close together, for them all, or even a majority of them, to have been taverns. In Norwich, where there are fifty-four late-medieval brick undercrofts (and records of over thirty more), (fig. 155) and in Chester, where long ranks of them form high bases for the Rows, their efficacy in supporting timber-framed buildings must have been matched by their suitability for all kinds of commercial uses well beyond the needs of the bibulous. (fig. 156) Most of them were combinations of shop and warehouse, devoted to a wide range of goods.

By reason of its size and the possibilities for decoration, an undercroft could provide surroundings that matched the luxury of the goods on sale within. It was well suited to displaying silks and any sort of fine cloth whose bright dyes would last longer away from strong light. Subdued lighting was no impediment, since the area immediately behind the entrance was well enough lit for showing luxuries to discerning customers, and lamps made up some of the deficiency further inside.[39] Despite this, the damp interior was far from ideal for storing cloth, which rapidly deteriorates if not kept completely dry.

In Chester, the rebuilding of the city within the Roman walls, which began in the middle of the thirteenth century, was possibly given fresh impetus by a reportedly disastrous fire of 1278, and more certainly spurred on by the wealth brought by Edward I's armies, first of soldiers and then of castle-builders.[40] The deep rubble of Roman Chester facilitated the formation of a grid of sunken streets based on the Roman crossing of what became Northgate Street, Eastgate Street, Bridge Street and Watergate Street, which lie just above the bedrock. Rows of fireproof undercrofts, containing shops, were built immediately along these streets, and are reached from them down short flights of stairs. Being so high, they form a podium along the street, but, being dug into built-up rubble, they are entirely below ground at their

155. Plans of eight Norwich undercrofts, demonstrating their great variety, from left to right, top to bottom: 15 Bedford Street; 4 Tombland; Chapel-in-the-Fields, Theatre Street; 13–17 St Giles Street; the Guildhall; 9 Princes Street; 24 Lower Goat Lane; 91 King Street. After R. Smith, and Carter 1983, fig. 2. © Vernacular Architecture Group

156. 12 Bridge Street, Chester. The impressive pointed rib-vaulting of the mid-thirteenth-century undercroft, now used as a bookshop

151

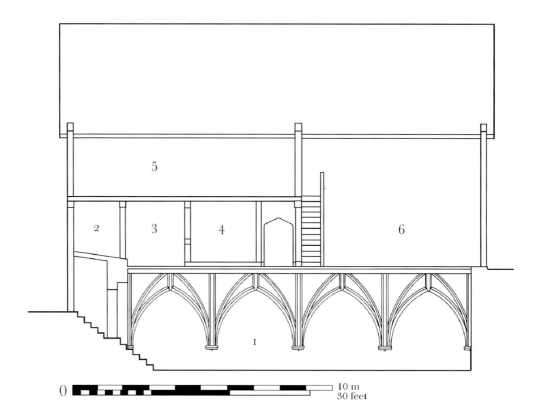

backs. (fig. 157) The buildings that they support are arcaded at the front and incorporate a row of stalls above the flight of stairs leading down into each undercroft and a public gallery between these and the shops that line the inner side, thus forming Chester's unique Rows. Meanwhile, the upper storeys continue forward over the gallery, thus sheltering it as any common arcade would do.

This comprehensive undertaking and the enclosed public right of way that it brought into being suggest that it might have resulted from specific and unusual action that prescribed the form of rebuilding.[41] There is no evidence for this, and it is just as likely, if not more so, that a combination of circumstances particular to Chester was responsible, including both its terrain and its wealth as a garrison and market town. Where the idea for the scheme came from is unknown. Trajan's Markets in ancient Rome had a similar arrangement of shops at two levels, with public rights of way above the lower ones, and the Emperor Constantine took this arrangement to Byzantium, but to trace a line across Europe and a thousand years is to stretch a point, despite the international talent that Edward I's craftsmen brought to Chester. Yet a combination of men in the know and enterprising burgesses could have developed this unique form of building and, having proved its efficacy, impressed it on Chester's main streets.[42] An alternative and, perhaps, more likely possibility is that the first houses to be built along these streets were raised above them on the embanked rubble, and were entered not from the streets but from raised paths immediately in front of them. When these houses came to be rebuilt, not as a single act of civic improvement, but one at a time, an undercroft was first dug out beneath them and reached from street level. The path had to be maintained so that neighbouring houses could still be reached, and this passed over the top of the new undercroft. It only remained for the upper storeys of the house to extend forward over the path to protect it from the weather. Soon neighbouring houses were rebuilt in the same way, and thus, by a process of accretion, produced the Rows.[43]

12

Cloud-capp'd towers, and gorgeous palaces

The palaces and halls of magnates

After the Conquest the Crown built halls of increasing magnificence, as wealth and craftsmanship allowed, to reach a zenith late in the Middle Ages in the incomparable rebuilding of Westminster Hall. (Fig. 158) What individual kings commanded at their palaces, bishops, the next wealthiest class, commanded for theirs. These were the more significant for being in towns. While kings favoured palaces in the countryside, where they could enjoy the hunt, bishops built their palaces beside their cathedrals, which were now all in towns, and, as a consequence of their powerful political role, also built houses near the seat of government at Westminster, just as other great magnates did. The Norman aristocracy, like the king, established its political power through building castles at strategic sites, in both town and countryside, and this newly adopted form of building contained halls of various sorts within its confines.

What resulted from all this activity was two sorts of hall. One of these, the open hall, had an ancient German pedigree and was built directly on the ground and open to the roof. The other, the upper hall, had a very mixed pedigree, partly Roman and partly new, conceived to meet the needs of changed circumstance; it was built over an undercroft and often as part of a complex building that incorporated other rooms beside or above it. Both forms of hall eventually merged to some extent, and descended to lower rungs of society, notably to the burgesses of the expanding towns.

By the middle of the thirteenth century open halls were in the grasp of this lower stratum of society. But, for at least a century before this, prosperous burgesses had been building stone houses of a different kind that included a large heated room, an upper hall of sorts, raised over an undercroft. These houses had affinities with the upper halls whose pedigree had originated among Continental emperors, kings and magnates before being passed on to lesser citizens. This pedigree, by then some three centuries old, already had several strands.

From the seventh century onwards masonry was bringing to the Church in north-west Europe a material permanence that proclaimed its eternal truths. What it thereby gained as an institution for the purpose of accommodating its acts of worship, the secular and ecclesiastical lords, who protected and administered it, came to covet for their formal and domestic needs as well.

This ambition took a while to cross the Channel to Britain, but already in the 790s it brought stone to the construction of Charlemagne's royal palace at Aachen. Its very existence exacerbated the uneasy relationship between Church and State, which came to a head with Charlemagne's confrontation with Pope Leo III.[1] Charlemagne intentionally based his palace on the papal Lateran Palace in Rome as a means of demonstrating his assumed equality with the successors of the Roman emperors. He meant Aachen to become a *Roma secunda*, and, to this end, the stone he brought from Rome as a symbolic relic of the Holy City sanctified and validated his works for all who understood its meaning. Leo, naturally, viewed these works askance: he was apprehensive about what he interpreted as a scheme to draw him into the threatening clutches of the Frankish monarchs.

The old Lateran Palace comprised among other rooms a *loggia*, an *aula Concilii* or Council hall, and a *triclinium* or great dining room.[2] Likewise, Charlemagne's palace came to include state and private apartments, set around an open courtyard to the north of his chapel. The

158. The Palace of Westminster, from Wyngaerde's *Panorama, c.* 1544. A landing stage leads through the Water Gate into the Outer Ward; to the right are the Conduit House and Clock Tower; to the left the northern entrance to Westminster Hall, flanked by the Exchequer building, and, in the background, Westminster Abbey; further to the left is St Stephen's Chapel. See Colvin & Foister 1996, drawing 1. © Ashmolea Museum, Oxford

most important of these was the *sala regalis*, a large hall with apses, evidently designed as a Roman basilica.[3] This Charlemagne called his Lateran.[4] Similar Roman motifs appear again in the royal monastery at Lorsch (fig. 163) and his palace at Ingelheim. Not only the style of their halls, but also the way in which they were incorporated within large, extended structures along with other separate rooms serving various purposes, is a clear revival from Rome. As Charlemagne intended, these owe little to the old Germanic tradition of the open hall, separate and apart from its attendant chambers and ancillary rooms.

Charlemagne's successors again included suites of rooms within their palaces. This was in direct contrast to the open halls with detached ancillary buildings that contemporary English monarchs preferred. The turbulence that despoiled Carolingian Europe, eventually splitting it into the relatively stable European monarchies of the eleventh century, significantly modified royal buildings by raising their basilican halls over undercrofts as a means of protecting them from casual violence. Hence the imperial palace at Paderborn was rebuilt by its Ottonian inheritors with its great hall set above an undercroft supported by a spinal arcade of columns

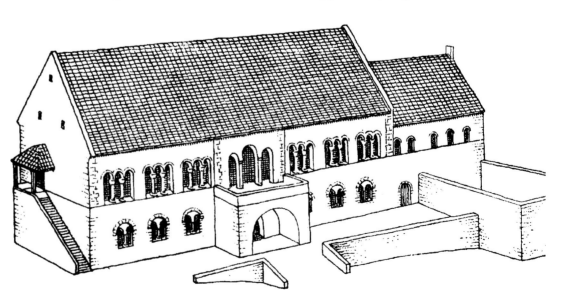

159. The hall or *Kaiserhaus* of the imperial palace at Goslar, as it probably was in its original state *c.* 1050, before rebuilding and enlargement. After Conant 1959, fig. 23

and probably a stone vault. So, before the ninth century was out, the form of the classic Continental hall raised over an undercroft had arrived. This was repeated elsewhere in the Empire, notably at Ingelheim, and at Goslar. (fig. 159)

This so-called upper hall soon became the norm among magnates from Germany to Spain, and, as time passed, entered the aspirations of ever lesser men.[5] The dukes of Normandy built what Dawson Turner described as a 'great hall' at their palace at Lillebonne, when he and the artist John Sell Cotman visited it early in the nineteenth century. (fig. 160) This was raised over an undercroft, which was arcaded and partly open to one side. Here, significantly for what came later in Britain, the Conqueror held court among his assembled nobles (had this hall been built already), and, according to tradition, here again he mustered his forces before setting sail for England in September 1066.[6]

By the middle of the tenth century, yet another new but related type of building emerged in Continental Europe, again resulting from the years of struggle. Its analogous form was closely related to the hall raised over an undercroft, and, because of its seigneurial ownership, became known as a donjon. It took the form of a tower, at once defensive and domestic, which responded to the new conditions of warfare inaugurated by the appearance of mounted knights. By building donjons, the emerging feudal rulers of France and the Rhineland extended and maintained their power after the collapse of Charlemagne's empire.

Apparently in the second quarter of the tenth century, Theobald, Count of Blois, rebuilt an undefended open hall of stone at Doué-la-Fontaine, which had been burnt in an attack. The hall's entrances were blocked, and it was converted into a high basement or undercroft over which an upper chamber was raised so as to form a strong, defensible building with domestic accommodation.[7] If this simple structure is not the very first donjon, within a century donjons had spread across France from the Loire valley into the duchy of Normandy, which the Conqueror's ancestors had founded in 911. William himself would command the building of another donjon at Caen as part of its fortification.[8] Rectangular in plan and constructed with thick walls that rose high enough to support a basement with one or more floors above, these donjons are redolent of strength and power: they were not to be rapidly overborne. No doubt they quickly gained a formidable reputation for impregnability, a reputation possibly strengthened by their similarity to the ancient towers and gateways scattered around western Europe by the forces of Rome.[9]

Donjons, or towers or keeps as they variously came to be called, developed in sophistication, sometimes by embracing two or three floors of heated rooms, as was already achieved about 1000 by the notoriously violent Fulk Nerra at Langeais, and again at Loches many decades before the Conquest.[10] In both these and the raised halls of the Ottonian palaces lies the origin of the architectural alternative to the open hall, the so-called upper hall, a large formal room with a prominent, enclosed fireplace accommodated on an upper floor.

While the upper hall lacked the ancient Germanic character of the open hall, it probably functioned in a similar way. Nevertheless it was not so obviously public as the open hall. The staircase by which it was entered and, in several cases, the anterooms that were set before it acted as a means of control that might have to make up for the lack of a clearly expressed high and low end. These, so obvious in an open hall with its linear arrangements and a central, open hearth, could not be so readily expressed inside an upper hall: the hearth, set within a fireplace built into one of the walls, would be a natural focus within the room, but might compete with the human focus, against another wall, of a throne or a high table set on a dais. (figs 56 and 202) No doubt the arrangement of furniture and fittings solved this problem; but these were removed after every lordly visitation, so their effect is far from clear today. Moreover, the upper floor contained at least one further room, and there might well be a second upper floor too, and some of these were private by intention. Yet, while the particular uses to which the rooms of donjons or keeps were put is often obscure – it is sometimes hard to distinguish from their physical remains between rooms that functioned as semi-public halls and those as semi-private chambers – they went much further than Charlemagne's palace so far as they integrated several rooms for all kinds of uses on two or more floors within a rectangle of all-embracing external walls.

It was the Conquest that brought the donjon to England as a permanent feature of the landscape. The comparatively simple keep that William's close political colleague and companion in arms William FitzOsbern raised on a precipice overlooking a bend in the Wye and called Estrighoiel,[11] later Chepstow, can be dated between 1067 and perhaps 1071, and probably no later than 1075. This makes it the first datable secular building of stone to survive in medieval Britain. Low and oblong in plan, its great hall was set above an undercroft with a floor resting on stout joists between them. (fig. 161) FitzOsbern's models were probably Lillebonne, which he may have known personally, and donjons like Doué, Langeais, and particularly Falaise, the Conqueror's birthplace, since the architectural forms that they embrace appear again together at Chepstow. Significantly, the keep was built of robbed Roman stone from Caerwent: neatly coursed, squared sandstone ashlar, and a few courses of red tile that ring the building roughly at the level of the upper floor, their use in this way being a common feature of Roman ruins in France.[12]

The masons were no more than following contemporary practice in their use of robbed stone, but more than simple robbery seems to be their purpose, as though FitzOsbern were appealing symbolically to Roman power. How this great building was used is a matter of surmise: its great upper hall could serve all the public functions accommodated in an open hall, but the room partitioned off its northern end may less clearly have been either a private chamber, or a chapel, or even an audience chamber; and lesser members of the household probably made do with the undercroft. Ancillary buildings of a semi-permanent character presumably completed the ensemble.

Similar uncertainties bedevil an understanding of several other early keeps; that they were symbols of Norman power is nevertheless certain.[13] So, where William FitzOsbern led, other Norman magnates followed. The first building works of Bishop Remigius (or Remi) at Lincoln, started between 1072 and 1075, seem to fit precisely into this innovating context, yet are far more outlandish and less readily pinned down. Remigius was not only the newly appointed bishop but also the principal secular lord of Lincoln. As well as a new cathedral, he needed a stronghold to deter bellicose Danes, who had their eyes on his territory. Following the transfer of the see to Lincoln, he converted the upper city, the former Roman fortified precinct that became the *colonia*, into a centre of secular and ecclesiastical power that had all the greater political importance following the Conqueror's 'harrowing of the north'.[14]

The Bail, as it became known, was both strategically ideal and symbolically imbued with a thousand years of power. Here Remigius built an extraordinary tower. (fig. 162) Now incorpo-

162. Lincoln Cathedral, the west front in its possible original form as a free-standing tower. The latest research suggests that there may have been twin roofs running from side to side instead of three running front to back, reflecting the division of the space below into a ceremonial hall and antechamber. From a drawing by W. T. Ball in Gem 1986, fig. 3, incorporating minor modifications. © British Archaeological Association

163. The Königshalle at Lorsch. The attached half-columns flanking the arches, the arcading of the upper storey, and the octagonal blocks of masonry demonstrate a detailed knowledge of Roman forms

rated within the west front of the cathedral, its three great arches embellish entrances to the high nave and flanking aisles that lie immediately within. Its former use is obscure: the remains of machicolations and openings in the arch jambs strongly suggest that it had a defensive capability, and the likelihood of domestic usage is implied by a tall arched opening on its north side that appears to have been the pit of a huge garderobe or latrine.[15] These features are more akin to a donjon than to a cathedral, and indeed this part of the west front may have been built to be quite separate from the first cathedral.[16] Even so, no donjon or keep was ever penetrated by three immense arched recesses quite so deep. However, a defensive capability should not necessarily be equated with absolute impregnability.[17]

The interior may have resembled contemporary donjons in the likely division of its upper storey into two transverse parts, perhaps a great hall and privy hall with an antechamber, and in the provision of intra-mural chambers, including the putative garderobe. As such, it could have served as the lord-bishop's formal residence, an upper hall of magnificent proportions, served by the adjacent garderobe on its north side and subsidiary chambers in a storey above, reached by a spacious newel.

This leaves the three large recesses of the west front unexplained. Great halls set over triple arches in an ecclesiastical context are well known in Carolingian Europe, the Königshalle alias Michaelskapelle in the centre of the atrium before the monastery at Lorsch being a celebrated example. (fig. 163) Probably built for ceremonial liturgy by Abbot Richbod (784–804), it recalls the propylaeum of Old St Peter's where visiting dignitaries were received.[18] However, the source for Lincoln may well be more direct. In 1071 and again in 1076 Remigius went to Rome, in part to gain Pope Alexander III's confirmation of his appointment as bishop, but Remigius had also come to the shrine of St Peter. As well as visiting the Lateran he may have made his obeisance at the venerable basilica. Founded by Constantine, Old St Peter's comprised the church itself with an atrium before it, entered by way of the likely source of the Lorsch hall, a triple-arched propylaeum as could be found at the entrance to a Roman forum. This might have been in his mind when he started to build at Lincoln. But what of that greater arch, the one that bore the name of Constantine himself?

The Arch of Constantine was erected in 315 to commemorate his victory over Maxentius, the victory that, famously, was inspired by Constantine's vision of the Cross and his words 'In hoc signo vinces'.[19] (fig. 5) This won for Constantine the imperial throne and, with the Edict of Milan the next year, Christianity the Empire. There is no record of Remigius examining this powerful symbol of the triumph of the faith any more than of what passed between him and

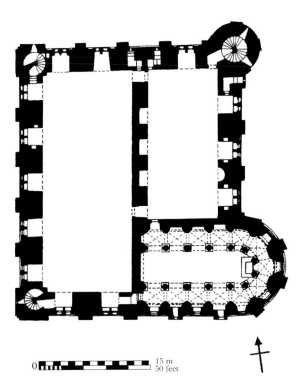

164. White Tower, Tower of London. Plan of the second floor: the main newel in the north-east corner (top, right) leads up from a lower suite of two large rooms; the L-shaped spaces within the walls just below and to the left of the newel are garderobes; the apsidal chapel occupies the eastern half of the south side. Circulation and a hierarchy of spaces can only be readily explained at this level if the large room, lying north of the chapel, is partitioned off from the newel, and only therefore reached by way of the larger room on the west side, perhaps a grand hall, with the partitioned southern end of the eastern room acting as a kind of presence or throne room, with direct access to the chapel. After Drury 1982, fig. 40. © Royal Archaeological Institute

0 ⊢▮▮▮▮⊣ 15 m / 50 feet

the mason commissioned with the task of building his new works. Yet a comparison between the Arch of Constantine and the west front of Lincoln Cathedral goes further than the symmetrical arrangement of their three arched openings and embraces the similar width and spacing of the arches themselves.

This congruency is surely significant. What better way for Remigius to symbolize his secular power as the Conqueror's lieutenant in Lincoln, and to affirm his ecclesiastical power as bishop of the immense midland see than to refer, architecturally, to an ancient conquest by which Christianity triumphed? The west front of Lincoln Cathedral, therefore, may have started life as a keep-like citadel, palace, vestibule, triumphal arch and, above all, sign by which the Norman Conquest of Lincoln and the Midlands over the Danelaw was broadcast from the high hill that later on would give the cathedral a prominence second to none.[20]

Other great clerical magnates followed in their different ways, the most renowned being Bishop Gundulf of Rochester, who, it seems, directed operations at Colchester and the Tower of London for the Conqueror as well as at Rochester itself. The White Tower of the Tower of London and the great keep of Colchester Castle became the largest of all donjons in England.[21] Though the construction of the White Tower followed that of Colchester, William had ordered the fortifications of the future Tower of London in the winter of 1066. Both here and, later, at Colchester the chosen sites have strong Roman associations, the eastern termination of the Roman wall at London, the podium of the ruined temple of Claudius at Colchester. Whatever constructional or strategic advantage prompted these choices, the notion of building on Rome cannot have escaped those in the know. Moreover, in their similar plans and elevational treatment Rome seems to be a source of inspiration yet again.[22]

Construction of the White Tower probably only began after Gundulf's arrival in England from Normandy and appointment to the bishopric of Rochester in 1077.[23] How quickly work progressed is unclear, but William never saw the White Tower finished. His son Rufus turned his attention to the great hall at Westminster, and it was probably only Henry I who finally entered a roofed Tower in the first years of the twelfth century.

This White Tower could be entered at ground level into its undercroft, or, formally, at first-floor level into one of two great rooms which shared this floor with the crypt of a chapel. The second floor, reached by a wide newel staircase built into the north-east corner, was similarly disposed, the chapel rising into an upper stage, as it still does, the two great rooms being roofed at a lower level than today. (fig. 164) All these rooms were heated, and the north wall, furthest from the entrances on the south side, was penetrated by chutes for garderobes. These four

165. The Keep, Colchester Castle. The apsidal end of the chapel (left), which juts forward in a manner reminiscent of Roman gateways and incorporates reused Roman brick and stone

rooms seem to have served as rooms of increasing elaboration through which those attending court passed until they reached the royal presence in a throne room. The complexity of the planning, including the sophisticated arrangement of intra-mural passages, secondary chambers and garderobes, brought the keep to a new peak of development. Meanwhile, the apsidal projection of the chapel, the main feature that breaks the overall rectangularity of the plan (if one excepts the lesser curved projection of the newel), as it also does at Colchester, (fig. 165) may depend on forms taken from Rome, perhaps from the likes of Constantine's Porta Nigra at Trier (Augusta Treverorum) or some other Roman gateway that had caught Gundulf's eye. Roman, too, are the round arches that adorn the walls between the pilaster buttresses.

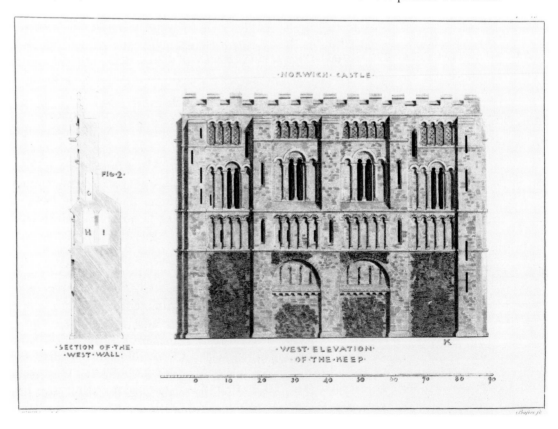

166. Norwich Castle. The unrestored west elevation of the keep as recorded before 1795 by William Wilkins senior, together with a section through the wall showing two stages of intramural passages. After Wilkins 1796, Pl. 11. © Society of Antiquaries of London

160

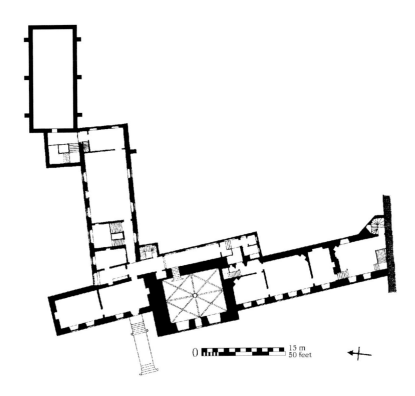

167. Bishop's Palace, Norwich. Plan of principal floor. The north wall of the nave of the cathedral is on the extreme right; a long range links this to the thick walls of the keep-like main block; a second range extends to the north-east, terminating in a chapel (top, left). After Whittingham 1980, fig. 17. © Royal Archaeological Institute

The White Tower came to be known as *arx palatina*, a palatial citadel. So far as military invincibility is concerned, this is as much a consequence of monumentality as of impediments to entry. Colchester was no less. As combined strongholds and palaces, they were intended to symbolize power as well as being a means of formally wielding it. The flat buttresses that articulated their walls stood for strength, and the Romanesque style of the round arches decorating the spaces between the buttresses at the Tower demonstrated the universal debt that western European architecture of the time owed to Rome. The heavy, round-arched arcades of its chapel did likewise, and this was probably true of the destroyed chapel at Colchester as well.

The great keep in the royal castle at Norwich and the smaller royal keep at Canterbury,[24] both attributed to Henry I, have similar qualities. Work at Norwich may well have begun in the last years of William Rufus, although little had been achieved at the time of his death in 1100. (fig. 166) Politically it was to be a royal counterpart of the new cathedral, and, as such, probably complete in time for a crown-wearing festival at Christmas 1121, when, following Henry I's second marriage, Adeliza of Louvain was consecrated as queen there. Even more so than Colchester and the White Tower, the external elevations were embellished with blind arcading[25] that exemplifies an almost classical sense of symmetry, order and proportion, based on an identifiable unit of 5 feet 6 inches (1.68 m). The interior, all swept away but for the shell, suggests a similarly complex disposition of formal and service rooms as the White Tower provided.[26]

Formality and symbolism stand like a pair of rampant bearers to the escutcheon of medieval monarchic power. Nowhere are they better seen than in these great keeps, which, like an achievement of arms, signify the status of lordship and its role as the temporal guardian of Christianity. Indeed the keeps of London and Colchester owe a debt to the fountainhead of the Church Militant through their being metaphorically built on Rome and using debased Roman architectural forms. They also broke free of the ancient Germanic tradition of the open hall and its detached attendant buildings. In doing so, they brought to England the discontinuous thread of sophisticated planning that Charlemagne had taken from Rome and passed on to the Frankish kingdoms that succeeded his empire.

This Carolingian thread appears again on a small scale in Bishop Herbert de Losinga's palace at Norwich. This comprised a range of private rooms built over a tunnel vault that also carried a processional route from the palace to the gallery on the north side of the cathedral. (fig. 167) This upper entry distinctly recalls the arrangements of the palatine chapel at Aachen, although what use Herbert made of the cathedral gallery (for instance to house a throne?) is unclear. Herbert's palace terminated at its northern end in a keep-like structure with a large heated room in its upper storey in the form of an upper hall. These works were completed before his death in 1119, and were presumably self-sufficient since they predate an open hall added by Bishop Turbe after 1146.[27] This form of entry at upper level was repeated in Paris by the route from Archbishop Sully's palace into Notre Dame, and, a century later, from the royal palace into the Sainte-Chapelle, and it became almost standard practice thereafter.

Keeps of a more or less standard pattern were raised in great numbers during the next hundred years as Norman lords and their successors secured their grip on the land. In 1127–39 William de Corbeil, archbishop of Canterbury, built the keep at Rochester, the tallest of all at 113 feet (34.5 m) to the top of its parapet, with finely appointed accommodation on three floors above the basement. Scotland's first keep was built at this time too,[28] and their vertical form remained popular on both sides of the Border for the tower-houses that responded to the hostility between the English and Scots in the fourteenth, fifteenth and sixteenth centuries.

Besides these early keeps, a number of castles also saw the construction of small analogous suites of rooms within their perimeter walls. How far the keep or the Ottonian raised hall

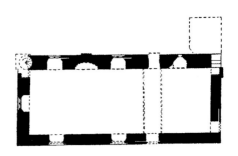

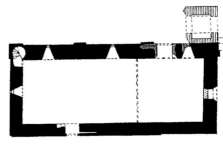

might stray from its origins is uniquely exemplified by Castle Acre, initially William de Warenne's monumental country house in Norfolk. Seemingly complete by 1085, its two storeys of rooms were arranged as a double pile, set within rectangular walls that only later were made thicker and converted into a keep of the standard kind.[29]

Less unusual are the domestic buildings, akin to keeps but distinctly lower and less strongly defensible, like the Ottonian upper halls, which were built at a few castles. Perhaps the earliest of them was Scolland's Hall at Richmond Castle, built about 1080 over an undercroft as the first domestic block of stone to rise on the site.[30] The similar hall at Framlingham Castle may have originated in the middle of the twelfth century in the works of Hugh Bigod, first earl of Norfolk, where it is placed on an upper floor, complete with an enclosed fireplace, with a heated room below it as well.[31] The hall of Christchurch Castle, (fig. 168) probably built by one

168.   (above) Christchurch Castle. Plans of the hall range: undercroft (below), and upper hall (above), showing access between them from the newel in top left corner, and later garderobe (in outline) top right. After Wood 1935, fig. 5. © Royal Archaeological Institute

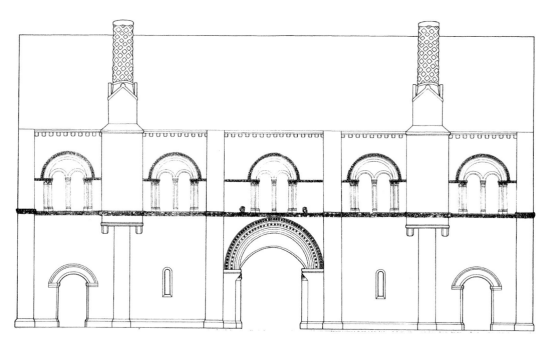

169.   St Mary's Guildhall, Lincoln. Elevations of the symmetrical west wall, outside and inside, showing the heated undercrofts, flanking the arched entrance, and the long upper hall with its twin fireplaces. After Stocker 1991, figs 36 and 37. © City of Lincoln Archaeology Unit

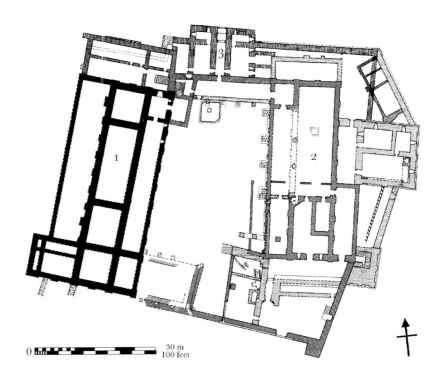

170. Winchester, Wolvesey Palace. Plan showing West Hall (solid – 1) and East Hall (hatched – 2) with a courtyard between them formed by later medieval works, including Woodman's Gate (3), a precinct wall and other works. After Biddle 1986. © English Heritage

0 ▮▮▮▮▮▮▮▮▮▮▮▮▮▮ 30 m / 100 feet

of the earls of Devon between 1155 and 1180, comprises a basement floor, perhaps partitioned, and an upper floor reached by an external stairway and also by a newel stair in the north corner; this floor is apparently divided by a lobby into a heated hall and a chamber with an attached garderobe.[32] These halls were possibly complete in themselves, and were certainly the most sophisticated and grandiose structures on their sites when new.

Similar in form but quite divorced from any defensive context is St Mary's Guildhall, in High Street, Wigford, Lincoln's southern mercantile suburb. (fig. 169) Built apparently in the years immediately following the middle of the twelfth century, it looks forward to the city's numerous merchant houses of the later twelfth century. Its grand scale embraces a central entrance arch set symmetrically between two vaulted rooms, each with its own fireplace. Above this undercroft are the remains of a magnificent hall, its 'aula Magna', which was reached by newel stairs at each end, heated by two great fireplaces, and arcaded at one end, if not both. A rear wing provided ancillary accommodation, again on two storeys. Both the size and the carved decoration suggest a royal origin, perhaps as the house (hospicium) that Henry II is known to have owned in 1157, and the site of his crown-wearing feast at Christmas that year. This great ceremony had an important political significance for the young king after the anarchy of Stephen's reign, and may have reflected Lincoln's growing economic importance as well. In the thirteenth century this use was at an end and the hall became a wine store until 1251/2 when it was sold to St Mary's Guild.[33] Had Henry's ceremony taken place here, it is hard to imagine how the hall was arranged. There is no obvious high or low end to provide a focus, and the two fireplaces split the interior, making one end a mirror-image of the other, so perhaps the king's throne was placed between them.

Even further from the castle keep, and also less urban so far as they were not built close to the street frontage, are two unusually large upper halls at Oxford and Cambridge. St Mary's College, at Oxford, later Frewin Hall, of which three groin-vaulted bays of its undercroft remain, began its life in the twelfth century inhabited by an important family of burgesses.[34] Far more survives of Merton Hall at Cambridge, which is half as large again.[35] Over a formerly aisled and vaulted undercroft, its large hall has a fireplace to one side and was probably once partitioned from a second room at the north-eastern end, these two rooms generously providing a combined area of 1,675 square feet (156 m²). A small wing opening off the hall accommodated a further small room, but both the original arrangements and the circumstances of its construction about 1200 are unclear.

Standing alone for its extreme complexity was the West Hall at Wolvesey Palace. (fig. 170) Following his elevation to the see in 1100, and fresh from overseeing the rebuilding of Westminster Hall for William Rufus, Bishop Giffard gave this stone building a very different form and truly Roman proportions and complexity in an endeavour to improve his episcopal residence. Its suite of private chambers was raised up on a solid base so far above ground level that they at once made an imposing sight and enjoyed a sweeping view of the surrounding landscape. Lower and to the side there were rooms for clerks, and at the southern end was a three-storeyed tower for the bishop's treasury and exchequer.[36] Its eminence could not be doubted, nor could its relative privacy when compared with the public character of its equally eminent neighbour, which would shortly be raised to its east.

However distantly, the West Hall recalls the former episcopal palace at Auxerre, which is a likely descendent of the Kaiserhaus or Pfalz built about 1050 at Goslar with a raised balcony.[37] The palace was built in the 1130s on steeply sloping ground to the east of Auxerre Cathedral, with an open gallery, set over an undercroft and adjoining a suite of private rooms.[38] Sumptuously decorated, its arcaded promenade resembles a cloister walk, and confers on the chosen few not a private view of an enclosed garth, but a public panorama of the splendid sweep of the river Yonne. These arrangements became more common in France than England. Even so, attached to Henry III's open hall of about 1240 at the Tower of London, there was a similar gallery overlooking the Thames.[39]

The form of large hall built over an undercroft became common in France. Greatest of all was the hall of the Palais Royal in Paris, built in 1302–13 over a vaulted undercroft,[40] just as contemporary churches were built over crypts. Similarly, the Salle Synodale which Archbishop Gauthier Cornut built as a seat of ecclesiastical pomp and administration about 1230–40 for his palace at Sens[41] gave the Church in France a hall on an upper floor to challenge the open hall of his colleagues at Canterbury.

This form was adopted for one of the Scottish kings' greatest halls, and also one of the earliest. Long before

171. Kirkwall, Bishop's Palace. The interior of the ruined hall set over the undercroft of *c.* 1200, modified and raised by Bishop Reid *c.* 1550, with his tower beyond and the crossing tower of St Magnus's cathedral to the right. © Royal Commission on the Ancient and Historical Monuments of Scotland

Orkney was incorporated into Scotland it had at Kirkwall a cathedral, begun in the 1130s, in the manner although not the size of Durham, possibly by an English mason, at the instigation of Earl Rognvald and Bishop William the Old. Here, a later bishop, perhaps Bjarne Kolbeinsson, built a great hall over an undercroft for his new palace in about 1200. (fig. 171) Only the undercroft remains, but the palace is interesting because it had room enough to accommodate both the bishop and King Haakon Haakonssen in 1263 after the king had retreated from his defeat at Largs, the king dining in state in the apartments on the upper floor, the retainers of both bishop and king dining together, on separate tables, in the hall below.[42]

The upper hall came to dominate Scottish planning, leaving no place for the open hall of Anglo-Saxon and English tradition. The hall of Stirling Castle was built over a great vaulted undercroft in the later fifteenth century and completed either at the end of James III's reign or more probably early in that of James IV. (figs 172 and 173) Measuring 126.5 feet in length and 36.5 feet in width (38.5 by 11.1 m), it was arranged in the usual way with entrances on either side at its north end, linked by a passage screened from the main body of the hall, and a dais at its south lit by two rib-vaulted oriel windows, while a fine hammerbeam roof spanned it. No less than five fireplaces were set into the walls, and, half way down the east side, a staircase built into

172. Stirling Castle. Plan, showing (1) the King's Old Building (probably built for James IV *c*.1496), (2) the Chapel Royal (rebuilt 1591), (3) the Great Hall, (4) the Gatehouse, (5) the Prince's Tower, and James V's Palace, (6) the main entrance, (7) the Gallery, (8) the palace courtyard, (9) the King's Guard Hall, (10) the King's Presence Chamber, (11) the King's Bed Chamber, (12) the Queen's Guard Hall, (13) the Queen's Presence Chamber, and (14) the Queen's Bed Chamber. The palace is typically disposed with its rooms progressing from public to private, and divided into king's and queen's quarters. After MacGibbon and Ross 1897, 1, fig. 406

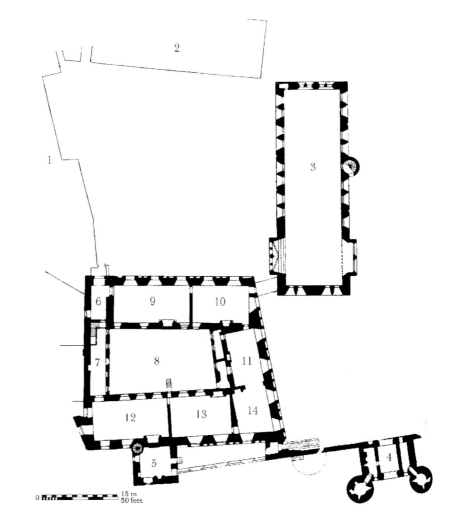

173. The Great Hall of Stirling Castle, newly restored and finished in a coat of buff-tinted protective limewash. View from the south-east, showing the outside of the newel that links the hall with the services in the undercrofts, the stacks for two of the fireplaces on each side of the newel, and the oriel window that lights the high table

a tower allowed servants to enter from below. Here the Scottish kings held court; and it was the scene of the coronation festivities of both James V and Mary Queen of Scots, and the baptism and coronation of James VI. The Union of the Crowns in 1603 changed this abruptly: James deserted Stirling for London; General Monk seized the castle in 1651, and it was defended in the rebellions of 1715 and 1745, following which the hall was used as barracks until the 1960s.[43]

Meanwhile, in England the age-old Germanic open hall remained remarkably unaffected by the importation of the sophisticated upper hall. Open halls were increasingly built of stone and certainly became more ornate, but they retained their essentially atavistic qualities. Rather than bowing to a superior form, the open hall was so greatly esteemed that it became entirely naturalized in a way that did not occur in France. The clear-cut linear order of its open interior, which was fully developed by the thirteenth century, gave it an undisputed prestige that was readily visible outside as well as in. For this reason it had the edge over the upper hall, which arranged its hall and attendant rooms within a large structure of two or more storeys, in such a way that both comprehensible linear arrangements and a recognizable external appearance were readily obscured.

The low end of an open hall, with its entrances and routes to service rooms, was for servants and people of low degree; its high end, with its formal table raised on a dais, conferred merit on all who sat there and had access to the inner sanctum of private chambers that lay beyond. This allowed clearly defined, specific places for men and women of all classes and stations. Just as important, in their midst was an open hearth, aligned centrally and sometimes rather nearer the high end, its fire symbolizing hospitality, if not life itself. So successful was this archaic arrangement that the earliest descriptions of its use in *Beowulf* and Bede differ little from what occurs in guildhalls and college halls even today. The symbols of formality went hand in hand with the practicalities of usage, if indeed they could ever be distinguished from each other at all, and, over the centuries, hardened into precious fossils.

This tangible symbolism reinforced a mythical prestige. When Geoffrey of Monmouth pressed the claim of that greatest son of the House of Constantine, King Arthur himself, as British monarch and Christian champion, he furnished him with a royal hall as splendid as *Beowulf*'s Heorot. The open hall consequently gained a renewed significance for English monarchs, particularly from the time of the Angevins, that was not echoed beyond the English Channel. Indeed the open hall offered both the legitimacy of history and the romance of a chivalrous age.[44]

This is borne out by the great hall that Henry II in his role of duke of Anjou built at Saumur, and utilized for Christmas festivities the year before his death in 1189.[45] That feast was not recorded in detail, but another feast was, one that took place there in 1241 long after Anjou had fallen into the hands of Louis IX. 'The king', Louis's chronicler Jean Sire de Joinville recalled, 'held his banquet in the hall of Saumur which it was said was built by the great Henry of England so he could hold feasts there.' Louis, so the account continues, sat at the high table in a blue satin tunic with a vermilion surcoat trimmed in ermine, flanked by a host of nobles, including the king of Navarre and nine counts; other nobles acted as servers and regal guards; and attending them was a great company of knights and serjeants, all arrayed in bright tunics and surcoats. This splendour stretched the length of the hall, as Joinville remembered with amazement long afterwards:

> The hall is made in the form of a Cistercian cloister, but I think none is so big. There was room for a table for twenty bishops and archbishops. The queen mother [Blanche de Castille, Regent during Louis's youth] sat at another table at the side of the cloister. She was served by the Comte de Boulogne, the Comte Hughes de St Pol and a young German of eighteen years.
>
> At the far end of the cloister were the kitchens, the wine cellars, the pantries and butteries, from where the king and queen mother were served. Down either side and in the middle so many knights were dining that I could not count them. Many said that they had never seen so many surcoats of silk and gold . . .[46]

Indeed Joinville recalled 3,000 knights in all, an immense throng for any hall. The curious misuse of the word cloister for hall probably results from his confusion of a form of hall so strange to a Frenchman, with the aisled chapter house that typically opened off a Cistercian cloister; but, for the rest, here is a scene that, with the substitution of white tie and tails for tunics and

surcoats, and with somewhat up-dated protocols, could be found on state occasions in the City Guildhall today.

These archaic qualities prompted the reconstruction of numerous open halls without greatly altering their arrangements. Winchester Palace, burnt out in 1065 and replaced by the Conqueror in 1069–70 as his *palacium cum aula sua* (his palace with a hall),[47] was burnt again by Bishop Henry of Blois in 1141 during Stephen and Matilda's contested reign, and again replaced.[48] The Confessor's hall at Westminster was rebuilt by William Rufus under the direction of his chancellor, William Giffard, later to become bishop of Winchester, and completed by 1099. Vast even by European standards, its aisled interior spanned 67.5 feet (20.6 m) and extended to 240 feet (73.2 m), dimensions which astonished all but the king, who thought it not large enough. The great size of Westminster Hall is evident today, though the walls were largely refaced and their upper parts rebuilt in the closing years of the fourteenth century for Richard II in order to support Hugh Herland's outstanding arched hammerbeam roof.[49] Royal formalities required an open hall throughout the Middle Ages, and this, despite all the encumbrance of attached ancillary rooms, still stood out as a demonstrable entity of the utmost import.

After the king, the bishops of Winchester were the richest and most powerful men in medieval England, their palace the grandest. Already by about 1000 they occupied a hall, perhaps the creation of Bishop Ætholwold, on the island of Wolvesey south of the cathedral. This did not satisfy Bishop Henry of Blois, who built a new open hall beside Giffard's West Hall which, known as the East Hall, was probably complete in time to accommodate a legatine council in 1139. (fig. 174) On each of its sides ran low galleries, requiring it to be lit by clerestory windows; at its southern end it continued into a large chamber block of two or three storeys, thus bringing under one set of roofs what previously had been separate and under two or more. The West Hall and the East Hall between them catered for the bishop's more private and more public roles respectively. This significant pointer to the future augmented the overall splendour of what was recorded at the time as his *domus quasi palatium*. Together with Henry's other buildings, the new Wolvesey Palace caused Giraldus Cambrensis to praise his 'wonderful works, most sumptuous palaces, vast ponds, difficult aqueducts, and hidden passages in different places' – the latter surely a reference to what was for its time unusual complexity in Wolvesey's planning.[50]

174. Winchester, Wolvesey Palace. The remains of the East Hall, showing its north wall replete with the arcading that once graced the end above the high table

Until the fourteenth century, the construction of wider halls, like Westminster, had to rely on internal arcades to support the span of the roof. Since arcades came to be associated with large halls, and perhaps also the solemnity of wide churches, they became an object of esteem in their own right. In the second half of the twelfth century the aisled hall enjoyed its heyday. It was probably Henry who, shortly after the East Hall at Winchester was complete, built an aisled hall in his other palace at Farnham, and this had timber arcade-posts. King Henry II followed the aisled hall he built in 1181–3 at his palace at Clarendon[51] with the one at Saumur. The aisled hall that was probably built by Robert de Beaumont, Earl of Leicester, at Leicester Castle shortly before his death in 1168, had a high main roof and lower side roofs, like a Roman basilica or a contemporary church, leaving space between them for clerestory windows and consequently a better distribution of daylight inside.[52]

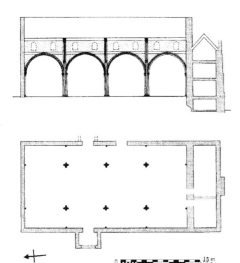

175. The Bishop's Palace, Hereford. The restored plan and elevation of Foliot's hall, showing the round-arched timber arcades, and the storeyed block attached to the southern end. After Blair 1987, fig. 4. © Society for Medieval Archaeology

The great aisled hall built in 1179 or soon after by Bishop Robert Foliot (1173–86) of Hereford is similar, but here the three round-arched bays, the survivors of four, are of timber, not stone.[53] (fig. 175) It seems to have followed the East Hall at Wolvesey Palace by terminating in a narrow chamber block, only 14 feet (4.3 m) wide, but rising three storeys over a basement or undercroft. This was too small for principal chambers, which were probably accommodated within a separate block to the north-east, but a step towards their ultimate integration into one range.[54] Walchelin de Ferrers's contemporary aisled hall at Oakham Castle included a low service block comprising buttery and pantry attached at the south end, with a kitchen beyond, leaving the hall itself appearing rather less encumbered. (fig. 176) Apart from the jollity and rowdiness in place of silence and solemn reading from holy scripts, these halls differed little from the monastic refectory. When kitchens, wine cellars, pantries and butteries, and also private chambers were added to one or both ends of a hall, a pattern evolved that would accentuate its high and low ends, with chambers and services placed opposite each other in a recognizable way at its extremities.

Ancillary rooms were usually differentiated from the hall by setting them under smaller roofs, sometimes as clearly dependent wings, which hardly reduced the visual impact of the hall, and hence its status, at all. As for the hall itself, the low end was marked out by its entrance, sometimes with a prominent porch, and the high end, eventually, by a large window lighting the high table, a window that might take the form of a grand oriel. There was no mistaking which end was which. This form, raised over an undercroft, was taken up by a number of upper halls, such as that at Stirling, even though their service rooms were augmented or displaced by the undercroft.

At Lincoln, Bishop Chesney started a new palace on the south side of the cathedral on a sloping site he acquired in 1155. (fig. 177) For this he seems to have pledged the cathedral jewels to Aaron the Jew, but gained little save odium for his efforts. Before his death in 1166 he may have begun a small hall which, after his time, was completed over an undercroft, and this continued southwards into a small chamber block with an attached garderobe complete with privies of remarkable size. Known as the Eastern Hall, it served as a comfortable private residence once Bishop Hugh put in hand a second, aisled hall for ceremony, after 1186. This Western Hall was completed by about 1224 on a larger scale, being some 90 feet (27 m) from the high end, down its four bays to the low end, where the structure continued with two service rooms, a buttery and pantry, built over an undercroft used for storage. Later, a covered passage led over a bridge to a large detached kitchen with five fireplaces, also built on an undercroft. To complete the scheme,

176. Oakham Castle, its aisled interior divided by arcades of round piers with capitals carved with crockets – a distant memory of the Roman Corinthian capital

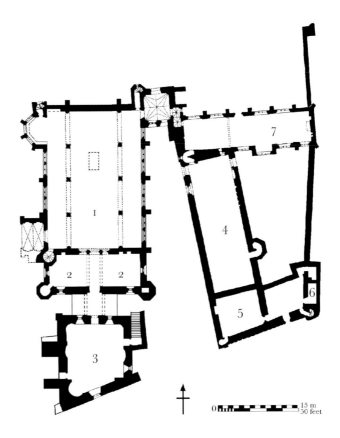

177. The Bishop's Palace, Lincoln. Plan of upper level, showing Bishop Hugh's ceremonial West Hall (1), with a passageway to a pair of service rooms (2) and, beyond these, a separate kitchen (3), and, to the right, the remains of the East Hall (4), its great chamber (5) and garderobes (6), and a chapel to the north (7). After Faulkner 1974a figs 19 and 20. © Royal Archaeological Institute

a ceremonial way led from its elaborate porch to the cathedral Galilee porch, the whole ensemble providing a sophisticated architectural setting for the bishop's private and public life.[55]

The developing sense of high and low ends with their attendant chambers and service rooms found expression about 1200–20 in the largest of all ecclesiastical halls, the work of archbishops Hubert Walter and Stephen Langton at Canterbury. (fig. 178) Second only to Westminster Hall, it measured 165 by 60 feet (50 by 18 m), its great overall roof being supported

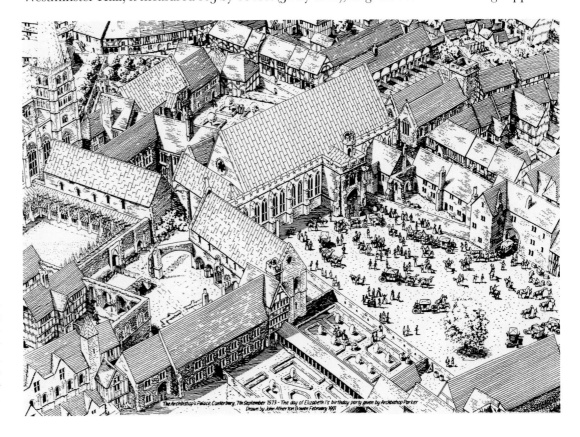

178. The Archbishop's Palace, Canterbury, in a reconstructed view by John Bowen as it might have appeared on 7 September 1573, the occasion of the birthday party given by Archbishop Parker in honour of Queen Elizabeth, whose coach is seen arriving before the entrance porch of the great hall. After Rady, Tatton-Brown and Bowen 1991. © Canterbury Archaeological Trust

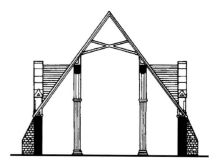

179. Winchester Castle hall. Cross-section and north elevation as originally built in 1225–35, and before general fourteenth-century reconstruction raised the aisles thus removing the dormer windows. After drawings by Philip Marter in T. B. James 2000, fig. 40b

0 |███| 15 m / 50 feet

by arcades of eight bays, marked outside by buttresses and, between them, pairs of two-light lancet windows with foils over them that rose into gables breaking the roof line. Running along the full width of the hall beyond its high end was an undercroft with a great chamber above; a second chamber filled the upper storey of a large projecting porch marking the main entrance, and close by was a detached kitchen.[56]

Meanwhile the Conqueror's hall at Winchester had been burnt in 1140 during Matilda's siege, and by the end of the disputed reign even Winchester itself was grievously damaged. The Crown abandoned its former palace and looked to the castle for greater security. Here, within the protection of its walls, Henry III built in about 1222–36 a new aisled hall, like a smaller version of Canterbury, with tall windows rising into prominently gabled dormers to break the line of the overall roof.[57] (fig. 179)

Because of his continuing disputes with the City of London, Henry III also improved his domestic accommodation at the Tower of London, as well as its defences. About 1240 he put in hand the construction of another aisled hall and two towers, one at each end, as lodgings for himself and his queen. (fig. 180) That to the east, for Eleanor of Provence, was three storeys high and comprised a vaulted basement with two magnificent chambers above, one over the other, connecting with secondary chambers in an attached rectangular block. This was where Lanthorn Tower now stands, and his own lodgings, probably similar but grander, are now Wakefield Tower. While their detailed arrangements are conjectural, they set a much copied precedent for future royal and lordly apartments in this formal separation.[58]

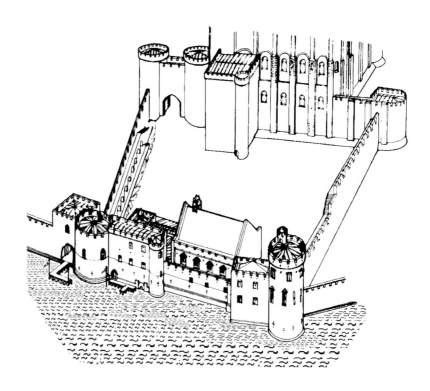

180. Henry III's new hall overlooking the Thames at the Tower, with its attached suites for himself (to the left) and for Queen Eleanor (to the right). After David Honour's drawing in Thurley 1995, fig. 3. © Society of Architectural Historians of Great Britain

181. Winchester Castle hall. The aisled interior with its raised aisles and the round table hanging on the east wall. © Hampshire County Council

Little remains of these, but Henry's hall at Winchester served a ceremonial role until well after the Middle Ages,[59] particularly in promoting the Arthurian legend. (fig. 181) In 1272 Edward I retired from Louis IX's failed Crusade and embarked on his conquest of Wales. To bolster his Britishness at the expense of the Welsh princes he played the Arthurian card, now all the stronger following the recent supposed discovery of Arthur's grave at Glastonbury. It can hardly be coincidence that about 1290 a round table was constructed at Winchester, probably as 'evidence' of the antiquity of the city's role as capital and the continuity of the British monarchs in England since Arthur's time. Two hundred years later, Henry VII not only claimed descent from King Arthur but also baptized his eldest son and heir Arthur. Death kept this name from the throne, but the Tudors capitalized on it so as to justify their rule as monarchs and defenders of the faith, eventually in defiance of the pope. The centre of the table was painted with a Tudor rose, and, like a darts board, radiating segments bear the names of twenty-four Arthurian knights and depict a bearded Arthur looking suspiciously like Henry VIII. He displayed the table in this guise within the hall when he entertained the Emperor Charles V there in 1522, and there it can still be seen.[60]

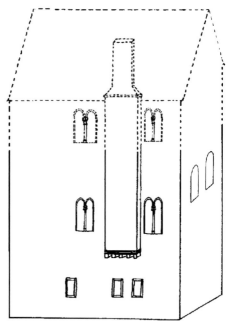

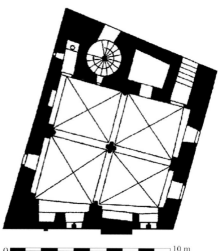

182. Hôtel de la Buffette, Provins. Plan and restored elevation. After Garrigou Grandchamp 1999, fig. 15

The additive process whereby a hall and its high and low ends were developed in the twelfth century, for example at Hereford and Canterbury, to provide services and chambers, and then duplicated so as to separate private and public functions, became typical of English and indeed Welsh episcopal palaces. By the Reformation there were about a score of them. These had been built up with private and public suites, as time went by, embracing an ever-increasing multitude of ancillary rooms in separate ranges, rather than in one great ensemble in the French way, much as British cathedrals differed from the French. But the confusion of styles, often evident in English cathedrals, less affected the palaces, where the great halls were clearly distinct from their ancillary ranges. The ancillary ranges nevertheless demonstrated the growing size of episcopal households, the aggrandizement of formalities and, at once, the need of individual bishops to escape from these into private apartments. Bishops simultaneously built about a score of London inns, palaces in miniature, where smaller households were accommodated in tighter circumstances that still required an escape into privacy.

When William Rufus described Westminster Hall as 'too big for a chamber, not big enough for a hall',[61] it was size that determined his choice of words, not function. Alexander Necham, writing about 1200, thought differently: size was not the principal distinguishing factor; a hall meant an open hall, not any large upper room with a hearth and a formal use; a chamber meant a room containing curtains, drapes, a bed and bed-clothes. Moreover, a hall should be aisled and divided into distinct bays by posts.[62] Several documented cases support his view that both these forms and roles differentiate the two sorts of room.[63] But these cases refer to establishments that incorporated both chambers and open halls, which, of course, were clearly differentiated. When a lordly establishment did not include an open hall, but did include one or more large rooms on upper floors with a public role, as those of the White Tower did, the distinction between hall and chamber is far less clear, and perhaps unimportant.

For all its forward-looking qualities, this lack of distinction may have been a drawback to the upper hall, and a reason why builders kept faith with the older Germanic form. Far from being condemned for old-fashioned arrangements, the antique had a special quality of its own. The open hall might not be Roman in origin, but it had been the centre of royal life for Christian kings for half a millennium by the time of the Conquest. While the innovating upper hall captured the imagination for a while, the open hall was not neglected, as the hall Rufus commanded at Westminster shows.[64] It embraced a clear hierarchical form that continued to be prized until long after the Middle Ages were done. By contrast, the accommodation incorporated within a storeyed block seems to have had a variable and ambiguous role. Essentially more private than the open hall, its principal room was often designed for a public role, and this required control. Moreover, this room was often hardly expressed outside, from where appearances also counted. Symbolically powerful the keep may have been, but, in the manner of innovations, the upper hall within had its day, and, as time passed, was reserved for special occasions. The open hall better expressed traditional values, however romantically these were held, so it remained as the defining building of the Middle Ages, eventually accommodating rich and poor alike.

The upper hall, meanwhile, took on the formal arrangement of the open hall, although it was built over an undercroft. It was adopted lower in society too: what began in imperial Paderborn within three centuries became for a while the object of esteem of anyone who had turned a penny or two in the prospering towns and cities of Norman and Angevin England. British bishops built several upper halls in their palaces, although usually for their private use, retaining larger open halls for public ceremony. In France, too, there were several mundane developments of the upper hall in which the twin elements of domestic apartments set over some kind of basement were employed on both large and small scales within buildings that lacked strong defensive capability. The Hôtel de la Buffette at Provins was built in the twelfth century as a three-storeyed tower, with its undercroft and lower storey vaulted, and a high degree of comfort overall. (fig. 182) Entered up a flight of steps from the street, the rooms were well lit and enjoyed the benefits of large fireplaces, basins for washing, and subsidiary rooms and latrines in the thickness of the walls. Like the arrangements of a donjon, the rooms took the form of a storage room at ground level, a hall above, and a chamber or solar at the top.[65] From such noble houses the French would develop the *maison polyvalente*, and English burgesses would build small houses in a similar manner.

13

Houses small and not lofty

Merchants' and Jews' houses

While Norman magnates set themselves up in great stone citadels and palaces, and built themselves lesser houses of stone for occasional use, the evident status of these buildings led affluent burgesses and other town dwellers to build in stone on their own account. It was cheaper to build in timber, but timber was the lot of poorer people, and the craft of carpentry had yet to develop far enough to offer status, strength and durability. Stone was now obtainable at an affordable price, even in some places that lacked good quarries, so this was their way forward.

The marked development in house building during the twelfth century is characteristic of much of western Europe. The Flemish cloth industry was producing its first mercantile nobility in the late eleventh century, and these men built great stone houses of up to four or five storeys. The undercrofts and ground floor served for storage and warehousing, and perhaps an upper floor did so as well, while an intermediate *piano nobile* was reserved as a form of public hall where they would do business. Over this was the living space on two or more floors that rose into the garret, and sometimes there was more in a further, separate block at the back. Such houses were built end-on to the street, where there were steps and entrances into the lower floors, and windows above.[1] The Spijker house at 10 Graslei, Gent, is an early survivor of these great houses, built about 1200 with five storeys, and this and its neighbours show how the tradition continued despite changing architectural fashions right to the end of the Middle Ages and beyond. (fig. 183)

Along the coast of the North Sea and the Baltic similar houses came to be built, with local differences but the same general layout. The multi-storeyed houses of Baltic merchants (fig. 184) were characterized by a public hall or *Diele* on the ground floor, which was used for trading.[2] This was reached directly from the street and occupied about two thirds of the floor, the rest being given over to a living room. The *Diele* was overlooked by an office in a mezzanine, spanning one of its long sides, and also a kitchen that probably provided refreshments for the traders. Meanwhile, the upper floors contained family sleeping rooms. Sometimes, for example in a finely restored house at Stralsund, the *Diele* was heated by a hearth of its own, set on one side, and a fifteenth-century *Diele* at Tallinn has a huge hooded fireplace which looks as though it were used for cooking[3] (fig. 185).

British practice was more modest, but parallel so far as goods were manufactured, stored and sold on the ground floor and living accommodation was above. After the anarchy of Stephen and Matilda's reign had been resolved with the accession of the Angevin King Henry II in 1154, economic circumstances advanced so favourably that richer citizens could afford to construct modest stone houses in great numbers. These had a potential lifespan so long, thanks to their masonry, that several of them still survive: when those known from excavation or records are added, their number well exceeds a hundred. Longevity, nevertheless, was probably not a primary concern.

Lifespan was different. The previous generation inhabited houses that would last for the length of a working life or marriage. Now, in lasting longer, a house became part of one's capital: it could be traded and was inheritable, something to bequeath along with one's skills and connections in trade and craft. Strength also counted, particularly in terms of fireproof qualities, since the preservation of worldly goods mattered each and every day. This security probably embraced the need to escape from the rowdiness of the street below. But perhaps status counted most, for these stone houses were a decided novelty in the urban scene.

183. Spijker, Graslei, Gent, its bold crow-stepped gable standing out beside those of its later, more refined neighbours. © Christopher Wakeling

They were built in Scotland too, although survivors there are more fragmentary, and in that troubled kingdom it is possible that security counted for more than it did south of the Border. In essence the use of an upper floor for private domestic accommodation was a faint echo of the main, first-floor rooms of a donjon or keep, and designed as a practical symbol of deterrence against casual intrusion.

Size does not seem to have been an issue, even though stone provided an opportunity to build on several storeys. These houses were sometimes built over an undercroft, and comprised two storeys above, but seldom more.[4] They were often planned with just two rooms on the upper floor, one with a fireplace, set over less important rooms or shops beneath.[5] The lower rooms and undercroft were usually let out, if their separate access be taken at face value. Usually it is only the upper rooms that count for domestic purposes. A few of these stone

184. (below, left) Tallinn, Lai 23, a fifteenth-century Baltic merchant's house. © Andor Gomme

185. (below, right) Tallinn, Lai 23, the interior of the *Diele*, with the living accommodation beyond and upstairs. © Andor Gomme

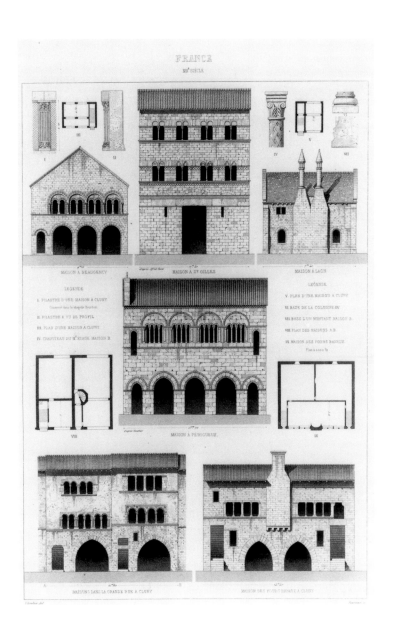

houses are, nevertheless, confined to one storey only, and perhaps had three rooms, with a loft or solar at one end.[6] Larger houses could have one large room at the front and another one or even two at the rear, divided by a spine wall like that of a donjon.[7]

Because the relative grandeur of the heated upper room has been associated with the upper halls found in donjons and palaces, they are seen as fulfilling a similar role through emulation.[8] This is questionable. The accommodation of these stone houses is limited, the smallest having no more than 370 square feet ($35\,m^2$) or half that of a small family home today,[9] and many having little more than 500 square feet ($45\,m^2$),[10] although larger ones were double this size.[11] Because many of these houses were so small, the single heated rooms that they contain must have been simply a communal family living room, whatever formalities it also served, and perhaps a sleeping room for lesser members of the family and servants. In many cases only a plain wooden partition divided it from a smaller private chamber, which probably had to double as a sleeping room for the head of the house, and a store, office and strong room.

This pattern of building in England is ubiquitous and age-old. The world over, where constructional techniques favour building on two or more floors, practicality demands that shops must go downstairs and lodgings upstairs or at the rear. This was the way of ancient Rome;[12] this was the way of ancient Gaul; now it was the way of medieval France, where such houses are called *maisons polyvalentes*. (fig. 186) The type produced many variants. Aymar Verdier recorded numerous houses like this, such as 4–6 rue des Farges, Périgueux, where three large arches open into commercial accommodation, and two narrower, flanking arches form

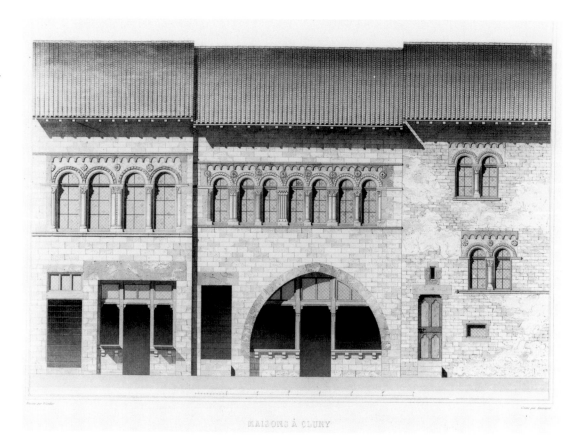

entrances to staircases and the domestic upper storey, which is ostentatiously lit by arcaded windows.[13] In Provence the traditional birthplace of Guy Foulque, Pope Clement IV (1265–8), in St-Gilles-du-Gard, has a two-storeyed lodging over ground-floor shops.

The merchants' houses of Burgundy are the clearest evidence of what ordinary traders and craftsmen could afford to occupy when the economic climate was at its most favourable. The strategic importance of Burgundy, abetted by the presence of the abbey and the freedom from external control it had gained, made Cluny a haven for artisans, merchants and professional men. The abbey's masons gave them both the skills and the taste for building stone houses that would display their wealth with fashionable ostentation and the most up-to-date architectural features. (fig. 187) Nearly fifty of their houses survive from the twelfth century and rather more from the thirteenth and fourteenth centuries.[14]

They generally comprise a ground-floor shop with one or two storeys of domestic accommodation above. The ground floor had no domestic use at all: it served as a workshop, a warehouse, and a retail shop. The great arch, which advertised its presence, was usually flanked by a doorway that led directly upstairs to the *logis*. In smaller houses this comprised a pair of rooms, a heated living room and an unheated chamber. Between them they provided a living space of some 650 square feet (60 m²), but many houses had further rooms, sometimes beyond an internal courtyard or on a second upper floor, and their living space might then amount to 1,400 square feet (130 m²) and more.

The *logis* was advertised externally by an ornate arcaded clerestory. Its immediate source was the abbey church, but, more distantly, the fragments of Roman architecture that remained in Burgundy. Whether the arrangement of lodging over shop was also the result of emulation of Roman practice or traditional practicality is open to question but perhaps unimportant in a region that knew the classical Mediterranean.

Such houses were also built in Normandy, more importantly for the English context, for instance in Rouen where fragments survive in the former Clos aux Juifs and elsewhere in the city.[15] A destroyed house in rue Malpalu had a groin-vaulted undercroft, lit by small round-headed windows with deep internal splays, and an upper floor with a corbelled chimney breast and a two-light window of a characteristic Romanesque type.[16] (fig. 188) These houses are close

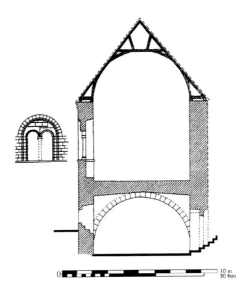

188. Rue-Malpalu, Rouen. Section and detail of a window of a destroyed twelfth-century house, with its main room set over an undercroft. After Pitte & Lescroart 1994–5

to English practice, and their size is similar too: while the smallest of the Rouen lodgings only provided about 500 square feet (45 m²), like the smaller English houses, the house in rue Malpalu went to some 800 square feet (75 m²) and others extended to over 1,100 square feet (100 m²).

What France adopted, England and Wales accepted, and so did Scotland. Perhaps the upper halls of the first English castles and houses of magnates also influenced the design of these small stone town houses, but architectural ideas travelled quickly in the twelfth century and so these houses were more probably prompted by French practice, their basic design being imported by merchants or clerics, or wandering Jews.

Because so many of these stone houses were associated with Jews, they became known as Jews' houses and seemed through their solid construction and height to offer much-needed protection from casual violence.[17] For similar reasons they were called merchants' houses. Both Jews and merchants certainly occupied houses of this type in Lincoln,[18] and they may have sought protection from violence in the strong stone walls, although a greater threat was probably fire. Bullion and stock tallies were particularly at risk, and the upper floor of a stone house served better in this respect than a room in a timber house could do.

The earliest survivors of these houses generally date from a century after the Conquest, but London was precocious: its first stone houses followed so hard on the heels of the first stone houses of magnates – indeed about 1100, as the Conquest produced its first economic dividend – that an imported source from Normandy is quite likely. There were stone houses on the north side of Cheapside, and also along Thames Street close to the river. One possibly survived long enough to be recorded by the surveyor Ralph Treswell in 1612.[19] Archaeological fragments of undercrofts probably supported stone buildings set end-on to the street and larger rectangular buildings sited away from the street on larger plots. Among the latter was the so-called Norman House recorded in 1870 at Corbet Court, Gracechurch Street, which had an undercroft, roughly square in plan, of two aisles, each of three bays, which supported a stone building rising directly from it. The smaller rectangular buildings placed end-on to the street are best represented by the remains of one of them in Milk Street, a street later associated with a colony of Jews.[20]

Norwich was precocious too. Wensum Lodge alias the Music House, in King Street, was built in the earlier twelfth century as a two-storeyed stone house, set end-on to the street, with an entrance directly into the end of the surviving vaulted undercroft. (fig. 189) This was originally at street level and is in two parts. The two bays nearer the street are ornately finished with roll-moulded and hollow-chamfered diagonal ribs; a stone wall with a round-arched doorway separates these from the remaining three bays, which have a plain groin-vault. The front bays,

189. Wensum Lodge, King Street, Norwich. Plans and schematic view of: (left) original house, with its two-celled vaulted undercroft and a porch on the south side containing a staircase to the upper storey; and (right) after the addition of a single-aisled hall on the south side. The outline shows the extent of the house after a wing had been built out from the hall on the south side and the gap between this and the original building had been filled in. King Street lies along the west side. Based on Carter 1980, fig. 7, and VAGCP 1997

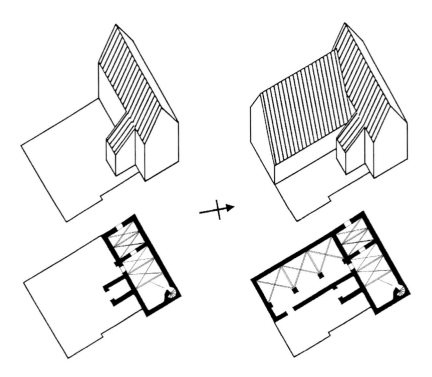

therefore, seem to have had a public use since show was important, while the rear bays were perhaps used for warehousing. Lighting came from loop windows on the south side. A newel stair in the end further from the street led into the smaller of two rooms above, and an external stair led into the larger, heated room, which extended right to the front. In this form it was a classic example of an upper hall, all the rooms on both floors forming a single entity, with about 540 square feet (50 m²) of floor space to each storey.[21]

Moyse's Hall in Bury St Edmunds is another house associated with Jews, though on very slight evidence. (fig. 190) Perhaps the house really was a synagogue or belonged to a Jew called Moyse, this being a corruption of Moses; but Moyse was a gentile name in medieval Suffolk, and the building may well have been one of the stone houses built or purchased by Abbot Samson about 1198.[22] At all events, this was an expensive house, commanding one corner of the market place. It comprises two ranges, both with vaulted undercrofts and important chambers set over them. Little of the exterior survives except for buttresses at each end and between the ranges, and the remains of a pair of two-light windows under round arches, typical of the late twelfth century. The lost external grandeur is reflected in the groin-vaults of the undercrofts, three bays with arches set on responds to the west, and two aisles each of three square bays to the east with a pair of supporting cylindrical piers between them. (fig. 154) The rooms above correspond to the spaces below: a larger room to the east, measuring 38 by 27 feet (11.6 by 8.25 m) and once lit by five fair-sized windows, was perhaps a hall, and a narrow one to the west perhaps a heated solar chamber.

The early occupants of these modest stone houses are well recorded in Canterbury, where Jews and money-

190. Moyse's Hall, Bury St Edmunds, mutilated and much altered, yet still dominating the north side of the market place

men were clearly to the fore. About thirty stone houses are known from the city's documents, among them Jacob the Jew's large stone house which occupied three holdings on the corner of High Street and Stour Street (formerly Hethenmanne Lane). He obtained these about 1180 and built his house straight away. His sons Aaron and Samuel were living there in 1205 and still were in 1216, but soon afterwards they sold out to Christ Church; the monks then leased it to another Jew, Cressel, who paid them an annual rent of 11s. Following the expulsion of the Jews in 1290, there were no suitable tenants and the house was divided up. Cogan House, 53 St Peter's Street, where enough of the stone walls remain of the rebuilt front range to suggest that in the late twelfth century this contained an upper hall, was reputedly occupied by Luke the Moneyer. Lambin Frese built and occupied another stone house in Stour Street. He originally lived over his mint and workshop in the cramped alley before Christ Church Gate, where in September 1174, if rumour be true, the heat of his furnace set fire to neighbouring premises, three of which were burnt down before the fire was extinguished. Unseen, sparks were blown into the roof of the cathedral choir and, fanned by a strong wind, blazed up and destroyed it. Thanks to Frese the cathedral gained a new choir, the celebrated work of William of Sens, the mason who thereby brought French Gothic to England. Frese gained the site of his new house – a less celebrated architectural work. This was the gift of the Christ Church monks, who were understandably anxious to remove him and the other crowded workshops from the edge of their precinct, and went so far as to give him 10 marks and secure a charter from Henry II confirming the deal.[23]

191. Jew's House, The Strait, Lincoln, a potent symbol of twelfth-century urban wealth, despite its small size

192. Flaxengate, Lincoln. Hypothetical reconstruction drawn by Stanley Jones of excavated stone houses, showing the earliest twelfth-century house found on the site (bottom), with a later rear wing, and a later house, end-on to the street (top left), shown with a decorative chimney-pot on the roof ridge. After R. H. Jones 1980, fig. 41. © Lincoln Archaeological Trust

Canterbury's early stone houses have been swept away, and the details of their appearance and arrangements are largely lost. In Lincoln, two such houses survive with much of their original form visible. The transition between the timber houses built at about the time of the Conquest, which themselves superseded more primitive timber houses,[24] and the stone houses that followed seems to have taken place quite rapidly, as it did elsewhere. Whole sites were cleared of their former timber buildings before new stone ones took their place.[25] The house at 46–7 Steep Hill, mistakenly called Aaron's House, (fig. 63) and, lower down at 15 The Strait, Jew's House, (fig. 191) which was in fact occupied by the Jewess Belaset in the late thirteenth century, were built about 1170 with strength, safety and status made concrete in their form. Local oölitic limestone was at hand, and so was the mason's skill in design as well as construction.

These were not unusual houses for their time: while the exorbitantly rich Aaron lived more grandly within the protection of the Bail, and died there in 1186, many Jews and equally many merchants known for their wealth lived in other similar houses in the lower town around Grantham Street (fig. 192) and in the suburb of Wigford, further south, where quays on the river Witham and the Fossdyke provided their trading links with Torksey and Boston. Wigford boasted several stone houses: one faced St Benedict's Square at the north end of the suburb, and there were others such as Scots Hall and St Andrew's Hall. Opposite St Mary's Guildhall lay the fancifully named John of Gaunt's Palace, and also Broadgate House.

Lincoln was at the height of its prosperity in the mid and later twelfth century, ranking just after York and Norwich, and on a par with Cluny. When the deep recession that followed in the fourteenth century removed the pressure for redevelopment, many of these houses remained since no one wanted to replace them with anything more modern. Celia Fiennes, visiting in 1697, noted that the houses were 'small and not lofty nor the Streets of any breadth', but the eighteenth-century antiquary Edward King was impressed by the 'vast number of beautiful Saxon [i.e. round-arched] and Norman doorways' of its private houses.[26]

Only Aaron's House and Jew's House survive in a recognizable form that demonstrates the living conditions of Lincoln's affluent citizenry in its heyday.[27] This begins with the carved entrances, particularly that of Jew's House, where the crocket capitals and interlaced chain-link

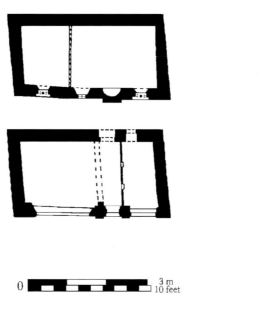

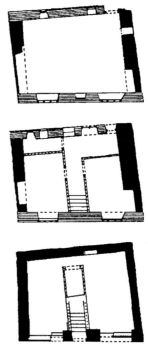

193. Jew's House, The Strait, Lincoln. Detail of the entrance, showing the decorated mouldings that spring from the inner and outer colonettes (now all but one removed), and the moulding (extreme right) that formed part of the jamb of a shop window

194. Jew's House (left) and Norman (formerly Aaron's) House, Lincoln. Plans of the ground and upper floors, with the undercroft of Norman House (bottom right); original masonry is shown solid. After Wood 1935, figs 8 and 9. © Royal Archaeological Institute

ornament around the arch caught King's eye. (fig. 193) Rising prominently above them, the corbelled bases of the chimney breasts again demonstrate the unusual wealth of the occupants at a time when most people could hardly afford the benefit of an open hearth, let alone an enclosed fireplace with a chimney. (fig. 194) Beside the entrance, arched openings (now replaced) served self-contained shops occupying each side, while the entrances led to stairs and the upper storeys, where an ornate window lit each of the two rooms. One of these had a fireplace and was divided from the other by a simple partition. So steep is Steep Hill that the otherwise similar Aaron's House rests on a tunnel-vaulted undercroft with its own entrance.

Although there are several significant differences between them in planning and detail, these houses are clearly similar to numerous others whose fragments survive in both Lincoln and several other cities and towns, or are otherwise known through illustration. While the Cluny houses do not generally have ornate doorways, as some of these do, the magnificence of the Cluny clerestories is way beyond the decoration of English windows, or the similar ones in Normandy, which have a form typical of contemporary Romanesque churches. Interestingly, the corbelled-out chimney breast, a distinctive feature in England and Normandy, is directly matched in Cluny and elsewhere in France. Rich people wanted their chimneys to show.

After Lincoln, Southampton has the best surviving fragments of stone merchants' houses in England. These replaced timber buildings of the eleventh and early twelfth centuries whose posts were simply set into the earth. Shortly before the end of the twelfth century the expanding Gascon wine trade was doing well enough to allow a major rebuilding campaign of the kind that Lincoln experienced. This also established the west shore line where ships would berth. As a result, the new stone houses include warehouses in one form or another, usually as undercrofts. They were also rather varied in plan and some were remarkably large.[28]

The remains of three houses, the romantically named King John's Palace in Blue Anchor Lane, Norman House in Cuckoo Lane, and 79½ High Street, all have a similar pattern comprising a warehouse at ground level and a dwelling above. (fig. 195) The warehouses were divided by an arcade of either stone arches or timber posts, and the domestic ranges above were similarly divided, forming a kind of double pile. The warehouse of King John's Palace may have been open to the quay before it, while its upper storey contained a large heated room to one side and two smaller rooms to the other, possibly an office or counting house and a private chamber. This was one of the larger stone houses, less by virtue of its three rooms than its floor area of 1,720 square feet (160 m²). Norman House in Cuckoo Lane was probably a good deal larger still, with a floor area of perhaps 2,500 square feet (270 m²), but its plan is less clear,

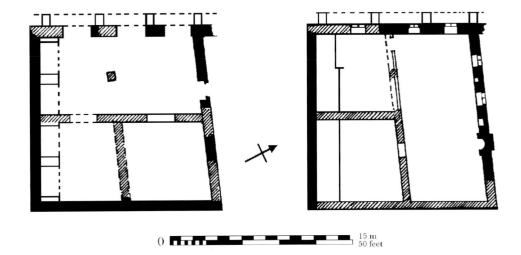

195. King John's Palace, Southampton. Plan, showing remains of ground floor (left), and upper floor with a heated hall on the right and two adjacent secondary rooms. After Faulkner 1966, fig. 87. © Royal Archaeological Institute

0 ▮▮▮▮▮▮▮▮▮▮▮▮▮▮▮▮ 15 m / 50 feet

196. Norwich, St Martin-at-Palace Plain. David Dobson's reconstruction of an excavated Norman house with two storeys of domestic accommodation over the undercroft (see fig. 10). Norfolk Archaeological Unit, *Annual Review*, 1998–9, 39. © Norfolk Museums and Archaeology Service

although a fine two-light window attests its former glories. At 79½ High Street the fireplace was, unusually, in the smaller upper room of a house whose arrangements are now mostly lost. (fig. 106) The even more romantically named Canute's Palace in Porter's Lane began life with domestic accommodation on both floors, a heated room and a chamber both upstairs and down, and included a warehouse in an attached block with a counting house above it; but, later, both ground-floor rooms of the main block were converted for yet more warehousing. All of these houses had round-headed two-light windows with a relieving arch over them of the common pattern, and these were left unglazed and simply shuttered.[29]

Bennet's Hall in Pride Hill, Shrewsbury, traditionally known as the Old Mint, had its fireplace unusually but sensibly placed for the efficient dispersal of its heat against the stone transverse wall separating the upper hall from the adjacent chamber, which is reached by two flanking arched doorways. The fireplace itself has stone jambs and carved foliated capitals with, once, a hood of wattle and daub.

While York's earlier stone houses may have arrived in the 1150s, their one survivor was built twenty years later behind 48–50 Stonegate, with a two-light window in its upper storey very similar to those at Lincoln and Southampton, and this probably flanked a chimney breast.[30] It is well set back from the street, suggesting that it belonged to a more spacious age in the city's history and represents a type once common among the city's affluent merchants and Jews.[31] Even more fragmentary are the remains of similar houses in Stamford.[32]

Apart from Wensum Lodge, there were once perhaps at least another fifteen stone houses in Norwich, several of them close to the river Wensum in King Street, or near St Martin-at-Palace Plain where one has been excavated (fig. 196) and two others, known from documents, were on 'Land with quay and quayside building'.[33] The excavated house had a floor area of about 1,025 square feet (95 m²), so it was rather larger than Wensum Lodge. Both of the entrances into its undercroft were protected by draw-bars. Elsewhere in Norfolk there are fragments of more of these houses embedded in later structures: 28–32 King Street, King's Lynn, was first built with an upper hall in the late twelfth century; a similar but slightly later house stood at 28–34 Queen Street until its demolition in 1977; and ten more are known here.[34]

The fragmentary evidence of the east coast is matched by Norwich's West Country counterpart Bristol. A fairly large stone house excavated in Tower Lane was probably as early as Wensum Lodge and predated the surviving Lincoln houses by several decades. The lower floor had the form of an undercroft, apparently used for storage, and its trapezoidal plan, measuring 52 by 23 feet (16 by 7 m), fronted the street with steps leading down into its east end; the floor above seems to have been reached by an external staircase and was divided into a room with a stone hearth and an unheated second chamber in the usual way. A coin of Henry I found on the site suggests that this was a merchant's house of the first half of the twelfth century, and perhaps that of Robert FitzHarding, who was Bristol's reeve at the time.[35]

Apart from Southampton, the smaller ports of the south coast tell a similar story. There are fragments of the entrance to a stone house in Preston Street, Exeter,[36] and the remains of a stone

197. 3 King's Yard, Sandwich. The ruins of an early thirteenth-century stone house, the further, two-light window marking the principal room, the nearer window perhaps a chamber

house at 3 King's Yard, Sandwich, include a single lancet to light a chamber and paired lancets for its hall, suggesting a rather later date for its construction, perhaps about 1230. (fig. 197) Two more fragments belong to what may have been similar houses nearby, and other houses in the town built of flint with suggestions of antiquity bring their number to perhaps six.[37]

These stone houses were not always built over undercrofts or ground-floor shops. Nos 3–4 West Street, New Romney, one survivor of apparently several stone houses built before a fateful storm in 1287 filled the town with mud and sand and raised its ground level, has just the one storey, and comprises an open hall with a single aisle at the rear, a cross-passage entered through a two-centred arch, with a service room beside it, and, beyond the hall, a heated chamber raised above a very low undercroft.[38] (fig. 198)

198. 3–4 West Street, New Romney. Reconstruction of elevation, section and plan, showing an open hall at centre with rear aisle, cross-passage to the left, with service room beyond, and, over a low undercroft, an upper chamber to the right with a fireplace on the end wall. Based on Parkin 1973

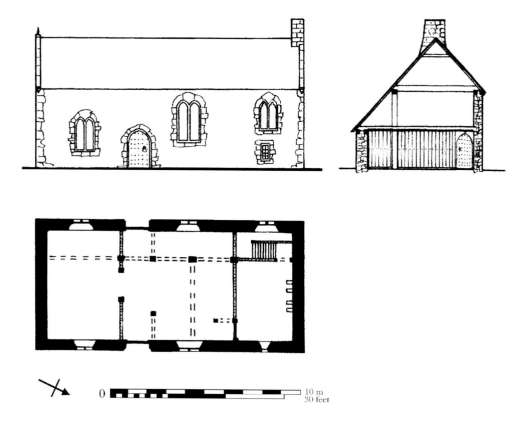

199. Aberconwy House, Conwy. With Owain ab Gruffydd's rebellion at an end in the second decade of the fifteenth century, Wales got the green light for a modest house-building campaign, perhaps inaugurated here about 1420. © National Trust

Wales once boasted several early stone houses. Their remains have been recorded in Abergavenny,[39] and in Conwy,[40] where fragments of a large stone building in Mill Gate may mark the site of the Lodging of the Master of the King's Works. However, Aberconwy House is far more demonstrative on account of its timber-framed top floor, which is jettied over the lower storeys, which are of stone. (fig. 199) Once thought to be of the sixteenth century, this likely merchant's house is now known to have been built all of a piece about 1420; it has a hall and inner room set, in the usual way, over a high undercroft that was probably in commercial use, and chambers in the unusual framed upper storey. Stone houses of this early sort, however late in date, are fairly common in South Wales, particularly in that bastion of Anglo-Norman culture, Pembrokeshire, where merchants of Tenby, Pembroke and Haverfordwest lived in stone houses built over vaulted undercrofts.[41] The Old House in Tenby has many of the characteristics of these houses, although its alternative name Tudor Merchant's House suggests the

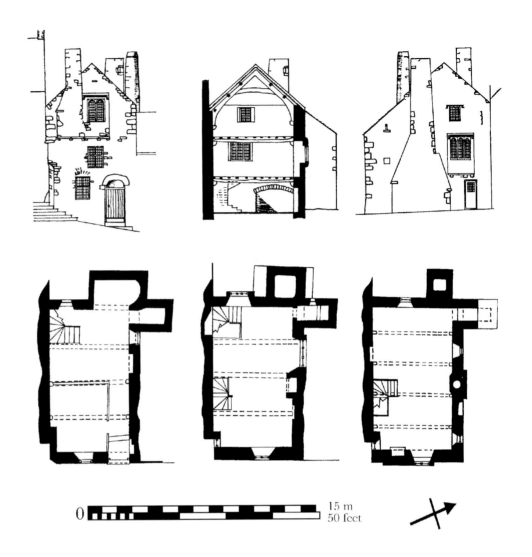

200. Tudor House, Tenby. From left to right, front elevation, cross-section and rear elevation (above), and (below) plans of ground, first and top floors. After Thomas 1962b, fig. 4. © Royal Archaeological Institute

0   15 m / 50 feet

survivor of a tradition rather than one of its makers. (fig. 200) The entrance is into the under-croft beside a partition that separates a store from the main part of the room. On account of the large size of its fireplace this must have been a kitchen. Both the main floor above and the garret have fireplaces, in separate positions and with their own chimney stacks, and again, all three floors have privies, with an external chute placed beside the kitchen stack, of all places.[42]

This vertical arrangement of services, hall and chamber suggests the Scottish practice of building towers with a similar vertical arrangement. The earliest of these stone houses in Scotland is in fact horizontally arranged. It was apparently built by the Church at St Andrews before the end of the twelfth century. Wrongly called Dean's Court, since it was built for the archdeacon, its upper storey measured 38 by 28 feet (11.6 by 8.6 m) so it was on the large side. Separate from its undercroft, it was probably entered by an external staircase.[43]

In a sense Dean's Court was more significant for Scotland than the more numerous stone houses south of the Border were for England. Status and fashion are fickle masters. These modestly sized stone houses were beginning to seem old hat when the Jews were expelled in 1290. Their houses were generally taken up by new gentile occupants, but, as a type, they were no longer built in numbers except where good stone was cheap. Three disadvantages turned people away from them. With walls 3 feet (1 m) thick and accommodation often restricted to only two rooms, they were not readily adaptable or extendable. Their supposed upper halls were small and lacked the formal and symbolic qualities that people increasingly esteemed in the thirteenth century. Finally cost: stone had lost its edge to timber, which had now developed far enough to provide strength and durability at a far lower cost than stone, and at the same

201. The later, fashionable timber-framed front of 29–32 King Street, King's Lynn, which originated as a stone house built in the twelfth century on the quayside before this and the river Ouse moved further to the west and left it stranded facing the new street and open to shoppers

time could provide a more adaptable building. This marked change was not confined to Britain, and is readily apparent in France wherever timber was to hand and urban economies were thriving.

Large town houses were still to be built of stone, although to a different plan, particularly where stone was abundant, but, where it was not, timber took over. In Lincoln the stone houses survived, as much thanks to economic downturn as to a poor supply of local timber, and indeed long enough for their antique qualities to attract attention,[44] though not to save them. Many were extended,[45] but ultimately their small size was against them. In Norwich continuing prosperity culled the smaller stone houses. Wensum Lodge, however, was quickly extended: well before the twelfth century was out an open hall was added to its south-east side running along King Street, and following Sir John Paston's purchase of the property in 1488 it was greatly altered and again extended, thus giving the house its present U-plan.[46]

At 28–32 King Street, King's Lynn, a conventional open hall superseded the upper hall, which was divided longitudinally in the fifteenth century, and its street front was fashionably recast in timber so as to include shops (fig. 201).[47] A similar fate befell Cogan House in Canterbury when an aisled hall was built at its rear to serve a new use as part of a hospital, founded by William Cokyn in 1203 and, about 1230, united with Eastbridge Hospital; eventually the original building was refaced in timber and converted into a shop with a fashionable jetty and chambers above.[48] Several more of Canterbury's houses, according to the record, ended up of mixed construction: one man has a house, 'half stone, half timber'.[49]

Most of these stone houses fared worse. They were torn down, their undercrofts alone remaining, now to support timber houses that might be taller, embrace more storeys and extend further to the rear. In the fourteenth century the stone house in Tower Lane, Bristol, was demolished and rebuilt, partly in timber. This was the fate of many of Bristol's other stone houses, for instance one built against the church of St Mary-le-Port, and the so-called Jews' houses recorded in Wine Street in the thirteenth century, and indeed all but a sole survivor at 24–5 Broad Street, part of whose stone walls still rise two full storeys.[50] The widespread urban dereliction of the later Middle Ages caused many of these houses to fall. A twelfth-century stone house with an upper hall in Staple Gardens, Winchester, was in a state of utter collapse three centuries later, its site empty but for fragments of broken roof tiles in the remains of its chalk-walled groined cellar.[51]

The future lay with timber, and with the open hall, not the upper hall. That introduced a complication, seemingly at odds with efficient urban planning. Efficiency, however, has seldom had a chance when faced with the temptations of status and form. So far as the later Middle Ages are concerned, these won the day.

14

A HOUSE FOR ROYAL BUSINESS AND OTHER AFFAIRS

The houses of royalty, magnates and wealthy merchants

In the towns of the thirteenth and later centuries the detached, spread-out form of house, typical of a rural manorial establishment, was increasingly reserved for those magnates who could afford large plots of land. Nevertheless, these plots had limits, and magnates were often tempted to fill up the available space with a jumble of buildings, and to construct shops and lodgings along the margins for letting out at a nice profit. Together these formed their mansions, which could be indiscriminately called palaces, houses, inns, or just places. Splendid though their hall might be, its stately impact was often hedged around by all sorts of ancillary buildings.

These grew in number and importance as households increased and privacy raised its modest head. In the two hundred years from the later thirteenth to the later fifteenth century, when the growing affluence of a lordly household might be expressed in a fourfold increase in its members,[1] the number of rooms in a large establishment multiplied accordingly, both to accommodate the extra bodies and to satisfy the desire of the privileged few for greater privacy. This is said to have brought about the decline of the hall. Yet the reality is different, particularly since halls were built in ever-increasing numbers. Rather than declining, the hall's all-purpose role was sometimes relinquished in favour of a more specialized role as the main room in which formal occasions were concentrated. (fig. 202) To achieve this, it still needed to be at the physical centre of an establishment, and, indeed, there it remained until the end of the Middle Ages and for at least a century thereafter. This increased formality along with changing episcopal roles, as already noted, led bishops to require two halls, one for formal quasi-state occasions, the other for lesser, semi-private dining with their episcopal household and staff.

The inherent formality of the high and low ends of later halls is emphasized by the specific uses of the ancillary rooms attached to them. These suggest an increased provision and sophistication in the hospitality on offer, as well as a desire for greater privacy of a sort, particularly on the part of the head of the household, both for himself and for his favoured guests. The hall, meanwhile, became progressively more important as a means of displaying the largesse of his everyday hospitality as well as the ritual of a great feast. While feasting continued to take place in a domestic context, it was also institutionalized and became a major social event for the members of guilds, colleges and inns of court. The feast itself required a battery of rooms for storing, preparing and cooking food; and it was the formalities of such events that necessitated the multiplicity of informal rooms, particularly a great chamber or parlour, where, following a feast, the host and chosen guests could unbutton themselves. Lesser occasions may well have been unbuttoned from the start, hence the use of a great chamber for entertaining small parties in private, and, perhaps, also when a lord had no desire to display largesse to voracious outsiders.

There is only a little indication, despite these overtones of formality, of particular rooms being set apart for the sole use of either men or women. Henry III's separate towers for himself and for his queen at the Tower of London are an indication of what would become common lower in society in a few centuries' time, and in Scotland as well. Women sometimes sat at

202. Dining at High Table. A thirteenth-century illustration of Sobriety and Gluttony (top), and (below, centre) a lord and lady seated at table, attended by servants and musicians eating their fill, while (left and right) a guest and a leper are given food and drink. © British Library. MS Add 28,162 f10v

their own tables in the great hall,[2] but furnishings moved around with peripatetic households, so what other evidence there once was for a separation of the sexes has now vanished. Children, part of the female domain, were another matter, and might have private quarters of their own, tucked out of the way.

The issue of how a hall and parlour should be used famously inked Langland's pen with black ire. Despairingly he complained of modern manners:

> Swiche lessons lordes sholde lovye to here,
> And how he myghte moost meynee manliche fynde –
> Noght to fare as a filthelere or a frere for to seke festes,

Homliche at othere mennes houses · and hatien hir owene.
'Elenge is the hall · ech day in the wike,
Ther the lord ne the lady liketh noght to sitte.
Now hath ech riche a rule—to eten by hymselve
In a pryvee parlour for povered mennes sake,
Or in a chambre with a chymenee · and level the chief halle
That was maad for meles · men to eten inne,
And al to spare to spille that spende shal another.'[3]

This is usually taken as evidence of a widespread desire for the greater privacy of a heated chamber and the consequent decline of the open hall. Yet Langland was also, if not mostly, carping about men who ate freely at other men's public tables, but refused the hospitality of their own hall to others by shunning it themselves and eating in private when at home so as not to attract unwelcome guests.[4] But there was a catch in this behaviour: the order of precedence within a lordly household was crucial to its cohesion; and, so that it might be properly maintained, it had to be made visible. This was most readily achieved by the family regularly taking communal meals in the hall, each member in his or her formally allotted place, with the lord commanding all from the centre of the high table and dispensing hospitality to all who were subservient to him.

However much traditional hospitality might be reduced by the mean habits of the selfish rich, and whatever the effects of occasional privacy on the overall usage of the hall, these did not lead to its immediate decline. In lordly and institutional establishments it remained at the centre, although joined to multiplying ancillary ranges. In lesser establishments, the houses of merchants and yeomen alike, halls were built in greater numbers than ever before. When deep purses ran to large sites and determined minds to lucid plans, these needs paved the way to triumphs of artistry. More often a succession of empirical decisions confused the endeavour. Worse, succeeding generations, viewing a stately establishment with greed, built and rebuilt over it with similar consequences.

The first and largest medieval halls had been built for kings and bishops, the rich and powerful. They led peripatetic lives, and so needed several establishments where they and their entourage might lodge in comfort and entertain guests with a lavishness appropriate to their status, and, when they were not in residence, where their constables could maintain the household estate and the power it symbolized. Often generously sited in whole quarters of towns, as Wolvesey was in Winchester, the halls and the ancillary buildings that together comprised these establishments came by processes of both accretion and clearance to embrace courtyards. So far as a monumental building and a wide open space tend to complement each other, the appearance of hall and courtyard came to be the measure by which an establishment would be judged. Often the two came together by hazard, building being at the cost of open space; but, just occasionally, the two were put together as a planned ensemble, and the whole became greater than a sum of their parts.

Less at hazard, the evidence suggests, was the idea of the courtyard as a semi-private space where circulation could be controlled. A gatehouse kept the public at bay, but, even were there none, the surrounding effect of ranges of buildings would deter the unwelcome, and the central position of the hall, with its high and low ends clearly visible from outside, would impress on visitors which parts were appropriate to their status. Even the greater formality of a ceremonial hall would be distinguished from the more domestic usage of a secondary hall by its siting at one end of a processional route, which usually related to a gatehouse or some other feature.

In the realm of the episcopal palace, already in the first decades of the twelfth century Bishop Flambard of Durham had cleared away all the houses that lay between his new cathedral and the royal castle which had been granted to his predecessor, together with vice-regal powers, as a bastion against the Scots. This set the scene for a unique episcopal enclosure in which cathedral and castle-palace – a true *arx palatina* – would each make a better show, one from the other, with the processional route between the two clearly established.

(fig. 203) He and his successor Bishop Puiset proceeded to lay out the castle bailey with halls and a chapel that form the basis of the courtyard that remains today.[5]

Early in the thirteenth century Bishop Jocelyn began a new palace at Wells, to the south of the cathedral, on what would become a proud, moated and crenellated site, akin to a castle, but now in a more chivalrous than defensive mood. (figs 204 & 205) Eventually the palace comprised a loose group of ranges set around a courtyard. His upper hall at the centre was accompanied by the chapel and much larger open hall of his successor Bishop Burnell to the south, and offices to the north, as well as a gatehouse. Both the upper hall and its vaulted undercroft were subdivided laterally and longitudinally into subsidiary rooms, leaving the main upper room to cater for the semi-private needs of the episcopal household, once Burnell had built the open hall at the end of the thirteenth century for ceremonial needs. For all the irregular layout, each building received its due, and, without losing its identity, contributed to the greater effect of the whole, both stylistically and symbolically.[6]

While Wales is famed for the magnificence of its Edwardian castles, its episcopal palaces are similarly distinguished. The unified design of St David's, its clever planning and remarkable decoration are uniquely impressive. The palace was begun in the twelfth or early thirteenth century, and foundations from this period survive on the west side of what is now a great rectangular courtyard, which was probably started in earnest by Bishop Bek in the 1280s. The eastern and southern sides of this courtyard are quite a different matter, for these comprise two-storeyed ranges of remarkable homogeneity, possibly begun by Bek in response to a visit of Edward I and Eleanor of Castile in 1284,[7] but almost certainly built afresh by Bishop Henry of Gower between his appointment in 1328 and death in 1347.[8] (fig. 206)

Bek's comparatively modest beginnings, perhaps of timber and hardly comprising a working palace, Henry of Gower transformed into an outstanding architectural ensemble. Across the east side of the courtyard he built a large domestic range; across the south a grander ceremonial range, each with undercrofts and an upper hall as its centrepiece, entered by way of a staircase rising through a porch. (fig. 207) The service ends of both halls were screened off, and here stairs led down to the undercrofts, which were used as service rooms, and up to parapets, while independent staircases led to separate kitchens. The high end of each hall had a raised dais, beyond

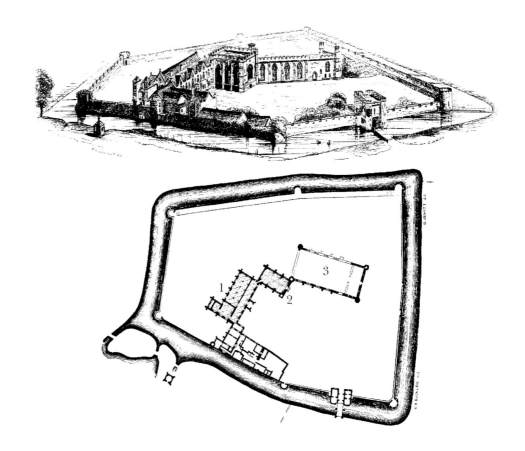

204. Bishop's Palace, Wells. Bird's-eye view from the north-west and plan, drawn by Charles Alban Buckler and engraved by O. Jewett, showing (1) Bishop Jocelyn's upper hall, now converted into a modernised residence, (2) Bishop Burnell's chapel, and (3) his open hall, now a ruin. After J. H. Parker 1861–2, Plates 1 and 2

205. Bishop's Palace, Wells. View from the west, showing the residence (left), the chapel, and the ruined Great Hall (right). © Andor Gomme

which were retiring chambers, a bedchamber, a latrine and a chapel. Meanwhile, the west range was rebuilt to accommodate suites of lodgings. Significantly, the smaller, domestic hall in the east range was heated by a fireplace set into the long, east wall, but the great ceremonial hall in the south range had an open hearth, perhaps two of them, which would have added a sense of archaic symbolism to his ceremonial feasts. Moreover, the route from its kitchen was remarkably narrow, suggesting that food was brought to the high table in a symbolic procession.

The walls of the main buildings that faced the courtyard were plastered, those of the ceremonial south range apparently coloured with red ochre, while the east range was a contrasting

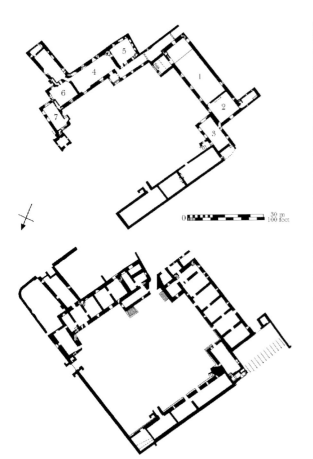

206. Bishop's Palace, St David's. Plan of the basement and the upper floor, showing the Great Hall (1) with its attendant Great Chamber (2) and Chapel (3), and the Bishop's Hall (4), Kitchen (5), Solar (6) and Chapel (7); service rooms are in the lower floor, and the west range of lodgings is at the top. After Turner 2000, fig 8. © Society of Antiquaries)

207. Bishop's Palace, St David's. View from the top of the cathedral tower, showing the Bishop's Hall in the east range nearer the camera, and the Great Hall beyond. © Cadw: Welsh Historic Monuments. Crown Copyright

white. All these works were finished with a distinctive arcaded parapet, mounted on corbels carved with heads, and further embellished by a chequer-work of sandy white and purple stone. This crowning stroke – Gower's architectural signature – bound together the various ranges facing the courtyard. If it lessened the impact of individual parts to the benefit of the whole, the great ceremonial hall was distinguished from the rest by its magnificence, its central position, its colour and lead-clad rather than slated roof. Its interior was plastered too, and possibly painted with a figurative scheme, and its great timber roof was again painted. This has all gone, but a twelve-spoked wheel window with a quatrefoil as its hub remains at the western end of the hall, strategically placed over the service end, and in direct line of sight from the high table.[9]

This was the apogee of the episcopal palace, its former military associations now abandoned or translated into chivalrous references. The ceremonial range faced the gateway that led to the cathedral, the domestic range faced the lodgings on the west side, in a clearly expressed architectural hierarchy that matched the purposes to which the palace was put. Stately pomp was the hallmark, not military power.

The formal arrangement of hall, chapel and lodgings scaled another peak of integration at the bishop of Winchester's New College, Oxford, founded by William of Wykeham in 1379 and built between 1380 and 1386. The first Oxford and Cambridge colleges were content with loose aggregations of refectory, chapel, library[10] and lodgings,[11] assembled piecemeal as space and benefactions allowed. Front Quad of Merton College, which the chancellor and future bishop of Rochester Walter de Merton founded between 1262 and 1274 (and hence the oldest of Oxford's colleges) is just such a loose assemblage of hall, chapel and scholars' lodgings.[12] It was not at Oxford but at Cambridge that the first regularly laid-out university quadrangle was formed. This is at Corpus Christi College, which the town guilds founded in 1352, where the quadrangle with a hall on its south side was completed by 1377.[13]

The novel arrangement at New College, Oxford, completed ten years later, of chapel and hall forming one great range facing lodgings for warden, fellows and students across a practically symmetrical Great Quadrangle, is probably due to Wykeham's master-mason at

208. New College, Oxford, in Loggan's bird's-eye view of 1675 from the west. The chapel lies behind the central window, one of three with ostentatious Perpendicular tracery (lower left) that light an antechapel, the roof merging into that of the hall, which continues the range, and has a low louver; to their right lies Great Quad, flanked by lodgings; this is reached from New College Lane (bottom, centre) by way of a gateway; another gateway on its further side leads into Garden Quad; bounding the college (left and above) is the thirteenth-century city wall, together with a series of projecting bastions. Loggan 1675, vol. 2, 126. © Society of Antiquaries of London

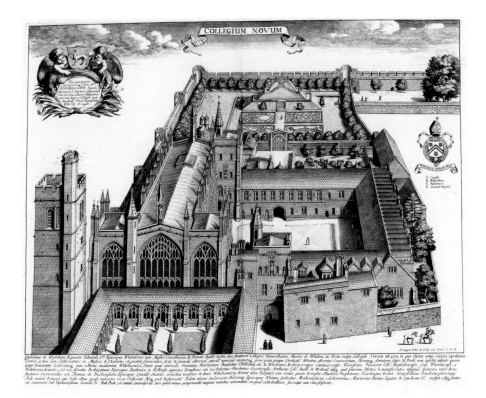

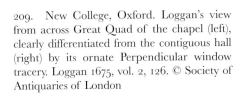

209. New College, Oxford. Loggan's view from across Great Quad of the chapel (left), clearly differentiated from the contiguous hall (right) by its ornate Perpendicular window tracery. Loggan 1675, vol. 2, 126. © Society of Antiquaries of London

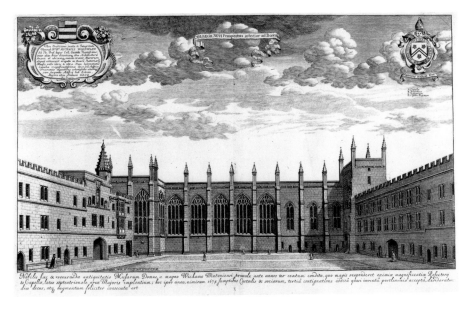

Winchester, William Wynford.[14] (fig. 208) The architectural integration of food for the body and food for the soul that it initiated had the effect of properly reducing the hall to no more than *primus inter pares*, and hardly that since the chapel was emphasized no less than the hall, and has more ornate Perpendicular tracery as well. (fig. 209) Repeated again at St John's and All Souls, founded at the instigation of Archbishop Chichele in 1437 and 1438 respectively,[15] the arrangement was modified for another bishop of Winchester, William of Wayneflete, who founded Magdalen College in 1459. Its Great Quadrangle was built about 1473–80 with one side devoted to the chapel and hall, the latter set once again over an undercroft.[16]

These episcopal foundations raised the domestic courtyard with its dominating hall to a peak of development. The remarkable combination of ambition and opportunity on which they capitalized, together with a lavishly conceived architectural aim, set them apart from other courtyards with a domestic purpose. In the more crowded and transient realm of their London lodgings, ecclesiastics had to make do with either as little as a commodious but rather small

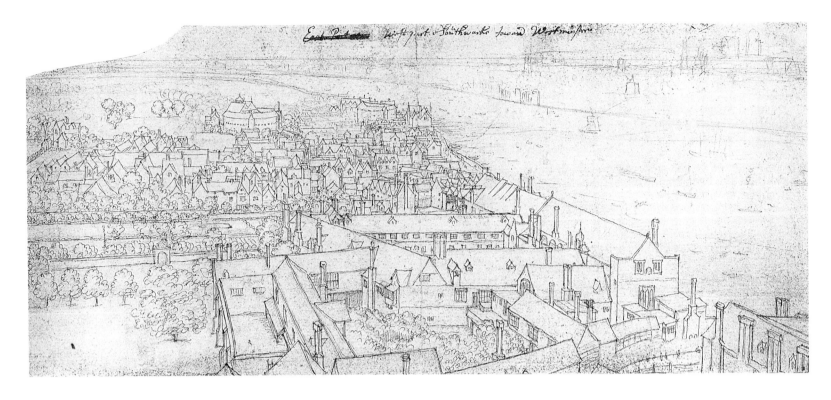

210. Winchester House, Southwark. Hollar's view of 1647, showing the Great Hall on the right, overlooking the river, with the service block beyond it, and extending to its left, a courtyard formed by two ranges accommodating the squire's chamber on the further side, and the knight's chamber on the nearer side, flanked by the chapel; in the centre foreground is a privy courtyard and the bishop's quarters, and to the left part of the extensive gardens. © Yale Center for British Art, Paul Mellon Collection

211. Winchester House, Southwark. The Great Hall showing the oculus and triple service doors. After a view by F. T. Dollman in the Guildhall Library, London. © Society of Antiquaries of London

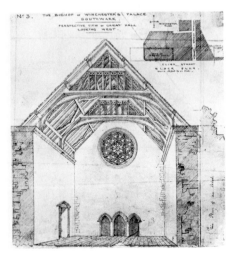

house, perhaps purchased from some other magnate when he had done with it, or an inn, usually embracing a courtyard, that grew with changing needs over the centuries until the Reformation put a brake on the Church and its medieval ways.

Well before the Conquest, magnates of all kinds felt drawn to London on account of its pre-eminent wealth. Whatever their relationship with the monarch of the day, bishops and lesser churchmen needed to attend court. As this increasingly met at Westminster, particularly with the construction of William Rufus's new hall at the end of the eleventh century, they built themselves palaces, or inns as they were commonly called, nearby to fit their station. By the end of the Middle Ages both archbishops, all the bishops except St Asaph's, and at least twenty-two abbots and six priors had built themselves a town house in London or its suburbs. This accommodated a permanent establishment that dealt with the economic business and administration of the see and, when they were in residence, provided all the worldly symbols of their rank and the necessary luxury for themselves and their guests. The bishop of Winchester Henry of Blois spoke for them all when he explained that he built in town so as to find a remedy for 'many inconveniences and losses that I and my predecessors have sustained through the lack of a house to use for royal business and other affairs in the neighbourhood of London'. Therefore, he continued, 'I have procured the house and land that were of Orgar the Rich and many other lands lying around them of the soke of the church and monks of Bermondsey.'[17]

None did so well as the powerful abbots of Cluny in Paris. They set up house on the left bank of the Seine, close to the bridge leading to the Palais Royale and Nôtre Dame, on a site that had the symbolically powerful advantage of allowing them to build their *hôtel* against the remains of the Gallo-Roman baths of Lutetia Parisiorum, thus giving it an air of ancient yet mysterious validity.[18]

While a few of the English episcopal inns were in the City itself, most bishops avoided the jurisdiction of the bishop of London. Wanting to live beside the Thames so that they could proceed in state to Westminster by barge, they chose the north bank along the Strand or the south bank at Southwark. The archbishop of Canterbury settled at Lambeth, upstream from the royal palace, and the archbishop of York at Westminster itself, presumably to upstage Canterbury, and preferring to process from what is now Whitehall rather than trust the waters of the Thames.[19]

Extensive records of these great houses survive, and even substantial fragments of a few of them. On the Southwark bank of the Thames the bishops of Winchester built up a new establishment close to the priory of St Mary Overie,[20] with a small quay for their barge between them. Winchester House appears in several seventeenth-century views, notably Wenceslaus Hollar's of 1647, by which time it had grown to include several ranges of buildings set around inner and outer courtyards. (fig. 210) Beside the river lay the great hall, raised over an undercroft as were all the ranges adjacent to it, as a precaution against floods and to make a greater show. On the landward side two ranges comprising a squire's chamber to the west and a knight's chamber and a chapel to the east embraced an inner court, beyond which Hollar shows an outer court and ranges with a more lowly function, opening on to pleasant gardens.[21]

The only substantial fragment to survive includes the walls of the vaulted undercroft that lay beneath the great hall and most of its western wall. (fig. 211) This still retains the triple doorways that led into the service range, while filling the gable above is a traceried oculus that stands comparison with the wheel at St David's. It makes great play of cusped triangles, a fashionable device in the early fourteenth century with symbolic implications. At its centre is a hexagonal wheel comprising twelve daggers, alternately six large and six small, like a miniature version of the St David's wheel, and around this are eighteen interlocking cusped equilateral triangles, six based on the hexagon and pointing outwards, twelve arranged as six pairs and pointing inwards. Were the coloured glass still in place, the symbolism of these numbers might be explicit, since the bishop who commanded it was surely interested in more than showing off his mason's artistic skill.

Beyond Winchester House lay a few cottages, occupied by watermen and some of the women known as the bishop's 'geese', before un-reclaimed marsh took over the great curve in the south bank. Then, upstream at Lambeth, near the landing place of an ancient river ferry, lies the archbishop of Canterbury's palace. (fig. 212) Like the bishops of Winchester, the archbishops had owned their site from the later twelfth century, having already had a lease from long beforehand. Notwithstanding the recent completion of the new works to Canterbury in 1184, Archbishop Baldwin determined to replace his cathedral in far away Kent with a new one closer to the centre of power at Westminster, so building was started here in Lambeth. However, the fate of the Holy Land was also on his mind, and, before construction had progressed far, he took off on the third Crusade only to fall sick and die in 1190 before the walls of Acre. His church was eventually abandoned.[22]

Early in the thirteenth century a chapel undercroft was built,[23] probably in Archbishop Langton's time, and the chapel itself, rebuilt after wartime destruction, retains a doorway, window openings and shafting of about 1230. These lie on the north side of a small courtyard facing the principal hall on the south, which was rebuilt after destruction during the Commonwealth. On the east side of the courtyard there is a further hall, a small affair of four bays, raised over an undercroft and rebuilt in the nineteenth century but reusing a fourteenth-century arch-braced timber roof. This was part of the archbishop's private residence, which extended further eastwards, now all replaced. Opposite lay a large outer court, open to the Thames, with the great hall flanked by a gatehouse and three towers clustered around the chapel.

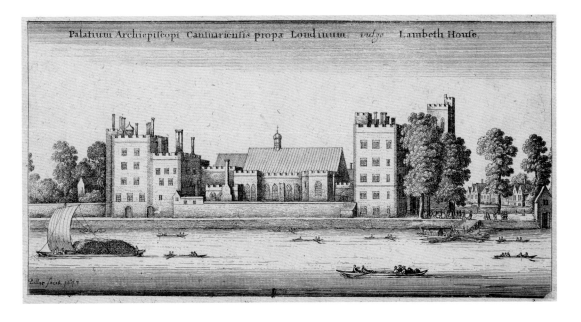

212. Lambeth Palace. Hollar's view of 1647, showing the medieval Great Hall in the centre flanked by Chichele's Water Tower (left) and Morton's gatehouse tower (right); further to the right is the tower of Lambeth parish church. © Lambeth Palace Library

213. The tower of Pountney's (Pulteney's) Inn (centre), with his Great Hall behind it and the steeple of the church of St Lawrence Pountney (above right). From Wyngaerde's *Panorama, c.* 1544, see Colvin and Foister 1996, drawing 7. © Ashmolean Museum, Oxford

The pedigree of the gatehouse began in classical times, and may be traced through openings in Saxon town walls, the towers that often accompanied these,[24] and, latterly, the fortified entrances to castles. Traditionally they were the lodging of a castle's constable, who needed to control entry, but they came to be lodgings for any important servant and guests as well. Archbishop Morton's five-storeyed gatehouse, which was built as lodgings for senior members of his household, is notable for its construction in red brick, proudly diapered in black, an innovation even in the last decade of the fifteenth century when Morton, a notable protagonist of brick, ordered its construction.

Of the towers set around the chapel the earlier four-storeyed Lollards' Tower or Water Tower formerly projected from the banks of the river and, from the time of its completion in 1435, allowed Archbishop Chichele and his successors unparalleled views of Westminster.[25] Many establishments were embellished with a tower of this kind, a well-established badge of a noble residence. Henry III, after all, had already built two towers for the royal chambers in about 1240 at his new residence at the Tower.[26] In 1305 William Servat had a licence to crenellate a tower which he built over the gate to his house in Bucklersbury, and Sir John de Pulteney's City inn was graced with an embattled tower, to which a licence to crenellate of 1343 may apply. (fig. 213) At about this time, the widow of Aymer Valence, Earl of Pembroke, was responsible for building yet another tower at the family inn near Ludgate, which was reported to be encroaching on Ave Maria Lane in 1358.[27] While halls might have an embattled parapet, a sign of chivalrous rather than military intent, a tower was understood to symbolize magnificence even though its progenitors were the defensive towers of the internecine nobility that blooded the streets of Italian city states.

Symbolic towers, complete with suites of rooms, were popular on the Continent, for instance the two built respectively after 1363 and in the 1440s by the dukes of Burgundy at their palace in Dijon,[28] just as they were in London in such long-vanished Thames-side establishments as the second Baynard's Castle and the second Coldharbour. In Bristol at Canynges's House, which was occupied by a prominent mercantile family in the fourteenth and fifteenth centuries, the younger William Canynges had built a tower by 1455 with four bay windows looking out over Redcliffe Back and the Avon.[29]

Still the most spectacular of these otherwise mostly lost towers was built at Thomas Burgh's command to enhance Gainsborough Old Hall, probably in time for Richard III's visit in October 1483, soon after which Burgh was created Knight of the Garter. (fig. 214) He was one of the few courtiers crafty enough to square his political ambitions with both Lancastrians and Yorkists, finally to be summoned as Baron Gainsborough to parliament by Henry VII as his councillor.[30] In 1462 he began the construction of his house at Gainsborough, probably as a result of marriage to Margaret Roos. In essence 'a major country house in an urban setting',[31]

214. Gainsborough Old Hall. The north front with the brick tower on the left and the hall with its prominent, later stone oriel window in the centre

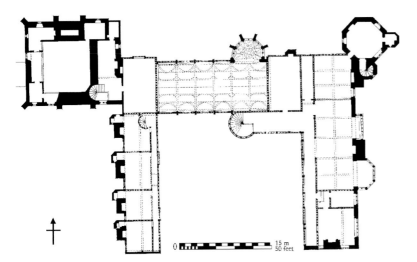

215. Gainsborough Old Hall. Plan, showing the Great Hall (centre), with its roof timbers (hatched); in the west wing (left) a corridor serves the four bays of lodgings, each one with a projecting fireplace and adjacent privy; the north-west corner block contains the large kitchen; this is balanced in the north-east corner by the octagonal tower; and in the east wing are the state apartments, again served by a corridor. After Faulkner 1970, fig. 7. © Royal Archaeological Institute

216. Gainsborough Old Hall. The south front, with the west wing of lodgings on the left

its spacious grounds took in a whole quarter of this small port on the banks of the river Trent. Apart from its site, Gainsborough Old Hall's rural qualities show in its outward-facing appearance, its north side open to the river and the parish church, its southern side in the form of an open courtyard facing the town; but much of its outer buildings together with an encircling moat have gone. While it lacks an enclosed yard faced with shops and an entrance gate, its overall accommodation could be found in many a magnate's town house.[32]

The first phase of Gainsborough Old Hall, completed by 1470, comprises a central timber-framed open hall in a range that continues at each end. (figs 215 and 216) Beyond the hall's screens passage, entrances and triple service doors, the west end accommodated a buttery and pantry with a chamber above, and further on lay a large, formerly detached kitchen, built of brick, partly with safety in mind. The east end accommodated a great parlour with an upper chamber. Beyond this in a great southerly-projecting two-storeyed wing are the elaborate state apartments in which Richard probably stayed in 1483. By that time, however, Burgh had fallen foul of the county's envious Lancastrians, who had rebelled and damaged the house, if not destroying parts of it. Reinstated, Burgh made repairs, joined the kitchen to the main range to form a servery, and was completing, if not rebuilding, a balancing range of apartments in a wing projecting southward on the western side, and also 'the lowe towre'[33] of three storeys at the north-east corner.

While the timber framing lacks carved decoration, the brick chimney stacks and tower cut a dash, even though brickwork was by no means new in the county. More significantly, the domestic arrangements must have been both up to date and singularly lavish, and included much wall-painting. How the eastern wing was first arranged is unclear, but it seems to have accommodated a large heated room flanked by smaller ones connected by a corridor on the upper floor with a simpler arrangement below. Some of the unheated rooms were probably bedchambers, the heated rooms parlours. Following the addition of the three-storeyed tower in the early 1480s the ensemble formed three suites of ascending magnificence, their rooms linked by corridors, themselves a remarkable innovation. The lowliest suite was a single chamber on the ground floor at the southern end of the wing, which could have been for the personal servant of the occupants of the second suite. This comprised a heated outer chamber and an inner chamber in the rest of the wing with access to a third chamber in the base of the tower, which was both heated and served by a garderobe. On the floor above, the southernmost chamber was partitioned to form an anteroom and a small closet. This probably served the most splendid suite of all, comprising four rooms: a heated outer chamber and an inner chamber that led directly onwards to the first-floor chamber in the tower, and a further chamber on the second floor, and, finally, the look-out on the tower roof. Which were the state apartments and which for Burgh and his family is unclear, but he certainly occupied part of this wing and did so in style.

The arrangements in the west wing are quite different, (fig. 217) and based on the repetition on three floors of four units per floor, each comprising a single chamber with a fireplace and an

217. Gainsborough Old Hall. Section showing the apartments in the west wing, with a fireplace and the entrance to a privy on its right in each of the four bays on all three storeys. After Lindley 1991, 52, fig. 13. © The Society of Lincolnshire History and Archaeology, and M. V. Clark

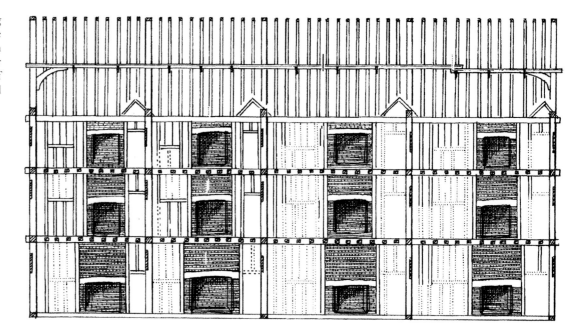

218. Gainsborough Old Hall. The chimney-stacks and garderobes of the west wing

adjacent garderobe built into a projecting brick stack.[34] (fig. 218) The position of the staircases and yet more corridors suggest that the resulting twelve units formed five suites; a suite of 4 chambers on the top floor; one of 2 chambers on the middle floor; with another of 2 chambers on the ground floor beneath; and two more suites, each of 2 chambers set one over the other on the ground and middle floors. Here Burgh accommodated the senior members of his household, each according to status, and probably some of his guests as well.

These complex and varied arrangements, based on a central hall, could be found in London and many a provincial town. The advancing standards of the late Middle Ages and the increasingly large households of the time could not be served without them. The bishop of Bath's inn[35] came perhaps as close as any to Gainsborough Old Hall's lavish arrangements.[36] It occupied a large site between the Strand and the Thames, with its gatehouse set well back from the street and opening into a large courtyard. On the further side was the hall, which had probably been built in the first half of the fourteenth century rather archaically as a free-standing

219. Arundel House (formerly the bishop of Bath's Inn). Hollar's view of 1646, showing the main courtyard from the south, with the hall towards the right, behind the group of three men

Aula Domus Arrundeliana Londini.   Septentrionem versus.

structure of five bays with a large entrance porch at its low end. (fig. 219) There seems to have been a parlour block and, contemporary with the hall, a vaulted undercroft. Beyond the hall, extensive orchards and gardens swept down to the river. Both the courtyard and the gardens were flanked by ranges of buildings, mostly rebuilt after the bishops had departed, such as an extensive service wing and a kitchen court, partly built over an ancient undercroft, and lodgings, storehouses, stables and a barn; but there were also several tenements, recorded in 1509 as the Tabard, le Cardinal's Hat and the Keeper's Mansion. By this time the inn was in a state of transition, the tenements serving commercially for travellers, and the very name 'inn' was superseding the older term 'hospice' for lodgings of this sort.

The abbot of St Augustine's, Canterbury, the abbots of Battle and Hyde, the priors of Lewes and of Christ Church, Canterbury, and the Earl of Warenne were among the principal magnates who built their inns in the borough during the later twelfth and thirteenth centuries, and these grew with the needs of their occupants. Many of them had extensive accommodation for guests which was let out during their master's absence, even to

Men so disorder'd, so debauch'd, and bold,
That this our court, infected with their manners,
Shows like a riotous inn: epicurism and lust
Make it more like a tavern or a brothel,
Than a graced palace.[37]

Southwark was well placed to accommodate all the needs of travellers, and its inns readily evolved into commercial undertakings. Long vanished, they are known for their undercrofts, halls and chapels, gateways, chambers and lodgings, service rooms and kitchens, gardens, orchards and even vineyards.[38] The most celebrated of these was the abbot of Hyde's inn,[39] part of which became 'this gentil hostelrye, That highte the Tabard, fastè by the Belle', where 'The chambres and the stables weren wyde, And wel we weren esèd attè beste'.[40]

What the fourteenth century began, the Dissolution completed. It quickly put paid to ecclesiastical ownership and converted inns to commercial use. The prior of Christ Church's inn became the Flower de Luce, a commonly adopted anglicization of *fleur-de-lis* that was invested with the quaint etymology *fleur delice* and hence erotic connotations,[41] and Lewes's Inn 'is now a common hosterie for travellers, and hath to sign the Walnut Tree'. Was that name erotic too?[42]

The remainder of Southwark's medieval inns followed the pattern quickly established on the further side of the river by passing into the hands of the new Tudor aristocracy, to be split up and rebuilt for their new owners. At the start of the sixteenth century, London's western suburbs were dominated by the inns of Church dignitaries, many of these having grown venerable during at least three hundred years of service while room was piled upon room. Five small inns lay within the City on the west side of the Fleet river around St Bride's, but the greater ones were closer to Westminster. The inns of the bishops of Bath, Carlisle, Durham, Exeter and Norwich all enjoyed the salubrious atmosphere of the Strand and pleasant views up and down

220. Lincoln's Inn, Holborn. The old hall of 1489–92, from an engraving of 1805 by Samuel Rawle, showing the unusual symmetrical arrangement of oriel windows, those at the screens end (to the left) being an addition together with an extension of the hall executed in 1583. Comprehensively restored in 1924–8, the hall now looks rather different (i.e. with an embattled parapet and a Gothic lantern). To the right are the three bays of the chapel, built in 1619–23, again in Gothic, 'answerable' to neighbouring buildings in the Inn. © The Treasurer and the Masters of the Bench of Lincoln's Inn

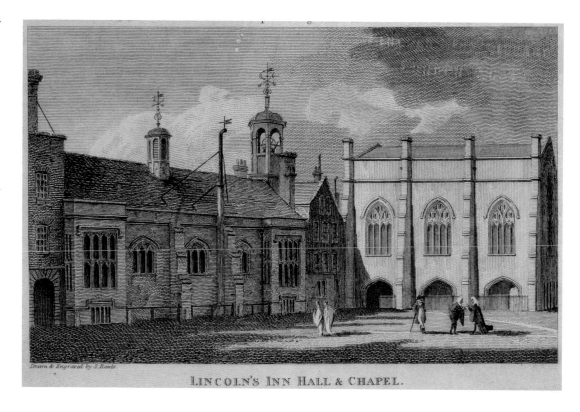

Drawn & Engraved by S. Rawle.

LINCOLN'S INN HALL & CHAPEL.

stream. They survived long enough to appear in Hollar's bird's-eye view of west London of about 1656 and had by then been bought up by secular magnates or become commercial inns.

A different fate befell the inn of the bishops of Chichester. This lay to the north of the Strand and to the west of a new street which became Chancery Lane on a site that Henry III had granted to his chancellor, Bishop Neville, in 1227. In 1422 one of his successors leased the inn, which already seems to have included a chapel or did so soon afterwards, to apprentices of the Common Law who called themselves the Society of Lincoln's Inn. (fig. 220) Before the century was out they had built eleven new chambers and, in 1489–92, rebuilt the hall in brick with four bays set over an undercroft. Early in the new century, the brick-maker John Frankham had manufactured 200,000 bricks from clay dug on site and, in 1506–8, these went into the construction of a new range that included a council chamber. There followed a four-storeyed brick court of chambers and a gatehouse, completed by 1520, which echoed the archbishop's gatehouse at Lambeth with diapering in vitrified header bricks, and further chambers were added, forming a south range in 1525–34. Despite the piecemeal construction, Lincoln's Inn had all the ingredients of a university college, the only difference being that the chambers doubled as offices. Largely rebuilt, the external form and a little of the fabric of all these buildings survive, including the hall's arch-braced roof.[43]

Inns of court were not the only urban institutions that required large establishments of this sort for the accommodation of their members and the formalities that bolstered their prestige. The easy extensions of meaning resulting from the lack of distinguishing features in the buildings themselves allowed grand medieval inns comprising a large hall and attendant service rooms, private rooms and chambers to be put to the uses of city companies, as well as those of the law, of academic learning, and of travellers. A magnate's inn would concentrate on a grand hall for show, and a principal suite of chambers for himself, perhaps a state suite as well, and ancillary suites for his entourage and guests. An episcopal inn might stretch to two halls. An institutional inn would require a fine hall for its formal gatherings, but it also catered for the needs of business in its provision of private parlours where this would be conducted, but had few or no chambers for domestic occupation. An inn for travellers would instead concentrate on rooms for entertainment, large chambers or dormitories where many beds could be set up for those who had no use for privacy, and smaller chambers for sleeping in private, all these at the expense of a lavish hall, which might become little more than a public drinking and eating room.

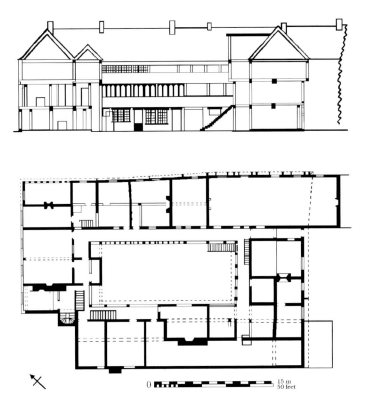

221. New Inn, Gloucester. General plan and section and elevation of the eastern range of the galleried courtyard. Based on Pantin 1961, figs 9.2 and 9.3

The plan that was particularly favoured for large commercial inns for travellers embraced a semi-public courtyard, entered from the street, with the hall sited along one side of the yard, facing parlours and ale rooms opposite.[44] The hall was not of prime importance since formality and a hierarchy of spaces mattered to neither innkeeper nor travellers, and so could do without the status of a central position. This left the front of the inn free for a wide carriage entrance set between more ale rooms or shops, and the rear for stabling and coaches. Ale rooms came in all sizes so that they might cater for those who were 'Hail, fellow, well met, all dirty and wet', and those who preferred intimacy, wit, and dry, wry natter. Some of them were therefore partitioned to form 'dryngkynge bowers', as recorded in the 1540s in the Tabard at Southwark, and fitted with benches.[45]

A large inn with its accommodation arranged around a courtyard well suited the needs of pilgrims, merchants and other visitors, or travellers who needed to stop for a night along a major coaching route. None was greater than Gloucester's New Inn. It lies close to the abbey of St Peter[46] and was rebuilt 'from the foundations' in 1432 or soon afterwards by one of its monks, the laudable John Twynnyng, for the abbey's benefit,[47] and known in 1455 as '*magnum et novum hospitium vocatum "Newyn"*'. It retains much of its original framing as well as four galleried ranges that form a courtyard. (fig. 221) This is still reached from Northgate Street through an archway, flanked by shops. Three of the ranges are of three storeys, but the south side is different. Here, the eye of faith can make out what remains of a small, possibly open hall, with a parlour at one end and services and perhaps a kitchen at the other, while the north side of the yard was entirely devoted to parlours where parties of guests, large or small, could eat and drink with a degree of intimacy. At the further, eastern end of the yard there is a gateway that once led to a rear yard with stabling and further galleries with chambers opening off them, all now disappeared, but once extending 137 feet (41.8 m) in all from Northgate Street. Additionally, at one time, there were gardens and a passage, lined with lodgings, leading to Eastgate Street.

A flight of stairs, now moved to a new position in the yard, rises to an open gallery which runs right around the first floor, and to further stairs rising to another open gallery along three sides of the yard at the top, but not along the putative hall range. Galleries of this kind were to become an abiding feature of inns for several centuries to come. (fig. 222) They were also used by the audiences of plays that took place in the yards they overlooked, as they did at the New Inn in the sixteenth century. Soon they were adapted for the new round theatres. The New

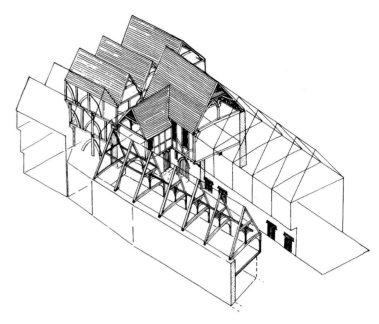

222. The Tabard Inn, St Albans. The fourteenth-century galleried courtyard as recorded by J. C. Buckler in 1824 before alterations left only a small part recognizable. © Hertfordshire Archives and Local Studies

223. The New Inn, Cornmarket, Oxford. View showing the three surviving shops on Cornmarket (top), with the two destroyed houses in outline, and the long, narrow courtyard of the inn (right), with its two ranges of accommodation. After Munby 1993 fig. 10. © Oxford Architectural Survey

Inn's courtyard and galleries had another, occasional purpose: public announcements were made and celebrated there, most notoriously, in view of its outcome, when the hapless Lady Jane Grey was proclaimed Queen in 1553.[48] The galleries gave access to at least forty chambers, each about 17 feet (5.2 m) in depth and between 12 and 17 feet (3.5 and 5.2 m) wide, and large enough to accommodate four or more guests.[49] In all, the inn could accommodate two hundred guests and probably many more in the lost yard at the back.

The New Inn, like another inn on the site of the present Fleece Hotel whose vaulted undercroft survives, was admirably placed for such large numbers of guests. Many of them were travellers, since the lowest crossing of the river Severn was at Gloucester, and the town served routes in all directions. Traditionally, however, these inns were built to accommodate pilgrims, who were attracted in droves by the tomb of King Edward II. Murdered in notorious circumstances at Berkeley Castle in 1327, Edward was refused burial by the abbots of Bristol, Kingswood and Malmsbury, who were no doubt outraged by his and his camp followers' perverse extravagance. However, Abbot Thokey brought his body to Gloucester, where his tomb attracted pilgrims, second in number only to those going to Becket's tomb at Canterbury. Perhaps they went to lay yellow lilies on it, as they do today, or perhaps because it was said that Edward had died reverently, a hermit, in Lombardy.[50]

The courtyards of private and ecclesiastical inns were readily adapted for commercial inns for travellers in the later fourteenth century. The northern part of Marshall's Inn in Cornmarket, Oxford, was progressively built up around a courtyard before 1380 when it was still a private house, but the vintner John Gibbes began his commercial New Inn further north in Cornmarket shortly after 1386 with a fully fledged courtyard in mind from the first. (fig. 223) The timber-framed front range comprised five shops (of which three have been restored) and an entry to a yard, which was flanked by stone and timber ranges to north and south. The north range, of which hardly a third survives, may have accommodated the inn's public rooms and, above, a single open room, shown in J.C. Buckler's drawing of 1864 as unpartitioned and open to the roof, which was probably a public dormitory. A gallery joined this range to the south range, of which less is known, although its two floors may have contained a hall and another dormitory.[51] (fig. 224)

By the fifteenth century, landowners had realized the potential for profit in building timely inns on well-frequented routes. Winchester College, for instance, built the Angel at New Alresford, on the route to Farnham and London, under a contract of 1418 made with the carpenter Thomas Wolfhow, by which he would undertake to build within a year a hall, a gatehouse, and a chamber over it with a bay window overlooking the street, a plain window overlooking a garden, and a latrine behind a partition. There would be a further partitioned room, including a parlour and a larger chamber, set over an existing cellar (*selarium*), with an additional room jettied over this, and, in a separate building, a shop, a hall and a kitchen, with

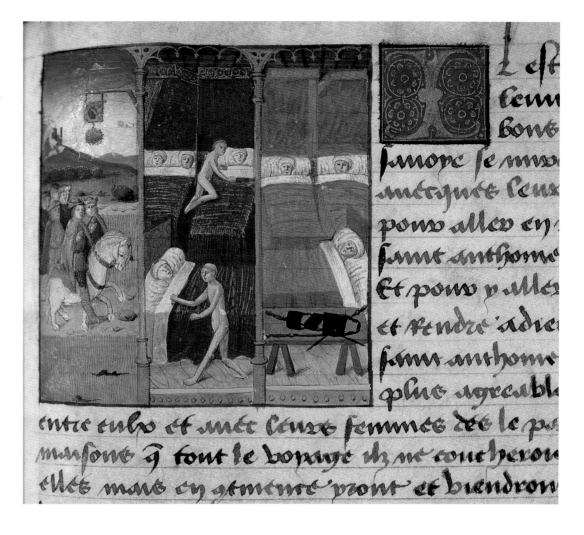

224. Fifteenth-century travellers arriving at an inn, and, in the remaining scenes, climbing, naked, into closely spaced single and double beds in a dormitory; the beds themselves offer the comforts of bolsters, linen sheets and coloured coverlets. From *Les cents nouvelles nouvelles*, Glasgow University Library, MS Hunter 252, f70r. Reproduced by kind permission of the Librarian, Glasgow University Library, Department of Special Collections

225. Eastbridge Hospital, St Peter Street, Canterbury. The aisled hall where pilgrims might stay for two nights, but no more. © Andor Gomme

a chamber above it. Winchester College would provide the timber and pay Wolfhow £50 for the job. In 1444–5 the college entered into another contract, with the carpenters John Hardyng and Richard Holnerst, to build an inn at Andover on the roads to Oxford and Bath, and, more importantly, the road between London and Salisbury. This was to have four ranges set around a courtyard, two of them with a gateway, a cellar, a hall and chambers, the other two with stables, a kitchen and more chambers.[52]

Travellers were an everyday sight on the roads of Europe, particularly pilgrims seeking numberless shrines for simple devotion or miraculous cures. The miracles associated with the shrine of the murdered Thomas à Becket attracted huge numbers to Canterbury. The first building designed to accommodate them was Eastbridge Hospital, founded in Becket's honour about 1175 by a Canterbury alderman, Edward son of Odbold. (fig. 225) It comprised an undercroft, supporting a chapel and a hall with a single aisle, in which a mural of Christ, his hand raised in blessing, is surrounded by the symbols of the Evangelists. Here poor pilgrims might stay two nights, but not more, since the last thing the hospital wanted was squatters.[53] One of its final uses before Archbishop Parker converted it to an almshouse was to serve as barracks for soldiers on their way to and from defending Calais before its fall in 1558.

Canterbury's Chequers of Hope, 'that many a man doth knowe',[54] was built in 1392–5 for £867 14s 4d as a courtyard inn, whose jettied, three-storeyed east range facing Mercery Street survived a devastating fire in 1865.[55] (fig. 226) It accommodated a 'dormitory of a hundred beds' as well as chambers, drinking rooms, and parlours. To one side lay a garden where herbs for soup and surgery grew and guests took the air:

> The wyf of Bath was so wery, she had no will to walk;
> She toke the Priores by the hond: 'madam, wol ye stalk
> Pryvely into the garden, to se the herbis grow?

226. Mercery Lane, Canterbury. The stone corner together with its openings, and the jettied ranges above are the surviving remains of the Chequers of Hope

227. Bull Inn, Burgate, Canterbury, as drawn by John Bowen. © Canterbury Archaeological Trust, 1983–4

228. Bull Inn today

And aftir, with our hostis wyff, in hir parlour rowe,
I woll gyve yewe wyne, and yee shull me also;
For tyll wee go tu soper wee have naught ellis to do.'[56]

Fully aware of the profit it could make from pilgrims and travellers, the Church invested heavily in such inns and taverns. During Prior Goldstone's time, 1449–68, Christ Church built a series of lodging chambers on the site of a stone house known as the Bull which it had built at the end of the twelfth-century. The new Bull Inn[57] comprised some thirty-eight single-roomed lodgings built around a courtyard. (fig. 227) Unlike Gloucester's New Inn, access was by a series of individual staircases, like those of college lodgings, which led up to nine separate groups of chambers on each floor, rather than by gallery, floor by floor. The north side, facing Burgate, largely survives as a three-storeyed jettied timber range, built over an undercroft, with shops on the ground floor, (fig. 228) the eastern range being similar but of only two storeys. Meanwhile, the lodgings in the western range were probably the best and may have been arranged back to back, those facing the yard perhaps having enclosed hearths set into brick chimney stacks. Lacking evidence for a hall, parlours, services and kitchen (which might have been accommodated in the lost southern range), the Bull may not have been a commercial inn in the fullest sense but just a large lodging house or hospice.[58]

The Maison Dieu that Hubert de Burgh founded about 1221 at Dover for the benefit of poor infirm pilgrims was again a response to the attraction of Becket's shrine at Canterbury, as well as Dover's role as the prime cross-Channel port. By the fourteenth century this included a hall, set over a vaulted undercroft, that served in a similar way to a monastic dorter or dormitory. Another similar inn, of which a little survives as the priory at Cricklade, was founded before 1231 as the Hospital of St John the Baptist, a *senodochium* or hostel for poor travellers on the ancient road to Cirencester.

These hostels or hospices were widespread. The framed building of Coffee Yard, just off Stonegate in York, now called Barley Hall, comprises a three-storeyed range of 1359–60 and an open hall of the late fifteenth century attached at right angles. (fig. 229) The older range was the town house of Nostell Priory, and probably served as a hospice with its main accommodation for travellers in a single chamber occupying all the six bays on the first floor and reached by an external stair.[59]

Probably the earliest hospice in Scotland was set up in St Andrews by royal and episcopal clerks, known as culdees, to accommodate six pilgrims to the shrine of St Andrew. In 1144

Bishop Robert enlarged it and put it into the care of the cathedral's Augustinian canons. So it remained until the fifteenth century when it became an almshouse for aged women. They 'gave little or no return in devotion or virtue' so in 1512 it was converted into the College of Poor Clerks for the education of Augustinian novices, and its buildings – a rather makeshift arrangement of the old hospital and chapel around a long courtyard with all the recent additions – became part of the university.[60]

Visiting merchants, as well as pilgrims and travellers, needed accommodation, and most ancient market places therefore have at least one inn overlooking them. Among these, the King's Head at Aylesbury is memorable for the magnificent window of its fifteenth-century hall: a mullion and a transom quarter it, and each quarter contains five lights, the upper ones with four-centred heads and stained glass with angels and the arms of Henry VI and Margaret of Anjou.[61] The Booth Hall at Evesham, clearly built as an encroachment on the Market Place, has all the appearance of a market hall, its ground floor accommodating shops and its twin two-storeyed gabled ranges suggesting a civic use. (fig. 230) According to tradition, however, it was built in the late fifteenth century as an inn, and accommodated cloth merchants, not their trade. In the 1580s it gained notoriety for the town court that met there in opposition to what had been the abbot of Evesham's separate court, which, after the Dissolution, Sir Philip Hoby had purchased from the Crown.[62]

By far the most impressive inn is the White Hart at Newark, where travellers dealing in market trade jostled with those on the Great North Road. (fig. 102) An ornate three-storeyed timber-framed range facing the street, probably built in the mid 1460s,[63] comprises shops and an entrance arch to a courtyard. Painting, carving, and bands of windows stretching the whole width of the two upper storeys are as impressive as those of any late medieval framed building

230. Booth Hall, Evesham

FACING PAGE
232. The Angel, Grantham, as it is today

233. The Angel, Grantham, an ideal setting for medieval hospitality (below), contrasting with a faceless Georgian gin palace, the Angel at Oxford, an open door to inebriation, licentiousness and crime, as depicted in Pugin's *Contrasts*. © Society of Antiquaries of London

in the land. The buildings within the yard include the remains of an earlier range, probably including a hall, built shortly after 1313,[64] on the south side, and, on the north, galleries with two storeys of chambers, of the later fifteenth century.[65]

London was a special case because of its multitude of affluent visitors and the pressures on space. It too had its courtyard inns, the Crowne being one of those recorded by Ralph Treswell early in the seventeenth century.[66] (fig. 231) By then the inn had a long history of ownership beginning in the late twelfth century when Holy Trinity Priory granted a long strip of land in Aldgate to a succession of owners. It comprised a front yard opening off Aldgate flanked by a hall, parlour and kitchen, while a yard at the rear served eight stables with hay lofts and small warehouses. In all, there were twenty individual chambers, most of them with fireplaces when the survey was made.

The ranges of chambers, as opposed to the open dormitories of earlier inns, were the most important innovation of the fifteenth century, giving visitors privacy for business as well as pleasure. A surviving range of chambers, perhaps rather like those at Alresford, added to the Blue Boar Inn at Salisbury, was the subject of a contract of 1444 between the city's most important fifteenth-century landowner William Ludlow and the carpenter John Fayrebowe. The upper floor contained a small heated chamber reached by one staircase, probably for visitors willing to pay a premium for the luxury of a fire and privacy, and a much larger unheated room reached by a second stair that probably served as a communal dormitory.[67]

231. The Crowne Inn, Aldgate, London. The entrance to the inn is on the right (1) beside a pair of chambers (2); this gives on to a small yard, with entrances to a newel staircase and to the hall (3), which is separated from a parlour (4) by a brick chimney-stack with back-to-back hearths heating both rooms; beside this there is a kitchen (5) and then a chamber (6); after this, the yard opens out to be lined with stables and hay lofts, and a small passage (7) leads out into a garden on the extreme left. After a survey by Thomas Treswell, reproduced in Schofield 1987, fig. 6

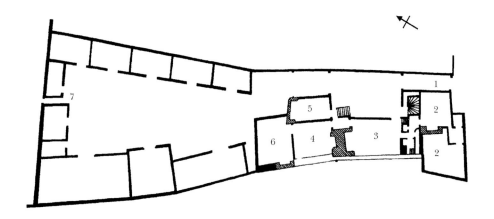

ANGEL INN OXFORD

Smaller inns put all their goods in the front window, and their yards at the back were reserved for service rooms and stabling. The Angel at Grantham was celebrated by Welby Pugin as an exemplar of 'Pointed or Christian Architecture' that served the needs of honest travellers on the Great North Road seeking a simple bed, roast beef and a flagon of real ale.[68] (figs 232 and 233) It was founded by the Knights Templars, taken over by the Hospitallers, and built in its present form in the later fifteenth century as a two-storeyed stone gatehouse with a central archway flanked by prominent buttresses and canted bay windows to each side. The ground-floor windows lit two main rooms, that to the left rather more elaborately finished, perhaps serving as a private parlour, the other being a public hall, and there were probably chambers upstairs. Everything to the rear was built much later, but may have replaced earlier services and stables.[69]

Lacking the Angel's near symmetry, the contemporary George Inn at Glastonbury is nevertheless more ornately decorated. (fig. 234) Built by Abbot Selwood for pilgrims, it carries the arms of Edward IV, and two shields, one blank, the other bearing the cross of St George. A bay-windowed public room to the left of the entrance arch is matched by a single narrow room on the other side. The bay rises the full three storeys, continuing the line of the overall traceried Perpendicular panelling that makes this inn so appealing. Unlike the Angel, the George was planned as a double pile, with a large heated room at the rear and, on the opposite side of the archway, a newel staircase to the chambers above. Behind the inn, facing a courtyard, lay a single range, again probably for services and stables, but not coaches. The entrance passage, little over 7 feet (2 m) wide, is unable to admit them, but only horses and pedestrians, like the entrance passage at the similar Fleur-de-Lys at Canterbury. The Fleur-de-Lys, however, was built early in the sixteenth century of timber, not stone, and its fireplaces were built in the newly adopted way of south-east England. Their back-to-back hearths, serving both front and back rooms, were enclosed in a single brick stack, standing free of the frame, while a newel staircase took advantage of its support and wound up its side to the upper rooms, which were similarly heated.[70]

The dean and chapter of Lincoln either built an inn or converted a stone house at the junction of High Street and Grantham Street to give it a similar plan in the fifteenth century. Known as the Cardinal's Hat, perhaps to commemorate Bishop Thomas Wolsey's appointment as a cardinal in 1515, it formerly had a long stone range running back from High Street beside a yard and comprising an open hall with a screens passage, a buttery, kitchen, brew-house, and beer-house, and, later, a timber-framed range facing the street with parlours, and chambers on the two upper floors.[71]

From the fourteenth century onwards, if not beforehand, commercial inns had detached themselves from

234. The George, Glastonbury. © Andor Gomme

the ecclesiastical establishments that gave them their birth. The lodgings for travellers that monasteries provided beside and within their gatehouses continued to serve travellers who could plan their journeys with stops wherever there was a suitable monastery, but their accommodation was limited, both in amount and in the services they offered, and their location in any case ruled out several towns.

Winchester's abbeys were not without accommodation of this kind, but demand had moved on. Its innkeepers are first recorded exploiting this trade in 1361, but that is long after they had set up their first commercial houses under the signs of the Tabard and the Chequer. The record is confusing because similar names were also applied to purely domestic inns, which were readily put to commercial use, and also to taverns, to which lodgings for travellers were easily added. Nonetheless, early in the fifteenth century commercial inns were concentrated in the central part of High Street, where they served the city's trade. None approached the accommodation of Gloucester's New Inn, nor had more than half its frontage or probably more than a dozen or so bedchambers each. Even when the Chequer absorbed the Tabard next door about 1600 it only boasted twenty-six chambers, each one with a coy name such as 'Adam and Eve', or 'Flower de Luce'. Another was the Bell's 'Maydenhead Chamber', which, for all it may have attracted customers looking for one or delighted couples intent on leaving one behind, in fact referred to the saucy name of an adjacent latrine.[72]

An inventory of 1639 records the names of rooms in Oxford's inns and taverns as the Crown, the Rose, the Flower de Luce, the Sun, the Three Tuns, the Angel, the Cross Keys, the Bell, the Lyon, the Fountain, the Castle, the Star, and the Moon, and these popular names, though they sound like the inns themselves, may have been given to either bedchambers or drinking parlours,[73] a practice that still continues. By 1639 the commercial inn was enjoying a long-lasting heyday, and had a near monopoly of the word 'inn'. Besides, like the monasteries, the monastic inn had been suppressed for a century.

Below the level of the inns of great magnates and the related academic colleges, inns of court and traveller's inns, there came the numerous houses of well-to-do clerics, civic dignitaries, merchants and craftsmen that embraced a yard of sorts and were a cut above the houses that were built directly on to the street or with the merest passages for access. Such houses abound in the cathedral close, although their yards took time to evolve and sometimes to vanish through being filled in. At Salisbury the North Canonry at 60 The Close grew between the thirteenth and sixteenth centuries through successive building and rebuilding campaigns to embrace an open courtyard.[74] Meanwhile at the Bishop's Palace, Poore's Hall was rebuilt further to the east at some time before 1470, and this allowed a yard to be formed between it and the formerly attached undercroft, but by 1663 the hall had become ruinous and the yard had been filled in piecemeal by new building.[75]

The Bishop's House and the interlocking Priory House at Ely again embraced a series of courtyards as they extended with ancillary buildings joining their halls and undercrofts between the twelfth and sixteenth centuries.[76] The house that Antony Bek, chancellor of Lincoln, built up after 1321 'for recreation and enjoyment after continual preaching and study' was on the grandest scale, comprising a great hall dividing a front courtyard from another at the back.[77] John Gunthorpe, dean of Wells (1472–98) and in 1480 Edward IV's Lord Keeper of

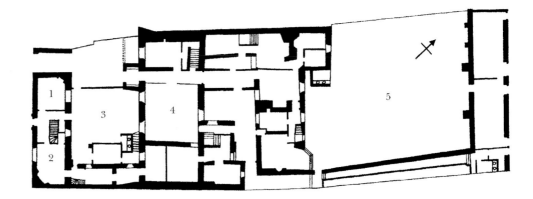

235. 7 The Close, Exeter. Plan showing gateway from the cathedral close on the left, with a parlour (1) and kitchen (2) facing outward and a small yard and garden (3) behind them, set before the entrance porch to the open hall (4), beyond which are private service rooms and parlours with chambers over them, and then a large garden (5) separated from Egypt Lane at the rear by a stable block. © D. Portman 1966, fig. 9

236. Hampton Court, King's Lynn. Perspective showing warehouse range in foreground, hall range behind it, and street range with entrance archway at the rear. © V. Parker 1971, fig. 8

237. Hampton Court, King's Lynn. Plan, showing the arcade beneath the warehouse in the western range (1), a counting-house (2) and chamber (3) in the southern range, to the left of an open hall (4) with a fireplace set into a partition wall, and, beyond three arched doorways, service rooms (5) to its right, and, in the eastern range, a row of shops flanking the entrance from the street (6); the later, northern range contains further service rooms. After Pantin 1962–3b fig. 75. © Society for Medieval Archaeology

the Privy Seal, built himself a splendid deanery with a gatehouse opening on to an outer court formed by stores and service rooms and perhaps a private chapel, and an inner court with a hall on one side and a kitchen, services and chambers completing it.[78] In Exeter there is a sequence of courtyard houses in the Close, starting at No. 7, (fig. 235) and then 8–9a, a canon's house, which has an archway leading to the hall, at right angles to the street. The archdeacon of Barnstaple's house at 10–11 began in the fourteenth century as a simple range along the street that included a hall, but was expanded about 1500 to form a courtyard with a new hall and a rear two-storeyed range for parlours with chambers over them.[79] Finally comes the gate-house of the abbot of Buckfast's courtyard house at No. 12.[80]

Affluent merchants applied a similar process to their houses as they built up their fortunes. Some of them included commercial premises around yards that took on an important role as the heart of the establishment's activities. The clearest example of this is Hampton Court at King's Lynn, which fronts Nelson Street with a row of shops and a central archway leading to a courtyard. (figs 236 and 237) On one side of the yard lies a fourteenth-century hall with service rooms adjoining it at the street end and, at the other, private rooms comprising a parlour

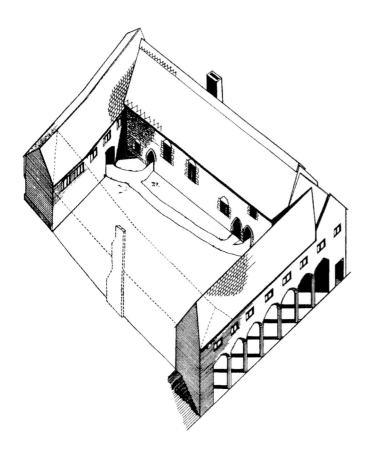

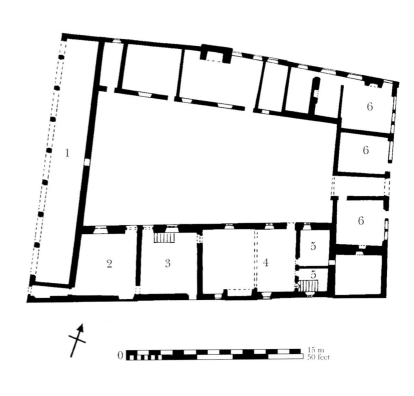

238. Hampton Court, King's Lynn. The arcade (now blocked) of the warehouse range, once directly facing the quayside

239. (below, left) The Steelyard, London, shown in Wyngaerde's *Panorama*, *c.* 1544, immediately above the tower of St Mary Overie, with a framed building beside a long range set beside a wharf, and a tower at the rear. See Colvin and Foister 1996, drawing 5. © Ashmolean Museum, Oxford

240. (below, right) 35 The Close, Newcastle upon Tyne. Ground plan, showing house to the left set between two long ranges of warehouses; the River Tyne is to the left, the street to the right. Based on VAGCP 1998, fig. 40. © Royal Commission on the Historical Monuments of England/English Heritage

and counting-house or office with solar chambers above them. The disposition of the hall range along the side of the yard leaves the further end free for a range of warehouses, which face on to South Quay and are set above an open arcade designed for sorting goods awaiting shipment. (fig. 238) The fourth side of the yard was probably taken in from an adjoining plot for further buildings, perhaps a kitchen among them, which, after a series of building campaigns, completed a singularly grand version of a widespread arrangement.[81]

Only a short way from Hampton Court, a narrower courtyard served Lynn's Steelyard, one of four such houses that Hanseatic traders established in England following the treaty of 1475 that so favoured them in the Baltic trade.[82] This was essentially a long narrow courtyard with warehouses down both sides as well as at the end, leaving the front for domestic accommodation.[83] London had a similar steelyard: 'The said Merchauntes of the Hanze, shuld have a certeyn place within the Citee of London, called the Stylehof, otherwise called the Stileyard',[84] and this was established close to the end of London Bridge in 1475.[85] (fig. 239) There were probably similar ones at

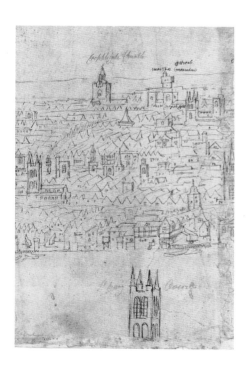

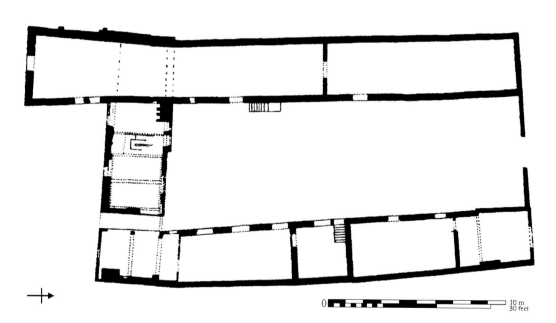

0 [scale bar] 10 m
30 feet

Great Yarmouth, Boston and Hull. For all that they served foreigners, these steelyards were not related to the storeyed Baltic houses with their ground-floor *Dielen* any more than English traders turned to their native forms with open halls when they built houses abroad.

Although nothing of medieval date now survives and it was never a steelyard occupied by a Hanseatic trader, 80 Fore Street in Ipswich has much the same arrangements. An archway through a sixteenth-century range leads from the street to a yard which has a long range of buildings running down one side. These comprise, firstly, a dwelling house, dated 1636, and then two stages of warehouses that run along to the quay-side, the first stage predating the house, the second resulting from an extension of the quay out into the river.[86]

In Newcastle upon Tyne, 35 The Close is the last survivor of a similar tradition of building in the north, certainly as old as the Hanseatic trade, in which merchants arranged their properties along narrow courtyards, (fig. 240) with warehouses stretching to the riverside in long ranges that also included a counting house, an office and workshops, in this case with their dwellings running parallel to the river close to the quay between one range of warehouses and the next, while a wall closed off the further end of the yard from the street.[87]

Far more normal are the city-centre houses of affluent merchants and craftsmen, which generally had a single, main entrance on to the street, and sometimes a secondary, service entrance at the back or to one side. Henry Tudor House in Wyle Cop, Shrewsbury, is probably part of a prosperous merchant's house of this sort. It was rebuilt some while after a fire destroyed most of the street in 1392.[88] The earliest part is a three-storeyed range, built shortly after 1426 to one side of a yard at the rear, probably to accommodate work rooms and stores associated with the local wool industry. Once more extensive than today, it became known as the Trotting Horse, and now the Lion Tap to record a former use as a tap room for the Lion Inn. Then in 1431, or shortly after, came the domestic range at the front (fig. 241), which has shops at ground level, divided by an archway leading to the yard, and two jettied storeys of rooms above. The name records the legend that the future Henry VII stayed a night here in 1485 on his way from Wales to defeat Richard III at Bosworth.[89] (fig. 242)

241. Henry Tudor House, Wyle Cop, Shrewsbury. The front range of *c.* 1431. © Andor Gomme)

242. Henry Tudor House, Wyle Cop, Shrewsbury. The traceried window of one of the upper chambers

243. Dragon Hall, King Street, Norwich. An aerial view from the rear during excavation, showing the remains of the fourteenth-century hall-house projecting on the left, and the main range across the top; originally a roadway ran through the centre down to the river, and a further projecting wing comprising ranges of the thirteenth and fifteenth century faced on to it. Photo Jason Dawson. © Norfolk Museums and Archaeology Service

244. Dragon Hall, King Street, Norwich. The two-storeyed street range

245. Dragon Hall. The crown-post roof over the long front range

Dragon Hall in King Street, Norwich, had a rather different arrangement of commercial and domestic ranges. The earliest fragment is of a fourteenth-century hall fronting Old Barge Lane, the alley that runs from King Street down to the river Wensum. (fig. 243) In the common Norwich way, its service end stretched forward to the street over an undercroft, but this was partly rebuilt and incorporated into a two-storeyed range, fronting King Street, which was apparently added soon after 1427.[90] (figs 244 and 245) The original arrangements of the brick and flint ground floor are obscure, but the open, timber-framed upper floor is little altered: it is fitted with extensive windows, and the opulent decoration of its four northern bays include a braced tie-beam with a dragon carved in its spandrel that was once painted as well (hence the building's present name). Its association with the rich clothier Robert Toppes suggests that the most likely use of this upper floor was as a trading hall for fine cloth, the southern, unheated bays serving as a public showroom, the northern, heated bays being used more privately to entertain valued customers and to strike deals. A route was especially cleared to and from the Wensum, behind the original hall, and led through a timber archway into the ground floor of the hall so that goods landed from the river could be readily brought inside.

It is seldom that the arrangements of medieval merchants' houses can be so readily understood, although the general pattern of an open hall, sometimes built over an undercroft, and ancillary ranges for domestic and commercial use are widespread. Stranger's Hall, at

246. Foxe's Court, London. An entrance in St Nicholas Lane (1) between warehouses and a shop leads into a large courtyard lined by more warehouses on the south side, and a hall (2), parlour (3) and kitchen (4) with a flanking chamber (5) on the north side; the west side of the property is lined by rows of small shops, facing Abchurch Lane, with stores behind them and probably solar chambers above. After a survey by Ralph Treswell. © Schofield 1994, fig. 50

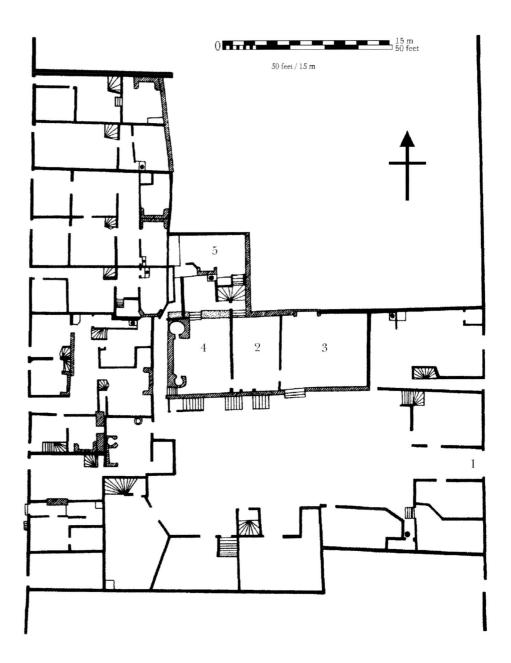

Norwich, slowly took on its present form as a result of many changes to an early-fourteenth-century building, set over a three-bay undercroft, within a courtyard that could be entered from the street and also privately from the further end. The hall was realigned in the middle of the fifteenth century, probably when it was occupied by the merchant William Barley, and a parlour and solar were fitted into the end of the old hall. A buttery and a further chamber were added in a west wing, and later extended for a kitchen, and another range was added to the hall. In 1621–2, the house was the residence of the mayor Francis Cook, and alterations have continued ever since, leaving a very confused pattern of building.[91]

Although their specific patterns of usage are lost, this arrangement was common in London among such large establishments as Crosby Place and Pulteney's Inn,[92] and numerous smaller ones known from the surveys of Ralph Treswell, including one at 115 and 118 Fenchurch Street and 12–14 Billiter Street, and another at Foxe's Court opening off St Nicholas Lane.[93] (fig. 246) These were probably similar in many ways to the framed houses facing Market Place at Faversham, from which arched entrances lead to small yards that were typically built up in stages. At 5–6 Market Place an open hall, set back parallel to the street, has before it three shops and an archway with an undercroft below and chambers over them fronting the street to form a double pile. (figs 247 & 248) Behind the hall, there is a yard embraced by two ranges with a pentice in the form of a protective roof covering the way to service rooms and work

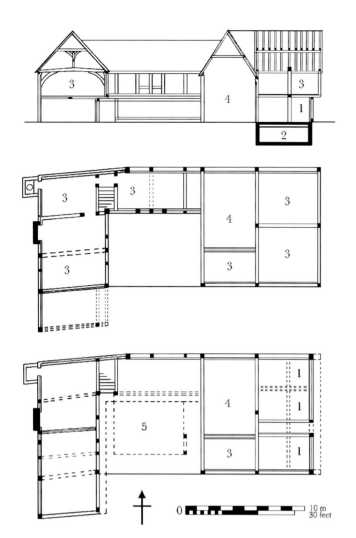

247. 5–6 Market Place, Faversham. Plans of ground and upper floors, and cross-section, showing (right to left) entrance from street between shops (1) built over an undercroft (2) with jettied solar chambers (3) above, open hall (4), and courtyard (5) flanked by services and workrooms with jettied chambers above. After Faulkner 1969. © Royal Archaeological Institute

248. 5–6 Market Place, Faversham, with a stone arch beside the shops leading to the courtyard

rooms with chambers over them.[94] The yard, it seems, served as a centre for the establishment's commercial activity, with goods being received and despatched from here, as well as being a focus for people with business in different parts of the ranges that embraced it.

Although the courtyard of Staircase House at Stockport must have served as a social and commercial focus in a similar way, this wealthy establishment had a less usual arrangement of public and private spaces, possibly because its site slopes down steeply from Market Place, which lies on the crest of a hump-backed ridge. This seems to have determined the position of the hall, which lies at the highest point on the plot, facing directly on to the street. Already by 1460 this took the form of a three-bay cruck-framed open hall, lying along the frontage in a very public position, which its owner, a prominent but un-named Stockport merchant, may have found convenient for business. The remainder of the frontage was occupied more normally by shops. Behind the hall lay a service range with a staircase leading up to a solar, and a counting house lay further back still. These overlooked a courtyard behind the shops, which provided private access to all the rooms and also to a warehouse at the rear. Despite the rebuilding of the hall in 1618 to provide an upper storey and more space, and many improvements after that, this pattern is still evident today.[95] Its particularities aside, the arrangements at Staircase House with a courtyard at its heart represent a universal solution to the specific needs of a medium-sized commercial and domestic establishment.

Throughout the later Middle Ages a small number of merchants' houses were built without the usual open hall. The earlier ones may be survivors of the old tradition of building halls in upper storeys, the later ones from a precocious rejection of everything that the open hall stood for. Vaughan's Mansion in Shrewsbury, one of the early ones, was built around an open courtyard in the later thirteenth or early fourteenth century with its hall still on an upper floor and grandly finished with a hammerbeam roof with two tiers of purlins, supported above and below by cusped wind-braces that form decorative quatrefoils, bay by bay.[96]

249. Governor's House, Stodman Street, Newark. The fireplace of the principal room, which retains fragments of a scheme of painted stripes and diaper

Governor's House in Stodman Street, Newark, may be much later since its three-storeyed street range was built about 1474[97] with an ornately painted great chamber taking up all the first floor over the ground-floor shops and the wagon entrance that led to a range at the back. Here there is a hall, heated by a hearth in an enclosed chimney stack, and in the jettied upper storey are further heated chambers and a garderobe.[98] (fig. 249) Paycocke's at Great Coggeshall is similar, its front range being full storeyed and penetrated by a wagon entrance. The hall occupies the upper floor and the garret overhead is divided into two chambers.[99] Extending to the rear and embracing a fair-sized yard are two ranges designed to accommodate the clothing industry that paid for this luxurious house shortly before 1505, and beyond that the river Blackwater served for the transhipment of goods as well as providing the water necessary to their manufacture. (fig. 250)

250. Paycocke's House, Great Coggeshall. The front elevation, showing the arched entrance to the rear courtyard, formed by two ranges of workshops

The stone house that the Plymouth merchant Thomas Yogge built in Finewell Street about ten years before he died in 1509[100] is less usual: it has a courtyard with galleries overlooking it for access to the rooms of the upper two storeys, just like the arrangements of an inn, and there is no evident hall or main room at all.[101]

The courtyard still had a long future ahead of it. A sizeable yard continued to offer the best means of making sense of a series of ranges that combined the domestic and commercial activities of a moderately sized house, as well as facilitating circulation between them. It was a haven from the turbulence of public places too, and, setting the scene for the hall of a more formal house, lent a sense of occasion to all who entered, particularly where ceremony remained in place. To this day, when ceremony is involved, one commonly sees its occupants robed so archaically that this needs a word of explanation. But no word is necessary to understand that this antiquity is prized, along with the antiquity of the architectural forms around them, all to validate the encumbrances of the past on the present so as to safeguard the future.

15

For dignity compos'd

Guildhalls, hospitals, almshouses and colleges

The palaces and inns of medieval magnates served all kinds of civic roles as well as domestic ones. While they assumed such charitable functions as the provision of hospitality for both the needy and those of suitable rank, they were also centres of power, and therefore housed the financial and administrative management of extensive estates, together with the dispensation of justice. Some of these functions gave rise to specialized civic buildings, specifically conceived for their accommodation.

Characteristically of the Middle Ages, the form of these buildings was based on the hall. Ancillary rooms played their part too, but the relationship between them and the hall was never precisely fixed, even though certain general principles were involved. Among these developments, and above all others, the halls that medieval guilds built as the physical centre of their activities became a blatant object of civic pride.[1]

The express purpose for which a guild was founded was the social and economic welfare of its members, as ever, within a strong religious context. Guildhalls came from humble origins, being whatever room a guild could afford to hire or rent. Established guilds set their eyes on a hall, and the grander it was the better it would reflect their standing. Here they held the ritualized feasts that symbolized the Last Supper, and that incorporated the ingrained ceremonials which gave a guild its identity and its members their exclusivity. Affluence brought influence and, eventually, civic power. Ambition consequently built upon this modest foundation an imposing edifice.

The guildhall took on many of the attributes of the purely domestic hall: its focus was the high end where a dais and ornate framing or other decoration or hangings conferred dignity on both the office and person of the master of the guild. There would be adjacent service rooms for the preparation of the feasts, a council chamber where its members deliberated over its affairs, and private parlours where its records were kept and the mysteries of the trade or fraternity were passed on to its brothers and occasional sisters. The charitable works that guilds undertook sometimes found expression in an associated hospital or almshouse for the infirm, with a chapel for their spiritual comfort. So there was plenty of scope for a lavish hand.

The hall's splendours reflected a guild's success. This was often achieved through a process of amalgamation and absorption that in many towns and cities led the most powerful guilds into the corridors of power. This was a happy outcome. Although several guilds had advanced this far long before the end of the Middle Ages, the Dissolution was applied to all kinds of religious institution, fraternal guilds among them. They were suppressed, but not their members, who, in the newly secularized Tudor state, applied their vowed allegiance to the Holy Trinity to the new role of civic government.[2]

From the time that the Guild of St Mary's acquired its twelfth-century hall in Lincoln in 1251/2, guilds favoured the symbolic elevation of upper halls. Three of York's four guildhalls have upper halls. The most famous and least changed, the Merchant Adventurer's Hall, was built about 1357–68 for the Guild of Our Lord Jesus and the Blessed Virgin Mary in the form of a twin-aisled, eight-bay, timber-framed hall, set over a similarly aisled undercroft, whose brick walls are

251. Merchant Adventurer's Hall, York. View from the south, showing the close-studded upper storey over the brick and stone undercroft

252. Merchant Adventurer's Hall, York. The twin aisles of the interior. © Woodmansterne

among the earliest in York. (figs 251 & 252) In 1372 a hospital or almshouse was established in the undercroft for thirteen poor people, this number reputedly symbolizing Christ and His Disciples; and, for the benefit of its inmates, a chapel with stone walls was added about 1411, opening directly off the undercroft, so that, from their beds, they could see the Holy Sacrament on its altar. By 1432 the guild had been absorbed into the city's powerful Guild of Mercers and Merchants, and its fraternal role was subordinated to serving the city's most powerful craft guild.[3]

The Merchant Taylor's Hall was built with a conventional open hall about 1413, and, though encased in brick later, has the distinction of being York's only surviving hall that originally served a craft guild.[4] The rather later hall of the Guild of St Anthony, founded in 1446 for the religious and social benefit of its members, was completed in 1453 very differently, with a chapel in its stone undercroft, beneath the hall; and, later in the century, an extension provided

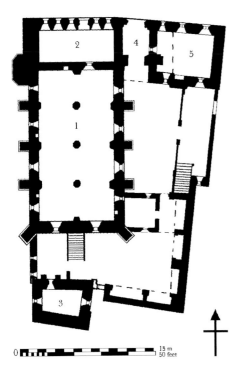

253. St Mary's Hall, Coventry. Plan at ground level, showing the undercroft of the main hall (1), with smaller undercroft beneath the hall dais to its north (2), and, beyond a flight of stairs, the base of 'Caesar's Tower' (3); a gateway from the street (4) has a lodge (5) beside it, both of them with a parlour above. After Rigold 1971, fig. 12. © Royal Archaeological Institute

254. St Mary's Hall, Coventry. The interior of the hall, showing the tapestry hanging below the Perpendicular window, and the angel roof. © The Herbert Art Gallery and Museum, Coventry

space for a hospital for the infirm.[5] The last of York's great halls, the Guildhall, was built by the mason Robert Couper about 1449–59 for the Corporation and the Guild of St Christopher, so it served York's civic authority as well as a fraternal guild. All but destroyed in 1942, and now restored, it has a stone undercroft supporting a wide aisled hall of six bays, comparable to the nave of the finest Perpendicular churches.[6]

The thriving commercial status of late medieval Coventry is fully exemplified by St Mary's Hall, whose arrangements closely approach those of an affluent merchant's inn. (fig. 253) An entrance gateway with a flanking lodge, later a chapel, opens on to a small courtyard, beside which is the undercroft of a magnificent and showy five-bay hall, the trusses of its timber roof bearing carved angels with outstretched wings. (fig. 254) The hall has a dais at the high end and an adjacent parlour above the entrance arch; at the low end there are a kitchen and service

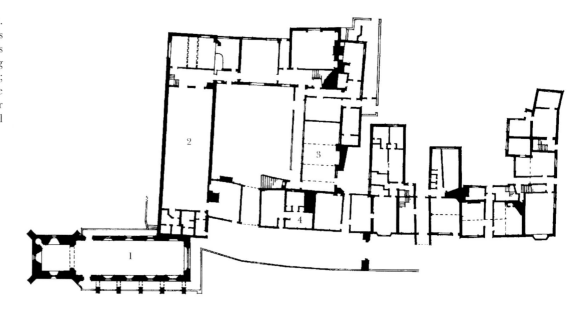

255. Lord Leycester's Hospital, Warwick. Plan, showing the chapel (1), with the King's Hall (2) extending from it; across a courtyard is the undercroft of the East Hall (3), and along the bottom the undercroft of the Guildhall (4); the rest of the buildings are given over to the lodgings of the master and inmates. After Faulkner 1971, fig. 9. © Royal Archaeological Institute

room, with a council chamber over it, and also a gallery, and, beyond this, 'Caesar's Tower' with a treasury in the upper part.[7] This is all the result of the powerful Trinity Guild's absorption of the Guild of St Mary (and also the guilds of St John the Baptist and St Catherine), confirmed in 1392, following which the hall was built to accompany the earlier tower and at least part of the kitchen block.[8] Unusual if not unique survivals are the Arras tapestry, and the Guild Chair. The tapestry, which hangs at the high end of the hall below the glowing contemporary stained glass of the north window, depicts the Assumption of the Virgin with the Apostles and a kneeling Henry VI or VII and his Queen. The Guild Chair, elaborately carved in the mid-fifteenth century with Gothic tracery, also bears a representation of the Virgin.[9] Like many guildhalls, when its fraternal role came to an end with the Dissolution, it assumed a civic role and became the exclusive office of the mayor. Here Coventry's lord mayors are still elected and here they hold their civic banquets.

Leicester Guildhall, again, is like an affluent merchant's inn. (fig. 123) Its builder, the Guild of Corpus Christi, was founded in 1343, and soon became the most important civic authority in the town. The hall itself, which was part of the first build, was extended in the late fifteenth century when a west range containing parlours was built. A gabled and jettied east range at the low end of the hall connected it to a now replaced south range which contained kitchens. Unusually, the hall was not raised on an undercroft and faced directly on to the street, rather than being placed on the further side of a courtyard, as it might have been in a merchant's inn. Nevertheless, its base-cruck trusses as well as close-studding demonstrate its standing, however sombrely grand, but this was probably ameliorated by fittings and furnishings, now lost.[10]

The remains of the Brotherhood House erected by the Fraternity of the Virgin Mary in 1472–3 at Aylesbury show the extent to which a guild would seek to decorate its hall. The timbers of its open roof are finished with hollow mouldings and its stub-ties carried carved heads. Moreover, the walls (of which one largely remains) have a fine scheme of painting with a repeating pattern of black hexagons and lozenges enlivened with a motif of fleurs-de-lis and other flowers, finished with a frieze of alternating hearts and knots.[11] (fig. 103)

The complicated history of guilds and their relationships within a town give Lord Leycester's Hospital in Warwick its particular labyrinthine quality. (fig. 255) In 1571 Robert Dudley, Earl of Leicester, took over no less than three vacant halls and various associated buildings belonging to a suppressed guild and adapted these for his hospital. Originally they belonged to two religious colleges which had united in 1128, and whose chapel was assigned to the Guild of St George in 1383. This guild almost immediately amalgamated with the Guild of the Holy Trinity and the Guild of the Virgin Mary, which had both recently built halls and various ranges of chambers near the chapel. These were combined to form an enclosed courtyard and a second, open courtyard, enclosed by a superfluity of accommodation until Leicester brought them together.[12]

The commercial roles that some guilds promoted were occasionally expressed in the uses to which parts of a guildhall were put. The Guildhall of St George at King's Lynn was founded in 1406 and built in the following decade over an undercroft, which, lying between King Street and the river quay, made a convenient warehouse to serve its mercantile members.[13] The civic power of a few guilds became so great that their halls became the centre of a town's or city's government. Corpus Christi Guild had already allowed Leicester's mayor and the Corporation to meet in its Guildhall before the end of the fifteenth century, so that when the guild was finally suppressed the Guildhall could in 1563 be legally conveyed to them and this ensured its survival.

While trade guilds generally survived the Reformation, the suppression of religious guilds and fraternities jeopardized the future of their buildings. Although several of these became in effect town halls, this was not their only future. Stratford-upon-Avon Grammar School[14] gained its independence as well as its buildings as a consequence of the suppression of Holy Cross Guild. (fig. 256) Until the sixteenth century the Master and Fraternity of the Holy Cross governed Stratford-upon-Avon. In 1269 Bishop Godfrey Giffard of Worcester had granted this guild a licence to found a hospital at Stratford. In 1403 Henry IV confirmed its amalgamation with the Guilds of the Blessed Virgin and St John the Baptist, and fourteen years later they built a timber-framed hall beside the Guild Chapel in Church Street. This was unusual in having its principal feasting hall on its ground floor and the less important Over Hall in the jettied upper storey. Here the Grammar School started its life. A *rector scholarum* had been ordained in the town as long beforehand as 1295, and in 1427 the guild, wishing to promote the benefits of education, spent about £10 to build the Pedagogue's House for its pupils at the back of the site. This was where many boys who later reached the highest rank in the land received an education in Latin grammar. Meanwhile, a slightly lower, jettied range of two-storeyed almshouses was added to the group shortly afterwards.[15] Then, probably in 1492, a former pupil and Stratford's most influential citizen, Sir Hugh Clopton, builder of the bridge that bears his name, began the rebuilding of the Guild Chapel, which in his will of 1496 he committed to the Bailiffs of Stratford. When the guild was suppressed in 1547, the chapel was granted to the mayor and Corporation, and, in 1553, Edward VI re-endowed the school. Although the chapel was meant for the Grammar School's use, which now occupied the Over Hall, its vicar was accused of having

prophaned the Chapple by suffering his children to play at Bale and other sportes therein. And his servants to hange clothes to drye in it. And his pigges and poultrie to lye and feed in it, and alsoe his dogge to lye in it and the pictures therein to be defaced and the windowes broken.

256. King Edward's Grammar School, Stratford-upon-Avon. The front range of the former Guildhall with its main feasting hall on the ground floor and the Over Hall above

257. The Guild Chapel, Stratford-upon-Avon. The pigs have been turned out and fragments of the wall painting that Shakespeare's father covered in whitewash are now visible

258. Norwich Guildhall. Although refaced in flint in 1835, the two ranges behind the porch with embattled parapets include the council chamber and are part of the original early fifteenth-century building and its partial rebuilding in the 1530s after a collapse; the two lower ranges flanking the porch, itself rebuilt in 1861, belong to later extensions, that to the right replacing the former chapel

The mural pictures – the Last Judgement, St George and the Dragon, the Martyrdom of St Thomas à Becket, St Modwenna, and St Ursula – were no more than covered in a good coat of whitewash. (fig. 257) The culprit was John Shakespeare, acting as chamberlain to the Corporation, and the date 1563, the year before the birth of his son and the Grammar School's most famous pupil.[16]

The civic power wielded from the hall of influential guilds led to the very term guildhall becoming synonymous with town or city hall. London was first in the field, and Norwich followed. (fig. 258) After the amalgamation of its English and French boroughs, Norwich was administered from the Tollhouse. The grant of full powers of self-government in 1404 prompted its new Guildhall. Built in 1407–12, and then extended, it accommodated a free or unchained prison for those awaiting trial at the next sessions, separate male and female debtors prisons within a brick, rib-vaulted undercroft that was probably part of the old Tollhouse, a solar with a chapel, dedicated to St Barbara, a great hall for full meetings of the town council and also the sheriff's court, a guest hall, and a smaller hall for the use of the mayor's court and the inner court of aldermen. Here, in effect, was one of the new breed of town hall, its architecture appropriately symbolizing dignified civic authority. Indeed the Guildhall makes a powerful show, with Perpendicular tracery to the windows of its two storeys overlooking the Market Place, flint and stone chequer-work to the upper storey, and an embattled parapet.[17]

While many guilds founded and built hospitals and almshouses for their poor members in the later Middle Ages, often as part of their main premises, the hospital had already come into its own as a refuge for the sick and poor, the infirm and elderly. Another term for this was almshouse, a building of similar form and use until the sick tended to be excluded from almshouses in favour of the merely infirm. The general confusion of terms was aggravated by how indiscriminately the word 'hospitium' could be applied to all the various kinds of extensive urban house, and when it was eventually superseded by the vernacular term 'inn', as well as 'hospice', 'hospital' and 'almshouse', these terms diverged very slowly to gain their present distinctions.

Sickness, poverty, infirmity or age were not clearly differentiated conditions where charity was concerned, but worthiness was. Hospitals, in the sense most nearly approximating to today's, were founded to alleviate the sufferings of the worthy, though not of epileptics or those with violent mental diseases associated with possession by the Devil. They provided shelter, food, cleanliness, and spiritual comfort, rather than medical attention. The founders, or donors, could be individuals or groups of individuals, such as bishops, magnates or members of guilds, who wished to engage in public charity, sometimes for its own sake, and often as a means of atoning before God for the pleasures of wealth.

Spiritual comfort lay in the hands of the hospital chaplain and also the nursing sisters. According to Bishop Suffield's statutes of 1257 for St Giles's Hospital at Norwich, 'Sisters are required to tend the sick very gently and considerately, to console them in their adversity and to exhort them to recognise in everything the chastisement of the Lord.' The success of their care was not measured in the number of cures and therefore of discharges, but in the number of souls reclaimed from the Devil and thus eased on their way to the gates of heaven.[18]

Here lay a problem. The Church found women difficult: remember Eve! Women not only posed the medical and theological dangers of menstruation, but also aroused the moral dangers of lust. 'For she that liveth in pleasures, is dead while she is living', as St Paul reminded the bishop of Ephesus; and, he warned, 'the younger widows avoid. . . . they learn to go about from house to house: and are not only idle, but tattlers also, and busibodies, speaking things which they ought not. . . . For some are already turned aside after Satan.'[19] Nurses, therefore, should be beyond the menopause and thus (so the priests who wrote the statutes believed) beyond lust; male and female inmates had to be segregated. Consequently Suffield insisted that the sisters be 'of good life and honest conversation approved over many years, being fifty years or a little less', and the whole community could then rely on them as skivvies.[20]

These attitudes remained from Suffield's time throughout the Middle Ages. The statutes of 1514 for Wyggeston's Hospital in Leicester provided for twelve poor unmarried men, who were to be 'blind, decrepit, paralytic, or maimed in their limbs, and idiots wanting in their natural senses, so that they be peaceable, not disturbing'; and the women were to be 'poor, aged, and of good report, and honest conversation, not married'. Two of the women had to be more able and strong than the others so that they could prepare food, make beds, bury the dead, and 'rid their clothes of vermin'.[21]

While hospitals had to provide clearly segregated accommodation for men and women, another problem confronting their design was their dual need to care for the souls of donors as well as inmates. A chapel in sight of the inmates would serve both needs, and here they were encouraged to pray for the soul of the hospital's founder. The more glorious the chapel, the better it would please God. Magnificence became the order of the day, particularly in the last two troubled centuries of the Middle Ages.

The famous Hôtel Dieu at Beaune (fig. 259) stands out because its lavish buildings, fittings and furnishings exemplify both the highest artistic aspirations of British hospitals, which are

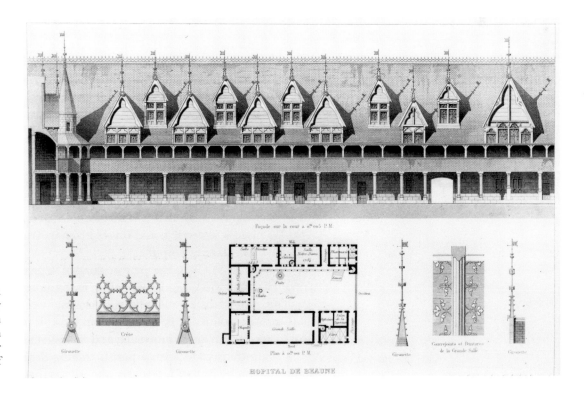

259. Hôtel Dieu, Beaune. The elevation shows the arcaded courtyard with ancillary rooms and lodgings in its upper floors, sited on the further side of the infirmary hall, which appears in the lower part of the plan. After Verdier and Cattois 1855, 1, 1. © Society of Antiquaries of London

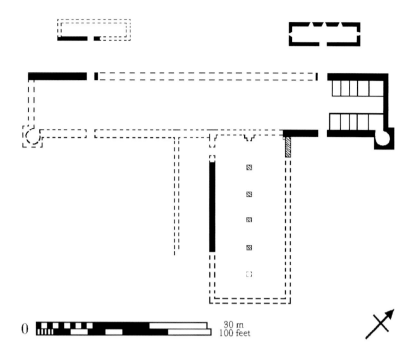

260. St John's Hospital, Northgate, Canterbury. Plan showing remaining walls (solid) and suppositional walls of the undercroft of the infirmary hall, the chapel to the south-east of it, and two multi-seat latrine blocks or reredorters (male and female) to the north-west. After a plan in Canterbury Archaeological Trust 1983–4, 51 [31]

now all desecrated if not destroyed, and the lengths to which its founder Nicolas Rolin went to save his soul. As chancellor to the Valois dukes of Burgundy, Jean sans Peur and Philippe le Bon, he was unusually tainted with the riches of this world and needed powerful intercession to gain entry to the next. To this end he paid for the hospital in the 1440s, and its splendid fittings, including Roger van der Weyden's *Last Judgement* – one of the finest paintings on this theme – which depicts Rolin, as donor, in the hope of weighing lightly in the Archangel Michael's scales on Doomsday.[22] Lesser works eased the way of British donors, but their needs are still evident in the provision of lavish accommodation for the priests charged with praying for their souls, rather than for the ancient women charged with washing the sick.

The first hospitals specifically intended for the sick, infirm and poor of which there is a cogent record were founded soon after the Conquest by the Church. Archbishop Lanfranc founded St John's Hospital in Northgate, Canterbury, (fig. 260) in 1084 or early 1085, and also a separate leper house, with its own chapel, well away from the city at Harbledown. The hospital's symmetrical arrangement may imply equality between the sexes. In the shape of a T, it had an infirmary range, some 200 feet (60m) long, which sheltered thirty men and thirty women, presumably at opposite ends. From the middle of this range projected a chapel, while two *necessaria* or multi-seat privies lay separately to the rear, presumably again one for men, one for women, and these drained into the river Stour.[23] At about the same time, Bishop Gundulf of Rochester founded the Hospital of St Bartholomew at Chatham, and again, just then, St Wulfstan is said to have founded his hospital at Worcester outside the town walls.

Within a little over a century 250 hospitals were in existence, such as the Hospital of St Cross at Winchester, which Henry of Blois founded in 1136 for thirteen poor and infirm men, with provision for daily meals for yet more paupers. By 1250 the number of hospitals had risen to over four hundred, about a quarter of these being devoted to lepers, who were kept separate because of their shocking disfigurement. The numbers continued to grow as sympathy with the plight of the sick and disabled prompted founders in the direction of what was often their primary motive, remission of their sins and a speedy journey through purgatory.

Bishop Herbert de Losinga founded the first hospital in Norwich at the end of the eleventh century to shelter lepers, and dedicated it to St Mary Magdalen, who, for her sins, always had to care for the outcasts of society. Built of stone a mile outside the city's gates, the leper house took the form of a two-cell church, comprising an infirmary housing the inmates and a chapel containing the Blessed Sacrament for their spiritual comfort. Together with Lanfranc's at Harbledown, this was among the first of such charitable institutions, which were usually run by monks outside city gates so that lepers and other disfigured men and women could find shelter without inflicting their appearance or their disease on the growing population within the gates.[24]

St Paul's Hospital, the first within the walls of Norwich, was founded during the twelfth century with about twenty beds for 'the sick, infirm and child-bearing poor'. This became so crowded that a local merchant, Hildebrand le Mercer, set up another refuge for poor people in 1201. Yet more was needed, and this led Bishop Walter Suffield to found what was to become Norwich's most lasting hospital.

Dedicated to St Giles, the patron saint of lepers, cripples and nursing mothers, Suffield's Great Hospital was begun soon after its foundation in 1249. (fig. 261) Much rebuilt and extended, it nevertheless still reflects its original intentions better than any other surviving hospital, and does so on a scale grander than most. It now comprises a range, over 200 feet (60m) long, formed by an aisled infirmary, and an aisle-less chapel. To this were added a south porch and a south transept to form a parish church, dedicated to St Helen, and a west tower. The chapel, rebuilt by Bishop Despenser about 1380, had an intermediate floor built into it so as to

261. The Great Hospital, Norwich. Plan, showing the infirmary range to the south, with the tower (1) in the south-west angle, the infirmary (2), with its destroyed south aisle (hatched), the central section converted for use as St Helen's Church (3), with a porch and two chapels, and the chancel (4); on the north side lie a cloister, refectory (5) and, further north, lodgings for the master (6) and chaplains, and the site of the kitchen. © Rawcliffe 1999, map 3

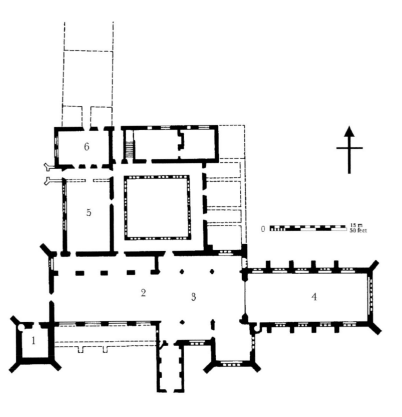

262. The Great Hospital, Norwich. A corner of the cloister, designed for the corporeal succour of the master and chaplains. Above, to the left, is the upper part of the infirmary range, and, to the right, the refectory or hall of the master's lodging

divide it into two wards for women, while, at the same time, the original infirmary was given over to men, and its east end was divided off to become part of the parish church. In the middle of the fifteenth century a cloister was added to the north, (fig. 262) where the hall of the master's lodgings was sited along with what was by then necessarily convenient accommodation for the priests who were charged with the onerous task of praying for the souls of the benefactors, and a kitchen and other ancillary buildings that gave them the physical strength and the incentive of comfort to spend their lives interceding with Almighty God in this way. Sumptuously finished, the Great Hospital (as it became known after the Reformation) still shelters the infirm, and only lacks the spiritual solace of a living chapel with the Eucharist reverently displayed in a candle-lit, incense-heavy setting that rings with the chanting of prayers and the tinkling of bells.[25]

This linear arrangement of infirmary and chapel characterized medieval hospitals from the start, and, although sometimes elaborated, it remained the commonest form.[26] Royal Garrison Church at Portsmouth was built with an aisled infirmary and chapel as a multi-purpose God's House (or Domus Dei), following its foundation by Bishop Peter des Roches about 1212. Its dedication to St Nicholas (and also St John) was a suitable choice since he was patron saint of seafarers, as well as children, merchants and pawnbrokers, among others, and a noted saviour of women threatened with prostitution. The hospital possibly tended all of these, but was specifically for travellers and sick and aged people.[27]

One of the best-appointed hospitals was founded in 1331 by the third Earl of Lancaster and Leicester as the Hospital of the Annunciation of Mary the Virgin (rededicated to the Trinity in 1614), and built in the Newarke, Leicester, for fifty aged men of whom twenty were resident, with a master, four chaplains, two clerks, and five female nurses. (fig. 263) His son, the Duke of Lancaster, made additions at the time when he was also founding the College of St Mary the Great in 1354 so that 'in it were maintained one hundred infirm poor persons, the third part of them to be women, and also ten other poor women to be keepers and washers of the said hundred.' Originally Trinity Hospital took the form of an aisled infirmary hall of ten bays, with an eastern chapel, graced by an east window of four stepped lancets. This the duke extended perhaps to seventeen bays (200 feet or 60 m) to house the augmented numbers, and later an upper storey was inserted into the infirmary before its partial destruction.[28]

How the men there were separated from the women is unclear, but in Wyggeston's Hospital, also at Leicester, and founded in 1513, each of the twelve men had 'one chamber apart by himself, to abide and lodge all night only there', and, according to the statutes, he was forbidden to go upstairs 'into the chambers of the women, but by two and two', and then only with the master's or the confrater's permission. The individual chambers or cells were about 8 feet (2.4 m) square, and partitioned to form two rows of six facing each other across a corridor that led from the confrater's chamber to the chapel; the upper floor was similarly arranged for twelve women, except that their corridor led from a kitchen over the confrater's chamber to a gallery opening on to the chapel; and a timber-framed wing contained service rooms. The statutes also provided for gowns of frieze for the inmates, 'handsome priestly garments' for the master and confrater, and 'a chalice, bread, wine, wax, provisions, and ornaments for the altar, and all things else to the solemnizing the mass, as pitchers, phials, bells, and bell ropes, salt for the holy water, and also a lamp burning in the hospital every night from the feast of St Michael to the feast of Easter.'[29]

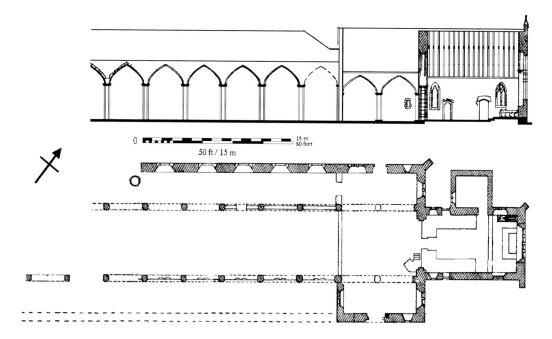

263. Trinity Hospital, The Newarke, Leicester. Plan and section showing (left) the curtailed remains of the infirmary (its demolished south aisle hatched), and (right) the chapel. After a survey by Albert Herbert in Godfrey 1933

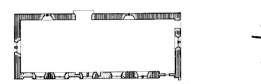

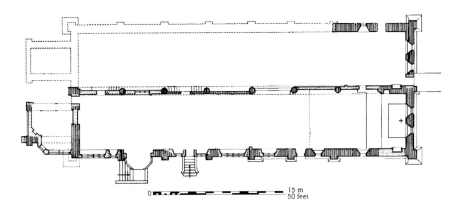

By the end of the Middle Ages this arrangement was commonplace: segregation was assured, although it gave women poorer access to the chapel. A rather more equitable but far less common arrangement was apparently tried at Salisbury, where, long beforehand, Bishop Bingham's St Nicholas Hospital was built about 1231. (fig. 264) An obligation to care for both sexes caused its unusual infirmary to be given two equal aisles, divided by an open arcade, their five bays running directly into two further bays comprising the double-aisled chapel.[30] Meanwhile, a further separate range, perhaps 'the old hospital towards the north', now redundant as an infirmary, was converted for the warden and chaplains.[31]

One of the most elaborate medieval hospitals was founded in Stamford by 'a merchant of very wonderful richnesse', Alderman William Browne, 'for the invocation of the most glorious Virgin Mary, and All Saints, to the praise and honour of the Name Crucified'. (fig. 265) Construction began in 1475 and the work was completed by Browne's brother-in-law Thomas Stoke, a canon of York. While Browne's Hospital adopted the usual arrangement of infirmary and chapel in one range, this was grandly conceived on a raised terrace with the infirmary proper in its undercroft and, above it, an audit room, anteroom and confraters' room. The infirmary was finished with five cubicles on each side of the central corridor for the ten poor brothers, and both this and the confraters' room open on to a square, double-height chapel beyond a screen to the east, which has large, richly traceried Perpendicular windows. This wonderfully prominent range was reached through a gateway,[32] and beyond it lay a cloister. The chapel is no less magnificently fitted-out, with stalls enriched with angels on the arm-rests, more angels and birds, a mermaid and other figures carved on the misericords, an alms box, and coloured glass with figures of saints, and, elsewhere, figures of King David, King Solomon and St Paul, and Browne's arms.[33] (fig. 266)

Occasionally hospital infirmaries were separate from their chapel. This was the case in Bristol when, in 1220, one of the Berkeley family 'Maurice de Gant founded the faire hospitall of St Marke of Billeswyke . . . endowing it with ample possessions', although not a chapel. The homeless, sick and destitute who sheltered there had to wait ten years before Gant's nephew Robert de Gournay provided the benefaction for a chapel to be built separately.[34] When the Hospital of St Wulfstan at Worcester was rebuilt at the end of the fifteenth century its elaborate plan included a suite of rooms for the so-called commander and two chaplains, and a wing for the infirm, in which one room has a series of wall paintings representing saints associated with various illnesses, which were intended to comfort inmates on the point of death.[35]

265. Browne's Hospital, Stamford. South elevation and section looking south, showing the audit room set over the infirmary, and the end chapel. After Dollman and Jobbins 1863, 2, Pl. 2. © Society of Antiquaries of London

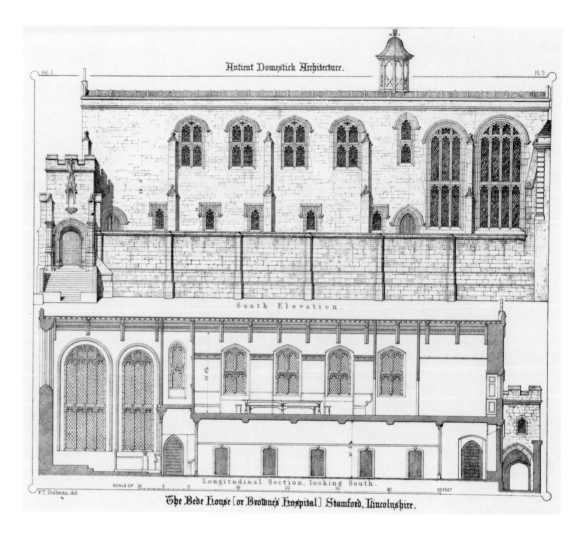

266. Browne's Hospital, Stamford. Stained glass windows from the Audit Room, showing (left to right) King David, St Paul, King Solomon and a composite figure with the head of a saint in a doctor's cap, implying that a cure comes from heaven. © National Monuments Record

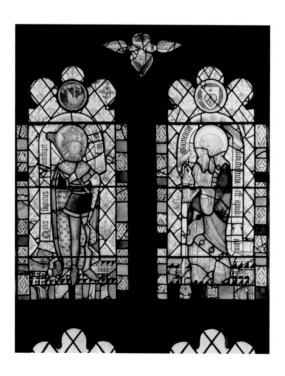 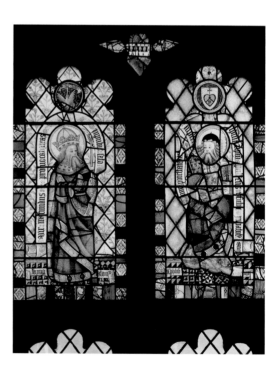

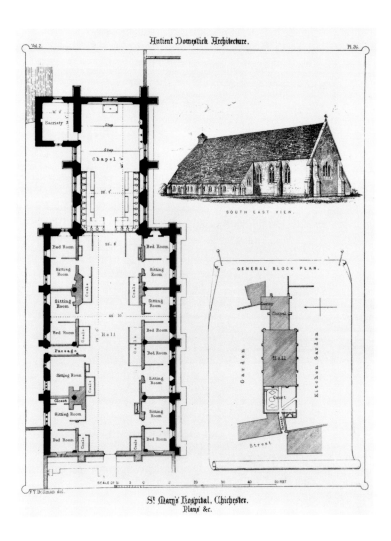

St Mary's Hospital at Chichester shares with the Great Hospital at Norwich the distinction of having been occupied by the needy ever since it was founded, perhaps in 1158. (fig. 267) Between 1269 and 1285 it removed to its present site, where its infirmary range was built with a timber-framed arcade of six bays and an immense roof running in one fell swoop from ridge across nave and aisles to low eaves just above head height, with an attached chapel at the east that retains its original screen and stalls with misericords carved with mythical creatures.[36]

The vague distinctions between who were classed as sick, who as old, and who as merely poor and infirm, are reflected in the lack of distinction between medieval hospitals and almshouses. They shared the charitable purpose of sheltering those who were unable to care for themselves and at once the personal desire of their donors to glorify God so as to avoid the torments of purgatory. Some donors gave a whole range of institutional buildings for good measure. While the fortunes of Higham Ferrers waxed through the patronage of the House of Lancaster, it was Archbishop Chichele who embellished the town in the early fifteenth century with its most magnificent architecture. He was born there about 1362 and the parish church contains the monuments of his parents, brother and sister-in-law. As an act of filial piety, he endowed a college of priests in 1422, together with a school and the Bede House. (figs 268 and 269) This was built soon after 1428 for twelve old men, who prayed for his soul, and a woman attendant who cared for them. While it has the characteristic arrangement of an infirmary, its partitioned cubicles for the men's beds and lockers gave them a little privacy. A chapel at the east end stands out for the fine Perpendicular tracery of its east window, and even more so for the multicoloured stone walls which are banded in buff oölitic limestone and deep gold ironstone.[37]

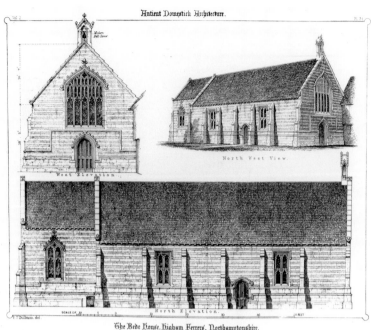

268. Bede House, Higham Ferrers, seen from the parish church, together with the fourteenth-century churchyard cross

269. Bede House, Higham Ferrers. Elevations and perspective. After Dollman and Jobbins 1863, 2, Pl. 34. © Society of Antiquaries of London

Like Chichele's Bede House, St Mary's Hospital at Glastonbury, founded in the thirteenth century as an almshouse for men, followed the classic lines of a hospital,[38] with an infirmary hall divided up into five cubicles on each side of a central corridor, and an entrance lobby and an office at the eastern end before a rectangular chapel. The division into cubicles would be a significant development for the future, when diverging aspirations gave almshouses ranges of separate lodgings, while hospitals remained distinguishable by their open wards.

Demonstrating the vague use of terms, the elaborate almshouse (*domus elemosinarum*) dedicated to St John the Baptist and St John the Evangelist at Sherborne was a hospital in all but name. Founded in 1437–8, with practically every inhabitant of Sherborne listed among the benefactors, so concerned were they for their souls, it was completed in 1448 for the separate

270. The Almshouse of the two St Johns, Sherborne. The central panel of the triptych, depicting the raising of Lazarus. © National Monuments Record

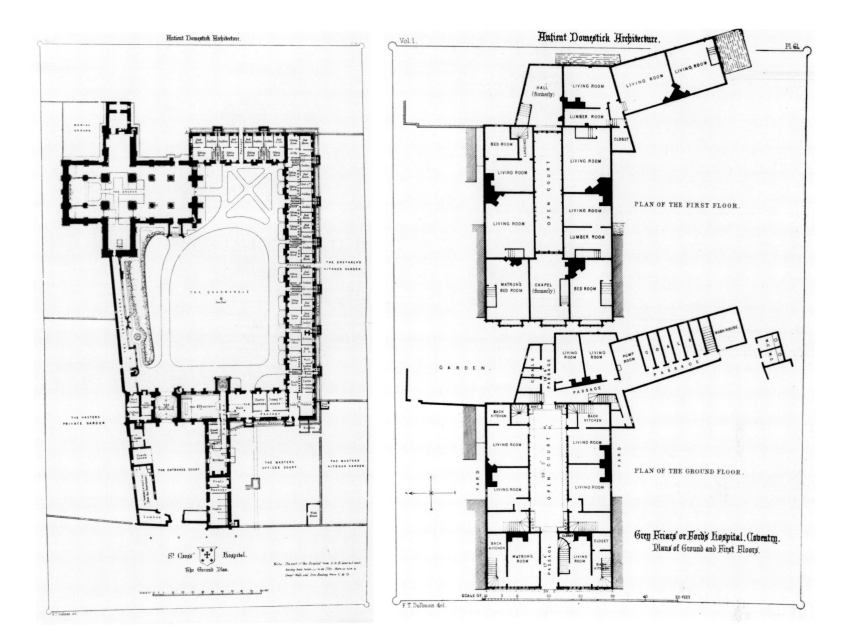

PLAN OF THE FIRST FLOOR.

PLAN OF THE GROUND FLOOR.

Grey Friars' or Ford's Hospital. Coventry.
Plans of Ground and First Floors.

St. Cross' Hospital.
The Ground Plan.

271. St Cross, Winchester. Plan showing the church (top left), the identical brethren's lodgings and (at bottom) the entrance court, refectory, hall and master's house. After Dollman and Jobbins 1861, 1, Pl. 16. © Society of Antiquaries of London

272. Ford's Hospital (Greyfriars), Coventry. Plans of ground and first floor, showing the individual living rooms for the pensioners. After Dollman and Jobbins 1861, 1, Pl. 61. © Society of Antiquaries of London

accommodation of 'twelfe pore feble and ympotent men and foure pore feble and ympotent wommen', since the manifold snares of lust, despite impotence, were best avoided. The men apparently occupied cubicles in a single room on the lower floor, while the women lived above. A perpetual priest cared for their souls and a 'Hosewyfe of St John is House' made beds, cooked, and washed for them. These needs thus fulfilled, the chapel has a triptych for their spiritual solace,[39] depicting the miraculous raising of Lazarus, the casting out of the Devil from the dumb man, the restoration of sight to the blind man, the calling to life of the widow's son at the gate of Nain, and the raising of the daughter of Jairus. (fig. 270) No soul in peril could fail to gain the celestial haven before the sight of this.[40]

When Cardinal Beaufort re-founded the Hospital of St Cross at Winchester in 1446 for 'noble poverty', in effect for infirm priests of gentle birth who had fallen on hard times, his scheme, even in its incomplete state, is indistinguishable from a magnificent almshouse. (fig. 271) Its southern and western ranges comprised forty separate Brethren's Dwellings, its northern range comprised the master's lodging, the Hundred Mens' Hall and service rooms; these and the great cruciform church itself formed a large courtyard, with further ancillary buildings set around another, smaller yard to the north.[41]

The almshouse that the merchant William Ford founded in Coventry in 1509, originally for six poor people, but eventually to include single rooms for seventeen women, points even more strongly to future distinctions. (fig. 272) Built by 1517, or possibly 1529, Ford's Hospital com-

prised a pair of two-storeyed ranges facing each other across a very narrow courtyard with an entrance gateway at one end flanked by two sets of twin rooms for a matron and chaplain with a chapel in the storey above, and, at the other end, a small common hall, again on the upper floor. There was no open infirmary range at all.[42]

Although largely rebuilt in the seventeenth century, Christ's Hospital or Long Alley Almshouses at Abingdon, founded in 1446 and built as a long range of individual houses within the parish churchyard, has an arcaded pentice like a cloister,[43] similar to the gallery of Greenway's Almshouses at Tiverton, and a predecessor of countless future houses. (fig. 273)

It is no more than a short step from these later almshouses with ranges of individual rooms for the aged and infirm to the lodgings for vicars and other middle-ranking priests, who often associated in colleges. Unlike monks, they came to expect all the comforts of individual accommodation, and their dwellings were usually set out in rows. Like colleges for academics, colleges of vicars and closes for vicars attached to a cathedral tended to follow a courtyard plan derived from the cloister.

In 1280 Bishop Oliver Sutton initiated the conspicuously generous Vicars' Court at Lincoln, next to his palace, and this was completed by his successor Bishop Buckingham in 1309–10. Intended for twenty-six senior vicars and laid out around a quadrangle with an attendant hall and kitchen, the ranges provided single, heated rooms on each of their two storeys, the upper ones served in pairs by newel stairs. The south range exploits the fall of the land on its southern side, which is heavily buttressed, and has monumental garderobe towers, surely a model for the garderobe towers at Gainsborough Old Hall, to serve the individual chambers.[44]

Vicars' Close at Wells, the best-known of such ranges, was begun as an ideal scheme by Bishop Ralph of Shrewsbury about 1347, and modified by Bishop Beckington (1443–65) or his executors. (fig. 274) In 1334 the archdeacon of Bath Walter de Hulle gave some property in Wells so that thirteen chantry priests might live in common together, but what Bishop Ralph began Beckington completed on a grander scale. The Close comprises two rows of identical, self-contained houses, for forty-two vicars in all, facing each other across a long, slightly tapering courtyard that starts with a gatehouse, hall and kitchen, perhaps the work of Bishop Ralph, and terminates in a chapel and library at the northern, narrower end.[45] (fig. 275)

Vicars' Cloister at Hereford suggests an inclination to keep the vicars under greater control. The College of Vicars Choral was founded in 1396 to accommodate twenty-six vicars and a

274. Vicars' Close, Wells. The east range looking towards the chapel and library

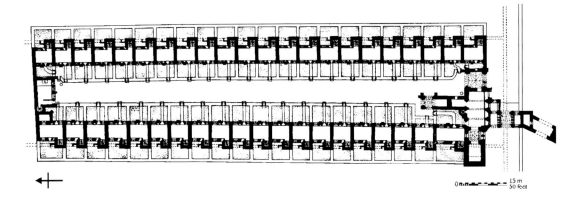

275. Vicars' Close, Wells. Plan of the two facing terraces of forty-two houses, with the entrance through Chain Gate at the southern end (right), together with a hall and kitchen and, at the north end (left), a chapel and library. After plan given in Godfrey 1950. © Royal Archaeological Institute

custos, and land was granted within the close in 1473 for four ranges of not entirely self-sufficient lodgings, arranged around a rectangular cloister with a hall in the south range, together with a chapel, and a link to the south transept of the cathedral. The model might well have been the similar Cloister Court at Eton College, founded by Henry VI in 1440, where a contract for construction is dated 1443.[46]

The twenty-one timber-framed houses built about 1480 for vicars around Horseshoe Cloister at Windsor Castle are planned as short ranges, angled to form a polygon. Vicars' Close at Chichester, perhaps dating from the late 1460s, is possibly another similar scheme, where, significantly, the houses replaced a common dwelling and gave thirty-two vicars some privacy in a layout comprising two facing ranges and a short third range across one end divided by a gatehouse.[47]

Many of these ecclesiastical colleges were suppressed at the Dissolution, among them what became Chetham's Library and School at Manchester. This college began life in the form of a tiny monastery in 1421 when Thomas de la Warre, Lord of Manchester and rector of the parish, rebuilt his church[48] and founded a college for eight fellows, four clerks, six lay choristers and a warden beside it. He gave his baronial hall for the purpose, and here the college took shape around a small cloister from which a long, two-storeyed eastern wing extends to termi-

276. Chetham's Library and School, Manchester. Plans of ground (below) and upper floor: entry is by way of a gatehouse (1), which is joined to the main accommodation by a long wing that formerly accommodated guests, servants and a kitchen (2); the open hall (3) lies beyond a screen, with the warden's apartment (4) at its high end; the sets for the fellows (5) lie on the further side of the cloister, with their sleeping cubicles (6) above, and the cubicles for the clerks adjacent. After H. Taylor, 1884, Pl. 8

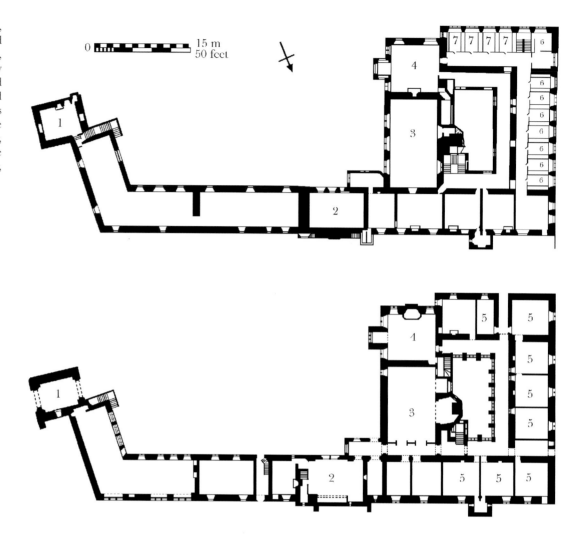

nate in a gatehouse. (fig. 276) This wing, which was intended for servants and guests, included a kitchen, built beside the screens passage of the hall. This took up the east side of the cloister, together with the wardens room beyond the dais at its high end. The other three ranges, again of two storeys, were devoted to the fellows, who had individual sets for daytime use, each with its own door opening off the cloister walk, but they slept in individual cubicles within a communal dormitory on the upper floor. Following the dissolution of the college in 1547, its subsequent conversion into a private house, reconversion as a college during Mary's reign, closure under Elizabeth and a reopening in 1578, the executors of Humphrey Chetham's will finally converted it in 1654 as a school for forty poor boys and a public library 'within the town of Manchester for the use of scholars'.[49]

16

Houses most of timber work

Small town houses in the later Middle Ages

When urban populations reached a peak at the start of the fourteenth century, most people were under intense pressure to hang on to house and home. Life was difficult and they were never so wretchedly accommodated. Migration brought in unprecedented numbers, hunting a roof as well as work. Sagging fever-dens, run up for subletting in the angle of a house or garden, augmented poor incomes, and dragged down all but the hardy.

Pestilence resolved the problem. The rookeries of the Middle Ages fell into ruin, together with much good housing, in the depressed years that laid waste whole neighbourhoods. Even so, a significant number of better houses survived: their intrinsic value and reduced pressures on redevelopment gave them a chance. Their happy face suggests that the past was less a burden for some people than it was for the majority, especially in the later fifteenth century when the economy was rebuilding and new houses were put up in prospering towns.

For all the hardship, the princely festivities that royal halls accommodated were emulated at ever lower levels of society. This descent eventually came to transform feasting into no more than everyday meals formally set at a high table in the glow of an open fire; the performance of bards and harpers into the repetition of old family tales and local gossip; matters of state into discussions of market trends and produce; and justice into a fuss about the ceremonies of the guilds. For all these affairs, anyone who was anyone and many who were not looked to an open hall, just like the king.

Halls now served everyday houses, and by Chaucer's time were as common as his poor widow.[1] The open hall had become the defining domestic room of the Middle Ages. Why it should have done so, and reached almost the lowest levels of society, may be explained by a general desire to emulate the chivalrous social fashions of the nobility, and to follow their patriarchal attitudes to the family. In other respects the descent of the hall into the sphere of the smaller urban house was at odds with the practicalities of everyday life, practicalities that the restrictions imposed by urban circumstances often greatly aggravated.

The greatest restriction was the comparatively high cost of land and the consequent need to use it as efficiently as possible, even after the Black Death had emptied many urban streets. Scotland found a solution, generally in line with European practice, by building upward in horizontal layers. In England the increasing desire for an open hall made this difficult, if not impossible, and determined the pattern of even modest houses. Reflecting the heavy premium on frontage, the typically narrow burgage that urban pressure encouraged limited the means of lighting the interior and restricted circulation within a house, particularly when it incorporated an open hall in its midst.

In the countryside even the tofts or homesteads of a densely occupied village were spacious enough to let feudal tenants arrange their modest houses, animal sheds and barns in a convenient way around an irregular yard so that none of these impinged unduly on the others. An open hall might be a luxury, but it was not an obstacle.

Early buildings in the new and re-founded towns had followed suit, and many were hardly distinguishable from rural buildings, although they might be grouped more compactly. As urban land became more scarce, this changed: after the Conquest the luxury of the detached

277. Booth Mansion, Chester. Built about 1260–80 over an undercroft aligned perpendicularly with Watergate Street. The house comprised part of the row with a shop behind it and a solar chamber above, and an open hall behind these reached by a passage from the front. Graham Holme's view in A. Brown 1999, Pl. 12. © English Heritage

forms of rural houses increasingly became the preserve of either those who could afford large plots, or those who inhabited small unpopulous towns or the margins of towns where economic matters were not pressing business. For everyone of small means the typically narrow burgage was the limit of their aspirations. This brought into existence the row house, a form that took advantage of the whole frontage and was therefore contiguous with one if not both of its neighbours.

Where plots were reasonably wide, a house could front the street in the rural way, its service rooms, hall and chambers all facing both forward to the street and rearward to a garden or yard, but this inefficient use of frontage usually resulted in wings being added at the back to increase the accommodation. (fig. 88) Many plots in the centre of busy towns were less wide, and so the rooms within each house were planned end-on to the street with some kind of access passageway running to the rear, either inside the house or outside. (fig. 277) This arrangement simply turned the layout of rooms through 90 degrees, with the service rooms at the front, where they could be put to commercial use and profit, and the chambers or parlours at the rear, where they could enjoy the pleasures of a garden ground.

This inwardly turned arrangement offered some respite from the hurly-burly of the street, just as the courtyard arrangement of greater establishments did, but so simple and practical a scheme often failed to work out. Further service rooms, and perhaps workshops and warehouses, had to be accommodated at the rear, as well as paddocks for animals, means of disposing of waste, access to a watercourse or well, and, with obvious hazards to health, to a privy or latrine.[2]

This solution of building end-on to the street was widespread in northern Europe, but always it raised the problem of lighting were a house of any depth. This was especially true of England, where the crux of the problem was the open hall in the centre, which, from the thirteenth century onwards, increasingly came to dominate the plan of all but the smallest houses. Even so, in London, where urban pressure was at its greatest, in Bristol too, and occasionally elsewhere, the open hall was sometimes spurned, an upper room serving in its place.[3] Had this tradition of building a principal room or hall into an upper storey won the day, as it seemed to be doing in the twelfth century, the way the English urban house eventually developed during the later Middle Ages might have more closely resembled French practice. But this was not to be, and the resulting urban hall-houses came to be built in a great variety of patterns instead.

This was not simply a matter of emulation. While the hierarchical formality, atavistic symbolism and mythical tradition that prompted royalty and the highest levels of society to adopt the hall were passed down to burgesses and their lesser fellows, if only as a vaguely understood chivalrous fashion, there was another reason for adopting the open hall. By cutting a vertical swathe through a house, an open hall set up a barrier between upper floors on each side of it, and its need of lighting required it to have at least one free wall, though that was not always attained. This barrier nevertheless had a singular advantage. Almost as though it were taking the place of the courtyard of a larger establishment, its open space, from floor to roof, became a fulcrum between the connotations of work before it at the front end of the house, and what little privacy individual members of a family might enjoy beyond it at the back.

In the end-on arrangement, the front of the house, where it accommodated retailing, was devoted to a public role and open to strangers without hindrance; where it accommodated manufacturing it was still open to strangers. The central hall, by distinction, might serve guests as well as family, but, however far this allowed the entry of strangers by invitation, they were bound by common formalities, and, in that sense, tamed. Here, the head of the family, man or woman, ruled, and this central basis of the household was properly represented by the physically central role of the hall.

Before the last century or so of the Middle Ages there was no question of any but favoured visitors penetrating to the private zone beyond, except in unusual circumstances. Nevertheless, this slowly changed. In some of Bristol's grander houses, such as Canynges's House, the hall had become little more than a symbolic place of welcome by the end of the fifteenth century, and hospitality was on offer more privately beyond.[4]

Here, where space allowed, there was also a hierarchy. By the sixteenth century the open hall of larger houses was increasingly a formal space and sometimes little else, the parlour becoming the centre of family life. In London, and indeed elsewhere, this private end of the house often overlooked a garden whose economic benefits were matched by its eternal pleasures. The occasional gallery enhanced the view, and the long progress of rooms from the street, punctuated by the caesura of the hall, ensured its privacy.[5] The best chamber was devoted to the head of the family, and was so placed, particularly in relation to hall and staircases, as to allow him or her some control over the other members of the family when they entered and left the lesser chambers. This arrangement was particularly valuable at night to ensure that sexual morality meant more than mere decorum.

The smaller houses of less important towns continued to follow tradition. Inventories made in the 1560s of the contents of three houses in Ashford and Canterbury record their halls as containing a table each, a chair or two, stools and benches, cupboards and hangings, all in the age-old way, while their parlours and chambers, upstairs and down, were indiscriminately furnished with beds of various kinds, ancient and modern, and the newly introduced luxuries of pillows, bolsters, sheets, blankets and coverlets, towels and napkins, as well as chests and tables, and painted cloths and hangings.[6]

That much, at least, may be inferred from the physical arrangements of a majority of row houses and the occasional probate inventory. This generality is nevertheless dangerous. Not all small urban houses followed this arrangement, and the distinctions between public and private in those houses that were arranged with their rooms lying along the street, instead of at right angles to it, must have been weaker. After all, there was apparently no breach of social etiquette when Absalom serenaded Alison and Nicholas just outside the ground-floor chamber of the Oxford carpenter's house – he was just a nuisance.[7] Furthermore, private chambers and service rooms were not always kept distinct and separated by the *cordon sanitaire* of an open hall: often chambers were in the form of solars set above service rooms or shops, and only a plank door and ladder-stair separated them. It was easy to peep in. While a later age viewed a front door that opened directly on to the street as a clear-cut division between public and private that would brook no transgression without invitation, the gregariousness of medieval society may have had no truck with the sensibilities that the forms it inhabited seem to imply. Moreover, in the fluid society of towns, the hierarchy that generally seems to underlie medieval society and finds expression in the layout of the characteristic hall-house may have been no more than a Sunday-best to be donned for feasts but too fine for everyday use.

Generally these smaller houses were either compactly sited so that their ends faced the street, or they lay along the street so that the hall, service end and chamber end all faced on to it. This latter arrangement eased the problem of lighting, but there were disadvantages. It lacked security and privacy, and took up valuable space that might otherwise be given over to shops. Worse, so far as the street frontage was concerned, there was little differentiation other than in its architectural detail between its three parts: the central hall, the working zone in the service end, and the private zone in the chamber end.

Unusual for so central a site, the fifteenth-century Beam Hall in Oxford has its formerly open hall and services with a solar above aligned with Merton Street.[8] (fig. 278) Survivors of the arrangement are more commonly found in those small towns which have developed little since the Middle Ages, or in the side streets or suburbs of larger towns where time has passed them by. (fig. 279) In Bury St Edmunds 61–3 Whiting Street was built up in this way and survived the devastating fire of 1608. (fig. 280) The timber-framed 19, 21 and 23 Bradford Street, Bocking,[9] and the Woolpack Inn at Great Coggeshall, typically of three-part Essex hall-houses, have their end blocks treated as gabled wings as well as lying along the street. Clare, Lavenham,[10] Chipping Camden,[11] Cranbrook and many similar towns whose prosperity rose and fell with cloth still retain several houses of this kind. The same form was used for the Duke of Wellington in Cowbridge, one of three substantially medieval houses to survive in this small Welsh town, but they are small and comprise only a pair of rooms on each floor.[12]

These urban hall-houses suited all kinds of people with money, not just clothiers and innkeepers. Coincidentally, two houses, both named after Anne of Cleves, whose property they became, have this form. One, at Melton Mowbray, was built in stone in the later fourteenth century, possibly to support chantry priests, and came

into the hands of the Cluniacs of Lewes Priory who appropriated the living of the parish church.[13] The other was built for the priory at Lewes itself, in the suburb of Southover, probably a century later, and of timber with an open hall recessed between two jettied wings.[14] Following the Dissolution both houses became Crown property and in 1541 formed part of Henry VIII's nullity settlement on the former Queen Anne.

While gables distinguished the storeyed chamber and service ends of many houses, sometimes the gable was reserved for the chamber end so as to accentuate its greater importance within the social hierarchy of spaces that the house embraced. The Merchant's House from Bromsgrove, which was occupied by the Lyllye family of dyers and clothiers early in the sixteenth century, has a gabled wing, containing a parlour and shop on the ground floor, according to an inventory of 1558, with a single chamber above, but the low end, which continued the line of the hall,[15] contained two service rooms in the usual way with a smaller chamber above.[16] (fig. 281) Across the border, White Hall at Presteigne not only exemplifies this plan well but also is the one almost complete medieval town house in central Wales.[17] (fig. 282) It was the forerunner of many more similar Welsh houses, both in town and country.

Another of these houses, the Old Vicarage at Tadcaster, was built about 1474 with an open hall, cross-passage, services and solar in a single range, which continues via a passage into a kitchen, open to the roof, while, at the other end of the hall, a storeyed cross-wing contains a parlour and chamber, both of them having their own fireplaces. How these lavish arrangements were used is not recorded, but it is easy to see the open hall physically separating the services, where women may have worked, from the heated parlour and chamber where the vicar could have lived in private, professing celibacy, and led not into temptation.[18]

In the West Riding of Yorkshire the seemingly archaic form of aisled hall dominated building traditions around Halifax from the middle of the fifteenth century until nearly the end of the sixteenth century. This seems to have been a practical response to local needs, rather than an old-fashioned attitude. White Hall on the outskirts of Halifax at Ovenden was among the earliest of these houses and had aisles on each side of its hall, but later houses such as Bankhouse at Skircoat had only a rear aisle. (fig. 283) These comparatively large houses had a typical three-part plan, sometimes with gabled ends, but the local weaving industry required great quantities of wool to be stored in the house, and this took up the space normally devoted to service rooms, and the rear aisle apparently served their function instead. Moreover, the hearth, which usually had a reredos backing the cross-passage, was also provided with a hood, even though the hall was open.

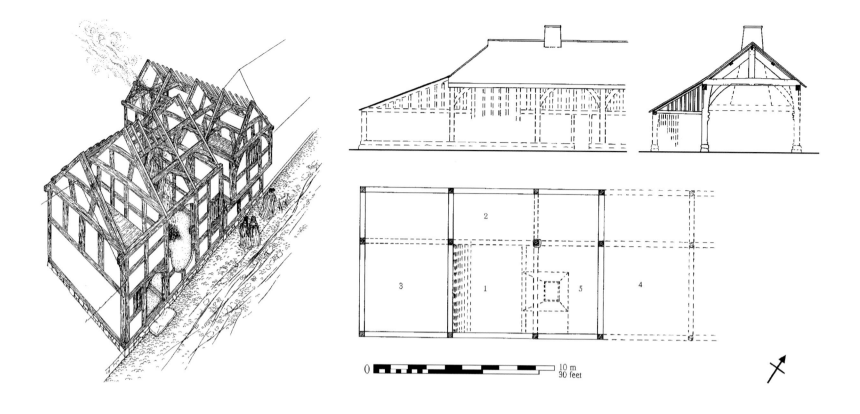

282. White Hall, Presteigne. Perspective view of the original frame (now concealed behind a rendered front), prepared for the forthcoming RCAHMW volume on medieval houses in Radnorshire. The two-bay open hall lies at the centre, with a single bay to the left, comprising an entrance, services and solar, and a jettied cross-wing at the high end containing private chambers. © Crown copyright: Royal Commission on Ancient and Historical Monuments in Wales

283. Bankhouse, Skircoat, Halifax. Plan, section and partial restoration of front elevation (with removed timbers shown hatched), showing central hall or housebody in Yorkshire terminology (1), with aisle (2), flanked by a parlour (3) and a wool store (4); the entrance is into a passage (5) behind a large hood, set over the hearth, while, at the further end of the hall, a cove rises above the position of the hall table. After RCHME *W. Yorks* 1975, figs 13 and 14. © Crown copyright

This seems to have been because the abundant coal of the region was burnt instead of wood, and the hood ensured that the acrid, poisonous smoke was safely removed.[19]

The three-part arrangement of medieval hall-houses is so ubiquitous that it is readily taken for granted. However, while the merchant's house known as Greyfriars, which was built in Friar Street, Worcester, in the late fifteenth century and possibly owned by Thomas Grene,[20] has gabled ends in the typical way, these were separated not by an open hall, but by a storeyed central range that continued the line of their jetties, and it seems that the open hall was in a rear wing instead.[21] (fig. 284)

Given the premium on frontage, it is hardly surprising that the more compact single-ended arrangement of solar chamber set above service rooms was favoured for lesser houses in towns where land was expensive. These two-part hall-houses are, if anything, even more ubiquitous than those of three parts with a chamber end. There are several in the little towns of west Kent, notably 49–51 High Street, Westerham, which started with a two-bay open hall with a cross-passage, and its services and solar chamber were combined in a single cross-wing.[22] (fig. 285) The Ancient House at Clare and a smaller house at 6–7 Lady Street, Lavenham, had a similar plan.[23] Ownership is hard to trace in Lavenham, but it was probably a family of clothiers, the well-to-do Caustons, who occupied the much more ostentatious Little Hall, whose open hall occupies two bays together with the entrance and cross-passage in a close-studded main range, while the services and solar are housed in a jettied and gabled cross-wing, made all the more magnificent by the play of its herringbone bracing.[24] (fig. 286)

Such two-part hall-houses need not be of little consequence. Great Porch House at 6–8 Monday Market Street, Devizes, was built with some panache early in the fifteenth century to comprise an open hall, unusually of three bays; an adjacent cross-passage with a narrow chamber over it; and a cross-wing, set over an undercroft, jettied at the front, with service rooms below and two chambers above, front and back, the great chamber at the front, perhaps once having an oriel window. (fig. 287) Decoratively applied curved braces, a carved head and flowers, as well as foiled window tracery suggest its likely construction for the Coventry family, who were prominent merchants in Devizes at the time and also counted mayors and members of parliament among their numbers.[25]

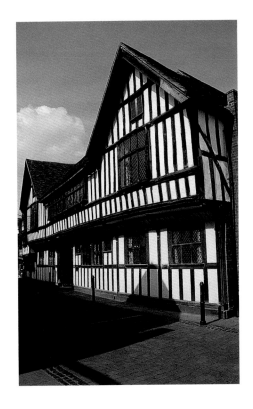

284. Greyfriars, Friar Street, Worcester. The original continuous jetty signifies the storeyed centre, rather than an open hall, between the two gabled wings

285. 49–51 High Street, Westerham. The services and solar are in the gabled wing, the hall beyond them

286. Little Hall, Lavenham, is essentially similar in arrangement to the house at Westerham, but larger and more lavish externally

287. Great Porch House, 6–8 Monday Market Street, Devizes. Section, showing (to left) the three bays of its formerly open hall with a cross-passage in part of the right-hand bay (1), and the cross-wing with services (2) built over an undercroft, and solar chamber above (3), spanned by an arch-braced truss. Based on a survey by Dan Miles and Richard Warmington in VAGCP 1990, 33. ©Wiltshire Buildings Record

288. Cloth Hall (alias Turk Farm), Smarden. Although extended to the left, partly in brick, and altered by the insertion of a raised upper-storey window, the characteristic jettied ends and recessed central hall under a continuous roof are clearly evident

289. Clarendon House, East Grinstead. Until 1939 the timber frame of this standard, four-bay Wealden hall-house in the heart of the Sussex Weald was hidden by plaster; its restoration exposed the frame (the timber was felled c. 1438–67), but it still needs an experienced eye to strip away the projecting gables and continuous upper floor (inserted in the 1560s) to recognize the central open hall set between the jettied service end (left) and chamber end (right)

Both three-part and two-part hall-houses appear in the characteristic form of the so-called Wealden house. This comprises a single range, with a central hall and storeyed end bays, all in a line. (fig. 288) The ends are jettied at the front, like vestigial wings, and rise to the same height as the open hall, which therefore appears to be set back between them. An overall roof usually spans the jettied ends and the recessed hall, where the deep eaves are supported on brackets.

Wealdens are very common in most of rural Kent and Sussex, where probably a thousand of them survive, if not more, but they are far less common in other counties. The Wealden is again less common in towns, partly through destruction, but also because many are hidden by alterations and accretions. (fig. 289) Urban examples are not confined to this south-eastern homeland, several appearing in the Midlands, and there is one in York. Many of these are two-part hall-houses, with only one jettied end, known as half-Wealdens (sometimes as two-thirds Wealdens). (figs 290 and 291)

The oldest Wealdens are of the 1380s, and seem to be descended from the hall and cross-wing plan of the thirteenth and fourteenth centuries, but the wings are suppressed so that they are only expressed in the jetties, and, occasionally, in the form of the roof-framing. The suppression of the wings might suggest an adaptation designed to serve the needs of urban sites in the centre of such towns as Canterbury or Maidstone.[26] Indeed, an apparently very early

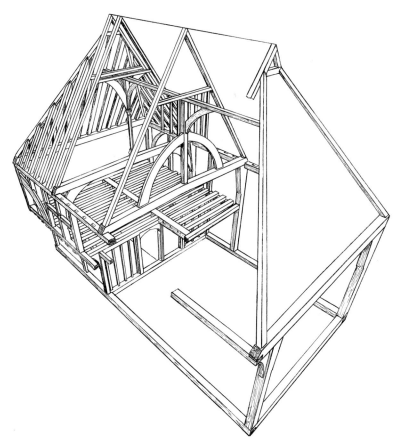

290. 81 St Dunstan's Street, Canterbury. Cutaway perspective of a half-Wealden, with the nearer bay containing the open hall, and the further bay with two doors to the service rooms, a characteristic front jetty, and upper chamber open to a typical crown-post roof. After John Bowen, © Canterbury Archaeological Trust 1982–3, 32

291. 81 St Dunstan's Street, Canterbury, its original form partly hidden by modern alterations and a large doorway driven into its formerly open hall

Wealden at 35 High Street, Winchester, seemingly dates from 1340, but nearly all the other surviving evidence points to a rural origin. The wealthy yeomen farming the Wealden vale to the south of Maidstone seem to have provided the incentive for the construction of the greatest concentration of these houses, as well as most of the oldest survivors.[27]

The form has much to recommend itself architecturally, being particularly distinctive, and its storeyed end-bays and recessed hall are well articulated. It enjoyed an outstanding popularity among rich and prosperous Kentish yeomen, particularly in the closing years of the fifteenth century. Popularity alone may account for its appearance outside its native homeland, particularly for inns and taverns, where a fashionable face counted.

This fashionable face is precisely where the Wealden scores. Because the determining features of the Wealden hall-house do indeed face the front, the design is particularly suited to an urban setting, and, moreover, with no projections at ground level, it can be readily built along the street frontage or even beside a passage in a way that a house with the impediment of a projecting cross-wing cannot.

Carpenters who were employed by the Church may possibly have been the first to develop the design; they were certainly building Wealdens by the start of the fifteenth century. In Robertsbridge, of a dozen surviving hall-houses, five were built about 1390–1430 as Wealdens with standard measurements, probably through the auspices of the Cistercians of Robertsbridge Abbey and the craftsmen of a single carpenters' yard.[28] (fig. 292) Between 1406 and 1414, Richard Curteys, the beadle of Battle Abbey, built a Wealden fronting High Street.[29] In Smarden, where four of the surviving halls are of Wealden form, one, the Cloth Hall, formerly Turk's Farm, was probably built about 1470–1500 by the Church (Turk being a corruption of Church). Another, the Old Vicarage at Westerham, was perhaps built under the auspices of Christ Church, Canterbury, during the period 1460–1500.[30]

Several of the Wealdens at Robertsbridge either were or became taverns, but there was little to differentiate this particular usage. The hall became a drinking room and the buttery an ale-store and servery or tap room. The Maiden's Head, Wincheap, in a suburb of Canterbury, was built opposite a market place, and, before alterations, had an extended chamber end, possibly

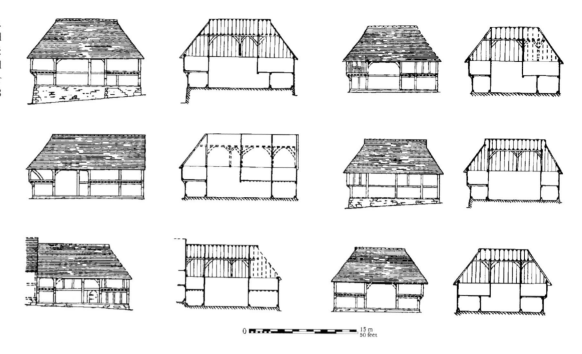

292. Six Wealden houses at Robertsbridge. Partially restored front elevations and longitudinal sections (left to right) of: Androwes and Le Angell (top), Smytholts and Cradocks (middle), Brokers and Le Checker (bottom). © Martin & Mastin 1974, figs 6 and 8

0 ⬛⬛⬛⬛⬛⬛⬛⬛⬛⬛ 15 m
50 feet

serving as drinking parlours, and a large framed building at the rear may have been a combined malt-house and brew-house.[31] At Edenbridge, the Old Eden Inn was built about 1470–1500 as one of three Wealdens in the town, set among other hall-houses with projecting cross-wings,[32] and the King and Queen is another. At 13–23 Upper Lake, Battle, a Wealden was leased out in the late 1470s as an alehouse, and was flanked by rows of half-Wealdens of which two more were similarly leased.[33] So too in the Midlands: the Woolpack Inn in Stodman Street, Newark, is a half-Wealden[34] always used as an alehouse as well as a lodging for travellers, and may be the sole survivor of a longer range.

The Wealden became remarkably popular in the western Midlands, particularly in Warwickshire, where there are a handful at Stratford-upon-Avon,[35] Warwick,[36] Henley-in-Arden[37] and Alcester.[38] (fig. 293) In Coventry they are legion, but very small; there are two pairs and a row of six half-Wealdens in Spon Street, and between seventeen and perhaps even thirty

293. Mason's Court, 11–12 Rother Street, Stratford-upon-Avon. A Wealden hall-house, far from home

294. Blue Boar Inn, St John's Street, Winchester. The continuously jettied upper floor extends round the corner, and is now rendered white, partly to distinguish the repairs after extensive fire damage, and partly to accord with the medieval practice of using limewash to preserve timber and plaster alike

295. 2 Market Place, St Albans. Cross-section showing its three storeys built over an undercroft. After J. T. Smith 1992, fig. 236. © Crown copyright

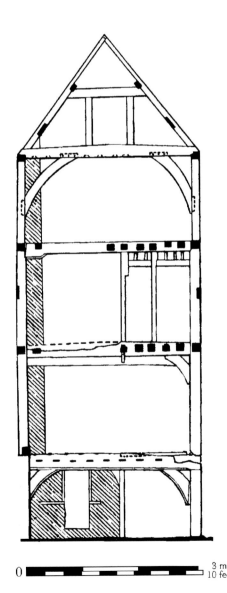

0 ▄▄▄▄▄▄▄▄▄▄ 3 m / 10 feet

more are known to have been scattered around the city's suburban streets. Fifteenth-century prosperity may have prompted speculators to build large numbers of permanent houses in the suburbs for the first time, land being both available and cheap enough to encourage intensive development, and the Wealden design added a dash of distinction.[39]

An unusual and presumably late variation of the Wealden form, particularly favoured in Hampshire, included a gallery jettied across the front of the hall, consequently obscuring its characteristic recessed appearance. Despite fire damage in 1968, this can still be seen outside Winchester's city walls at the Blue Boar Inn in St John's Street, where it served drinkers going to St Giles's Fair. (fig. 294) The gallery was designed not for the practical purpose of linking the separate upper chambers, but probably to give the inn a fashionable exterior, suggesting a complete upper storey, and to serve entertainers inside.[40]

When pressure of space enforced the typical pattern of long narrow burgage strips on builders it was a simple matter to turn the three-part plan of a hall-house round so that it lay end-on to the street against one boundary and to form a passage along the other. The range fronting the street might contain shops with chambers over them as well as an entrance to the rear of the property. The hall would normally lie end-on to the front range, while the passage or narrow yard continued to a back lane.

A majority of houses built on comparatively narrow burgages resulted from several campaigns of work, and these forced compromises so that the resulting arrangements are endlessly varied. The route through from front to back might be no more than a mean passage, just wide enough for a single person, but it could accommodate wagons and swell into a small yard. The plot would need to be significantly wider than the hall, 20 feet (6 m) being roughly a minimum, with the width of the hall taking up 16.5 feet (5 m). This would allow space for one or two narrow shops and the entrance, with two or three solar chambers above. The shops could belong to the household, and be devoted to the craft or trade that supported it, and similarly the chambers above them might double as stores; but often the front range of shops and chambers was leased out separately.

Occasionally a whole range might be in commercial use, such as at 2 Market Place, St Albans, where an unusually tall building, two bays in depth, comprised an undercroft, a ground-floor shop where both retailing and manufacture were probably undertaken, and two upper storeys that served for warehousing, not occupation.[41] (fig. 295) Most shops advertised their presence with one or more large openings, often arched, which had fold-down counters

296. 34–50 Church Street, Tewkesbury.
Perspective showing a typical interior, with a
shop on the ground floor at the front (right),
with fold-down counters, a chamber above,
and a small open hall (left) at the rear; many
houses in the row had a room added behind
this, thus blocking its windows to direct light.
Redrawn from a survey exhibited on site

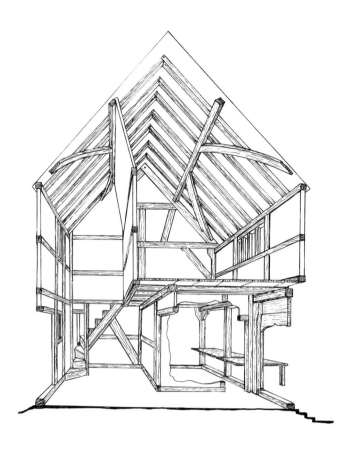

297. 34–50 Church Street, Tewkesbury. Part
of the row, showing one house with a restored
shop window and shutters

298. High Street, Tewkesbury, seen from
Tolzey Lane, framing a typical late medieval
shop set over an undercroft, with two jettied
storeys of solar chambers above

where goods were displayed. (fig. 296) Sometimes the main entrance served shoppers as well,
but often, beside the shop windows, there was a characteristically narrow door that would only
admit one person at a time, presumably to deter thieves. Internal doors to shops were again
particularly narrow.[42] While the chambers might well provide accommodation for the tenants
of the shops beneath them, the shops could as easily be let as separate lock-ups, and the chambers be devoted to the use of the main householder or to other tenants. (figs 297 and 298)

299. Comparative shop fronts, showing (from left to right, top to bottom): a projecting solar set over an open arcade to form porches for an entrance to the main house, an entrance down steps to an undercroft, and a place to view a shop window (based on 58 French Street, Southampton); a pentice sheltering entrances and shop windows on a house lacking a jetty (based on 29–32 High Street, King's Lynn); a jetty offering minimal shelter (based on the Green Dragon, 6 Church Street, Wymond-ham); an arcade of a Chester Row, with shops to the left and a place for stalls on the right, built over an undercroft and beneath a solar (based on a section of Watergate Street); and a fully developed arcade, with solars projecting well forward of the shops beneath them (based on The Pentice, High Street, Winchester)

Occasionally the upper chambers were not only jettied out over the shops, but also extended further out still to cover an arcade of the kind that came into existence from the late thirteenth century onwards to form the Chester Rows. Arcades sheltering shops are common in Europe, but not in Britain. The Pentice, which runs along the front of 30–41 High Street, Winchester, is as good an example as can be found in England. (fig. 299) It was apparently built after 1450, perhaps to make permanent the former awnings over temporary stalls, or perhaps in emulation of some half-remembered Continental example, and then piecemeal, rather than as a single project.[43] The colonnaded walks at Totnes may well be later still, but, despite their obvious advantages in a land of variable weather, and even the example of Inigo Jones's fashionable arcades of the 1630s at Covent Garden, arcades of this sort have never become popular.

The arrangement of shops fronting a private house became increasingly common in the late thirteenth and fourteenth centuries. It was widely adopted in Winchester, where the characteristics of a courtyard house were scaled down to suit the pattern of burgages. From the early twelfth century, archaeological evidence shows that the main part was built of stone at the rear and may have incorporated a hall.[44] The front buildings, which stretched back some 33 feet (10 m) from the street, were often rebuilt during the Middle Ages and more likely to have been of timber.

This arrangement suited men of substance, who valued its seclusion. Entry was by way of an arch set between what were often shops fronting the street and under the solar chambers of an upper storey. Both William Dunstaple and William le Spycer owned property of this sort in High Street early in the fourteenth century. Larger frontages allowed a full wagon entrance, but frontage was so precious that access this wide was usually from the rear, where gateways were placed within rows of smaller shops with rooms above that lay along the back lane.

Between the hall and the rear of the plot there were subsidiary buildings used as quarters for servants, stores and workrooms, stables and wagon sheds. Kitchens were sometimes placed there too since this reduced the risk of fire – but not all risks: in 1280 Roger Stygant was killed in his kitchen while attempting to separate a mare from two overheated stallions. For the most part, kitchens were closer to the main accommodation, and could be surrounded by other rooms within the main part of a house when cooking was not undertaken over the fire of an open hall.[45]

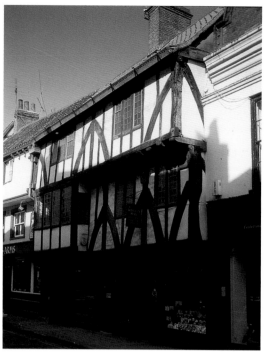

300. Flore's House, Oakham. © Andor Gomme)

301. 49–51 Goodramgate, York

While narrow frontage suggests a certain meanness, this was not invariable. William Canynges's stone house in Redcliffe Street, Bristol, was built on the grandest scale even though it had a frontage of only 28 feet (8.5 m). To make up for this, the depth of over 200 feet (60 m) allowed for shops or service rooms at the front and a magnificently finished open hall, 33 feet long and 22 feet wide (10 by 6.7 m). This remained a festive place, and, like his associate Gaywood's hall, was hung with tapestries and lit by candles at Christmas. On ordinary days it increasingly became a place of welcome, and part of the elaborate entry to an ornately tiled family parlour at the rear, beyond which was his tower overlooking the river.[46]

Far more modest is the house that one of Oakham's richest inhabitants, William Flore, the Controller of Works at Oakham Castle (or perhaps his son Roger Flore, merchant and one time Speaker of the House of Commons), began towards the end of the fourteenth century. (fig. 300) It faces an alley running off High Street without an intervening archway; its cross-wings, which apparently came later, respectively contain services, unusually away from the street in comparative privacy, and a parlour toward the street where commercial pressure eventually made a shop of it.[47]

The front range of 49–51 Goodramgate, York, comprises shops and a narrow archway in the common way, with two jettied storeys of chambers above. (fig. 301) These front a complete three-part hall-house, the most northerly of Wealden design, running away from the street beside an alley wide enough to provide plenty of daylight.[48] Less generously, 126 High Street, Oxford, was built about 1500 with an undercroft, and, over it, a shop and chamber block rising through three full storeys into a garret, behind which lay an open hall (since rebuilt), reached by a passage through the front to a narrow open yard before it.[49]

A different interpretation of a similar plan made necessary by the narrowest of passages or gaps between one house and the next put all the emphasis on the front and ignored the side. In Southampton, 58 French Street has plain stone side and rear walls, which would hardly have shown, leaving only its jettied front wall of fashionable timber. (fig. 302) Built over a separate undercroft, its front door leads to a passage that runs within the house past a shop to the hall, and this is spanned at high level by a gallery that connects the upper chambers, front and rear.[50]

The halls of these houses were hard to light, a problem readily solved were the plot wide enough for a double-pile with the hall placed not at right angles but parallel to a row of shops facing the street. Tackley's Inn at 106–7 High Street, Oxford, was built about 1320 with a front range comprising five individual shops with solar chambers, set over an undercroft, and a rear range, reached through a passageway between the shops, comprising an open hall and a large chamber. (fig. 303) The front block was lit only from the north, the rear only from the south, but

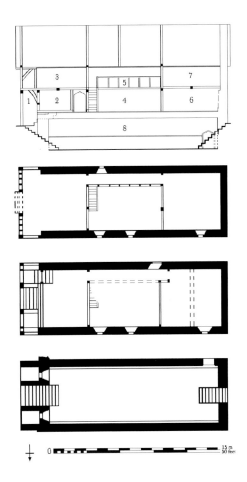

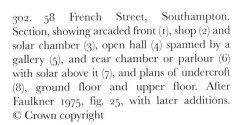

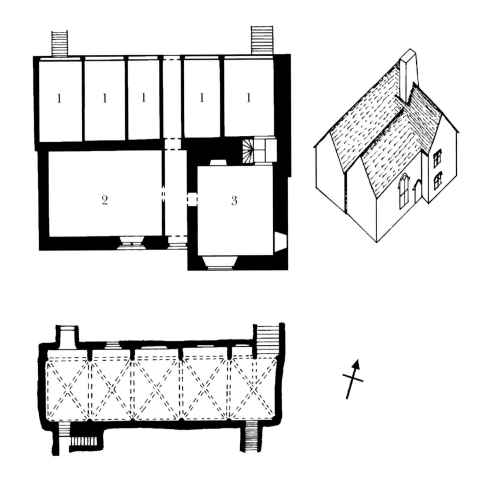

302. 58 French Street, Southampton. Section, showing arcaded front (1), shop (2) and solar chamber (3), open hall (4) spanned by a gallery (5), and rear chamber or parlour (6) with solar above it (7), and plans of undercroft (8), ground floor and upper floor. After Faulkner 1975, fig. 25, with later additions. © Crown copyright

303. Tackley's Inn, 106–7 High Street, Oxford. Plan of undercroft (below), and reconstructed plan of building above, showing five shops (1) facing the street (at top) with, at the back, an open hall (2), cross-passage, and heated chamber (3). On the right-hand side is a hypothetical perspective of the whole building. After Pantin 1942 and 1947, and Faulkner 1966, fig. 5

304. 38–42 Watergate Street, Chester. Graham Holme's cutaway perspective showing the row at the front (right) with a shop behind it and the hall at the rear, set over part of two timber-roofed undercrofts. A. Brown 1999, Pl. 1. © English Heritage

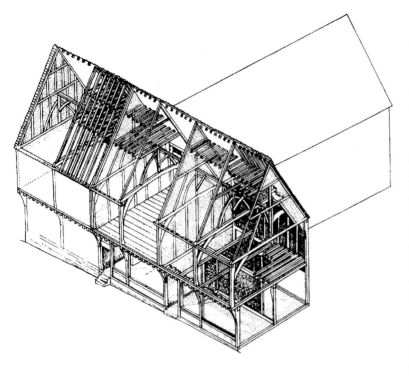

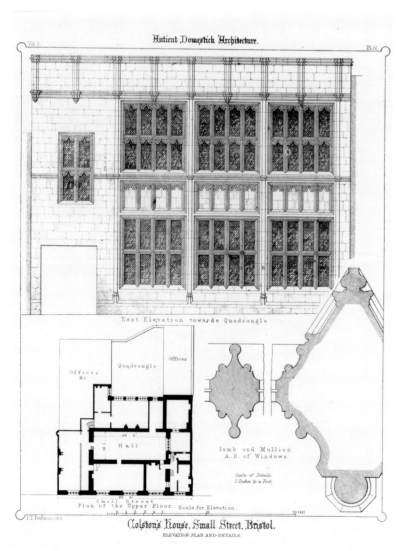

East Elevation towards Quadrangle

Antient Domestick Architecture.

Offices &c.

Quadrangle

Offices

Hall

Jamb and Mullion
A.B. of Windows

Scale of Details
2 Inches to a Foot.

Small Street
Plan of the Upper Floor. Scale for Elevation

20 FEET

Colston's House. Small Street, Bristol.
ELEVATION, PLAN AND DETAILS.

this was an expensive stone building and, with glazed windows that kept out bad weather, lighting from one side only was no impediment, since shutters only went up for security.[51] In another variation at 38–42 Watergate Street, Chester, the hall is built over the rear part of two undercrofts, and the chamber block extends forward along the whole of a third.[52] (fig. 304) A simpler variation, exemplified by 28–30 Steep Hill, Lincoln, placed the hall in a rear wing. (fig. 305)

This general arrangement of hall and chamber block set behind shops was common among cheaper timber-framed houses too, for instance in Jordan Well and Gosford Street, Coventry, and in Tudor House, Southampton. It appeared again, though possibly with private rooms rather than shops at the front, in Colston's House at 20 Small Street, Bristol. This house never belonged to the city's famous merchant of that name, and was built in the 1540s by another outstandingly successful merchant John Smythe. Its hall, emulating those of magnates, was a place where those of lesser estate displayed obsequiousness to Smythe and his like.[53] (fig. 306)

When they were built end-on to the street many houses were contiguous and formed rows (in Latin *rangiae*). If they were built against their neighbours on each side, access beyond the shops at the front must be by an internal passage. Such row houses survive in substantial numbers in England's medieval towns. They were convenient, economical of space, relatively cheap to build, and found ready tenants. As a result they were eventually to become one of the commonest forms of medieval urban dwelling, and their progeny, much adapted, became a ubiquitous element in urban building.

When a plot was too narrow to embrace any more than the width of an open hall there was no other recourse than to cram it in against the neighbouring houses. It might lie behind shops, where an entrance led to a passage through to the hall and then on to a chamber range at the rear. The hall then suffered from lack of light, receiving only what filtered in from the rooms, front and back.

In the west this plan was used for houses which characteristically had stone party walls dividing them from neighbouring houses, which was a sensible precaution against fire, and timber-framed walls spanning them and adorning the front. A passage would normally run from front to back, beside a shop at the front, with a storey or two of chambers over it – usually with prominent jetties, oriel windows and a gable – and then past the hall, which might have windows high up, and finally reaching service rooms at the back, again with a chamber built over them. Beyond this there might be a separate kitchen further to the rear past a small yard, and sometimes attached to the rear of the main block by a timber gallery.

The grandest examples of these houses, 36 and 38 North Street, Exeter,[54] had fireplaces in their open halls, and so were probably the last of a medieval tradition. (fig. 307) This was passed on to the later sixteenth century and the houses that line Fore Street and High Street in Totnes, where the hall is floored over. The difficulty in lighting the halls must have made these houses difficult to modernize in this way, since flooring over the halls would make them darker still. It was easier to take down the timber frame and rebuild it between the stone party walls with less depth so that light could penetrate to the centre more readily from front and back.[55]

307. 38 North Street, Exeter. Plan and section, showing shop (1) and solar chamber with side passage (2) leading to open hall (3), with fireplace on side wall, and probable chamber or parlour (4) and detached kitchen (5). After Laithwaite 1995, fig. 5.10. © Devon County Council

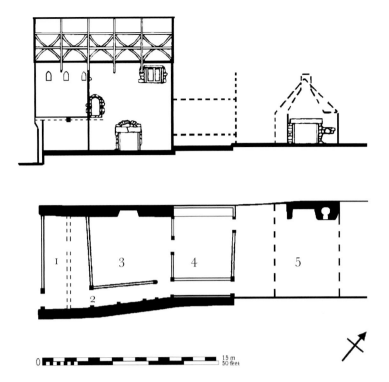

Many lost houses of Bristol had this form.[56] Similarly, in Winchester, 33 and 34 High Street were built like this between 1459 and 1463. Before them was the covered walkway, known as the Pentice, that protects the shops at the front, rather like the galleries of Chester's Rows, but makes the inside of the hall darker still. (fig. 299) Over the walkway are solar chambers, which are linked to those at the back by galleries. These extend across the open halls above the passages that link the shops to the ground-floor rooms at the back.[57] In Wales, 47 High Street, Presteigne, was built as a row house with an internal access passage. Unusually it has an undercroft which was furnished with a fireplace and could be reached directly from the house above.

Corner houses were an exception. Both of their exposed sides were of timber so as to make a good show. A corner house in Stepcote Hill, Exeter, was framed on both of its sides in this way and had just one room on each of its three floors and garret, probably serving as a shop, a hall, a bedchamber and store respectively; likewise the Cherub, 13 Higher Street, Dartmouth, though its ground-floor room was provided with a fireplace so must have been a living room, not a shop; it has jetties on both sides and prominent dragon-posts and beams to support them at the corner.

The problem of lighting the hall of a row house was made all the worse when, as in Winchester, direct communication was sought between the upper floors at front and back by bridging one side of the upper part of the hall with a gallery. The Golden Lion in High Street, Worcester, took this form when it was built about 1400 over a stone undercroft, which had separate access to the street and was used as a tavern. At the front there was a shop with the entrance passage beside it, and two jettied chambers as well as a garret above. The hall was finished with very high mullioned windows and a louver in the centre of its roof, while a gallery, spanning one of its sides over the entrance passage, linked the lower front chamber with one in the storeyed rear range. While these arrangements are clear enough, it is a puzzle to work out how they incorporated the rooms indicated by the probate inventory of its occupant John Walsgrove alias Flytt of 1567. In addition to the hall and undercroft, there were two parlours, a buttery, a wool chamber, a maiden's chamber, a press chamber, and a kiln (kyell) chamber as well as three other chambers, another tavern, a kitchen and a boulting house. Only too evident from its smell must have been the 'Lyttell howthce under the stayr'.[58]

Beneath the level of these houses came those of the commonest sort. Many were of only one room, some of two, and their accommodation was augmented by little more than what a garret could offer. Even these houses on occasion sported an open hall. In Coventry little houses

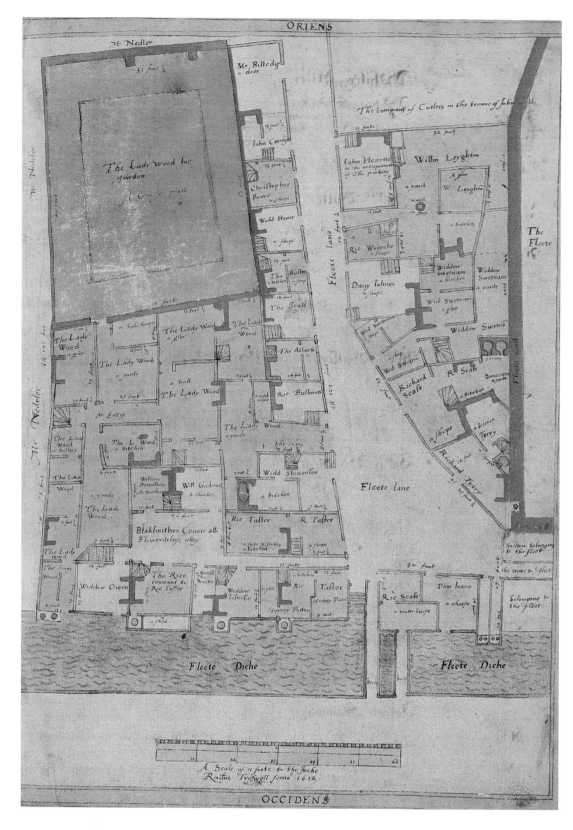

were built with open halls but no service room as such, and a solar, doubling as a store, was perched over the entrance passage and jettied out into the hall in the manner of two houses removed from Much Park Street to Spon Street.[59] This was so restricted a form that additional rooms were invariably added at the rear to take the pressure off the solar. Sometimes the service block was built behind the hall in the first instance so as to reduce the pressure on frontage a little.

Another way of exploiting a single framed bay was to divide it in half with a shop and solar at the front and an open hall at the rear. This form appears in Church Street, Tewkesbury, (fig.

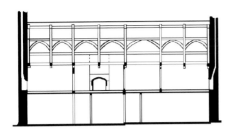

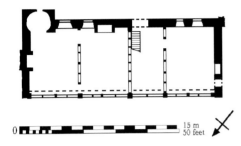

309. 16 and 18 High Street, Bruton. Plan and section of a pair of small houses with heated upper chambers. After Penoyre 1997, p. 109. © Jane and John Penoyre

296) and again at 39 High Street, Kingston upon Thames. This house dates from before 1500, and may have been part of the neighbouring but structurally separate building, but could readily have stood alone.[60] The similar house at 7 West Street, Dunstable, is a little larger and its two framed bays comprise a shop with a chamber over it at the front and a windowless open hall at the rear with a louver in the roof. All the light comes from two shop windows, which could be shut by downward-hinged shutters that served as counters.[61]

A few of these tiny houses survived in the West Country until they were demolished in the 1970s because of their small size. No. 33 North Street, Ashburton, had two rooms divided by a cross-passage, and no upper rooms or even a loft. At Newton Abbot, 15–17 Highweek Street was smaller still, being only 25 feet (7.5 m) across inside, and had a shop at the front and a hall with an enclosed fireplace on the rear wall.[62] Bristol's shop-houses were so small that they lacked a hall, and had no provision for cooking or heating.[63] Similarly, small rows of houses still stand in Much Wenlock, some of them built in the middle of the fifteenth century with only a single room.[64]

These houses are as rare today as once they were common. They probably filled every space in crowded towns, making permanent temporary shops and stalls, crowding against the walls of larger houses that faced inwards on to courtyards, and lining back lanes where no one of substance would want to live. This was the commonest type of house in the City before the Great Fire. Ralph Treswell surveyed dozens of them – in Billiter Lane, in Fleet Lane, in Bishopsgate and Cock Lane, and along Haywharf in Upper Thames Street. (fig. 308) Some have a single room, others two; most by the time of his surveys in the early seventeenth century had brick chimney stacks, and those beside the Fleet were fitted with privies jutting out over the ditch. Many had stairs to upper floors, a timely reminder that, though small on plan – they might have a floor area of only around 200 square feet (20 m²) – they could have cellars and rise through several floors, five with a garret being the top limit.[65]

The house in Fleet Lane occupied by Thomas Atherton in 1612 had a total floor area of only 345 square feet (32 m²), and this was divided into two chambers, the upper one slightly larger on account of its jettied floor. In 1611 Stephen Woodford occupied an old house in Bread Street called The Ship, which was built over a cellar and measured about 30 by 15 feet (9 by 4.5 m) on plan. This also seems fairly small, but it had three storeys comprising a hall, a kitchen and three chambers, and there was a privy in the garret. Size is not the only measure since multiple occupancy reduced both space and privacy, and what the occupants did for a living perhaps added further complications. Several 'widows' kept house in Blacksmiths Court alias Flower de Luce Alley, close by the Fleet, for instance one incorporating 'A chamber over Widow Johnson's chamber, with a chimney 15½′ × 14½′ with a little house of office over the Fleet ditch, in which chamber dwelleth George Priest . . . a garret over the same'.[66]

Although the open hall became obsolescent in the sixteenth century, several earlier houses made do without one. Many of these houses were too small to embrace so much formal open space, but there were others that were large enough for an open hall but did without for no apparent reason, and certainly not because they were advanced in any particular way.

Many of the City's houses comprised a heated room on the ground floor, perhaps behind a shop, with several storeys of chambers above. In small towns the circumstances were very different, but still there might be no open halls. The earlier houses of Bruton, a Somerset wool and cloth town, were rebuilt in the middle of the fifteenth century using stone, leaving the only exposed timber on the front where its fashionable status would count most. (fig. 309) The houses were fairly small and, despite the comparatively low cost of stone, not all their party walls were made of it. The internal timber trusses were set at right angles to the street and incorporated a jetty at the front, the ground floor accommodating shops, the upper floor chambers. Some houses were three or four bays wide, and 16 and 18 High Street were built as a pair, with a closed timber truss dividing them. Neither of these houses had an open hall, but, instead, both of them had hearths built into the upper part of their stone end-gables, and No. 16 had a second hearth on the rear wall.[67]

In the middle of the fifteenth century the carpenter Nicholas Coksegge agreed to build a new house for John Brasyer of Bury St Edmunds (who died in 1468) between two others in the

310. Abbot's House, Butcher Row, Shrewsbury. Front elevation and details of dragon post, doorways and shop windows. After Dollman and Jobbins 1863, 2, Pl. 125. © Society of Antiquaries of London

311. Abbot's House today

town. It was to be 34.5 feet (10.5 m) from side to side, and would have 'a kechen' at the back and a 'halle', the angle between them being covered by a 'tresaunce', and there was also to be a parlour. These were to be 'all soleryd over with a gete into the weyeward'. In short, the house would have a jetty along the street, and there would be a continuous upper floor containing solars over the hall and parlour at the front and the kitchen at the back, which would have a pentice linking it to the rear of the hall. No mention is made of chimneys, nor of smoke-hoods, but the cost of the timber and all the carpentry is given as 20 marks (£13 16s 8d), which was to be paid in stages as work progressed.[68] The house was not cheap, and the lack of an open hall is a pointer to the future.

Some houses had their halls on the first floor. At 21–2 Steep Hill, Lincoln, the former Harlequin Inn, a complete timber-framed hall-house, comprising an open hall (really an upper hall), chamber end, and services, the latter contained in a gabled cross-wing, is jettied over a row of five shops, partly dug into the steeply sloping ground. This is a neat solution to the problems of a difficult site. (fig. 364) A more curious arrangement that seems to abandon the open hall for Continental and even Scottish practice occurs in Abbot's House, Butcher Row, at Shrewsbury. (figs 310 and 311) This L-shaped timber-framed range was built for one of the later fifteenth-century abbots of Lilleshall who attended a building ceremony, together with his carpenter and borough officials, in 1459.[69] The lower part is conventionally arranged with chambers jettied over the ground-floor shops, which have well-restored windows for the display of goods, but the third storey is very differently planned from the individual units below, and comprises a three-bay hall or great chamber and smaller private rooms that together form an independent apartment which admirably fulfilled the needs of a visiting dignitary such as the abbot.

From this great multiplicity of urban houses, time would pick the row house as the most likely source of future endeavour; stripped of its open hall, its general arrangements served well right through the Industrial Revolution and thereafter. It would also provide the basis for the terrace, the most successful house type of all.

17

One frame called the 'Lady Rowe'

Terrace houses

By the later seventeenth century London was booming. One evident sign of this was the construction of row upon row of uniform houses. These were designed to attract a growing population that had done well from the professional, commercial and industrial ventures which London made possible. Many towns throughout Britain followed this lead at an ever-growing pace, through the eighteenth century, into the nineteenth and beyond.

In the Middle Ages these were simply called 'rows', as were other groups of houses built together along the street frontage with some kind of common identity, such as the Chester Rows. There was no need of differentiation because rows of uniform houses were neither common enough nor special enough to need a word of their own. They were also called 'rents', since they were usually built by speculators for renting out for profit, and hence termed '*domus rentales*' in legal documents.

The current word for them, 'terrace', originated with a speculative development that Robert and James Adam began in 1769 in which they treated a long row of commodious houses as a single architectural composition. Because of the sloping site between the Strand and the Thames, the houses were raised on a terrace above high water. First known as 'The Royal Taras', later as Adelphi Terrace, this was the height of fashion, and, though it ruined the Adam brothers financially, the name stuck. So the word 'terrace' can usefully distinguish a row of several houses that were conceived as a single unit, and built on a single extended plot of land, usually in a short space of time, to a uniform design. Meanwhile, the term 'row' means any set of adjoining houses aligned along a street with a common identifying feature.

The terrace already had a long ancestry when the Adam brothers began the Adelphi. This was far from illustrious. The terrace was not particularly common in the Middle Ages: in terms of both the class of person for whom it was intended and the parts of town where it was usually built, it was demonstrably marginal. On occasion a terrace was built relatively grandly, but then always with a special class of person in mind, usually vicars.

Because most medieval row houses were built individually on separate plots, they were as easy to finance as to build. These advantages set them apart from the superficially similar terraces of uniform houses that were built as single constructions on single plots of land with a long frontage. Although one individual terrace house might cost no more than an equivalent row house, overall they required a greater investment, and all at once. A terrace had to be planned, capital had to be found, a plot obtained, and the whole operation overseen until completion, all in the hope of finding a number of ready tenants. In short, a terrace needed a confident speculator.

A terrace required a frontage of at least some 10–13 feet (3–4 m) per house, and usually more, so a modest terrace of five small houses would have a frontage of about 50–65 feet (15–20 m). This was not readily found along main streets in the centre of town, nor easily created by amalgamation. Conversely, a terrace needed little in depth. While a number of long thin burgages could be consolidated into a frontage wide enough for the construction of a terrace, the financial and legal problems that this involved deterred speculators in a type of house

312. Lady Row, Goodramgate, York. Part of Britain's oldest dated surviving terrace

that was not a particularly profitable investment unless there was much to gain in the back land. When a plot with so long a frontage did appear in such a location, it was usually laid out for an important civic building or a rich merchant's establishment, that is to say for a building important enough for financial and legal considerations to be no stumbling block, and part of the frontage might then be given over to a terrace.

There were nevertheless two major sources of land in the centre of town that could be tapped: the fringes of churchyards and market squares. Both of these were traditionally linked with trade, and this was an important consideration. There were also side lanes and the out-skirts of towns, where land values and therefore rents were lower simply because property there was less conveniently sited. It is precisely in these locations that long frontages could most easily be created, and that is where most medieval terraces are found.

Churchyards were widely used in the twelfth century as market places before these grew in thriving towns to such an extent that they needed a specific, permanent site of their own.

Sometimes, when a church and its yard overlooked a newly formed market place, stalls might be set up along the edge to take advantage of the opportunities for profitable trade. This is well illustrated by Hemel Hempstead, where, on the east side of the churchyard, there were 'Twelve sheddes used for staules for Butchers'; and similar circumstances prevailed at Watford and Hitchin.[1] It was relatively easy to replace such stalls with a row of permanent shops, built to a uniform design with a domestic room in an upper storey, as occurred in Ludlow. By developing its churchyards in this way, the Church exploited an age-old partnership with manufacture and retailing.

Churchyards had the added advantage of being owned by an institution with a particular desire to exploit its possessions for the purpose of augmenting its income. These were ideal for terraces. They had the necessary undivided space, and they were sited close enough to town centres to command a good rent, but not so close as to be better suited to a grander class of house and occupant. This gave the Church the edge over other landowners to make it apparently the earliest to build terraces.

The Church's ability to build repetitively is exemplified by the lodging houses, and the domestic quarters of colleges and inns. None of these is a prototype of the terrace as it first appeared in the fourteenth century. More significant are the rows of small lodgings set around cloisters to accommodate the special needs of monks, particularly Carthusians, who were devoted to individual seclusion and could not enjoy the fruits of communal life. Soon after the countess of Salisbury founded their monastery in 1232, the Carthusians of Hinton Priory in Somerset built themselves fourteen identical houses, each with a main heated room and a subsidiary room set in a regular way around a cloister.[2] These served all the domestic needs of the monks in isolation. While the houses were not contiguous as terrace houses were to be, the uniformity of their planning was a herald of things to come.

Rows of more or less identical houses were built in London early in the fourteenth century.[3] These are all lost, however, and the most numerous survivors are in York,[4] where the oldest terrace to be securely dated was built on church land fronting Goodramgate in 1316 and called Lady Row. (fig. 312) The Church exploited York's growing population by developing its churchyards with the intention of devoting the ensuing rents to support the foundation of new chantries or other works. Lady Row is dated by a deed of October 1315 whereby the archbishop of York granted William de Langetofte, vicar of Holy Trinity, Goodramgate, permission to construct buildings 'in the southern part of the cemetery . . . from the King's Street towards the church'. Although well within the city walls, Goodramgate was little more than a meandering lane leading northward from the city centre, and not the kind of street to command high rents. Overall the plot measured 18 feet (5.59 m) in width and 128 feet (39 m) in length, and a chantry survey of 1548 records the fact that it had been taken 'owte of the churche yerde there by the parochainers'.

In 1585 the terrace was described as 'one frame called the "Lady Rowe" conteyning vj tenements and iij cottages . . . abuttying toward Trenytie church yerd on the north'. (fig. 313) 'One frame' is significant: Lady Row comprises a long continuous timber frame running along the street, divided up into bays in the customary manner. Originally there were ten bays, each large enough to provide adequate space for a single house with a room at ground level and a second one over it, although one house extended across two bays. The frame itself rose into two storeys, the upper one jettied out at the front. Each bay, therefore, provided space for one room on each floor, and, taking the two rooms together, that provides about 500 square feet (45 m²) of floor space.

This is modest accommodation by any standard, and apparently designed for the small needs of tenants of limited means. The poll tax returns of 1381 list five possible householders of Lady Row as *laborarius* and one as a mercer. The Latin term *laborarius* – labourer – may instead be translated in this urban context as journeyman, someone working in a trade or craft for a daily wage. Among these people were two women and Johannes de Wharrom, a mercer, who might have employed them.

This suggests that Lady Row was used for domestic purposes rather than as lock-up shops for commercial purposes. The most likely inference is that the ground-floor room was a general

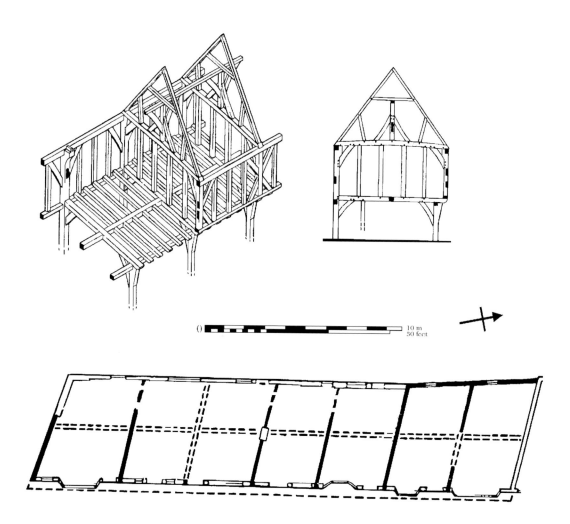

313. Lady Row, York. Perspective showing part of two bays of the frame, a cross-section of a truss and partition, and a plan of the seven surviving bays. After RCHME *York* 1981, fig. 86. © Crown copyright

living-room and work place, the upper room a private chamber and store. This minimal accommodation would suit people who expected the best from urban life because they were well enough established to want a work-place and the comfort of individual quarters, as opposed to a lodging, but had yet to make enough to allow them to move into something larger. Lacking an open hall, or fireplaces served by chimney stacks, they had to forego the luxury of a hearth, so could only warm themselves at winter braziers and take their food to York's bakeries to be cooked, just as the urban poor used to do until well into the twentieth century.

Another early terrace at 54–60 Stonegate is a three-storeyed version of Lady Row's single-bay plan, and built at much the same time.[5] (fig. 314) Once again, the cross-framing seems to have divided this terrace into five or six dwellings of one bay each, perhaps with a single house of two bays. The terrace was probably in the jurisdiction of the dean and chapter of York Minster. It may have originated as a combined speculation of the prebends of Barnby and Ampleforth, just as the adjacent houses at 46–52 Stonegate were of the prebend of Osbaldwick, but the more likely builders were York's Vicars Choral. The 1381 poll tax suggests that among the occupants of these houses were Willelmus de Aynderby, a moderately prosperous tailor, Willelmus Gunnays, a scrivener, and Witkynus Goldesmyth, perhaps indeed a goldsmith. They were a cut above those of Lady Row, being not journeymen but craftsmen who could reasonably expect to enter the lowest ranks of the city council. Their houses provided them with a shop and two private chambers above, the lower one probably taking some of the more public functions of a hall, although both were without the comfort of a hearth.

This simple arrangement of terrace planning with one bay per house became standard for the Church's later speculations in York. While chambers might be upstairs or down, economy in the use of scarce urban frontage tended to raise them upstairs, thus leaving the ground floor free for a shop; circulation simply relied on a front door, perhaps a back door as well, and a ladder-stair or tight newel between storeys. Similarly, all the needs of lighting were satisfied by windows at the front and back on each storey. Already in the first quarter of the fourteenth century it seems that builders and tenants alike recognized that the most useful way of putting scarce urban land to efficient use was not only to build upwards, but also to live within a vertical arrangement of rooms. In no other way could a work room or shop and a private chamber be incorporated within a single bay of a timber frame so easily without compromising either circulation or lighting. By these means, tenants of modest income could be induced to pay enough rent to satisfy the needs of the Church and to obtain a decent dwelling that would satisfy their own domestic and occupational needs as well.

The social pattern of employment played a role too. No one would build for labourers since their economic worth was too low. Journeymen were a different matter: their daily pennies gave them enough for rent and a few other necessities of life. So, while the specific uses of shop and chamber might be amplified by further rooms and more storeys, the basic premise of one up and one down set the pattern for what would become the standard terrace house of later years. It suited the practice of builders; it suited the living patterns of the occupiers. The speculating Church took the profit and made 'mighty things from small beginnings grow.'

These small beginnings in York at the start of the fourteenth century led to the erection of several more terraces or rents during the next few decades. At least eight terraces went up during the 1330s, comprising some fifty small houses, and there were probably many others. This was a sizeable augmentation of the city's available accommodation. The reasons for this building boom are clear enough. York had become the richest city of the north. Its cloth industry had advanced rapidly, particularly during the second quarter of the fourteenth century, giving work to more than weavers. Upwards of five hundred people paid poll tax in 1381; York's new terrace houses could have accommodated a fifth of these people at least, and their dependents.

What people would have been looking for was decent but modest accommodation that they could rent cheaply while they set themselves up, and this meant at least a workshop and a chamber. Were this contained within a house that was built economically, as York's

314. 54–60 Stonegate, York. A three-storeyed terrace (on the left) with greater amenities than those of Lady Row, and, being worth more, rather more altered

terraces were, on a small plot of land facing a side street or lane, as many churchyards did, then the speculator could make a decent profit by charging a monthly rental of one or two shillings, and this lay within the budget of a journeyman who might expect to earn three or four times as much. If a fifth of York's craftsmen and tradesmen were living in terrace houses by the end of the fourteenth century, the terrace house had filled a significant niche in the housing market.

As well as the terrace houses that survive, many others are known through documents. For instance seven houses built on a confined site in St Martin's Lane, which ran off Coney Street down to the river, were the subject of a contract of 1335 between the parishioners of St Martin's (presumably acting for the Church) and the carpenter Robert Giles that required him to build '*septem domos rentales*', of which six were to have a continuous roof, suggesting a terrace, and conform with the pattern of a house in North Street. The specification stated that the ground-floor room of each house was to have a door and a window facing St Martin's Lane with a jetty extending 2 feet (0.6 m) above; and each upper room (*solarium*) was to have a single window on the opposite, un-jettied side, that is facing the church, and, unusually, be fitted with a plastered chimney. The six houses were to have a marginally greater floor area than the houses of Lady Row, and be higher too.[6] When the 1381 assessment was made, the six houses were occupied by artisans, people of slightly superior standing to *laborarii*.

The Church built many more terraces in York during the 1330s, some in Stonegate and others in Mickelgate, that seem to have been intended for artisans once again. A terrace in

Newgate on a rather larger scale, the houses having jetties to both front and back, owe their existence to a licence granted by the archbishop of York to the chaplain Sir Hugh le Botoner in 1337, which specified part of a church cemetery, 130 feet long by 20 feet deep (39.6 by 6.09 m). The twin jetties added architectural status and a width of 21.5 feet (6.5 m), considerably more than that of Lady Row and of Mickelgate.

Despite the double jetties, the light, undecorated timber frame accords more with the likely status of the early occupants, which apparently included three tailors and a tapiter (a tapestry-maker) in 1381, who were taxed at 8d and 4d respectively. The latter, the lowest sum permitted in the assessment, was usual among labourers, whereas tailors were ordinarily assessed at a sum between 2s and 5s. These, then, were poor tailors, but the tailors of this parish were known to be among the poorer brethren of their craft.

Finally, among York's smaller medieval terraces is one formed by three houses in North Street. Similar to the St Martin's Lane houses, with one room up and one room down, they may have been built up to seventy-five years later to support a chantry in All Saints' Church on whose land they are sited. If the early fifteenth century is indeed when these three houses were built, they were among York's last medieval terraces. The economy fell into deep recession, and houses into decay and dereliction. This long sleep had one benefit for at least some of York's small houses: there was no pressure to redevelop them, so many survive as valuable evidence of its fourteenth-century heyday.

Surviving medieval terrace houses with a single room per storey are fairly uncommon. Small size reduced their chance of survival, but they were probably never as widespread as in York, where special circumstances favoured them. There are no signs of medieval terraces of any sort in many towns where plenty of medieval houses of other kinds survive. Stamford, for instance, prospered from weaving in a similar way to York, but, despite particularly close scrutiny, no evidence has come to light for the building of terrace houses of any sort there until long after the Middle Ages.[7]

Bombing and re-planning have ruined Bristol's medieval quarters, but surviving evidence suggests a lack of medieval terraces, and that its medieval shop-houses were individually built,

315. Middle Row, Dunstable. Perspective, showing framing of one pair of back-to-back houses, and the remaining three in outline. © Bailey 1980b

often with stone party walls in the West Country style of Exeter and Totnes.[8] Exeter, which again suffered bombing and post-war demolition, seems to have had one medieval terrace in Preston Street, where a box-framed house, isolated when recorded, had formerly been part of a continuous row that extended on each side of it.[9]

A surprising and puzzling terrace of five cottages survives at Much Wenlock, where 25–8 Barrow Street are framed by six cruck-trusses and comprise a ground storey measuring 15 by 25 feet (8 by 5 m), with a loft and no sign of heating. Built about 1435,[10] they may have been intended for combined shops and dwellings of the smallest sort, or perhaps as chantry priests' houses, or even as almshouses.[11]

A few terraces varied the basic arrangement of one bay per house laid out as a continuous row. Apparently now a unique survivor is the double pile of houses built on land taken from the market place at Dunstable.[12] (fig. 315) This kind of encroachment, with permanent buildings taking the place of temporary stalls, is common enough, but these are without parallel. For a start, the houses are as early as the second decade of the fourteenth century.[13] Then the plan: where Watling Street opens up to accommodate a wide market there was just enough space to squeeze in a group of houses with access on both sides. This was achieved by building two pairs of four houses, one backing the other, thus forming Middle Row. Each house comprises a single small bay with a shop on the ground floor and two jettied floors above. The windows of the two middle houses had to be at the front, because the back partition is a party wall dividing each house from its opposite counterpart, just as the side partitions divide it from its neighbours. It is on the back party wall that the staircase is placed. Constructionally, Middle Row is treated not as two frames running along the street and forming a double pile, but as four contiguous frames set perpendicular to the street, one for each opposing pair, and terminating in gables with windows. In all, this was a remarkably effective way of providing the greatest floor area on the smallest plot. Their first tenants may have been traders who were glad to move from their temporary lock-up shops to live where they worked, but it is possible that Middle Row began life as shops and warehouses and their domestic use only came later.

This back-to-back arrangement is very uncommon indeed, even though it allows good access to each house.[14] Far more common were the terraces fronting a large establishment which, for the rest, faced inwards on to a courtyard for the sake of privacy. This is particularly evident in Oxford, where the parson of Tackley paid for a row of five shops with solars set over a separately occupied undercroft in High Street, behind which was a hall, reached by way of a passage between shops 2 and 3.[15] (fig. 303) A similar row, of which three of the original five shops with solars are well restored, was built by the vintner John Gibbes to front his New Inn in Cornmarket. The inn is divided from the street frontage by a stone wall that seems to have belonged to an earlier building, and between this and the street are the shops, built over undercrofts. (figs 223 and 316) Although not identical, these are framed together as one build, and follow the pattern already established in York, except for having neither doors nor windows at the rear. The upper storeys are jettied and gabled along the front, the jetties continuing around the corner of Cornmarket and the former Somenour's Lane (now Ship Street). Each house had a staircase to the two upper floors, the top one being open to the roof, and originally there were no chimney stacks or other means of accommodating hearths. John Gibbes probably did not live to see them finished, and in 1396 his grandson granted the 'Neweyn within the Northgate and five shops' to feoffees.[16]

316. New Inn, Cornmarket, Oxford. The three restored shops and solar chambers facing the street

317. Vicars' Close, Wells. A restored house, showing the clear division between the service end, to the left of the chimney-stack, and the hall and solar chamber to the right

318. Vicars' Close, Wells. The front of one of the houses. After Parker 1863, Pl. 7

The one-room terraced plan was put to spectacular use at Wells, with walls of stone and window and door openings carved with pointed Gothic heads forming the two facing terraces of Vicars' Close.[17] This ideal scheme was begun about 1349 and completed in a more regular form by Bishop Beckington (1443–65) or his executors as a telling demonstration of Church money spent on its own. The ground-floor room served as a hall, and, from it, a projecting newel staircase leads to the upper room, probably a combined bed-chamber and private study; both have the advantage of enclosed fireplaces, their chimney breasts and stacks being a proud external feature of the forty-one houses. (figs 274, 275, 317, 318 and 319) Their floor area of about 570 square feet (52 m²) is rather greater than that of Lady Row, but these houses accommodated neither handicraft nor artisans and their families, but men who were devoted, as far as canon law was concerned, to lives of celibacy, and had for entertainment small gardens, front and rear.

Ranges of dwellings for vicars often took the form of terraces of uniform houses. Vicars' Cloister at Hereford comprises four ranges of similar lodgings, each one with rooms on two floors, arranged around a cloister. Horseshoe Cloister at Windsor Castle has four houses simi-

larly planned to those of Vicars' Close, their entrances, sheltered within a cloister, leading to a cross-passage and back door, while the newel staircase opening off the passage is partitioned from the hall, and a closet may have taken further adjacent space from the hall.[18]

The terrace house quickly took root in the capital and began its long process of development. In 1369 the carpenters Roger Fraunkeleyn and Johan Page agreed with the dean and chapter of St Paul's Cathedral to build a range of twenty houses with shops, their windows and doors all to one design,[19] and in 1370 it was the turn of the mason Pieres Webbenham, who agreed with St Paul's to build eighteen shops, which were to have chimneys with flues of 'Flandrisch Tyle', that is brick.[20] Then in 1373 the Southwark carpenter William Wyntryngham agreed with the prior of Lewes to build two rows of five and six shops beside the gatehouse of his inn in Southwark, and these were to have a jettied upper floor on the pattern of the 'Rente de Adam Fraunceys' across the Thames at Austin Friars.[21]

The rear ground-floor room of later terrace houses in London was probably used as a kitchen and replaced a separate structure in the yard, but there was no hall. Numerous examples are recorded in Ralph Treswell's surveys late in the sixteenth century and early in the seventeenth.[22] It was quite feasible to partition the single bay of a terrace house to form a separate shop at the front and parlour or kitchen at the back, but this produced very small rooms. Shortly before or in 1390 the draper John Basse built a terrace of nine shops with solars in Abchurch Lane in the City of London, with their two rooms aligned perpendicularly to the street frontage. (fig. 246) These were later recorded as comprising a shop and warehouse, with a kitchen beyond a narrow yard. The front room on the first floor may well have served as a hall with a principal chamber behind it and another storey of chambers above. These terraces houses were spacious, with about 390 square feet (35 m^2) on each floor.[23]

A half-sized version of this two-roomed plan survives in Canterbury at 5–8 Turnagain Lane, where the shorter depth from front to back allows the frame to be aligned along the

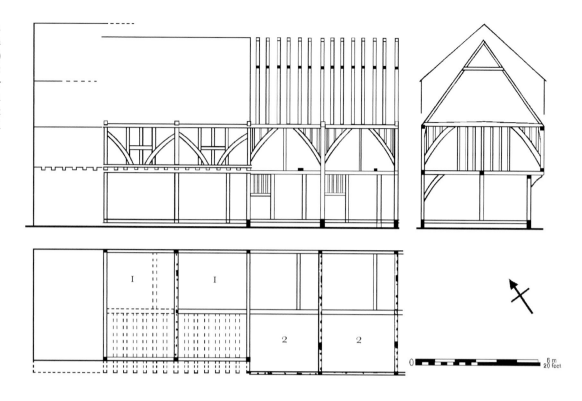

320. 5–8 Turnagain Lane, Canterbury. Above: reconstructed elevation (two bays on left), longitudinal section (two bays on right) and cross- section (separate, far right). Below: plan, of ground floor with open hall (1) at rear (two bays on left), and upper floor (two bays on right), with solars (2) towards front, upper part of hall at rear. © Canterbury Archaeological Trust 1983–4, 46–7 [46]

321. Turnagain Lane, Canterbury. The houses have now been reduced in number and raised by a storey, and their framing has been concealed

street. (figs 320 and 321) These are the remains of perhaps seven or eight houses, arranged bay by bay as a terrace near the corner with Palace Street. They backed St Alphege's Church, whose clergy probably built them for the sake of an enhanced income that would accrue from their rents. The ground-floor bay of each house was apparently divided by a partition into a shop or service room at the front, with a jettied solar over it, and a rear room that may have been ceiled over but could as easily have extended into the upper storey to form an open hall.[24]

This terrace was probably built in the fifteenth century, as was another in Canterbury recorded by a building agreement of 1497 whereby a Canterbury carpenter, John Browne, agreed to build four houses on a site belonging to the Augustinians. The individual houses were of the same width, but slightly greater depth, than those in Turnagain Lane, and, apart from two small additional rooms, were to be similarly planned, with

> iiij halles to be devyded and conveniently made wᵗ their lyghtes on the South syde. And a staire ledying fro the halle to the chambr' in euery house. . . . And with iiij Shoppez next to the said strete. And iiij Chambers wᵗ their Wyndowes ouer. . . . And at euery ende of the said shoppez a Buttery. . . . And to euery of the said Tenementes a Kechyn . . . to be gabeled in and vpon the halle. . . . And the same tenementes to be getied in length lxxx fote . . .[25]

So the shop had to share the width of each house with a small buttery, but the kitchen apparently projected from the back of the hall and had a separate gabled roof, probably to provide a small modicum of safety from fire.

This arrangement of two rooms arranged perpendicularly to the street had to be fitted into the bay-by-bay framing, and this meant a space which seldom exceeded 20–22 feet (6–6.5 m). If that became a bit of a squeeze when more than two rooms were involved, it was nevertheless adequate, and has remained so for terraces to this day. A terrace of at least twenty-three houses was built about 1450 at 34–50 Church Street, Tewkesbury, on the abbey's land in just this way.[26] (figs 47, 296 and 297) Their regular appearance is emphasized by the line of the jetty and height of the central house which rises into a further gabled storey. The front half of each house contains a shop with a jettied solar chamber above; a passage beside the shop leads to an open hall in the rear half. A restored house has a shop window with a shutter that can be folded downwards to form a counter. The hall is lit by a shuttered window framed in the rear wall; and a ladder-stair ascends to the solar. This arrangement must have been quite convenient in its day, but limited space caused extensions to be added to the rear of most of the houses shortly after they were built, and these reduced the lighting within their halls to what filtered through the open partitions between it and the shop at the front and the newly added room at the back.

An interesting variation of the Tewkesbury arrangement reversed its order: at 119–23 Upper Spon Street, Coventry, again of the 1450s, the open hall is at the front and a service and solar, jettied out above, are at the rear.[27] Yet another variation of this plan, at 22–5 Frankwell in Shrewsbury, had a shop with a jettied solar fronting a hall for each of its three houses, and at the back there was a communal workshop. This, once again, caused difficulty with the lighting at the centre. In fact lighting remained a perennial problem, until the advent of gas and electric lighting in the nineteenth century, in the many terrace houses which were built with more than two rooms per storey, set in a line like these were, perpendicular to the street.

The problem of lighting could be resolved if all the rooms were set in a line parallel to the street, instead of perpendicular to it, since all of them could be lit from front or back. Possibly the majority of surviving medieval terrace houses with two or more rooms per floor have their halls and service and solar bay aligned with the terrace itself along the street, in the rural way, even though this was not the most economical use of frontage.

The Wealden form was readily adapted to form a terrace. Six half-Wealdens form a speculative terrace at 157–62 Spon Street, Coventry,[28] and there are pairs of joined full Wealdens in the city's inner suburbs as well. (fig. 322) Attached pairs of half-Wealdens are also common, for instance 19–21 St Andrew's Street and 20–2 West Street, Hertford, and 31–3 Bancroft, Hitchen. These are Hertfordshire's only endeavour in the direction of medieval terrace building, unless an unheated row of shops at 59–61 High Street, Royston, also had a domestic role.[29]

The longest terrace of Wealdens is appropriately in their south-eastern homeland, at Battle, where the abbot built a row of nine houses some time between 1460 and 1477 on the site of a

322. 157–62 Upper Spon Street, Coventry. A terrace comprising half-Wealden hall-houses and tiny one-roomed shops and solars

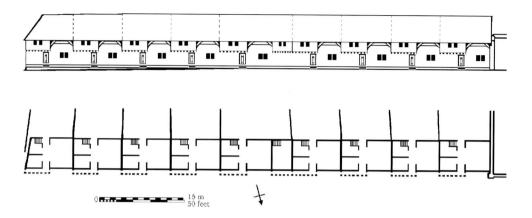

323. 13–23 Upper Lake, Battle. Schematic plan and elevation of four half-Wealden hall-houses, a central full Wealden, and four more half-Wealden houses, forming Quarry Rents. © Martin & Martin 1987, 16

quarry adjacent to the abbey's precinct in Upper Lake.[30] (fig. 323) From the start of the century Wealdens had been built on the abbey's land in the town, but the Newrents or Quarryrents were special. Two ranges of half-Wealdens were designed to flank a full Wealden in a remarkably symmetrical arrangement some 275 feet (84 m) long. The half-Wealdens had two bays of framing each – one for the hall, one for the service rooms and cross-passage and the jettied solar – while the central Wealden had three bays, the third bay containing a ground-floor chamber and jettied solar. This house was leased out at 16s per annum and served as an alehouse. The four smaller houses that stood between it and the abbey gatehouse and the start of the High Street brought in 10s each, while the four to the east, therefore further from the gatehouse and the centre of town, brought in 8s. Two of the smaller houses were also alehouses in the 1470s. All the houses were entered beside the two service rooms, the front one being a shop in the central house and probably in other houses too.

This lengthwise planning of the houses, parallel to the street, made only one concession to the premium of frontage by compressing the three-part arrangement of the hall-house into two parts. (fig. 324) With about 590 square feet (55 m²) of floor area and a frontage of 28 feet (8.5 m), they were not cramped, but Battle was little more than a village and the virgin site unrestricted. The houses in the Spon Street terrace in Coventry are noticeably smaller, even though they are marginally deeper, and treat the site in a more urban way with each house set out within two narrower framed bays forming a frontage of 16.5 feet (5 m), and between them are even narrower bays for yet smaller shops and dwellings.

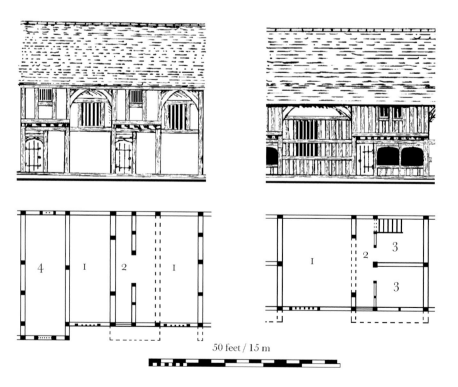

324. Wealden terraces compared: elevations and plans of lower and upper floors at Spon Street, Coventry (left), and lower floor at Upper Lake, Battle (right), showing open halls (1), cross-passages (2), service rooms (3) and solar chambers (4) carried over the cross-passages. © after Pantin 1962–3b, fig. 70, and Martin and Martin 1987, 16

Like the Wealden design, stone brought status, and so did a chimney stack. In the former market town of Silverton, Devon, 6–12 Fore Street, and probably also 4–5, were built in the late Middle Ages as a continuous row of houses, each one comprising a hall and service room fronting the street, with an inner room at the rear. (fig. 93) The hall has its hearth at the front, served by a chimney stack built for show against the front wall in the characteristic West Country way.[31]

Abbot Selwood of Glastonbury adopted a similar plan when about 1470 he began to re-plan Mells in Somerset. (fig. 325) Believing that he could exploit the newly found potential of the West Country clothing industry, he 'reedified the townelet with mene houses of square stones to the figure of an Antonie Cross; whereof yn deade he made but one streatelet.' This, New Street, the only one that came to fruition, runs between the High Street and the parish church, and here he built two facing terraces of more or less uniform houses. Each house comprises a cross-passage giving access to a hall on one side, a service room on the other, and a back door in the usual way; the hall, like the halls of the Vicars' Close at Wells, is confined to the ground storey and heated by a hearth set within a chimney stack backing the passage, and adjacent to it on the rear wall is a projecting newel stair, which leads to a pair of upper chambers and a closet. Not only were these terraces built of squared stone, but they are also thoroughly up to date, so determined was Selwood to attract master-weavers to Mells. The individual houses have a wide frontage, for the same reason, and this can hardly have been at a premium. Moreover, they are very spacious, having a total floor area of about 1,300 square feet (120 m²); one of them is even larger, and has a three-part plan just like the central house of the Battle Newrents, with a parlour beyond the hall and a third chamber above. Some seventy years after they were built the antiquary John Leland noted that Mells 'hath bene a praty townelet of clothing', and well he might, for it never became more despite the attraction of the New Street terraces.[32]

Norwich was far more than a pretty townlet and its continuing prosperity may have discouraged terrace builders. Its only surviving terrace is on a plot of land taken from St Augustine's churchyard to form 2–13 Gildencroft, (fig. 326) which comprises six houses, aligned with the street as three pairs with mirror-image plans. The rubble-built ground floor of each has two rooms, with an entrance into a hall heated by a hearth built into a chimney stack against the party wall, and a second room, which may have been a service room, but was certainly not a shop since the only access was from the churchyard; a staircase beside the stack in the hall led to the upper rooms, which were framed and jettied on the churchyard side where they would be seen.[33]

The terrace house is a singularly English invention. It did not immediately penetrate north of the Border to Scotland, which had other ways of exploiting confined urban space that owed much to France. The terrace house did nevertheless reach France, and, significantly, in the provision of fairly modest houses with a single room on each floor on the English pattern. At Tours, 2–18 rue de la Madeleine were built about 1520–30 as a row of four mirror-image pairs (with an extra house at one end), with a single heated room on each of the two main floors and an unheated garret. The 484 square feet (45 m²) of space on each floor was entirely domestic, since they lacked shops, so they were both comfortable and commodious.[34]

In all, the medieval terrace was a good idea before its time. The provision of enclosed hearths towards the end of the Middle Ages was a pointer towards the future, as it was for all types of house. Cheap brick and enclosed multi-flue chimney stacks were to be the liberating factor, since these obviated the need for an open hall; but they only arrived in significant numbers in the seventeenth century, and the main problems of circulation, heating and lighting were only finally solved in the 1680s.[35] Until then, the terrace found a niche in urban house building because it could provide an acceptable and necessary

325. New Street, Mells. © Andor Gomme

form of accommodation for people of fairly modest means. They would pay a good rent, so, needing to increase its income or to find new incomes for new ventures, the Church saw the terrace as a sound speculation. It also had access to suitably wide plots of land, and these were the first physical prerequisite for planning a terrace.

Despite their apparent advantages, there was a hiatus in the construction of terraces in the sixteenth century. Economic changes had put a brake on town development, so the need for new houses was less pressing than it had been two centuries beforehand. Even so, the most likely change to have stalled terrace building was probably more a result of failed supply than failed market, notably the removal of the Church as an economic force and hence as a speculator. This role was eventually taken up by the landed aristocracy, men who had profited from the break-up of the Church estates by their valued support of the Tudor monarchy. During the later sixteenth and early seventeenth centuries they had concentrated their efforts on developing the agriculture of their former monastic estates. But a few aristocratic speculators moved in on former Church land, as Sir Henry Rich did on the land of the former priory of St Bartholomew in the City, where he started to build rows about 1598, many of them with one room on each floor in the way established at Lady Row in York nearly three hundred years beforehand.[36]

It still remained to modernize the elevations, which came about in the 1630s when the fourth earl of Bedford developed his estate to the west of London (which once had been the garden of the convent that supplied Westminster Abbey with fruit and vegetables) and employed the court architect Inigo Jones in the design of a square – the Piazza – and a grid of streets in the latest Italian manner, which were lined with terraces of houses to suit all classes of persons. What had been the convent's became Covent Garden, and that for a while was a really desirable address. So novel was the Piazza that the arcaded terraces lining it became popularly known as the piazzas. But perhaps for a twist of fate, the uniform row house might, today, have become known as a 'piazza' and not a 'terrace' at all.

18

Housses mirk and steepy

Scotland from the late Middle Ages to the Union of the Crowns

About 1500 the poet William Dunbar wrote of Scottish town houses, 'Your forestairis makis your housses mirk'. Repeating this complaint nearly two centuries later Thomas Morer thought forestairs unsightly and inconvenient: 'being built out of the street for the service of every storey, they are sometimes so steepy, narrow and fenceless that it requires care to go up and down for fear of falling.'[1] Yet open stairways and stair towers, rising to even four storeys and often projecting at the front, became a common feature of Scottish houses in the sixteenth century. Like a badge of height, they were worn with pride.

This emphasis on height sets Scottish houses apart from their English counterparts, which seldom went above three storeys, but not from houses on the Continent. Continental influence was strong in Scotland in the later Middle Ages, with ideas variously taken from France, the Netherlands and even Italy.[2] Late-medieval framed houses in Normandy and elsewhere in France often reach four storeys, with two more as garrets in the roof. Stair towers, too, are a common feature of French houses, often in their courtyards, and, where they are built of stone, also on the front elevation.[3] So too was the tradition of building towers as a form of magnate's house.[4] There was little use for the English style of open hall, built low on the ground with no upper storey.

The instability that Scotland suffered as a result of English invasions and, following these, rivalries between monarch and baron, led to the development of the characteristic tower-house of the later Middle Ages.[5] Based on the example of the Norman keep, it became ubiquitous in Scotland and was commonly adopted in northern England as well. Wherever bloody conflict was a tangible threat, magnates erected towers both to demonstrate their power and ownership of land, and their will to defend it. Towers spread to parts of Wales, and, encouraged by a £10 subsidy introduced in 1429, far more so to Ireland,[6] but Scotland is their real homeland.

Here they are legion. Like keeps, they were occasionally built in towns, without gaining an urban character. The keep, and castles generally in England, encouraged towns to grow up in their shadow, but it took more than the building of a tower-house to quicken the slow and late development of towns in Scotland. Most tower-houses are found where the needs of defence were important, namely beside the coast on the eastern side of the country and along the Border, not in town. The tower did nevertheless demonstrate the efficacy of its vertical arrangement of rooms and impressed this on the planning of Scottish town houses.

Although there are tower-houses far south of the Border, their form finds a strong echo both in the Scottish landscape and among her people:

> In the ingenuity of their planning, in the skill with which the conflicting demands of comfort and defence are harmonized, and in the economy which is studied in all these structures, whether large or small, the practical commonsense, logical outlook, shrewdness and frugality of the Scottish character is demonstrated to us in the most vivid manner.[7]

The tower-house took the three-part arrangements of the hall-house and set them vertically. (fig. 327) Service rooms were therefore placed in the ground-floor undercroft, the hall was above, and private chambers were at the top. The entrance was into the main upper floor by

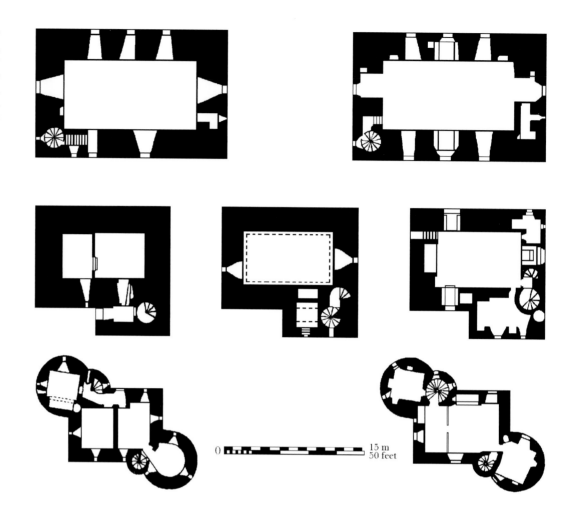

327. Comparative plans of: Alloa Tower (top), showing the upper stage of the hall (left), before alteration, and the solar chamber (right); the tower of Craigmillar Castle (middle), showing (left to right) ground floor, entresol, and first floor (hall); and Claypotts Castle (bottom), showing the ground floor (left) and first floor (right). After Alloa Guidebook; Simpson 1964, fig. 18, and Stewart 1991, figs 6 and 7. © Royal Archaeological Institute respectively

way of an external stair or ladder, and from here newel stairs, or, as the Scots graphically call them, turnpikes, ran down and up, usually in the thickness of the walls, but sometimes in a tower or projecting wing, known by the Scottish term 'jamb'. These became the forestairs of the urban scene. Fireplaces, together with their flues, and privies with their chutes were similarly built into walls. Thus was convenience harmonized with defence.

When the needs of defence seemed less pressing than convenience the entrance was at ground level, but it would be defended by gun loops and the internal arrangements would be designed to confuse intruders by doubling back, changing direction or exposing them to attack from a floor above. The hall on the main upper floor was always the centrepiece, and when jambs augmented the basic rectangular plan, it remained at the centre, while the jambs accommodated the ancillary rooms that brought an increase in comfort as well as vantage points from which the walls could be covered by defenders. Sometimes a single jamb gave the tower an L-plan or a T-plan, and two jambs, often in the form of circular turrets placed diagonally on opposite corners, produced the characteristic Z-plan. This arrangement, again, may owe something to France: the massive embattled tower of the Hôtel de Saint-Livier, at Metz, was augmented by a pair of turrets at its corners,[8] and patrician houses like this set a powerful example.

The first tower-houses were built in the middle of the twelfth century on coastal sites, reached from the sea. Again, many of the later ones are by the sea or close to the shore of a loch or firth as a means of deterring invasion as well as securing easy access in a land of slow roads. The first recorded tower was built as 'a fine stone castle' in 1140 on Wyre, the smallest of the Isles of Orkney, by the Norse chieftain Kolbein Hruga (Cubbie Roo), who also owned extensive estates in western Norway.[9]

Despite these early beginnings, tower-houses were only built in great numbers during the struggle for independence from England in the fourteenth and fifteenth centuries. Proving themselves to be economical to build, efficacious in defence, and comfortable for everyday life,

328. Alloa Tower, its patched walls a consequence of restoration following the removal of the great house that was added to it in the eighteenth century

they entered the Scottish tradition of lordly building as a symbol of power, and claimed the sixteenth and seventeenth centuries for themselves too.

Alloa Tower, (fig. 328) possibly among the early ones, was built either in the later fourteenth century or in the 1490s,[10] with all the characteristic arrangements at their simplest, incorporated within a rectangular plan. The ground floor was given over to storage and service rooms, and reached by a turnpike which descended in one corner from the double-height floor above. This contained the hall, which was heated by fireplaces in the thickness of the walls. The turnpike led upward to a great chamber on the top floor, which had window seats, fireplaces and, opposite the stair, a privy. Then it continued further up to the parapet, where open bartizans at the corners and in the middle of one long side provided look-out points from where defenders could hurl missiles at attackers.

King David II built a more developed form of tower in 1368–77 during his remodelling of Edinburgh Castle. This was part of the defensive perimeter wall on the vulnerable eastern side of the castle, and for a while was a residence incorporating private apartments just as a solitary tower-house would have done. Until its destruction in the siege of 1573 it was the highest point on the Edinburgh skyline and its L-plan highly influential. A turnpike provided access to vaulted lobbies and main rooms, and the tower had a water supply from a cistern as well as a privy. A 'lord's hall' and 'mid chamber' are recorded in the tower and also a 'cloisset' or oratory, but the exact plan is lost.[11]

329. Craigmillar Castle

330. Craigmillar Castle. The hall, and the corbels that once supported the floor-joists of the vaulted chamber above

This general arrangement was copied by several tower-houses built around Edinburgh, notably the bishop of Dunkeld's tower at Cramond, and others belonging to the city's nobility at Merchiston, Liberton, and, most instructively, Craigmillar. Craigmillar Castle was built within three miles (4 km) of the city centre as the suburban retreat of the Prestons, who were granted the barony in 1374. (fig. 329) The builder of its first phase, a solitary tower-house, may be Sir Simon Preston or his grandson, Sir George Preston, who died in 1424. Their descendant Sir William Preston, who succeeded to the estate in 1442, may have added a protective curtain wall. He presented an arm bone of St Giles to Edinburgh High Church (St Giles's Cathedral) about 1450, an act of munificence that prompted the slow construction of the aisle that bears his name.[12] The tower-house he inherited is in many ways like David's Tower. It has a single, small jamb, with the main entrance set into its ground floor and covered by a single gun loop. A tunnel-vaulted lobby, originally divided by a timber floor into two storeys, leads into a similarly divided barrel-vaulted undercroft, and also to a turnpike. This turns one way to reach the upper floor, and then the other way, so as to surprise an intruder, to reach another lobby on the main floor. Here there was a hall, heated by a huge ornate fireplace set into its west wall with coupled shafts supporting a sloping hood, (fig. 330) and served by a small chamber in the thickness of the walls as well as a small store and a privy. A kitchen, once with a wide fireplace, lay beside the hall in the jamb.[13] (fig. 331) The beams supporting the floor overhead have gone, and the ruined hall is now open to the barrel-vault of the room above, formerly a bedchamber, with a great chamber beside it in the jamb.[14]

The Dalmahoys probably built Liberton Tower shortly afterwards, with similar arrangements, but lacking a jamb.[15] The tower-house of the Napiers, Merchiston Castle, which they had built by 1495, has an L-plan, and five storeys, formed by doubling the undercroft floors in the manner of Craigmillar, though none of these was vaulted.[16]

Tower houses also claimed the border counties of England, where two prominent urban towers belonged to the archbishop of York in his capacity as Lord of the Liberty and Regality of Hexham. They lie close to the priory church, and are both early and unusual. One, remarkably, was built in 1330–2 as a prison; the other, the Moot Hall, came later in the fourteenth cen-

331. Craigmillar Castle. The kitchen in the jamb, later converted into a chamber where Mary Queen of Scots grieved for Rizzio

tury and certainly before 1415, when it was included in the castle list of that year. It served as the archbishop's court house, but its three storeys and higher southern wing have been heavily remodelled. What remains from the original tower are a tunnel-vaulted passage running through the ground floor, and evidence of an entry into the floor above, a main chamber on the next floor up with a garderobe, a recess that might have been a buffet for displaying plate, and a chapel and other small chambers.[17]

The more developed form of Z-plan tower-house appeared in the late fifteenth century, and, when over-sailing garrets with crowstepped gables set on projecting brackets, or skewputts as the Scots call them, were also included, would take on an amazingly jagged form. Claypotts Castle[18] on the outskirts of Dundee is exactly this. (fig. 332) Its vaulted undercrofts are given

332. Claypotts Castle from the east. © Malcolm Airs

333. Townhead, Glasgow. The Bishop's Palace, with Bishop Cameron's tower in the foreground and the cathedral beyond, as it was in 1790, before demolition to make way for Robert Adam's Royal Infirmary. From Joseph Swan, *Select Views of Glasgow and Environs*, 1829

over to store rooms and its south-west turret contains a kitchen. The entrance, at ground level, provides access to a newel that ascends to the main floor where there is a cross-passage before the heated hall; within the turrets there are parlours, each one with its own garderobe. This floor was for entertaining, and food could be brought up to it directly from the kitchen below. There is also a service stair diagonally opposite the main stair, rising from the store rooms below up to the next floor which contained the main living quarters in a suite of heated chambers; above these, in the garrets, were the servants' rooms.

Claypotts was built by John Strachan, a younger son of the line, who obtained a lease of land appropriated from Lindores Abbey at the Reformation of 1560. Although the castle was apparently conceived of as a whole, the south-west turret is dated 1569 and the north-east turret 1588 – building was slow. The times, though, were more settled, and this accounts for the ground-floor entry. It was well protected by gun loops, and the circular turrets allowed the walls of the rectangular main block to be covered by fire. Square corbelled-out garret chambers perched over the turrets gave watchmen a view over the surrounding countryside and down to the base of the walls, while the interior plan provided an additional measure of defence against successful intruders, who would have to cross at least one of the rooms before they could reach the upper floors. The castle was, even so, designed for comfort: the walls were plastered and woollen hangings would have reduced draughts. For all its proximity to Dundee, it was built as a country house, and lived off its estates rather than the trade of the town.

The tower at the Bishop's Palace at Glasgow, the work of Bishop John Cameron (1426–46) and known as its Great Hall, took the form of a large oblong tower-house, three or four storeys high, with a corbelled parapet and saddleback roof. (fig. 333) Archbishop James Beaton (1508–22) raised the tower and built an embattled wall around the palace grounds, and then Gavin Dunbar added a gatehouse with round turrets at the corners and crowstepped gables.[19] The tower that Bishop Robert Reid added about 1530 to the Bishop's Palace at Kirkwall is round, unusually, and well provided with gun loops. (fig. 334) It is five storeys high with a caphouse; the basement is vaulted, and all but the third of the three floors above have fireplaces, with the first floor also having a garderobe. But, such were the times, Glasgow is gone, Kirkwall a ruin.[20]

334. Bishop's Palace, Kirkwall. Reid's round tower, finished with a cap-house. © Crown copyright, Historic Scotland

Just as in England, and France, the larger establishments in Scotland set their buildings around a courtyard of some sort or other. Although precious little survives, St Andrews followed the precedent established by its English counterparts at Oxford and Cambridge.[21] In 1419 the new university received its first grant of land, and, as the College of St John, was 'to build, construct, and repair buildings, halls, and chambers' for students.[22] These were all replaced in the seventeenth century. In any event, the revival of the university thirty years later with Bishop Kennedy's foundation of St Salvator's College prompted an altogether more substantial response. (fig. 77) Unlike the colleges of Oxford and Cambridge, this put its main goods in the front window. The splendid buildings of about 1450–60 comprised an entrance tower, facing North Street, flanked by a collegiate church and a domestic range, and, behind these, two courts of further domestic ranges – a smaller one with a cloister backing the church, and a larger one to the west which included the Common Hall and Schools. These courts and their ranges were progressively rebuilt between 1829 and 1906, but the chapel and the sheer entrance tower remain, and so does the three-storeyed domestic range, now called Hebdomadar's Building. Since the level of its vaulted undercroft suggests a building date at the start of the fifteenth century, this apparently predated the foundation and was incorporated within it.[23] Later, it may have been refaced to match the tower and chapel, their rugged rubble walls of carboniferous limestone exactly catching the seriousness for which Scottish education is well known.

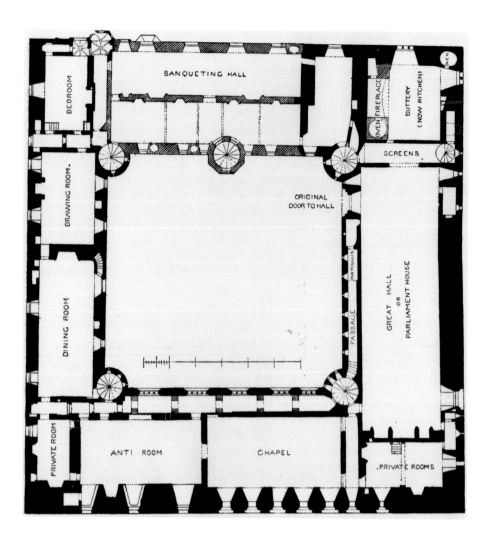

This pattern had already been established in St Andrews by Dean's Court, where a small courtyard developed as buildings were added to the original house, and this kind of development was to continue into the future with increasing frequency. Several greater courtyards were started in Scotland at about the same time as St Salvator's, although these took longer to take effect. The irregular accretions of halls, chambers and other buildings at the royal palace at Stirling and at Edinburgh Castle eventually formed open courtyards that at least enhanced the architecture of their surrounding buildings. Holyroodhouse, meanwhile, was built up beside the abbey to embrace an internal residential courtyard, and Linlithgow Palace grew piecemeal with four ranges which, uniquely, were set regularly around a square courtyard.[24]

While the appearance of Linlithgow's courtyard, with its regularly placed corner turrets, suggests a comprehensive plan, it in fact results from long, disjointed campaigns of building for the Stewart monarchs.[25] (fig. 335) These began after the destruction of a former royal manor house in 1424, and ended about 1629 with a regular courtyard, unique in Scotland, that owes much to English practice. Begun in 1425 for James I as a defensible house, the first works ended about 1437; the second major campaign came in 1490–1513, and a third from about 1534 to 1541, by which time the palace was essentially complete. However, the north range collapsed, and a fourth campaign was needed to rebuild it in 1618–20, and this continued with the rearrangement of some of the interiors.

The original main entrance on the east side, (fig. 336) where a drawbridge led to an archway, or pend, into the courtyard, had already proved unsatisfactory before James V's death in 1542, and been replaced by another entrance through a pend on the south side. The ground floor was then occupied with guard rooms, service rooms and wine cellars, and in each corner were turnpikes. One in the south-west corner led to the king's apartments on the first floor of the west range, a second in the north-west corner led to the queen's in the north range, but after their collapse these were rebuilt to a different plan, thus confusing the earlier arrangements.

336. Linlithgow Palace. The original entrance on the east side showing the position of the destroyed outworks and drawbridge

337. Linlithgow Palace. The Great Hall, open to the sky

When the rebuilding and redecorating were complete in 1629 the king's apartments comprised a hall, a presence chamber and a bedchamber with an attached oratory at the north end. These were aligned with access from one room to the next and also by way of the turnpike from the service rooms below. The great hall occupied the upper floor of the east range over the original entrance (fig. 337) and was served by a kitchen in the north-east corner, and the south range comprised a chapel and an attendant hall over the new entrance. The late-medieval carving that decorates part of Linlithgow is partly French and partly English in style, but time moved on and the palace was finished with Renaissance details such as the window surrounds of the north range.

338. Linlithgow Palace. The courtyard showing the turnpike in the north-east angle, the east range together with the original entrance to its right, the rebuilt north range to its left, and the fountain, apparently commemorating the marriage of James V and Marie de Lorraine, at its centre. © Crown Copyright, Historic Scotland

Linlithgow was a favoured residence of the Stewart kings, particularly James V. He was born there in 1512, and a fountain erected in the centre of the courtyard is said to have carried his arms and those of Marie de Lorraine, whom he married in 1538. (fig. 338) Their daughter Mary Queen of Scots was born here in 1542. Like her father and most of the Stewarts she came to an unhappy end, as did nearly everything the Stewarts touched, for Linlithgow was used as barracks by Cumberland's troops, following his suppression of the Young Pretender's cause, and they burnt the place.

The melancholy history of Holyroodhouse began when a guest house was attached to King David's Abbey of the Holy Rood.[26] Robert Bruce held a parliament here in 1326, and accounts for wining and dining a few years later imply a burgeoning domestic use. Here James II was born in 1426, crowned in 1437, and married to Mary of Gueldres in 1449. Thereafter the abbey was intimately associated with the Stewart monarchs, and they with lost causes and untimely death. James espoused the Lancastrian cause and lost his life in 1460 at the siege of Roxburgh. It was to the abbey that his body was brought back for burial.

His rooms lay in a range lying to the west of the abbey church, which was rebuilt in 1501–5 by James IV. Only then was a separate dwelling acknowledged as 'the Palace beside the Abbay of Holy Croce'. James IV's works concluded with the formation of a courtyard with, disposed around it, a southern tower, a chapel, a gallery, a gatehouse, and a pair of suites for himself and for his new Queen, Margaret Tudor, these recalling the duplicated apartments that Henry

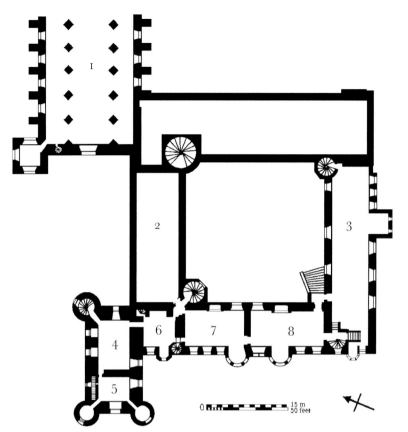

339. Holyroodhouse, Edinburgh. Plan as in James V's time (mid-sixteenth century). To the north-east lies the nave of the abbey church (1), attached to the east quarter; below this are the north quarter (2) and chapel (3), forming a courtyard with James IV's works. To the left is James V's tower with a newel staircase in one turret leading up to an outer chamber (4) on each of the main floors; this leads to an inner chamber (5) with closets in the two remaining turrets, and the intramural staircase on the left-hand side. Extending to the right is his front range or Forework, comprising a wardrobe (6), beside the tower, and a mid-chamber (7) and an outer chamber (8) with access to staircases and the chapel. After Dunbar 1963, fig. 1. © Royal Archaeological Institute

340. Holyroodhouse, Edinburgh. James V's Great Tower, with its two floors of apartments

III of England had built as long before as 1240 at the Tower of London. In what was by now a common European pattern, each suite comprised a hall, great chamber and inner chamber where king and queen spent their separate but similarly arranged lives. Before their marriage ceremony in 1503, King James received the English delegation in his great chamber, sitting 'in a Chayre of Cramsyn Velvett . . . under hys Cloth of Astat', as the English herald John Young recalled. 'Ther wer also in the sam Chammer a riche Bed of Astat, and a riche Dressor after the Guyse of the Countre'. Separate receptions took place in Margaret's suite, both before and after the ceremony, and, while these were similar to the king's, unlike his they were characterized by a notable parsimony. Mixing with the pope, the emperor, the king of Spain and the king of France, James thought himself secure. Unwisely, he allowed himself to quarrel with his brother-in-law Henry VIII, who, at Flodden, disposed of him and half the Scottish nobility.

His son James V left a more enduring mark on Holyroodhouse. (fig. 339) The Great Tower that he added at the north-west corner between 1528 and 1532 is unlike other tower-houses with their lop-sided jambs, since its three round turrets project regularly from its free corners. (fig. 340) One of these contains a turnpike, with access to the outer chamber on each of the two main floors, and the other two at the front contained closets opening off the inner chamber. The two suites of rooms thus formed, one above the other on the two main floors, exemplify the separate apartment, or 'flat', at the highest level of society. These were opulently decorated for himself and his intended queen. Unlike his father's arrangement of separate suites on the same floor, but in two distinct ranges, the arrangement at Holyroodhouse made the division less inviolable. While the turnpike provided access between them and for servants from below, a narrow intramural stair linked the two inner chambers for more intimate communication.[27]

Having completed the Great Tower at Holyroodhouse in 1532, James proceeded to remodel the south and west ranges of his father's courtyard to provide a new chapel and a ceremonial suite of chambers that led to his private suites in the tower. (fig. 341) Pillage and fire during the Earl of Hertford's invasion (the start of England's so-called 'rough wooing' of Scotland), followed by patching and repair, and another fire when Cromwell's troops occupied the palace in the 1650s finally led to all but the west range and Great Tower being rebuilt, and even they were redecorated, so little remains of the earlier Stewart palace and all its unhappy memories.[28]

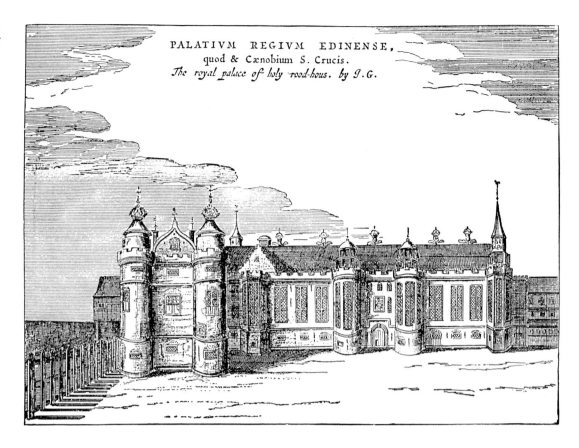

PALATIVM REGIVM EDINENSE,
quod & Cænobium S. Crucis.
The royal palace of holy rood-hous. by J.G.

It was notable for its up-to-date decoration, even so, and a little of this survived the ruin. The renewal of the 'auld alliance' with France and James V's marriage to Madeleine de Valois in January 1537, and, following her death but months later, a second marriage, to Marie de Lorraine, had brought French craftsmen and masons to Scotland at his command. With them came stylistic innovations, 'first begun and used in Scotland at this tyme, eftir the fassione quhilk thay had sene in France'. Indeed James V's façades at Stirling (fig. 342) and Linlithgow, and, above all, in the courtyards of Falkland Palace are among the earliest coherent Renaissance designs in Britain.[29]

If only James had been as effective a politician as he was a connoisseur! The Great Tower of Holyroodhouse was not just a symbol of power. It exemplified James's assertion of kingship after the fifteen years of his minority that began with his father James IV slain on the field of Flodden. It projected bravely forward from the west end of the abbey and the various domestic works of his ancestors that he reshaped, presenting him as a monarch in the mould of Henry VIII, his English rival. Fate dealt cruelly with this confidence. Overwrought, James V died suddenly in 1542, his independent policies in tatters and the English set on an invasion that would bring widespread destruction to Scotland yet again. No other Scottish tower stands for so much sought, so much lost.

The way Scottish towns were planned with alleys, wynds and vennels threading their way back between the riggs lining main streets, often to broaden into sizeable yards, tended to promote the formation of irregular domestic courtyards. Far from the importance of the royal court-yard houses there is a whole range of smaller houses, set around these yards, with occasional survivors reaching back to the sixteenth century to recall this ancient practice. In Edinburgh they are legion. In Kirkwall, Tankerness House began as a pair of manses for the cathedral's clergy, one of them built with a T-plan in 1574 for Gilbert Fulzie, archdeacon of Orkney.[30] (fig. 343) The pair were eventually united around a courtyard, enlivened by their harled crow-stepped gables and turnpike stair-towers, his initials and those of his wife Elizabeth Kinnaird appearing on a skewputt at the top of the turnpike. The date is given by a panel carved with the inscription:

PATRI[A]E ET POSTERIS

NISI DOMINUS CVSTODI

ERIT FRVSTAR SEMEN

NOSTRVM SERV[I]ET IPS[I]

ANNO SALUTIS 1574

In but a few years Scots would have abandoned Latin for their version of the English tongue and have written instead: 'For country and posterity. If the Lord be not the guardian our seed will serve in vain.'

The tradition of building tower-houses spread to lesser builders who arranged their smaller houses with halls set over undercrofts with chambers above, and indeed this practice continued well beyond the Middle Ages. Queen Mary's House at Jedburgh was built by the Wigmore

343. Tankerness House, Broad Street, Kirkwall, showing the archway into the courtyard formed by the three-storeyed northern range with the crow-stepped gable (to its right), the southern jamb to the rear, these all apparently Fulzie's works of 1574, and later extensions and remodelling to the left. © Leslie Burgher, Pentarq

344. Queen Mary's House, Jedburgh

345. Kelly Lodging, Pittenweem. The turnpike and cap-house

family whose arms are carved on the house, impaled with those of the Scotts. (fig. 344) The Wigmores were already a prominent Edinburgh family in the fourteenth century, but, since their house at Jedburgh was built and rebuilt countless times as a result of its destruction by invaders, the present construction with its sixteenth-century detailing is really no more than the latest guise in which it has appeared. A characteristic tunnel-vaulted undercroft carries the principal rooms above and a top storey of private chambers. These are reached by way of a prominent turnpike corbelled out in the re-entrant angle between the main range and an extensive jamb. Its conical roof and crowstepped gables complete what is a typical house of middling size that was probably fairly common from the fourteenth century onwards, although only a very few with a pretence to medieval date survive today.[31]

Kelly Lodging, another of these houses, was built for the earls of Kellie at Pittenweem, a tiny fishing port made a royal burgh in 1541. (fig. 345) The house probably dates from shortly afterwards, and again has a prominent stair turret at the front rising through three storeys to a cap-house, the Scottish term for a small chamber at the head of a turret, more often seen in tower-houses.[32] The Old Manse in Anstruther Easter followed in 1590 for the minister of Kilrenny, a village a short way up the coast, with harled walls and crowstepped gables, an L-plan and a corbelled stair turret in the angle which rises from the first to the third floor.[33] (fig. 346) The Abbot's House in Dunfermline, a fifteenth-century house that was remodelled about 1571, has four vaulted undercrofts and two stair turrets, and over the entrance the inscription:

346. The Old Manse, Anstruther Easter. The jamb and the corbelled-out turnpike

347. 75 North Street, St Andrews. The turnpike rising up the Georgianized front

SEN·VORD·IS·THRALL·AND·THOCHT·IS·FRE
KEIP·VEILL·THY·TONGE·I·COINSELL·THE[34]

Until the fifteenth century practically all the common houses of Scotland's burghs were made of timber with wattle and daub walls and thatched in straw. Apart from lordly houses, the few exceptions were the occasional manse, such as Dean's Court at St Andrews, where a stone undercroft supported an upper storey. This pattern, typical of England in the twelfth and thirteenth centuries, was largely abandoned there, but not in Scotland.

By the middle of the fifteenth century, when Scotland's burghs were enjoying a period of modest prosperity, the first of their former timber houses were at last rebuilt in stone. For some, this meant no more than a stone ground storey, over which there might be two jettied upper floors framed in timber, as was the case of Kinnoul Lodging at Perth. This house was demolished in 1966, and others of probably similar form include a late fourteenth-century house fronting Cants Close in Edinburgh that lasted only a hundred years or so. Practically all the surviving houses were eventually built or rebuilt entirely of stone – either with an undercroft and a hall, and sometimes a chamber above, forming three storeys in all like a miniature tower house, or comprising a front range with a vaulted passage (or pend) leading through it to a yard (or close) where a rear wing contained an upper hall with a fireplace built over a barrel-vaulted ground floor that contained a kitchen and service room.

348. 71 North Street, St Andrews

349. The Roundel, South Street, St Andrews

St John's House at 67–9 South Street, St Andrews, was rebuilt in this way about 1450 with a three-storeyed front range and an upper hall at the rear. Several other houses in both South Street and North Street gained a similar form during the next century and a half. No. 75 North Street, for instance, has a vaulted undercroft in its rear wing, and at the front a cylindrical tower with a conical roof contains a turnpike leading to its upper floors. (fig. 347) The staircase tower or forestair of 71 North Street doubles as the main entrance to the house, and is provided with defensive gun-loops. (fig. 348) Another forestair gives the Roundel at 1 South Street its name, (fig. 349) and the late sixteenth-century Geddie plan of St Andrews shows several more houses like this with turnpikes in the form of forestairs.[35]

Stair towers became common architectural features of Scottish town houses, despite Dunbar's criticism. In Dundee, Tendall's Wynd had a forestair set into a tower in the form of a canted bay, and another long-demolished house had a round stair tower prominently turning the corner of Overgate and High Street, corbelled out over the ground floor and rising through four floors to a look-out. Dundee's only concrete evidence of these early houses is the carcass of Gardyne's House, ruggedly built of hewn stone about 1600, but with an internal staircase leading to its five floors, many of them decorated with tempera ceilings painted with poems and mottoes, in what was by then a common Renaissance way.

The pattern of a vaulted undercroft and one or two storeys and garret over it became increasingly common in Scottish burghs in the fifteenth century. If Hebdomadar's Building in

350. Provand's Lordship, Glasgow. The three gables are part of the later extension to the main range behind them. © Andor Gomme

St Andrews was already built with this pattern early in the century, the Glasgow manses come at the end. Provand's Lordship is the only survivor of several houses built in Glasgow for prebendaries of the cathedral. (fig. 350) It was built in 1471 by Bishop Andrew Muirhead as part of St Nicholas's Hospital, but was soon acquired by the prebendary of Barlanark, and was subsequently enlarged as its manse. Initially each of its three floors comprised three equal square rooms with fireplaces on their southern walls. The first floor was the best, its fireplaces being elaborately finished, and its windows were fitted with seats. The upper floors were probably reached by way of external stairs and galleries on the west side, but such an arrangement was swept aside in 1670 when the house was extended and a turnpike was set against the middle rooms. The foundations of two of the other thirty-two prebendaries' houses suggest that they were generally similar, and views of the High Street in the seventeenth century show more houses of this kind.[36]

Both Church and commercial wealth were invested in houses of this form. Of all the prosperous burghs on the Fife coast, Culross stands out for its large numbers of harled houses with crowstepped gables and the occasional forestair. One of these in the town centre is dated 1577, and there are several others with seventeenth-century date-stones. Culross grew up below a Cistercian abbey, which the earl of Fife founded about 1217 on a hilltop, and became a burgh of barony in 1490. In 1575, following its suppression, the abbey's lay commendator sold a lease of its disused coal workings to George Bruce, who reopened and extended the colliery, thus

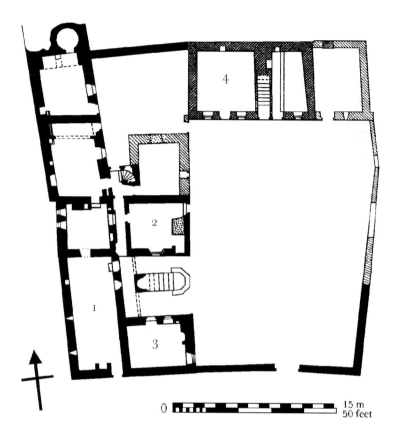

351. Culross Palace. Ground plan showing staircase leading from the courtyard up into Bruce's west range (1); to the north lies the undercroft of Bruce's hall block (2), dated 1597, and to the south a later answering range (3); further north are vaulted undercrofts containing services; and to the north-west is a separate block (4) dated 1611. After Apted 1964, fig. 11. © Royal Archaeological Institute

giving the burgh fifty years of modest prosperity that also grew on the export of fish, and salt to the Netherlands. In 1592 James VI made Culross a royal burgh, and granted it a monopoly of the manufacture of iron girdles for baking scones.

Bruce seems to have built, or more probably taken over, a modest stone house which he extended until it became large enough to be called the Great Lodging, and now Culross Palace. (figs 351 and 352) The original house comprised a kitchen and store on the ground floor with a hall and chamber above. These bear the date 1597 and his initials on the central dormer, probably recording the first works, or enlargement, formed by raising this block and adding an L-shaped main range and jamb to the south, thus making a U, with the original part balancing the new jamb. Soon the range was also extended northwards with the addition of a turnpike

352. Culross Palace. View from the quay, showing main range (left) of 1597 and the later block (right) of 1611. © photo Andor Gomme

286

353. The Bay House, Pan Ha', Dysart, with the tower of the ruined parish church behind it

and a vaulted kitchen and bakery. Later on, Bruce inserted a fine panelled ceiling into the former hall, and had it painted with allegories, biblical subjects and moralizing texts. Indeed both the wooden panelling and painting, which eventually extended to eight rooms in all, are the most unusual feature of this modest place, and include a Judgement of Solomon and fourteen representations taken directly from Geoffrey Whitney's *A Choice of Emblems and Other Devices*, which was published in Leyden in 1586. A separate three-storeyed range, added to the north-east to embrace a small courtyard, has yet more painting, and above two of its dormer windows appear the date 1611 and the initials S.G.B – Bruce had become Sir George Bruce the year beforehand.[37]

Dysart, a royal burgh from 1535, has a few sixteenth-century houses, notably the harled and crowstepped 31 East Quality Street, which has a date-stone of 1589 and a corbelled-out stair turret leading to its garret. Several other houses in the town are similar, notably those in Pan Ha'. The Bay House, which was built here for Patrick Sinclair, has a corbelled-out chimney stack, human heads carved on the skewputts, and, over the back door, a timber lintel inscribed MY HOIP IS IN THE LORD 1583. (fig. 353) Three ground-floor rooms comprised a kitchen and store rooms, and there is a hall on the floor above, open to the roof, flanked by chambers, which once had painted ceilings, and garrets.[38]

The restrictions imposed by Edinburgh's topography on the steeply sloping riggs facing Castlehill, Lawnmarket and High Street caused their builders to pile storey on storey in the typical Scottish way, and add galleries above the sordid wynds and stinking closes that separated range from range. The lofty tenements, or lands as they were called, had narrow gabled fronts, but the galleries projected more and more, the higher they were built.

In the earlier sixteenth century, Edinburgh's houses were still mostly of two storeys with a garret, like the old mansion in High Street that John Stanlie inherited, 'containing a hall, chamber, kitchen and lofts above and three cellars below.' Later in the century there was little change, although Isobel Ker's house in Canongate also had 'a gallery or wooden balcony with a small house under the same.'[39] In 1508 Edinburgh's citizens had been encouraged to extend their houses by constructing these galleries, since it was in the burgh's interest that they should buy timber from its estates. So the town council enacted that 'whoever should buy a quantity thereof sufficient to new front the Tenement he, she, or they dwelt in, should be allowed to extend the new front, the space of seven feet into the street; whereby the High Street was reduced fourteen feet in breadth; and the buildings which before had stonern fronts were now converted into wood'.[40] This seems to have become common practice only after the earl of Hertford's attack on the city in 1544. (fig. 42) Galleries, usually with a shop or stable beneath them, rapidly spread as builders repaired the damage. Practically all of the tenements of that time have been rebuilt and their galleries removed, so, with two celebrated exceptions, High Street has 'stonern fronts' once again. Even so, internal beams, posts and panelling in a few survivors reveal a little of Edinburgh's appearance at the end of the sixteenth century.

Writing in 1598 the traveller Fynes Moryson remarked on the ubiquity of the timber galleries 'built upon the second storey of the houses: yet these galleries give the owners a fair and pleasant prospect' – and did so safely removed above the filth and squalor of the street. By then, and well into the seventeenth century, the internal timber and woodwork of these tenements provided

354. Old Fishmarket Close, Edinburgh, from John Ewbank, *Picturesque views of Edinburgh*, 1823

355. Henry Duguid, *Head of the West Bow.* © National Gallery of Scotland)

another fair and pleasant prospect, being commonly painted in a characteristic Renaissance style with patterns of foliage, biblical scenes and inscriptions, heraldry, myth and allegory.[41]

Just how ramshackle the constant building, enlargement and extension became is captured in views of old Edinburgh as it was two hundred years ago. The Royal Scottish Academician John Ewbank caught this over and over again in his *Picturesque views of Edinburgh*,[42] published in 1823. He juxtaposed the ancient tenements of Old Fishmarket Close, their jettied fronts rising

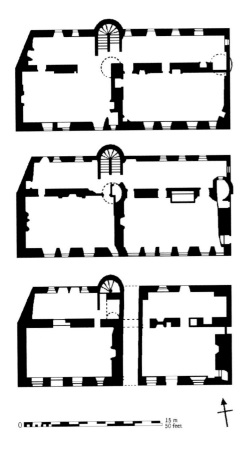

356. Abbey Strand, Edinburgh. Plans, from bottom to top, of ground, first and second floors, showing original two rooms on each floor and (in hatched outline) position of fifteenth-century turnpikes, and extension northwards in the sixteenth century with new, central turnpike and two extra rooms on each floor. After RCAMS *Edinburgh* 1951, fig. 318. © Crown Copyright: Royal Commission on the Ancient and Historical Monuments of Scotland

357. Abbey Strand. View from the north showing the new turnpike of post 1544

through three or four storeys to deeply overhanging gabled cap-houses, against a foreground of single-storeyed hovels encroaching on the mess of the market and, looming in the background, the tenements of his own day, their sheer walls, seven and eight storeys high, made jagged by crowsteps and piled-up, smoking chimney stacks. (fig. 354) Shortly afterwards, the romantic topographical artist Henry Duguid recorded *Head of the West Bow, Edinburgh*,[43] where several narrow houses with three main storeys set over a ground floor are built up against the slope on undercrofts. (fig. 355) Above the main floors are various sorts of attic and garret, either framed in timber and precariously over-sailing the harled wall below, like cap-houses, or rising up in stone to crowstepped gables. A framed corner house facing on to Lawnmarket has three main floors jettied to both the front and side over a ground floor, which is deeply inset behind a timber arcade, and there is a jettied attic with dormer windows and finally a low garret under the roof with windows in the gable. The view extends to the contrastingly uniform tenements of James Court, which, in 1795, had been rebuilt on the further side of Lawnmarket with six regulated storeys and plain attic.[44]

This apparent regularity nevertheless still hides a mass of building in the courts and closes behind the façades of Lawnmarket, and those of the rest of the Royal Mile and the adjacent streets and wynds. Gladstone's Land, Shoemakers' Land, Bible Land, Playhouse Close, Advocates' Close, World's End Close, Fleshmarket Close, Old Fishmarket Close, North Foulis Close and all the other suggestive names give just an inkling of what lies behind.

Most significantly, the habit of building separate apartments on the French pattern, floor by floor, was clearly established in Edinburgh well before the end of the Middle Ages. Close by James V's Great Tower at Holyroodhouse are the remains of a late-fifteenth-century three-storeyed tenement with an attic in Abbey Strand, which had a pair of two-room dwellings comprising the basic Scottish domestic unit of a hall and chamber on each floor. (figs 356 and 357) These were reached by a corresponding pair of stairs, starting with a forestair to the first floor, and a corbelled-out stair to the floors above. The block was reconstructed after Hertford sacked Edinburgh in 1544, and greatly extended by the addition of another storey and a replacement stair tower at the back serving all the apartments, but the former pattern is not entirely obliterated.[45]

At the higher end of the Royal Mile in Lawnmarket, the gabled façade of Gladstone's Land stands out beside the taller uniform façades of James Court. (fig. 358) It owes its front as well as its name to its purchase in 1617 by the merchant Thomas Glaidstanes,[46] but a rear block of the sixteenth century (and possibly earlier) comprises four storeys with a vaulted undercroft and a garret, a stair turret built out from the back, and a jettied and double-gabled outshot of plastered timber, while inside there are relics of the windows and balcony of the original galleried front of the house. When the galleries were removed in 1620 and the house was extended forward it was given a stone arcaded front, a solid development of the former timber gallery, and the last one to survive in Edinburgh.[47]

It is these fragmentary relics that explain the totality of Edinburgh's lands as they were at the end of the Middle Ages. For instance, in High Street a pair of roll-moulded doorways dated 1581 show that the rear wing of North Gray's Close survived the rebuilding of the front range because, being less for show, the back was not so important.[48] Where fronts are concerned, there is still evidence for the galleries that once ran at first-floor level across Roman Eagle Hall, a substantial late-sixteenth-century three-storeyed mansion in Lawnmarket, and also across the front of 306–10 Lawnmarket, but these were removed along with other hazardous timber constructions from Edinburgh's tenements long ago.[49]

Just two houses near the lower end of High Street – Moubray House and John Knox House – are far from fragmentary, and owe their survival to an unlikely or, at least, disputed connection with the famed protagonist of the Scottish Reformation. (fig. 359) In 1529 Andrew Moubray, a wright, rebuilt a new apartment of stone rubble beside Trunk's Court, perhaps the rear block of the present house, with three storeys and a garret, crowstepped gables and a massive corbelled projection for a stair. The addition of timber galleries later in the century may have extended the front forward to High Street, but this newer part of the house is now of stone and contains a plaster ceiling dated 1630.[50]

John Knox House, meanwhile, originated as a medieval two-storeyed house, probably with a projecting stair, that was raised and given a new front block, probably when Christina Arres conveyed the house to her son John in 1525, or, if not then, perhaps after the sack of 1544. This made it a rectangular three-storeyed block, with a two-roomed apartment on both the first and second floors (just like James V's Great Tower at Holyroodhouse), and also an attic and garret. These are reached by two turnpikes, one serving the apartments, the other rising from the first-floor entrance to the attic. Above a fireplace in the southern gallery are three panels with a lion rampant and the date 31 October AD 1561. Timber galleries projected from the rubble stone

358. Gladstone's Land, Edinburgh

359. Moubray House and John Knox House, Edinburgh. Plans (from left to right) of undercrofts of both houses, ground floor of John Knox House, and first floor and second floor of both houses, with the two-roomed apartments of John Knox House marked 1a and 1b, 2a and 2b. After RCAMS *Edinburgh* 1951, fig. 257. © Crown copyright: Royal Commission on the Ancient and Historical Monuments of Scotland

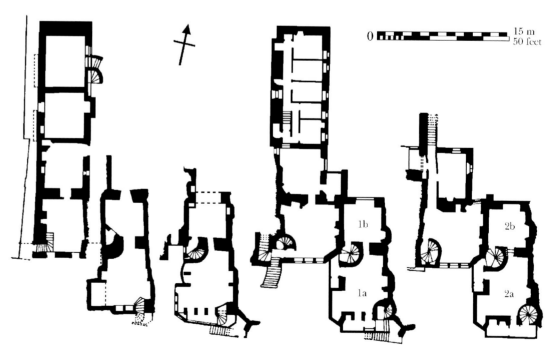

360. John Knox House, Edinburgh, from a lithograph made shortly after 1840 when the house to the right collapsed and before the west front was partly refaced in stone

361. Moubray House (left) and John Knox House, Edinburgh, showing the partial refacing in stone that largely follows the lines of the framing shown in fig. 360; a further jettied and gabled garret room has also been added since its time

walls from the start, but the present southern one may be later and has all the appearance of being an encroachment over the street. (figs 360 and 361) It nevertheless precedes the ashlar refacing of part of the west front that replaced the galleries at the corners and permanently incorporated into the ground floor three stalls, which were leased to street traders who previously used wooden lock-ups or luckenbooths. These works are dated by a coat of arms and the initials of James Mosman, goldsmith to Mary Queen of Scots, and his wife Mariot Arres, and were therefore undertaken between 1556 when Mariot inherited the house and 1573 when Mosman was executed for treason. What consolation had he then in the inscription carved over the three shop windows: LYFE·GOD·ABVFE·AL·AND·YI·NYCHTBOVR·AS·YI·SELF.[51]?

By the end of the sixteenth century the pressure to rebuild was becoming irresistible. Regent Morton's House in Blackfriars Street had been built early in the sixteenth century with four storeys, but a hundred years later it was raised to five, and its projecting timber galleries survived until 1860.[52] (fig. 362) Huntly House Museum at 154–66 Canongate was rebuilt with a timber frame, and part of this survives, albeit hidden behind the stone front, to emerge in the jettied top storey and gabled garret. (fig. 363) It comprised three small houses in 1517, built side by side, their upper floors reached by forestairs. In 1570 the houses were thrown together and extended forward to the street, and the eastern house was rebuilt over a vaulted pend closer to the street, which allowed space at the back for a large two-storeyed extension with a kitchen.[53]

362. Regent Morton's House, 8 Blackfriars Street, Edinburgh. A view by James Drummond, inscribed 'Blackfriars' Wynd' and dated 13 June 1857, showing the house before the removal of its timber galleries, and with its surviving ogee-arched entrance into the base of its stair tower (later published as a lithograph in *Old Edinburgh*, 1879). © Crown copyright: Royal Commission on Ancient and Historical Monuments of Scotland

In 1590 Bailie John McMorran, reputedly Edinburgh's richest merchant at the time, was anxious to rebuild 'ane auld ruinous hous', namely Riddle's Court in Lawnmarket. This in fact is dated 1587, and comprises two L-shaped three-storeyed blocks, each of which contains a house, enclosing a tiny yard. The principal rooms are on the first floor, and one has its ceiling beams painted in tempera with a stencilled pattern of cherubs' heads and double-headed eagles which fit McMorran's time.[54] Tweddale House is another sixteenth-century house that came to be enlarged. It was inherited in 1585 by Neil Laing, Keeper of the Signet, and has a lintel inscribed with his initials and those of his wife Elizabeth Danielstoune. By 1602 he had added a 'dwelling hous', probably to convert his father's house into a double pile, and carved on it the motto: THE·FEIR·OF·THE·LORD·PRESERVITH·THE·LYF[55].

Well before the end of the sixteenth century, Edinburgh's citizens had taken to adding personal mottoes of this sort to their houses in prominent positions. This widespread practice is clear evidence of a profound change in attitude towards Divine purpose and individual responsibility that came about through the collapse of authority within the Catholic Church as a result of the Reformation. So when Clement Cor built Advocates Close in High Street as a six-storeyed tenement in 1590, he had his initials carved on a moulded door piece together with those of his wife Helen Bellenden, as well as one lintel inscribed BLISSIT·BE·GOD·OF·AL·HIS·GIFTIS and another SPES·ALTERA·VITÆ·1590.[56] Boswell's Court was built about 1600 in Castlehill with a shield, a merchant's mark and the initials TL on its stair tower, and on another panel are the initials RM and RY and the motto O LORD [IN THE] IS A[L] MI TRAIST.[57]

By 1600 Edinburgh was in the middle of another process of change, one that turned it from the medieval city it had been before 1544 into a modern city. For all the tumble-down appearance of its galleries and the putrescence of its darker wynds, it was now a jump ahead of London. When James VI left for England and complained about the overweening size of its metropolis, he found a city that was still essentially medieval and had yet to come fully to terms with the suppression of the open hall. Only the Great Fire brought the radical modernization that Edinburgh in its smaller way was already achieving, and, moreover, in a way that was more recognizably European in character. Edinburgh had no open halls, and its apartments were full of promise for the future.

363. Huntly House Museum, Canongate, Edinburgh

CONCLUSION

Restoring intellectual day

The Reformation was one of the great turning points of European history.[1] Ever since the fourteenth century the Roman Church had been in a state of peril. Corruption was rampant; schism divided it. Yet it survived, and the basic tenet of faith on which the Middle Ages were founded withstood the battery of plague on bodies and humanism on minds.

When the sixteenth century unleashed the full force of the Reformation, this was not universally welcomed, nor did the Church founder. Henry VIII's claim to be 'the Supreme Head of the Church of England'[2] served his *raison d'état*; and the 'extirpation, abolition and extinguishment, out of this realm . . . of the pretended power and usurped authority of the Bishop of Rome, by some called the Pope'[3] would at the stroke of a pen lay down the law with a high-flown statement of intent. Nonetheless, if this authority, as Henry claimed, 'did obfuscate and wrest God's holy word', his actions provoked a heated rejoinder, causing the blood of martyrs to mingle with their Saviour's before a new commonwealth was woven from the shreds of the old medieval kingdom.

Thoughtful people did eventually come to accept that they were responsible for their own salvation, and that this was not to be purchased through a timely endowment. The burning issues of the sixteenth century were reduced to no more than dampened embers by the start of the eighteenth. Religion by this time waited on the state, rather than vice versa. The principle of functional qualification now required power to serve the tangibles of earthly wealth, instead of the mysteries of celestial riches. This attitude was dressed up as a noble ideal, particularly by Britain's landed oligarchy, who inherited the Church's suppressed role as well as its wealth, and invested in a vast new artistic and intellectual heritage to replace the old. It was over these fertile acres that the Age of Reason dawned.

> As steals the morn upon the night,
>   And melts the shades away;
> So truth does fancy's charm dissolve,
>   And melts the shades away;
> The fumes that did the mind involve,
>   Restoring intellectual day.[4]

Truth nourished the learned; intellectual day gave science the mind of Newton. In its vulgate translation, the Bible became propaganda to suit the age: the tale of Judas Maccabaeus, for instance, was re-spun to celebrate Cumberland's victory over the Jacobites at Culloden. 'See, the conqu'ring hero comes!' sang Handel's chorus of youths and virgins. And London rejoiced.[5]

For all the trumpets and all the drums, the fumes of the Middle Ages had not entirely blown away. Maybe the mystical rituals of the Church were confined, as the shades of night, yet religion comforted people of all persuasions. The ancient style of its architecture, too, was still revered. In 1623, when considering how to adorn the new library at St John's College, Cambridge, Bishop Cary of Exeter persuaded the master that 'the old fashion of church window' was 'most meet for such a building'; and so it came about that Gothic tracery was used.[6] That learned minds should keep faith with Gothic in this way is a paradox in an age that equated ancient Rome with reason, not medieval Christendom. But traditional symbols were still potent: they had a romantic appeal; and the new men of both Oxford and Cambridge employed the Gothic style from time to time throughout the next three centuries, content that this re-asserted their scholastic ideals in tangible form.

They were not alone. Before the seventeenth century was done, Sir Christopher Wren, a man of the highest intellect, would adopt the Gothic style magisterially, not just as an occasional dressing where he deemed it appropriate, but for its structural value too. While Gothic's fanciful charm worked architectural wonders, there had been no constructional advances, so far as architecture's rational side was concerned, beyond what it had inaugurated in the twelfth and thirteenth centuries, nor would there be until the Industrial Revolution proved the worth of iron framing and Portland cement. For all its baroque grandeur, St Paul's Cathedral owes a constructional debt to the Middle Ages, and indeed its plan does too. Unlike his City churches, which Wren designed for preaching, he bowed to its clergy's desire for dignified ceremony, causing the cathedral's general arrangements of long nave and choir and prominent transepts to follow a precedent set soon after the Conquest. In this, as in all kinds of other works, Gothic continued to serve the Vitruvian notion of firmness, convenience and delight.

Nevertheless, just as the Reformation was a matter of Church and state, and this affected the control of power and therefore money, it reformed the way people thought and eventually the way they lived. This slowly changed the form of their houses. Those who accepted the Reformation understood that their religion was now guided by personal responsibility, not by paying for indulgences. This prompted many builders, in England as in Scotland, to inscribe their houses with mottoes of faith: 'Unless the Lord buildeth the house, he buildeth in vain'. This demonstrated a significantly different attitude to the Deity from the building of chantries to save one's soul.

The architectural style of these houses changed at the same time, with classical motifs at first fleshing out Gothic skeletons and eventually building the whole body. This was tentatively achieved, step by step, until Inigo Jones exhibited the full meaning of classicism in his royal works at Whitehall and Greenwich. These signalled a radical shift in attitude, and, significantly, were designed for James I, a descendant of the Stewart line whose aesthetic credentials were already well proved at Falkland, Linlithgow and Stirling.

Those who built lesser houses were slower to respond. They were increasingly the inheritors of the wealth that before the Reformation belonged to the Church. Many were institutions, the secular inheritors of guilds, colleges and hospitals. The open hall remained crucial to their efforts. Its high and low ends had the benefit of necessary formality and offered a romantic link with those ancient traditions that gave their functions a seemingly eternal validity. The open hall itself, built directly on the ground, soon passed away in the urban context, at least so far as new buildings were concerned. But, as bishops had discovered in their inns and palaces as long beforehand as the thirteenth century, the upper hall could readily adopt high and low ends, with additional services in its undercroft, and was well suited to the new conditions. Not a decade passed from the sixteenth to the twentieth century when some city company or borough council, legal inn, charitable hospital or academic college did not demonstrate the continuing vitality of its affairs with a brand-new hall of this kind.

These institutions favoured the medieval courtyard arrangement too, since less formal accommodation had to be fitted in as well, and they appreciated the hierarchy that a courtyard displayed as well as its control of circulation. They would continue to employ this arrangement, as they did the upper hall, until the present day. Nevertheless, symmetry of form crept in, and this obscured the hierarchy of its parts by emphasizing such main elements as halls and chapels, and obscuring such lesser ones as services and anterooms. What Wykeham and his mason Wynford had inaugurated at New College, Oxford, took greater effect in the early seventeenth century in the courts of Oriel College,[7] and Clare College, Cambridge.[8] This also applied to almshouses. Wren's Royal Naval Hospital at Greenwich and the petty Fisherman's Hospital in Great Yarmouth, both of about 1700 or so, are evidence of the abiding efficacy of this arrangement on widely differing scales, both now subject to the discipline of classical symmetry.

Nevertheless, the supposed picturesque and symbolic qualities of medieval architecture asserted themselves, either for the propriety of a specific context or for romantic effect, and sometimes for both. Hawksmoor's North Quadrangle of All Souls, Oxford, is a case in point.[9] Designed in 1714–15 in his own interpretation of the Perpendicular style of the fifteenth-century chapel that forms its south side, its north side is given over to the Codrington Library, which balances the chapel, and, with two further ranges, embraces a classically symmetrical layout, despite its Gothic dress. A century later, Lincoln's Inn, above all other legal institutions, went from strength to strength, classical and Gothic, eventually with an extensive campaign of building that gave it a magnificent new hall in 1843 with an attendant library embracing an irregular open courtyard in the best Gothic style of the early Victorian years.

Individual magnates were at first similarly disposed. Many episcopal inns passed into secular hands, and some were rebuilt so as to give them a new lease of life that lasted for at least half the seventeenth century. The bishop of Bath's inn passed to Sir Thomas Seymour and then quickly on to the earl of Arundel, during whose time it was subject to much rebuilding along traditional lines to improve its accommodation. More radically, William Cecil completely rebuilt Exeter House in the Strand, with a great hall as an integral part of its extensive suite of formal reception rooms, and with open courtyards that embraced a formal garden, stables, a kitchen garden, and a tennis court. He could afford to do so, and needed to, since, as Lord Burleigh, Queen Elizabeth's chief minister, he counted her as his principal guest and his status required no less.[10]

These needs nevertheless died with him, and the house fell a hundred years after it had been completed. Significantly, his country mansion at Stamford, Burleigh House, survives with its similarly disposed suites of rooms very much as he left it. Such prodigious London houses, however, no longer suited the needs of Stewart and Georgian court life, and their sites were too valuable to resist the pressure of speculative development. The example of the fourth earl of Bedford's mansion, north of the Strand, comes to mind. However, when he employed Inigo Jones in the 1630s to develop the grounds of Bedford House as Covent Garden, this was based around another form of courtyard to become the first regular London square, even though its direct antecedents were Italian *piazzi* and French *places*. The square has provided the best address in British towns ever since.

In general, the medieval open courtyard took too much space in London for most magnates. They turned to smaller houses that stood either like suburban villas within their own grounds – smaller versions of the Parisian *hôtel* with a small courtyard, front and back – or like large versions of the row house with an even smaller yard at the back, separating the main dwelling from stabling that opened on to a mews. Both of these types were well-established forms long before the end of the Middle Ages, although they were now distinguished by their lack of accretive irregularity. The independent town house, as it emerged in the seventeenth century, was therefore more compact, and endeavoured to adopt a classical symmetrical form that was designed to engage directly with the street.

Such houses are found the length of the kingdom. Argyll Lodging exemplifies how the French style of *hôtel* was built up from medieval beginnings in Stirling, while the late seventeenth-century remodelling of Provost Skeane's House in Aberdeen takes typical Scottish features, particularly its dramatic turnpikes, one stage further into this new modern realm. Plas Mawr, at Conwy in Wales, and, in England, Whitehall at Shrewsbury, are just two among countless more examples of these new compact urban houses where local characteristics stamp an individual mark on classical features.

The smaller row house followed a similar course, particularly now that the central break caused by an open hall was removed. Once again, it still had all the semblance of its medieval forebears in such grand framed houses as the mansions built for the Shrewsbury merchants Robert Ireland, Richard Owen and Roger Rowley in the last quarter of the sixteenth century. Within fifty years the giant classical pilasters set over the rusticated ground storey of Lindsey House, in Lincoln's Inn Fields, London, made these provincial houses seem hopelessly old fashioned. Nevertheless, they all built on the idea of the formal first-floor suite of rooms. Both in London and in the provinces these smaller houses particularly changed in the sphere of increasing comfort and privacy – at least for those who could afford it. Once again, this tendency had operated throughout the Middle Ages, and was hardly new; it just continued apace, eventually into uncharted territory. The enclosed hearth, confined by a chimney stack, completed its conquest of the open fire – an obvious necessity when coal replaced wood as fuel. With its open hall forsaken, a house could now readily have a continuous upper storey, with all kinds of attendant benefits. This was not a feature unknown in the Middle Ages, yet it became a defining difference between medieval and modern.

For all it remained as a room of state, the hall did go out of fashion in the purely domestic establishment, to have its role split among parlours, dining rooms and lobbies in smaller houses, and to be reduced to a formal place of welcome in rather larger ones. This liberated the terrace house. These were no longer built as marginal properties for the purpose of supporting chantries out of their rents. Instead they found a new niche, one that precisely suited the times, and made them the most popular house form of all. The new secular class of capitalist landowner took on the role of builder for its own worldly profit, as did the earl of Bedford, often through the efforts of a rising breed of middlemen, who frequently went bankrupt in the process. These were to be the real speculators of the future, men like the 'able, but far from amiable' Nicholas Barbon.[11] Thus the popular Georgian terrace house emerged out of its tentative medieval beginnings, piling floor upon floor, usually with two main rooms on each, and more in a back extension. There was a great future here, especially for unscrupulous scoundrels; and yet, despite all the advances, this type of house and the speculative way in which it was built were founded on the bedrock of medieval practice.

The adoption and development of all the various features that became popular in the sixteenth and later centuries – they could hardly be called innovations – led to a slow and quiet transformation of all kinds of dwelling. For such reasons as the advance of fashionable brickwork and the substitution of classical decorative motifs for Gothic ones, a modern house of the eighteenth century looked utterly different from a late medieval one. Its planning upheld this view. Even so, these changes were more of degree than kind.

Scotland moved in a different direction. It developed the established form of apartment in which individual dwellings were confined to a single floor of a multi-storeyed building. Confusingly, this came to be called a tenement, an old term put to new use. The tenement would dominate Scottish housing until the twentieth century. This form of horizontal dwelling was quite distinct from the English vertically arranged terrace house. Nevertheless the terrace house was readily split into semi-independent suites of rooms, floor by floor, when it was not occupied by a single family. Even a single household usually split itself in the name of privacy and propriety so that the servants occupied the basement and attic levels, and did most running up and down stairs, the master and mistress, meanwhile, confining themselves to the principal floors in the middle. Impressed by this compromise, the Scots took to the terrace and brought it back to Edinburgh as a sign of the sophistication that could be found south of the Border. Yet by the middle of the nineteenth century the English had turned to Scotland, and, in a countermove, brought the tenement south so as to provide blocks of flats, at first for the deserving poor, and by the 1870s as urban lodgings for middle-class professionals and businessmen.[12]

The Middle Ages, it turns out, had plenty to offer as a foundation for the future. Many of its forms, like genes, were passed down to succeeding generations. These would be modified but not obliterated. As an instance of this, there is the English form of universal *maison polyvalente*, as exemplified by those two surviving twelfth-century stone houses in Lincoln. This ultimately found expression in the mid-twentieth century, not only in the shop-house, which remained common enough, but also in what house agents call the 'town-house', an innovating form dependent in general arrangement on its twelfth-century ancestor except that the ground-floor shop is given over to the twentieth century's pride and joy, a motor car.[13]

That sounds radical. Yet nothing, in fact, had changed so radically since the end of the Middle Ages as the medieval re-establishment of the Roman practice of including several different sorts of room, each with its distinct uses, within the overall fabric of an individual house – unless it were the re-establishment of constructional techniques that enabled a house to last indefinitely, and hence become part of a capital inheritance. These fundamentals are the greatest legacy of the Middle Ages – and the most easily overlooked. They allowed a Scotsman to call a house 'auld' in 1590 because it was small and ruinous, not because it was built with no thought for permanence or the convenience of several rooms. By the seventeenth century these were well-established benefits, and have remained so.

Then there is style. From the end of the Middle Ages until well into the twentieth century style was firmly founded on the past. This was accepted as the norm, so much so that, when the international modern style emerged in the 1920s, its novelty lay as much in its denial of the past as in its glad welcome to the future. A small band of connoisseurs embraced it, but it never became universally accepted. The stylistic attributes of an older house, with their conscious reference to ancient traditions, tipped the balance against international modern. Bright young things may at first desire the spanking new, but a growing awareness of the past turns many aspiring house-owners, as they establish their lives, towards an identifiable image taken from the past that expresses their self-esteem and assumption of social position.

There is a saying that houses are too difficult for architects. This slander is only to say that houses are more than a convenient shelter or, in Le Corbusier's notorious phrase, 'a machine for living in'.[14] Yet convenience and efficiency became the principal tenets of modernism. These qualities may serve a transient city dweller a month or two, but a longer stay needs more. A house needs its household gods, however these are expressed, and all the lesser touches of form and decoration that relate it to the living culture that brought it forth. The medieval house, whether of archbishop or artisan, was as full of symbolic intangibles as of material substance. Nearly forgotten, the shade of these symbols still haunts the wreckage of past centuries and gives what little survives of Britain's medieval houses their particular poignancy.

It is that shade as well as the stylistic and constructional remnants of its period that differentiate medieval houses as they are known today from the confident, worldly Georgian style of the eighteenth century or from the extraordinarily eclectic flourish of retrospective styles that convert an otherwise utilitarian modern dwelling into a desirable home for our new millennium.

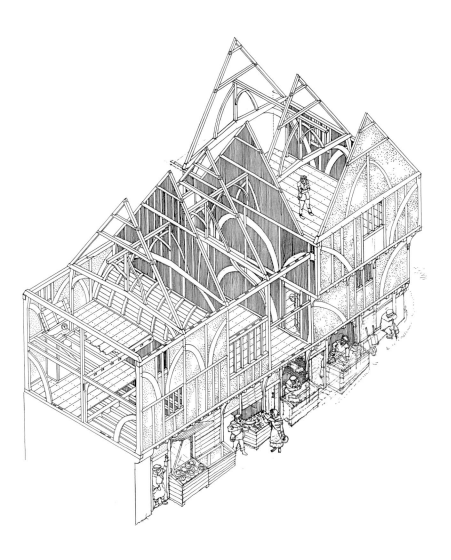

364. The former Harlequin Inn, Steep Hill, Lincoln. Stanley Jones's reconstruction of a fairly standard timber-framed hall-house, probably built about 1400, with a two-bay open hall, flanked by a storeyed chamber end (left), and a storeyed service end in a gabled wing (right). Unusually these are built over a range of five shops, which are partly set into the steeply sloping site towards the right-hand side, and terminate in thick stone walls that also support the framed ends of the house above. The fire in the open hall must have burned on a hearth stone, and the floor must have been plastered as a fire precaution. © Stanley Jones

ABBREVIATIONS

Archaeol.	Archaeological, Archaeology
Archit.	Architectural, Architecture
Assoc.	Association
BAA	British Archaeological Association
BL	British Library
BM	British Museum
Brit.	British
CBA	Council for British Archaeology
HMSO	Her Majesty's Stationery Office
Hist.	History
Inst.	Institute
J.	Journal
Med.	Medieval
Proc.	Proceedings
RAI	Royal Archaeological Institute
RCAHMW	Royal Commission on the Ancient and Historical Monuments of Wales
RCA[H]MS	Royal Commission on the Ancient [and Historical] Monuments of Scotland
RCHME	Royal Commission on the Historical Monuments of England
Rep.	Report
Ser.	Series
SMA	Society for Medieval Archaeology
Soc.	Society
Soc. Antiqs	Society of Antiquaries of London
Trans.	Transactions
Trd	Tree-ring date list
VAG	Vernacular Architecture Group
VAGCP	Vernacular Architecture Group Conference Programme
Vernac.	Vernacular
VCH	*Victoria History of the Counties*

Note: textual references cite author and date of publication; where appropriate, volume and page numbers follow; catalogue entries are in square brackets [ ].

Notes

INTRODUCTION: *In the beginning was the Word*

1 Milton, *L'Allegro* (1632), 1, 117.
2 *Genesis*, 11, 1–9.
3 Ullmann 1955, 2 *et passim*.
4 St Ambrose, *Explanatio psalmi 40*, 30, in *Corpus Scriptorum Ecclesiasticorum Latinorum*, 64, 250.
5 Ullmann 1955, 59–66.
6 Defoe 1701, 1, 1, 374.
7 Bede 1955, Ch. 14–20.
8 Fernie 1989; Phythian-Adams 1998.
9 Tawney 1938, 68.
10 Tawney 1938, 42, quoting Coulton, *A medieval garner*, 68–73.
11 Locke 1690, Ch. 9, p. 124.
12 Vitruvius 1914, 1, 3.
13 Fernie 1989.
14 Fisher 1935.
15 Schofield 1995, *passim*.
16 For example at Gloucester, where buildings statutorily listed for their special architectural or historic interest were demolished by the dozen in the name of modernization.
17 Platt 1976, 125–47.
18 The village of Long Crendon in Buckinghamshire, for instance, has a guildhall.
19 Urry 1967, 113.

1 VENERABLE MARKS OF ANTIQUITY: *The Anglo-Saxon inheritance*

1 Myres 1986, 217.
2 Frere 1967, 32–8, 65–6, 73–4, if one accepts that the Romans invaded via Pegwell Bay in Kent, rather than further west, cross the Channel via Chichester – pers. com. Mark Hassall.
3 Merrifield 1990; Martin Millett tells me that 100 persons per hectare was the norm for a crowded Roman town, this giving London a maximum population of only 13,500.
4 Frere 1967, 87, 257–8, 305–14.
5 Schofield & Vince 1994, 12–16.
6 Salway 1981, 542–52, suggests 5–6 million; Martin Millett pers. com. the lower figure.
7 Darby 1976a, 45–7.
8 Biddle, Lambrick & Myres 1968.
9 Stenton 1947, 1–4.
10 Ebner 1991, in Schofield & Vince 1994, 14–15.
11 In his own *Historia Britonum*, which he completed in 1139. The case for Arthur's historical existence is most fully made by Leslie Alcock (1971), the case against by David Dumville (1977).

12 Bede 1955, 3, 1.
13 Hawkes 1969.
14 Webster & Cherry 1979, 240; for *Grubenhäuser* see Chapter 10 below.
15 Stenton 1947, 59–60, 105–6.
16 Bede 1955, 2, 3.
17 W.O. Hassall 1962, 31.
18 Gravett 1994.
19 RCHME *Northants*. 1985, 41–4, [8]; J.H. Williams *et al*. 1985.
20 Bede 1955, 2, 14.
21 Stenton 1947, 177–99.
22 Defoe 1724–6, 4, 256–7.
23 Adams & Carley 1991.
24 Arrol 1988.
25 Wilson & Hurst 1957, 170.
26 Wade 1988.
27 Bede 1955, 2, 3.
28 Hobley 1988; Merrifield 1990,
29 Holdsworth 1976; Youngs & Clark 1981, 184–5; Youngs, Clark & Barry 1983, 178–9; Andrews 1997.
30 Bencard 1981; de Groot 1996.
31 Radley 1971; Kemp 1996, 75–83.
32 Stenton 1947, 261, 267–73.
33 Biddle 1976, 289 *et passim*.
34 W.O. Hassall 1962, 32.
35 Hill 1969.
36 Biddle & Hill 1971; T.G. Hassall 1978.
37 W.O. Hassall 1962, 32.
38 Merrifield 1990.
39 Colvin 1963, 1, 9–11.
40 R.A. Hall 1996, 37, 86–9.
41 M.W. Beresford & St Joseph, 1979, 200, 204–213, 322; Saunders 1980.
42 M.W. Beresford 1967, 459.
43 Rigold 1962–3, 1980; Davison 1967; Heywood 1980.
44 Davison 1967.
45 Ayers 1994b.
46 Stenton 1947, 362–5.
47 M.W. Beresford 1967, 326.
48 Carver 1979.
49 Colvin 1963, 1, 11–17.

2 NEW MASTERS IN ANCIENT PLACES: *Norman and Angevin England*

1 Postan 1944.
2 Thompson 1986.
3 M.W. Beresford 1967, 55–97.

4 Searle 1963; Beresford 1967, 492.
5 M.W. Beresford 1967, 492–8.
6 I was told this by Tim Tatton-Brown.
7 M.W. Beresford 1967, 405, 411–13; Saunders 1984.
8 Cherry & Pevsner 1989, 779–80.
9 Carus-Wilson 1962–3.
10 M.W. Beresford 1967, 511–12, 515–16; Leland 1964, 1, 53.
11 M.W. Beresford 1967, 333–8.
12 T.A. Heslop 1994, 6–7.
13 Ayers 1994b. In fact there were at one time over sixty churches, and, despite the destruction of nearly half of them, Norwich today has more medieval parish churches than any other city in Europe.
14 Bishop 1948.
15 M.W. Beresford & St Joseph 1979, 173–6.
16 Carus-Wilson 1941.
17 W.O. Hassall 1962, 63.
18 Gem 1986; Stocker & Vince 1997; Quiney 2001.
19 Donkin 1976, 123–9.
20 M.W. Beresford 1967, 263–5, 327–38.
21 RCHME Cambridge 1959, [33], 147; attributed to A.E. Housman on coming to Cambridge from Oxford, *The Penguin Dictionary of Modern Quotations* (1976), 159.
22 Cant 1946, 2; the Scots were again numerous enough to form a 'nation' at the University of Orléans, and few other European universities were without a group of Scotsmen.

3 BEYOND THE BORDERS OF AN EASY LIFE: *Wales and Scotland*

1 M.W. Beresford 1967, 37–8, 551–2.
2 Knight 1991.
3 W.G. Thomas 1962a.
4 M.W. Beresford 1967, 528.
5 M.W. Beresford 1967, 527–74; Soulsby 1983; Butler 2000. The Welsh lords of Powys perhaps founded Machynlleth, Llanidloes, Newtown in Montgomeryshire, and Caerswys; and Prince Llywelyn ab Gruffydd possibly founded Dolforwyn, but its location is unclear and English intervention may have caused it to be stillborn.
6 Soulsby 1983.
7 Longley 1998.
8 Soulsby 1983.
9 A.J. Taylor 1961.
10 Colvin 1963, 293–408.

11 A.J. Taylor 1975; for *The Dream of Macsen Wledig*, see Jones & Jones 1949, 69–74.
12 Radford 1967.
13 Perhaps the bones – reputedly St Andrew's arm-bone, three fingers, a tooth and a knee-cap – were brought by the Augustinians together with the myth of St Regulus (alias St Rule) to validate the foundation of their abbey in 1144.
14 Cant 1991, 8.
15 Pryde 1965, 3–12.
16 Cant 1991.
17 Stevenson 1988.
18 Colvin 1963, 409–22.

4 MONEY MAKYTHE THE MAN: *The commerce of towns*

1 Bland *et al.* 1914, 116–19.
2 Tittler 1991, 76. King's Lynn, for example, only freed itself from the control of the bishops of Norwich in the sixteenth century through royal intervention and thus gained its present name.
3 M.W. Beresford 1959.
4 Leland 1964, 5, 91–2; Pevsner 1968b, 134.
5 McNeil 1983; Leland 1964, 7, 82.
6 M.W. Beresford 1959.
7 Defoe 1724–6, 7, 408–9.
8 Adams 1978, 38.
9 Urry 1969, 108.
10 Grenville 1988.
11 Keene 1985, 335–6.
12 Schofield 1984, 60.
13 Keene 1990.
14 M.W. Beresford 1967, 195.
15 J.T. Smith 1992, 135–40.
16 M.W. Beresford & St Joseph 1979, 180–3.
17 Fisher 1935.
18 C.T. Smith 1967, 303–4; Werweke 1971, 37–40.
19 Platt & Coleman-Smith 1975, 35.
20 W.O. Hassall 1962, 92–3.
21 Jessup & Jessup 1952.
22 Leland 1964, 4, 47.
23 M.W. Beresford & St Joseph 1976, 210–12.
24 H. Parker 1965.
25 Carus-Wilson 1962–3.
26 M.W. Beresford 1967, 337–8, 346.
27 M.W. Beresford 1967, 534–74.
28 M.W. Beresford 1967, 327–31, 403–4, 457–9, 465–6.

5 WHAT IS THE CITY BUT THE PEOPLE?: *The society of towns*

1 Latin *familia*, household or establishment, never parents and children.
2 E.g. Drewett 1979 for the Bronze Age.
3 As formalized in the Elizabethan Prayer Book and set down by a more puritan age in *The Book of Common Prayer* (1662), *The Form of Solemnization of Matrimony*. The sacrament of marriage was not codified in the Middle Ages, marriage itself only requiring of the couple an exchange of words that signified consent and also that there was no impediment of incest or bigamy between them.
4 Chaucer 1893, *Canterbury Tales, Prologue* 649–65.
5 Chaucer 1893, *Canterbury Tales, Miller's Tale*, 3187ff.
6 Chaucer 1893, *Canterbury Tales, Reeve's Tale*, 4122.
7 Chaucer 1893, *Canterbury Tales, Reeve's Tale*, 3974.
8 Mertes 1988, summarized in Appendix C; this general increase was subject to much local and temporary fluctuation.
9 Girouard 1978, 14–15.

10 Girouard 1978, 27–8.
11 Le Roy Ladurie 1980, 24–34.
12 Stone 1979, 37–8, 69–76.
13 Few did as well in this last respect as Baldwin, the penniless younger son of the Comte de Boulogne, who set out on the first Crusade in 1097, and by a remarkable combination of luck and skill was ultimately crowned king of Jerusalem on Christmas Day 1100; countless other lords and knights fell victim to disease or died in battle, and the survivors found spiritual solace more readily than worldly gain – see Runciman 1951, 1, books 3–5.
14 Tawney 1941.
15 Stone 1979, 44.
16 Chaucer 1893, *Complaint of the Death of Pity*, 99–105.
17 Titow 1962.
18 Stone 1979, 51–5.
19 Rawcliffe 2000.
20 Rawcliffe 1999, 6–7, and on diseases more generally, see Rawcliffe 1995, and 1999, 8–18.
21 Rawcliffe 1999, 18–29.
22 *The Gospel of St Luke*, 16, 19–31.
23 Dixon-Smith 1999. There is no record of the logistical problem of achieving this or of guarding against benefit scroungers.
24 Keene 1985, 371–9.
25 Keene 1989.
26 Platt 1976, 97–8; Keene 1985, 371–9.
27 Platt 1976, 97–8.
28 Rawcliffe 1999, 8–9.
29 Chaucer, *Canterbury Tales, Prologue*, 363–4.
30 Newman 1976, 409.
31 Bland *et al.* 1914, 148–50.
32 Walton 1991, 346.
33 Salzman 1964, 71–82.
34 Stocker 1991, 4.
35 Moran 1992.
36 Faraday 1991, 77–95; *VCH Shropshire* 1973, 134–40.
37 Trd 54, [13].
38 Keene 1985, 332–4.
39 Unwin 1908, 370–1.
40 Pantin 1962–3b, 232.
41 Platt 1973, 240, 248, 253; Platt 1976, 107–8; Carus-Wilson 1967, 86–7; Verey & Brooks 1999, 228–31.
42 Platt 1976, 108–10.
43 Girouard 1978, 2.
44 Platt 1973, 261, fig. 10.
45 G. Williams 1963, 75, 318, table d.
46 Platt 1976, 103–7.
47 Schofield 1995, [22].
48 RCHME *Salisbury* 1980, xxxvii.
49 Pers. com. Julian Munby.
50 Bradley, Gaimster & Haith 1999, 270.
51 Schofield 1995, 158–9.
52 Kirk 1900, 4, vii; the name 'Chaucer' possibly derives from the French *chaussure* and their ancient occupation as shoemakers, in medieval English 'cordwainers' – the Chaucers settled in Cordwainer Street, but so did many vintners.
53 Platt and Coleman-Smith 1975, 18–24.
54 Keene 1985, 380–4.
55 Tawney 1938, 45.
56 Roth 1964.
57 The monks were Benedictine, the archbishop was Cistercian; he disapproved of their dissolute rule, but they were supported by the pope and various European princes as well as the Jews.
58 A mark was nominally valued at 13s 4d.
59 Urry 1967, 119–20.

60 Keene 1985, 384–7.
61 Wood 1965, 6.
62 Johnson & Vince 1992.
63 Stocker 1986, 109; this emotive subject inspired Chaucer's *Prioress's Tale*, which is dedicated to the memory of little St Hugh.
64 R.H. Jones 1980; Keene 1985, 387; Wood 1935.
65 Bland *et al.* 1914, 45.
66 Bland *et al.* 1914, 50.
67 E.g. in Guildford – Nenk *et al.* 1997, 290–2.
68 M. Roberts 1992.
69 Bland *et al.* 1914, 34.
70 Tawney 1938, 41–2.
71 Langland, *Piers the Ploughman*, 5, 245, 238–40.
72 Postan 1928.
73 Chaucer, *Canterbury Tales, Prologue*, 282.
74 Thomas Aquinas, *Summa Theologica*, $2^a 2^{ae}$, Q 83, art 6, quoted in Tawney 1938, 44.
75 Morris 1989, 172–5; Biddle & Keene 1976, 329–35.
76 Soulsby 1983, 45–6.
77 Ewan 1990, 10–11.
78 Butler 1984.
79 Urry 1967, 70.
80 Postan 1928.
81 Munby *et al.* 1992.
82 Cowie 1893, 4–9.
83 Schofield 1995, [114].
84 See generally Thrupp 1948, 169–74; Power 1975; Gilchrist 1994.
85 M.W. Beresford 1967, 18; Short 1980; Keene 1985, 387–9.
86 Urry 1967, 42–5, 107–8 *et passim*.
87 Salzman 1964, 71–2.
88 Cherry 1991, 193.
89 Holkham Bible, BL MS Add. 47,682, f31, in Cherry 1991, 186–8.
90 Cherry 1991, 186.
91 Cherry 1991, 186–7.
92 Cherry 1991, 187–8.
93 Walton 1991, 323–31.
94 Chaucer, *Canterbury Tales, Prologue*, 448–9.
95 Anon., *The Tale of Beryn, Prologue*, 23–9.
96 Keene 1990. Both Orford and Shrewsbury, Tom Beaumont James tells me, had their Gropecuntlanes, the latter now discreetly reduced to Grope Lane.
97 Langland, *Piers the Ploughman*, 5, 308–14.
98 Slang term for brothel, from stew = fishpond, for which Southwark was equally noted.
99 Riley 1868, 47–8.
100 Chaucer, *Canterbury Tales, Prologue*, 3109–854.
101 Keene 1985, 390–2; 1990.
102 *The Book of Common Prayer*, 1662, *The Form of Solemnization of Matrimony*.
103 Nenk *et al.* 1991, 226–7.

6 FROM PLAGUE, PESTILENCE, AND FAMINE: *The late Middle Ages*

1 Campbell 1990.
2 Lucas 1930.
3 Donkin 1976.
4 For which archaeological evidence remains. See D.M. Wilson & Hurst 1961, 322; Webster & Cherry 1979, 239.
5 Laithwaite 1995, 97. St. Thomas's church at New Winchelsea may have been only half completed, rather than half destroyed by the French, see M.W. Beresford & Cherry 1979, 239.

6 That was despite several new charters, its strategic site at the western entrance to the Solent, and the construction there of a fortress in the 1540s and a grand house for the Captain of the Island in the 1660s.

7 Rawcliffe 2000. Whether the Black Death was really bubonic plague or some other form of pestilence remains a debating point.

8 T.B. James & Roberts 2000.

9 D.M. Wilson & Hurst 1966, 198; T.B. James 1997, 75–85.

10 Bartlett 1959–60.

11 Verey & Brooks 1999, 228–32.

12 Pounds 1992.

13 Cherry and Pevsner 1989, 779–80, 808–9.

14 Quiney 1993, 262–3; RCHME *Kent* 1994a, 167–8; 1994b, 111–15.

15 A.R.H. Baker 1976, 239–40.

16 Carus-Wilson 1962–3.

17 Pryde 1965.

18 Cant 1946, 1–4.

19 Murray & Murray 1993.

20 Adams 1978, 49–51.

21 Spence 1980.

22 Dixon 1979.

23 *Jock o' the Side* from *Border Ballads*, Child Collection 187; first recorded in 1774, Jock was traditionally a raider of the 1560s who came from Liddesdale (the Side); there are several versions of this ballad.

24 P. Williams 1963.

7 FOR THE COMMON UTILITY OF THE CITY: *The regulation of towns*

1 M.W. Beresford & St Joseph 1979, 180–8.

2 Cruden 1964.

3 Cant 1991.

4 Frere *et al.* 1982.

5 Schofield 1995, 8–11.

6 Great Yarmouth is a classic example, its pattern still entirely clear despite destruction in the Second World War and subsequent clearances; see Carter 1980a.

7 Milne & Hobley 1981. The process was not confined to the Middle Ages: further west the Strand is now truly stranded by Victorian reclamations and the typically inventive combination of underground railway, intercepting outfall sewer and carriageway that together form the Victoria Embankment.

8 Webster & Cherry 1979, 240.

9 M.W. Beresford 1967, 16–18.

10 Wade 1988.

11 M.W. Beresford 1967, 151–2.

12 Cant 1991.

13 Spearman 1988.

14 Gifford 1988, 108–9, 175, 357–9.

15 M.W. Beresford & St Joseph 1979, 245–6; Hey 1980.

16 RCHME *Salisbury* 1980, xxxiii–xxxvi.

17 Slater 1980; D.M. Wilson & Moorhouse 1971, 156–7.

18 M.W. Beresford & St Joseph 1979, 219–20; Leland 1964, 1, 69.

19 M.W. Beresford 1967, 504.

20 Just as, on the Isle of Wight, a widening of one of the streets forming Yarmouth's grid served its market.

21 Salisbury's planners likewise kept the whole of one large island on the west side of the town free

for the market. Overlooked by the parish church of St Thomas's, half of the market chequer in fact belongs to the other parish of St Edmund's so as to keep everyone happy – RCHME *Salisbury* 1980, xxxviii–xl. Of New Buckenham's fragmentary six or perhaps eight quarters, half of one was reserved for the church and half of another for the market, which, lying on the Bury–Norwich road, was optimistically designed to attract pilgrims as well as local custom – M.W. Beresford 1967, 14–28, 148; M.W. Beresford & St Joseph 1979, 215–17, 226–8; Rutledge 1980.

22 Urry 1967, map 2(b).

23 Keene 1985, 152–4.

24 Samuel 1989.

25 Keene 1985, 195, figs 153–5. Ale was the common English medieval beverage, beer the German. Beer is distinguishable from ale by the use of hops to preserve it, rather than wormwood; Caxton knew this, but he was probably unaware that Flemish immigrants had been growing hops on a small scale in England since the fourteenth century and by 1490 this was becoming rather more widespread.

26 M.W. Beresford 1959.

27 Keene 1985, 180–2.

28 Radley 1971.

29 Hansen 1976.

30 Ersland 1994.

31 Slater 1980.

32 VAGCP 1983, 22–3.

33 VAGCP 1982; Trd 64, 29, 30, 83.1.

34 Cant 1991.

35 Cruden 1964.

36 R.H. Jones 1980.

37 Urry 1967, 185–92, map 2(b).

38 M.W. Beresford 1967, 14–28.

39 Slater 1980.

40 Davison 1967.

41 D.M. Wilson & Hurst 1966, 168.

42 Perring 1981; R.H. Jones 1980.

43 Urry 1967, maps 1 and 2.

44 Biddle 1976, 345.

45 Ayers 1987.

46 Slater 1980.

47 Colvin 1958, 69.

48 Schofield 1995, 4, 95.

49 Heslop & Truman 1993, 11.

50 Heslop *et al.* 1995.

51 Laithwaite 1995, 95–7.

52 According to its surviving records covering 1301–1427.

53 Schofield 1995, 4.

54 i.e. windows below 16 feet overlooking someone else's property.

55 Schofield 1995, 59, 95.

56 Salzman 1967, 268–9; Tatton-Brown 1983.

57 Salzman 1967, 268.

58 Bradley *et al.* 1999, 257.

59 Salzman 1967, 272; Bradley *et al.* 1999, 239–40.

60 Portman 1966, 16.

61 Wood 1965, 369–72.

62 Salzman 1926, 86–7; 1967, 273.

63 Keene 1985, 179.

64 Fiennes 1949, 5.

65 RCHME *Salisbury* 1980, xxxiii–xxxvi.

66 Portman 1966, 15.

67 Salzman 1967, 282–3.

68 Salzman 1926, 87.

69 Keene 1985, 179–80.

70 Wood 1965, 385.

71 Schofield & Vince 1994, 68.

72 Salzman 1967, 282–5.

73 Salzman 1967, 282–5.

74 Portman 1966, 15.

75 Keene 1985, 179–80.

8 SQUARED STONES, EVENLY JOINTED: *Walls, floors and roofs*

1 Vitruvius 1914, 1, 1 *et passim*.

2 Salzman 1967, 1–29; Harvey 1984, *passim*.

3 Christie *et al.* 1979; Trd 80, [29].

4 Innocent 1916, 134–8; Clifton-Taylor 1972, 287–93.

5 Atkin & Carter 1977.

6 Anderson 104, 106; J.R. Harrison 1984; 1989; 1991.

7 Turner & Parker 1851–9, 1, 281.

8 From the French *torchis*, 'mud', but plasterer may be meant.

9 Riley 1868, 30.

10 Clifton-Taylor 1972, 288; Schofield 1994, 152.

11 'an earthen hall, a chamber, a stable, a shop or booth at the front', RCAMS *Edinburgh* 1951, lxvii.

12 Portman 1966, pl. 9.

13 Laithwaite 1995, 97; Thorp 1982.

14 Atkin 1985.

15 D.M. Wilson & Hurst 1964, 263–4, 267.

16 Salzman 1967, 88, 540.

17 Webster & Cherry 1973, 159–61; *Current Archaeol.*, 1972, 312, 318; Department of the Environment 1973, *Archaeological Excavations 1972*, 73.

18 Carver 1979.

19 Radley 1971.

20 Carver 1979.

21 Salzman 1967, 148.

22 Webster & Cherry 1972, 187–8. The Dutch scholar and traveller Erasmus was writing to Cardinal Wolsey's physician some time before 1530, in Latin as follows: 'Tum sola fere sunt argilla, tum scirpis palustribus, qui subinde sic renovantur, ut fundamentum maneat aliquoties, annos viginti, sub se fovens sputa, vomitus, mictum canum et hominum, projectam cervisiam, et piscium reliquias, alias que sordes non nominandas.' See N. Lloyd 1931, 80.

23 The late second millennium BC.

24 Clifton-Taylor 1972, 32 *et passim*.

25 The very name of the apostle who had brought Christianity to Rome, Peter, in Latin *Petrus*, meant rock, hence the pun on his name as the rock on which the Christian Church was founded.

26 'lapideam ecclesiam iuxta Romanorum quem semper amabat morem', Bede, *Historia Abbatum*, 5, quoted in Plummer 1896, 1, 368; for this and other early stone churches see Bede 1955, 5, 21; Salzman 1967, 1; H.M. Taylor 1969; Tatton-Brown 1991.

27 Knoop & Jones 1967; Salzman 1967, 1–29; Harvey 1984.

28 'aulis et cambris regalibus, lapideus et ligneis', according to Alfred's biographer Asser, see Parsons 1991, 14.

29 RCHME *Northants.* 1985, 41–4, [8]; J.H. Williams *et al.* 1985.

30 Parsons 1991, 11–18. Eaton 2000; which supports this view; appeared too late to be taken into account.

31 Stocker & Everson 1990.

32 Colvin 1963, 13–17.

33 Parsons 1991, 18–21.

34 Jope 1964.
35 Salzman 1967, 119.
36 R.H. Jones 1980, 46–7.
37 Tatton-Brown 1990.
38 Ayers 1987, 156; for stone supply in Norfolk, see A.P. Harris 1990.
39 Ayers 1987, 172–4.
40 D.M. Wilson & Hurst 1959, 314.
41 Radley 1971.
42 RCHME *York* 1981, 5, [469].
43 Keene 1985, 169–70, 178.
44 E.g. Burgundy, see Quiney 1999a.
45 Bony 1939.
46 P. Smith 1975, 392–3.
47 Salzman 1967, 140.
48 Moore 1991, 212.
49 Quiney 1998, 280.
50 Bilson 1896.
51 Pantin & Sturdy in *VCH Oxon* 1964, 144–7; quoted in Moore 1991, 214.
52 Keene 1985, 175.
53 Chaucer, *Canterbury Tales, Miller's Tale*, 5927–8, 5931–2.
54 Harden 1961, 39–44.
55 Harden 1961, 34.
56 Faulkner 1975, 78–9, [8], [9], [10], [11].
57 Keene 1985, 175.
58 Armstrong 1977.
59 Chaucer 1893, *Booke of the Duchesse*, 321–5.
60 Marks 1991, 282–93.
61 Now in the British Museum.
62 D.M. Wilson & Hurst 1961, 323; Cherry 1991, 198–9.
63 M. Hall 1992.
64 Chaucer, *Booke of the Duchesse*, 232–4.
65 Innocent 1916, 188–222; Letts 1999, 3–27 *et passim*; Stanford 2001.
66 T.H. Turner & Parker 1851–9, 1, 282.
67 From the Old German *Dach*, roof.
68 Bede 1955, 3, 10; 1, 19.
69 Salzman 1967, 223.
70 '*arundine*, . . . *junco*, . . . *aliquo modo straminis neque stipula*', Turner & Parker 1851–9, 1, 282; Salzman 1967, 223–9.
71 Urry 1967, 194.
72 RCAMS *Edinburgh* 1951, lxvi.
73 Moir & Letts 1999, 9–12.
74 Laithwaite 1995, 97.
75 Schofield 1995, 96.
76 Colvin 1963, 527.
77 Keene 1985, 173–4.
78 Samuel 1989.
79 Salzman 1967, 228–9.
80 Knight 1991.
81 For the process, see Cherry 1991, 190.
82 Cherry 1991, 193–4.
83 Hare 1991.
84 R.H. Jones 1980, 49.
85 Urry 1967, 192–4.
86 Salzman 1967, 230.
87 Cherry 1991, 194–5.
88 Keene 1985, 173–4.
89 Salzman 1967, 231; Jope 1951.
90 Dunning 1961, 79; Cherry 1991, 196.
91 Laithwaite 1995, 97.
92 Moorhouse 1900.
93 Hare 1991.
94 From the French *l'ouvert*, opening; Wood 1981, 277–80.
95 Keene 1985, 174.

96 Bailey 1980a.
97 HMSO *Salisbury* 1993, 204–7; Holton-Krayenbuhl 1999.
98 Keene 1985, 174.
99 Wood 1965, 279.
100 Dunning 1961.
101 Keene 1985, 174–7.
102 Salzman 1967, 430–2, 443–4.
103 Dunning 1961, 78.
104 Harrison, *Description of England*, ed. Furnivall 1877, 239–40.
105 Winthrop Papers, quoted in Cummings 1979, 4.
106 Even as late as 1700, see Quiney 1993, 176–9.

9 LIKE SEASONED TIMBER, NEVER GIVES: *Framed walls and roofs*

1 Orme 1982; Munby 1991, 379–82.
2 Goodburn 1994.
3 West 1985.
4 Millett & James 1983, 227–36.
5 Slater 1994.
6 Radley 1971.
7 R.A. Hall 1984.
8 D.M. Wilson & Hurst 1969, 231.
9 Webster & Cherry 1975, 245.
10 D.M. Wilson & Hurst 1964, 264–5.
11 Keene 1985, 170–1.
12 Carver 1979.
13 Davison 1967.
14 And in many other places such as Steyning, see Nenk, *et al.* 1993, 285; and Winchester, see Perring 1981, 36–40.
15 Keene 1985, 171.
16 Rackham 1972; Rackham 1982; Currie 1983.
17 '*et erit conformatum per omnia edificio Ricardi de Briggenall in North Stret*', Salzman 1967, 430–2.
18 Harvey 1984, 20.
19 Charles & Down 1970–2.
20 For terminology, see Alcock *et al.* 1996.
21 Colvin 1963, 529.
22 For the study of how timber framing developed in the Middle Ages, see Quiney 1994; for the development itself, see Quiney 1992, 41–59.
23 Trd 32, [1a].
24 Blair 1987; S.R. Jones & Smith 1960; Radford *et al.* 1973.
25 Goodburn 1994.
26 R. Harris 1989.
27 R. Harris 1989.
28 R. Harris 1989.
29 Aitkens 1999.
30 As a *getticium*, Schofield 1995, 147.
31 R. Harris 1990. I am grateful to Richard Suggett for bringing Aberconwy House to my notice and discussing its jetty with me; Conwy Castle was incidentally taken during Owain ab Gruffydd's rebellion, so it is possible that temporary fortifications at that time may have prompted the jettied top floor of the house; see also Trd 121 [1.]
32 Munby, Sparks & Tatton-Brown 1983; Warren 1992.
33 Alcock 1981.
34 For a summary of the controversy surrounding the origin of crucks and their distribution, see Quiney 1994.
35 Charles 1967, 17–25.
36 And also in Ireland, see Alcock 1981, 87–92.
37 Alcock & Blair 1986.
38 Youngs & Clark 1981, 206–7.

39 N.W. Jones 1998; Leland 1964, 6, 115 (J.T. Smith 1964, 3, 10).
40 Moran 1992; Trd 56, [14], [15].
41 Alcock 1981, 140.
42 Thame is similarly endowed with medieval crucks, but other prosperous towns in the Thames valley such as Cirencester have none. Similarly the Severn estuary is flanked by numerous cruck-framed houses, but, again, its towns are all but devoid of them (Gloucester 1; Tewkesbury 3), see Alcock 1981, 117–19. An exception is Tudor House in Hatters Lane at Chipping Sodbury, which was remodelled in Tudor times, but nevertheless retains a three-bay cruck – framed hall, probably of the fourteenth century, in which the four pairs of crucks are raised high on the stone walls to gain the necessary height, and joined by cambered collars – Youngs & Clark 1982, 170.
43 Alcock 1981, 137, and also four more in the village of Old Malton.
44 Hayes & Rutter 1972; RCHME *N. York Moors* 1987, 138–44.
45 Alcock 1981, 112.
46 J.T. Smith 1981.
47 Siddington barn, Gloucestershire, built with timber felled in 1245–7, see Trd 23, [44].
48 Alcock & Barley 1972; Alcock 1997.
49 Mercer 1996.
50 Trd 117 [6], which supersedes the earlier date given in Trd 14 [F23].
51 Crook 1982.
52 Highfield 1971.
53 Nevertheless, there is a drawing in Villard de Honnecourt's famed notebook of about 1235 (*Carnet* f. 17v shows a roof truss, inscribed '*Or poé veir 1.bon conble legier por hierbegier deseur und chapele a volte* [*Ici vous pouvez voir un bon comble léger pour couvrir une chapelle voûtée* – Here you can see a good light truss to cover a vaulted chapel]) with what may either be interpreted as hammerbeams supporting posts, or sole-pieces extending inwards supporting ashlar-pieces; the inscription suggests the latter.
54 Colvin 1963, 930–7, 527–33; Waddell 1999.
55 Fox 1957; Portman 1966, [8], fig. viii; Cherry & Pevsner 1989, 411–13.
56 Gifford *et al.* 1984, 95–9; for Scottish hammer-beams more generally, see Gomme 2002.
57 RCHM *Salisbury* 1980, [351], [132].
58 Munby *et al.* 1983.
59 Short 1980.
60 Nenk *et al.* 1991, 164–5.
61 Chaucer, *Canterbury Tales, The Miller's Tale*, 3836–9.
62 Hewett 1969, 134–7.
63 Hewett 1985, 28.
64 Penoyre 1998; Trd 93, [8], [9].
65 Trd 27, [6].
66 Schofield 1995, [47].
67 Roberts 1996.
68 Lewis *et al.* 1988.
69 D.M. Wilson & Hurst 1965, 198.
70 Biddle 1976, 345.
71 Keene 1985, 171–2.
72 Laithwaite 1995, 90.
73 P. Smith 1975, 392–3.
74 Salzman 1967, 68–81.
75 Munby 1991, 386–9.

10 THE SHADOW OF A FLEETING DREAM: *Impermanent houses*

1 Tacitus, *Germania*, 16.
2 Tacitus, *Germania*, 16.
3 Literally German for 'sunken house'.
4 Tacitus, *Germania*, 16.
5 M.U. Jones 1979; M.U. Jones & Jones 1974; Hamerow 1993.
6 Rahtz 1976.
7 West 1969; 1985.
8 Pers. com. West.
9 Hawkes 1969; Canterbury Archaeol. Trust 1982–3, 9–13.
10 Webster & Cherry 1980, 225–7; Youngs & Clark 1981, 171–2.
11 D.M. Wilson & Hurst 1965, 168–9.
12 Davison 1967.
13 The earliest signs of Anglo-Saxon occupation at well over a dozen other towns are the excavated remains of *Grubenhäuser*, e.g. Abingdon, Aylesbury, Dorchester (Dorset), Dorchester-on-Thames, Dunstable, Eynsham, Ipswich, Leicester, Letchworth and Norwich, as well as those of Lydford and Thetford; see Webster & Cherry 1972, 147; 1973, 148; 1974, 174; 1975, 220; Youngs *et al.* 1987, 160; Gaimster *et al.* 1989, 196; Nenk *et al.* 1991, 180, 183; Nenk *et al.* 1994, 231–2, 235; Nenk *et al.* 1996, 245, 258.
14 Schofield 1984, 28.
15 Slater 1994.
16 For the use and survival of *Grubenhäuser*, see also Myres & Dixon 1988. 'Sunken-floored buildings' of the late tenth or early eleventh century have recently been excavated between King Street and Gresham Street in the City of London; see Bradley & Gaimster 2000, 267.
17 E.g. also Portchester, where two such groups have been excavated, see D.M. Wilson & Hurst 1970, 157.
18 Addyman *et al.* 1972; Addyman & Leigh 1973.
19 James *et al.* 1984; Alcock & Walsh 1993.
20 Millett & James 1983.
21 Bede 1955, 2, 13.
22 Hope-Taylor 1977.
23 Cramp 1957.
24 Rahtz 1979.
25 Colvin 1963, 1–17, 42–8.
26 G. Beresford 1975; 1987; Thompson 1995, 50–73.
27 RCHME *Northants.* 1985; J.H. Williams *et al.* 1985.
28 For a discussion of the word 'palace', see Thurley 1997, 93–4.
29 Biddle 1976, 323–8; 1986.
30 Cramp 1969; 1976.
31 Conant 1968, figs 6–8.
32 Cramp 1957.
33 Edward the Martyr; he was assassinated in 978. Colvin 1963, 5.
34 Davison 1967.
35 Addyman & Hill 1968/9.
36 Holdsworth 1976; Youngs & Clark 1981, 184–5; Youngs, Clark & Barry 1983, 178–9; de Groot 1996.
37 Yeoman 1995, 60–1.
38 Perring 1981, 12–18, 36–44. Similar remains of early medieval buildings have been uncovered at Melbourne Street, Southampton, at Lion Walk, Colchester and at 62–4 High Street, Maldon, and in Northampton, Bristol, Bedford, Chelmsford, and Hull, among many other places; see Webster & Cherry 1972, 155; 1973, 140–1; 1975, 225–6, 242–5.

39 Wade 1994.
40 D.M. Wilson & Hurst 1970, 157–8.
41 Biddle & Keene 1976, 345. Similar early-eleventh-century houses have been found in Oxford at St Ebbe's Corner, see D.M. Wilson & Hurst 1961, 324–5; and in Bristol near the church of St Mary-le-Port Street, where there were sunken hearths and a cess pit and evidence of iron smelting, see D.M. Wilson & Hurst 1964, 264–5.
42 Yeoman 1995, 54–60.
43 This excavation has never been fully published. *Current Archaeol.* 1972, 3.12, 318; Webster & Cherry 1973, 159–61; Department of the Environment 1973, 73.

11 VAULTES STRONGLYE AND SUBSTANCIALLYE WROUGHT: *Undercrofts*

1 M.W. Beresford 1967, 27. The town was losing the battle to keep its port and livelihood. The term 'undercroft' is used on account of its greater neutrality than that of such terms as 'cellar', 'crypt' or 'vault' which imply specific types or uses.
2 Further timber-lined sunken buildings have been found near Cheapside and Eastcheap; see Schofield 1995, 74, [31], [32].
3 Schofield 1984, 28.
4 Schofield 1984, 54–5; 1994, 74, [138], [174].
5 Quiney 1999a.
6 Similar undercrofts once existed in Southwark, in or close to Tooley Street, at what may have been the earl of Warenne's inn, recorded in 1829, and again at the prior of Lewes's inn, recorded in 1831; see Schofield 1995, [91], [198], [199].
7 As St James's Hermitage – Schofield 1984, 56–7; 1994, [140].
8 E.g. Bishop Poore's Palace at Salisbury, see RCHME *Salisbury* 1993, 53–4, 57–9; Bishop Jocelyn's Palace at Wells, the former Abbot's House, now the Bishop's Palace at Peterborough.
9 Barron 1974; Schofield 1995, 16–17.
10 Keene 1985, 166.
11 P. Smith 1975, 22–3.
12 Cant 1975.
13 S.R. Jones, Major & Varley 1990, 67–85.
14 A.N. Brown 1999, 15–18, 183–4. This was probably extended by one more post to form an arcade of five bays which used to be answered by a second one, now replaced, making three aisles in all; the timber of one samson-post was felled in about 1260, so this is among the oldest to support one of Chester's Row buildings yet to be recognized. See also Turner 1988.
15 Faulkner 1966.
16 Schofield 1984, 78; 1995, [13]. It was demolished to make way for the extension of Cannon Street in 1852.
17 Schofield 1995, 75–6, [119].
18 Urry 1967, 192–4.
19 Turner 1988; A.N. Brown 1999, 183–4.
20 Urry 1967, 192–4.
21 D.M. Wilson & Hurst 1964, 268–9.
22 Faulkner 1975, 113.
23 R.B. Harris 1998.
24 Garrigou Grandchamp 1998; Quiney 1999a.
25 D.M. Wilson & Hurst 1962–3, 329; Faulkner 1975, 97.
26 Schofield 1995, [174].
27 D. Heslop & Truman 1993; D. Heslop *et al.* 1995. The three houses were re-fronted in timber in the

sixteenth century and, later still, raised to four or five storeys, and, in the case of Milbank House, re-fronted yet again in brick as fashion succeeded fashion.
28 Urry 1967, 192–4.
29 Carter 1980b; Ayers 1987, 158; Pevsner & Wilson 1997, 274.
30 Schofield 1984, 77–8.
31 Barley 1986, 69.
32 R.B. Harris 1998.
33 Pantin 1957.
34 At least after Adam de Brome, chancellor of Durham Cathedral, had acquired the property so that he could make it the home of his foundation, Oriel College, see Pantin 1962–3b, [14]; VAGCP 1987.
35 D.M. Wilson & Hurst 1962–3, 329–30.
36 Pantin 1961, 188–9.
37 Keene 1985, 166.
38 Defoe 1724–6, Letter 8, 451–2.
39 Faulkner 1966.
40 Brown 1999, especially Chs 1–5. Despite the report, no archaeological evidence has been found of a disastrous fire in 1278.
41 Lawson & Smith 1958.
42 Grenville 1988; A.N. Brown 1999, 55–62.
43 Alcock 2001.

12 CLOUD-CAPP'D TOWERS, AND GORGEOUS PALACES: *The palaces and halls of magnates*

1 Ullmann 1955, 87–118.
2 It was demolished 1585–6; Conant 1959, 225, Pl. VIII B
3 Buchkremer 1940–55; Conant 1968.
4 '*Fecit ibi et palatium, quod nominavit Lateranis*', see Ullman 1955, 95. The use of the word 'palace' as well as Lateran has clear imperial overtones.
5 Thompson 1995, 41–5.
6 Cotman & Turner 1822, 75. Interestingly, in view of a possible source for the west front of Lincoln Cathedral (see below), Turner describes the hall's features as 'distinctly Roman', noting the resemblance of its cornice to those of the Tomb of Cecilia Metella, the Arch of Constantine and the Colosseum. Edward Impey (1993, 83–4) believes that this was not a hall but a chamber block, which, though unusually early, post-dates the Conquest, and presumably served an undiscovered open hall.
7 Bouard 1973–4.
8 R.A. Brown 1976, 24–5.
9 E.g. the so-called Temple of Janus at Autun (Saône-et-Loire).
10 Mesqui 1993, 220.
11 Welsh for 'bends of the river'.
12 Knight 1991, 4–5, 37–9. This early date for Chepstow has recently been questioned, but without a final conclusion. I am grateful to John Goodall for telling me this.
13 Stocker 1992.
14 Owen 1983.
15 Gem 1986.
16 Stocker & Vince 1997; Stocker 2001. Gem disagrees with the view that this was a separate structure, even though accepting its range of possible functions. A full archaeological investigation may decide the issue, and, David Stocker tells me (December 2001), this now increasingly seems to favour two separate structures.

17 A number of keeps have been shown to be less impregnable than symbolically strong, Castle Hedingham in Essex being the classic case, see Dixon & Marshall, 1993. Similar views now embrace the Conqueror's White Tower, Henry II's keep at Dover and a range of other keeps built during the intervening years. For the White Tower, see Parnell 1998; for Dover, see Goodall 1999.

18 Minst & Huth 1965. See also Conant 1959, 297, n. 21: 'Richbod, a member of the Palatine School at Aachen, friend and pupil of Alcuin, archbishop of Trier from 798, served as Abbot of Lorsch 784–804, the period of Charlemagne's epic struggle of conquest against the Saxons (788, 804), the Avars (805), and the Bavarians. Tassilo, Duke and King of the Bavarians, became a monk at Lorsch, and died there about 797. It is easy to see how the idea of a triumphal arch could arise under these circumstances'.

19 Eusebius, *Life of Constantine*, 1, 28. It is not clear how the arch was perceived in the late eleventh century: it was commonly viewed in the Middle Ages as pagan, but Constantine's name and his role were revered by educated men within the Church.

20 Quiney 2001.

21 R.A. Brown & Curnow 1984; Parnell 1998; Drury 1982.

22 It was also a source of myth. Visiting Colchester in April 1722, Daniel Defoe (1724–6, Letter 1) reported: 'The castle of Colchester is now become only a monument showing the antiquity of the place, it being built as the walls of the town also are, with Roman bricks; and the Roman coins dug up here, and ploughed up in the fields adjoining, confirm it. The inhabitants boast much that Helena, the mother of Constantine the Great, first Christian Emperor of the Romans, was born there, and it may be so for aught we know'.

23 This and much of what follows was the general consensus of the White Tower Conference, held by the Society of Antiquaries of London and Historic Royal Palaces, Burlington House, on 16 April 1999.

24 Colvin 1963, 753–5; 588–90.

25 Ponderously restored by Antony Salvin in the 1830s.

26 Wilkins 1796; T.A. Heslop 1994.

27 Whittingham 1980; Fernie 1993, 54–5 *et passim*.

28 Cubbie Roo's Castle, Orkney – see Chapter 18 below.

29 Coad & Streeten 1982.

30 Peers 1953.

31 Raby & Reynolds 1973.

32 Wood 1956b.

33 Stocker 1991.

34 RCHME *Oxford* 1939, [124]; Blair 1978b.

35 Gray 1932; RCHME *Cambridge* 1959, xc–xci, [292].

36 Biddle 1976, 323–8; 1986.

37 Conant 1959, 44, 77–8, 260.

38 Garrigou Grandchamp 1996, 47. The palace is now the préfecture.

39 Thurley 1995. Similarly placed, the great hall of Archbishop Sully's palace looked across the Seine from the south side of Nôtre Dame; and there is a magnificent view from the gallery of the palace at Laon.

40 The only surviving part and now called the Salle des Gens d'Armes.

41 Collette *et al.* 1980, 55–65; Quiney 1999a.

42 Gifford 1992, 327–9. Haakon's defeat at the hands of King Alexander III freed Scotland from the threat of Norwegian domination, but Orkney, a dependency of Norway and Denmark, only became part of Scotland in 1468 when Christian I of Denmark married his daughter Margaret to King James III, and gave the islands as a dowry.

43 Dunbar 1964.

44 Thompson 1995, 100–1.

45 Thompson 1995, 31–2.

46 Joinville, book 2, translated Evans 1938, 29–30. Louis IX's *Ordinatio hospicii et familiae* demonstrates the problems of imposing a formal hierarchy on a seigneurial household – see Jervis 2000, 32.

47 An early use of the word 'palace' in Britain and a possibly conscious reference to the Emperor Augustus's house on the Palatine Hill in Rome.

48 Biddle 1976, 289–302.

49 This probably being the direct result of competition with the hall of the French royal palace, which, though wider, was divided by an arcade into two, whereas Richard's remodelling removed the aisles to provide a single immense span. See Colvin 1963, 45–7, 527–33.

50 Biddle 1976, 323–8; 1986.

51 Colvin 1963, 910–18.

52 Alcock & Buckley 1987.

53 S.R. Jones & Smith 1960; Radford *et al.* 1973; Blair 1987; Trd 32. 1989, [1].

54 Blair 1987.

55 Faulkner 1974a.

56 Canterbury Archaeol. Trust 1982–3; Rady *et al.* 1991. The great chamber led to further private accommodation for the archbishop and an entrance into the cathedral at an upper level in the by-now established way.

57 Colvin 1963, 854–64.

58 Thurley 1995.

59 Colvin 1963, 45.

60 The Arthurian card did little for Henry VIII's game: it was no ace and the round table failed to reward his diplomatic aspirations in Europe with success. For the table itself, see Biddle 2000. It is both curious and dispiriting to note how continuing bad luck has dogged members of the royal line who have been given the name Arthur.

61 '*In aula sint postes debitis interstitiis distincti*'.

62 Blair 1993, 4–5.

63 Nevertheless the possibility of an undercroft here – and descent from Paderborn – cannot be ruled out. See Thompson 1995, 84–6.

64 Garrigou Grandchamp 1992, 47; 1999.

13 HOUSES SMALL AND NOT LOFTY: *Merchants' and Jews' houses*

1 Laleman 1994.

2 *Diele* means a deal board, and, presumably by extension, a board on which goods were displayed, hence the room itself; Muret-Sanders's German Dictionary also gives 'vestibule' and 'entrance hall'.

3 Pers. com. Andor Gomme.

4 Aaron's House, Lincoln; excavated house at St Martin-at-Palace Plain, Norwich.

5 Jew's House, Lincoln.

6 3–4 West Street, New Romney.

7 King John's Palace, Southampton.

8 Faulkner 1958.

9 Flaxengate site, Lincoln.

10 Jew's House and Aaron's House, Lincoln.

11 St Martin-at-Palace Plain, Norwich.

12 As the ruins of Ostia Antica can verify, see Meiggs 1973, 236–8, 272–3.

13 Verdier & Cattois 1857, 2, 204–6.

14 Garrigou Grandchamp *et al.* 1997, *passim*.

15 Pitte & Lescroart 1990–1; Pitte & Cailleux 1998.

16 Pitte & Lescroart 1994–5.

17 N. Lloyd 1931, 19; Wood 1965, 1–6.

18 R.H. Jones 1980, 46.

19 Schofield 1987, [11].

20 Schofield 1995, 29–32, [91], [138].

21 Carter 1980b; Pevsner & Wilson 1997, 274–5.

22 Wood 1935, 203–5. The surviving external fragments are set in the upper storey of the eastern range; its eastern return wall has been rebuilt, but at least until the eighteenth century this was also divided by buttresses into three bays, of which the outer two still had similar two-light windows, and there was a third blocked one in the centre.

23 Urry 1967, 113, 150–2.

24 Perring 1981, 18–33.

25 R.H. Jones 1980, 46.

26 Fiennes 1949, 71; King 1782, 261; R.H. Jones 1980, 46–54; Stocker 1991, 3.

27 Wood 1935, 194–8.

28 Platt & Coleman-Smith 1975, 25.

29 Faulkner 1975, 78–9, [8], [9], [10], [11].

30 RCHME *York* 5 1981, [469].

31 RCHME *York* 3 1972, lxi.

32 RCHME *Stamford* 1977, l–lii; ten of their plans are shown in fig. 8.

33 Ayers 1987, 172–4.

34 Clarke & Carter 1977, 411–49; Richmond *et al.* 1982; Taylor & Richmond 1989.

35 Youngs & Clark 1981, 205–6.

36 Wood 1935; Portman 1966, [26]. It was bombed in 1942.

37 Quiney 1993, 260.

38 Parkin 1973.

39 Webster & Cherry 1972, 173.

40 Wilson & Hurst 1964, 269–70. Pers. com. Richard Suggett and Trd 121. [1].

41 P. Smith 1975, 23.

42 W.G. Thomas 1962b.

43 Cant 1997. For Scottish stone houses in the form of a tower, see Chapter 18 below.

44 King 1782, 261.

45 R.H. Jones 1980, 46–50.

46 Carter 1980b; Pevsner & Wilson 1997, 274–5.

47 Pevsner & Wilson 1999, 504.

48 Parkin 1970; Canterbury Archaeol. Trust 1979–80.

49 Urry 1967, 192–4.

50 D.M. Wilson & Hurst 1964, 264; Webster & Cherry 1976, 187; Youngs & Clark 1981, 205–6; 1982, 167, 170.

51 D.M. Wilson & Hurst 1961, 322–3.

14 A HOUSE FOR ROYAL BUSINESS AND OTHER AFFAIRS: *The houses of royalty, magnates and wealthy merchants*

1 Mertes 1988, Appendix C.

2 Some institutional halls were confined to men, a few to women. James IV and his queen Margaret Tudor lived and dined separately at Holyroodhouse at the time of their marriage in

1503, for which see Chapter 18 below. Precedence in a stately hall at meal times had always been imperative to such an extent that a display of this in where one sat was a significant function of a meal; precedence, according to *The Boke of Curtasye* (*c.* 1460), was sometimes ordered by a marshal: 'In hall marshalle alle men shalle sett, After here degré, with-outen lett.' – see Jervis 2000, 31–3.

3 Langland, *Piers Ploughman*, 10, 92–102. 'Lords should be glad to hear these lessons, and consider how they might provide for as many men as possible – and not seek out the hospitality of feasts, as fiddlers and friars do, in other men's houses while despising their own. "For their hall is deserted, each day of the week, when the lord and lady do not wish to sit there. The rich nowadays have a habit of eating by themselves in a private parlour for the sake of the poor, or in a chamber with a chimney, and to abandon the main hall, which was made for men to eat meals in, and all to save what another will squander"'.

4 Grenville 1997, 197; Quiney 1999b.

5 Leyland 1994.

6 J.H. Parker, 1861–2; Brakspear 1950. In January 2003 the Society of Antiquaries of London reported the discovery within the palace of a well-preserved wall painting of 'a woman dressed in the height of fashion in a low-cut, tight-waisted gown with her hair drawn back tightly into a net, on which there are extensive remains of gilding.' According to Jerry Sampson, 'a pale fawn area of drapery seems to belong to a butterfly headdress which, with the gown, suggests a date of around 1470 to 1485. Both the dress and position of the hands can be related to monumental brasses of the period . . . It seems likely that the lady belongs either to a narrative sequence, such as that of Susannah and the Elders, or conceivably is a depiction of Mary Magdalene, who was generally shown dressed in the height of fashion.

7 Radford 1934.

8 Turner 2000.

9 Turner 2000.

10 Newman 1978.

11 Blair 1978a.

12 RCHME *Oxford* 1939, [16].

13 RCHME *Cambridge* 1959, [25].

14 RCHME *Oxford* 1939, [17].

15 RCHME *Oxford* 1939, [6], [22].

16 RCHME *Oxford* 1939, [15].

17 Schofield 1995, 34, [193]; *Survey of London* 1950, 46–56.

18 Jacques d'Amboise reconstructed the thirteenth-century Hôtel des Abbés de Cluny at the end of the fifteenth century with fashionable new ranges set around an open courtyard.

19 Tatton-Brown 2000, 15 *et passim*; Thurley 1999.

20 Later Southwark Cathedral.

21 Youngs *et al.* 1984, 232–3.

22 Pers. com. Tim Tatton-Brown; Tatton-Brown 2000, 19–22. Baldwin, who led the English contingent to Acre, had played a prominent but unsuccessful role in trying to reconcile the dying King Henry II of England to his heir Richard, who was allied with Phillip II of France against him, all of whom had vowed to go on Crusade to recapture Acre from Saladin – see Runciman 1951–4, vol. 3, book 1, Ch. 1.

23 Tatton-Brown 2000, 23–58; and see Chapter 11 above.

24 Audouy *et al.* 1995.

25 *Survey of London* 1951, 81–103; Tatton Brown 2000, 23 *et passim*.

26 Thurley 1995.

27 Schofield 1995, [11], [42], [114].

28 Quiney 1999a.

29 Now reduced to a small fragment. See Pantin 1962–3b, 232; Youngs *et al.* 1984, 206.

30 Gunn 1991.

31 Emery 2000, 242.

32 Faulkner 1970, 138–40, inc. plan; Faulkner 1974b; Lindley 1991b; Emery 2000, 242–50.

33 Burgh's will, see Emery 2000, 244.

34 M.V. Clark 1991.

35 Purchased by the Earl of Arundel in 1549 and accordingly shown by Hollar as Arundel House.

36 Schofield 1995, [157].

37 *King Lear*, 1, 4. Shakespeare knew full well the fate of Southwark's medieval inns, hence these remarks about the palace that Lear had bequeathed to Regan and Goneril, albeit at the hands of his own retinue.

38 Schofield 1995, [197–201].

39 Schofield 1995, 41.

40 Chaucer, *Canterbury Tales, Prologue*, 28–9.

41 For which also see Edmund Spenser, *Faerie Queen* (1596), c XII.lxxv.

42 Schofield 1995, 232, [199]. Langland (*Piers Ploughman*, 11, 251), in an early reference to walnuts, remarked that within their bitter shell was a kernel of strengthening food; for that reason a walnut tree might possibly be a suitable sign for an inn; Shakespeare (*Merry Wives of Windsor*, 4, 2, 171) spoke of a hollow walnut concealing a wife's lover.

43 Schofield 1995, [47].

44 Pantin 1961, 169–76.

45 Pantin 1961, 188.

46 Since 1541 Gloucester Cathedral.

47 'magnum emolumentum ac proficuum'. The recent dendrochronological study of two timbers suggests the primary building date of 1432 or soon after – see Trd. 125 [1].

48 Frith 1965a.

49 Pantin 1961, 169–73, suggests slightly different sizes.

50 Tom Fenton, to whom I am grateful for discussing this with me, says that Thokey may have been forced to take Edward II's body, rather than gladly accepting it, in which case the story of a hermit's death may have been a convenient cover for his embarrassment.

51 Pantin 1962–3b, [24]; Munby *et al.* 1993.

52 Salzman 1967, 493–5, 517–19.

53 Rawcliffe 2000.

54 *Tale of Beryn, Prologue*, 14.

55 Canterbury Archaeol. Trust 1983–4, 33, [7].

56 *Tale of Beryn, Prologue*, 281–6, also quoted in Pantin 1961, 188.

57 'unum aedificium lignium plures mansiones constituens vocatum anglice Le Bole'.

58 Canterbury Archaeol. Trust 1983–4, 37–8, [26].

59 RCHM *York* 1981, [485]; Trd 44, [21].

60 Cant 1946, 32; Gifford 1988, 386. The remaining buildings are now part of St Leonard's School for Girls.

61 Pevsner & Williamson 1994, 163.

62 For the complicated story of this dispute, see Tittler 1991, 94–5. Among numerous other medieval inns, the Crown at Faringdon is among the oldest, part of one range of its courtyard apparently dating from the early fourteenth century, see Pevsner 1966, 141. The Birdcage at Thame is another early inn, with a stone vaulted undercroft. The White Hart and the Bull at Henley-on-Thames, the Bell Inn at Nottingham and the Christopher at St Albans, whose remains are now built into 1–5 French Row, are others with substantial medieval remains.

63 With timber felled about 1463. See Trd 12, [16].

64 With timber felled in 1312–13. See Trd 39, [9].

65 Charles & Charles 1978.

66 Schofield 1987, [3].

67 Spanning each of these was a roof truss with arched collars rising from stub-beams, or false hammer-beams, to give a dash of class. See Drinkwater & Mercer 1963; Salzman 1967, 516–17; RCHME *Salisbury* 1980, [344].

68 As opposed to the nondescript late Georgian inns of his own day that would, of course, have been serving gin, which, by contrast, led to insobriety, incontinence and criminality. See Pugin 1836.

69 Pantin 1961, [3].

70 Pantin 1961, 181–2. The George at Glastonbury is first mentioned in 1439 but was rebuilt or refronted *c.* 1456–74, possibly by the mason John Stowell, whom Harvey (1984, 286) records as working in Wells at that time, though living in Glastonbury.

71 D.L. Roberts 1974.

72 Keene 1985, 167–9.

73 Pantin 1961, 187.

74 RCHME *Salisbury* 1993, 193–201.

75 RCHME *Salisbury* 1993, 53–73.

76 Holten-Krayenbuhl 1999.

77 S.R. Jones 1974.

78 Godfrey 1950.

79 Thorp 1990.

80 The only part to have survived the war. See Portman 1966, [5], [6], [7], [8], [9]; Cherry & Pevsner 1989, 411–13; Laithwaite 1995, 111–13.

81 Pantin 1962–3a.

82 Steelyard is a derivation of *Stalhof*, a yard or house for samples or patterns – *Stal* – and hence warehouse; it has no connection with *Stahl* meaning steel.

83 Pantin 1962–3a.

84 Parliamentary Rolls vi 123/1 quoted in *OED*: I owe this reference to Andor Gomme.

85 Schofield 1984, 118–20.

86 Cooper & Kindred 1998.

87 The dwelling in this case was demolished for road widening but the warehouse ranges survive, one of stone, the other framed, using timber felled in 1514: Trd 39, [10]; VAGCP 1998, 40.

88 Trd 56, [19].

89 Arrol & Snell 1981; Trd 64, [33].

90 Pers. com. Brian Ayers. Trd 104, [31].

91 Carter 1980c.

92 *Survey of London* 1908; Schofield 1995, [22], [114].

93 Schofield 1987, [21], [31].

94 Faulkner 1969.

95 I am grateful to Robina McNeil for bringing this house to my notice. See McNeil 1999.

96 VAGCP 1982 *Shropshire*, 17.

97 Trd 18, [3].

98 Barley 1986, 74.

99 Hewett 1980, 211.

100 Erroneously believed to be the Prysten or Priest's House.

101 Cherry & Pevsner 1989, 611; Laithwaite 1995, 111–13.

15 For dignity compos'd: *Guildhalls, hospitals, almshouses and colleges*

1 Giles 1998.
2 Tittler 1991, particularly Chs 1, 4 and 5.
3 RCHME *York* 1981, [37]; Trd 47, [8].
4 RCHME *York* 1981, [38]; Trd 47, [9].
5 RCHME *York* 1981, [39].
6 RCHME *York* 1981, [36].
7 After the guild had been disbanded, Mary Queen of Scots was imprisoned here in 1569.
8 Trd 80, [61].
9 Rigold 1971b. The tapestry is now thought to have originated in Tournai rather than Arras.
10 Fosbrooke & Skillington 1923–4.
11 Chenevix Trench & Fenley 1991.
12 Faulkner 1971.
13 Trd 80, [57]; Pevsner & Wilson 1999, 505.
14 King Edward VI's School.
15 Originally not contiguous, as now, a further bay having been subsequently added to the range to join them.
16 Pevsner & Wedgwood 1966, 418–19; Rouse 1971. Only part of the the Last Judgement survives in recognizable form, the remaining painting being now very fragmentary. For schools generally, see Seaborne 1971.
17 Dunn & Suttermeister 1978; R. Smith & Carter 1983. For the lesser and initially commoner breed of town hall incorporating a hall built over an open arcade that derives from the form of a market cross, see Tittler 1991, Ch. 2.
18 Rawcliffe 1999, 169–76 *et passim*, Appendix 1. Statistics are equally unavailable for cures and conversions.
19 First epistle of St Paul to Timothy, 5, 6–15.
20 Rawcliffe 1999, 169–76 *et passim*.
21 Cowie 1893, 13–14.
22 Rawcliffe 1999, 5.
23 Canterbury Archaeol. Trust 1983–4, 31, 50–3, [10].
24 Rawcliffe 1999, 1–4.
25 Rawcliffe 1999, 103–32 *et passim*.
26 St John's Hospital at Cirencester, founded in 1168–9, and built soon afterwards in this form, had a four-bay aisled infirmary similar to a monastic infirmary. Verey & Brooks 1999, 270–1.
27 Pevsner & Lloyd 1967, 404–5. Only the infirmary and chapel remain after a long run of post-Dissolution mutilation ending in the bombing of the Second World War that left it partly roofless.
28 Godfrey 1933; Pevsner & Williamson 1984, 219–20.
29 Cowie 1893, 12–15. The hospital was recorded in detail before its demolition in 1875 by H. Dryden: I am grateful to Tim Schadla-Hall for showing me the set of drawings in Leicester Record Office.
30 The northern aisle has been demolished leaving the former arcade built into a new wall.
31 RCHME *Salisbury* 1980, [26].
32 Now rebuilt as an entrance porch.
33 RCHME *Stamford* 1977, [48]; Pevsner & Harris (rev Antram) 1989, 697–8.
34 The nave of this cruciform building survives as the Mayor's Chapel, but the hospital itself fell into ruins after it was suppressed in 1539. Quiney 1977.
35 Known as the Commandery after the masters of the hospital, who called themselves commanders, it has a five-bay open hall at the centre with a hammerbeam roof that once had two louvers; the timber was felled in 1491. See VAGCP 1995 *Worcestershire*.
36 *Archaeol. J.* 1935, 92, 393–4. The formerly open aisle bays (now reduced to four each side) have been converted into independent dwellings, each complete with its own fireplace and chimney stack, in a similar way to the conversion of the Heiligengeist Hospital at Lübeck. Meanwhile, the chapel still retains its original character, largely unaltered.
37 *VCH Northants.* 1906, 177–9; Pevsner 1961, 251–2; Thompson 1967.
38 Before alteration in the sixteenth century.
39 It has a two-storeyed infirmary range opening into a square chapel at the east end, with a small refectory on the ground floor and a common room continuing the range to the west. The painting in the chapel, of about 1480, is said to be of the school of Roger van der Weyden, no doubt because of his triptych at the Hôtel Dieu at Beaune.
40 Godfrey 1930; RCHME *Dorset* 1952, 212–14, and Sherborne [7]; Gibb 1983.
41 Harvey 1966.
42 Rigold 1971a. Ford may have been prompted in his foundation by Thomas Bond, a Coventry draper, who in 1506 founded his hospital as an almshouse for aged men and women with a two-storeyed range forming part of a less private open courtyard with Bablake School.
43 Pevsner 1966, 59.
44 S.R. Jones *et al.* 1987 [S31]; Trd 80, [56].
45 Pantin 1959; Penoyre & Penoyre 1999.
46 Pantin 1959.
47 Pantin 1959. A range of lodgings for chantry priests in the Cathedral Close at Lichfield comprised fifteen chambers, each assessed at the time of its suppression in 1548 at between 12d and 20d, see Tringham 1984–5. The ten priests who served the Palmers' Guild in Ludlow seem to have been accommodated in the fifteenth century behind College Street in a two-storeyed stone range which comprised ten chambers and five studies, built on two sides of a courtyard, with timber felled in 1393. See Trd 54, [12]; *VCH Shropshire* 1973, 139–40.
48 Now Manchester Cathedral.
49 Cornish 1884; Powell 1987; Trd 122, [3].

16 Houses most of timber work: *Small town houses in the later Middle Ages*

1 Chaucer, *Canterbury Tales, Nuns Priest's Tale*, 12.
2 Pantin 1962–3b.
3 Leech 1998; Schofield 1998; Leech 2000. The ground floor was usually a shop, devoted to manufacturing and retailing, as it already had been for some centuries.
4 Leech 1998; Leech 2000.
5 Schofield 1998.
6 Melling 1965, 20–3.
7 Chaucer, *Canterbury Tales, Miller's Tale*.
8 RCHME *Oxford* 1939, [79]. Merton Street was little more than a side street when compared with the nearby High Street, where all the houses were built end-on.
9 VAGCP 1984 *Essex*, 72–85.
10 Nos 8 and 9 Market Place, see VAGCP 1972 *Suffolk*; VAGCP 1984 *Essex*, 72–85.
11 Grevel's House.

12 Newman 1995, 332, and pers. com. Richard Suggett.
13 Pevsner & Williamson 1984, 319–20; Trd 75, [3].
14 H. Poole 1999.
15 Not rebuilt with the rest of the house in the Avoncroft Museum at Stoke Prior, since it had already been destroyed.
16 VAGCP 1995 *Worcestershire*, 1.8.
17 With timber felled in 1462–3, see Trd 103, [7]. I am extremely grateful to Richard Suggett of the RCAHMW for telling me about this and other Welsh houses before publication of the Commission's own volume on Radnorshire houses.
18 Trd 60, [18]. The walls of the Old Vicarage are of the local Magnesian limestone, and the timber roof-trusses are varied according to the status of their position in the house, both the central trusses of the hall and the chamber having superior arch-braced collars.
19 RCHME *W. Yorks* 1986, 27–36, [184].
20 Recently renamed Greyfriars.
21 VAGCP 1995 *Worcestershire*, 2.14.
22 Quiney 1993, 164, 178.
23 VAGCP 1972 *Suffolk*.
24 Pounds 1992.
25 VAGCP 1990 *Wiltshire*, 31–3.
26 Rigold 1969b.
27 RCHME *Kent* 1994a, 80–1; but 35 High Street, Winchester, a puzzling fragment of a Wealden dendro-dated to 1339–40 (see Lewis *et al.* 1988, [11]; Trd 72, [16]; T.B. James & Roberts 2000), reopens the question of the timing and source of this design – perhaps Stuart Rigold was right after all.
28 Martin & Mastin 1974.
29 Martin & Martin 1987, [1].
30 RCHM *Kent* 1994b, 112–13, 132.
31 Canterbury Archaeol. Trust 1983–4, [27].
32 RCHME *Kent* 1994b, 57–8.
33 Martin & Martin 1987, [3].
34 Said to date from 1489, but built from timber felled in 1452, see Trd 57, [9]; Pevsner & Williamson 1979, 196.
35 Mason's Court, 11–12 Rother Street.
36 74 Smith Street and 105 West Street.
37 47 High Street.
38 Further west in Herefordshire there are three Wealdens in Weobley (inc. 38 High Street and 37 Portland Street); see S.R. Jones & Smith 1960–1.
39 S.R. Jones & Smith 1960–1. The half-Wealden form was well suited to this kind of speculation, but other, less ambitious forms could have been more practical for such small houses. The distinctiveness of the design in the context of speculative building in peripheral urban sites seems to account for a full Wealden which was built in 1459 on the corner of Hollybush Row and St Thomas High Street, Oxford, and survived to be recorded by J.C. Buckler before its destruction about 1841, see Munby 1974.
40 Lewis *et al.* 1988, 18–19, [13].
41 J.T. Smith 1992, 143–4. The lack of fireplaces does not however necessarily preclude a domestic use.
42 For which, see Myddleton Place, Saffron Walden; the Woolpack, Great Coggeshall; and Lady Street, Lavenham. Stenning 1985; D. Clark 2000.
43 T.B. James & Roberts 2000. The arcaded front of 58 French Street, Southampton, is a half-way-house between a full arcade of this and the

44 Although the Latin term *aula* was not used, this may have been an upper hall.
45 Keene 1985, 154, 156–7.
46 Pantin 1963, 470–3; Leech 1998; Leech 2000.
47 VAGCP 1974 *Leicester*; Pevsner & Williamson 1984, 500.
48 RCHM *York* 1981, [194].
49 Munby 1975; RCHME *Oxford* 1939, [73]; Trd 3, [F6].
50 Faulkner 1966.
51 Munby 1978.
52 A. Brown 1999, 184, Pl. 1.
53 Pantin 1962–3b, [14–23]; Leech 1998; 2000.
54 Portman 1966 [28–9]; they were demolished in 1972.
55 Laithwaite 1995, 106–8.
56 Leech 1998; 2000.
57 Lewis *et al.* 1988, [12]; Trd 72, [15]; Trd 114, [11]; T.B. James & Roberts 2000.
58 VAGCP 1995 *Worcestershire*, 2.15.
59 Pantin 1962–3b, [9], [10].
60 Author's survey for the GLC, 1974, see Cherry 1975, 247, and Trd 115, [9].
61 Bailey 1980a.
62 These seem to have been matched by their neighbour at 13 Highweek Street; see Laithwaite 1971.
63 Leech 1998; 2000.
64 Moran 1992; Trd 56, [14], [15].
65 Schofield 1987, [21], [22], [25], [38], [39].
66 Schofield 1987, [10], [22].
67 Penoyre & Penoyre 1997; Trd 84, [2], [3], [4], [5].
68 Dymond 1998.
69 Timber felled in 1458: Trd 56, [18].

17 ONE FRAME CALLED THE 'LADY ROWE': *Terrace houses*

1 J.T. Smith 1992, 142–3.
2 D. M. Wilson & Hurst 1958, 191 and fig. 48.
3 Schofield 1984, 88; 1987, 11–15.
4 Short 1980; RCHME *York* 1981, [222].
5 Short 1980; RCHME *York* 1981, [471]; Trd 114, [24]. For a while thought to date from 1270, timber felled in 1322/3 was used for No. 60, and this house together with the rest of the terrace was probably rebuilt at that time by the Vicars Choral of York.
6 Salzman 1967, 430–2; Short 1980.
7 RCHME *Stamford* 1977.
8 Leech 1998; 2000.
9 Laithwaite 1995, 113.
10 Nos 25–8 Barrow Street were built using timber felled in 1435, see Trd 56, [15].
11 Moran 1992; part of a similar terrace has been discovered at 18–21 Abbey Foregate, Shrewsbury, which has two pairs of cruck-framed bays, using timber felled in 1408 and 1430–3, respectively; see Trd 109, [7].
12 Bailey 1980b.
13 Middle Row was built with timber felled in the period 1310–20; see Trd 19, [1].
14 The back-to-back came into its own in the nineteenth century when the Industrial Revolution put greater pressure on urban land than the Middle Ages experienced, and then mostly in the northern weaving towns. Lighting and ventilation were always a problem, as the houses could only be one room deep and were confined on three sides, but their notoriety is not entirely justified,

however much the one-roomed plan is associated with poverty.
15 RCHME *Oxford* 1939, [69]; Pantin 1942; Munby 1978.
16 Munby *et al.* 1992.
17 Pantin 1959; Penoyre & Penoyre 1999; Trd 110, [5].
18 Pantin 1959.
19 Salzman 1967, 441–3.
20 Salzman 1967, 443–4.
21 Salzman 1967, 446–8.
22 Schofield 1987, 14–16, 100–3.
23 Schofield 1987, 100–3; Schofield 1994, [142].
24 Canterbury Archaeol. Trust 1983–4, [46].
25 Salzman 1967, 554–6.
26 *VCH Gloucestershire* 1968, 129–30.
27 Trd 100, [14].
28 S.R. Jones & Smith 1960–1, 23–5.
29 J.T. Smith 1992, 148–9.
30 Martin & Martin 1987, [3] and 16–17. All the houses are now concealed behind brick fronts.
31 Thorp 1982.
32 Pantin 1959; Leland 1964, x, 5.
33 R. Smith & Carter 1983.
34 Garrigou Grandchamp 1992, 36.
35 Kelsall 1974.
36 Leech 1996.

18 HOUSSES MIRK AND STEEPY: *Scotland from the late Middle Ages to the Union of the Crowns*

1 McKean & Walker 1982, 16. Forestairs might be in the form of either a simple open flight of stairs rising up to a doorway at first-floor level, or an enclosed newel set within a tower serving several floors.
2 Fawcett 1996.
3 E.g. up to seven storeys by the early seventeenth century in Rouen's framed houses; stair towers are common in Dijon's courtyards and on such front elevations as that of the Maison de Sires de Domecy, Place Saint-Lazare, and in the Grande rue-Aristide-Briand, Avallon, and elsewhere in Burgundy.
4 Such as the Hôtel de Saint-Livier at Metz.
5 W.D. Simpson 1961.
6 P. Smith 1975, 21–4, 338–9.
7 W.D. Simpson 1961, 229.
8 Garrigou Grandchamp 1996, 23.
9 Gifford 1992, 377. Cubbie Roo's Castle.
10 Alloa Tower, the stronghold of the Erskmes, earls of Mar, who were granted Alloa in 1363, was until recently said to date from about then; it was, however, first recorded in 1497, roughly when its timber roof was constructed, so may be of this later date.
11 C. Wilson 1984; Gifford *et al.*, 1984, 92–3.
12 Gifford *et al.*, 1984, 110–11; Pringle 1996.
13 When a larger kitchen was built elsewhere, this became a parlour where Mary Queen of Scots is said to have recuperated following the murder of her lover David Rizzio in 1566.
14 Gifford *et al.* 1984, 538–43.
15 Gifford *et al.* 1984, 489–50; Bradley & Gaimster 2000, 332.
16 Gifford *et al.* 1984, 497–8.
17 Grundy *et al.* 1992, 329.
18 Stell 1991; Stewart 1991.
19 Gomme & Walker 1987, 17.
20 Gifford 1992, 328–9. The palace of the bishop of Dornoch, however, survives. Built about 1500 as a five-storeyed tower with a jamb and a projecting, full-height turnpike, it survived its transfer into sec-

ular hands after 1557, being eventually put to civic use as a county court and jail, and is now a hotel.
21 Nothing at all survives of the medieval Glasgow University, which was founded in 1450–1. King's College Chapel, begun in 1500, is the only surviving medieval building of the two independent colleges that were eventually united to form Aberdeen University. For Glasgow, see Billings 1845–52, 2, 57–9; for Aberdeen, see Billings 1845–52, 1, 6–8.
22 Cant 1946, 14.
23 Cant 1946, 22–7.
24 Dunbar 1984; Dunbar 1999.
25 Apted 1964a; McWilliam 1978, 291–301. Stewart is the original Scottish spelling of the name, Stuart the later French spelling.
26 RCAMS *Edinburgh* 1951, [87]; Dunbar 1963; 1984. These early buildings have long since vanished. The economies that Queen Margaret suffered during the coronation festivities included making do with used candles at her separate dining table, for which see Dunbar 1999.
27 Interestingly, a similarly private stair was designed in the nineteenth century to link the similarly disposed private suites of the Duke and Duchess of Sutherland at Dunrobin Castle.
28 Dunbar 1984; Gifford *et al.* 1984, 125–48.
29 Dunbar 1984; 1999.
30 Gifford 1992, 338–9.
31 Renilson 1937. Mary Queen of Scots is said to have stayed here, hence the name.
32 Gifford 1988, 351.
33 Gifford 1988, 73.
34 Gifford 1988, 194. The inscription, which loosely means 'Since word is binding and thought is free, guard well thy tongue, I counsel thee', comes from James I's *The Kingis Quair*. It may have been carved on a former hearth lintel, and been reset in this position when Abbot's House was rebuilt. This was probably undertaken by James Murray of Perdieu, after the Reformation left it 'ruinous in sundry parts'. The appearance of mottoes in English at the same time as the Bible was first printed in English is surely not just coincidental.
35 Cant 1997, 4–5. All of these houses have been modernized in various ways, and most of them now have regularized Georgian fronts.
36 Gomme & Walker 1987, 17–20; Williamson *et al.* 1990, 107, 142–3.
37 He entertained James VI several times at the Great Lodging, a remarkable achievement given its lack of state apartments and entirely domestic character. Bruce paid for repairs to the former parish church of Carnock, a hamlet a short way inland (Apted 1964b); at his death in 1625 Bruce was commemorated by his son with a fine three-tiered monument in the most magnificent Jacobean taste, made by the mason John Mercer, and inscribed 'THIS IS SIR GEORGE BRUCE OF CARNOCK HIS LADY HIS THREE SONS AND FIVE DAUGHTERS THIS TOMB WAS PROVIDED BY GEORGE BRUCE OF CARNOCK HIS ELDEST SON', and there they are, all ten of them, he and his wife recumbent on a tomb chest, 'both looking very dead', and the children kneeling at prayer before it (Gifford 1988, 149, 154–7).
38 Gifford 1988, 289–90.
39 RCAMS *Edinburgh* 1951, lxvii.
40 McKean & Walker 1982, 24.
41 Cruden 1964.
42 Ewbank 1823.

43 National Gallery of Scotland, Edinburgh.

44 RCAMS *Edinburgh* 1951, [13].

45 RCAMS *Edinburgh* 1951, [90]; Gifford *et al.* 1984, 218.

46 Or perhaps 1631 – RCAMS *Edinburgh* 1951, [14].

47 RCAMS *Edinburgh* 1951, [14]; Gifford *et al.* 1984, 195.

48 RCAMS *Edinburgh* 1951, [31]; Gifford *et al.* 1984, 205.

49 RCAMS *Edinburgh* 1951, [19]; Gifford *et al.* 1984, 200.

50 RCAMS *Edinburgh* 1951, [38]; Gifford *et al.* 1984, 205–7.

51 RCAMS *Edinburgh* 1951, [39]; Gifford *et al.* 1984, 207–8; D. Smith 1996.

52 RCAMS *Edinburgh* 1951, [42]; Gifford *et al.* 1984, 220.

53 RCAMS *Edinburgh* 1951, [104]; Gifford *et al.* 1984, 213–14.

54 RCAMS *Edinburgh* 1951, [18]; Gifford *et al.* 1984, 198–200.

55 RCAMS *Edinburgh* 1951, [41]; Gifford *et al.* 1984, 209–10.

56 RCAMS *Edinburgh* 1951, [21]; Gifford *et al.* 1984, 201–2.

57 RCAMS *Edinburgh* 1951, [11]; Gifford *et al.* 1984, 193.

CONCLUSION: *Restoring intellectual day*

1 Particularly if history is seen as a record of human progress. See, for instance, H.A.L. Fisher's *A history of Europe* (London: Eyre & Spottiswood, 1935), vol. 1 *Ancient and medieval*, and vol. 2 *Renaissance, Reformation, Reason*, whose opening chapter is entitled 'The new Europe'.

2 *Act of Supremacy*, 1534.

3 *Act against Papal Authority*, 1536.

4 Charles Jennens, *Il Moderato*, 1740.

5 Handel's oratorio, *Judas Maccabaeus*, with a libretto by Thomas Morell, was completed in August 1846, four months after the Duke of Cumberland's violent defeat of the Jacobites the previous April, and opened in April 1747 at Covent Garden 'with very great Applause'.

6 RCHME *Cambridge* 1959, [37], 196–7. The chapel of Lincoln's Inn, which was built in the Gothic style in 1619–23, is an analogous, though less-known, example (see fig. 220).

7 Front Quad, 1620–42, Gothic in detail, but classical in its symmetry; see RCHME *Oxford* 1939, [18].

8 From 1638, see RCHME *Cambridge* 1959, [24].

9 RCHME *Oxford* 1939, [6]. Moreover, the design of the library, in a wonderfully sophisticated volte-face, turns from the external Gothic to a severe classical inside.

10 Husselby & Henderson 2002.

11 Summerson 1962, 50, and more generally on Barbon, 44–50.

12 Flats for the English middle class were in reality inspired by Parisian practice rather more than by Scottish, see for example Saint 1976, 194–201.

13 And a 'utility room' containing, in place of servants, such 'white goods' as a washing machine and freezer.

14 'Machine à habiter', from *Vers une architecture* (1923), translated by Frederick Etchells as *Towards a new architecture* (London, 1927), 124–5.

BIBLIOGRAPHY

Adams, I.H. 1978. *The making of urban Scotland.* London: Croom Helm

Adams, L., and J.P. Carley (eds). 1991. *The archaeology and history of Glastonbury Abbey: essays in honour of the ninetieth birthday of C.A. Raleigh Radford.* Woodbridge: Boydell Press

Addy, S.O. 1898. *Evolution of the English house.* London: Swann Sonnenschein

Addyman, P.V.A. 1981. 'Cruck buildings', in Alcock 1981, 37–9

——, and V. Black (eds). 1984. *Archaeological papers from York presented to M.W. Barley.* York: York Archaeol. Trust

——, and D.H. Hill. 1968–9. 'Saxon Southampton: a review of the evidence', *Proc. Hampshire Field Club*, 25, 61–93; 26, 61–96

——, and D. Leigh. 1973. 'Anglo-Saxon village at Chalton, Hants.', *Med. Archaeol.*, 17, 1–25

——, D. Leigh and M.J. Hughes. 1972. 'Anglo-Saxon houses at Chalton, Hants.', *Med. Archaeol.*, 16, 13–31

Aitkens, P. 1999. *Twelfth and thirteenth-century houses and their carpentry in Suffolk – and some comparisons with other parts of southeast England.* Unpublished paper presented on 17 April to Anglo-French Seminar on 12th and 13th-century buildings, Norwich, for Norfolk Archaeol. Unit

Alcock, L. 1971. *Arthur's Britain: history and archaeology AD 367–634.* London: Alan Lane

Alcock, N.W. 1997. 'A response to: "Cruck distribution: a social explanation" by Eric Mercer', *Vernacular Archit.*, 28, 92–3

—— 2001. 'The origin of the Chester Rows: a model', *Med. Archaeol.*, 45, 226–8

—— (ed.). 1981. *Cruck construction*, CBA Research Rep., 42. London: CBA

——, and M.W. Barley. 1972. 'Medieval roofs', *Antiquaries J.*, 52, 132–68

——, M.W. Barley, P.W. Dixon and R.A. Meeson. 1996. *Recording timber-framed buildings: an illustrated glossary.* York: CBA

——, and J. Blair. 1986. 'Crucks: new documentary evidence', *Vernacular Archit.*, 17, 36–8

——, and R.J. Buckley. 1987. 'Leicester Castle: the great hall', *Med. Archaeol.*, 31, 73–9

——, and D. Walsh. 1993. 'Architecture at Cowdery's Down: a reconsideration'. *Archaeol. J.*, 150, 403–9

Anderson, R. 1804. *Cumberland Ballads and Songs*, centenary edn, ed. T. Elwood. Ulverston: W. Holmes

Andrews, P. 1997. *Excavations at Hamwic, 2, Excavations at Six Dials.* York: CBA

Anon. *The Tale of Beryn*, ed. F.J. Furnivall and W.G. Stone, 1887. London: Chaucer Society

Apted, M.R. 1964a. 'Linlithgow Palace', *Archaeol. J.*, 121, 176–7

—— 1964b. 'Culross Palace', *Archaeol. J.*, 121, 190–2

Aquinas, St T. see Thomas, Aquinas, St.

Armstrong, J.R. 1977. 'The closure of unglazed windows', *Vernacular Archit.*, 8, 832–3

Armstrong, P., and B. Ayers. 1987. 'Excavations in High Street and Blackfriargate', Hull Old Town Rep. Ser. 5, *East Riding Archaeologist*, 8

Arrol, A. 1988. 'Much Wenlock', *Annual Conference Programme*, Soc. of Archit. Historians of Great Britain, 39–40

——, and A. Snell. 1981. 'The Trotting Horse, Shrewsbury', *Archaeol. J.*, 138, 41

Aston, M., and J. Bond. 1997. *The landscape of towns.* 2nd edn. Gloucester: Alan Sutton

Atkin, M.W. 1985. 'Excavations on Alms Lane', in Atkin, Carter and Evans 1985, 144–260

——, and A. Carter. 1977. 'Excavations in Norwich, 1976/7', *Norfolk Archaeol.*, 36, 296–8

——, A. Carter and D.H. Evans. 1985. 'Excavations in Norwich 1971–8, Pt 2', *East Anglian Archaeol.*, 26, 144–260

Audouy, M., B. Dix and D. Parsons. 1995. 'The tower of All Saints' Church, Earls Barton, Northamptonshire: its construction and context', *Archaeol. J.*, 152, 73–94

Ayers, B. 1985. 'Excavations within the north-east bailey of Norwich Castle, 1979', *East Anglian Archaeol. Rep.*, 28

—— 1987. 'Excavations at St Martin-at-Palace Plain, Norwich, 1981', *East Anglian Archaeol. Rep.*, 37

—— 1990. 'Building a fine city: the provision of flint, mortar and freestone in medieval Norwich', in Parsons 1990, 217–27

—— 1994a. 'Excavations at Fishergate, Norwich, 1985', *East Anglian Archaeol. Rep.*, 68

—— 1994b. *English Heritage book of Norwich.* London: Batsford and English Heritage

Bailey, J.M. 1980a. 'Nos 7 and 9 West Street, Dunstable', *Bedfordshire Archaeol. J.*, 14, 91–8

—— 1980b. 'Nos 26–32 Middle Row, Dunstable', *Bedfordshire Archaeol. J.*, 14, 98

Baker, A.R.H. 1976. 'Changes in the later Middle Ages', in Darby 1976, 186–247

Baker, N. 1994. 'House-plots and houses in English medieval towns'. Unpublished paper presented in April to *Houses and Households in Towns 100–1,600*, University of Birmingham

Ballard, A., and J. Tait (eds). 1923. *British borough charters, 1216–1307.* Cambridge: Cambridge University Press

Barley, M.W. 1961. *The English farmhouse and cottage.* London: Routledge and Kegan Paul

—— 1974–5. 'Flore's House, Oakham, Rutland', *Trans. Leicestershire Archaeol. and Hist. Soc.*, 50, 37–40

—— 1979. 'The double pile house', *Archaeol. J.*, 136, 253–64

—— 1986. *Houses and history.* London: Faber and Faber

—— (ed.), 1976. *The plans and topography of medieval towns in England and Wales.* CBA Research Rep., 14. London: CBA

Barlow, F., *et al.* 1976. *Winchester in the early Middle Ages: an edition and discussion of the Winton Domesday*, Winchester Studies, 1, ed. M. Biddle. Oxford: Clarendon Press

Barron, C.M. 1974. *The medieval guildhall of London.* London: Corporation of London

Bartlett, J.N. 1959–60. 'The expansion and decline of York in the later Middle Ages', *Economic History Review*, Ser. 2, 12, 17–31

Beacham, P. (ed.). 1995. *Devon building.* 2nd edn. Tiverton: Devon Books

Bede. 1955. *A history of the English church and people*, translated L. Sherley-Price. Harmondsworth: Penguin

Bencard, M. (ed.). 1981. *Ribe excavations 1970–76*, 1. Esbjerg: Sydjysk Universitetsforlag

Beowulf, translated M. Alexander. 1973. Harmondsworth: Penguin Books

Beresford, G. 1975. *The medieval clay-land village: excavations at Goltho and Barton Blount.* SMA Monograph, Ser. 6. London: SMA

—— 1987. *Goltho: the development of an early medieval manor c. 850–1150*, Historic Buildings and Monuments Commission (England), Archaeol. Rep. 4. London: HMSO

Beresford, M.W. 1959. 'The six new towns of the bishops of Winchester, 1200–55', *Med. Archaeol.*, 3, 187–215

—— 1967. *New towns of the Middle Ages: town plantations in England, Wales and Gascony.* London: Lutterworth Press

———, and J.K. St Joseph. 1979. *Medieval England: an aerial survey.* 2nd edn. Cambridge: Cambridge University Press

Biddle, M. 1976. 'The evolution of towns: planned before 1066', in Barley 1976, 19–32

———. 1986. *Wolvesey. The old bishop's palace, Winchester*, English Heritage Guide. London: HMSO

———. 1990. *Object and economy in medieval Winchester*, Winchester Studies, 7, 2. Oxford: Oxford University Press

——— (ed.). 1976. *Winchester in the early Middle Ages*, Winchester Studies, 1. Oxford: Clarendon Press

——— (ed.). 2000. *King Arthur's Round Table: an archaeological investigation*. Woodbridge: Boydell Press

———, and D. Hill. 1971. 'Late Saxon planned towns', *Antiquaries J.*, 51, 70–85

———, and D.J. Keene. 1976. 'Winchester in the eleventh and twelfth centuries', in Barlow *et al.* 1976, 241–448

———, H.T. Lambrick and J.N.L. Myres. 1968. 'The early history of Abingdon, Berkshire, and its abbey', *Med. Archaeol.*, 12, 26–69

Billings, R.W. 1843. *Architectural illustrations and description of the cathedral church at Durham*. London: T. and W. Boone

———. 1845–52. *The baronial and ecclesiastical antiquities of Scotland.* 4 vols. Edinburgh: William Blackwood and sons.

Bilson, J. 1896. 'The North Bar, Beverley', *Trans. East Riding Archaeol. Soc.*, 4, 38–49

Binski, P. 1996. *Medieval death. Ritual and representation.* London: BM Press

Bishop, T.A.M. 1948. 'The Norman settlement of Yorkshire', in *Studies in medieval history presented to F. M. Powicke*, ed. R.W. Hunt *et al.*, 1–14. Oxford: Clarendon Press

Blair, W.J. 1978a. 'Monastic Colleges in Oxford', *Archaeol. J.*, 135, 262–7

———. 1978b. 'Frewin Hall, Oxford: a Norman mansion and a monastic college', *Oxoniensia*, 43, 48–99

———. 1982. 'St John's Hospital, Bedford', *Archaeol. J.*, 139, 60–1

———. 1984. 'Posts or crucks?', *Vernac. Archit.*, 15, 39

———. 1987. 'The twelfth-century Bishop's Palace at Hereford', *Med. Archaeol.*, 31, 59–72

———. 1993. 'Hall and chamber: English domestic planning 1000–1250', in Meirion-Jones and Jones 1993, 1–21

Blair, W.J., and N. Ramsay (eds). 1991. *English medieval industries.* London: Hambledon Press

Bland, A.E., P.A. Brown and R.H. Tawney. 1914. *English economic history. Select documents.* London: Bell

Bony, J. 1939. *La technique Normande du mur épais à l'époque romane*, Société Français d'Archaéologique pamphlet. Paris: Société Français d'Archaéologique

Bouard, M. de. 1973–4. 'De l'*aula* au donjon, les fouilles de la motte de la Chapelle à Doué-la-Fontaine (Xᶜ–XIᶜ siècles)', *Archéologie Médiévale*, 3–4, 5–110

Brachman, H., and J. Herrmann (eds). 1991. *Frühgeschichte der europäischen Stadt.* Berlin: Akademie Verlag

Bradley, J., and M. Gaimster. 2000. 'Medieval Britain and Ireland', 1999', *Med. Archaeol.*, 44, 235–54

———, M. Gaimster and C. Haith. 1999. 'Medieval Britain and Ireland, 1998', *Med. Archaeol.*, 43, 226–302

Brakspear, H. 1950. 'Bishop's Palace, Wells', *Archaeol. J.*, 107, supplement 74–6

Brisbane, M. 1988. 'Hamwic (Saxon Southampton): an eighth-century port and production centre', in Hodges and Hobley 1988, 101–8

Brooke, C. 1975. *London 800–1216: the shaping of a city.* London: Secker and Warburg

Brown, A.N. (ed.). 1999. *The Rows of Chester.* London: English Heritage

Brown, R.A. 1976. *English castles.* London: B.T. Batsford

———, and P. Curnow. 1984. *Tower of London*, Department of the Environment Official Handbook. London: HMSO

Buchkremer, J. 1940–55. *Beiträge zur Baugeschichte*, 3 vols.

Bulmer-Thomas, I. 1979. 'Euclid and medieval architecture', *Archaeol. J.*, 136, 136–50

Butler, L.A.S. 1976. 'The evolution of towns: planted towns after 1066', in Barley 1976, 32–48

———. 1984. 'The houses of the mendicant orders in Britain: recent archaeological work', in Addyman and Black 1984, 123–36

———. 1987. 'Domestic building in Wales and the evidence of the Welsh Laws', *Med. Archaeol.*, 31, 458

———. 2000. 'Dolforwyn Castle, Powys: nineteen years of excavation'. Unpublished paper read in March to the RAI

Campbell, R.M.S. 1990. 'People and land in the Middle Ages, 1066–1500', in Dodgshon and Butlin 1990, 69–122

Cant, R.G. 1946. *The University of St Andrews. A short history.* Edinburgh: Oliver and Boyd

———. 1991. 'The medieval city of St Andrews', *Archaeol. J.*, 148, supplement 7–13

———. 1997. 'Burg planning and early domestic architecture: the example of St Andrews (*c.* 1130–1730)', in Mays 1997, 1–12

Canterbury Archaeol. Trust. 1979–80. *Annual Rep.*

———. 1982–3. *Annual Rep.*

———. 1983–4. *Annual Rep.*

Carley, J.P. (ed.). 2001. *Glastonbury Abbey and the Arthurian tradition.* Woodbridge: Brewer

Carter, A. 1980a. 'Great Yarmouth', *Archaeol. J.*, 137, 300–7

———. 1980b. 'The Music House and Wensum Lodge, King Street, Norwich', *Archaeol. J.*, 137, 310–12

———. 1980c. 'Stranger's Hall, Norwich', *Archaeol. J.*, 137, 360–1

Carus-Wilson, E.M. 1941. 'An industrial revolution of the thirteenth century', *Economic Hist. Review*, 11, 1–21

———. 1954. *Medieval merchant venturers.* London: Methuen

———. 1962–3. 'The medieval trade of the ports of the Wash', *Med. Archaeol.*, 6–7, 182–201

Carver, M.O.H. 1979. 'Three Saxo-Norman tenements in Durham City', *Med. Archaeol.*, 23, 1–80

——— (ed.). 1983. 'Two town houses in medieval Shrewsbury: the excavations and analysis', *Trans. Shropshire Archaeol. Soc.*, 61

Chapman, M., P. Davenport and E. Holland. 1995. 'The precincts of the Bishops' Palace at Bath, Avon', *Archaeol. J.*, 152, 95–108

Charles, F.W.B. 1967. *Medieval cruck building and its derivatives.* SMA Monograph, Ser. 2. London: Soc. for Med. Archaeol.

———. 1979. 'Timber-framed houses in Spon Street, Coventry', *Trans. and Proc. Birmingham and Warwickshire Archaeol. Soc.*, 89, 91–122

———, and M. Charles. 1978. 'White Hart, Newark (Nottinghamshire)', *Archit. East Midlands*, 76, 36–40

———, and K. Down. 1970–2. 'A sixteenth-century drawing of a timber-framed town house', *Trans. Worcestershire Archaeol. Soc.*, Ser. 3, 3, 67–79

Chaucer, G. *The complete works of Geoffrey Chaucer*, ed. W. Skeat, 1893. Oxford: Clarendon Press

Chenevix Trench, J., and P. Fenley. 1991. 'The County Museum Buildings, Church Street, Aylesbury', *Records of Buckinghamshire*, 33, 1–43

Cherry, B., and N. Pevsner. 1989. *The buildings of England: Devon.* 2nd edn. London: Penguin Books

Cherry, J. 1975. 'Post-medieval Britain in 1974', *Post-Medieval Archaeol.*, 9, 240–60

———. 1991. 'Pottery and tile', in Blair and Ramsay 1991, 189–209

Chew, H.M., and W. Kellaway 1973. *London Assize of Nuisance 1301–1431*, London Record Soc., 10

Christie, H., O. Olsen and H.M. Taylor. 1979. 'The wooden church of St Andrew at Greensted, Essex', *Antiquaries J.*, 59, 92–112

Clark, D. 2000. 'The shop within: an analysis of the architectural evidence for medieval shops', *Archit. Hist.*, 43, 58–87

Clark, M.V. 1991. 'The west range [of Gainsborough Old Hall]: survey and analysis', in Lindley 1991b, 43–56

Clark, P. 1984. *The English alehouse: a social history 1200–1830.* London: Longman

Clarke, H. 1981. 'King's Lynn', in Milne and Hobley 1981, 132–6

———, and A. Carter. 1977. *Excavations at King's Lynn 1963–70.* SMA Monograph, Ser. 7. London: SMA

Clifton-Taylor, A. 1972. *The pattern of English building.* 3rd edn. London: Faber and Faber

Coad, J.G. 1971. 'Recent excavations within Framlingham Castle', *Proc. of the Suffolk Inst. of Archaeol.*, 32, 152–63

———, and A.D.F. Streeten. 1982. 'Excavations at Castle Acre Castle, Norfolk, 1972–7; country house and castle of the Norman earls of Surrey', *Archaeol. J.*, 139, 138–301

Collette, B., *et al.* 1980. *Viollet-le-Duc dans l'Yonne. Les cahiers des archives*, 2. Auxerre: Département de l'Yonne

Colvin, H.M. 1958. 'Domestic architecture and town-planning', in Poole 1958, 1, 37–97

——— (ed.). 1963. *The history of the king's works*, 1 and 2, *The Middle Ages.* London: HMSO

———, and S. Foister. 1996. 'The Panorama of London *circa* 1544 by Anthonis van den Wyngaerde', London Topographical Society Publication 151

Combe, T. 1821. 'An account of some Anglo-Saxon pennies found at Dorking, in Surrey', *Archaeologia*, 19, 109–19

Conant, K.J. 1959. *Carolingian and Romanesque architecture 800–1200.* 2nd edn. Harmondsworth: Penguin Books

———. 1968. *Cluny. Les églises et les maisons du chef d'ordre.* Mâcon: Protat Frères (for Medieval Academy of America)

Cooper, S., and B. Kindred. 1998. 'Isaac Lord's Premises, 80–80a Fore Street [Ipswich]', *Annual*

Conference Programme, Soc. of Archit. Historians of Great Britain, 59–61

Corpus Scriptorium Ecclesiasticorum Latinorum. 1866 – continuing. Vienna: Oesterreichesche Akademie der Wissenschaft

Cotman, J.S., and D. Turner. 1822. *Architectural Antiquities of Normandy*, 2 vols. London: J. and A. Arch and J.S. Cotman

Cowie, G. 1893. *The history of Wyggeston's Hospital, the Hospital Schools and the Old Free Grammar School, Leicester, AD 1511–1893*. London: Simpkin, Marshall, Hamilton, Kent

Cramp, R. 1957. '*Beowulf* and archaeology', *Med. Archaeol.*, 1, 57–77

——. 1969. 'Excavations at the Saxon monastic sites of Wearmouth and Jarrow, County Durham: an interim report', *Med. Archaeol.*, 13, 22–66

——. 1976. 'Jarrow Church and Monkwearmouth Church', *Archaeol. J.*, 133, 220–8, 230–37

Crook, J. 1982. 'The Pilgrims' Hall, Winchester', *Proc. Hampshire Field Club and Archaeol. Soc.*, 38, 85–101

——. 1991. 'The Pilgrims' Hall, Winchester: hammerbeams, base-crucks and aisle-derivative roof structures', *Archaeologia*, 109, 129–59

Cruden, S.H. 1964. 'The Royal Mile', *Archaeol. J.*, 121, 184–5

Cummings, A.L. 1979. *The framed houses of Massachusetts Bay, 1625–1725*. Cambridge, Mass.: Belknap, Harvard University Press

Cunliffe, B. 1976. *Excavations at Porchester Castle*, 2 vols. London: Soc. Antiq.

Currie, C.R.J. 1983. 'Timber supply and timber building in a Sussex parish', *Vernac. Archit.*, 14, 52–4

Daniels, R. 1990. 'The development of medieval Hartlepool: excavations at Church Close, 1984–5', *Archaeol. J.*, 143, 260–304

Darby, H.C. 1976a. 'Domesday England', in Darby 1976b, 39–74

——. 1976b. *A new historical geography of England before 1600*. Cambridge: Cambridge University Press

Davison, B.K. 1967. 'The late Saxon town of Thetford: an interim report on the 1964–6 excavations', *Med. Archaeol.*, 11, 189–202

de Bièvre, E. 1996. *Utrecht, Britain and the Continent: archaeology, art and architecture*. BAA Conference Trans., 18. London: BAA

de Groot, H.L. 1996. 'Utrecht and Dorestad: fifteen miles apart, a world of difference', in de Bièvre 1996, 12–21

Decaëns, J. 1993. 'De la motte au château de pierre dans le nord-ouest de la France', in Meirion-Jones and Jones 1993, 65–81

Defoe, D. 1701. *The True-Born Englishman, a satyr*. Published anonymously

——. 1724–6. *A Tour through the whole island of Great Britain*. London: G. Strahan

Department of the Environment. 1973. *Archaeological excavations 1972*. London: HMSO

Dixon, P.W. 1979. 'Tower-houses, pelehouses and border society', *Archaeol. J.*, 136, 240–52

——. 1993. '*Mota, Aula et Turris*: the manor-houses of the Anglo-Scottish border', in Meirion-Jones and Jones 1993, 22–48

——, and P. Marshall. 1993. 'The great tower at Hedingham castle: a reassessment', *Fortress*, 18, 16–23

Dixon-Smith, S. 1999. 'The image and reality of alms-giving in the greater halls of Henry III', *J. BAA*, 152, 79–96

Dodgshon, R.A., and R.A. Butlin (eds). 1990. *An historical geography of England and Wales*. 2nd edn. London: Academic Press

Dollman, F.T., and J.R. Jobbins. 1861–3. *An analysis of ancient domestic architecture in Great Britain*. 2 vols. London: B.T. Batsford

Donkin, R.A. 1976. 'Changes in the early Middle Ages', in Darby 1976b, 75–135

Drewett, P. 1979. 'New evidence for the structure and function of Middle Bronze Age round houses in Sussex', *Archaeol. J.*, 136, 3–11

Drinkwater, N., and E. Mercer. 1963. 'The Blue Boar Inn, Salisbury. An existing fifteenth-century building and the contract for its erection', *Archaeol. J.*, 120, 236–41

Drury, P.J. 1982. 'Aspects of the origins and development of Colchester Castle', *Archaeol. J.*, 139, 302–419

Dumville, D.N. 1977. 'Sub-Roman Britain: history and legend', *History*, 62, 173–92

Dunbar, J.G. 1963. 'The Palace of Holyroodhouse during the first half of the sixteenth century', *Archaeol. J.*, 120, 242–54

——. 1964. 'Stirling Castle', *Archaeol. J.*, 121, 178–80

——. 1984. 'Some aspects of the planning of Scottish royal palaces in the sixteenth century', *Archit. Hist.*, 27, 15–24

——. 1999. *Scottish royal palaces: the architecture of the royal residences during the late medieval and early renaissance periods*. East Linton: Tuckwell Press

Dunkley, J.A., C.G. Henderson and J.P. Allan. 1985. 'Survey of 5 East Street and 15 Stepcote Hill', *Exeter Archaeol. 1984–5*, 36–8. Exeter: Exeter Museums Archaeol. Field Unit

Dunn, I., and H. Suttermeister. 1978. *The Norwich Guildhall*. Norwich: City of Norwich with the Norwich Survey

Dunning, G.C. 1961. 'Medieval chimney-pots', in Jope 1961, 78–93

Dymond, D. 1998. 'Five building contracts from fifteenth-century Suffolk', *Antiquaries J.*, 78, 269–87

Eaton, T. 2000. *Plundering the Past: Roman stonework in medieval Britain*. Stroud: Tempus

Ebner, H. 1991. 'Die Frühgeschichte Wiens', in Brachman and Herrmann 1991, 60–7

Emery, A. 1996. *Greater medieval houses of England and Wales 1300–1500, 1, Northern England*. Cambridge: Cambridge University Press

——. 2000. *Greater medieval houses of England and Wales 1300–1500, 2, East Anglia, Central England and Wales*. Cambridge: Cambridge University Press

Ersland, G.A. 1994. 'Non-familial households, Bergen 1200–1600'. Unpublished paper presented in April to *Houses and Households in Towns 100–1600*, University of Birmingham

Eusebius. 1891. *Eusebius's Life of Constantine*. London: Pilgrims' Text Soc.

Ewan, E. 1990. *Town life in fourteenth-century Scotland*. Edinburgh: Edinburgh University Press

Ewbank, J.W. 1823. *Picturesque views of Edinburgh*. Edinburgh: Daniel Lizars

Faraday, M. 1991. *Ludlow, 1085–1680*. London and Chichester: Phillimore

Faulkner, P.A. 1958. 'Domestic planning from the 12th to 14th centuries', *Archaeol. J.*, 115, 150–83

——. 1966. 'Medieval undercrofts and town houses', *Archaeol. J.*, 123, 120–35

——. 1969. 'No. 6 Market Square, Faversham', *Archaeol. J.*, 126, 249–52

——. 1970. 'Some medieval archiepiscopal palaces', *Archaeol. J.*, 127, 130–46

——. 1971. 'Lord Leycester's Hospital, Warwick', *Archaeol. J.*, 128, 233–5

——. 1974a. 'Lincoln Old Bishop's Palace', *Archaeol. J.*, 131, 340–44

——. 1974b. 'Gainsborough Old Hall', *Archaeol. J.*, 131, 366–8

——. 1975. 'The surviving medieval buildings [in Southampton]', in Platt and Coleman-Smith 1975, 56–124

Fawcett, R. 1991. 'St Andrews Castle', *Archaeol. J.*, 148, supplement 33–4

——. 2001. *Stirling Castle: the restoration of the Great Hall*. York: CBA

Fehring, G.P. 1989. 'Archaeological evidence from Lübeck for changing material culture and socio-economic conditions from the thirteenth to the sixteenth century', *Med. Archaeol.*, 33, 60–81

Fernie, E.C. 1985. 'Anglo-Saxon lengths: the "Northern" system, the perch and the foot', *Archaeol. J.*, 142, 246–54

——. 1989. 'Archaeology and iconography. Recent developments in the study of English medieval architecture', *Archit. Hist.*, 32, 18–29

——. 1991. 'Anglo-Saxon lengths', *Med. Archaeol.*, 35, 1–5

——. 1993. *An Archit. Hist. of Norwich Cathedral*. Oxford: Oxford University Press

Fiennes, C. 1949. *The journeys of Celia Fiennes*, ed. C. Morris. London: Cresset Press

Fisher, F.J. 1935. 'The development of the London food market, 1540–1640', *Economic Hist. Review*, 5, 46–64

Fosbrooke, T.H., and S.H. Skillington. 1923–4. 'The Old Town Hall of Leicester'. *Trans. Leicestershire Archaeol. Soc.*, 13, 5–72

Foster, I.Ll., and L. Alcock (eds). 1963. *Culture and environment, essays in honour of Sir Cyril Fox*. London: Routledge and Kegan Paul

Fox, C.F. 1957. 'The Law Library', No. 8 The Close, Exeter', *Archaeol. J.*, 114, 161

Frere, S.S. 1967. *Britannia. A history of Roman Britain*. London: Routledge and Kegan Paul

——, S. Stow and P. Bennett. 1982. *Archaeology of Canterbury, 2, Excavations on the Roman and medieval defences of Canterbury*. Canterbury: Canterbury Archaeol. Trust

Frith, B. 1965a. 'The New Inn [Gloucester]', *Archaeol. J.*, 122, 219

——. 1965b. 'Bishop Hooper's Lodgings [Gloucester]', *Archaeol. J.*, 122, 220–1

Furnivall, F.J. (ed.). 1877. *Harrison's description of England*. London: New Shakespeare Society

Gaimster, D., and P. Stamper (eds). 1997. *The age of transition. The archaeology of English culture 1400–1600*. SMA Monograph, 98. Oxford: Oxbow Books

Gaimster, D.R.M., C. Haith and J. Bradley. 1998. 'Medieval Britain and Ireland in 1997', *Med. Archaeol.*, 42, 107–190

——, S. Margeson and T. Barry. 1989. 'Medieval Britain and Ireland in 1998', *Med. Archaeol.*, 33, 161–241

Gardiner, M. 2000. 'Vernacular buildings and the development of the late medieval domestic plan in England', *Med. Archaeol.*, 44, 159–79

Garrigou Grandchamp, P. 1992. *Demeures médiévales, coeur de la cité*. Paris: R.E.M.P.ART

——. 1998. 'Domestic architecture from the twelfth to the fourteenth century in the countries to the north of the Loire and Rhône rivers', *Towns and their buildings – 1100–1650*. Vernac. Archit. Group, winter conference, December

——. 1999. 'Twelfth and thirteenth-century domestic architecture north of the Loire: a summary of recent research', *Vernac. Archit.*, 30, 1–20

——, M. Jones, G. Meirion-Jones and J.-D. Salvèque. 1997. *La ville de Cluny et ses maisons*. Paris: Éditions A. et J. Picard

Geddes, J. 1991. 'Iron', in Blair and Ramsay 1991, 167–88

Gem, R.D.H. 1986. 'Lincoln Minster: Ecclesia pulchra, Ecclesia Fortis', *BAA Conference Trans.*, 8, *Medieval art and architecture at Lincoln Cathedral*, 9–28

Geoffrey of Monmouth (Galfridus). 1844. *Historia Britonum*. London: Caxton Soc.

Gibb, J.H.P. 1983. 'Sherborne Almshouse', *Archaeol. J.*, 140, 20

Gifford, J. 1988. *The buildings of Scotland. Fife*. London: Penguin

——. 1992. *The buildings of Scotland. Highlands and Islands*. London: Penguin

——. 1996. *The buildings of Scotland. Dumfries and Galloway*. London: Penguin

——, C. McWilliam and D. Walker. 1984. *The buildings of Scotland. Edinburgh*. London: Penguin

Gilchrist, R. 1994. *Gender and material culture: the archaeology of religious women*. London: Routledge and Kegan Paul

Giles, K. 1998. 'The archaeology of public buildings – York's medieval guildhalls'. Unpublished paper presented in September to *Medieval Urban Buildings: aspects of current research*, joint conference of the RAI and the Department of Archaeology, University of York

Gillyard-Beer, R. 1970. *Fountains Abbey*, Department of the Environment Official Handbook. London: HMSO

Giraldus Cambrensis. 1951. *Topography of Ireland*, translated J.J. O'Meara. Dundalk: Dundalgan Press

Girouard, M. 1978. *Life in the English country house*. London and New Haven: Yale University Press

Godfrey, W.H. 1930. 'The Hospital of St John the Baptist and St John the Evangelist, Sherborne; St Mary's Hospital [Glastonbury]; St Saviour's Hospital, Wells', *Archaeol. J.*, 87, 427–9, 462–4

——. 1933. 'Trinity Hospital (The Newarke) [Leicester]', *Archaeol. J.*, 90, 368–9

——. 1950. 'The Deanery; Vicars' Close [Wells]', *Archaeol. J.*, 107, 110–13

——. 1955. *The English almshouse, with some account of its predecessor, the medieval hospital*. London: Faber and Faber

Gomme, A.H. 2002. 'Scottish hammerbeam roofs, and one that isn't', *Archit. Heritage* 13, 20–35

——, and D. Walker. 1987. *Architecture of Glasgow*. Revised edn. London: Lund Humphries

Goodall, J. 1999. 'The key of England: in the powerhouse of Kent', *Country Life*, 193, 44–7, 110–13

Goodburn, D. 1994. 'The form and construction methods of vernacular dwellings in London 100–1600'. Unpublished paper presented in April to *Houses and Households in Towns 100–1600*, University of Birmingham

Grant, L. (ed.). 1990. *Medieval art, architecture and archaeology in London*. BAA *Conference Trans.*, 10, for the year 1984

Gravett, K.W. 1994. 'Fordwich quay and town hall'. 'The Canterbury area', *Archaeol. J.*, 151, supplement 50–1

Gray, J.M. 1932. *The School of Pythagoras (Merton Hall), Cambridge*. Cambridge: Cambridge Antiquarian Soc.

Grenville, J. 1988. 'Recent research on the Rows of Chester'. Unpublished paper presented on 7 December to the RAI

——. 1997. *Medieval housing*. Leicester: Leicester University Press

Grundy, J., *et al.* 1992. *The buildings of England. Northumberland*. Revised edn. London: Penguin

Gunn, S.J. 1991. 'The rise of the Burgh Family, *c.* 1431–1550', in Lindley 1991b, 8–12

Hall, M. 1992. 'Painting the town reddle', *Country Life*, 186 (3 September 1992), 58–60

Hall, R.A. 1984. 'A late-pre-Conquest urban building tradition', in Addyman and Black 1984, 71–7

——. 1996. *York*. English Heritage Ser. London: B.T. Batsford

Hamerow, H. 1993. *Excavations at Mucking*, 2, *The Anglo-Saxon settlement*. London: English Heritage

Hansen, V. 1976. 'The pre-industrial city of Denmark. A study of two medieval founded market-towns', *Geografisk Tidskritt*, 75, 50–7

Harden, D.B. 1961. 'Domestic window glass: Roman, Saxon and medieval', in Jope 1961, 39–63

Hare, J.N. 1991. 'The growth of the roof-tile industry in later medieval Wessex', *Med. Archaeol.*, 35, 86–103

Harris, A.P. 1990. 'Building stone in Norfolk', in Parsons 1990, 207–16

Harris, E. 1958. 'A medieval undercroft at 50 Mark Lane, London, E.C.3.', *Med. Archaeol.*, 2, 178–82

Harris, R. 1989. 'The grammar of carpentry', *Vernac. Archit.*, 201–8

——. 1990. 'Jetties', *Vernac. Archit.*, 21, 33–6

Harris, R.B. 1994. *The origins and development of English medieval townhouses operating commercially on two storeys*. Unpublished University of Oxford DPhil thesis

——. 1998. 'The English medieval townhouse, 1100–1350', *Towns and their buildings – 1100–1650*. VAG, winter conference, December

Harrison, J.R. 1984. 'The mud wall in England at the close of the vernacular era', *Trans. Ancient Monuments Soc.*, new Ser. 28, 154–74

——. 1989. 'Some clay dabbins in Cumberland, Pt 1', *Trans. Ancient Monuments Soc.*, new Ser. 33, 97–152

——. 1991. 'Some clay dabbins in Cumberland, Pt 2', *Trans. Ancient Monuments Soc.*, new Ser. 35, 29–88

Harrison, W. *Description of England* – see Furnivall

Hartley, C. 1992. *Gladstone's Land*. Edinburgh: John Donald

Harvey, J.H. 1966. 'Church and Hospital of St Cross [Winchester], domestic buildings', *Archaeol. J.*, 123, 216–17

——. 1971. *The master builders: architecture in the Middle Ages*. London: Thames and Hudson

——. 1984. *English medieval architects. A biographical dictionary down to 1550*. Revised edn. Gloucester: Alan Sutton

Hassall, T.G. 1976. 'Excavations at Oxford Castle, 1965–73', *Oxoniensia*, 43, 232–308

——. 1978. 'Wallingford, the defences', *Archaeol. J.*, 135, 291–2

——, C.E. Halpin and M. Mellor. 1989. 'Excavations in St Ebbe's, Oxford, 1967–76, Pt 1, Late Saxon and medieval domestic occupation and tenements, and the medieval Greyfriars', *Oxoniensia*, 54, 71–278

Hassall, W.O. 1962. *How they lived. 55 BC – 1485*. Oxford: Basil Blackwell

Hawkes, S.C. 1969. 'Early Anglo-Saxon Kent', *Archaeol. J.*, 126, 186–92

Hayes, R.H., and J.G. Rutter. 1972. *Cruck-framed buildings in Ryedale and Eskdale*, Scarborough and District Archaeol. Soc. Research Rep. 8. Scarborough: S and DAS

Heighway, C.M. 1983. 'Tanner's Hall, Gloucester', *Trans. Bristol and Gloucestershire Archaeol. Soc.*, 101, 83–109

Herteig, A.E. 1959. 'The excavation of "Bryggen", the old Hanseatic wharf in Bergen', *Med. Archaeol.*, 3, 177–186

Heslop, D., G. McCombie and C. Thomson. 1995. *Bessie Surtees House. Two merchant houses in Sandhill Newcastle upon Tyne*. Soc. of Antiquaries of Newcastle upon Tyne

Heslop, D., and L. Truman. 1993. *The Cooperage: a timber-framed building in Newcastle upon Tyne*. Soc. of Antiquaries of Newcastle upon Tyne

Heslop, T.A. 1994. *Norwich Castle Keep: Romanesque architecture and social context*. Norwich: Centre of East Anglian Studies

Hewett, C.A. 1961. 'Timber building in Essex', *Trans. Ancient Monuments Soc.*, new Ser. 9, 33–56

——. 1962–3. 'Structural carpentry in medieval Essex', *Med. Archaeol.*, 6–7, 240–71

——. 1966. 'Jettying and floor-framing in medieval Essex', *Med. Archaeol.*, 10, 89–112

——. 1969. *The development of carpentry 1200–1799*. Newton Abbot: David and Charles

——. 1976. 'Aisled timber halls and related buildings', *Trans. Ancient Monuments Soc.*, new Ser. 21, 45–99

——. 1980. *English historic carpentry*. London and Chichester: Phillimore

——. 1985. *English cathedral and monastic carpentry*. London and Chichester: Phillimore

——. 1989. 'Evidence for an intermediate stage between earth-fast and sill-mounted posts', *Trans. Ancient Monuments Soc.*, new Ser. 33, 181–92

Hey, D. 1980. 'Bawtry Town', *Archaeol. J.*, 137, 420–22

Heywood, S. 1980. 'North Elmham cathedral, a second interpretation', *Archaeol. J.*, 137, 328–9

Highfield, J.R.L. 1971. 'The Aula Custodis', *Postmaster*, 4, no. 4, 14–22

Hill, D. 1969. 'The Burghal Hidage: the establishment of a text', *Med. Archaeol.*, 13, 84–92

Hilton, R.H. 1966. *A medieval society: the West Midlands at the end of the thirteenth century*. London: Weidenfeld and Nicolson

Hobley, B. 1988. 'Lundenwic and Lundenburh: two cities rediscovered', in Hodges and Hobley 1988, 69–82

Hodges R., and B. Hobley. 1988. *The rebirth of towns in the west AD 700–1050*, CBA Research Rep. 68. London: CBA

Holdsworth, P.E. 1976. 'Saxon Southampton: a new review', *Med. Archaeol.*, 20, 26–61

Holton-Krayenbuhl, A. 1999. 'The Prior's Lodging at Ely', *Archaeol. J.*, 156, 294–341

Hope-Taylor, B. 1977. *Yeavering: an Anglo-British centre of early Northumbria*. London: HMSO

Horn, W. 1956. 'On the origin of the medieval bay system', *J. Soc. Archit. Historians*, 17, 2–23

Husselby, J. and P. Henderson. 2002. 'Location, location, location! Cecil House in the Strand', *Archit. History*, 45, 159–93

Impey, E. 1993. 'Seigneurial domestic architecture in Normandy, 1050–1350', in Meirion-Jones and Jones 1993, 82–120

Innocent, C.F. 1916. *The development of English building construction*. Cambridge: Cambridge University Press

James, S., A. Marshall and M. Millett. 1984. 'An early medieval building tradition', *Archaeol. J.*, 141, 182–215

James, T.B. 1997. *Winchester*. London: B.T. Batsford for English Heritage

——, and E. Roberts. 2000. 'Winchester and late medieval urban development: from palace to pentice', *Med. Archaeol.*, 44, 181–200

Jervis, S. 2000. 'The Round Table as furniture', in Biddle 2000, 31–57

Jessup, R., and F. Jessup. 1952. *The Cinque Ports*. London: Batsford

Johnson, C., and A. Vince. 1992. 'The South Bail Gates of Lincoln', *Lincolnshire Hist. and Archaeol.*, 27, 12–16

Joinville, J.S. de. 1938. *The history of St Louis, by Jean Sire de Joinville*, text reconstructed by Natalis de Wailly, 1874, translated J. Evans. Oxford: Oxford University Press

Jones, G., and T. Jones (eds). 1949. *The Mabinogion*, Everyman edn. London: J. and M. Dent

Jones, M.U. 1979. 'Saxon sunken huts: problems of interpretation', *Archaeol. J.*, 136, 53–9

——, and W.T. Jones. 1974. 'The early Saxon landscape at Mucking, Essex, in Rowley 1974', 20–35

Jones, N.W. 1998. 'Excavations within the medieval walled town at New Radnor, Powys', 1991–2, *Archaeol. J.*, 155, 134–206

Jones, R.H. 1980. *The archaeology of Lincoln*, 11, 1, *Medieval houses at Flaxengate, Lincoln*. London: CBA

Jones, S.R. 1974. 'The Chancery, Lincoln', *Archaeol. J.*, 131, 322–3

——, and J.T. Smith. 1960. 'The great hall of the Bishop's Palace at Hereford', *Med. Archaeol.*, 4, 69–80

——, and ——. 1960–1. 'The Wealden houses of Warwickshire and their significance', *Trans. and Proc. Birmingham and Warwickshire Archaeol. Soc.*, 79, 24–35

——, K. Major and J. Varley. 1984. *Survey of ancient houses in Lincoln*, 1, *Priory Gate to Pottergate*. Lincoln: Lincoln Civic Trust

——, —— and ——. 1987. *Survey of ancient houses in Lincoln*, 2, *Houses to the south and west of the Minster*. Lincoln: Lincoln Civic Trust

——, —— and ——. 1990. *Survey of ancient houses in Lincoln*, 3, *Houses in Eastgate, Priorygate, and James Street*. Lincoln: Lincoln Civic Trust

——, ——, —— and C. Johnson. 1996. *Survey of ancient houses in Lincoln*, 4, *houses in the Bail: Steep Hill, Castle Hill, and Bailgate*. Lincoln: Lincoln Civic Trust

Jope, E.M. 1951. 'The development of pottery ridge-tiles in the Oxford region', *Oxoniensia*, 16, 86–8

——. 1964. 'The Saxon building-stone industry in southern and midland England', *Med. Archaeol.*, 8, 91–118

—— (ed.). 1961. *Studies in building history*. London: Odhams Press

Keene, D. 1985. *Winchester Studies*, 2, *Survey of medieval Winchester*, ed. M. Biddle. Oxford: Clarendon Press

——. 1989. 'Medieval London and its region', *London J.*, 14, 99–111

——. 1990. 'Shops and shopping in medieval London', in Grant 1990, 29–46

Kelsall, A.F. 1974. 'The London house plan in the later seventeenth century', *Post-Med. Archaeol.*, 8, 80–91

Kemp, R.L. 1996. 'Anglian settlement at 46–54 Fishergate', in *The archaeology of York*, 7, *Anglian York*, ed. P.V. Addyman. York: CBA

Kidson, P. 1990. 'A metrological investigation', *J. Warburg and Courtauld Insts*, 53, 71–97

King, E. 1782. 'Sequel to observations on ancient castles', *Archaeologia*, 6, 231–374

Kirk, R.E.G. 1900. *Life records of Chaucer*. London: Chaucer Soc.

Knight, J.W. 1991. *Chepstow Castle*. Revised edn. Cadw guide. Cardiff: Cadw

Knoop, D., and G.P. Jones. 1967. *The medieval mason*. 3rd edn. Manchester: Manchester University Press

Laithwaite, J.M.W. 1971. 'Two medieval houses in Ashburton', *Proc. Devon Archaeol. Soc.*, 29, 181–94

——. 1995. 'Town houses up to 1660', in Beacham 1995, 95–116

Laleman, M.C. 1994. 'Housing in medieval Ghent – a methodological case study'. Unpublished paper presented in April to *Houses and Households in Towns 100–1600*, University of Birmingham

Laver, H. 1909. 'Ancient type of huts at Athelney', *Proc. of the Somerset Archaeol. Soc.*, 55, 175–80

Lawson, P.H., and J.T. Smith. 1958. 'The Rows of Chester; a problem and two interpretations', *Chester Archaeol. Soc. J.*, 45, 1–42

Laxton, R.R., and C.D. Litton. 1989. 'Construction of a Kent master dendrochronological sequence for oak, AD 1158 to 1540, *Med. Archaeol.*, 33, 90–8

Leech, R.H. 1996. 'The prospect from Rugman's Row – the row house in late-16th and early-17th-century London', *Archaeol. J.*, 153, 201–42

——. 1998. 'Bristol – house and household in the medieval and early modern period'. Unpublished paper presented on 5 November to the Soc. Antiqs

——. 2000. 'The symbolic hall: historical context and merchant culture in the early modern city', *Vernac. Archit.*, 31, 1–10

Leland, J. 1964. *The Itinerary of John Leland in or about the years 1535–1543*, ed. L. Toulmin Smith, 5 vols. London: Centaur Press

Le Roy Ladurie, E. 1980. *Montaillou, Cathars and Catholics in a French village 1294–1324*, translated B. Bray. Harmondsworth: Penguin

Letts, J.B. 1999. *Smoke Blackened Thatch*. Reading: University of Reading and English Heritage

Lewis, E., E. Roberts and K. Roberts. 1988. *Medieval hall-houses of the Winchester area*. Winchester: Winchester City Museum

Leyland, M. 1994. 'The origins and development of Durham Castle', in Rollason *et al.* 1994, 407–24

Lindley, P.G. 1991a. 'Structure, sequence and status: the architectural history of Gainsborough Old Hall to *c.* 1600', in Lindley 1991b, 21–6

—— (ed.). 1991b. *Gainsborough Old Hall*, Occasional Papers in Lincolnshire History and Archaeology, 8. Lincoln: Soc. for Lincolnshire Hist. and Archaeol.

Lipman, V.D. 1967. *The Jews of medieval Norwich*. Cambridge: Cambridge University Press

Lloyd, D., and M. Moran. 1978. 'The Corner Shop'. *Ludlow Research Papers*, 2, 28

Lloyd, D.W. 1988. *The making of English towns*. London: Gollancz

Lloyd, N. 1931. *A history of the English house from primitive times to the Victorian period*. London: Archit. Press

Locke, J. 1690. *Second treatise on civil government: an essay concerning the true original, extent and end of civil government*, in *The Social Contract*, World's Classics edn (1947). London: Geoffrey Cumberlege for Oxford University Press

Loggan, D. 1675. *Oxonia illustrata*. Oxford: Bodleian Library

Longley, D. 1998. 'Llanfaes and Rhosyr, two Maerdrefi of the Welsh Princes of Gwynedd'. Unpublished paper presented on 11 March to the RAI

Lucas, H.S. 1930. 'The great European famine of 1315, 1316 and 1317', *Speculum*, 5, 343–77

Lynch, M., M. Spearman and G. Stell (eds). 1988. *The Scottish medieval town*. Edinburgh: John Donald

MacGibbon, D., and T. Ross. 1887–92. *Castellated and domestic architecture of Scotland from the twelfth to the eighteenth century*, 5 vols. Edinburgh: D. Douglas

McGrail, S. (ed.). 1982. *Woodworking techniques before AD 1500*. Brit. Archaeol., Reps, International Ser. 129. Oxford: CBA

McKean, C., and D. Walker. 1982. *Edinburgh: an illustrated architectural guide*. Edinburgh: RIAS Publications

——. 1984. *Dundee: an illustrated introduction*. Edinburgh: RIAS Publications

McNeil, R. 1983. 'Two 12th-century wich houses in Nantwich, Cheshire', *Med. Archaeol.*, 27, 40–88

——. 1999. 'Staircase House, Stockport', *Current Archaeol.*, 165, 346–53

McWilliam, C. 1978. *The buildings of Scotland: Lothian, except Edinburgh*. Harmondsworth: Penguin Books

Manley, J. 1987. 'Cledemutha: a late Saxon burh in north Wales', *Med. Archaeol.*, 31, 13–46

Marks, R. 1991. 'Window glass', in Blair and Ramsay 1991, 265–94

Martin, D., and B. Mastin. 1974. *An Architectural History of Robertsbridge*. Hastings Area Archaeol. Papers, No. 5. Robertsbridge

——, and B. Martin. 1987. *Historic buildings in eastern Sussex*, 4. Robertsbridge: Rape of Hastings Archit. Survey

Mays, D. (ed.). 1997. *The architecture of Scottish cities*. East Linton, Scotland: Tuckwell Press

Meiggs, R. 1973. *Roman Ostia*. Oxford: Oxford University Press

Meirion-Jones, G., and M. Jones (eds). 1993. *Manorial domestic buildings in England and northern France.*

Occasional Papers of the Soc. Antiqs, 15. London: Soc. Antiqs

Melling, E. 1965. *Kentish Sources*, 5, *Some Kentish Houses*. Maidstone: Kent County Council

Mercer, W.E.R. 1996. 'Cruck distribution: a social explanation', *Vernac. Archit.*, 27, 1–2

Merrifield, R. 1990. 'The contribution of archaeology to our understanding of pre-Norman London, 1973–1988', in Grant 1990, 1–15

Mertes, K. 1988. *The English noble household, 1250–1600: good governance and politic rule*. Oxford: Oxford University Press

Mesqui, J. 1993. *Châteaux et enceintes de la France médiévale*. Paris: Picard grands manuels

Millett, M., and S. James. 1983. 'Excavations at Cowdery's Down, Basingstoke, Hants., 1978–81', *Archaeol. J.*, 140, 151–279

Milne, G. 1992. *Timber building techniques in London c.900–c.1400*, London and Middlesex Archaeol. Soc. Special Paper, 15

——, and B. Hobley (eds). 1981. *Waterfront archaeology in Britain and Northern Europe*. CBA Research Rep., 41

Minst, K.J. 1949. *Das Königskloster zu Lorsch. Sein Entstehen, Bestehen, und Vergehen*. Mannheim

——, and Huth, H. 1965. *Kloster Lorsch*. Berlin: Deutscher Kunstverlag

Moir, J., and J. Letts. 1999. *Thatching in England, 1790–1940*. English Heritage Research Trans., 5. London: James and James

Moore, N.J. 1991. 'Brick', in Blair and Ramsay, 1991, 211–36

Moorhouse, S. 1990. 'The quarrying of stone roofing slates and rubble in west Yorkshire during the Middle Ages', in Parsons 1990, 126–46

Moran, M. 1992. 'A terrace of crucks at Much Wenlock, Shropshire', *Vernac. Archit.*, 23, 10–14

Morris, R. 1989. *Churches in the landscape*. London: Dent

Morris, R.K. 1991. 'Hereford, the Vicars Choral', *West Midlands Archaeol.*, 34, 39–41

——. 1994. *The Abbot's House, Shrewsbury*. Hereford Archaeol., Ser. 200, 8

Munby, J. 1974. 'A fifteenth-century Wealden house in Oxford', *Oxoniensia*, 39, 73–6

——. 1975. '126 High Street: the archaeology and history of an Oxford house', *Oxoniensia*, 40, 254–308

——. 1978. 'J.C. Buckler, Tackley's Inn and three medieval houses in Oxford', *Oxoniensia*, 43, 123–69

——. 1991. 'Wood', in Blair and Ramsey 1991, 379–405

——, et al. 1992. 'Zacharias's: a medieval Oxford inn at 26–8 Cornmarket', *Oxoniensia*, 57, 245–309

——, M. Sparks and T. Tatton-Brown. 1983. 'Crown-post roofs and king-strut roofs in south-east England', *Med. Archaeol.*, 27, 123–35

Murphy, K. 1994. 'Excavations in three burgage plots in the medieval town of Newport, Dyfed, 1991', *Med. Archaeol.*, 38, 55–82

Murray, H.K., and J.C. Murray. 1993. 'Excavations at Rattray, Aberdeenshire. A Scottish deserted burgh', *Med. Archaeol.*, 37, 109–218

Myres, J.N.L. 1986. *The English settlements*. Oxford: Clarendon Press

——, and P.H. Dixon. 1988. 'A nineteenth-century *Grubenhaus* on Bucklebury Common, Berkshire', *Antiquaries J.*, 58, 115–22

Nenk, B.S., C. Haith and J. Bradley. 1997. 'Medieval Britain and Ireland in 1996', *Med. Archaeol.*, 41, 241–328

——, S. Margeson and M. Hurley. 1991. 'Medieval Britain and Ireland in 1990', *Med. Archaeol.*, 35, 126–238

——, —— and ——. 1992. 'Medieval Britain and Ireland in 1991', *Med. Archaeol.*, 36, 184–308

——, —— and ——. 1993. 'Medieval Britain and Ireland in 1992', *Med. Archaeol.*, 37, 240–313

——, —— and ——. 1994. 'Medieval Britain and Ireland in 1993', *Med. Archaeol.*, 38, 184–293

——, —— and ——. 1995. 'Medieval Britain and Ireland in 1994', *Med. Archaeol.*, 39, 180–293

——, —— and ——. 1996. 'Medieval Britain and Ireland in 1995', *Med. Archaeol.*, 40, 234–318

Newman, J. 1976. *The buildings of England. West Kent and the Weald*. 2nd edn. Harmondsworth: Penguin

——. 1978. 'Oxford Libraries before 1800', *Archaeol. J.*, 135, 248–57

——. 1995. *The buildings of Wales. Glamorgan*. London: Penguin

——, and N. Pevsner. 1972. *The buildings of England. Dorset*. Harmondsworth: Penguin

Norman, P., and W.D. Caröe. 1908. *Crosby Place*, Survey of London Monograph, 9. London: Batsford

Orme, B.J. 1982. 'Prehistoric woodlands and woodworking in the Somerset Levels', in McGrail 1982, 79–84

Owen, D. 1983. 'The Norman cathedral at Lincoln', *Anglo-Norman Studies (Proc. of the Battle Conference)*, 6, 188–99

Packham, A.B. 1924. 'The Marlipins, New Shoreham', *Sussex Archaeol. Collections*, 65, 158–95

Palliser, D.M. 1976. 'Sources for urban topography: documents, buildings and archaeology', in Barley 1976, 1–6

Pantin, W.A. 1942. 'Tackley's Inn', *Oxoniensia*, 7, 80–92

——. 1947. 'The development of domestic architecture in Oxford', *Antiquaries J.*, 27, 120–50

——. 1957. 'Medieval priests' houses in south-west England', *Med. Archaeol.*, 1, 118–46

——. 1959. 'Chantry priests' houses and other medieval lodgings', *Med. Archaeol.*, 3, 216–58

——. 1961. 'Medieval Inns', in Jope 1961, 166–91

——. 1962–3a. 'The merchants' houses and warehouses of King's Lynn', *Med. Archaeol.*, 6–7, 173–81

——. 1962–3b. 'Medieval English town-house plans', *Med. Archaeol.*, 6–7, 202–39

——. 1963. 'Some medieval town houses: a study in adaptation', in Foster and Alcock 1963, 445–78

——, and E.C. Rouse. 1955. 'The Golden Cross, Oxford', *Oxoniensia*, 20, 46–89

Parker, H. 1965. 'A medieval wharf in Thoresby College, King's Lynn', *Med. Archaeol.*, 9, 94–104

Parker, J.H. 1861–2. 'The bishop's palace at Wells', *Proc. Somersetshire Archaeol. and Natural Hist. Soc.*, 11, 143–58

——. 1863–4. 'The ecclesiastical buildings of Wells', *Proc. Somersetshire Archaeol. and Natural Hist. Soc.*, 12, 25–39

Parker, V. 1971. *The making of King's Lynn. Secular buildings from the 11th to the 17th century*. King's Lynn Archaeol. Survey, 1. Chichester and London: Phillimore

Parkin, E.W. 1970. 'Cogan House, St Peter's, Canterbury', *Archaeol. Cantiana*, 85, 123–38

——. 1973. 'The ancient buildings of New Romney', *Archaeol. Cantiana*, 88, 117–28

Parnell, G. 1998. 'The White Tower: the Tower of London', *Country Life*, 192, 86–9

Parsons, D. 1991. 'Stone', in Blair and Ramsay 1991, 1–27

—— (ed.). 1990. *Stone: quarrying and building in England AD 43–1525*. Chichester: Phillimore with the RAI

Peers, C. 1953. *Richmond Castle*, Ministry of Public Buildings and Works Official Handbook. London: HMSO

Penoyre, J. 1998. 'Medieval Somerset roofs', *Vernac. Archit.*, 29, 22–32

——, and J. Penoyre. 1997. 'Nos 16 and 18 High Street, Bruton, Somerset', *Vernac. Archit.*, 28, 108–10

——, and ——. 1999. 'The Somerset dendrochronolgy project: phase 5', *Vernac. Archit.*, 30, 54–5

Perks, J.C. 1967. *Chepstow Castle*, Ministry of Public Buildings and Works Official Handbook. 2nd edn. London: HMSO

Perring, D. 1981. *The archaeology of Lincoln*, 9, 1, *Early medieval occupation at Flaxengate, Lincoln*. London: CBA

Pevsner, N. 1958a. *The buildings of England. North Somerset and Bristol*. Harmondsworth: Penguin

——. 1958b. *The buildings of England. South and west Somerset*. Harmondsworth: Penguin

——. 1961. *The buildings of England. Northamptonshire*. Harmondsworth: Penguin

——. 1963. *The buildings of England. Herefordshire*. Harmondsworth: Penguin

——. 1966. *The buildings of England. Berkshire*. Harmondsworth: Penguin

——. 1968a. *The buildings of England. Bedfordshire, Huntingdon and Peterborough*. Harmondsworth: Penguin

——. 1968b. *The buildings of England. Worcestershire*. Harmondsworth: Penguin

——, and D. Lloyd. 1967. *The buildings of England. Hampshire*. Harmondsworth: Penguin

——, and A. Wedgwood. 1958. *The buildings of England. Warwickshire*. Harmondsworth: Penguin

——, and E. Williamson. 1979. *The buildings of England. Nottinghamshire*. 2nd edn. London: Penguin

——, and ——. 1984. *The buildings of England. Leicestershire and Rutland*. 2nd edn. London: Penguin

——, and ——. 1994. *The buildings of England. Buckinghamshire*. 2nd edn. London: Penguin

——, and B. Wilson. 1997. *The buildings of England. Norfolk*, 1, *Norwich and north-east*. 2nd edn. London: Penguin

——, and ——. 1999. *The buildings of England. Norfolk*, 2, *North-west and south*. 2nd edn. London: Penguin

Phythian-Adams, M. 1998. 'Some thoughts on the design and iconography of St Mary the Virgin, Iffley, Oxfordshire'. Unpublished paper presented on 9 December to the RAI

Pitte, D., and P. Cailleux. 1998. 'L'habitation rouennaise aux XII⁰ et XIII⁰ siècles'. Unpublished paper presented on 16–17 October to Table ronde franco-anglaise, *L'architecture civile des XII⁰ et XIII⁰ siècles*, Rouen

——, and Y. Lescroart. 1990–1. 'Rouen, rue St-

Romain: découverte d'un maison médiévale en pierre (début du XIIIe siècle)', *Bulletin des Amis des Monuments Rouennais*, 1990–1, 65–70

——, and ——. 1994–5. 'Un édifice roman disparu, rue Malpalu, à Rouen', *Bulletin des Amis des Monuments Rouennais*, 1994–5, 73–83

Platt, C. 1973. *Medieval Southampton: the port and trading community, AD 1000–1600.* London: Routledge and Kegan Paul

——. 1976. *The English medieval town.* London: Secker and Warburg

——. 1996. *King Death. The Black Death and its aftermath in late-medieval England.* London: University College London Press

——, and R. Coleman-Smith. 1975. *Excavations in medieval Southampton, 1953–1969.* Leicester: Leicester University Press

Plummer, C. 1896. *Venerabilis Baede Historium Ecclesiasticam Gentis Angbrum, Historiam Abbatum, Epistolam ad Eabertum.* Oxford: Clarendon Press

Poole, A.L. (ed.). 1958. *Medieval England.* Revised edn. Oxford: Clarendon Press

Poole, H. 1996. *Anne of Cleves House.* Lewes: Sussex Archaeol. Soc.

Portman, D. 1966. *Exeter houses 1400–1700.* Exeter: University of Exeter Press

Postan, M.M. 1928. 'Credit in medieval trade', *Economic Hist. Review*, 1, 2–26

——. 1944. 'The rise of a money economy', *Economic Hist. Review*, 14, 123–34

——. 1972. *The medieval economy and society. An economic history of Britain 1100–1500.* London: Weidenfeld and Nicolson

—— et al. (eds). 1971. *The Cambridge Economic History of Europe*, 3, *Economic organization and policies in the Middle Ages.* Cambridge: Cambridge University Press

Pounds, N.J.G. 1992. 'Lavenham', *Archaeol. J.*, 149, supplement 48–9

Powell, M.R. 1987. 'Chetham's Library and School [Manchester]', *Archaeol. J.*, 144, 46–8

Power, E. 1975. *Medieval women.* Cambridge: Cambridge University Press

Prescott, E. 1992. *The English medieval hospital, c. 1050–1640.* London: B.A. Seaby

Prescott, R.G.W. 1991. 'Anstruther Easter and the Scottish Fishing Museum', *Archaeol. J.*, 148, supplement 61–2

Price, R., and M. Ponsford. 1998. *St Bartholomew's Hospital, Bristol: the excavation of a medieval hospital.* York: CBA

Pringle, D. 1996. *Craigmillar Castle.* 2nd edn. Edinburgh: Historic Scotland

Pryde, G.S. 1965. *The burghs of Scotland*, ed. A.A.M. Duncan. Oxford: Oxford University Press

Pugin, A.W.N. 1836. *Contrasts: or, a parallel between the noble edifices of the Middle Ages and corresponding buildings of the present day . . .* London: Charles Dolman

Quiney, A.P. 1977. 'St Mark's Chapel [Bristol]', *Archaeol. J.*, 134, 372–3

——. 1992. *Traditional buildings in England.* London: Thames and Hudson

——. 1993. *Kent houses.* Woodbridge: Antique Collectors' Club

——. 1994. 'Vernacular Architecture', in B. Vyner ed. *Building on the Past. Papers celebrating 150 years of the Royal Archaeological Institute.* London: RAI

——. 1998. 'Bax Farmhouse, Tonge, Kent: materi-

als, planning and style of a sixteenth-century manor house', *Archaeol. J.*, 155, 252–91

——. 1999a. 'Burgundy: medieval town houses', *Archaeol. J.*, 156, 404–16

——. 1999b. 'Hall or chamber? That is the question. The use of rooms in post-Conquest houses'. *Archit. Hist.*, 42, 24–46

——. 2001. 'In hoc signo: the west front of Lincoln Cathedral', *Archit. Hist.*, 44, 162–71

Raby, F.J.E., and P.K. Baillie Reynolds. 1973. *Framlingham Castle*, Ministry of Public Buildings and Works Official Handbook. London: HMSO

Rackham, O. 1972. 'Grundle House', *Vernac. Archit.*, 3, 3–8

——. 1982. 'The growing and transport of timber and underwood', in McGrail 1982, 199–218

Radford, C.A.R. 1934. *The Bishop's Palace, St David's, Pembrokeshire*, Ministry of Works Official Guidebook. London: HMSO

——. 1967. 'The early church in Strathclyde and Galloway', *Med. Archaeol.*, 11, 105–26

——. 1970. 'The later pre-Conquest boroughs and their defences', *Med. Archaeol.*, 14, 83–103

——, E.M. Jope and J.W. Tonkin. 1973. 'The great hall of the Bishop's Palace at Hereford', *Med. Archaeol.*, 17, 78–86

Radley, J. 1971. 'Economic aspects of Anglo-Danish York', *Med. Archaeol.*, 15, 37–57

Rady, J., T. Tatton-Brown and J. Bowen. 1991. 'The Archbishop's Palace, Canterbury, *J. BAA*, 144, 1–60

Rahtz, P.A. 1976. 'Buildings and rural settlement', in Wilson 1976, 49–98

——. 1979. *The Saxon and medieval palaces at Cheddar. Excavations 1960–2.* Brit. Archaeol. Reps, Brit. Ser. 65. Oxford: CBA

Rawcliffe, C. 1995. *Medicine and society in later medieval England.* Stroud, Glos.: Sutton Publishing

——. 1999. *Medicine for the soul. The life, death and resurrection of an English medieval hospital: St Giles's, Norwich, c. 1249–1550.* Stroud, Glos.: Sutton Publishing

——. 2000. 'Tending bodies and healing souls: form and function in the medieval hospital'. Unpublished paper presented on 13 December to the RAI

RCAHMW *Glamorgan*. 1982. *An inventory of the ancient monuments in Glamorgan*, 3, *Medieval secular monuments*, 2, *non-defensive.* Cardiff: HMSO

RCAMS *Edinburgh*. 1951. *An inventory of the ancient and historical monuments of the city of Edinburgh.* Edinburgh: HMSO

RCHME *Cambridge*. 1959. *An inventory of the historical monuments in the city of Cambridge.* London: HMSO

RCHME *Dorset*. 1952. *An inventory of the historical monuments in the county of Dorset*, 1, *West Dorset.* London: HMSO

RCHME *Kent*. 1994a. *The medieval houses of Kent: an historical analysis.* London: HMSO

——. 1994b. *A gazetteer of medieval houses in Kent.* London: HMSO

RCHME *Northants*. 1985. *An inventory of the historical monuments in the county of Northampton*, 5, *Archaeological sites and churches in Northampton.* London: HMSO

RCHME *N. York Moors*. 1987. *Houses of the North York Moors.* London: HMSO

RCHME *Oxford*. 1939. *An inventory of the historical monuments in the city of Oxford.* London: HMSO

RCHME *Salisbury*. 1980. *Ancient and historical monuments in the city of Salisbury*, 1. London: HMSO

——. 1993. *Salisbury: the houses of the Close.* London: HMSO

RCHME *Stamford*. 1977. *An inventory of the historical monuments. The town of Stamford.* London: HMSO

RCHME *W. Yorks*. 1975. *Rural houses of West Yorkshire 1400–1830*, Supplementary Ser. 8. London: HMSO

RCHME *York*. 1972. *An inventory of the historical monuments in the city of York*, 3, *South-west of the Ouse.* London: HMSO

RCHME *York*. 1975. *An inventory of the historical monuments in the city of York*, 4, *Outside the city walls east of the Ouse.* London: HMSO

RCHME *York*. 1981. *An inventory of the historical monuments in the city of York*, 5, *The central areas.* London: HMSO

Renilson, J. 1937. 'Queen Mary's House', *Trans. Howick Archaeol. Soc.*, 5, 9

Renn, D. 1997. *Framlingham and Orford Castles.* English Heritage Official Handbook. 3rd edn. London: HMSO

Richmond, H., R. Taylor, and P. Wade-Martins. 1982. 'Nos 28–34 Queen Street, King's Lynn', *East Anglian Archaeol. Reps*, 14, 108–24

Rigold, S.E. 1962. *Temple Manor, Strood*, Ministry of Housing and Public Works Guidebook. London HMSO

——. 1962–3. 'The Anglian Cathedral of North Elmham, Norfolk', *Med. Archaeol.*, 6–7, 67–108

——. 1963. 'The distribution of the "Wealden" house', in Foster and Alcock 1963, 351–4

——. 1969a. 'The Roman haven of Dover', *Archaeol. J.*, 126, 78–100

——. 1969b. 'Timber-framed buildings in Kent', *Archaeol. J.*, 126, 198–200

——. 1971a. 'Ford's Hospital, Coventry', *Archaeol. J.*, 128, 251–2

——. 1971b. 'St Mary's Hall, Coventry', *Archaeol. J.*, 128, 253–5

——. 1980. 'North Elmham cathedral', *Archaeol. J.*, 137, 328–9

Riley, H.T. 1868. *Memorials of London and London life in the 13th, 14th and 15th centuries.* London: Longmans, Green

Roberts, D.L. 1974. 'The Cardinal's Hat, 268 High Street, Lincoln', *Archaeol. J.*, 131, 344–5

Roberts, E. 1996. 'A thirteenth-century king-post roof at Winchester, Hampshire', *Vernacular Archit.*, 27, 65–8

Roberts, M. 1992. 'A Northampton Jewish tombstone, c.1259 to c.1290, recently rediscovered in Northampton Central Museum', *Med. Archaeol.*, 36, 173–8

Rollason, D., M. Harvey, and M. Prestwich (eds). 1994. *Anglo-Norman Durham, 1093–1193.* Woodbridge: Boydell Press

Roth, C. 1964. *A history of the Jews in England.* 3rd edn. Oxford: Oxford University Press

Rouse, E.C. 1971. 'Guild Chapel, Stratford-on-Avon', *Archaeol. J.*, 128, 218

Rowley, T. (ed.). 1974. *Anglo-Saxon settlement and landscape.* Brit. Archaeol. Reps, Brit. Ser. 6. Oxford: CBA

Runciman, S. 1951–4. *A history of the Crusades*, 3 vols. Cambridge: Cambridge University Press

Rutledge, P. 1980. 'New Buckenham', *Archaeol. J.*, 137, 352–4

Ryder, P. 1995. *Buildings of Northumberland*, 1, *The two towers of Hexham, Hexham Moot Hall and the Old Gaol*. Newcastle upon Tyne: Soc. of Antiquaries of Newcastle upon Tyne

Saint, A. 1976. *Richard Norman Shaw*. London and New Haven: Yale University Press

Salway, P. 1981. *Oxford history of England*, 1a, *Roman Britain*. Oxford: Clarendon Press

Salzman, L.F. 1926. *English life in the Middle Ages*. Oxford: Oxford University Press

——. 1964. *English trade in the Middle Ages*. London: Fordes

——. 1967. *Building in England down to 1540, a documentary history*. 2nd impression. Oxford: Clarendon Press

Samuel, M. 1989. 'The fifteenth-century garner at Leadenhall, London', *Antiquaries J.*, 69, 119–53

Sandall, K. 1975. 'Aisled halls in England and Wales', *Vernacular Archit.*, 6, 19–27

——. 1986. 'Aisled halls in England and Wales', *Vernacular Archit.*, 17, 21–35

Saunders, A.D. 1973. 'Launceston Castle', *Archaeol. J.*, 130–4

——. 1980. 'Lydford Castle, Devon', *Med. Archaeol.*, 24, 123–86

——. 1984. *Launceston Castle*, Department of the Environment Guide. London: HMSO

Schofield, J. 1984. *The building of London from the Conquest to the Great Fire*. London: BM

——. 1995. *Medieval London houses*. New Haven and London: Yale University Press for the Paul Mellon Centre for Studies in Brit. Art

——. 1998. 'Living and working in British towns, 1350–1600', *Towns and their buildings – 1100–1650*. VAG, winter conference, December

—— (ed.). 1987. *The London surveys of Ralph Treswell*. London Topographical Soc., No. 135

——, and A. Vince. 1994. *Medieval towns*. London: Leicester University Press

Seaborne, M. 1971. *The English school: its architecture and organization, 1370–1870*. London: Routledge and Kegan Paul

Searle, E. 1963. 'Hides, virgates and tenant settlement at Battle Abbey', *Economic Hist. Review*, Ser. 2, 16, 290–300

Short, P. 1980. 'The fourteenth-century rows of York', *Archaeol. J.*, 137, 86–136

Simpson, A.D., and S. Stevenson. 1981. *Historic St Andrews*. Scottish Burgh Survey. Glasgow

——, and —— (eds). 1980. *Town houses and structures in medieval Scotland: a seminar*. Scottish Burgh Survey. Glasgow

Simpson, W.D. 1961. 'The tower-houses of Scotland', in Jope 1961, 229–42

——. 1964. 'Craigmillar Castle', *Archaeol. J.*, 121, 205

Slater, T. 1980. *The analysis of burgages in medieval towns*, Working Paper 4, Department of Geography, University of Birmingham.

——. 1994. 'Types and distribution of medieval German town-houses'. Unpublished paper presented in April to *Houses and Households in Towns 100–1600*, University of Birmingham

Smith, C.T. 1967. *An historical geography of western Europe before 1800*. London: Longmans

Smith, D. 1996. *John Knox House. Gateway to Edinburgh's old town*. Edinburgh: John Donald

Smith, J.T. 1955. 'Medieval aisled halls and their derivatives'. *Archaeol. J.*, 112, 76–94

——. 1958. 'Medieval roofs', *Archaeol. J.*, 115, 111–49

——. 1964. 'Cruck construction', *Med. Archaeol.*, 8, 119–51

——. 1965. 'Timber-framed building in England', *Archaeol. J.*, 122, 133–58

——. 1974. 'The early development of timber buildings', *Archaeol. J.*, 131, 238–63

——. 1975. 'Cruck distributions: an interpretation of some recent maps', *Vernac. Archit.*, 6, 3–18

——. 1981. 'The problems of cruck construction and the evidence of distribution maps', in Alcock 1981, 5–24

——. 1992. *English Houses, 1200–1800: the Hertfordshire evidence*. London: HMSO for RCHME

Smith, P. 1975. *Houses of the Welsh countryside. A study in historical geography*. London: HMSO

Smith, R., and A. Carter. 1983. 'Function and site: aspects of Norwich buildings before 1700', *Vernac. Archit.*, 14, 5–18

Smith, T.P. 1985. *The medieval brickmaking industry in England 1400–1450*, Brit. Archaeol. Rep. 138. Oxford: BAR

Soulsby, I. 1983. *The towns of medieval Wales*. Chichester: Phillimore

Sperman, M. 1988. 'The medieval townscape of Perth', in Lynch *et al.* 1988, 116–32

Spence, R.T. 1977. 'The pacification of the Cumberland borders, 1593–1628', *Northern Hist.*, 13, 59–160

——. 1980. 'The Graham clans and lands on the eve of the pacification', *Trans. of the Cumberland and Westmorland Antiquarian and Archaeol. Soc.*, new Ser. 80, 79–102

Speed, J. 1676. *The theatre of the empire of Great Britaine*. London: Thomas Bassett and Richard Chiswell

Stanford, C.P. 2001. *Thatching in Cambridgeshire*. Unpublished PhD thesis, University of Greenwich

Stell, G. 1980. 'Scottish burgh houses, 1560–1707', in Simpson and Stevenson 1980, 1–31

——. 1991. 'Castles and towers [in the St Andrews area]', *Archaeol. J.*, 148, supplement 13–15

Stenning, D.F. 1985. 'Timber-framed shops 1300–1600: comparative plans', *Vernac. Archit*, 16, 35–9

Stenton, F.M. 1947. *Anglo-Saxon England*. 2nd edn. Oxford: Clarendon Press

Stevenson, A. 1988. 'Trade with the south', in Lynch *et al.* 1988, 180–206

Stewart, F. 1991. 'Claypotts Castle', *Archaeol. J.*, 148, supplement 25–7

Stocker, D.A. 1986. 'The shrine of Little St Hugh', *BAA Conference Trans.*, 8, *Medieval art and architecture at Lincoln Cathedral*, 109–17

——. 1991. *The archaeology of Lincoln*, 12, 1, *St Mary's Guildhall, Lincoln*. London: CBA

——. 1992. 'The shadow of the general's armchair', *Archaeol. J.*, 149, 415–20

——. 2001. *The Lord's Tower, or Towers of the Lord?*, Maurice Barley Lecture, June

——, and P. Everson. 1990. 'Rubbish recycled: a study of the re-use of stone in Lincolnshire', in Parsons 1990, 83–101

——, and A. Vince. 1997. 'The early Norman castle at Lincoln and a re-evaluation of the original west tower of Lincoln Cathedral', *Med. Archaeol.*, 41, 223–32

Stone, L. 1979. *The family, sex and marriage in England 1500–1800*. London: Penguin

Summerson, J.N. 1962. *Georgian London*. Revised edn. Harmondsworth: Penguin Books

Survey of London. 1908. *Crosby Place*, Philip Norman. London: Committee for the Survey of the Memorials of Greater London

——. 1950. Vol. 21: *Bankside (the parishes of St Saviour and Christchurch Southwark)*, ed. H. Roberts and W.H. Godfrey. London: London County Council

——. 1951. Vol. 23: *The parish of St Mary, Lambeth, Pt 1 (South Bank and Vauxhall)*, ed. H. Roberts and W.H. Godfrey. London: London County Council

Tatton-Brown, T.W.T. 1983. 'The precinct's water supply', *Canterbury Cathedral Chronicle*, 77, 45–52

——. 1990. 'Building stone in Canterbury c. 1070–1525', in Parsons 1990, 70–82

——. 1991. 'The buildings and topography of St Augustine's Abbey, Canterbury', *J. BAA*, 144, 61–91

——. 2000. *Lambeth Palace: a history of the Archbishops of Canterbury and their houses*. London: SPCK

Tawney, R.H. 1938. *Religion and the rise of capitalism*. 2nd edn. Harmondsworth: Penguin

——. 1941. 'The rise of the gentry 1558–1640', *Economic Hist. Review*, 11, 1–34

Taylor, A.J. 1961. 'Castle-building in Wales in the later thirteenth century: the prelude to construction', in Jope 1961, 104–33

——. 1975. 'Caernarvon Castle and town walls', *Archaeol. J.*, 132, 287–9

Taylor, H. 1884. *Old Halls in Lancashire and Cheshire*. Manchester: J. Cornish

Taylor, H.M. 1969. 'The special role of Kentish churches in the development of pre-Norman (Anglo-Saxon) architecture'; 'Reculver Church'; and 'St Augustine's Abbey', *Archaeol. J.*, 126, 102–8, 225–7, 228–33

——. 1974. 'St Peter-at-Gowts, Lincoln', *Archaeol. J.*, 131, 348–50

Taylor, R., and H. Richmond. 1989. '28–32 King Street, King's Lynn', *Norfolk Archaeol.*, 40, 260–85

Thomas Aquinas, St. 1911–22. *Summa Theologica*, translated L. Shapcote, 18 vols. London: R. and T. Washbourne

Thomas, C., C. Phillpotts, B. Sloan, and G. Evans. 1989. 'Excavation of the priory and hospital of St Mary Spital', *London Archaeol.*, 6, 87–93

Thomas, W.G. 1962a. 'Tenby', *Archaeol. J.*, 119, 316–18

——. 1962b. 'The Old House [Tenby]', *Archaeol. J.*, 119, 324–5

Thompson, M.W. 1967. 'A contraction in plan at Archbishop Chichele's College in Higham Ferrers, Northants', *Med. Archaeol.*, 11, 255–7

——. 1986. 'Associated monasteries and castles in the Middle Ages: a tentative list', *Archaeol. J.*, 143, 305–21

——. 1995. *The medieval hall. The basis of secular domestic life, 600–1600 AD*. Aldershot: Scolar Press

——. 1998. *Medieval bishops' houses in England and Wales*. Aldershot: Ashgate

Thorp, J.R.L. 1982. 'Two hall-houses from a late medieval terrace, 8–12 Fore Street, Silverton', *Proc. Devon Archaeol. Soc.*, 40, 171–80

——. 1990. '10 The Close, Exeter', *Archaeol. J.*, 147, supplement 47–50

Thrupp, S. 1948. *The merchant class of medieval London*. Ann Arbor: University of Michigan Press

Thurley, S. 1993. *The royal palaces of Tudor England: architecture and court life 1460–1547*. London and New Haven: Yale University Press for the Paul Mellon Centre for Studies in Brit. Art

——. 1995. 'Royal lodgings at the Tower of London 1216–1327', *Archit. Hist.*, 38, 36–57

——. 1997. 'Whitehall Palace and Westminster 1400–1600: a royal seat in transition', in Gaimster and Stamper 1997, 93–104

——. 1999. *Whitehall Palace: an architectural history of the royal apartments, 1240–1698*. London and New Haven: Yale University Press

Tittler, R. 1991. *Architecture and power: the town hall and the English urban community 1500–1640*. Oxford: Oxford University Press

Titow, J.Z. 1962. 'Some differences between manors and their effects on the condition of the peasant in the thirteenth century', *Agricultural Hist. Review*, 10, 1–3

Trd 3. 1980. *Vernac. Archit.*, 11, 34

Trd 14. 1984. *Vernac. Archit.*, 15, 69

Trd 18. 1986. *Vernac. Archit.*, 17, 52–3

Trd 19. 1986. *Vernac. Archit.*, 17, 53–4

Trd 23. 1988. *Vernac. Archit.*, 19, 43–4

Trd 32. 1989. *Vernac. Archit.*, 20, 46–9

Trd 44. 1992. *Vernac. Archit.*, 23, 51–6

Trd 47. 1992. *Vernac. Archit.*, 23, 59–61

Trd 54. 1993. *Vernac. Archit.*, 24, 54–60

Trd 55. 1994. *Vernac. Archit.*, 25, 25–7

Trd 56. 1994. *Vernac. Archit.*, 25, 28–36

Trd 57. 1994. *Vernac. Archit.*, 25, 36–40

Trd 64. 1995. *Vernac. Archit.*, 26, 60–74

Trd 75. 1997. *Vernac. Archit.*, 26, 124–7

Trd 80. 1997. *Vernac. Archit.*, 28, 138–58

Trd 83. 1997. *Vernac. Archit.*, 28, 168–71

Trd 93. 1998. *Vernac. Archit.*, 29, 123–6

Trd 100. 1999. *Vernac. Archit.*, 30, 98–105

Trd 103. 1999. *Vernac. Archit.*, 30, 111–13

Trd 104. 1999. *Vernac. Archit.*, 30, 113–28

Trd 109. 2000. *Vernac. Archit.*, 31, 105–7

Trd 110. 2000. *Vernac. Archit.*, 31, 108–9

Trd 114. 2000. *Vernac. Archit.*, 31, 118–28

Trd 115. 2001. *Vernac. Archit.*, 32, 70–7

Trd 117. 2001. *Vernac. Archit.*, 32, 79–81

Trd 118. 2001. *Vernac. Archit.*, 32, 81–2

Trd 120. 2001. *Vernac. Archit.*, 32, 84–6

Trd 121. 2001. *Vernac. Archit.*, 32, 86–7

Trd 122. 2001. *Vernac. Archit.*, 32, 87–92

Trd 123. 2001. *Vernac. Archit.*, 32, 92–8

Trd 125. 2002. *Vernac. Archit.*, 33, 78–81

Tringham, N.J. 1984–5. 'The Chantry Priests' House in Lichfield Cathedral Close', *South Staffordshire Archaeol. and Hist. Soc. Trans.*, 26, 36–43

Turner, R.C. 1988. 'Early carpentry in the Rows of Chester', *Vernac. Archit.*, 19, 34–41

——. 2000. 'St Davids Bishop's Palace, Pembrokeshire', *Antiquaries J.*, 80, 87–194

Turner, T.H., and J.H. Parker. 1851–9. *Some account of domestic architecture in England*, 3 vols. Oxford: J.H. Parker

Ullmann, W. 1955. *The growth of papal government in the Middle Ages*. London: Methuen

Unwin, G. 1908. *The gilds and companies of London*. London: Methuen

Urry, W. 1967. *Canterbury under the Angevin kings*. London: Athlone Press

——. 1969. 'A perambulation of Canterbury', *Archaeol. J.*, 126, 235–7

VAGCP. 1972. *Suffolk*

VAGCP. 1974. *Leicester*

VAGCP. 1975. *Surrey*

VAGCP. 1982. *Shropshire*

VAGCP. 1983. *North Avon and South Gloucestershire*

VAGCP. 1984. *Essex*

VAGCP. 1987. *Oxfordshire*

VAGCP. 1990. *Wiltshire*

VAGCP. 1995. *Worcestershire*

VAGCP. 1996. *Radnorshire*

VAGCP. 1997. *Norfolk and Norwich*

VAGCP. 1998 *Northumberland*

VCH Gloucestershire. 1968. *Victoria History of the Counties of England. Gloucestershire*, 8. London: Oxford University Press

VCH Northants. 1906. *Victoria History of the County of Northampton*, 2. London: Archibald Constable

VCH Oxfordshire. 1964. *Victoria History of the Counties of England. Oxfordshire*, 8. London: Oxford University Press

VCH Shropshire. 1973. *Victoria History of the County of Shropshire*, 2. London: Oxford University Press

Verey, D., and A. Brooks. 1999. *The buildings of England: Gloucestershire, 1, The Cotswolds*. 3rd revised edn. Harmondsworth: Penguin

Verdier, A., and F. Cattois. 1855–7. *Architecture civile et domestique du Moyen Age et à la Renaissance*, 2 vols. Paris: Librairie Archéologique de V. de Didron

Vince, A. 1990. *Saxon London: an archaeological investigation*. London: B.A Seaby

Vitruvius. 1914. *De architectura. Ten Books on architecture by Marcus Vitruvius Pollio*, translated M.H. Morgan. Cambridge, Mass.: Harvard University Press

Waddell, G. 1999. 'The design of the Westminster Hall roof', *Archit. Hist.*, 42, 47–67

Wade, K. 1988. 'Ipswich', in Hodges and Hobley 1988, 93–100

——. 1994. 'The buildings of Anglo-Saxon Ipswich, 600–1100'. Unpublished paper presented in April to *Houses and Households in Towns 100–1600*, University of Birmingham

Walker, F.A. 2000. *The buildings of Scotland: Argyll and Bute*. London: Penguin

Walker, J. 1999. 'Late-twelfth and early-thirteenth-century aisled buildings: a comparison', *Vernac. Archit.*, 30, 21–53

Walton, P. 1991. 'Textiles', in Blair and Ramsay 1991, 319–54

Warren, J. 1992. 'Greater and lesser Gothic roofs: a study of the crown-post roof and its antecedents'. *Vernacular Archit.*, 23, 1–9

Webster, L.E., and J. Cherry. 1972. 'Medieval Britain in 1971', *Med. Archaeol.*, 16, 147–212

——, and ——. 1973. 'Medieval Britain in 1972', *Med. Archaeol.*, 17, 138–88

——, and ——. 1974. 'Medieval Britain in 1973', *Med. Archaeol.*, 18, 174–223

——, and ——. 1975. 'Medieval Britain in 1974', *Med. Archaeol.*, 19, 204–60

——, and ——. 1976. 'Medieval Britain in 1975', *Med. Archaeol.*, 20, 158–201

——, and ——. 1977. 'Medieval Britain in 1976', *Med. Archaeol.*, 21, 204–62

——, and ——. 1979. 'Medieval Britain in 1978', *Med. Archaeol.*, 23, 234–78

——, and ——. 1980. 'Medieval Britain in 1979', *Med. Archaeol.*, 24, 218–64

Weddell, P.J. 1985. 'The excavation of medieval and later houses at Wolborough Street, Newton Abbot', *Proc. Devon Archaeol. Soc.*, 43, 77–109

Werweke, H. van. 1971. 'The rise of the towns', in Postan *et al.* 1971, 3–41

West, S.E. 1969. 'The Anglo-Saxon village of West Stow: an interim report on the excavations, 1965–8', *Med. Archaeol.*, 13, 1–20

——. 1985. *West Stow: the Anglo-Saxon village*, 2 vols. Ipswich: Suffolk County Planning Department

Whittingham, A. 1980. 'The Bishop's Palace, Norwich', *Archaeol. J.*, 137, 364–8

Wilkins, W. 1796. 'An essay towards the history of the Venta Icenorum of the Romans, and of Norwich Castle; with remarks on the architecture of the Anglo-Saxons and Normans', *Archaeologia*, 12, 132–80

Williams, G.A. 1963. *Medieval London: from commune to capital*. London: Athlone Press

Williams, J.H. 1979. *St Peter's Street Northampton, excavations 1973–76*. Northampton: Northampton District Council

——, M. Shaw, and V. Denham. 1985. *Middle Saxon Palaces at Northampton*. Northampton: Northampton Development Corporation

Williams, P. 1963. 'The northern borderland under the early Stuarts', *Historical essays 1600–1750 presented to David Ogg*, ed. H.E. Bell and R.L. Ollard, 1–17. London: A., and C. Black

Williamson, E., A. Riches, and M. Higgs. 1990. *The buildings of Scotland: Glasgow*. London: Penguin

Wilson, C. 1984. 'Medieval tower houses, castles and palaces [in Edinburgh]', in Gifford *et al.* 1984, 49–53

Wilson, D.M. (ed.). 1976. *The archaeology of Anglo-Saxon England*. London: Methuen

——, and J.G. Hurst. 1957. 'Medieval Britain in 1956', *Med. Archaeol.*, 1, 147–71

——, and ——. 1958. 'Medieval Britain in 1957', *Med. Archaeol.*, 2, 183–213

——, and ——. 1959. 'Medieval Britain in 1958', *Med. Archaeol.*, 3, 295–326

——, and ——. 1960. 'Medieval Britain in 1959', *Med. Archaeol.*, 4, 134–65

——, and ——. 1961. 'Medieval Britain in 1960', *Med. Archaeol.*, 5, 309–39

——, and ——. 1962–3. 'Medieval Britain in 1961', *Med. Archaeol.*, 6–7, 306–49

——, and ——. 1964. 'Medieval Britain in 1962 and 1963', *Med. Archaeol.*, 8, 231–99

——, and ——. 1965. 'Medieval Britain in 1964', *Med. Archaeol.*, 9, 170–220

——, and ——. 1966. 'Medieval Britain in 1965', *Med. Archaeol.*, 10, 168–219

——, and ——. 1967. 'Medieval Britain in 1966', *Med. Archaeol.*, 11, 252–319

——, and ——. 1968. 'Medieval Britain in 1967', *Med. Archaeol.*, 12, 155–211

——, and ——. 1969. 'Medieval Britain in 1968', *Med. Archaeol.*, 13, 230–87

——, and ——. 1970. 'Medieval Britain in 1969', *Med. Archaeol.*, 14, 155–208

——, and S. Moorhouse. 1971. 'Medieval Britain in 1970', *Med. Archaeol.*, 15, 124–79

Wood, M.E. 1935. 'Norman domestic architecture', *Archaeol. J.*, 90, 167–242

——. 1950. 'Thirteenth-century domestic architecture', *Archaeol. J.*, 105, supplement

——. 1956a. *Chepstow Castle*, Ministry of Public

Buildings and Works Official Handbook. London: HMSO

——. 1956b. *Christchurch Castle*, Ministry of Public Buildings and Works Official Handbook. London: HMSO

——. 1965. *The English medieval house*. London: J.M. Dent

Woolgar, C.M. 1999. *The great household in late medieval England*. London and New Haven: Yale University Press

Wrigley, E.A., and R. Schofield. 1981. *The population history of England, 1541–1871, a reconstruction*. Cambridge: Cambridge University Press

Yeoman, P. 1995. *Medieval Scotland, an archaeological perspective*. London: B.T. Batsford for Historic Scotland

Youngs, S.M., and J. Clark. 1981. 'Medieval Britain in 1980', *Med. Archaeol.*, 25, 166–228

——, and ——. 1982. 'Medieval Britain in 1981', *Med. Archaeol.*, 26, 164–227

——, —— and T.B. Barry. 1983. 'Medieval Britain in 1982', *Med. Archaeol.*, 27, 161–229

——, —— and ——. 1984. 'Medieval Britain in 1983', *Med. Archaeol.*, 28, 203–65

INDEX